Lecture Notes in Computer Science   3408

Commenced Publication in 1973
Founding and Former Series Editors:
Gerhard Goos, Juris Hartmanis, and Jan van Leeuwen

David E. Losada   Juan M. Fernández-Luna (Eds.)

Advances in Information Retrieval

27th European Conference on IR Research, ECIR 2005
Santiago de Compostela, Spain, March 21-23, 2005
Proceedings

 Springer

Volume Editors

David E. Losada
Universidad de Santiago de Compostela
Departamento de Electrónica y Computación
Campus sur s/n, Universidad de Santiago de Compostela
15782 Santiago de Compostela, Spain
E-mail: dlosada@usc.es

Juan M. Fernández-Luna
Universidad de Granada
E.T.S.I. Informática
Departamento de Ciencias de la Computación e Inteligencia Artificial
C/Periodista Daniel Saucedo Aranda, s/n, 18071 Granada, Spain
E-mail: jmfluna@decsai.ugr.es

Library of Congress Control Number: 2005921726

CR Subject Classification (1998): H.3, H.2, I.2.3, I.2.6, H.4, H.5.4, I.7

ISSN 0302-9743
ISBN 3-540-25295-9 Springer Berlin Heidelberg New York

Springer is a part of Springer Science+Business Media

springeronline.com

© Springer-Verlag Berlin Heidelberg 2005
Printed in Germany

Typesetting: Camera-ready by author, data conversion by Scientific Publishing Services, Chennai, India
Printed on acid-free paper   SPIN: 11406761   06/3142   5 4 3 2 1 0

Preface

Welcome to Santiago de Compostela! We are pleased to host the 27th Annual European Conference on Information Retrieval Research (ECIR 2005) on its first visit to Spain.

These proceedings contain the refereed full papers and poster abstracts presented at ECIR 2005. This conference was initially established by the Information Retrieval Specialist Group of the British Computer Society (BCS-IRSG) under the name "Annual Colloquium on Information Retrieval Research." The colloquium was held in the United Kingdom each year until 1998, when the event was organized in Grenoble, France. Since then the conference venue has alternated between the United Kingdom and Continental Europe, reflecting the growing European orientation of ECIR. For the same reason, in 2001 the event was renamed "European Conference on Information Retrieval Research." In recent years, ECIR has continued to grow and has become the major European forum for the discussion of research in the field of information retrieval.

ECIR 2005 was held at the Technical School of Engineering of the University of Santiago de Compostela, Spain. In terms of submissions, ECIR 2005 was a record-breaking success, since 124 full papers were submitted in response to the call for papers. This was a sharp increase from the 101 submissions received for ECIR 2003, which was the most successful ECIR in terms of submissions. ECIR 2005 established also a call for posters, and 41 posters where submitted. Paper and poster submissions were received from across Europe and further afield, including North America, South America, Asia and Australia, which is a clear indication of the growing popularity and reputation of the conference. All papers and posters were reviewed by at least three reviewers. Out of the 124 submitted papers, 34 (27%) were accepted; 17 (41%) posters were accepted.

Students are well represented, since 22 out of 34 full papers and 10 out of 17 posters involve a full-time student as the primary author, which means that the traditional student focus of the conference has been very well preserved.

The increasing presence of research papers from leading companies it is also remarkable.

We had an outstanding set of research contributions this year, reflecting the full range of information retrieval research areas. The proceedings start with two invited papers, from Keith van Rijsbergen and Ricardo Baeza-Yates. van Rijsbergen's work shows how logic emerges from the geometry of the popular vector space model. Baeza-Yates proposes two applications of analyzing and clustering queries stored in server logs of search engines and website logs. The topics covered by the papers and posters include peer-to-peer systems, formal models, text summarization, classification, fusion, user studies, evaluation, efficiency issues, image and video retrieval, web IR, and XML retrieval.

The success of ECIR owes a lot to many individuals involved in the reviewing tasks. We are deeply grateful to all involved in this process for their dedication and professionalism in meeting the very tight deadlines. We would like to extend our warm thanks to the researchers who submitted their results for consideration. Many thanks also to our keynote speakers Keith van Rijsbergen and Ricardo Baeza-Yates for agreeing to present at ECIR 2005. We are also extremely grateful to Fabio Crestani, Pia Borlund and Gianni Amati for facing the difficult task of deciding which student paper deserved the Best Student Paper Award. A special word of thanks is extended to Fabio Crestani, who has supported us from the very beginning of the bidding process.

We wish also to thank the companies and institutions who sponsored ECIR 2005: the Information Retrieval Specialist Group of the British Computer Society (BCS-IRSG), the University of Granada, the Council of European Professional Informatics Societies (CEPIS), Microsoft Research, Sharp Laboratories of Europe, Ltd., and the European Research Consortium for Informatics and Mathematics (ERCIM).

We would also like to thank the members of the Local Organizing Committee for their hard work over many months. They enthusiastically supported us in every small task related to the conference. Not all these persons may be visible to conference participants but the efforts of all are invaluable in making the conference a success.

Most of all, we would like to thank our wives, Maria and Nuria, for their endless patience and tolerance through the long hours dedicated to ECIR.

January 2005   David E. Losada
                                              Juan M. Fernández-Luna

Organization

ECIR 2005 was organized by the University of Santiago de Compostela, with the collaboration of the University of Granada, and under the auspices of the Information Retrieval Specialist Group of the British Computer Society (BCS-IRSG).

Local Organizing Committee

Abraham Otero, University of Santiago de Compostela
Adolfo Riera, University of Santiago de Compostela
Alberto Bugarín, University of Santiago de Compostela
David López Moreno, University of Santiago de Compostela
Félix Díaz Hermida, University of Santiago de Compostela
José Luis Correa, University of Santiago de Compostela
Juan Carlos Vidal, University of Santiago de Compostela
Manuel Mucientes, University of Santiago de Compostela
María Pilar G. Souto, University of Santiago de Compostela
Paulo Félix, University of Santiago de Compostela
Purificación Cariñena, University of Santiago de Compostela
Roberto Iglesias, University of Santiago de Compostela

Programme Committee

David E. Losada, University of Santiago de Compostela, Spain (Chair)
Juan M. Fernández-Luna, University of Granada, Spain (Chair)

Andrew MacFarlane, City University London, United Kingdom
Alan Smeaton, Dublin City University, Ireland
Alvaro Barreiro, University of A Coruña, Spain
Anastasios Tombros, Queen Mary University of London, United Kingdom
Andreas Rauber, Vienna University of Technology, Austria
Arjen de Vries, CWI, Netherlands
Ayse Göker, Robert Gordon University, United Kingdom
Barry Smyth, University College Dublin, Ireland
Claudio Carpineto, Fondazione Ugo Bordoni, Italy
Djoerd Hiemstra, University of Twente, Netherlands
Dunja Mladenić, Jožef Stefan Institute, Slovenia
Eero Sormunen, University of Tampere, Finland
Enrique Herrera-Viedma, University of Granada, Spain
Fabio Crestani, University of Strathclyde, United Kingdom
Fabrizio Sebastiani, National Council of Research, Italy

Gabriella Pasi, National Council of Research, Italy
Gareth Jones, Dublin City University, Ireland
Giambattista Amati, Fondazione Ugo Bordoni, Italy
Gloria Bordogna, National Council of Research, Italy
Henrik Nottelmann, University of Duisburg-Essen, Germany
Hugo Zaragoza, Microsoft Research, United Kingdom
Iadh Ounis, University of Glasgow, United Kingdom
Ian Ruthven, University of Strathclyde, United Kingdom
Jane Reid, Queen Mary University of London, United Kingdom
Jesús Vegas, University of Valladolid, Spain
Joe Carthy, University College Dublin, Ireland
Joemon Jose, University of Glasgow, United Kingdom
Josiane Mothe, Institut de Recherche en Informatique de Toulouse, France
Julio Gonzalo, UNED, Spain
Jussi Karlgren, Swedish Institute of Computer Science, Sweden
Kalervo Järvelin, University of Tampere, Finland
Kees Koster, Radboud University Nijmegen, Netherlands
Keith van Rijsbergen, University of Glasgow, United Kingdom
Leif Azzopardi, University of Glasgow, United Kingdom
Luis de Campos, University of Granada, Spain
Marcello Federico, ITC-irst, Italy
Margaret Graham, Northumbria University, United Kingdom
Mark Girolami, University of Glasgow, United Kingdom
Mark Sanderson, University of Sheffield, United Kingdom
Massimo Melucci, University of Padova, Italy
Matthew Chalmers, University of Glasgow, United Kingdom
Michael Oakes, University of Sunderland, United Kingdom
Micheline Beaulieu, University of Sheffield, United Kingdom
Mohand Boughanem, Université Paul Sabatier, France
Monica Landoni, University of Strathclyde, United Kingdom
Mounia Lalmas, Queen Mary University of London, United Kingdom
Norbert Fuhr, University of Duisburg-Essen, Germany
Peter Ingwersen, Royal School of Library and Information Science, Denmark
Pia Borlund, Royal School of Library and Information Science, Denmark
Ricardo Baeza-Yates, ICREA-Universitat Pompeu Fabra, Spain, and
    University of Chile, Chile
Sándor Dominich, University of Veszprém, Hungary
Sharon McDonald, University of Sunderland, United Kingdom
Stavros Christodoulakis, Technical University of Crete, Greece
Thomas Roelleke, Queen Mary University of London, United Kingdom
Tony Rose, Cancer Research UK, United Kingdom
Ulrich Thiel, Fraunhofer IPSI, Germany
Umberto Straccia, National Council of Research, Italy
Victor Poznanski, Sharp Laboratories of Europe, United Kingdom
Wessel Kraaij, TNO TPD, Netherlands

Best Student Paper Award Committee

Fabio Crestani, University of Strathclyde, United Kingdom (Chair)
Giambattista Amati, Fondazione Ugo Bordoni, Italy
Pia Borlund, Royal School of Library and Information Science, Denmark

Additional Reviewers

Alessandro Moschitti, University of Rome "Tor Vergata", Italy
Alex Bailey, Canon Research Centre Europe Ltd., United Kingdom
Amanda Spink, University of Pittsburgh, USA
Andreas Pesenhofer, Electronic Commerce Competence Center, Austria
Andrew Trotman, University of Otago, New Zealand
Antonio Ferrández, University of Alicante, Spain
Basilio Sierra, University of the Basque Country, Spain
Ben He, University of Glasgow, United Kingdom
Benjamin Piwowarski, University of Chile, Chile
Birger Larsen, Royal School of Library and Information Science, Denmark
Börkur Sigurbjörnsson, University of Amsterdam, Netherlands
Cathal Gurrin, Dublin City University, Ireland
Chris Stokoe, University of Sunderland, United Kingdom
Christof Monz, University of Maryland, USA
David Hull, Clairvoyance Corporation, USA
Dawei Song, Distributed Systems Technology Centre, Australia
Donald Metzler, University of Massachusetts, USA
Edda Leopold, Fraunhofer Gesellschaft, Germany
Edie Rasmussen, University of British Columbia, Canada
Fabio M. Zanzotto, University of Milano-Bicocca, Italy
Fernando Diaz, Center for Intelligent Information Retrieval,
    University of Massachusetts, USA
Fernando Llopis, University of Alicante, Spain
Fidel Cacheda, University of A Coruña, Spain
Filippo Portera, University of Padova, Italy
Franciska de Jong, University of Twente, Netherlands
Gabriella Kazai, Queen Mary University of London, United Kingdom
Giorgio M. Di Nunzio, University of Padova, Italy
Hyowon Lee, Dublin City University, Ireland
Jamie Callan, Carnegie Mellon University, USA
Jean-Pierre Chevallet, CLIPS-IMAG, France
Jesper Schneider, Royal School of Library and Information Science, Denmark
Jian-Yun Nie, University of Montreal, Canada
José M. Gómez Hidalgo, Universidad Europea de Madrid, Spain
Juan Huete, University of Granada, Spain
Leonardo Candela, National Council of Research, Italy
Luo Si, Carnegie Mellon University, USA

Manuel Lama Penín, University of Santiago de Compostela, Spain
Miguel A. Alonso, University of A Coruña, Spain
Nicola Orio, University of Padova, Italy
Oscar Cordón, University of Granada, Spain
Pablo de la Fuente, University of Valladolid, Spain
Pasquale Savino, National Council of Research, Italy
Patrick Gallinari, Université Pierre et Marie Curie, France
Patrick Ruch, University Hospitals of Geneva, Switzerland
Pavel Calado, INESC-ID, Portugal
Pertti Vakkari, University of Tampere, Finland
Rafael Berlanga, Universitat Jaume I, Spain
Roberto Basili, University of Rome "Tor Vergata", Italy
Roi Blanco, University of A Coruña, Spain
Ross Wilkinson, CSIRO, Australia
Ryen White, University of Maryland, USA
Theodora Tsikrika, Queen Mary University of London, United Kingdom
Toni Rath, Center for Intelligent Information Retrieval,
    University of Massachusetts, USA
Vanessa Murdock, Center for Intelligent Information Retrieval,
    University of Massachusetts, USA
Vassilis Plachouras, University of Glasgow, United Kingdom
Xiaoyong Liu, Center for Intelligent Information Retrieval,
    University of Massachusetts, USA

Sponsoring Institutions

Table of Contents

Keynote Papers

Peer-to-Peer

Information Retrieval Models (I)

Text Summarization

Information Retrieval Methods (I)

Information Retrieval Models (II)

Text Classification and Fusion

User Studies and Evaluation

Information Retrieval Methods (II)

Multimedia Retrieval

Web Information Retrieval

Posters

A Probabilistic Logic for Information Retrieval

C.J. 'Keith' van Rijsbergen

Department of Computing Science, University of Glasgow,
Scotland, UK
keith@dcs.gla.ac.uk
http://www.dcs.gla.ac.uk/~keith

Abstract. One of the most important models for IR derives from the representation of documents and queries as vectors in a vector space. I will show how logic emerges from the geometry of such a vector space. As a consequence of looking at such a space in terms of states and observables I will show how an appropriate probability measure can be constructed on this space which may be the basis for a suitable probabilistic logic for information retrieval.

1 Introduction

Why another paper on logic? There is now a substantial literature on the application of logic to IR [1], so what new can be said about this topic? For one thing there is no unique logic that is suitable for reasoning in IR, but a labyrinth of possible logics. The field narrows somewhat if one insists that a logic combines naturally with a measure of probability. It narrows even further if both the logic and probability can be seen to respect the geometrical structure of the space of objects in which one intends carry out plausible inference.

To model IR we need logic, probability and similarity. Usually each is treated separately within any model. Is it possible to combine naturally all three within one framework? Or, can one find a way of looking at things that takes all three paradigms into account? The answer is, yes, and this paper is a description of how one might go about doing this.

2 What Is Needed?

To open the discussion we will start by presenting a small number of building blocks in terms of which such a framework can be constructed. These are *states* and *observables*. Objects are modelled by states, and the measurement of properties such as 'relevance' and 'aboutness' are modelled by the values that observables can have with a probability. It is important to realize that properties do not belong intrinsically to a state, but rather that the value of a property emerges as a result of an interactive measurement of that property. This is an essential change from the traditional way of viewing 'relevance' or 'aboutness' as belonging to an object. Given a state one can ask a question about that state, such as a simple two-valued question. This may be

D.E. Losada and J.M. Fernández-Luna (Eds.): ECIR 2005, LNCS 3408, pp. 1–6, 2005.

a Yes/No question, such as, is this document relevant or not, and its answer will be either Yes, or No, with a corresponding probability for each.

The method of representation is as follows. Documents will correspond to state vectors, queries will correspond to operators, and relevance will correspond to an operator as well. All this takes place in a Hilbert space, which for all practical purposes can be thought as a finite-dimensional vector space with complex scalars. Let me empasise that we have identified relevance and queries with observables.

Observables will correspond to Hermitian operators [2] which are represented by self-adjoint matrices. It is a theorem in Hilbert space that any Hermitian operator can be represented as a linear combination of simple operators, drawn from a set of projectors one corresponding to each eigenvalue of the operator, and combined linearly with the eigenvalues as weights. Thus if a query is now represented by a matrix instead of a vector then it can be resolved into a set of Yes/No question, each question weighted appropriately. For a detailed discussion of this, see [3].

2.1 Properties of Observables

That observables are sensibly represented by Hermitian operators in Hilbert space is a long story derived from their introduction into Quantum Mechanics (see [3]). The most important properties that they have are that they have real eigenvalues, and that the corresponding eigenvectors form an orthonormal basis of the space. Hence, it can be shown that a measurement of an observable gives as an outcome a real number, and the probability of the outcome is a function of where the eigenvectors are in the space. This gives us the possibility of a perspective, or a point of view, from which to observe the objects in the space. In practice this means that any document is indexed (with probability) with respect to each eigenvector of the matrix representing the query. The default case is where an observable, such as a query, is represented as a vector with respect to the same basis that indexes the documents.

3 Enter John von Neumann

In the early part of last century John von Neumann realized that to calculate the probability associated with an observation in Quantum Mechanics it was essential to have a geometry on the Hilbert space from which the probability could be derived.

> 'Essentially if a state of a system is given by one vector, the
> transition probability in another state is the inner product of the
> two which is the square of the angle between them.' [4]

Such an inner product is like the cosine correlation from which the probability of a value of an observable can then be calculated. The same is true for IR if we represent our objects in the way described above. But von Neumann did more, he and Birkhoff [5] wrote a, now seminal, paper showing how the geometry of the space also produced a logic - a non-classical logic no less. Simply put, the set of subspaces in Hilbert space form an ortholattice which is isomorphic to a non-classical logic just like a Boolean lattice is isomorphic to a Boolean logic.

This analogy between the representations of a Boolean logic and a non-Boolean logic is closer than one would intuitively suspect. Boole[6] in his Laws of Thought stated as defining equation for his logic: $x(1-x) = 0$ for propositional variables x. The subspaces of Hilbert space can be seen as propositions, and the projectors P onto them as propositional variables. That is, corresponding to each subspace is a unique (orthogonal) projection. These projectors are of course idempotent operators satisfying, $P^2 = P$, which can be rewritten as $P^2 - P = 0$, or $P(P-I) = 0$ not unlike Boole's defining equation. These projectors are like simple questions, which have only, Yes, or No as an answer. As mentioned above any observable can be expanded as a linear combination of these Yes/No questions.

The set of projectors on a space – corresponding to the subspaces – in general, form a non-Boolean lattice. Once a point of view, the eigenbasis, has been chosen then the projectors on the eigenvectors can be combined to form a hierarchy of projectors. Any query is then expressible as a selection of these projectors.

4 What Is Different?

There is a famous example due to Wittgenstein [7] derived from Jastrow in which a drawing of the head of a duck-rabbit is shown. When presented with such a drawing, people will see it as either a rabbit or a duck. Of course once told of what it should be they will see it that way, and when shown it repeatedly in quick succession, the same decision is made. The above example, illustrates how 'rabbitness' or 'duckness' is not a property of the representation (figure). The seeing of one or the other emerges during the interaction.

The attribution of relevance or aboutness can be analysed in the same way. It is not that 'relevance' or 'aboutness' is a property of a document, it is rather that such a property emerges through the user interaction with a document mediated by his, or her, cognitive state.

In general the measurement of different observables will interact. Mathematically this comes down to assuming that the operators corresponding to the different observables do not commute. In IR this is quite natural, if one of the observables is relevance one would expect the outcome of a judgment of relevance followed by a judgment about contents, to be different from a sequence in reverse order simply because there is a cognitive state change between two such judgments.

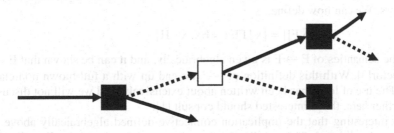

A document for assessment comes in at the left to be judged as to whether it is about 'ducks' (black box), assuming it is not (dashed line) and is then judged for relevance (white box) and is considered relevant (solid line). During the process of relevance judgment a user will have a cognitive state change, and when subsequently presented again with the same document for assessment as to whether it is about ducks or not, he may change his mind giving the possibility of either outcome. Thus the 'aboutness' assessment interacts with the 'relevance' assessment.

We are now quite used to this kind of interaction when considering counterfactual reasoning. For example, consider the following statements about a glass.

(1) will it break? -> yes
(2) is the floor made of rubber? -> yes
(3) will it break? -> no.

Examples are all very well but how does one formally capture this kind of interaction and reasoning? Fortunately, Hilbert space theory used to represent Quantum Mechanics can also be used to represent IR and will indeed give an appropriate method for handling non-commutative operators.

By choosing Hilbert space as a vehicle for representing objects in IR we are committing ourselves to a particular kind of logic. The logic associated with QM, is known as quantum logic and in general is non-distributative (see [8]). What breaks down in such a logic is the distribution law [9],

$$B \wedge (H \vee L) = (B \wedge H) \vee (B \wedge L)$$

5   Algebraic Considerations

One of the requirements for a reasonable logic is that it should have the usual connectives, especially an appropriate implication connective [10]. It can be shown quite readily that quantum logic does indeed have a sensible implication. The easiest way to do this is algebraically. Let us restrict our discussion to projection operators which correspond to propositions in quantum logic. Then if E and F are such operators, namely $E^2 = E$, and $F^2 = F$, then we can define in Hilbert space H,

$$[[E]] = \{x \mid Ex = x, x \in H\}$$
$$E \leq F \text{ if and only if } FE = E$$

The '$\leq$' is the natural ordering on the subspaces of H, or the equivalent projection operators. We can now define,

$$[[E \rightarrow F]] = \{x \mid FEx = Ex, x \in H\}$$

Then the semantics of $E \rightarrow F$ is given algebraically, and it can be shown that $E \rightarrow F$ is a projector[3]. With this definition of '$\rightarrow$' we end up with a full blown non-classical logic. The use of logic has been written about extensively, and we will not discuss this any further here, those interested should consult [1].

It is interesting that the implication connective defined algebraically above is the Stalnaker conditional. This implication was the basis for the probability kinematics developed for IR in [11]. There, a probability revision mechanism know as *imaging* was proposed. It is an open problem as to how imaging might be specified in Hilbert space. It may turn out to be a simple application of the following Theorem.

6 Enter Gleason

The purpose of this paper is to show how probability may be combined with logic to support plausible inference in IR. To complete the story we need one more piece of formal development, namely how to link probability in with the logic and geometry of Hilbert space. For this we need some more mathematics. But first an acknowledgment to Schrödinger whose interpretation of the state vector in QM foreshadowed precisely the introduction of probability.

> 'It [state vector] is now the means for predicting probability of measurement results. In it is embodied the momentarily-attained sum of theoretically based future expectation, somewhat as laid down in a catalogue'(for source, see [3]).

A possible reading of Schrödinger's remark is that the state vector encapsulates in it all the information for predicting the probabilities of measurement outcomes for any observable, like the possible future uses of a library catalogue. Another way of putting this is that the state vector induces a probability measure on the entire space by associating a probability with each subspace.

There is a famous theorem by Gleason[12] which gives an algorithm that specifies exactly how an special kind of operator will induce a probability measure on the space of objects, and conversely how any probability on the space can be capture algebraically by such an operator. The theorem goes as follows[13],

> Let μ be any measure on the closed subspaces of a separable (real or complex) Hilbert space H of dimension at least 3. There exists a positive self-adjoint operator T of trace class such that, for all closed subspaces L of H, $\mu(L) = \mathrm{tr}(TP_L)$.

The technical definitions do not matter here, one can look them up in [13], what does matter is that in this theorem all three probability, logic and geometry are combined. The logic is given by the projectors P_L, the probability by μ, and the geometry by the trace function $\mathrm{tr}()$. Tr(T) is defined as a sum of inner products, Σ [e_i |Te_i], where e_i is any orthonormal basis for H. Notice that this is an existence theorem, it claims the existence of a unique T once the probability measure has been specified.

To appreciate the power of this result. Assume that an a priori probability measure has been specified by using the query as an operator T. Now imagine that this probability measure is revised in the light of some feedback information, then the revised probability measure implies the existence, according to Gleason, of an operator T' which represents the new probability measure. This is a form of query expansion, T being expanded into T'. Another illustration is the use of conditional information such as $E \rightarrow F$, remember that this corresponds to a subspace, and so there is a projector $P_{E \rightarrow F}$ corresponding to that subspace. This projector can enter into the probability calculation as specified in the theorem.

7 Conclusions

In this paper I have presented a very sketchy introduction to how Hilbert space theory combined with Gleason's Theorem can be used to combine logic, probability, and geometry to generate a formal framework for specifying IR models. The interpretation of the measurement of relevance and aboutness deviates from the traditional one, and is more like the one adopted in quantum mechanics. The logic that arises in this was is non-standard and so is the probability theory. More information about this can be found in [3].

References

1. Crestani, C., Lalmas, M., Van Rijsbergen, C.J..: *Information Retrieval: Uncertainty and Logics: Advanced Models for the representation and Retrieval of Information*. Kluwer, Boston (1998)
2. Halmos, P. R.: *Finite-Dimensional Vector Spaces*, D. van Nostrand Company, Inc (1958)
3. Van Rijsbergen, C. J.: *The Geometry of Information Retrieval*, Cambridge University Press (2004)
4. Redei, M.., Stoltzner, M.: *John von Neumann and the Foundations of Quantum Physics*, Kluwer, Boston (2001)
5. Birkhoff, G., von Neumann, J.: The logic of quantum mechanics, *Annals of mathematics*, **37**, 823-843 (1936)
6. Boole, G.: *An Investigation of the Laws of Thought*, Dover, New York (1951)
7. Wittgenstein, L.: *Philosophical Investigations*, Blackwell, Oxford (1968)
8. Varadarajan, V. S.: *Geometry of Quantum Theory*, Springer-Verlag, New York (1985)
9. Hardegree, G. M.: An approach to the logic of natural kinds, *Pacific Philosophical Quarterly*, **63**, 122-132 (1982)
10. Hardegree, G. M.: The conditional in quantum logic, In *Logic and Probability in Quantum Mechanics*, P. Suppes (ed.), Reidel, Dordrecht (1976)
11. Crestani, C., van Rijsbergen, C.J.: A study of probability kinematics, *ACM Transactions on Information Systems*, **16**, 225-255 (1998)
12. Gleason, A. M.: Measures on the closed subspaces of a Hilbert space, *Journal of Mathematics and Mechanics*, **6**, 885-893 (1957)
13. Hughes, R. I. G,: *The Structure and Interpretation of Quantum Mechanics*, Harvard University Press, (1989)

Applications of Web Query Mining

Ricardo Baeza-Yates

Center for Web Research, Dept. of Computer Science,
Universidad de Chile, Santiago
ICREA Research Professor, Technology Department,
Universitat Pompeu Fabra, Spain
rbaeza@dcc.uchile.cl, ricardo.baeza@upf.edu

Abstract. Server logs of search engines store traces of queries submitted by users, which include queries themselves along with Web pages selected in their answers. The same is true in Web site logs where queries and later actions are recorded from search engine referrers or from an internal search box. In this paper we present two applications based in analyzing and clustering queries. The first one suggest changes to improve the text and structure of a Web site and the second does relevance ranking boosting and query recommendation in search engines.

1 Introduction

Nowadays, search tools are crucial for finding information on the Web. They range from Web search engines such as Google and Yahoo! to search boxes inside a Web site. However, the amount of information available to us in the Web is continuously changing and growing, and thus search technology is continuously being pushed to the limit. Several new techniques have emerged to improve the search process, and one of them is based on the analysis of query logs. Query logs register the history of queries submitted to the search tool, and the pages selected after a search, among other data.

The main goal of this paper is to show how valuable is to perform log query mining, by presenting several different applications of this idea combined with standard usage mining. Although past research in query mining has focused in improving technical aspects of search engines, analyzing queries has a broader impact in Web search and design in two different aspects: *Web findability* and *information scent*. Web findability or Web ubiquity is a measure of how easy to find a Web site is, where search engines are the main access tools. To improve findability there are several techniques, and one of them is to use query log analysis of Web site search to include on the Web site text the most used query words. Information scent [24] is how good it is a word with respect of words with the same semantics. For example, polysemic words (words with multiple meanings) may have less information scent. The most common queries are usually the ones with more information scent, so analyzing Web search queries we can find words that are found in a site but have more or similar information scent than words in the home page (which have to be replaced or added); and words that are not found that imply new information to be included [2].

D.E. Losada and J.M. Fernández-Luna (Eds.): ECIR 2005, LNCS 3408, pp. 7–22, 2005.

The search for certain groups of queries capturing common sets of preferences and information needs has been a recent trend in query log analysis [11, 36, 42]. Groups of related queries can be discovered by clustering queries using their related data in query logs. The clusters can then be used to improve search engines in several aspects. For example, search engines such as Lycos, Altavista, and AskJeeves, recommend related queries to the query submitted by a user. The related queries are computed by running query clustering processes. However, there is not much public information on the methods they use to do so.

A central problem that arises is how to represent the information needs represented by a query. Queries themselves, as lists of keywords, are not always good descriptors of the information needs of users. One reason for this is the ambiguity carried by polysemic words. On the other hand, users typically submit very short queries to the search engine, and short queries are more likely to be ambiguous. In order to formulate effective queries, users may need to be familiar with specific terminology in a knowledge domain. This is not always the case: users may have little knowledge about the information they are searching, and worst, they could be not even certain about what to search for.

The definition of an adequate way to model semantics of queries and similarity for queries is still an open problem. Query logs can heavily help in doing so. Previous works have proposed models to represent information needs related to queries based on data in query traces. We use this term to refer to the successive submissions of a query (usually by different users) in a period of time, along with the sets of URL's selected for them.

Another inherent problem to the use of query logs is that the clicked URL's are biased to the ranking algorithm of the search engine. The number of preferences on a particular answer depends on the position of the page in the answer list. Each successive page in the list is less likely to be selected by users. An adequate modeling for the preferences of users and for the semantics of queries should incorporate a method for reducing the bias caused by the current ranking produced by the search tool.

Our first example is a model for mining web site queries, usage, content and structure [2, 9]. The aim of this model is to discover valuable information for improving web site content and structure, allowing the web site to become more intuitive and adequate for the needs of its users. This model proposes the analysis of the different types of queries registered in the usage logs of a web site, such as queries submitted by users to the site's internal search engine and queries on external search engines that lead to documents in the web site. The words used in these queries provide useful information about topics that interest users visiting the web site and the navigation patterns associated to these queries indicate whether or not the documents in the site satisfied the queries submitted by the users. This model also provides a way to visualize and validate the web site's organization given by the links between documents and its content, as well as the correlation of the content to the URLs selected after queries.

Our second example is a new framework for clustering query traces [3, 4]. The clustering process is based on a term-weight vector representation of queries, obtained by aggregating the term-weight vectors of the selected URL's for the query. The construction of the vectors includes a technique to reduce and adjust the bias of the preferences to URL's in query traces. The vectorial representation leads to a a similarity measure in which the degree of similarity of two queries is given by the fraction of common terms in the URL's clicked in the answers of the queries. This notion allows to capture semantics connection between queries having different query terms.

Because the vectorial representation of a query trace is obtained by aggregating term-weight vectors of documents, this framework avoids the problems of comparing and clustering sparse collection of vectors, a problem that appears in previous work. Further, our vectorial representation of query traces can be clustered and manipulated similarly to traditional document vectors, thus allowing a fully symmetric treatment of queries and documents. This is important since we need to compute similarities between queries and documents for two cases: query recommendation and ranking boosting. The use of query clustering for query recommendation has been suggested by Beeferman and Berger [11], however as far as we know there is no formal study of the problem. Regarding ranking boosting, we are not aware of formal research on the application of query clustering to this problem. For both applications we provide a criterion to rank the suggested URL's and queries that combines the *similarity* of the query (resp. URL) to the input query and the *support* of the query (resp., URL) in the cluster. The support measures how much the recommended query (resp. URL) has attracted the attention of users. The rank estimate the *interest* of the query (resp., URL) to the user that submitted the input query. It is important to include a measure of *support* for the recommended queries (resp., URL's), because queries (URL's) that are useful to many users are worth to be recommended in our context.

The remainder of this paper is organized as follows. Section 2 presents the state of the art on query mining. In Section 3 we present a tool based on queries to improve a Web site. Section 4 shows the query clustering framework and its application to search engines. Finally, in Section 5 we outline some prospects for future work.

2   State of the Art

2.1   Characterizing Queries and User Behavior

Queries, as words in a text, follow a biased distribution. In fact, the frequency of query words follow a Zipf's law with parameter α, that is, the i-th most frequent query has $O(i^{-\alpha})$ occurrences. The value of α ranges from 0.6 [26] to 1.4 [7], perhaps due to language and cultural differences. However, this is less biased than Web text, where α is closer to 2. The standard correlation among the frequency of a word in the Web pages and in the queries is 0.15, very low [7]. That is, words in the content of Web pages follow a Zipf's distribution which order is very different from the distribution of query words. This implies that what people search is different from what people publish in the Web.

Table 1. Query statistics for four search engines

Measure	AltaVista	Excite	Fast	TodoCL
Words per query	2.4	2.6	2.3	1.1
Queries per user	2.0	2.3	2.9	–
Answer pages per query	1.3	1.7	2.2	1.2
Boolean queries	<40%	10%	–	16%

The search engine log also registers the number of answer pages seen and the pages selected after a search. Many people refines the query adding and removing words, but most of them see very few answer pages. Table 1 shows the comparison of four different search engines [29, 37, 33, 34, 35]. Clearly, the default query operation is dominant (in the case of TodoCL only 15% are phrase queries).

In addition, as an empirical study shows [29], the average number of pages clicked per answer is very low (around 2 clicks per query). Our own data shows the same. From navigational studies inside TodoCL we have found that advanced search is not used (but we must have it!), and less than 10% of the users browse the directory[1]. This means that instead of posing a better query, a trial and error method is used. Further studies of queries have been done for Excite [32, 33] and Fast [34], showing that the focus of the queries has shifted the past years from leisure to e-commerce. Other papers are focused in user behavior while searching, for example detecting the differences among new and expert users or correlating user clicks with Web structure [17, 6, 25].

2.2   Usage Mining for Web Site Design

Web site design based in usage mining is also called *user-driven design*. Previous work using Web mining for improving web sites, include the analysis of frequent navigational patterns and association rules based on the pages visited by users. In [10] they studied this in an on-line newspaper, with the main goal of discovering related newspaper sections, from the users points of view. In [18] new approaches are discussed for modeling user sessions and cluster analysis obtained from access logs.

WebSIFT [12] is a Web mining tool created to find interesting rules and patterns in a web site, defining as "interesting" rules and patterns that are new and unexpected. Other tools dedicated to the improvement of web sites using Web mining techniques are [21, 30, 31], most of these focused on improving the navigation (and sometimes the structure) of a web site dynamically and individually for each visitor. Also, [23] presents a method for mining patterns efficiently from access logs, and [40] improves the performance of the internal search engine.

Queries submitted to search engines can be a valuable tool for improving a web site. In [13] a method is proposed for analyzing similar queries on search

---

[1] TodoCL uses ODP (dmoz.org) as Google.

engines. The idea is to find queries that are similar to ones that directed traffic to a web site. This queries can contribute as new words for describing documents in the web site. Another kind of analysis, is the one presented in [2], that consists of studying queries submitted to a site's internal search engine. This approach proposes that valuable information can be discovered by analyzing the outcome of each query, in other words, if the user followed any of the results displayed by the search engine or not, or there was no answer.

2.3   Query Mining in Search Engines

Generic usage mining in search engines is surveyed in [8]. Few papers deal with the use of query logs to improve search engines, because this information is usually not disclosed. The exceptions deal with strategies for caching the index and/or the answers [38, 26, 20, 7] and query clustering as we see next. Recently, [27] weight different words in the query to improve ranking.

Some ranking algorithms such as DirectHit, PageRate [14], and MASEL [42] have included the analysis of query logs. Click-through data is also used by search engines to evaluate the quality of changes to the ranking algorithm by tracking them. DirectHit uses previous session logs of a given query to compute ranks based on the popularity (number of clicks) of each URL that appears in the answer of the query. This approach only works for queries that are frequently formulated by users, because less common queries do not have enough clicks to allow significant ranking scores to be calculated. For less common queries, the DirectHit rating provides a small benefit. Zhang and Dong [42] propose the MASEL (Matrix Analysis on Search Engine Log) algorithm which uses search engine logs to improve image search ranking. Clicks are considered positive recommendations on pages. The basic idea is to extract from the logs, relationships between users, queries, and pages. These relationships are used to estimate the quality of answers, based on the quality of related users and queries. The approach relies in the identification of users of a search engine, a task difficult to achieve in practice.

There is also recent related work on query clustering, and some approaches also consider data in query traces. Wen et al [36] propose to cluster similar queries to recommend URLs to frequently asked queries of a search engine. They use four notions of query distance: (1) based on keywords or phrases of the query; (2) based on string matching of keywords; (3) based on common clicked URLs; and (4) based on the distance of the clicked documents in some pre-defined hierarchy. Befferman and Berger [11] also propose a query clustering technique based on distance notion (3). This approach has limitations when it comes to identifying similar queries, because two related queries may output different URL's in the first places of their answers, thus inducing clicks in different URL's. As queries are short and the number of clicks is low, notions (1)-(3) are difficult to deal with in practice, because distance matrices between queries generated by them are very sparse. Notion (4) needs a concept taxonomy and requires the clicked documents to be classified into the taxonomy as well.

Fonseca et al [16] present a method to discover related queries based on association rules. Here queries represent items in traditional association rules.

The query log is viewed as a set of transactions, where each transaction represent a *session* in which a single user submits a sequence of related queries in a time interval. The method shows good results, but two problems arise. First, it is difficult to determine sessions of successive queries that belong to the same search process; on the other hand, the most interesting related queries, those submitted by different users, cannot be discovered. This is because the support of a rule increases only if its queries appear in the same query session, and thus they must be submitted by the same user. Zaiane and Strilets [41] present a method to recommend queries based on seven different notions of query similarity. Three of them are mild variations of notion (1) and (3). The remainder notions consider the content and title of the URL's in the result of a query. Their approach is intended for a meta-search engine and thus none of their similarity measures consider user preferences in form of clicks stored in query logs. Another approach adopted by search engines to suggest related queries is *query expansion* [5, 39]. The basic idea here is to reformulate the query such that it gets closer to the term-weight vector space of the documents the user is looking for.

3   Improving Web Site Design by Mining Queries

The Web has been characterized by its rapid growth, massive usage and its ability to facilitate business transactions. This has created an increasing interest for improving and optimizing web sites to better fit the needs of its visitors. Its more important than ever for a web site to be found easily in the Web and for visitors to reach effortlessly the contents they are looking for. Failing to meet these goals can result in the loss of many potential clients. In fact, this is an iterative process that can be modeled as in figure 1. Real usability and usage mining can only happen if the site is ubiquitous, that is, can be found easily by search engines first, and by people later.

Web servers register important data about the usage of a web site, this information generally includes visitors navigational behavior, the queries made to the web site's internal search engine (if one is available) and also the queries on external search engines that resulted in requests of documents from the web site.

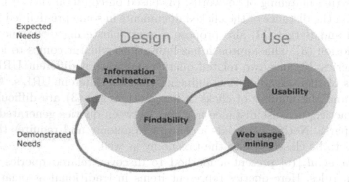

Fig. 1. Causal iterative model for Web design

All this information is provided by visitors implicitly and can hold the key to significantly optimize and enhance a web site.

This section presents a model for mining usage, content, and structure within a web site, centered in queries, to discover new and interesting information regarding ways to improve it [2, 9]. The model also allows to carry out a validation of the site's content organization in relation to the link organization between documents, as well as the URLs selected due to queries. The output consist of several reports and visualizations that make possible for the site's webmaster to decide how to modify the web site, which we do not cover here.

The suggestions generated by the model consist of: adding new contents to the site or broadening the current coverage of certain topics, changing or adding words to the hyperlink descriptions, adding new links between related documents, revise links between unrelated documents, and check the consistency of the content and the URLs selected after queries.

This model works on all types of web sites but is specially useful on large sites, in which the content is hard to manage for the site administrator, by pointing out the possible "problem areas" and ways to solve these conflicts, and improve its organization.

3.1   Model Description

This model develops different usage, structure and content mining tasks. Its input is the web site's access logs and the structure and content of its pages. The structure of the web site is obtained from the links between the documents and the content corresponds to the text associated to each document.

Figure 2 shows the description of the model, which gathers information about internal and external queries, navigational patterns and links in the web site to discover information scent that can be used to improve the site's contents. Also the link and content data from the web site is analyzed using clustering of similar documents and connected components.

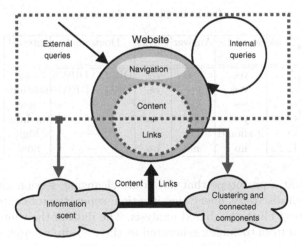

Fig. 2. Model description

3.2   Types of Queries

This model analyzes two different types of queries, which can be found in a web site's access registries, shown in figure 2. These queries are defined as follows:

External queries: These are queries submitted on Web search engines, after which users selected and visited documents in the web site.

Internal queries: These are queries submitted to a web site's internal search box. Additionally, external queries that are specified by the users for a particular site, will be considered as internal queries for that site.

For each query that is submitted in a search engine, a page with results is generated. This page has links to documents that the search engine considers appropriate for the query. The user can choose to visit zero or more documents from the results page, by reviewing the brief abstract of each document displayed, which allows the user to decide roughly if a document is a good match for her/his query.

By analyzing the users navigation within a web site, we can determine different types of pages. We divide the pages in two types: *documents reached without a search* (DRWS) and *documents reached only via queries* (DRQ). Note that DRWS and DRQ are not disjoint sets, because the same page can be reached using a search engine in one session, and without a search engine in another session. The important issue is to register how many times each of these different events occur. This classification is essential for discovering useful information from queries in a web site. Based on the different user actions we define five classes of queries as shown in table 2, where class B distinguishes queries associated to pages only visited by searching. Classes A and B can be further subdivided depending if they came from external or internal queries. All other classes are derived only from internal queries. Classes C' to E are classified either manually or with a thesaurus.

Table 2. Classes of queries

Class	Semantic exists	Answer	Clicks	Document type	Interest
A	yes	yes	yes	DRQ ∩ DRWS	low
B	yes	yes	yes	DRQ − DRWS	medium
C	yes	yes	no	—	low
C'	yes	no	no	—	medium
D	it should	no	no	—	high
E	no	no	no	—	none

We have built a prototype that does data cleansing, session and user identification, pattern discovery, query classification, separation of content and structure, and the text clustering based analysis. The data of the content and structure is extracted from the index generated by the web site's search engine crawler

Table 3. Examples for the different classes of queries

Class A	Class B	Class C	Class C'
admission tests	admission tests	scholarships	evening careers
universities	curriculum vitae	admission	diplomas
chat	bookstores	careers	Spain
employment	universities	sample tests	**Class D**
university scholarships	presentation letter	university chile	vocational test
admission exercises	English tests	law	scholarships Spain
thesis	university scholarships	admission results	compute score

[1], the tool used for the text clustering task was CLUTO [19], and the tool used for query pattern analysis was LPMINER [28]. The internal queries came from the internal search engine log and we considered only external queries from Google.

The prototype also includes a simple thesaurus, created from the user's feedback through a Web interface. This interface allows the user to group queries that have the same meaning. The thesaurus as well as the results of the manual classification of the queries C', D and E are saved permanently for each site, so the process does not need to be repeated for words previously classified.

As an example, Table 3 shows different examples taken from a one-week log from a portal targeted to university students. The log contained more than 56 thousand sessions, 355 thousand visited pages, 19 thousand external queries, and 4 thousand internal queries. On the left of this table, we show the most frequent queries for each class. Some suggestions that appear are to add information on scholarships in Spain or to provide a vocational test. Also, users do not like the answer for *law* or do not find information about night classes because the word *evening* is not used. Class E is not shown as many queries are not relevant for the portal (e.g. *msn* or *emotional intelligence*).

4   Query Clustering Framework

Following Wen *et al* [36], a *query session* consists of one query, a list of URLs, and the URLs the user clicked on. Figure 3 shows the relationships between the different entities that participate in the process induced by the use of a search engine. Our approach focuses in the relationship between queries, which will be defined using query traces, and the preferences/feedback of user about Web pages. The relationship between queries is obtained using the content of selected Web pages, which is indicated by the arrow from Web pages to queries.

The ranking and query recommender algorithms we present in this section consider only queries that appear in the query-log. Both algorithms follow ideas from a technique for building recommender systems called *collaborative filtering* [22]. Given a user searching for information, the idea is to first find similar users (via a k-neighborhood search or clustering process) and then suggest items preferred by the similar users to the current user. Since users are difficult to identify

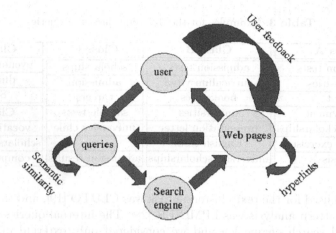

Fig. 3. Relationships of Entities in query logs

in search engines, we aggregate them in queries, i.e., sets of users searching for similar information. Thus the active user in our context is the input query. The items are respectively Web pages and queries in the ranking boosting and query recommendation algorithms.

Later we present experiments to evaluate the quality of our methods using a 15-day query-log from TodoCL. Currently the search engine has approximately 50,000 visits daily. The 15-day log contained over 6 thousand queries which have at least one click in their answers. There were over 22 thousand clicks in the answers, and these clicks were over 18,527 different URL's. The experiments consider the study of a set of 10 randomly selected queries. The 10 queries were selected following the probability distribution of the queries of the log.

4.1   Vector Representation of Query Traces and Query Similarity

In order to compute the similarity of two queries, we first build a term-weight vector for each query. Each term is weighted according to the number of occurrences and the number of clicks of the documents in which the term appears.

Given a query q, and a URL u, consider the popularity $\text{Pop}(u, q)$, that is, the number of clicks for page u when querying q. Let $\text{Tf}(t, u)$ be, as usual, the number of occurrences of term t in URL u. *Stopwords* are eliminated from the vocabulary considered. We define the *vector representation of a query trace*, q, as follows:

$$q[i] = \sum_{URLu} \frac{\text{Pop}(u, q) \times \text{Tf}(t_i, u)}{\max_t \text{Tf}(t, u)}$$

That is, Pop plays the role of *Idf* in the well-known tf-idf weighting scheme for the vector model.

We measure the similarity of two queries as the similarity of their trace vectors using the cosine function. Our notion of query similarity has several advantages. First it is simple and easy to compute. On the other hand, it allows to relate queries that happen to be worded differently but stem from the same information need. Therefore, semantic relationships of queries are captured. Another important advantage is that it avoids sparse similarity matrices which are usually generated using previous notions of query similarity.

4.2   Query Clustering

For the clustering process we used an implementation of a k-means algorithm, the CLUTO software package [43]. Each run of the algorithm computes k clusters, and to determine an adequate value of k we run the algorithm several times.

Many clusters represent clearly defined information needs of search engine users. Figure 4 shows details for three clusters, including the external and internal similarity. These examples, and many others found in our results, show the utility of our framework for discovering information needs related to queries.

Cluster Rank	ISim	ESim	Queries in Cluster	Descriptive keywords
84	0,697	0,015	office rental, rentals in Santiago, real state, apartment rental	office (11, 6%), building (7, 5%), real state (5, 9%), real state agents (4, 2%)
252	0,447	0,007	car sales, cars Iquique, cars used, diesel, new cars,	cars (49, 4%), used (14, 2%), stock (3, 8%), pickup truck (3, 7%), jeep (1, 6%)
497	0,313	0,009	stamp, serigraph inputs, ink reload, cartridge	print (11, 4%), ink (7, 3%), stamping (3, 8%), inkjet (3, 6%)

Fig. 4. Examples of clusters

4.3   Ranking Boosting

The algorithm operates in the following steps. Given an input query q, we find the cluster C to which the query belongs. Then the answer to q are the URL's that have been selected for the queries, ordered according to a rank score that considers two criteria: (a) the similarity of the page to the input query, it is measured using the notion of similarity based in equation 4.1. (b) the support or weight of the URL in the cluster. This is estimated as the popularity of the URL in the cluster. The rank score of a URL u is:

$$\text{Rank}(u) = \text{Sim}(q, u) \times \sum_{q_i \in C} \text{Pop}(u, q_i) \qquad (1)$$

This ranking can then be used to boost the original ranking algorithm, using a linear combination of the two ranks.

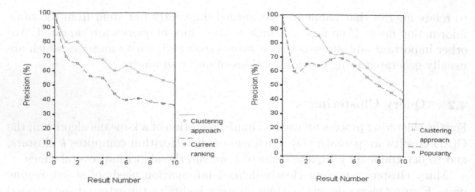

Fig. 5. Average retrieval precision of the proposed ranking algorithm (left) and the query commendation algorithm (right)

We compared our ranking algorithm with the algorithm provided by the search engine. The ranking algorithm of the search engine is based on a belief network which is trained with links and content of Web pages, and does not consider logs. Figure 5 (left) shows the average retrieval precision of the search engine and the proposed algorithm for ranking boosting. Only the top-10 answers of the queries studied are considered. The judgments of the relevance of the answers to each query were performed by different people. The graph shows that our algorithm can significantly boost the average precision of the search engine.

4.4   Query Recommendation

The query recommender algorithm is as follows. Given an *input query* q, again we first find the cluster C to which q belongs. Then we compute a rank score for each query in the cluster. The rank score of each query measures the *interest* of the query to users that submitted the input query. Finally, the related queries are returned ordered according to their rank score. The rank score of a query is based on notions of similarity to the input query and support of the query in the cluster. One may consider the number of times the query has been submitted as the support of a query. However, by analyzing the logs in our experiments we found popular queries whose answers are of little interest to users. In order to avoid this problem we compute the rank score of a query by aggregating the popularity and similarity (to the input query) of the URL's in the answer of the query. Let q be the input query, and let q_i be a query in the cluster C, and let U be the set of URL's in C, then the rank of q_i is:

$$\text{Rank}(q_i) = \sum_{u \in U} \text{Sim}(q, u) \times \text{Pop}(u, q_i) \tag{2}$$

In order to asses the quality of the query recommendation algorithm, we follow a similar approach to Fonseca *et al* [16]. The relevance of each query to the

Q	Ranking	Popularity
dress bride	house of bride	2
	dress wedding	7
	dress bridegroom	6
	wedding cake	3
	wedding rings	4
summer rental	rental apartments viña del mar owners	2
	rental apartments viña del mar	10
	viel properties	4
	rental house viña del mar	2

Fig. 6. Ranking of recommended queries for the input query dress bride

input query were judged by several people. They analyzed if the answers of the queries are of interest to the input query. Figure 6 shows the ranking of recommended queries for the input query *dress bride*. Notice that our algorithm finds queries with related terms, such as *wedding cake* and *bride dress*. Users looking for bride dresses are also interested in wedding cakes. In the other example we find that *Viña del Mar* is the top choice in Chile.

Figure 5 (right) shows the average precision for the queries considered in the experiments. We show precision vs. numbers of recommended queries. In average, we obtain a precision of 70% for the first six recommended queries. Therefore, the suggested queries are relevant to users that submitted the original queries. Our results also show that the rank scheme proposed is much better than the score obtained by considering only the popularity of the queries in the cluster.

5 Concluding Remarks

Our Web mining tool discovers in a simple way interesting words, by visualizing content that is relevant or not for the site. For example, class D queries may represent key missing content, products or services in a web site. Notice that the classification phase might be a drawback at the beginning, but in our own experience, it is almost negligible in the long run, as new queries seldom appear. Further study to evaluate the quality of the results is needed.

We have shown a clustering framework that allows to find groups of semantically related queries. Our experimental results show that our query clustering approach presents good results in two applications for improving a real vertical search engine. We have recently extended these results by adding techniques to unbias the distribution of clicks.

Traditional techniques for document retrieval can be used to handle queries in our framework. As an example, we could implement an inverted index scheme for terms in query traces to efficiently retrieve related queries. Such a scheme could also be used to recommend queries to input queries which do not appear in the logs.

Other measures for the interest of the queries in query recommendation are possible. For example, finding queries that share words but not clicked URL's.

This might imply that the common words have different meanings if the text of the URL's also are not shared. Hence we can detect polysemic words. On the other hand, if words are not shared and the many terms in the URL's are shared, that may imply a semantic relation among words that can be stored in an pseudo-ontology.

We are currently doing additional research in Web query mining to understand queries, find different type of users, as well as using queries to focus Web crawlers. For example, if we represent a given interest by a query vector Q using the vector model [5], a crawler can try to maximize the similarity of a retrieved vector page p with Q. We can extend the idea by representing all past queries in a search engine as a vector Q_t, which is updated using a time based average, with the last queries q by using a moving average: $Q_{t+1} = \alpha Q_t + (1 - \alpha)q$, where α weights past versus current queries.

References

1. Akwan Information Technologies. Myweb search. http://www.akwan.com.br.
2. R. Baeza-Yates. Excavando la web (mining the web, original in Spanish). *El profesional de la información (The Information Professional)*, 13(1):4–10, Jan-Feb 2004.
3. R. Baeza-Yates, C. Hurtado, and M. Mendoza. Ranking boosting based in query clustering. In *Atlantic Web Intelligence Conference*, Cancun, Mexico, 2004. LNCS Springer.
4. R. Baeza-Yates, C. Hurtado, and M. Mendoza. Query Recommendation Using Query Logs in Search Engines. In *Workshop in Web Clustering*, Greece, 2004. Current Trends in Database Technology - EDBT 2004 Workshops, LNCS 3268, Springer.
5. R. Baeza-Yates and B. Ribeiro-Neto. *Modern Information Retrieval*. Addison-Wesley & ACM Press, Harlow, UK, 1999.
6. Ricardo Baeza-Yates and Carlos Castillo. Relating web structure and user search behavior (extended poster). In *10th World Wide Web Conference*, Hong Kong, China, May 2001.
7. R. Baeza-Yates and F. Saint-Jean. A three level search engine index based in query log distribution. In *Proceedings of SPIRE 2003*, LNCS, Manaus, Brazil, October 2003. Springer.
8. Ricardo Baeza-Yates. Query Usage Mining in Search Engines. In *Web Mining: Applications and Techniques*, Anthony Scime, editor. Idea Group, 2004, 307–321.
9. R. Baeza-Yates and B. Poblete. A Web Usage and Content Mining Tool Centered in Queries, 2004, submitted.
10. P. Batista and M. J. Silva. Mining on-line newspaper web access logs, RPEC2-Workshop on recommendation and personalization on e-commerce, Spain 2002.
11. D. Beeferman and A. Berger. Agglomerative clustering of a search engine query log. In *KDD 2000*, Boston, MA, USA, 2000, 407–416.
12. R. Cooley, P. Tan, and J. Srivastava. Websift: the web site information filter system, 1999.
13. B. D. Davison, D. G. Deschenes, and D. B. Lewanda. Finding relevant website queries. In *Poster Proceedings of the Twelfth International World Wide Web Conference*, Budapest, Hungary, May 2003.

14. C. Ding and C. Chi. Towards an adaptive and task-specific ranking mechanism in web searching (poster session). In *Proceedings of the 23rd annual international ACM SIGIR conference on Research and development in information retrieval*, pages 375–376, Athens, Greece, 2000. ACM Press. http://doi.acm.org/10.1145/345508.345663.
15. DirectHit: Main Page. http://www.directhit.com, 1998.
16. B. M. Fonseca, P. B. Golgher, E. S. De Moura, and N. Ziviani. Using association rules to discovery search engines related queries. In *First Latin American Web Congress (LA-WEB'03)*, November, 2003. Santiago, Chile.
17. Christoph Hlscher, and Gerhard Strube. Web Search Behavior of Internet Experts and Newbies, WWW9, Amsterdam, Netherlands, May 15 - 19, 2000.
18. Z. Huang, J. Ng, D. Cheung, M. Ng, and W. Ching. A cube model for web access sessions and cluster analysis, 2001.
19. G. Karypis. CLUTO, a clustering toolkit. Technical Report 02-017, Dept. of Computer Science, University of Minnesota, 2002. Available at http://www.cs.umn.edu/~cluto.
20. Evangelos P. Markatos. On Caching Search Engine Query Results. In Proceedings of the 5th International Web Caching and Content Delivery Workshop, May 2000.
21. F. Masseglia, P. Poncelet, and M. Teisseire. Using data mining techniques on web access logs to dynamically improve hypertext structure, 1999.
22. M. Oconnor and J. Herlocker. Clustering items for collaborative filtering. Technical report, University of Minnesota, Minneapolis, MN, 1999. http://www.cs.umbc.edu/ ian/sigir99-rec/papers.
23. J. Pei, J. Han, B. Mortazavi-asl, and H. Zhu. Mining access patterns efficiently from web logs. In *Pacific-Asia Conference on Knowledge Discovery and Data Mining*, pages 396–407, 2000.
24. Peter Pirolli. Computational Models of Information Scent-Following in a Very Large Browsable Text Collection, In Human Factors in Computing Systems: Proceedings of the CHI '97 Conference. ACM Press, New York, 3-10, 1997.
25. Iko Pramudiono, Takahiko Shintani, Katsumi Takahashi, and Masaru Kitsuregawa. User Behavior Analysis of Location Aware Search Engine, Mobile Data Management, 139-145, 2002.
26. Patricia Correia Saraiva, Edleno Silva de Moura, Nivio Ziviani, Wagner Meira, Rodrigo Fonseca, and Berthier Ribeiro-Neto. Rank-preserving two-level caching for scalable search engines, In Proceedings of the 24th annual international ACM Conference on Research and Development in Information Retrieval, New Orleans, USA, 51-58, September 2001.
27. Andreas Schaale, Carsten Wulf-Mathies, and Sonke Lieberam-Schmidt. A new approach to relevancy in Internet searching - the SVox Populi Algorithm T, arXiv.org e-Print archive, August 2003.
28. M. Seno and G. Karypis. LPMINER: An algorithm for finding frequent itemsets using length-decreasing support constraint. In *Proceedings of the 2001 IEEE International Conference on Data Mining*, pages 505–512. IEEE Computer Society, 2001.
29. C. Silverstein, M. Henzinger, M. Hannes, and M. Moricz. Analysis of a very large alta vista query log. In *SIGIR Forum*, pages 6–12, 1999. 33(3).
30. M. Spiliopoulou and L. C. Faulstich. WUM: a Web Utilization Miner. In *Workshop on the Web and Data Bases (WebDB98)*, pages 109–115, 1998.
31. M. Spiliopoulou, C. Pohle, and L. Faulstich. Improving the effectiveness of a web site with web usage mining. In *WEBKDD*, pages 142–162, 1999.

32. Amanda Spink, Dietmar Wolfram, Bernard J. Jansen, and Tefko Saracevic. Searching the Web: the public and their queries. Journal of the American Society for Information Science and Technology, 52(3), 226-234, 2001.
33. Amanda Spink, Bernard J. Jansen, Dietmar Wolfram, and Tefko Saracevic. From E-Sex to E-Commerce: Web Search Changes. *IEEE Computer* 35(3): 107-109, 2002.
34. Amanda Spink, Seda Ozmutlu, Huseyin C. Ozmutlu, and Bernard J. Jansen. U.S. Versus European Web Searching Trends. SIGIR Forum 26(2), 2002.
35. Todocl - Todo Chile en Internet. http://www.todocl.cl/, 2002.
36. J. Wen, J. Mie, and H. Zhang. Clustering user queries of a search engine. In *Proc. at 10th International World Wide Web Conference*. W3C, 2001.
37. Dietmar Wolfram. A Query-Level Examination of End User Searching Behaviour on the Excite Search Engine. Proceedings of the 28th Annual Conference Canadian Association for Information Science, 2000.
38. Y. Xie, and D. O'Hallaron, Locality in Search Engine Queries and Its Implications for Caching, Infocom 2002.
39. J. Xu and W. B. Croft. Improving the effectiveness of information retrieval with the local context analysis. *ACM Transaction of Information Systems*, 1(18):79-112, 2000.
40. G-R. Xue, H-J. Zeng, Z. Chen, W-Y. Ma, and C-J. Lu. Log Mining to Improve the Performance of Site Search, 1st Int. Workshop for Enhanced Web Search (MEWS 2002), Singapore, Dec 2002, IEEE CS Press, 238-245.
41. O. R. Zaiane and A. Strilets. Finding similar queries to satisfy searches based on query traces. In *Proceedings of the International Workshop on Efficient Web-Based Information Systems (EWIS)*, Montpellier, France, September, 2002.
42. D. Zhang and Y. Dong. A novel web usage mining approach for search engines. *Computer Networks* 39(3): 303-310, April 2002.
43. Y. Zhao and G. Karypis. Comparison of agglomerative and partitional document clustering algorithms. In *SIAM Workshop on Clustering High-dimensional Data and its Applications*, 2002.

BuddyNet: History-Based P2P Search

Yilei Shao and Randolph Wang

Computer Science Department, Princeton University, NJ 08544, USA
{yshao,rywang}@cs.Princeton.edu

Abstract. Peer-to-peer file sharing has become a very popular Internet application. P2P systems such as Gnutella and Kazaa work well when the number of peers is small. Their performances degraded significantly when the number of peers scales. In order to overcome the scalability problem, numerous research groups have experimented with different approaches. We conduct a novel evaluation study on Kazaa traffic focusing on the interest-based locality. Our analysis shows that strong interest-based locality exist in P2P systems and can be exploited to improve performance. Based on our findings, we propose a history-based P2P search algorithm and topology adaptation mechanism. The resulting system naturally clusters peers with similar interests to each other and greatly improves the efficiency for searching. We test our design through simulations; the results show significant reduction in total system load and large speedup in search efficiency compared to random walk and interest shortcut schemes. In addition, we show that our system is more robust under dynamic situations.

1 Introduction

A decade after its birth, the Internet continues to deliver rapid growth and evolution in surprising ways. Peer-to-Peer (P2P) networks have become one of the fastest growing Internet applications [15] from the first introduction of Napster in 1999. Recent studies have shown a dramatic shift of the Internet traffic away from HTML pages to multimedia files shared in a P2P fashion. A March 2000 study at the University of Wisconsin found that the bandwidth consumed by Napster had surpassed the HTTP bandwidth [21]. Two years later, a University of Washington study showed that P2P file sharing dominates the campus network, consuming 43% of all bandwidth compared to only 14% for WWW traffic [22]. Without any doubt, P2P file sharing has already represented large portion of the Internet information needs and will continue to increase its dominance.

Today's P2P systems can be characterized into two classes. An *unstructured* P2P overlay network, such as Gnutella or Kazaa, builds an unstructured overlay network over the peers. A Gnutella-like system is simple and easy to adapt to dynamic situations when peers join and leave the system. Nevertheless, it is not scalable. When the number of peers increases, the number of messages propagated in this system increase dramatically and the latency to locate the content increases accordingly. Another class is *structured* P2P overlay networks. Most of them are based on the Distributed Hash

D.E. Losada and J.M. Fernández-Luna (Eds.): ECIR 2005, LNCS 3408, pp. 23 – 37, 2005.

Table (DHT) abstraction [6, 11, 12, 13, 14] . A DHT system organizes peers into a well-defined structure and controls the data placement and overlay topology. DHT's deterministic content locating and routing solve the scalability problem. However, DHTs require great effort to incorporate query models for keyword search [16].

The simplicity and adaptive features of unstructured overlay systems are very appealing for real-world P2P applications. The only obstacle is its scalability. Freely evolved P2P systems have shown tremendous similarity with social networks. User interactions and activities in P2P systems exhibit "small world" phenomena. [7,8,10]. We believe that there is a way we can utilize these characteristics to make unstructured overlay systems scalable. Our design philosophy originates from a simple observation: If a peer has satisfied a large percentage of queries originating from another peer, this peer is more likely to satisfy future queries from the same peer. Looking at real-life experiences, we can see this simple observation being exemplified in various social contexts: people continue buying goodies from their favourite stores, people rent movies following the same reviewer's recommendation and on Ebay [20], people bookmark their favourite sellers, etc. We also see that such interest-based localities are being harvested for all purposes: Retailers are diligent at sending catalogue to their past customers, book clubs periodically select new books for their customers based on their pervious purchases, web pages become more and more personalized. If P2P systems have so much resemblance with social networks, it may also be true that interest-based locality exists in P2P systems.

This simple observation sounds compelling, but to the best of our knowledge, there is no study that has proved its validity. We conduct a novel evaluation study on Kazaa traffic focusing on the interest-based locality property. Our analysis validates our observation and shows us how to harvest the interest-based locality to improve performance.

Based on our findings, we propose a history-based search algorithm and a self-organizing topology adaptation mechanism, called BuddyNet. The proposed system has two desirable features. First, BuddyNet is a loose structure on top of the underlying overlay; it does not impose any constraints on data placement and topology. As a result, it does not affect the correctness of the underlying system; it only tries to improve the performance of the system. Second, the information kept at each peer directly benefits that peer. Peers do not need to keep arbitrary information or perform extra operations for the common good. This conforms to each peer's selfish behavior [8].

We discuss our evaluation study in section 2, system design in section 3, simulation model in section 4 and its performance in section 5. We conclude our work in section 6 and compare it with some related work in section 7.

2 Does Interest-Based Locality Really Exist?

It has long been speculated that interest-based locality existed in P2P systems. Different schemes were proposed to harvest this kind of locality. [2, 5] However, to the best of our knowledge, there is no study performed on real world trace to validate this speculation. In this section we describe an evaluation study performed on a recently collected Kazaa trace and focus on the interest-based locality exhibited in this dataset. We show that our observation is backed by a sound proof.

We use data collected in [4]. The data collection process is as follows: A caching server is installed at the border between the local Kazaa user base of a large ISP and the Internet cloud. For each TCP connection, for both directions (in and out), a Layer 4 switch inspects the first few packets to detect Kazaa download traffics. If download traffic is detected then the switch redirects it through the caching server. Thus the caching server is able to log all downloads performed by local Kazaa users. The data collection period lasts for a year. There are no significant changes in traffic characteristics during this period. Therefore we use a part of the dataset for our analyses below. Table 1 summarizes the main characteristics of the collected data. *Consumer* describes a node that initiates download sessions. *Provider* describes a node that satisfies the query and provides the file for downloading. We use *peer, node* and *user* interchangeably in following sections.

Table 1. Characteristics of the collected Kazaa trace

Data collection period	2/5/03—2/11/03
Number of download sessions	$1.2 * 10^6$
Number of unique files	~130,000
Number of consumers	>90,000
Number of providers	>190,000
Bytes transferred	~6TB

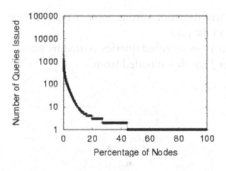

Fig. 1. User activity distribution   **Fig. 2.** User interaction distribution

Figure 1 shows the activity distribution of the peers. Y-axis shows the number of downloads for each user. On X axis, users are ordered in decreasing order of the number of downloads they initiate. Logarithmic scale is used on Y-axis.

The activity levels for different users are widely varied. With few users issuing as many as 10,000 requests, about 90% of the users issuing less than 10 requests. Who answers these queries? Does a user get data from a large group of random users or does it always get data from a small group of focused users?

We further look into how many different users a user actually gets data from. We plot the number of users that a user has downloaded data from over the user name space in figure 2. Logarithmic scale is used on Y-axis. From the graph, we see that more than 75% of the users have their queries satisfied by a single user. Over 85% of the users only need to keep two other users in their address book. About 95% of the users can satisfy their queries by asking less than 10 other peers. On the other hand, there are few users that get data from more than 100 other users.

From figure 2, we conclude that users can be classified into two categories. Users in the first category have focused interests and get data from a small group of other users. Recognizing their buddies and establishing direct links to them will most likely satisfy their future needs. Users in the second category have general interests and get data from a wide range of other users. It is not wise to keep direct links to all the peers that have answered its past queries. It is space inefficient to keep all of them in the address book and bandwidth consuming to ask all of them when future queries come. For users with general interests, we need to distinguish those buddies that have the highest probabilities to satisfy their future queries.

For each node, the probability that it will download from a node again if this node has satisfied N queries in the past is calculated as follows:

$$P(j,N) = \frac{\sum_{i \in G(j)} V(j,i,N+1)}{\sum_{i \in G(j)} V(j,i,N)} \qquad (1)$$

$$V(j,i,N) = \begin{cases} 1 & T(j,i) \geq N \\ 0 & T(j,i) < N \end{cases}$$

P(j,N) denotes the probability that peer *j* will download from another peer if peer *j* has downloaded *N* times from the same peer in the past.

T(j,i) denotes the number of times that peer *i* has satisfied queries issued by peer *j*.

G(j) represents the group of peers that peer *j* has downloaded from.

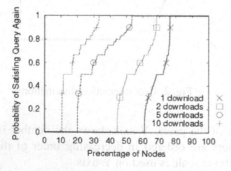

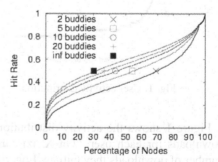

Fig. 3. Probability of satisfying query again   **Fig. 4.** Hit rate using different buddy list size

We plot the probability of satisfying query again in Figure 3. X-axis extends over the user name space. Y-axis shows the probability of satisfying query again. From the curve representing 1 past download (right most curve), when Y equals to 0.5, X is approximately 70%. It means that 30% of the users (from 70% to 100% on X-axis) will download from the same peer again with probability higher than 0.5. When there are 2 past downloads, about 50% of the users will download again with probability higher than 0.5. With more and more downloads in the past, such as 5 to 10 downloads, the probability to download again increases accordingly. With 10 downloads in the past, about 65% of the user will download from the same user again with probability 1. This result indicates that history information can help us identify those users that have the highest probability to satisfy future queries.

Until now, we prove the soundness of our observation. We demonstrate that higher number of past downloads is a good indication for peers that have high probability to download from in the future. We propose a history-based search algorithm and topology adaptation scheme based on our findings. We let every peer keep direct contacts to peers that have highest probabilities to answer future queries. We call these peers its *buddies*. Peers consult their buddies first when they issue queries. The next question is how many buddies a node should keep? If it is too small, frequent insertion and deletion may occur when the actually number of buddies exceed the size of the list. If it is too big, it not only takes space at user side, but also consumes a lot of bandwidth when using these direct links to locate content. We need to find a suitable size that maintains the balance between these two ends. We perform following experiment on the trace. We first selected from the trace those nodes that issued at least 10 queries in the whole period. We make every node keep a buddy list with maximum size N. The least recently used (LRU) entry is replaced when the list is full. We test value 2, 5, 10 and 20 for N. We also test a special case where N equals to infinite, which means a node can keep as many buddies as needed. If a node in the buddy list satisfies a new query, we call it a "hit". We plot the hit rate over the user name space in figure 4.

From figure 4, we see that with as few as two buddies in the list, nodes start to get benefit. Median hit rate is over 0.3, which means 30% of all the requests are satisfied by asking the two buddies. For the rightmost 10% of the nodes, the hit rates are over 0.8. The bigger the list size, the higher the hit rate. With list size equal to 20, the curve is very close to the optimal curve. We choose list size of 10 for our system. It not only provides decent hit rate, but also is small enough to add only negligible overhead.

3 System Design

From our analyses in section 2, we show that interest-based locality exist in Kazaa traffic. Queries should be directed to a focused set of nodes instead of flooding to all the nodes. We propose a history-based scheme to meet this goal. With very little bookkeeping of the past query statistics, each node is able to identify a subset of nodes that can satisfy its future queries with high probability. Furthermore, peers cluster together by their mutual interests as more and more queries are issued in the system.

3.1 Buddy Net Architecture

We add an additional layer on top of the peer-to-peer system's overlay. We call it BuddyNet. Besides keeping the links to their neighbors in the original overlay, peers also keep links to their buddies. Buddies are selected based on past query statistics. BuddyNet forms a loose overlay on top of the original unstructured overlay. The goal of the BuddyNet architecture is to let each peer contact those peers that have the highest probability of answering its future queries via these links, therefore decrease the system load and shorten the hop-by-hop delay. Furthermore, we adopt the one-hop replication technique into the BuddyNet architecture. The one-hop replication scheme used by Chawathe et al. [3] lets each node actively maintain an index of the content for each of its neighbors. We believe that instead of maintaining indexes for its neighbors, it is more appropriate for a peer to maintain indexes for its buddies. Storing indexes of neighbors' content requires a peer to maintain arbitrary data for the common good, while storing indexes of its buddies' content is directly self-beneficial.

Figure 5(a) shows the original unstructured overlay network. Peers communicate with each other via their overlay links. Figure 5(b) depicts two BuddyNet links for the top-left node. When this node issues a query, it tries to locate the content via BuddyNet links first. If the content is not found, the query is propagated in the system through the underlying overlay links. Figure 5(c) shows that of the two BuddyNet links, one link is in fact an index link (shown in bold), which means the top-left node keeps the index of the bottom-right node.

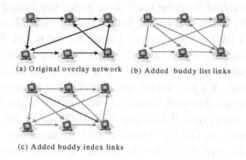

(a) Original overlay network   (b) Added buddy list links

(c) Added buddy index links

Fig. 5. BuddyNet architecture

3.2 Buddy List

Every node in the system keeps track of past query statistics by keeping a buddy list. The buddy list is a linked list. Every entry in the list is a tuple of (nodeID, responseCount). The buddy list is sorted based on reponseCount and the age of the entry.

Whenever a node receives a response for its query, it checks its buddy list to see whether that responding node is in the list. If it is in the list, it increases the response count of that node and re-inserts it into the list. If it is not in the list, a new entry is created as (nodeID, 1) and inserted into the list. If buddy list reaches its capacity, the oldest tuple with the lowest response count is removed. Figure 6 illustrates the insertion and deletion process of buddy list with an example.

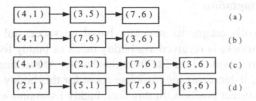

Fig. 6. Insertion/deletion for buddy list, size=4 : a) Before b) After receiving a response from node 3 c) After receiving a response from node 2   d) After receiving a response from node 5

For different search methods, the buddy selection process may be slightly different. For a random walk scheme, we could insert the first response that comes back. For a flooding method, we could choose a response to insert randomly from all the responses received. We can also insert all the responses into the list. Currently, we insert the first response into the buddy list. We explain how the buddy list adapts to load imbalance in a later session.

For any replacement algorithm, the main concern is whether the workload shows characteristics of sequential access. In our case, if a node continues receiving responses from a large number of peers randomly, its buddy list will constantly add new entries and expire old entries. We show in our simulation that after a short warm-up period, the buddy list becomes stable. Newly created entries only affect the head of the list. The tail of the list is relatively stable with buddies having high response count.

3.3 Buddy Index

Besides the buddy list, every node also keeps indexes for a subset of nodes. In order for node A to keep node B's index, node B must satisfy two requirements. First, node B must be in node A's buddy list at present. Second, node B must be in node A's buddy list for long enough time.

We checkpoint the buddy list at fixed interval. At every checkpoint, a special procedure is invoked to check and update the status of the buddy list and request the index from its buddies if needed. For every node in the buddy list, it checks whether it was also in the buddy list at the last checkpoint. If it was and we do not already have its index, an INDEX_REQUEST message is sent to the node. Upon receiving the INDEX_REQUEST message, the node sends its local index. We log the status of the buddy list to be used at the next checkpoint. When a node is removed from the buddy list, its index is also purged.

After the first transfer of the index, nodes periodically exchange indexes in an incremental fashion. An incremental index transfer can also be triggered when a peer finds out that its copy of a buddy's index is out-of-date by an incorrect response to its query or failed downloads.

Transferring indexes among peers can be an expensive operation. If it happens often, it will increase system load and cause the system to perform badly. We believe that since a peer only shares its index with peers that have similar interests, its buddy list will become stable after a short warm-up period. Transfers of indexes among peers will be very infrequent and utilize only a small fraction of available system resource. Our simulation result supports this hypothesis.

3.4 Dynamic Adaptation

BuddyNet dynamically adapts its structure based on successful or failed query response. When a response is received via buddy index or buddy list, the peer will subsequently attempt to download the file from this buddy. At this time, if it finds out that this buddy is down, it decreases the response count for this buddy in its buddy list and re-inserts it at the correct position. In this way, buddy list monitors the stability of the buddies. Under dynamic situations when nodes join and leave frequently, using the buddy list can shield peers from the instability of the network. It also prevents popular nodes from being overloaded. If a lot of nodes contact the popular node via their buddy links, the popular node can choose not to respond to some of the queries. The requesting nodes will treat this node as down and move it to a lower priority position in its buddy list and send queries to other buddies in its buddy list. Load balance is thus achieved.

3.5 Search Algorithm

A query is propagated in our system as follows:

When a node issues a query, it first checks its buddies' indexes kept locally. If the content is not found, it asks all the nodes in its buddy list by sending out a QUERY message with TTL equal to 1 to each of them. If no node in its buddy list responds to the query, it performs a random walk on its neighbors to locate the content.

Upon receiving a query, each peer checks its local storage to see whether it can satisfy the query. If it has the content, a RESPONSE message is sent back. If the content is not found in its local storage, it checks its buddy index. If one buddy's index satisfies the query, a RESPONSE message is sent back on behalf of that buddy. If it fails, the node uses a random walk to forward the query as long as the TTL of the message is greater than zero.

Sending extra messages to peers in the buddy list is only used at the query-originating node, not at intermediate nodes. In this way, even in the worst case, a single query will only generate as many extra messages as the size of the buddy list (we choose it to be 10) compared to the random walk scheme. We do not require any node in the system to take extra responsibility to delegate queries for others.

4 Simulation Model

In this paper, we use a trace-driven simulator on a subset of the dataset described in pervious sections. We randomly select 2,000 users who issue more than 10 queries in the trace. We filter out the sub-trace that contains only queries initiated by these users. There are 23,262 queries issued in total. There are 7,091 providers that supply the data. We now describe some basic features of the simulator.

Our simulator proceeds by having peers issue queries sequentially. At any time, a peer i in the network may be actively issuing queries, responding to queries or down. Upon issuing a query, a peer waits for incoming responses. Since we are interested in relative system load and average path length to locate the content, not absolute time, having queries executed in sequential order does not affect the correctness of our performance evaluation.

Freely evolving P2P networks have been shown to exhibit power-law network characteristics [18]. Hence, peer degrees in the simulation are governed by a power-law distribution. Upon joining the network, a peer connects to a node i with probability $\dfrac{d_i}{\sum_{j \in N} d_j}$, where N is the set of nodes currently in the network and d_i is the node degree of peer i. Every peer in the system maintains a minimal degree. Figure 7 shows the distribution of node degree for the simulated overlay network of 9,091 nodes with minimal degree equal to 4. Both X and Y-axes are log scaled

Figure 8 shows the content distribution of the simulated system. For each individual file in the system, we count how many peers possess a copy of the file. We plot the number of copies for each file. We see that in the simulation, file distribution is governed by a Zipf distribution. We assume a pool of N peers, and each peer has a certain probability of being online, assigned based on the statistics collected in [8].

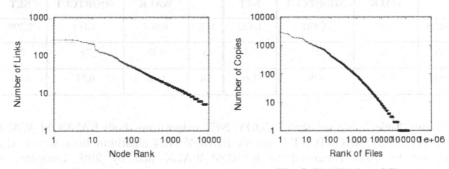

Fig. 7. Distribution of node degrees   **Fig. 8.** Distribution of files

5 Performance Evaluations

5.1 Performance Comparisons

In order to compare the performance of our algorithm with other search algorithms, we look at the following metrics:

1) Msg/query (M/Q): The average number of messages propagated throughout the system for each query, which represents the system load. Whenever a node receives a message, we increase the total number of messages in the system by one. If a message is seen by seven nodes, it will be counted seven times using our metric.

2) Path length (PL): The average hop counts to reach the first response for a query.

3) Success rate (SR): The percentage of queries that have gotten responses.

We compare the performance of following three search algorithms.

1) RANDOM_WALK: Query is forwarded to a randomly chosen neighbor until the first response is received. Originating peer sends out 16 walkers at a time with the TTL equal to 1024.

2) INTEREST_SHORTCUT: Nodes use the interest-based shortcuts scheme [5]. Peers keep shortcuts to other nodes that have similar interest.

3) BUDDY_NET: Peers keep track of past query history, including the buddy list and the buddy index, and perform history-based search during query propagation.

5.1.1 Baseline Performance Comparison

In the base line case, we assume all the nodes are always active and respond to all the queries that they receive. We discuss performance comparison under dynamic situations later. We run the simulator for the first 10,000 queries to warm up and record the result for query 10,001 to 20,000.

Table 2. Baseline performance comparison   Table 3. Performance under dynamic situations

	RANDOM WALK	INTEREST SHORTCUT	BUDDY NET		RANDOM WALK	INTEREST SHORTCUT	BUDDY NET
M/Q	3,842	1,370	1,122	M/Q	6,607	4,419	2,299
PL	88	31	28	PL	139	78	26
SR	0.97	0.98	0.98	SR	0.88	0.87	0.92

From Table 2, we see that BUDDY_NET outperforms both RANDOM_WALK and INTEREST_SHORTCUT Using the BUDDY_NET algorithm, the system load is reduced by 70% compared to RANDM_WALK and by 20% compared to INTEREST_SHORTCUT. BUDDY_NET also achieves a lower average path length.

5.1.2 Performance Under Dynamic Situations

In this section, we discuss the effects of participation dynamics. In the real world, peer-to-peer systems are highly dynamic, with nodes joining and leaving constantly. Dynamics can affect both the system load and the latency to locate the content. However, BuddyNet adapts to participation dynamics. Short-living nodes are more likely to age out, and stable nodes are more likely to accumulate higher response counts and stay in the list. Therefore, the buddy list is also an indicator of node stability. When a peer asks its buddies about a query, it is more likely to reach a responsive node. The BuddyNet algorithm greatly reduces the scope of query propagation. A query is more likely to be resolved within a small group of nodes; therefore, the dynamic behaviour at other nodes will not affect the query.

In Table 3, we show the simulation result under dynamic situations. We use the same setting as in last section, but assign each peer's uptime based on the uptime distribution in [8].

We see that in dynamic situations where nodes join and leave frequently, both RANDOM_WALK and INTEREST_SHORTCUT schemes degrade significantly. Both schemes generate significantly more messages; have longer path length and their success rates are dropped. On the contrary, BUDDY_NET still provides reasonable performance. We believe this is the contribution of the dynamic adaptation mechanism in BuddyNet system. It successfully shields nodes from the instability in the network and achieves robustness against participation dynamics.

5.2   Analysis of History-Based Algorithm

Our proposed system achieves its effectiveness by keeping track of past query history. However, keeping states in each node and exchanging information among nodes may be expensive. In the following section, we show that in our system we achieve good performance with every node keeping very small amount of history information. In addition, the information exchange among nodes happens infrequently and uses a very small fraction of the available system bandwidth. In this session, we refer to the simulation setting in section 5.1.1.

5.2.1   Effect of Keeping History Record
Every node in the system keeps two kinds of history information. First is the buddy list, which is a linked list that keeps track of its buddies. In our simulation, we choose the maximum size of the list to be 10, which yields very good performance. The second part is the buddy index. If peer A has stayed long enough in peer B's buddy list, peer B will request peer A to send its index to B. Since every node can only hold indexes for nodes in its buddy list, at any time, every node will hold indexes for at most 10 peers. However, if the buddy list is not stable, nodes might end up requesting index from other nodes and aging it out quickly. We show that in our simulation, the buddy list reaches a stable state quickly and transfers of indexes are kept to minimum.

Figure 9 plots the number of cumulative index transfers against the number of queries issued in the simulation. We can see that at the beginning of the simulation, nodes quickly accumulate buddy indexes and gather information for their buddy list. For the first 2000 queries, there are about 100 index transfers in the system. Which means out of the 2,000 consumers, about 5% of the nodes performed index transfers from their buddies. For the 10,000 warm up queries, 408 index transfers incurs. For query 10,001 to 20,000, there are 332 index transfers in total. This equals 0.166 index transfers per node on average. This result assures us that index transfer happens infrequently and its effect to the whole system is minimal.

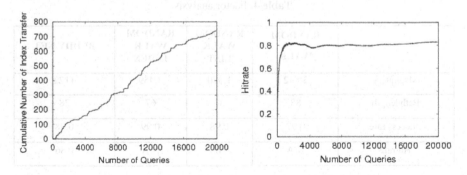

Fig. 9. # Index transfers vs. # queries   Fig. 10. Hit rate

5.2.2   Hit Rate

Now we look at how effective a buddy list is. In our simulation, we count how many queries are satisfied by either checking the buddy indexes kept locally at the originating node or directly asking its buddies. Figure 10 presents the hit rate curve for the 20,000 simulated queries. Within the first 2,000 queries, peers quickly gather information about its buddies and the hit rate continues to increase. At the end of query 2,000, the hit rate has exceeded 80%. For query 2,000 to 20,000, the hit rate remains at around 80%. It is larger than the hit rate we observed from the evaluation study in section II. This is because peers not only benefit from the indexes it kept locally and its buddy list, they also benefit from the indexes kept at its buddies. From this figure, we can see that with only 10 entries in the buddy list, the system achieves very high hit rate. 80% of the queries can be satisfied within one hop. And the high hit rate stays stable, which also indicates that there are few replacements for the buddy list, thus few index transfers are needed.

5.3   Factor Analysis

Our results in section 5 indicate that BUDDY_NET outperforms RANDOM_WALK and INTEREST SHORTCUTS in terms of system load and path length to locate the content. In this section, we pay special attention to how much each individual component of our algorithm contributes to the performance advantage. We show that simple addition of the one-hop indexing or the buddy list is not able to achieve the best performance. It is the *combination* of the buddy list, the buddy index and its dynamic adaptation mechanism that utilizes the distinct characteristics of P2P systems' workload and achieves large performance advantage.

We compare our system with following two algorithms. First, we add buddy list on top of RANDOM WALK and we call it RANDOM_WALK_LIST. This is similar to INTEREST SHORTCUTS [5]. Second, we add one-hop indexing into RANDOM WALK, in this case each node keeps indexes for 10 of its neighbors. We name this method RANDOM_WALK_INDEX.

Table 4 shows the result of these three algorithms under the same simulation setting as in section 5.1.1, with 9,091 nodes running for 20,000 queries. We also list the result for RANDOM_WALK from section 5.1.1 for comparison.

Table 4. Factor analysis

	RANDOM WALK	RANDOM WALK LIST	RANDOM WALK INDEX	BUDDY NET
Msg/query	3,842	1,370	3,459	1122
Path length	88	31	67	28
Success rate	0.97	0.98	0.99	0.98
Hit rate	N/A	0.85	N/A	0.86

Here, we see that adding the buddy list technique to random walk improves the performance. The system load is reduced from 3,842 M/Q to 1,370 M/Q. The average path length is shortened from 88 hops to 31 hops. This simple technique contributes to about 60% of the performance improvement. But as shown in section 5.2.2, this simple scheme does not perform as well in dynamic situations. Adding one-hop indexing to random walk, the system load is reduced to 3,459 M/Q and the average path length is shortened to 67 hops. This represents 10% performance improvement. This is because neighbors of a peer might not share similar interests as the peer; therefore indexing its neighbors content is not very effective. As we have said, queries should be directed to a focused set of peers who share similar interests, such as its buddies. BUDDY NET outperforms both RANDOM WALK LIST and RANDOM WALK INDEX.

6   Conclusions

We conduct the first evaluation study about the interest-based locality on a real-world P2P trace. Our analyses show that there is strong interest-based locality in P2P systems and it can be exploited by utilizing the history information of peer behaviors. We have thus proposed a history-based peer-to-peer search algorithm and self-organizing mechanism. We integrate the buddy list, one hop indexing and dynamic adaptation to improve the scalability and performance of Guntella-like systems. Our simulations suggest that these techniques provide significant reduction in system load and large speedup in search efficiency compared to the random walk and interest shortcut scheme. Moreover, our system is more robust at dynamic situations. We have demonstrated that with simple modifications to Gnutella protocol, the scalability problem can be overcome.

7   Related Work

Improving Gnutella-like system's scalability has become a hot research topic. Approaches based on expanding ring and random walk [1], where queries are forwarded to a randomly chosen neighbor, are designed to limit the scope of the queries and avoid the message explosion caused by the simple flooding mechanism. However, it does not outperform flooding scheme in finding rare items.

Kazaa [17] and Gia [3] both adopt super-node based architecture. A super-node takes the responsibility of indexing content located at other peers. When locating content, a peer contacts its super-node first. A super-node may subsequently contact other super-nodes. The super-node approach needs accurate accounting of peers' capacities that are not easy to acquire in real-world systems.

pSearch [9] and SETS [19] utilize techniques from information retrieval systems. SETS organizes peers into a topic-segmented topology, and data placement is strictly controlled. Queries are then matched and routed to the topically closest regions. pSearch distributes document indexes through the P2P network based on document semantics generated by Latent Semantic Indexing (LSI). Because of the controlled data placement and underlying topology, both systems can achieve low search cost.

However, when large portion of data has changed, LSI needs to be recomputed and data needs to be redistributed. This may cause a high maintenance cost.

Freenet [6] is a P2P system built on top of DHT. It utilizes query responses to dynamically adapt nodes' routing tables. Its goal is to make a node specialize in locating sets of similar keys. In order for the scheme to work, every node in the system needs to keep a fairly large routing table with hundreds or thousands of entries. And this information is not directly self-beneficial. Our approach goes the other way. Every node in BuddyNet only needs to keep very little information about its buddies. Our system achieves better performance through each peer's self-benefiting behavior.

More recently, associative overlays [2], and interest-based shortcuts [5] proposed different techniques to improve Gentella's performance based on interest-based locality. Associative overlay forms a guide-rules based overlay on top of Gnutella's network. Every peer participates in some guide-rules based on its interest. Search is carried out within the scope of a guide rule group. Associative overlay is effective, especially in finding rare items. However, it needs human effort to identify which guide rule to participate. Interest-based shortcuts technique keeps shortcuts to nodes that satisfied previous queries. It is similar to our buddy list. We have shown that with only this simple technique, the system does not perform well in real-world situations. Our system combines the buddy list, one hop indexing and dynamic adaptation techniques to utilize the interest-based locality and cluster peers by their mutual interests. We have shown that it is the combination of these techniques that achieves the biggest performance advantage.

References

1. Lv, Q., Cao, P., Cohen, E., Li, K., and Shenker, S. Search and Replication in Unstructured Peer-to-Peer Networks. In *Proceedings of ICS 2002*, June 2002.
2. Cohen, E., Fiat, A., and Kaplan, H. Associative Search in Peer-to-Peer Networks: Harnessing Latent Semantics. In *Proceedings of INFOCOM 2003*, March 2003.
3. Chawathe, Y., Ratnasamy, S., Breslau, L., Lanham, N., and Shenker, S. Making Gnutella-like P2P Systems Scalable. In *Proceedings of ACM SIGCOMM 2003*, August 2003.
4. Leibowitz, N., Pipeanu, M., and Wierzbicki, A. Deconstructiing the Kazaa Network. In Proceedings of *The Third IEEE Workshop on Internet Application*, June 2003.
5. Sripanidkulchai, K., Maggs, B., and Zhang, H. Efficient Content Location Using Interest-Based Locality in Peer-to-Peer Systems. In *Proceedings INFOCOM 2003*, March 2003.
6. The Free Network Project. In *http://freenet.sourceforge.net*, 2001
7. Krishnamurthy, B., Wang, J., and Xie, Y. Early Measurements of a Cluster-based Architecture for P2P Systems. In *Proceedings of ACM SIGCOMM Internet Measurement Workshop 2001*, November 2001.
8. Sariou, S., Gummadi, P., and Gribble, S. A Measurement Study of Peer-to-Peer File Sharing Systems. In *Proceedings of MMCN 2002*, January 2002.
9. Tang, C., Xu, Z., and Dwarkadas, S. Peer-to-Peer Information Retrieval Using Self-Organizing Semantic Overlay Networks. In *Proceedings of SIGCOMM 2003*, August 2003.
10. Gummadi, K., Dunn, R., Saroiu, S., Gribble, S., Levy, H., and Zahorjan, J. Measurement, Modeling, and Analysis of a Peer-to-Peer File-Sharing Workload. Appeared in *Proceedings of SOSP-19*, October 2003.

11. Ratnasamy, S., Francis, P., Handley, M., Karp, R., and Shenker, S. A Scalable Content-addressable Network. In *Proceedings of SIGCOMM 2001*, August 2001.
12. Stoica, I., Morris, R., Karger, D., Kaashoek, F., and Balakrishnan, H. Chord: A Scalable Peer-to-peer Lookup Service for Internet Applications. In *Proceedings of SIGCOMM 2001*, August 2001.
13. Zhao, B. Kubiatowicz, J., and Joseph, A. Tapestry: An Infrastructure for Fault-tolerant Wide-area Location and Routing. *Tech. Report, University of California, Berkeley*, 2001.
14. Rowstron, A., and Druschel, P. Pastry: Scalable, Distributed Object Location and Routing for Large-scale Peer-to-peer Systems. In *Proceedings of MIDDLEWARE 2001*, November 2001.
15. Konrad, R. Napster Among Fastest-growing Net Technologies, CNET news.com. In *http://news.cnet.com/2100-1023-246648.html*, October 2000.
16. Ratnasamy, S., Hellerstein, J., Shenker, S. Range Queries over DHTs. In *Intel Research Technical Report, IRB-TR-03-011*, June 2003.
17. KaZaA File Sharing Network. KaZaA. In *http://www.kazaa.com/*, 2002.
18. Ripeanu, M., and Foster, I. Mapping the Gnutella Network – Macroscopic Properties of Large-scale P2P Networks. *IEEE Internet Computing Journal, 6(1)*, 2002.
19. Bawa, M., Manku, G., and Raghavan, P. SETS: Search Enhanced by Topic Segmentation. In *Proceedings of SIGIR 2003*, July 2003
20. Ebay Online Marketplace. Ebay. In *http://www.ebay.com*, 2003
21. Plonka, D. Napster Traffic Measurement. Available at http://net.doit.wisc.edu/data/ Napster, March 2000
22. Saroiu, S., Gummadi, K.P., Dunn, R.J., Gribble, S.D. and Levy, H.M. An Analysis of Internet Content Delivery Systems. In *Proceedings of OSDI 2002*, Dec 2002

A Suite of Testbeds for the Realistic Evaluation of Peer-to-Peer Information Retrieval Systems

Iraklis A. Klampanos[1], Victor Poznański[2], Joemon M. Jose[1], and Peter Dickman[1]

[1] University of Glasgow, 17 Lilybank Gardens, G12 8QQ, Glasgow, U.K
{iraklis, jj, pd}@dcs.gla.ac.uk
[2] Sharp Labs of Europe Ltd., Edmund Halley Road,
Oxford Science Part, OX4 4GB, Oxford, U.K
vp@sharp.co.uk

Abstract. Peer-to-peer (P^2P) networking continuously gains popularity among computing science researchers. The problem of information retrieval (IR) over P^2P networks is being addressed by researchers attempting to provide valuable insight as well as solutions for its successful deployment. All published studies have, so far, been evaluated by simulation means, using well-known document collections (usually acquired from TREC). Researchers test their systems using divided collections whose documents have been previously distributed to a number of simulated peers. This practice leads to two problems: First, there is little justification in favour of the document distributions used by relevant studies and second, since different studies use different experimental testbeds, there is no common ground for comparing the solutions proposed. In this work, we contribute a number of different document testbeds for evaluating P^2P IR systems. Each of these has been deduced from TREC's WT10g collection and corresponds to different potential P^2P IR application scenarios. We analyse each methodology and testbed with respect to the document distributions achieved as well as to the location of relevant items within each setting. This work marks the beginning of an effort to provide more realistic evaluation environments for P^2P IR systems as well as to create a common ground for comparisons of existing and future architectures.

1 Introduction

Peer-to-Peer (P^2P) computing is a modern networking paradigm that allows for seamless communication of connected devices at the application level. In P^2P networks all participating processes are made equally capable, by exerting both server and client functionalities [1]. Because of this fact, and also because these networks are built on software, P^2P networking has become a fast-developing research field, since it can, potentially, provide cost-effective, efficient and robust solutions. Like in any distributed system, location and retrieval of relevant information and resources is of paramount importance. Therefore, depending on the application at hand, IR can be thought of as an important component of P^2P -based solutions. This follows from current P^2P applications (file-sharing, transparent interconnection of corporate sites etc. [2, 3]) as well as from potential uses (project collaboration, intelligent information sharing etc.). On the

D.E. Losada and J.M. Fernández-Luna (Eds.): ECIR 2005, LNCS 3408, pp. 38–51, 2005.

other hand, P^2P IR shares the aim of distributed IR, that is to achieve more effective IR than centralised solutions, through successful resource description, location and fusion of results[4].

P^2P IR networks have a number of inherent properties that render their evaluation a particularly hard task. First, they are usually assumed to be very large. Hundreds of thousands of computers participate typically in P^2P file-sharing networks. Researchers deal with such environments by simulating a carefully selected subset of their systems' intended functionality. Additionally, participating nodes are expected to join or leave unexpectedly and, moreover, nodes might leave willingly or simply crash, something which is easily resolvable in a medium-sized distributed system built on higher-end components. This effect is hard to simulate, however it is up to individual proposals to address how they deal with it.

On the IR side, in a P^2P network, the distribution of documents is, to a significant scale, a result of previous location and retrieval. However, this also depends on the application specification and/or on other non-functional requirements that may be imposed (such as copyright considerations etc.). Defining and simulating user behaviour, especially in a very large distributed system, is a complex and intimidating task. Indeed, most published P^2P IR solutions have dealt with this problem indirectly. Instead of simulating user behaviour, people have attempted to reflect it in the document distributions (or testbeds) they have used for their evaluation. The problem with such approaches is twofold. Firstly, there are cases where the distribution of documents does not reflect the application scenario successfully and therefore such evaluation results are hardly conclusive. Secondly, since individual proposals devise and use their individual testbeds, comparisons between different solutions, through their evaluation results, is impossible. Addressing these issues, we contribute a number of realistic testbeds, suitable for the evaluation of P^2P IR systems.

Emphasising on the fact that there may be many, diverse potential P^2P IR applications, we identify a number of possible scenarios and propose methodologies that can be used for the creation of realistic information-sharing testbeds. We have derived our testbeds using TREC's 10G Web collection (WT10g). This collection is an archive of 11,680 Web domains, 1.69 million documents and its relevance assessment comprises of 100 queries. This paper is organised as follows: The next Section is about related work of evaluating P^2P IR systems, which strengthens our reasoning in favour of the adoption of better thought-out evaluation environments. Section 3 presents a number of P^2P IR scenarios, their properties as well as a number of appropriate document testbeds that could address them. Section 4 presents an analysis of the obtained testbeds with respect to their document distributions among the derived peer-collections. Another aspect we have looked at is the distribution of the relevant, to the standard WT10G queries, documents. Finally, in Section 5, we present our conclusions regarding the current work and how this may relate to future P^2P IR systems.

2   Background and Motivation

The potential of P^2P architectures spans a number of possible applications. At the moment, the most popular ones are file-sharing (e.g. Limewire [5]) and distributed storage and retrieval systems (e.g. Freenet [6]). Future applications might include long-distance integrated development environments, virtual offices, P^2P photograph-sharing applications and other sophisticated information-sharing environments. This potential has been realised by the research community and there exist many ongoing projects that attempt to identify and solve related problems.

Properly evaluating research proposals, through simulation, as well as comparing, at least, systems that target at similar application domains, is a major part of research methodology. However, such provisions have not been taken for P^2P IR yet.

The research solutions that have been proposed to date, can be divided in two major fronts: Distributed-Hash-Table(DHT)-based [7, 8, 9] and content-based solutions [10, 11, 12, 13]. Although there has been some overlap between those two trends, the motivation behind them and, consequently, the solutions they propose focus on location and retrieval of different items of information. While a DHT is a convenient structure for location, routing and retrieval of items baring IDs or descriptions consisting of a few keywords, content-based approaches attempt to create informed networks by propagating knowledge and statistics about document collections. In many respects, DHT-based approaches fall within the realm of databases, while content-based approaches are, usually, IR-inspired. The work presented in this paper provides realistic testbeds for the effective evaluation of both types of systems. To the best of our knowledge, this constitutes the first attempt of its kind in the field of P^2P IR.

In this Section, we motivate our study by focusing on the evaluation of three content-based P^2P architectures. A summary of the evaluation characteristics of the following proposals can be found in Table 1. Although following different mechanisms, the main target of the following, cited, systems is to achieve effective resource selection and efficient routing, given a query. Success in achieving these goals translates directly into the retrieval being effective. We will not present the mechanisms these systems use in order to perform IR, since it is not within the intended focus of this paper. Instead we will be discussing their target application areas as well as the experimental testbeds in which they were evaluated.

2.1   SETS

SETS (Search Enhanced by Topics Segmentation) [11] is a P^2P IR system aimed at information-sharing (full-text search) over large, open P^2P networks. The idea behind SETS, and indeed other similar architectures, is to arrange peers in such a way that queries only have to traverse a small subset of the total participants in order to be effectively evaluated. SETS was evaluated in terms of query processing cost, that is the average number of sites that need to be contacted in order a query to be answered. The evaluation setup consisted of three different document sets, the TREC-1,2-AP, the Reuters collection as well as the CiteSeer database. Each site (peer) would hold documents of a particular author, therefore a very small number of mostly similar documents. In an open information-sharing network, however, such a setting could only occur during the network's bootstrapping phase. After that, users (authors in this paradigm), would be expected to search and download documents locally, which in turn would be searchable by others and so on. Therefore, in the end, the peer-collections would grow larger, the distribution of documents across the peers would start following more obvious power-law patterns, and replication of documents, through retrieval, would play a significant part in the effectiveness of any such P^2P IR system.

2.2   A Hybrid, Content-Based P^2P Network

Lu and Callan [12] proposed a hybrid P^2P network for addressing the problem of location, query routing and retrieval in a digital libraries setting. The term "hybrid" is used to distinguish between unstructured P^2P networks, where all nodes behave as equals in absolute terms, from structured ones, where there exists a division between administrative peers (directory nodes) and leaf peers. However, such separation of functionality does not imply a separation in capabilities. The network does not stop being a P^2P one, since at any given time and possibly depending on the nodes' characteristics, any leaf node can become a directory one and vice versa. In this proposal, certain directory nodes were made responsible for holding indices of specific interest areas. In essence, the information providers were clustered according to content, and if they fell within more than one topic of interest, they were assigned to more than one directory nodes.

The authors evaluated their architecture by using TREC's WT10g collection. For these experiments, 2,500 collections (domains) were randomly selected, containing 1,421,088 documents, and then they were clustered. The algorithm used was a soft-clustering [14] one, so that collections that were about more than one topic, got assigned to more than one clusters. By clustering, the authors managed to simulate the organisation of similar topics around their corresponding directory nodes in the network. The measurements taken were precision, recall and the number of messages generated for each query. Even though this testbed is suitable for a digital library scenario, it would be interesting to be able to evaluate this system in different settings, that exhibit different document distributions. Furthermore, the use of clustering might have enforced a more rigid organisation of content than the one observed in real-life digital library scenarios. However, recognising the importance of this testbed, we have included and analysed it in our study too.

2.3   IR in Semi-collaborating P^2P Networks

Same as the above, this system [13] is also a hybrid one. The intended target domain is large, information-sharing networks. The term "semi-collaborating" implies that, although peers do not need to share internal (and possibly proprietary) information, they do need to share information about their shared document collections. The testbed used for the evaluation of this architecture was based on the TREC adhoc collection, comprised of 556,077 documents. Also, the relevance assessments from TREC 6 and 7 were used, featuring 100 queries. The number of peers simulated was 1,500. Because of difficulties to cluster the whole collection using agglomerative approaches, the authors distributed the relevant documents of the topics to a small number of peers. The rest of the documents were assigned randomly to the peer population. Admittedly, this evaluation strategy has a number of serious drawbacks. Firstly, distributing the great majority of the documents randomly to peer-collections, is something unrealistic in an information-sharing scenario. On the other hand by assigning the relevant documents of the queries to some peers, and then by evaluating the system using the same queries, can produce results that are inconclusive and can even be considered as erroneous.

Table 1. An overview of the evaluation environments of three sample P^2P IR proposals. The incompatibilities are evident

Architecture	Collection(s)	Number(s) of Peers	Avg. Num. of Documents
SETS [11]	TREC AP / Reuters / Citeseer	1,834 / 2,368 / 83,947	43 / 44 / 5
HYBRID [12]	TREC WT10g	2,500	568
S-C P^2P IR [13]	TREC Adhoc	1,500	370

2.4   Summary

The evaluation of P^2P IR architectures is a complex task, which is usually done through simulation. However, in many proposed systems, the evaluation testbeds used only reflected a very small subset of possible application scenarios, and sometimes, even unrealistic ones. Hence, some of the results of such evaluations can be thought to be inconclusive. Additionally, the diversity of the evaluation testbeds used in different studies, prohibit the fruitful comparison between, even, systems that aim at similar information environments. For example, it would be interesting to compare the systems presented above in different experimental settings, as this would reveal their strengths and weaknesses at different information-sharing environments. We address these issues by providing a number of realistic testbeds for the evaluation of P^2P IR architectures. We reason in favour of our testbeds' appropriateness based on both the methodology used to derive them (described in the next section) as well as on their document distributions and other properties (presented in Section 4).

3   Testbeds for P^2P IR

By studying existing P^2P networks and various proposed solutions, such as the ones discussed in the previous section, we have identified a number of different features that could potentially affect IR. In this section, we present three high-level scenarios that should exhibit different characteristics, along with suitable testbeds that could be used for P^2P IR evaluation.

In P^2P information sharing networks, like in other distributed IR systems (such as the Web, digital libraries or P^2P file-sharing) each participating node shares documents about a limited number of topics. In other words, it is rather unlikely that random content will be placed into any node of such networks. Moreover, it has been shown that in file-sharing P^2P networks, files are distributed in power-law patterns across participating peers[15]. Therefore, these properties should be preserved in realistic P^2P IR testbeds as well.

Another important aspect of information-sharing environments is content replication. It has been shown by various studies that replication can affect retrieval and that it is even a desirable feature in some cases [16, 17]. Typically, replication occurs as a result of previous querying and retrieval. However, there are cases where retrieving content freely cannot be allowed because of either copyright issues or ethical considerations etc. An example of such a case could be a P^2P photograph-sharing application, where people might want to share their photographs with a limited number of people, family or others, at the time of their choosing, without compromising their privacy. Therefore, we feel that suitable testbeds for P^2P IR architectures should address both situations. Following from that, each of our testbeds comes in two flavours, one with included replication and one without. In this work, the names of the testbeds with replication have been suffixed by *WR*, while those without replication have been suffixed by *WOR*. The testbeds presented in this study can be reproduced by downloading the corresponding definitions from *http://www.dcs.gla.ac.uk/~iraklis/evaluation*.

3.1 Information-Sharing Environments

Currently, information-sharing scenarios are the most popular ones. They reflect settings analogous to the widely used file-sharing P^2P networks like Gnutella [2]. In such settings, the document distribution among the participating peers follows power law patterns [15]. The same is true for the world-wide Web, where there is a power-law distribution of documents within Web domains. In order to address this fact, we chose to represent each peer collection by one Web domain. By following this simple procedure we both get a power-law distribution of the documents in the network and also a large enough number of peers to drive potential simulations (11,680 for TREC's WT10g collection).

A replication effect can be achieved, if desired, by pulling into a peer-collection all other documents, residing at different domains, pointed by the documents of the current domain. In other words we exploit inter-domain links between Web domains in order to achieve meaningful replication in our P^2P IR testbed. The intuition behind this is straightforward: if a Web site links to another external Web page, these must be related in some way. Therefore, it would make more sense to replicate as described than to pull documents randomly into the peer-collections.

This set of testbeds was derived by using the Web domains unchanged and so it was named *ASIS*. Therefore, by following the naming convention described above, for the ASIS case, we have two testbeds: one with replication – *ASISWR* – and one without – *ASISWOR*.

3.2 Uniformly Distributed Information Environments

This testbed can be used for the simulation of systems where the documents are distributed uniformly across the peer population. Such distribution could result from limited I/O capabilities or memory of the participating devices, copyright issues or in the case of simulating IR behaviour in loosely controlled grid networks.

This testbed was obtained by dividing the available web domains into three buckets – under-sized, over-sized and properly-sized – according to the number of documents they share. Then, we moved each excessive document from the over-sized bucket into its closest under-sized domain; closeness defined as the cosine similarity between the page to be moved and the homepage of each of the under-sized domains. Once an under-sized domain or an over-sized domain reached the desired number of documents, they were moved into the properly-sized bucket.

We chose to use homepages because of efficiency reasons as well as because of the fact that homepages are written to be found and read and should, therefore, describe, to some extent, the rest of the Web-site. Some of them do that successfully and others do not; similarly, in a P^2P network we would expect some peers to share content consistently about a number of topics, in contrast to other peers. Using homepages provides us with an intuitive parallelism between Web-sites and peer-collections.

Like the ASIS testbed, this too has two versions: one with replication – *UWR* – and one without – *UWOR*. The replication method used is the same as in the ASIS testbed.

3.3   Digital Libraries

P^2P IR solutions could also aid the effective organisation and retrieval in distributed digital library (DL) environments. This fact has also been addressed in [12], as mentioned in Section 2. In a digital library setting we would, typically, expect to have fewer remote collections than in the other settings described above. However, we would also expect individual libraries to hold more documents, on average, than peer-collections would in an information-sharing scenario. The distribution of documents, therefore, would be expected to follow a power-law pattern, although perhaps not as an extreme one as in an open information-sharing environment.

In order to obtain this testbed, we first selected the 1,500 largest domains. Then, we pulled each one of the remaining domains to the closest of the larger ones. Again, closeness was computed as the cosine similarity between the homepages of the related domains.

Similarly to the testbeds described above, this also comes in one version with replication –*DLWR* – and one without – *DLWOR*.

As mentioned above, our digital library family of testbeds also includes the one generated and used by Lu and Callan in [12], herein referred to as *DLLC*.

4   Analysis and Results

In this Section, we analyse the six testbeds previously created as well as the one used by Lu and Callan [12] (*DLLC*). Our intention is to provide insight and justification for the usefulness of these testbeds, not to make comparisons between any two of them. We first present and discuss the document distributions that we obtained from the various testbeds (Section 4.1). Then, we look at the distributions of relevant documents within the testbeds from two perspectives. In Section 4.2 we look at the number of collections needed to reach 100% recall (for the topics used), while in Section 4.3 we look at precision levels for the same level of recall.

Some of the general properties of these testbeds are summarised in Table 2.

4.1   Document Distributions of the Testbeds

The distribution of the documents in a testbed reflects different possible scenarios, and can indeed affect the effectiveness of retrieval. While creating our testbeds, we took document distributions under consideration.

We already know that there is a power-law distribution of documents within the domains used in WT10g [18]. Therefore, exactly the same distribution of documents holds for the ASISWOR testbed. The imposition of replication via the method described

Table 2. General Properties

Testbed	Num. of Collections	Num. of Documents
ASISWOR	11,680	1,692,096
ASISWR	11,680	1,788,248
UWOR	11,680	1,692,096
UWR	11,680	1,788,041
DLWOR	1,500	1,692,096
DLWR	1,500	1,740,385
DLLC	2,500	1,421,088

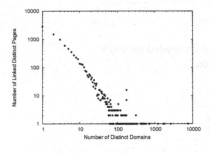

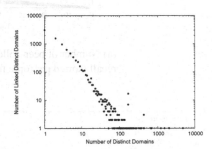

(a) Domain-to-page links distribution

(b) Domain-to-domain links distribution

Fig. 1. The distribution of inter-domain links in WT10g

in 3.1 did not alter this distribution, since the distribution of outgoing domain-to-page inter-domain links is also a power-law one (Fig. 1(a)), just like the domain-to-domain distribution of links is (Figure 1(b)).

Uniformity was imposed on WT10g in order to obtain the UWOR testbed (Section 3.2). Because of the distribution of inter-domain links, however, UWR has lost this uniformity, even though on a small scale. We consider this effect to be adding to the testbed being realistic. We would expect that the document distribution of any initially uniformly distributed network would start skewing, over time, towards power-law patterns. That would happen if free replication was allowed at some point during the lifetime of the network.

Finally, the digital-library testbeds (DLWOR, DLWR and DLLC), also exhibit power-law document distributions. For DLWOR and DLWR testbeds (Section 3.3), the initial largest domain exhibit power-law document distributions. The further agglomeration of the rest of the domains only adds to the asymmetry of the distribution. The reason behind this effect is that the larger domains are bound to be attached to smaller ones since they usually cover a broader range of topics, which are also usually reflected in their homepages. A homepage of a portal, like *Yahoo!* for instance, will typically contain keywords relevant to a very large number of topics. For DLLC, although a soft clustering algorithm was used, the same reasoning should hold.

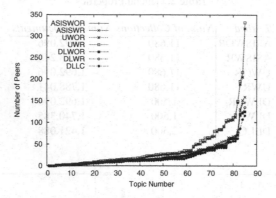

(a) Number of peer-collections needed for 100%
recall (sorted per topic figure).

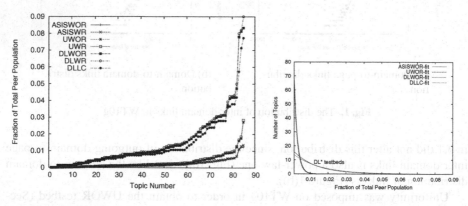

(b) Fraction of the peer population needed for
100% recall (sorted per topic figure).

(c) The distributions of the relevant
documents in the testbeds (Exponential fits of the data).

Fig. 2. The distribution of relevant documents

4.2 The Location of the Relevant Documents (Recall)

In the second stage of our analysis we investigate the location of relevant documents in the testbeds. In particular, we are interested in the number of peer-collections that a query would have to be forwarded to, in order to obtain 100% recall. In other words we need to know how the relevant documents get distributed in the testbeds, for any one topic. Such information may be important to P^2P IR architectures that might want to exploit it in their resource selection and routing algorithms.

Figure 2 shows the distribution of the relevant documents in the various testbeds. In Fig. 2(a), we have sorted the topics according to the number of peer-collections that contain at least one relevant document. It can be seen that in the uniformly distributed testbeds (UWOR and UWR), a significantly larger number of peers need to be reached in order to achieve 100% recall. The rest of the testbeds need a similar number of collection in order to reach the same amount of recall. This might be expected since the uniformity imposed on the UWOR and UWR testbeds means that each collection shares a relatively small number of documents, so there is a higher probability that the relevant documents for some topics will be scattered among a larger number of collections.

In Fig. 2(b) we see the same information, this time presented against the fraction of the total peer population that each topic needs to reach to satisfy 100% recall. From this perspective it can be seen that the DL testbeds need to reach a higher fraction of the population, while the U* and ASIS* testbeds need a significantly lower fraction. This can be explained by the fact that in the DL testbeds we have created a much smaller number of peer-collections (1,500 and 2,500) than in the rest (11,680). This is also reflected in Fig. 2(c), where we have plotted the exponential fits for the *WOR distributions as well as for DLLC. The *WR testbeds follow similar distributions hence they were omitted.

4.3   Coverage of the Topics (Precision)

Following the creation of the testbeds, another major aspect we looked at was the proportion at which topics were represented within the peer collections; in other words, the precision within the peer-collections. We have looked at precision from two different viewpoints[1]. Firstly, for each topic, we considered all the peer collections that had at least one relevant document and measured their average precision, *i.e.* $P_{\text{avg}} = 1/n \sum_{i=1}^{n} P_i$, where n is the number of peer-collections that have at least one relevant document and P_i is the precision as measured by the number of relevant documents over the total number of documents shared in the ith collection. These measurements are depicted in Fig. 3(a). Another way to look at precision was to consider the same peer-collections as one and then measure precision, *i.e.* $P_{\text{alt}} = \sum_{i=1}^{n} r_i / \sum_{i=1}^{n} total_i$, where r_i is the number of relevant documents of the ith collection and $total_i$ is the total number of documents shared by the ith collection. The alternative precision measurements are shown in Fig. 3(b).

The average precision measurements appear to be quite promising as to what a well designed P^2P IR architecture can potentially achieve. Although approximately half of the topics appear to be represented at a level of precision lower than 0.2, the rest follow an exponential increase, which reaches even 1 for one topic in the uniform testbeds. Overall, the uniformly distributed testbeds appear to perform a lot better, in terms of average precision, than the other ones. This can be explained by the fact that their collections share a small number of documents without great deviations. The second best-performing set of testbeds are the ASIS ones, and this is probably because of the cohesion that some domains demonstrate as to the topics they address. Finally, the DL* testbeds follow, whose collections share a larger number of documents.

In Fig. 4.3(b) we present the alternative definition of precision for the testbeds generated. The y-axis is presented in logarithmic scale for increased readability. Again the uniform distributions appear to be exhibiting higher levels of precision, although extremely lower than previously. The ASIS testbeds follow approximately the DLLC

---

[1] By the term "precision" we mean the coverage of specific topics in peer-collections. We do not imply that any actual retrieval took place.

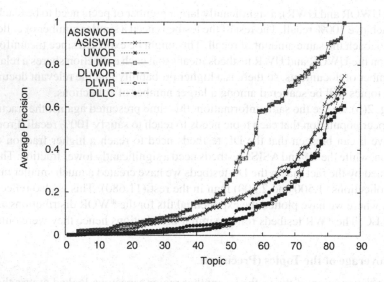

(a) Average precision (sorted per topic figure).

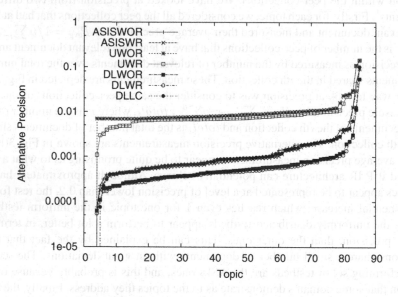

(b) Alternative precision (sorted per topic figure).

Fig. 3. Precision in collections that achieve 100% recall

testbed, while the DLWOR and DLWR appear to be the worst in that respect. It is interesting to note the reason why DLLC appears to have higher precision levels than DLWOR and DLWR. Two explanations can be given for this artifact: firstly, DLLC's collections share less documents in total, and secondly, DLLC was generated by applying a soft-clustering algorithm. Therefore, DLLC should have a better concentration of relevant content within its collection than the other DL testbeds.

4.4   Discussion and Summary

All testbeds described share a number of features. Any of the topics included, needs to reach only a small number of collections in order to be fully met. This fact clearly stresses the need for well informed networks that exhibit effective resource selection and routing. Additionally, a large number of irrelevant documents are bound to reside at the same peers, therefore impeding the local retrieval systems as well as fusion.

Analysing the coverage of all the relevant collections as a single one has the following significance. A system that wants to achieve 100% recall, will have to reach all these collections, for a given topic. At the end of a session, a significant number of results might be returned to the initiator of a query, which will then have to fuse them, before presenting them to the user. Both the large number of peers that will be returning responses as well as the fraction of relevant over the total number of responses can seriously impede effectiveness. Based on the results presented in this study, we believe that, regardless of the retrieval mechanisms used at the peers, the lack of a highly effective fusion technique will have a very negative impact on any P^2P IR application, especially those that require high precision and lower recall.

Summarising, we would like to emphasise on the scenarios targeted by our testbeds and reason towards their usefulness. The ASIS* testbeds are targeted on simulating openly available information-sharing P^2P networks, *i.e.* potential networks and applications where users can retrieve, download and replicate other documents, as well as introduce their own. The reasoning behind this assertion is that, the ASIS testbeds exhibit power-law document distributions, that are found in file-sharing P^2P networks, the Web and elsewhere. Additionally, since we have used the Web domains unchanged, the documents in the deriving collections are bound to be loosely organised on content, *i.e.* they are not randomly allocated. Thirdly, the addition of replication, in the ASISWR testbed, addresses a potentially significant side-effect of information-sharing networks. Lastly, by using the Web domains, we achieve to obtain a relatively large number of peer collections, suitable for adequate evaluation.

The uniform testbeds are suitable for evaluating P^2P IR systems targeted at a different class of information-sharing environments. Such possible application include grid-like environments, where an equal amount of load is imposed on all participating nodes. Other possible scenarios include systems whose peers have limited I/O and memory capabilities (for example mobile devices), and therefore the addition of large numbers of new documents is impossible. Another relevant situation would be where replication through retrieval is not permitted because of various non-functional requirements. We believe that the U* testbeds are suitable for the evaluation of such systems because they incorporate a sufficiently large number of peers, the documents are uniformly distributed across the peer population, but still the documents shared by any peers are loosely related without, however, having been properly clustered.

Finally, the DL* testbeds would be suitable for a number of digital-library instantiations of the P^2P IR problem. These might include P^2P networks that bridge corporate information sites, Internet meta-searching, academic P^2P networks etc. The document distribution in these testbeds follows power-law patterns, as one would expect in the aforementioned scenarios, but the average number of documents shared is significantly higher than the other testbeds. Content consistency has been preserved by having each peer-collection represented by a number of loosely related Web domains.

5   Conclusions and Future Work

Evaluating IR architectures and systems for P^2P networks is a demanding and neglected task. In this paper we address the importance of using realistic document testbeds for the evaluation of P^2P IR architectures, something which has been overlooked by many studies published so far. For this reason, we provide a number of realistic testbeds addressing different application scenarios (summarised in Section 4.4). These testbeds are derived from the TREC WT10g collection, by following different methods of distributing its documents into a sufficiently large number of smaller peer-collections. Subsequently, we analyse our testbeds from a number of different perspectives in order to understand their properties as well as to obtain justified hints on what would be needed by any architecture in order to provide effective and efficient IR over a P^2P network.

From our analysis we draw the following conclusions. Firstly, fusion needs to be seriously looked at if we want to achieve high effectiveness and user satisfaction in future P^2P IR systems. Additionally, the fact that only a small proportion of the total peer-population suffices in order to achieve high recall, is a promising fact with respect to the efficiency of these networks. On the other hand, in order for a system to be able to identify and properly use the resources available, a lot of effort will have to be put both into the content-based organisation of the network as well as into its resource selection and query routing algorithms. Even though these needs have been addressed repeatedly in the literature, we have managed to observe them in a number of different evaluation settings.

There are many ways in which this work can be used and extended. A first step would be to use the testbeds for evaluating existing or newly proposed P^2P IR architectures in order to observe how their effectiveness changes in different environments. The adoption of a set of standard testbeds could provide a strong lead towards benchmarking studies for P^2P IR systems. Additionally, we could start looking at some temporal properties of P^2P networks and their effect on IR. Such properties might be the generation and growth of the network as well as the joining and leaving of nodes. Finally, we could use these testbeds in order to derive a series of stress tests for potential systems. The dynamics of P^2P networks is an area still under heavy research and exploration, without mentioning the effects it might impose on IR.

References

1. Oram, A., ed.: PEER-TO-PEER: Harnessing the Power of Disruptive Technologies. O'Reilly & Associates, Inc., CA 95472, USA (2001)
2. OSBM LLC.: The homepage of gnutella. http://www.gnutella.org/ (2003)

3. Groove Networks: The homepage of groove networks. (http://www.groove.net/) As viewed on March 27 2004.
4. Callan, J.: 5 – Distributed Information Retrieval. In: Advances in Information Retrieval. Kluwer Academic Publishers (2000) 127–150
5. Lime Wire LLC.: The homepage of limewire. http://www.limewire.com/ (2003)
6. Clark, I.: The homepage of freenet project. http://www.freenet.sourceforge.org/ (2003)
7. Rowstron, A., Druschel, P.: Pastry: Scalable, decentralized object location, and routing for large-scale peer-to-peer systems. Lecture Notes in Computer Science **2218** (2001)
8. Hildrum, K., Kubiatowicz, J.D., Rao, S., Zhao, B.Y.: Distributed object location in a dynamic network. In: Proceedings of the Fourteenth ACM Symposium on Parallel Algorithms and Architectures. (2002) 41–52
9. Ratnasamy, S., Francis, P., Handley, M., Karp, R., Shenker, S.: A scalable content addressable network. In: Proceedings of ACM SIGCOMM 2001. (2001)
10. Cuenca-Acuna, F.M., Peery, C., Martin, R.P., Nguyen, T.D.: PlanetP: Using Gossiping to Build Content Addressable Peer-to-Peer Information Sharing Communities. In: Twelfth IEEE International Symposium on High Performance Distributed Computing (HPDC-12), IEEE Press (2003)
11. Bawa, M., Manku, G.S., Raghavan, P.: Sets: search enhanced by topic segmentation. In: Proceedings of the 26th annual international ACM SIGIR conference on Research and development in informaion retrieval, ACM Press (2003) 306–313
12. Lu, J., Callan, J.: Content-based retrieval in hybrid peer-to-peer networks. In: Proceedings of the twelfth international conference on Information and knowledge management, ACM Press (2003) 199–206
13. Klampanos, I.A., Jose, J.M.: An architecture for information retrieval over semi-collaborating peer-to-peer networks. In: Proceedings of the 2004 ACM Symposium on Applied Computing. Volume 2., Nicosia, Cyprus (2004) 1078–1083
14. Lin, K., Kondadadi, R.: A similarity-based soft clustering algorithm for documents. In: Proceedings of the 7th International Conference on Database Systems for Advanced Applications, IEEE Computer Society (2001) 40–47
15. Saroiu, S., Gummadi, P.K., Gribble, S.D.: A measurement study of peer-to-peer file sharing systems. In: Proceedings of Multimedia Computing and Networking 2002 (MMCN '02), San Jose, CA, USA (2002)
16. Lv, Q., Cao, P., Cohen, E., Li, K., Shenker, S.: Search and replication in unstructured peer-to-peer networks. In: ICS, New York, USA (2002)
17. Cuenca-Acuna, F.M., Martin, R.P., Nguyen, T.D.: Planetp: Using gossiping and random replication to support reliable peer-to-peer content search and retrieval. Technical Report DCS-TR-494, Department of Computer Science, Rutgers University (2002)
18. Soboroff, I.: Does wt10g look like the web? In: Proceedings of the 25th annual international ACM SIGIR conference on Research and development in information retrieval, ACM Press (2002) 423–424

Federated Search of Text-Based Digital Libraries in Hierarchical Peer-to-Peer Networks

Jie Lu and Jamie Callan

School of Computer Science, Carnegie Mellon University,
Pittsburgh, PA 15213, USA
{jielu, callan}@cs.cmu.edu

Abstract. Peer-to-peer architectures are a potentially powerful model for developing large-scale networks of text-based digital libraries, but peer-to-peer networks have so far provided very limited support for text-based federated search of digital libraries using relevance-based ranking. This paper addresses the problems of resource representation, resource ranking and selection, and result merging for federated search of text-based digital libraries in hierarchical peer-to-peer networks. Existing approaches to text-based federated search are adapted and new methods are developed for resource representation and resource selection according to the unique characteristics of hierarchical peer-to-peer networks. Experimental results demonstrate that the proposed approaches offer a better combination of accuracy and efficiency than more common alternatives for federated search in peer-to-peer networks.

1 Introduction

Peer-to-peer (P2P) networks are an appealing approach to federated search over large networks of digital libraries. The activities involved for search in peer-to-peer networks include issuing requests ("queries"), routing requests ("query routing"), and responding to requests ("retrieval"). The nodes in peer-to-peer networks can participate as clients and/or servers. Client nodes issue queries to initiate search in peer-to-peer networks; server nodes provide information contents, respond to queries with documents that are likely to satisfy the requests, and/or route queries to other servers.

The first peer-to-peer networks were based on sharing popular music, videos, and software. These types of digital objects have relatively obvious or well-known naming conventions and descriptions, making it possible to represent them with just a few words from a name, title, or manual annotation. From a Library Science or Information Retrieval perspective, these systems were designed for *known-item* searches, in which the goal is to find a single instance of a known object (e.g., a particular song by a particular artist). In a known item search, the user is familiar with the object being requested, and any copy is as good as any other. Known-item search of popular music, video, and software file-sharing systems is a task for which simple solutions suffice. If P2P systems are to scale to more varied content and larger digital libraries, they must adopt more sophisticated solutions.

A very large number of text-based digital libraries were developed during the last decade. Nearly all of them use some form of relevance ranking, in which term fre-

D.E. Losada and J.M. Fernández-Luna (Eds.): ECIR 2005, LNCS 3408, pp. 52–66, 2005.

quency information is used to rank documents by how well they satisfy an unstructured text query. Many of them allow free search access to their contents via the Internet, but do not provide complete copies of their contents upon request. Many do not allow their contents to be crawled by Web search engines. How best to provide federated search across such independent digital libraries is an unsolved problem often referred to as the "Hidden Web" problem.

This paper addresses the problem of using peer-to-peer networks as a federated search layer for text-based digital libraries. We start by assuming the current state of the art; that is, we assume that each digital library is a text database running a reasonably good conventional search engine, and providing individual documents in response to full text queries. Furthermore, we assume that each digital library cooperatively provides accurate resource description of its content upon request. We present in this paper how resource descriptions of digital libraries are used for efficient query routing, and how results from different digital libraries are merged into a single, integrated ranked list in P2P networks. It is worth noting that the general framework described in this paper for text-based federated search of digital libraries in cooperative environments also applies to uncooperative environments, although different approaches are required for acquiring resource descriptions and result merging.

In the following section we give an overview of the prior research on federated search of text-based digital libraries and P2P networks. Section 3 describes our approaches to federated search of text-based digital libraries in P2P networks. Sections 4 and 5 discuss our data resources and evaluation methodologies. Experimental settings and results are presented in Section 6. Section 7 concludes.

2 Overview

Accurate and efficient federated search in P2P networks of text-based digital libraries requires both the appropriate P2P architecture and effective search methods developed for the chosen architecture. In this section we present an overview of the prior research on federated search of text-based digital libraries, P2P network architectures, and text-based search in P2P networks in order to set the stage for the descriptions of our approaches to text-based federated search in peer-to-peer networks.

2.1 Federated Search of Text-Based Digital Libraries

Prior research on federated search of text-based digital libraries (also called "distributed information retrieval") identifies three problems that must be addressed:

- Resource representation: Discovering the contents or content areas covered by each resource ("resource description");
- Resource ranking and selection: Deciding which resources are most appropriate for an information need based on their resource descriptions; and
- Result merging: Merging retrieval results from a set of selected resources.

A directory service is responsible for acquiring resource descriptions of the digital libraries it serves, selecting the appropriate resources (digital libraries) given the query, and merging the retrieval results from selected resources into a single, integrated ranked list. Distributed information retrieval offers solutions to all three problems for the case of a single directory service. We briefly review them below.

Resource Representation. Different techniques for acquiring resource descriptions require different degrees of cooperation from digital libraries. STARTS is a cooperative protocol that requires every digital library to provide an accurate resource description to the directory service upon request [5]. Query-based sampling is an alternative approach to acquiring resource descriptions without requiring explicit cooperation from digital libraries [2]. The resource description of a digital library is constructed by sampling its documents via the normal process of submitting queries and retrieving documents.

Resource Ranking and Selection. Resource selection aims at selecting a small set of resources that contain a lot of documents relevant to the information request. Resources are ranked by their likelihood to return relevant documents and top-ranked resources are selected to process the information request.

Resource selection algorithms such as CORI [2], gGlOSS [6], and the Kullback-Leibler (K-L) divergence-based algorithm [21] treat the resource description of a digital library as a document and use techniques adapted from document retrieval for resource ranking. Other resource selection algorithms including ReDDE [17] and the decision-theoretic framework for resource selection [12] rank resources by directly estimating the number of relevant documents from each resource for a given query.

Deciding how many top-ranked resources to search ("thresholding") is usually simplified to use of a heuristic value (e.g., 5 or 10).

Result Merging. Result merging algorithms can be divided into two categories: Approaches based on normalizing resource-specific document scores into resource-independent document scores, and approaches based on recalculating resource-independent document scores at the directory service.

The CORI and the Semi-Supervised Learning result merging algorithm belong to the first category. The CORI merging algorithm uses a heuristic linear combination of the digital library score and the document score to produce a resource-independent document score [2]. The Semi-Supervised Learning result merging algorithm uses the documents obtained by query-based sampling as training data to learn score normalizing functions [16].

Usually in order to recalculate document scores, the directory service needs to download all the documents in the retrieval results. Downloading documents is not necessary if all the statistics required for score recalculation can be obtained alternatively. Kirsch's algorithm [9] requires each resource to provide summary statistics for each of the retrieved documents. It allows very accurate normalized document scores to be determined without the high communication cost of downloading.

2.2 P2P Network Architectures

As mentioned in Section 1, the activities involved for search in peer-to-peer networks include issuing queries, query routing, and retrieval. Query routing is essentially a problem of resource selection and location. Resource location in first generation P2P networks is characterized by Napster, which used a single logical directory service, and Gnutella 0.4, which used undirected message flooding and a search horizon. The former proved easy to attack, and the latter didn't scale. They also explored very different solutions: Napster was centralized and required cooperation (sharing of accurate information); Gnutella 0.4 was decentralized and required little cooperation.

Recent research provides a variety of solutions to the flaws of the Napster and Gnutella 0.4 architectures, but perhaps the most influential are hierarchical and structured P2P architectures. Structured P2P networks associate each data item with a key and distribute keys among directory services using a Distributed Hash Table (DHT) [13, 15, 18, 19]. Hierarchical P2P networks [8, 10, 20] use the top-layer of directory services to serve regions of the bottom-layer of digital libraries, and directory services work collectively to cover the whole network. The common characteristic of both approaches is the construction of an overlay network to organize the nodes that provide directory services for efficient query routing. An important distinction is that structured P2P networks require the ability to map (via a distributed hash table) from an information need to the identity of the directory service that satisfies the need, whereas hierarchical P2P networks rely on message-passing to locate directory services. Structured P2P networks require digital libraries to cooperatively share descriptions of data items in order to generate keys and construct distributed hash tables. In contrast, hierarchical P2P networks enable directory services to automatically discover the contents of (possibly uncooperative) digital libraries, which is well-matched to networks that are dynamic, heterogeneous, or protective of intellectual property.

2.3 Text-Based Search in P2P Networks

Most of the prior research on search in peer-to-peer networks only supports simple keyword-based search. There has been some recent work on developing systems that adopt more sophisticated retrieval models to support text-based search (also called "content-based retrieval") in peer-to-peer networks. Examples are PlanetP using a completely decentralized P2P architecture [4], pSearch using a structured P2P architecture [19], and content-based retrieval in hierarchical P2P networks [11].

In PlanetP [4], a node uses a TF.IDF algorithm to decide which nodes to contact for information requests based on the compact summaries it collects about all other nodes' inverted indexes. Because no special resources are dedicated to support directory services in completely decentralized P2P architectures, it is somewhat inefficient for each node to collect and store information about the contents of all other nodes.

pSearch [19] uses the semantic vector (generated by Latent Semantic Indexing) of each document as the key to distribute document indices in a structured P2P network. To compute semantic vectors for documents and queries, global statistics such as the inverse document frequency and the basis of the semantic space need to be disseminated to each node in the network, which makes this approach difficult to be extended to uncooperative and heterogeneous environments.

Content-based resource selection and document retrieval algorithms for a single directory service are extended to multiple directory services in [11]. Experimental results demonstrate that content-based resource selection and document retrieval can provide more accurate and more efficient solutions to federated search in P2P networks of text-based digital libraries than the flooding and keyword-based approaches.

3 Text-Based Federated Search in Hierarchical P2P Networks

The research described in this paper adopts a hierarchical P2P architecture because it provides a flexible framework to incorporate various solutions to resource selection and result merging. Following the terminology of prior research, we refer to text-based digital libraries as "leaf" nodes, and directory services as "hub" nodes. Each leaf node is a text database that provides functionality to process full text queries by running a document retrieval algorithm over its index of a local document collection and generating responses. Each hub acquires and maintains necessary information about its neighboring hubs and leaf nodes and uses it to provide resource selection and result merging services to a P2P network. In addition to leaf nodes and hubs, there are also "client" nodes representing users with information requests. Leaf nodes and client nodes only connect to hubs and hubs connect with each other.

Search in peer-to-peer networks relies on message-passing between nodes. A request message ("query") is generated by a client node and routed from a client node to a hub, from one hub to another, or from a hub to a leaf node. A response message ("queryhit") is generated by a leaf node and routed back along the query path in reverse direction. Each message in the network has a time-to-live (TTL) field that determines the maximum number of times it can be relayed in the network. The TTL is decreased by 1 each time the message is routed to a node. When the TTL reaches 0, the message is no longer routed. The initial value of TTL was 6 in our experiments.

When a client node has an information request, it sends a query message to each of its connecting hubs. A hub that receives the query message uses its resource selection algorithm to rank and select one or more neighboring leaf nodes as well as hubs. A leaf node that receives the query message uses its document retrieval algorithm (K-L divergence document retrieval algorithm in our experiments) to generate a relevance ranking of its documents and responds with a queryhit message to include a list of top-ranked documents. Each top-level hub (the hub that connects directly to the client node that issues the request) collects the queryhit messages and uses its result-merging algorithm to merge the documents retrieved from multiple leaf nodes into a single, integrated ranked list and returns it to the client node. If the client node issues the request to multiple hubs, it also needs to merge results returned by top-level hubs.

In this paper we assume a "static" network setting (i.e., fixed topology without node failure) so that we can focus on the solutions to resource representation, resource ranking and selection, and result merging for higher efficiency and accuracy in federated search of hierarchical P2P networks. Previous research has demonstrated that with a simple set of network reorganization protocols, content-based federated search in hierarchical P2P networks is robust in terms of unexpected hub failures [14].

3.1 Resource Representation

The description of a resource is a very compact summary of its content. Compared with the complete index of a collection of documents, resource description requires much less communication and storage costs but still provides useful information for resource selection algorithms to determine which resources are more likely to contain documents relevant to the query. The resource description used by most resource selection algorithms include a list of terms with corresponding term frequencies, and corpus statistics such as the total number of terms and documents provided or covered by the resource. The resource here could be a single leaf node, a hub that covers multiple leaf nodes, or a "neighborhood" that includes all the nodes reachable from a hub. Different methods are required to acquire different types of resources descriptions.

Resource Descriptions of Leaf Nodes. Resource descriptions of leaf nodes are used by hubs for query routing ("resource selection") among connecting leaf nodes. In this paper we focus on cooperative environments where leaf nodes provide accurate resource descriptions to connecting hubs (e.g., STARTS [5]).

Resource Descriptions of Hubs. The resource description of a hub is the aggregation of the resource descriptions of its connecting leaf nodes. Since hubs work collaboratively in hierarchical P2P networks, neighboring hubs can exchange with each other their aggregate resource descriptions. However, because the aggregate resource descriptions of hubs only have information for nodes within 1 hop, if they are directly used by a hub to decide which neighboring hubs to route query messages to, the routing would not be effective when the nodes with relevant documents sit beyond this "horizon". Thus for effective hub selection, a hub must have information about what contents can be reached if the query message it routes to a neighboring hub may further travel multiple hops. This kind of information is referred to as the resource description of a neighborhood and is introduced in the following subsection.

Resource Descriptions of Neighborhoods. A *neighborhood* of a hub H_i in the direction of its neighboring hub H_j is a set of hubs that can be reached by following the path from H_i to H_j. The resource description of a neighborhood provides information about the contents covered by all the hubs in this neighborhood. A hub uses resource descriptions of neighborhoods to route queries to its neighboring hubs.

Resource descriptions of neighborhoods provide similar functionality as routing indices [3]. An entry in a routing index records the number of documents that may be found along a path for a set of topics. The key difference between resource descriptions of neighborhoods and routing indices is that resource descriptions of neighborhoods represent contents with unigram language models (terms with their frequencies). Thus by using resource descriptions of neighborhoods, there is no need for hubs and leaf nodes to cluster their documents into a set of topics and it is not necessary to restrict queries to topic keywords.

Similar to exponentially aggregated routing indices [3], a hub calculates the resource description of a neighborhood by aggregating the resource descriptions of all the hubs in the neighborhood decayed exponentially according to the number of hops so that contents located nearer are weighted more highly. For example, in the resource description of a neighborhood $N_{i,j}$ (the neighborhood of H_i in the direction of H_j), a term t's exponentially aggregated frequency is:

$$\sum_{H_k \in N_{i,j}} \{tf(t,H_k)/F^{[numhops(H_i,H_k)-1]}\} . \tag{1}$$

where $tf(t, H_k)$ is t's term frequency in the resource description of hub H_k, and F is the average number of hub neighbors each hub has in the network.

The exponentially aggregated total number of documents in a neighborhood is:

$$\sum_{H_k \in N_{i,j}} \{numdocs(H_k)/F^{[numhops(H_i,H_k)-1]}\} . \qquad (2)$$

The creation of resource descriptions of neighborhoods requires several iterations at each hub and different hubs can run the creation process asynchronously. A hub H_i in each iteration calculates and sends to its hub neighbor H_j the resource description of neighborhood $N_{j,i}$ denoted by $ND_{j,i}$ by aggregating its hub description HD_i and the most recent resource descriptions of neighborhoods it receives from all of its neighboring hubs excluding H_j. $ND_{j,i}$ is calculated as:

$$ND_{j,i} = HD_i + \sum_{H_k \in directneighbors(H_i)\backslash H_j} \{ND_{i,k}/F\} . \qquad (3)$$

The stopping condition could be either the number of iterations reaching a predefined limit, or the difference in resource descriptions between adjacent iterations being small enough. The maximum number of iterations was 6 in our experiments.

The process of maintaining and updating resource descriptions of neighborhoods is identical to the process used for creating them. The resource descriptions of neighborhoods could be updated periodically, or when the difference between the old and the new value is significant.

For networks that have cycles, frequencies of some terms and the number of documents may be overcounted, which will affect the accuracies of resource descriptions. How to deal with cycles in peer-to-peer networks using routing indices is discussed in detail in [3]. We could use the same solutions described in [3] for cycle avoidance or cycle detection and recovery. For simplicity, in this paper, we take the "no-op" solution, which completely ignores cycles. Experimental results show that resource selection using resource descriptions of neighborhoods generated in networks with cycles is still quite efficient and accurate.

3.2 Resource Ranking and Selection

Query routing aims at an optimal cost-effective solution to directing the information request to those nodes that are most likely to contain relevant documents. In this paper, the cost of query routing is measured by the number of messages carrying the information request (query messages). The flooding technique guarantees to reach nodes with relevant information contents but requires an exponential number of query messages. Randomly forwarding the request to a small subset of neighbors can significantly reduce the number of query messages but the reached nodes may not be relevant at all. To achieve both efficiency and accuracy, each hub needs to rank its neighboring leaf nodes by their likelihood to satisfy the information request, and neighboring hubs by their likelihood to reach nodes with relevant information contents, and only forwards the request to the top-ranked neighbors. Because the resource descriptions of leaf nodes and those of neighborhoods are not in the same magnitude in vocabulary size and term frequency, direct comparison between leaf nodes and neighborhoods would not be fair. Therefore, a hub handles separately the ranking and selection of its neighboring leaf nodes and hubs.

In this paper all the hubs are required to use the same resource ranking/selection methods. In future work, we are interested in studying the performance of federated search in P2P networks when this requirement is relaxed.

Leaf Node Ranking. Adapting language modeling approaches for ad-hoc information retrieval, we use the Kullback-Leibler (K-L) divergence-based method [21] for leaf node ranking, which calculates the conditional probability $P(L_i | Q)$ of predicting the collection of leaf node L_i given the query Q and uses it to rank different leaf nodes.

$$P(L_i | Q) = \frac{P(Q | L_i) \times P(L_i)}{P(Q)} \propto P(Q | L_i) \cdot \tag{4}$$

with uniform prior probability for leaf nodes;

$$P(Q | L_i) = \prod_{q \in Q} \frac{tf(q, L_i) + \mu \times P(q | G)}{numterms(L_i) + \mu} \cdot \tag{5}$$

where $tf(q, L_i)$ is the term frequency of query term q in leaf node L_i's resource description (collection language model), $P(q | G)$ is the background language model used for smoothing and μ is the smoothing parameter in Dirichlet smoothing.

Leaf Node Selection with Unsupervised Threshold Learning. After leaf nodes are ranked based on their $P(L_i | Q)$ values, the usual approach is to select the top-ranked leaf nodes up to a predetermined number. In hierarchical P2P networks, the number of leaf nodes served by individual hubs may be quite different, and different hubs may cover different content areas. In this case, it is not appropriate to use a static, hub-independent number as the threshold for a hub to decide how many leaf nodes to select for a given query. It is desirable that each hub has the ability to learn its own selection threshold automatically.

The problem of learning the threshold to convert relevance ranking scores into a binary decision has mostly been studied in information filtering [22]. One approach to learn the threshold is to find an optimal threshold value that maximizes a given utility function based on the distributions of the scores of relevant and non-relevant documents. However, it requires user relevance feedback as training data, which is not easily available for federated search in peer-to-peer networks. Our goal is to develop a technique for each hub to learn the selection threshold without supervision based on the information and functionality it already has. In peer-to-peer networks, because each hub has the ability to merge the retrieval results from multiple leaf nodes into a single, integrated ranked list, as long as the result merging has reasonably good performance, we could assume that the top-ranked merged documents are relevant. If we further assume that when a hub merges the documents returned by all of its leaf nodes for a training query, a leaf node with at least n documents among the top-ranked merged documents at this hub is a relevant leaf node with respect to the query and non-relevant otherwise, then we can define a utility function based on the distributions of the normalized scores of relevant and non-relevant leaf nodes at this hub for a set of queries, and the leaf node selection threshold is one that maximizes the value of this utility function.

To be more specific, a linear utility function $U(\theta)$ is defined as below and the optimal value θ^* that maximizes $U(\theta)$ is used as the threshold for leaf node selection.

$$U(\theta) = N_{rel}(\theta) - N_{nonrel}(\theta) - w \times N(\theta) \ , \ \theta^* = \arg\max_\theta U(\theta) \ . \tag{6}$$

where $N_{rel}(\theta)$ and $N_{nonrel}(\theta)$ are the number of relevant and non-relevant leaf nodes respectively whose normalized scores are above threshold θ, $N(\theta)$ is the total number of leaf nodes with normalized scores above threshold θ, and w is the weight to control the tradeoff between accuracy and efficiency.

Because larger $N(\theta)$ leads to more selected leaf nodes and thus low efficiency, the term $w \times N(\theta)$ is included in $U(\theta)$ to penalize low efficiency since efficiency is equally important as accuracy for federated search in most peer-to-peer environments.

At a hub, the number of relevant and non-relevant leaf nodes with normalized scores above threshold θ can be calculated as:

$$N_{rel}(\theta) = \alpha \times \int_\theta^1 P(s \wedge rel)ds = \alpha \times \int_\theta^1 P(s \mid rel) \times P(rel)ds \ . \tag{7}$$

$$N_{nonrel}(\theta) = \alpha \times \int_\theta^1 P(s \wedge nonrel)ds = \alpha \times \int_\theta^1 P(s \mid nonrel) \times (1 - P(rel))ds \ . \tag{8}$$

where $P(s \wedge rel)$ is the probability of a leaf node having score s and being relevant, $P(s \wedge nonrel)$ is the probability of a leaf node having score s and being non-relevant, $P(s \mid rel)$ is the probability of a relevant leaf node having score s, $P(s \mid nonrel)$ is the probability of a non-relevant leaf node having score s, $P(rel)$ is the probability of a leaf node being relevant, and α is the total number of leaf nodes in training data.

The relevancy of a leaf node depends on whether it has at least n (empirically chosen to be 5 in our experiments) documents among the top-ranked merged documents at a hub. $P(s \mid rel)$ and $P(s \mid nonrel)$ at a hub can be estimated from the scores of relevant and non-relevant leaf nodes for a set of training queries. In information filtering, the score distributions of relevant and non-relevant documents are fitted using a Gaussian distribution and an exponential distribution respectively [1]. However, in our experience the score distributions of relevant and non-relevant leaf nodes at a hub $P(s \mid rel)$ and $P(s \mid nonrel)$ cannot be fitted very well by distributions such as exponential and Gaussian. For this reason, instead of fitting continuous distributions to the training data, each hub uses the empirical discrete score distributions learned from a set of training queries. Experimental results not shown in this paper verified that using the discrete score distributions had better performance (and was simpler) than using the fitted exponential score distributions.

Usually $P(rel)$ is estimated with maximum likelihood estimation using training data. However, in our experiments, because the amounts of training data for relevant and non-relevant leaf nodes are very unbalanced, using maximum likelihood estimation for $P(rel)$ yielded poor performance. Therefore, here we assume that all the leaf nodes connecting to a hub have equal probability of being relevant and non-relevant, i.e., $P(rel)$ is 0.5. This is a reasonable assumption when each hub covers a specific content area so that all of its connecting leaf nodes have somewhat similar contents.

$N(\theta)$ as a function of θ can be fitted quite well by an exponential function whose parameters are learned from the leaf node ranking results of a set of training queries.

Hub Ranking and Selection. The K-L divergence resource selection algorithm used for leaf ranking is also used for hub ranking. The resource descriptions of neighborhoods are used to calculate the collection language models needed by the resource selection algorithm. For hub selection, because selecting a neighboring hub is essentially selecting a neighborhood, using a prior distribution that favors larger neighborhood could lead to better search performance, which was indeed the case in our experiments. Thus the prior probability of a neighborhood is set to be proportional to the exponentially aggregated total number of documents in the neighborhood. Given the query Q, the probability of predicting the neighborhood N_i that a neighboring hub H_i represents is calculated as follows and used for hub ranking:

$$P(N_i \mid Q) = \frac{P(Q \mid N_i) \times P(N_i)}{P(Q)} \propto P(Q \mid N_i) \times numdocs(N_i) \cdot \tag{9}$$

$$P(Q \mid N_i) = \prod_{q \in Q} \frac{tf(q, N_i) + \mu \times P(q \mid G)}{numterms(N_i) + \mu} \cdot \tag{10}$$

where $tf(q, N_i)$ is the term frequency of query term q in the resource description of neighborhood N_i (collection language model), $P(q \mid G)$ is the background language model for smoothing and μ is the smoothing parameter in Dirichlet smoothing.

A fixed number of top-ranked neighboring hubs are selected. It remains to be future work to apply unsupervised threshold learning to hub selection.

3.3 Result Merging

As described earlier, result merging takes place at each top-level hub. Kirsch's algorithm [9] is extended for result merging in P2P networks which requires each resource to provide summary statistics for each of the retrieved documents, for example, document length and how often each query term matched. The corpus statistics come from the aggregation of the hub's resource description and the resource descriptions of neighborhoods for its neighboring hubs. Documents are merged according to the document scores recalculated by a K-L divergence retrieval algorithm using the above document and corpus statistics.

If the client node issues the request to multiple hubs, it also needs to merge the results returned by these hubs. Because client nodes don't maintain information about the contents of other nodes and corpus statistics as hubs do, they can only use simple, but probably less effective, merging methods. In this paper, client nodes directly use the document scores returned by top-level hubs to merge results.

4 Test Data

We used the P2P testbed [11] based on the TREC WT10g web test collection to evaluate the performance of federated search in hierarchical P2P networks of text-based digital libraries. The P2P testbed consists of 2,500 collections based on document URLs. The total number of documents in these 2,500 collections is 1,421,088. Each collection defines a leaf node in a hierarchical P2P network.

There are 25 hubs in the P2P testbed, each of which covers a specific type of content. The connections between leaf nodes and hubs were determined by clustering leaf nodes into 25 clusters using a similarity-based soft clustering algorithm, and connecting all the leaf nodes within a cluster to the hub associated with this cluster.

The connections between hubs were generated randomly. Each hub has no less than 1 and no more than 7 hub neighbors. A hub has on average 4 hub neighbors.

Experiments were run on two sets of queries. The first set of queries came from the title fields of TREC topics 451-550. The standard TREC relevance assessments supplied by the U. S. National Institute for Standards and Technology were used.

The second set of queries was a set of 1,000 queries selected from the queries defined in the P2P testbed. Queries in the P2P testbed were automatically generated from WT10g data by extracting key terms from the documents in the collection. Because it is expensive to obtain relevance judgments for these automatically generated queries, we treated 50 top-ranked documents retrieved using a single large collection for each query as the "relevant" documents ("single collection" baseline), and measured how well federated search in the hierarchical P2P network could locate and rank these documents. The single large collection was the subset of the WT10g used to define the contents of the 2,500 leaf nodes (WT10g-subset).

For each query, a leaf node was randomly chosen to act as a client node temporarily to issue the query and collect the merged retrieval results for evaluation.

5   Evaluation Methodology

A version of the JavaSim network simulator [7] was developed to evaluate the performance of text-based federated search in hierarchical P2P networks.

Both retrieval accuracy and query routing efficiency were used as performance measures. Precisions at document ranks 5, 10, 15, 20, 30, and 100 were used to measure retrieval accuracy. The efficiency of query routing was measured by the average number of query messages (messages to carry the information requests) routed for each query in the network.

6   Experiments and Results

A series of experiments was conducted to study text-based federated search in cooperative P2P environments. Three hub selection methods were compared: the flooding method (a hub broadcasting query messages to all of its hub neighbors), random hub selection (a hub randomly selecting some of its hub neighbors for query routing) and hub selection based on resource descriptions of neighborhoods. Two leaf node selection methods were compared: selecting a fixed percentage of top-ranked leaf nodes and selecting using the learned thresholds. Unsupervised threshold learning required a set of training queries. For each experiment that used threshold-based leaf node selection to run the 100 TREC queries, two runs were conducted with each using half of the 100 TREC queries for training and half for testing. The results from two runs were averaged to get the final results. For the experiments that used threshold-based leaf node selection to run the 1,000 WT10g queries, the 100 TREC queries were used as training data. Unsupervised threshold learning only used queries and the retrieved documents for training. The NIST relevance judgments for the 100 TREC queries were not used to learn thresholds. The weight w for unsupervised threshold learning was adjusted so as to yield similar overall query routing efficiency as selecting a fixed percentage (1%) of top-ranked leaf nodes. The number of top-ranked merged documents used for unsupervised threshold learning was 50.

Tables 6.1 and 6.2 show respectively the results of running the 100 TREC queries and the 1,000 WT10g queries for text-based federated search in a hierarchical P2P network using different methods. The column marked by "Msgs" shows the average number of query messages routed for each query. Precisions at different document ranks are shown in columns 4-9. The "single collection" baseline (Section 4) is also shown in Table 6.1 for the 100 TREC queries.

Because the "single collection" baseline was used as relevance judgment for WT10g queries, the retrieval performance on this set of queries directly measured the ability of federated search in the hierarchical P2P network to match the results from search in a centralized environment. The high precisions at top document ranks in Table 6.2 demonstrates that federated search in the hierarchical P2P network was able to locate most documents that were considered relevant by the centralized approach, which is an encouraging sign for federated search in peer-to-peer networks considering that only around 1% of the 2,500 digital libraries were actually searched.

If we compare the figures in Table 6.1 with those in Table 6.2, we can see that although the absolute values were quite different, the relative performance difference of different algorithms for the 1,000 WT10g queries was similar to that for the 100 TREC queries. Therefore the same conclusions drawn from the results of the 100 TREC queries could be drawn from the results of the 1,000 WT10g queries regarding the relative effectiveness of various algorithms, which indicates that the automatically generated queries and the "single collection" baseline are useful resources in studying federated search in peer-to-peer networks.

The results in Tables 6.1 and 6.2 demonstrate that compared with using the flooding technique for hub selection, hub selection based on resource descriptions of neighborhoods required around one third of the number of query messages with only a minor drop in search performance, irrespective of how hubs ranked and selected leaf nodes. Hub selection based on resource descriptions of neighborhoods and random hub selection gave similar query routing efficiency but the retrieval accuracy of the former was consistently higher than the latter.

Table 6.1. Search performance evaluated on the 100 TREC queries

Hub Selection	Leaf Selection	Msgs	P@5	P@10	P@15	P@20	P@30	P@100
Centralized	Centralized	N/A	0.324	0.287	0.255	0.241	0.208	0.175
Flooding	Top 1%	177	0.263	0.205	0.179	0.168	0.147	0.084
Flooding	Threshold	180	0.274	0.223	0.196	0.179	0.159	0.094
Random 1	Top 1%	63	0.240	0.191	0.170	0.154	0.130	0.066
Random 1	Threshold	65	0.252	0.205	0.177	0.159	0.137	0.067
Top 1	Top 1%	59	0.259	0.196	0.176	0.163	0.139	0.080
Top 1	Threshold	55	0.280	0.218	0.192	0.179	0.153	0.086

Table 6.2. Search performance evaluated on the 1,000 WT10g queries

Hub Selection	Leaf Selection	Msgs	P@5	P@10	P@15	P@20	P@30	P@100
Flooding	Top 1%	174	0.970	0.942	0.915	0.875	0.792	0.281
Flooding	Threshold	171	0.990	0.967	0.942	0.913	0.835	0.289
Random 1	Top 1%	60	0.874	0.809	0.753	0.698	0.595	0.198
Random 1	Threshold	55	0.891	0.831	0.773	0.718	0.616	0.195
Top 1	Top 1%	54	0.949	0.904	0.857	0.804	0.701	0.237
Top 1	Threshold	43	0.964	0.912	0.863	0.810	0.707	0.226

The power of the peer-to-peer system using the learned thresholds for leaf node selection lies in its ability to adapt the thresholds automatically to different hubs in order to obtain better performance. As shown in Tables 6.1 and 6.2, with the same hub
selection method, using leaf node selection with the learned thresholds in general
gave better performance for text-based federated search in the hierarchical P2P network than selecting a fixed percentage of top-ranked leaf nodes for each hub.

7 Conclusions and Future Work

This paper studies federated search of text-based digital libraries in hierarchical P2P
networks. Although some existing approaches to resource representation, resource
ranking and selection, and result merging for text-based federated search can be
adapted to P2P environments in a straightforward manner, new development is still
required to suit the solutions to the unique characteristics of hierarchical P2P networks. For example, in hierarchical P2P networks, hub ranking and selection should
be based on not only the hub's likelihood to provide relevant documents with its own
leaf nodes, but also its potential to reach other hubs that are likely to satisfy the information request. Thus new methods are needed to represent the contents covered
by the available resources in the networks. In this paper, we define the concept of
neighborhood and describe a method to create and use resource descriptions of
neighborhoods for hub ranking and selection. Experimental results demonstrate that
hub ranking and selection based on resource descriptions of neighborhoods offers a
better combination of accuracy and efficiency than the alternative flooding and random selection.

Another unique character of hierarchical P2P networks is that there are multiple
hubs and each hub must make local decisions on selecting from the leaf nodes it covers to satisfy the information request. Because hubs are different in the number of
leaf nodes and the content areas they cover, which could also change dynamically as
nodes come and leave or change connections, the ability for hubs to learn automatically hub-specific resource selection thresholds in the networks is much desired. This
motivated us to develop an approach for each hub to learn its own threshold in an unsupervised manner based on the retrieval results of a set of training queries. In our
experiments the proposed approach was consistently more accurate than the typical
method of selecting a fixed number of top-ranked leaf nodes with similar efficiency.

The results in this paper also provide additional support for using the automatically
generated queries and the "single collection" baseline to evaluate the search perform-

ance in P2P networks. The same conclusions on the relative effectiveness of various algorithms for federated search in P2P networks can be drawn from the results of the 1,000 WT10g queries and from the results of the 100 TREC queries. This is encouraging because the large number of queries automatically generated from WT10g (in the magnitude of 10^6) give us the opportunity to study in the future how the network can learn from past queries and evolve to improve the search performance over time.

Federated search in distributed environments is complicated, the main components of which include resource representation, resource selection, document retrieval and result merging. The overall search performance is affected by the performance of individual components as well as the interaction between them. P2P networks add further complexity to the problem due to factors such as dynamic topology, uncertainty in locating relevant information, and efficiency concerns. How the data are distributed over the network and how different nodes interact with each other also affect the use of different algorithms. Our next step is to further understand the unique characteristics of P2P networks and to develop practical algorithms that are more appropriate for search in dynamic and heterogeneous P2P networks.

Acknowledgements

This material is based on work supported by NSF grant IIS-0240334. Any opinions, findings, conclusions or recommendations expressed in this material are the authors', and do not necessarily reflect those of the sponsor.

References

1. A. Arampatzis, J. Beney, C. Koster and T. van der Weide. KUN on the TREC-9 Filtering Track: Incrementality, decay, and threshold optimization for adaptive filtering systems. In *Proc. of the 9th Text REtrieval Conference*, 2001.
2. J. Callan. Distributed information retrieval. W. B. Croft, editor, *Advances in information retrieval*, chapter 5, pages 127-150. Kluwer Academic Publishers, 2000.
3. A. Crespo and H. Garcia-Molina. Routing indices for peer-to-peer systems. In *Proc. of the International Conference on Distributed Computing Systems (ICDCS)*, July 2002.
4. F. Cuenca-Acuna and T. Nguyen. Text-based content search and retrieval in ad hoc p2p communities. Technical Report DCS-TR-483, Rutgers University, 2002.
5. L. Gravano, C. Chang, H. Garcia-Molina and A. Paepcke. STARTS: Stanford proposal for internet meta-searching. In *Proc. of the ACM-SIGMOD International Conference on Management of Data*, 1997.
6. L. Gravano and H. Garcia-Molina. Generalizing GlOSS to vector-space databases and broker hierarchies. In *Proc. of 21th International Conference on Very Large Data Bases (VLDB'95)*, pages 78-89, 1995.
7. Javasim. http://javasim.ncl.ac.uk/.
8. KaZaA. http://www.kazaa.com.
9. S. T. Kirsch. Document retrieval over networks wherein ranking and relevance scores are computed at the client for multiple database documents. U.S. Patent 5,659,732.
10. Limewire. http://www.limewire.com.

11. J. Lu and J. Callan. Content-based retrieval in hybrid peer-to-peer networks. In *Proc. of the 12nd International Conference on Information Knowledge Management*, 2003.

12. H. Nottelmann and N. Fuhr. Evaluation different methods of estimating retrieval quality for resource selection. In *Proc. of the 26th Annual International ACM SIGIR Conference on Research and Development in Information Retrieval*, 2003.

13. S. Ratnasamy, P. Francis, M. Handley, R. Karp, and S. Shenker. A scalable content-addressable network. In *Proc. of the ACM SIGCOMM'01 Conference*, August 2001.

14. M. Elena Renda and J. Callan. The robustness of content-based search in hierarchical peer-to-peer networks. In *Proc. of the 13rd International Conference on Information Knowledge Management*, 2004.

15. A. Rowstron and P. Druschel. Pastry: Scalable, distributed object location and routing for large-scale peer-to-peer systems. In *IFIP/ACM International Conference on Distributed Systems Platforms*, pages 329-350, 2001.

16. L. Si and J. Callan. A semi-supervised learning method to merge search engine results. *ACM Transactions on Information Systems*, 24(4), pages 457-491. ACM.

17. L. Si and J. Callan. Relevant document distribution estimation method for resource selection. In *Proc. of the 26th Annual International ACM SIGIR Conference on Research and Development in Information Retrieval*, 2003.

18. I. Stoica, R. Morris, D. Karger, M. Kaashoek, and H. Balakrishnan. Chord: A scalable peer-to-peer lookup service for internet applications. In *Proc. of the ACM SIGCOMM'01 Conference*, August 2001.

19. C. Tang, Z. Xu and S. Dwarkadas. Peer-to-peer information retrieval using self-organizing semantic overlay networks. In *Proc. of the ACM SIGCOMM'03 Conference*, 2003.

20. S. Waterhouse. JXTA Search: Distributed search for distributed networks. Technical report, Sun Microsystems Inc., 2001.

21. J. Xu and W. B. Croft. Cluster-based language models for distributed retrieval. In *Proc. of the 22nd Annual International ACM SIGIR Conference on Research and Development in Information Retrieval*, 1999.

22. Y. Zhang and J. Callan. Maximum likelihood estimation for filtering thresholds. In *Proc. of 24th Annual International ACM SIGIR Conference on Research and Development in Information Retrieval*, 2001.

'Beauty' of the World Wide Web—Cause, Goal, or Principle

Sándor Dominich, Júlia Góth, Mária Horváth, and Tamás Kiezer

University of Veszprém, Department of Computer Science,
8200 Veszprém, Egyetem u. 10, Hungary
{dominich, goth, kiezer}@dcs.vein.hu

Abstract. It is known that the degree distribution in the World Wide Web (WWW) obeys a power law whose degree exponent exhibits a fairly robust behaviour. The usual method, linear regression, used to construct the power law is not based on any, probably existing, intrinsic property of the WWW which it is assumed to reflect. In the present paper, statistical evidence is given to conjecture that at the heart of this robustness property lies the Golden Section. Applications of this conjecture are also presented and discussed.

1 Introduction

The experimental discovery by Faloutsos et al. [7] that the degree distribution for Web pages and Internet nodes follows a power law with a fairly robust degree exponent value was a basic milestone towards the emergence of a new science of the Web. The formulation of the principle of preferential attachment [5] triggered research into and stimulated ideas towards trying to explain, using generative models [13], why the Web link topology evolves according to a power law. Pennock et al. [15] as well as Adamic and Huberman [3] showed that this principle is not necessarily valid in the real Web; modified principles were proposed to better explain the development of a power law for degree distribution in the real Web.

Kahng et al [11] investigated the question of why the degree exponent exhibits a fairly robust behaviour, just above 2. Using a directed network model in which the number of vertices grows geometrically with time, and the number of edges evolves according to a multiplicative process, they established the distribution of in- and out-degrees in such networks. They arrived at the result that if the degree of vertex grows at a higher pace than the edges then the in-degree distribution is independent of the 'details' of the network.

The usual method, that of linear regression, used to construct the Power Law is not based on any 'internal' property of the Web network—it is a mere reflection of some deeper structure. The generative models proposed thus far are incomplete. They only model growth, and fail to take into account that nodes and links are also destroyed (not just added). It is not known how the processes of growth and extinction go on in the Web, how they relate to each other to give birth to what we observe as a power law.

D.E. Losada and J.M. Fernández-Luna (Eds.): ECIR 2005, LNCS 3408, pp. 67–80, 2005.

In the present paper, based on the robustness property of the degree exponent, a different approach is proposed: it is conjectured that, at the present scale of the Web, at the heart of this robustness property lies the Golden Section. The Golden Section is one of the most ancient and overdone yet evergreen topics in mathematics. It is also far-reaching in several other fields, e.g., art, architecture, biology, music, physics. There is a common agreement that it always relates — subjectively — to a notion of 'beauty' of the field. For example, it is believed that rectangles whose width-to-height ratio is the Golden Section are the most pleasing to the human eye, or that the timing of musical pieces is considered to be most pleasing to human ears when in Golden Section. In this paper, it is beleived that the evolution of the Web link topology may have an intrinsic property that is reflected in the Golden Section, and this is the expression of an inner beauty of the Web.

After a brief overview of several degree exponent values obtained experimentally, statistical evidence is given to conjecture that the degree exponent value varies around a Golden Section-based value. Using number theoretic results, this conjecture is then used, on the one hand, to propose a method, referred to as F-L method, for the construction of the Power Law for the real Web portion under focus, and, on the other hand, to give a theoretical underpinning for the application of high degree walks in crawling and searching in peer-to-peer networks. Also, formal relationships between the Golden Section and the LCD as well as Bollobás models are shown.

2 Power Law

If the probability P that a discrete random variable V assumes values equal to or greater than some value v is given by

$$P(V \geq v) = \left(\frac{m}{v}\right)^k, \quad m > 0, k > 0, v \geq m, \tag{1}$$

we say that V follows Pareto's Law [1, 10]. It follows from (1) that:

$$P(V < v) = 1 - \left(\frac{m}{v}\right)^k, \tag{2}$$

which is the distribution function $F(v)$ of V; it is differentiable with respect to v, the derivative is continuous (absolutely continuous). V has density function $f(v) = F'(v) = m^k \cdot v^{-(k+1)}$. The function $f(v)$ is referred to as a Power Law [18], and it is usually written in the following general form:

$$f(v) = C \cdot v^{-\alpha}, \tag{3}$$

where C is a — problem-dependent — constant, α is referred to as the degree exponent. For visualisation purposes, the Power Law is represented in a log-log plot as a straight line obtained by taking the logarithm of (3):

$$\log f(v) = \log C - \alpha \times \log v. \tag{4}$$

$\log v$ is represented on the abscissa, $\log f(x)$ on the ordinata, $-\alpha$ is the slope, $\log C$ is the intercept. Given two sequences of values $X = (x_1,..., x_n)$ and $Y = (y_1, ..., y_n)$. If the correlation coefficient $r(X, Y)$ suggests a fairly strong correlation — i.e., it is close to $|1|$ — between X and Y at a log scale, then a regression line can be drawn to exhibit a relationship between X and Y; using the slope and the intercept of the regression line the corresponding Power Law can be written.

3 Degree Exponent Values for the World Wide Web

Faloutsos et al. [7] arrived at the result that, using data provided by the National Laboratory for Applied Networks Research between the end of 1997 and end of 1998, the tail of the frequency distribution of an out-degree — i.e., the number of Internet nodes and Web pages with a given out-degree — is proportional to a Power Law. Their observation was that the values of the exponent seemed to be almost constant: 2.15; 2.16; 2.2; 2.48.

Barabási et al. [5] — using 325,729 HTML pages involving 1,469,680 links from the *nd.edu* domain — confirmed the earlier results obtained for the values of the degree exponent. They obtained the value 2.45 for out-degree, and 2.1 for in-degree.

In [6], two experiments are described using two web crawls, one in May and another one in October 1999, provided by Altavista, involving 200 million pages and 1.5 billion links. The results arrived at were the same in both experiments: the values of the degree exponent were estimated to be 2.1, 2.54, 2.09, 2.67, 2.72 for out-links distribution.

The values obtained earlier for the degree exponent were also confirmed by Pennock et al. [15], who found — using 100,000 Web pages selected at random from one billion URLs of Inktomi Corporation Webmap; they binned the frequencies using histograms — that the exponent for out-degree was 2.72, whereas 2.1 for in-degrees. Similar exponent values were obtained for the in-degree distribution for category specific homepages: 2.05 for companies and newspapers, 2.63 for universities, 2.66 for scientists, and 2.05 for newspapers.

Shiode and Batty [16] assessed the Power Law for Web country domain names in- and out-link distribution as of 1999. Their results for the Power Law exponent were the following values: 2.91, 1.6, 2.98, 1.46, 2.18, 2.

Adamic and Huberman [3] report on an experiment involving 260,000 sites, each representing a separate domain name. The degree exponent was estimated to be 1.94.

In [12], it is reported that a copy of the 1997 Web from Alexa (a company that archives the state of the Web) was used to estimate the degree exponent of the Power Law. The data consisted of about 1 Terabyte of data representing the content of over 200 million web pages. It was found that the degree exponent was 2.38.

In [4], it is reported that the value of 2.3 was found for the degree exponent, in [9] the values 2.1 and 2.38 are reported, while in [14] 2.1 and 2.7.

Friedman et al. [8], using a crawl on the *.hu* domain, assessed the power law for 11,359,640 pages and 95,713,140 links, and found the following values for exponent: 2.29 for in-degree, and 2.78 for out-degree.

70   S. Dominich et al.

Experiment 1. Using the "Barabási-data"[1], we repeated the fitting of a Power Law curve to out-degree distribution. Fig. 1 shows our results. (Computational details are given in the Appendix.)

Experiment 2. We generated the in-links frequency distribution for country domain names[2] as of January, 2004 (Fig. 2). The domain names *.gov, .org, .net, .edu, .us, .com, .mil, .um, .vi* were all considered as representing the USA, the domain names *.ac, .uk, .gb* as representing the UK, and *.fr, .fx* for France. The number of inlinks for every country domain name was identified using Altavista search engine's Webmasters option during 19-22 January, 2004. For example, the UK got a total of 30,701,157 in-links, the USA got 271,019,148; Albania got 2,041,573, Belgium got 3,386,900 in-links. The in-links were binned into 1,000 equally spaced intervals, the correlation coefficient was found to be −0.99 (at a log scale). The value for the Power Law exponent was found to be equal to $\alpha = 1.18$ using Mathcad's *linfit* linear regression command, the approximation error was equal to 14,509.

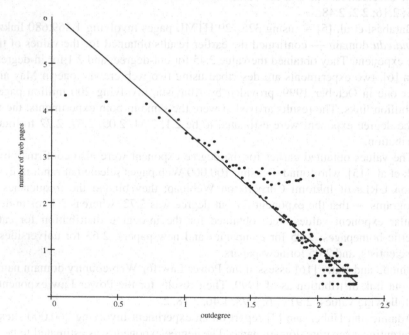

Fig. 1. World Wide Web Power Law. The frequency (i.e., number of Web pages) of the outdegrees of Web pages plotted at a log-log scale. The points represent real values, the straight line represents the regression line fitted to the real values. The correlation coefficient is equal to $r = -0.94$, the Power Law exponent is equal to $\alpha = 2.5$

The estimated values obtained experimentally thus far for the exponent of the Power Law for degree distribution in then Web Power Law are summarised in Table 1.

---

[1] Provided at http://www.nd.edu/~networks/database/index.html; downloaded January 2, 2004.
[2] Taken from http://www.webopedia.com/quick_ref/topleveldomains.

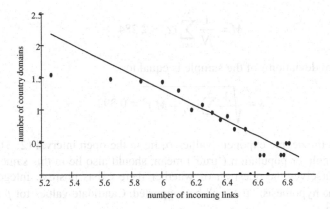

Fig. 2. Log-log plot of the Power Law for the in-links of country domain names as of January, 2004. The correlation between the number of in-links and the corresponding number of country domain names was found to be −0.99, whereas the value of the power law exponent was 1.18

Table 1. Estimated values obtained experimentally thus far for the exponent of the Power Law for degree distribution in the World Wide Web

Source (experiment)	Degree exponent value
Faloutsos et al. (1999)	2.15; 2.16; 2.2; 2.48
Barabási et al. (2000)	2.1; 2.45
Broder et al (2001)	2.1; 2.72; 2.09; 2.67; 2.54
Pennock et al. (2002)	2.1; 2.72, 2.05; 2.05; 2.63; 2.66
Kumar et al. (1998)	2.38
Adamic, Huberman (2000)	1.94
Shiode, Batty (2000)	2.91; 1.6; 2.98; 1.46; 2.18; 2
Albert (2000)	2.3
Gil et al. ()	2.1; 2.38
Pandarungan (2002)	2.1; 2.7
Friedman et al. (2003)	2.29; 2.78
Experiment 1 (see text)	2.5
Experiment 2 (see text)	1.18

4 Statistics of the Experimentally Obtained Degree Exponent Values

Let us conceive the different degree exponent values obtained experimentally (Table 1) as being a sample drawn from a population [17] consisting of degree exponent values (the population may consist, for example, of the degree exponent values obtained using the data of all Web crawlers, all domain names, etc.). Our sample has size $N = 34$. The mean M of the sample is equal to

$$M = \frac{1}{N} \sum_{i=1}^{N} \alpha_i = 2.284 \qquad (5)$$

The standard deviation s of the sample is equal to

$$s = \sqrt{\frac{1}{N} \sum_{i=1}^{N} (\alpha_i - M)^2} = 0.392 \qquad (6)$$

Because all the degree exponent values α_i lie in the open interval (2; 3), the mean μ, whether sample or population ('true') mean, should also lie in this same interval. We may ask ourselves the question of whether there exists positive integer numbers p such that the hypothesis: "$\mu = \sqrt{p}$" be supported. Candidate values for p are 4, 5, 6, 7, 8. Using the

$$z\text{-score}(\mu) = \left| \frac{M - \mu}{s / \sqrt{N - 1}} \right| \qquad (7)$$

the following values are obtained:

$$z\text{-score}(\sqrt{4}) = 4.163, \quad z\text{-score}(\sqrt{5}) = 0.7,$$
$$z\text{-score}(\sqrt{6}) = 2.43, \quad z\text{-score}(\sqrt{7}) = 5.309, \quad z\text{-score}(\sqrt{8}) = 7.988.$$

The 95% confidence interval for the score is $-2.035 < z\text{-score}(\mu) < 2.035$ ($t_{0.975} = 2.035$, $N - 1 = 33$ degrees of freedom), only $z\text{-score}(\sqrt{5})$ lies within this interval. Thus, the 95% confidence interval for the mean $\mu = \sqrt{5} = 2.236$ is as follows:

$$2.145 < \mu < 2.422 \qquad (8)$$

We may hence say that there is statistical support to assume that the sample comes from a population with mean $\mu = \sqrt{5}$. Thus, the Power Law for the degree distribution in the World Wide Web may be written in the following form:

$$f(x) \approx C \cdot x^{-\sqrt{5}} \qquad (9)$$

i.e., the number $f(x)$ of Web nodes having degree x is proportional to $x^{-\sqrt{5}}$.

5   Golden Section, Fibonacci and Lucas Numbers

In this part, those properties of the Golden Section, the Fibonacci and the Lucas numbers are recalled which are of interest to us in connecting them with the Web Power Law.

5.1   Golden Section

The Golden Section (*aka* Golden Ratio, Golden Mean, Divine Proportion) is denoted by φ, and defined as the smallest root of the equation:

$$x^2 - x - 1 = 0; \quad \varphi = (\sqrt{5} - 1)/2 \approx 0.61803398875$$

The other root is $\Phi = (\sqrt{5} + 1)/2 \approx 1.61803398875$. The following relationships hold:

$$\sqrt{5} = 2\varphi + 1, \quad \varphi \cdot \Phi = 1$$

A straightforward connection between the degree exponent as defined in (9) and the Golden Section is as follows:

$$\mu = \sqrt{5} = 2\varphi + 1$$

5.2 Fibonacci Numbers

The *Fibonacci numbers* are defined as $F_0 = 0$, $F_1 = 1$, $F_n = F_{n-1} + F_{n-2}$, $n \geq 2$, i.e., 0, 1, 1, 2, 3, 5, 8, 13, 21, 34, 55, 89, 144, ... The ratio of the consecutive numbers (i.e., 5/8 = 0.625; 8/13 = 0.615; 13/21 = 0.619;...) has limit equal to the Golden Section, namely:

$$\lim_{n \to \infty} \frac{F_n}{F_{n+1}} = \varphi \tag{10}$$

The Golden Section and the Fibonacci numbers are related by Binet's formula:

$$F_n = \frac{1}{\sqrt{5}} \left(\Phi^n - (-\varphi)^n \right) \tag{11}$$

from which it follows that:

$$(-1)^n \cdot \varphi^{2n} + F_n \cdot (2\varphi + 1) \cdot \varphi^n = 1, \quad n = 0, 1, 2, ... \tag{12}$$

5.3 Lucas Numbers

If the recurrence relation $L_n = L_{n-1} + L_{n-2}$, $n \geq 2$, is initialised with the numbers $L_0 = 2$, $L_1 = 1$, then one obtains the *Lucas numbers* L_n: 2, 1, 3, 4, 7, 11, 18, 29, 47, 76,... . It can be shown, e.g., using induction on n, that the Fibonacci and Lucas numbers are bound by the following relationship:

$$L_n = F_{n-1} + F_{n+1}, \quad n \geq 1 \tag{13}$$

6 Constructing the Web Power Law Using Fibonacci and Lucas Numbers

In this part, we propose a method based on the Golden Section, Fibonacci and Lucas numbers to construct the Web Power Law for a web portion under focus. Also, experimental evidence will be given to demonstrate the application of the method in practice.

6.1 Fibonacci-Lucas (F-L) Method

Taking into account the relationship (10), for sufficiently large values of n, we can write:

$$\sqrt{5} = 2\varphi + 1 \approx 2 \cdot \frac{F(n-1)}{F(n)} + 1 = \frac{F(n-1) + F(n-1) + F(n)}{F(n)}. \tag{14}$$

which — given the recursive definition of the Fibonacci numbers, and taking into account the relationship between The Fibonacci and Lucas numbers — becomes

$$\frac{F(n-2) + F(n-3) + F(n-1) + F(n)}{F(n)} = \frac{L(n-1) + L(n-2)}{F(n)} = \frac{L(n)}{F(n)} \tag{15}$$

Thus, the Web Power Law (9) re-writes in a form in which the exponent is expressed using both Fibonacci and Lucas numbers as follows:

$$f(x) \approx C \cdot x^{-\frac{L(n)}{F(n)}}. \tag{16}$$

Taking the logarithm of the relationship (16), one can write the following:

$$\log f(x) \approx \log C - \frac{L(n)}{F(n)} \log x \qquad \log f(x) + \frac{L(n)}{F(n)} \log x \approx \log C$$

$$F(n) \cdot \log f(x) + L(n) \cdot \log x \approx F(n) \cdot \log C \qquad f(x)^{F(n)} \cdot x^{L(n)} \approx C^{F(n)} \tag{17}$$

For real Web data, $f(x)$ is not a computed value but the actual frequency, while the Power Law exponent is slightly different from $L(n)/F(n)$. Let X_k denote the actual page degrees and Y_k denote the corresponding actual frequency ($k = 1, 2, ..., M$). Then, the relationship (17) becomes:

$$F(n) \cdot \log Y_k + L(n) \cdot \log X_k \approx F(n) \cdot \log C \tag{18}$$

Because the relationship (18) should hold for every $k = 1, 2, ..., M$, the mean of the left-hand side taken over all k should equal $F(n) \cdot \log C$ (of course, with an inherent approximation error):

$$\frac{1}{M} \sum_{k=1}^{M} (F(n) \cdot \log Y_k + L(n) \cdot \log X_k) \approx \frac{1}{M} \sum_{k=1}^{M} F(n) \cdot \log C = \tag{19}$$

$$= \frac{1}{M} \cdot M \cdot F(n) \cdot \log C = F(n) \cdot \log C$$

This property makes it possible to propose the following method for constructing a specific Power Law for given real Web data.

Fibonacci-Lucas (F-L) Method for constructing the Web Power Law for degree distribution

Step 1. Establish the number of degrees (e.g., out-links) X_k (in ascending order) and their corresponding frequencies Y_k, , $k = 1, 2, ..., M$, for the Web or Internet nodes under focus.

Step 2. Choose some n, e.g., $n = 8, 9$ or 19, and compute the corresponding Fibonacci number $F(n)$ and Lucas number $L(n)$ using, for example, Binet's formula (11) and formula (12) respectively (or other formulas available).

Step 3. Compute the left-hand side of the relationship (18), i.e.,

$$S_k = F(n) \cdot \log Y_k + L(n) \cdot \log X_k, \quad k = 1, 2, ..., M \tag{20}$$

Step 4. Compute the mean μ of S_k over all k, i.e.,

$$\mu = \frac{1}{M} \sum_{k=1}^{M} S_k \tag{21}$$

Step 5. Apply a correction equal to the standard deviation of S_k to compensate for the approximation errors:

$$\mu' = \mu + \text{stdev}(\mu) \tag{22}$$

Step 6. Compute the approximate value for the constant C as follows (using the relationship (17)):

$$C = 10^{\frac{\mu'}{F(n)}} \tag{23}$$

Step 7. Write the specific Power Law for the real Web or Internet portion under focus as follows:

$$f(x) \approx C \cdot x^{\frac{L(n)}{F(n)}} \tag{24}$$

where, as already seen, x denotes degree and $f(x)$ denotes frequency.

6.2 Experimental Evidence in Support of the F-L Method

We give now experimental evidence to support the applicability of the F-L method proposed above in practice.

Using the data of the Appendix, we applied the F-L method using the following pairs of $F(n)$ and $L(n)$:

$F(8) = 21,$	$L(8) = 47$
$F(19) = 4181,$	$L(19) = 9349$
$F(22) = 17711,$	$L(22) = 39603$
$F(29) = 514229,$	$L(29) = 1149851.$

For example, when $F(8) = 21$ and $L(8) = 47$, S_k assumes the values 115, 120, 122, 119, etc.. The means μ from Step 4 corresponding to the pairs $F(n)$ and $L(n)$ are as follows (rounded to integer values): 112; 22,332; 94,603; 274,6752, respectively, whereas the corrected means μ' of the Step 5 are as follows: 128; 25,576; 108,342; 3,145,661 (rounded to integer values). The application of the Steps 6 and 7 yielded the following Power Laws for the four $F(n)$ and $L(n)$ pairs respectively:

$$f(x) = 10^{\frac{128}{21}} \cdot x^{-2.23} \qquad = 1{,}324{,}3171 \cdot x^{-2.23}$$

$$f(x) = 10^{\frac{25576}{4181}} \cdot x^{-2.23} \qquad = 1{,}309{,}903 \cdot x^{-2.23}$$

$$f(x) = 10^{\frac{108342}{17711}} \cdot x^{-2.23} \qquad = 1,309,904 \cdot x^{-2.23}$$

$$f(x) = 10^{\frac{3145661}{514229}} \cdot x^{-2.23} \qquad = 1,309,904 \cdot x^{-2.23}$$

It can be seen that the values obtained for the constant are fairly stable and compare well with that obtained in the experiment of the Appendix using linear regression: $10^{6.1043} = 1,271,452$.

7 High Degree Seeking Walk

In a high degree seeking algorithm (HDS) an arbitrary node is chosen first, then a node with a degree higher than the current node; once the highest degree node has been found, a node of approximately second highest degree will be chosen, and so on. In a peer-to-peer (P2P) system, like GNUTELLA (which obeys a power law), a query is iteratively sent to all the nodes in a neighborhood of the current node until a matching is found. This broadcasting is costly in terms of bandwidth. If every node keeps adequate information (e.g., file names) about its first and second neighbors, then HDS can be implemented. Because storage is likely to remain less expensive than bandwidth, and since network saturation is a weakness of P2P, HDS can be an efficient alternative to usual searching. Adamic et al. show [2] that the expected degree $E(\alpha, n)$ of the richest neighbor of a node having degree n is given by

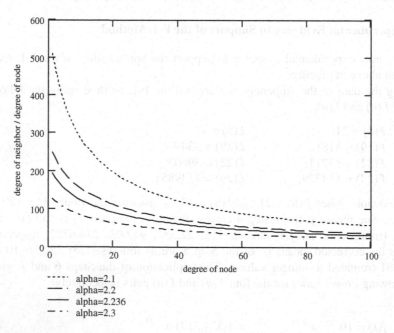

Fig. 3. Simulation of the ratio of the expected degree of the richest neighbor of a node with degree n for different values of the power law exponent alpha. The total number of nodes is equal to 100,000,000; and α = alpha = $2\varphi + 1 = \sqrt{5}$

$$E(\alpha, n) = \frac{n(\alpha - 2)}{(1 - N^{2/\alpha - 1})^n} \sum_{x=0}^{\lfloor N^{1\alpha} \rfloor} x(1 + x)^{1-\alpha} (1 - (x+1)^{2-\alpha})^{n-1} \tag{25}$$

where N denotes the number of nodes in the graph, α is the power law exponent. Fig. 3 shows simulation results for the ratio $E(\alpha, n)/n$. It can be seen that for the power law exponent between 2 and 2.3, the chance to find a richer neighbor is higher than the degree of the node itself within a relatively large interval of degree values, which means that HDS can be applied non-trivially. In Web search engines and retrieval, crawlers implement different strategies, e.g., breadth-first-search, to crawl the Web graph. However, it is becoming increasingly difficult to cope with scalability limitations. One possible way is given by an HDS-based crawling strategy which exploits the power law property of link distribution. From eq. (9) we have that $2 < \alpha < 2.3$, which may be viewed as a theoretical justification for the application of HDS to GNUTELLA or to crawling.

8 Formal Relationships Between the Golden Section, Degree and Probabilities in Generative Models

Based on results presented by Bollobás[3], we can establish the following formal relationships between the Golden Section and the degree distributions and link probabilities in generative models.

In the LCD model, it is shown that in a graph with n vertices and m edges the fraction $F = \#d/n$ of vertices having degree d is bounded as follows:

$$(1 - \varepsilon)\alpha \le F \le (1 + \varepsilon)\alpha,$$

where $\alpha = 2m(m + 1) / [(d + m)(d + m + 1)(d + m + 2)]$. Based on (9) and part 4.1, we take $F = d^{-(2\varphi + 1)}$, and thus we obtain (taking the logarithm of both sides and appropriately re-arranging) the following relationships between the Golden Section and degree:

$$1/[(1 - \varepsilon)\alpha d] \le d^{2\varphi} \le 1/[(1 + \varepsilon)\alpha d].$$

In the Bollobás model, the number $x_i(t)$ of nodes having in-degree i at step t is given by:

$$x_i(t) = C i^{-(1 + 1/c)}, \quad c = (\alpha + \beta)/[1 + \delta(\alpha + \gamma)], \quad \gamma \in \mathbb{R}_+$$

where α is the probability to add a new vertex together with an edge from it to an old vertex, β is the probability to add an edge between two existing vertices, and γ is the probability to add a new vertex and an edge from an old vertex to it (obviously $\alpha + \beta + \gamma = 1$). Based on (9) and part 4.1, we take $1 + 1/c = 2\varphi + 1$, thus we obtain:

$$\varphi = [1 + \delta(\alpha + \gamma)] / [2(\alpha + \beta)].$$

---

[3] Bollobás, B. (2003). Mathematical results on scale-free networks. http://stat-www.berkeley.edu/users/aldous/Networks (downloaded December, 2004).

9 Conclusions

After a brief summary of the numeric values obtained experimentally for the degree exponent in the Web Power Law, experiments are reported that assessed the Power Law, and confirmed earlier results. Then, using hypothesis testing, it was shown that the mean value of the degree exponent could be taken as being equal to $\sqrt{5}$ with a 95% confidence. The direct relationship between $\sqrt{5}$ and the Golden Section φ yielded to considering also the Fibonacci and Lucas numbers. Formal relationships were derived, which made it possible to express the Web Power Law using Fibonacci and Lucas numbers. Based on this result, a method was proposed, called F-L- method, to construct a specific Power Law for a real Web portion under focus. Experimental evidence was given to support the applicability of the method proposed. Also, it was shown, that the results obtained in this paper may serve as a theoretical underpinning for the application of high degree seeking walks in crawling and peer-peer-to searching.

The computationally useful and mathematically interesting relationship between degree frequencies, Golden Section, Fibonacci and Lucas numbers contained in this property can open up further possibilities to involve number theory into the computational study of Web topology. Because in this paper statistical evidence was given that supported the possibility that the mean value of the degree exponent in the Web Power Law can be expressed in terms of the Golden Section, it might be conjectured that, at very large scales, the link topology in the World Wide Web evolves in such a way as to exhibit a Golden Section-based behaviour. What we do not know is whether the **Golden Section** characteristic shown in the Web is a **cause** (i.e., the robustness of the value of the degree exponent — in other words: the evolution of link topology — stems from the Golden Section ultimately), a **goal** (i.e., the link topology evolves in such a way that a Golden Section-based degree exponent be reached), or a **principle** (i.e., the link topology develops according to some Golden Section-based rule 'hidden' in the structure somewhere).

References

1. Adamic, L. A. (2003). Zipf, Power-laws, and Pareto – a ranking tutorial. http://ginger.hpl.hp.com/shl/papers/ranking/ranking.html (visited: December 18, 2003)
2. Adamic, L., Lukose, R.M., Puniyami, A.R., Huberman, B.A. (2001). Search in power-law networks. *Physical Review*, The American Physical Society, vol. 64, pp: 046135(8)
3. Adamic, L.A., and Huberman, B.A. (2000). Power-Law Distribution of the World Wide Web. *Science*, vol. 287, March, p.2115a
4. Albert, R. (2000). PhD Dissertation, University of Notre Dame (visited December, 2003).
5. Barabási, A-L. Albert, R., and Jeong, H. (2000). Scale-free characteristics of random networks: the topology of the world-wide web. *Physica A*, 281, pp: 69-77.
6. Broder, A., Kumar, R., et.al. (2000). Graph structure in the Web. *Computer Networks*, vol. 33, pp: 309-320.
7. Faloutsos, M., Faloutsos, P., and Faloutsos, Ch. (1999). On Power-Law Relationship of the Internet Topology. *Proceeedings of the ACM SIGCOMM*, Cambridge, MA, pp: 251-262.
8. Friedman, E., Uher, M., Windhager, E. (2003). A magyar Web. (The Hungarian Web). *Híradástechnika*, vol. 58, no. 3., pp: 25-31 (in Hungarian)

9. Gil, R, Garcia, R, Delgado, J. (2004). Are we able to charaterize Semantic Web behaviour?
    http://dmag.upf.es/livingsw (downloaded December, 2004)
10. Guilmi, C., Gaffeo, E., and Gallegati, M (2003). Power Law Scaling in the World Income
    Distribution. *Economics Bulletin*, vol. 15, no. 6, pp: 1-7.
11. Kahng, B., Park, Y., and Jeong, H. (2002). Robustness of the in-degree exponent for the
    World Wide Web. *Physical Review*, vol. 66, 046107 1-6.
12. Kumar, R., Raghavan, P., Rajagopalan, S., and Tomkins, A. (1998). Trawling the web for
    emerging   cyber-communities.   *Proceedings   of   the   WWW8   Conference.*
    http://www8.org/w8-papers.
13. Menczel, F. (2002). Growing and navigating the small world Web by local content. *Pro-
    ceedings of the PNAS*, vol. 99, no. 22, pp: 14014-14019.
14. Pandurangan, G., Raghavan, P. (2002). Using PageRank to charaterize Web Structure.
    Lecture Notes In Computer Science, vol. 2387, Springer Verlag, pp: 330-339
15. Pennock, D.M., Flake, G.W., Lawrence, S., Glover, E., and Giles, L. (2002). Winners
    don't take all: characterizing the competition for links on the Web. *Proceedings of the New
    York Academy of Sciences*, April 16, vol. 99, no. 8, pp: 5207-5211.
16. Shiode, N., and Batty, M. (2000). Power Law Distribution in Real and Virtual Worlds.
    http://www.isoc.org/inet2000/cdproceeedings/2a/2a_2.htm (downloaded on December 18,
    2003.
17. Spiegel, M.R. (1961). *Theory and Problems of Statistics*. McGraw Hill.
18. Zipf, G. K. (1949). *Human Behaviour and Principle of Least Effort*. Addison Wesley,
    Cambridge, Massachussetts.

Appendix

Experiment 1. Using the "Barabási-data"[4], we repeated the fitting of a Power Law
curve to out-degree distribution. The data was provided as a zipped file; after unzip-
ping it the result was a text file which contained two numbers in each line: the leftmost number was the sequence number of Web pages (0; 1; 2; ...; 325,729), the other
number was the sequence number of the Web page pointed to by the page represented
by the leftmost number. A noteworthy observation is that the exponent of the Web
Power Law is slowly increasing from 1 with the number of pages (from a few hun-
dred up to several ten thousand pages), and is starting to stabilise around the value α
= 2.5 if the number of Web pages involved is fairly high, above 100,000. Thus, for
example, for 30,000 pages, the correlation — at a log scale — r between out-degree
and frequency was only $r = -0.892$, and the fitting of a Power Law curve $C \cdot x^{-\alpha}$ using
Mathcad's in-built curve fitting command *genfit* resulted in $\alpha = 0.867$ with an approximation error of the sum of the absolute values of differences of 3.7×10^6 at 10^{-4}
convergence error, whereas using linear regression yielded $\alpha = 1.47$ with an approximation error of 1,589,104 at 10^{-4} convergence error. Fig. 1 shows our results (see text)
for a number of 256,062 Web pages — involving 1,139,426 links — selected at random from the provided 325,729 pages. After processing this file the X data consisted
of the out-degrees of Web pages, whereas the Y data consisted of the corresponding
frequencies. For example, there were 2,206 pages having out-degree 13, and the out-

---

[4] Provided at http://www.nd.edu/~networks/database/index.html; downloaded January 2, 2004.

degree 14 had its frequency equal to 1,311. The empirical correlation coefficient — taking log scale data — r between out-degree and frequency was $r = -0.94$. The linear regression yielded the following values: $\alpha = 2.5$ for the exponent; and $C = 10^{6.1043}$ for the constant. The computation was performed using Matchcad's in-built *line* command; the numeric computation used in this command as well as the fact that we used 69,667 pages less may account for the difference of 0.05 in the exponent value compared to the value reported in [4]. Because of the strong correlation (see above) and power-like behaviour, and also due to inherently present numeric approximation errors, we believe that the difference of 0.05 is not an important one.

sPLMap: A Probabilistic Approach to Schema Matching

Henrik Nottelmann[1] and Umberto Straccia[2]

[1] Institute of Informatics and Interactive Systems, University of Duisburg-Essen,
47048 Duisburg, Germany
nottelmann@uni-duisburg.de
[2] ISTI-CNR, Via G. Moruzzi 1, 56124 Pisa, Italy
straccia@isti.cnr.it

Abstract. This paper introduces the first formal framework for learning map-pings between heterogeneous schemas which is based on logics and probability theory. This task, also called "schema matching", is a crucial step in integrating heterogeneous collections. As schemas may have different granularities, and as schema attributes do not always match precisely, a general-purpose schema map-ping approach requires support for uncertain mappings, and mappings have to be learned automatically. The framework combines different classifiers for finding suitable mapping candidates (together with their weights), and selects that set of mapping rules which is the most likely one. Finally, the framework with different variants has been evaluated on two different data sets.

1 Introduction

Federated digital libraries integrate a large number of legacy libraries and give users the impression of one coherent, homogeneous library. These libraries use different schemas (called source schemas). As users cannot deal efficiently with this semantic heterogene-ity, they only see one system-wide or personalized target (or global) schema, which is defined ontologically and independent from the libraries. Then, queries are transformed from the target (global) schema into the source schemas, and documents vice versa (which is out of the scope of this paper).

Our framework sPLMap (probabilistic, logic-based mapping between schemas) com-bines logics with probability theory describing schema mappings. In contrast to most of the approaches available so far, this allows dealing with schemas of different gran-ularity. If the target schema contains the two attributes "author" and "editor", and the source schema only the more general attribute "creator", this source attribute cannot be mapped onto "author" precisely but only with a specific probability. Systems with purely deterministic mappings fail in such settings.

Here, we focus on learning these schemas using documents in both schemas, but not necessarily the same documents. As a by-product, we also compute a theoretically founded measurement for the quality of a mapping.

For schemas, we adopt the document model presented in [7] with only slight modi-fications. Like in database systems, data types with comparison operators are explicitly modelled. However, vagueness of query formulations is one of the key concepts of

D.E. Losada and J.M. Fernández-Luna (Eds.): ECIR 2005, LNCS 3408, pp. 81–95, 2005.

Information Retrieval. Thus, it is crucial that comparison operators have a probabilistic interpretation. Vagueness is required e.g. when a user is uncertain about the exact publication year of a document or the spelling of an author name. These comparison operators are often called "vague predicates", we will use the term "operator" later to avoid confusion with logical predicates. For a specific attribute value the vague predicate yields an estimate of the probability that the condition is fulfilled from the user's point of view — instead of a Boolean value as in DB systems. The schema mapping rules also cover the problem of converting one query condition, a triple of attribute name, operator and comparison value, in another schema, where potentially also the operator or the comparison value has to be modified.

The paper is structured as follows: The next section introduces a formal framework for schema mapping, based on a special probabilistic logic. Section 3 presents a theoretically founded approach for learning these schema mappings which combines the results of different classifiers. This approach is evaluated on two different test beds in section 4. Then, section 5 describes how this work is related to other approaches. The last section summarizes this paper and gives an outlook over future work.

2   Formal Framework for Schema Mapping

This section introduces sPLMap, a formal, logics-based framework for schema mapping. It shares a lot of ideas from other approaches, e.g. [5], but is different as it is the first one which also takes data types, predicates and query mapping into consideration. It is also the first framework which is able to cope with the intrinsic uncertainty of the mapping process. The framework is based on probabilistic Datalog [8].

2.1   Probabilistic Datalog

Probabilistic Datalog (pDatalog for short) is an extension to Datalog, a variant of predicate logic based on function-free Horn clauses. Negation is allowed, but its use is limited to achieve a correct and complete model (negation is not required in this paper anyway). In pDatalog every fact or rule has a probabilistic weight $0 < \alpha \leq 1$ attached, prefixed to the fact or rule:

$$\alpha A \leftarrow B_1, \ldots, B_n .$$

Here, A denotes an atom (in the rule head), and $B_1, \ldots, B_n$ $(n \geq 0)$ are atoms (the sub goals of the rule body). A weight $\alpha = 1$ can be omitted. Each fact and rule can only appear once in the program, to avoid inconsistencies. The intended meaning of a rule αr is that "the probability that any instantiation of rule r is true is α". The following example pDatalog program expresses the fact that a person is with probability of 50% male:

person(mary) ←

0.8 person(ed) ←

0.5 male(X) ← person(X)

Thus, $Pr(\texttt{male(mary)}) = 0.5$, and $Pr(\texttt{male(ed)}) = 0.8 \times 0.5 = 0.4$. Formally, an interpretation structure (w. r. t. the Herbrand universe) in pDatalog is a tuple $\mathscr{I} = (\mathcal{W}, \mu)$.

Here, $\mathcal{W}$ denotes a possible world (the instantiation of a the deterministic part of a pDatalog program plus a subset of the probabilistic part, where all probabilities are removed in the latter), and μ is a probability distribution over $\mathcal{W}$. An interpretation is a tuple $I = (\mathcal{I}, w)$ such that $w \in \mathcal{W}$. The notion if truth w.r.t. an interpretation and a possible world can be defined recursively:

$$(\mathcal{I}, w) \models A \text{ iff } A \in w,$$
$$(\mathcal{I}, w) \models A \leftarrow B_1, \ldots, B_n \text{ iff } (\mathcal{I}, w) \models B_1, \ldots, B_n \Rightarrow (\mathcal{I}, w) \models A,$$
$$(\mathcal{I}, w) \models \alpha r \text{ iff } \mu(\{w' \in \mathcal{W} : (\mathcal{I}, w') \models r\}) = \alpha.$$

An interpretation is a model of a pDatalog program iff it entails every fact and rule. Given an n-ary atom A for predicate $\bar{A}$ and an interpretation $I = (\mathcal{I}, w)$, the instantiation A^I of A w.r.t. the interpretation A is defined by all $\alpha \bar{A}(c_1, \ldots, c_n)$ with $I \models \alpha \bar{A}(c_1, \ldots, c_n)$. With abuse of notation, we typically consider a relation instance as a set of probabilistically weighted tuples (the arguments of the ground facts), and do not distinguish between a relation R (an n-ary predicate) and the relation instance R^I.

2.2 Data Types

We first assume a finite set $\mathbf{D}$ of elementary data types. The domain $dom(d)$ for a data type $d \in \mathbf{D}$ defines the set of possible values for d. Examples are Text (for English text), Name (person names, e.g. "John Doe"), Year (four digit year numbers, e.g. "2004") or DateISO8601 for the ISO 8601 format of dates (e.g. "2004-12-31"). We further use a set $\mathbf{O}$ of operators (sometimes also called "data type predicates"). An operator is a binary relation $o \subseteq dom(d_1(o)) \times dom(d_2(o))$ defined on two data types $d_1(o), d_2(o) \in \mathbf{D}$, e.g. contains for text (searching for stemmed terms), > or = for years, or sounds-like for names. The operator relations have a probabilistic interpretation (which is the probability that the first value matches the second one) for supporting vague queries. In our scenario, $\mathbf{D}$ contains the data type DOCID (the set of all document ids); only the identity operator $\mathrm{id}_{\mathrm{DOCID}}$ is defined on it.

As we want to use variables for operators, we use a bijective mapping between operators $o \in \mathbf{O}$ and new constants $\delta \in \hat{\mathbf{O}}$ for a set of constants $\hat{\mathbf{O}}$. Then, these operators are combined in a ternary predicate op:

$$\mathrm{op} = \bigcup_{o \in \mathbf{O}} \{\hat{o}\} \times o.$$

Again, we do not explicitly distinguish between the operators o and their constants $\hat{o}$, and use the former notation for both of them. In addition, we use a predicate conv for value conversion between operators:

$$\mathrm{conv}^I \subseteq \bigcup_{o_1, o_2 \in \mathbf{O}} \{\hat{o}_1\} \times dom(d_1(o_1)) \times dom(d_2(o_1)) \times$$
$$\{\hat{o}_2\} \times dom(d_1(o_2)) \times dom(d_2(o_2)).$$

The informal meaning of $\mathrm{conv}(O, X, Y, O', X', Y')$ is that $\mathrm{op}(O, X, Y)$ can be transformed into $\mathrm{op}(O', X', Y')$. Also conv can be uncertain, where the weight denotes the probability that this is a correct conversion. For example, conv may contain the tuples for the data types Year2 (2-digit year numbers), Year4 (4-digit year numbers), *FirstName* (only first names) and Name (complete names):

$$(\mathtt{id}_{\mathtt{Year2}}, ``04'', ``04'', \mathtt{id}_{\mathtt{Year4}}, ``2004'', ``2004'') \,,$$

$$(\geq_{\mathtt{Year2}}, ``04'', ``06'', >_{\mathtt{Year4}}, ``2005'', ``2005'') \,,$$

$$(\mathtt{id}_{\mathtt{FirstName}}, ``John'', ``John'', \mathtt{id}_{\mathtt{Name}}, ``John\ Doe'', ``John\ Doe'')\ \text{with probability} < 1 \,.$$

2.3   Schemas and Schema Mappings

A schema $\mathbf{R} = \langle R_1, \ldots, R_n \rangle$ consists of a non-empty finite tuple of binary relation symbols. Each relation symbol R_i has a data type $d_{R_i} \in \mathbf{D}$. Then, for a (potentially uncertain) interpretation I, a schema instance is a tuple $\mathbf{R}^I = \langle R_1^I, \ldots, R_n^I \rangle$, where each relation symbol R_i is mapped onto a relation instance with the correct data types:

$$R_i \subseteq \mathtt{DOCID} \times dom(d_{R_i}) \,.$$

Informally, this is the relational model of linear schemas with multi-valued schema attributes. Each attribute is modelled as a binary relation, which stores pairs of a document id and a value for that attribute.

We use the following two schemas throughout this presentation:

$$\mathbf{T} = \langle \mathtt{creator}, \mathtt{date} \rangle \,,\ d_{\mathtt{creator}} = \mathtt{Name} \,,\ d_{\mathtt{date}} = \mathtt{DateISO8601} \,,$$

$$\mathbf{S} = \langle \mathtt{author}, \mathtt{editor}, \mathtt{created} \rangle \,,\ d_{\mathtt{author}} = d_{\mathtt{editor}} = \mathtt{Name} \,,\ d_{\mathtt{date}} = \mathtt{DateEnglish} \,.$$

The following example documents are used for explaining the schema matching algorithm:

$$\mathbf{T}^J := \{\mathtt{creator}(\mathtt{d}, ''\mathtt{Miller}''), \mathtt{creator}(\mathtt{d}, ''\mathtt{Smith}''), \mathtt{date}(\mathtt{d}, ''2004-12-31'')\},$$

$$\mathbf{S}^I := \{\mathtt{author}(\mathtt{d}, ''\mathtt{Miller}''), \mathtt{editor}(\mathtt{d}, ''\mathtt{Smith}''), \mathtt{date}(\mathtt{d}, ''\mathtt{Dec31}, 2004'')\}.$$

Schema mappings follow the GLaV approach [6]: A mapping is a tuple $\mathcal{M} = (\mathbf{T}, \mathbf{S}, \Sigma)$, where $\mathbf{T}$ denotes the target (global) schema and $\mathbf{S}$ the source (local) schema with no relation symbol in common, and Σ is a finite set of mapping constraints (pDatalog rules) of one of the forms (T_j and S_i are target and source attributes, respectively):

$$\alpha_{j,i}\ T_j(D,X) \leftarrow S_i(D,X_1), \mathtt{conv}(id_{d_{T_j}}, X, X, id_{d_{S_i}}, X_1, X_1)$$

$$\mathtt{op}(O,X,V) \leftarrow \mathtt{conv}(O,X,V,O_1,X_1,V_1), \mathtt{op}(O_1,X_1,V_1) \,.$$

For simplicity of representation, we drop the conv literal in the remainder of this paper.

In our example, creator subsumes both authors and editors, thus we have these mapping rules:

$$\mathtt{creator}(D,V) \leftarrow \mathtt{author}(D,V) \,,$$

$$\mathtt{creator}(D,V) \leftarrow \mathtt{editor}(D,V) \,,$$

$$\mathtt{date}(D,V) \leftarrow \mathtt{date}(D,V) \,.$$

For a schema mapping instance of a mapping $\mathcal{M} = (\mathbf{T}, \mathbf{S}, \Sigma)$ and a fixed interpretation I for $\mathbf{S}$, an interpretation J for $\mathbf{T}$ is a solution for I under $\mathcal{M}$ if and only if $\langle J, I \rangle$ (the combined interpretation over $\mathbf{T}$ and $\mathbf{S}$) satisfies Σ. The minimum solution is denoted by $J(I, \Sigma)$, the corresponding relation instance with $\mathbf{T}(I, \Sigma)$ (which is also called a minimum solution). Using pDatalog rules, the minimum solution $\mathbf{T}(I, \Sigma)$ is exactly the result of applying the rules Σ onto the instance $\mathbf{S}^I$. In our example, we have $\mathbf{T}^J = \mathbf{T}(I, \Sigma)$.

3   Learning Schema Mappings

This paper only deals with learning schema mappings, i.e. finding associations between attributes. The assumption is that a set of data types **D** and a set of operators **O** with the corresponding relations op and conv are both already given. Learning schema mapping in sPLMap consists of four steps: (i) we guess a potential schema mapping, i.e. a set of rules Σ_k of the form $T_j(x) \leftarrow S_i(x)$ (rules without weights yet); (ii) we estimate the quality of the mapping Σ_k; (iii) among all possible sets Σ_k, we select the "best" schema mapping according to our quality measure; and finally (iv) the weights α for rules in the selected schema mapping have to be estimated.

3.1   Estimating the Quality of a Schema Mapping

For two schemas $\mathbf{T} = \langle T_1, \ldots, T_t \rangle$ and $\mathbf{S} = \langle S_1, \ldots, S_s \rangle$ and two interpretations I for **S** and J for **T**, the goal is to find a suitable set Σ of mapping constraints. In many cases, there is no correspondence between the tuples in both instances, so that no non-trivial mapping $\Sigma \supset \emptyset$ exists. Thus, the goal is to find the "best" set of mapping constraints Σ which maximizes the probability $Pr(\Sigma, J, I)$ that the tuples in the minimum solution $\mathbf{T}(I, \Sigma)$ under $\mathcal{M} = (\mathbf{T}, \mathbf{S}, \Sigma)$ and the tuples in **T** are plausible. Here, $\mathbf{T}(I, \Sigma)$ denotes a schema instance, and $T_j(I, \Sigma)$ the instance of relation T_j formed by the minimum solution. The set Σ can be partitioned into sets Σ_j with common head T_j, whose minimum solutions $T_j(I, \Sigma_j)$ only contain tuples for T_j:

$$\Sigma_1 = \{\texttt{creator(D, V)} \leftarrow \texttt{author(D, V)}, \texttt{creator(D, V)} \leftarrow \texttt{editor(D, V)}\},$$
$$T_1(I, \Sigma_1) = \{\texttt{creator(d, "Miller"), creator(d, "Smith")}\},$$
$$\Sigma_2 = \{\texttt{date(D, V)} \leftarrow \texttt{date(D, V)}\},$$
$$T_2(I, \Sigma_2) = \{\texttt{date(d, "2004} - 12 - 31")\}.$$

As a consequence, each target relation can be considered independently:

$$Pr(\Sigma, J, I) = \prod_{j=1}^{t} Pr(\Sigma_j, J, I).$$

The instances $T_j(I, \Sigma_j)$ and T_j are plausible if the tuples in $T_j(I, \Sigma_j)$ are plausible values for T_j, and vice versa. Using Bayes' theory, $Pr(\Sigma_j, J, I)$ can be computed as:

$$Pr(\Sigma_j, J, I) = Pr(T_j | T_j(I, \Sigma_j)) \cdot Pr(T_j(I, \Sigma_j) | T_j)$$
$$= Pr(T_j(I, \Sigma_j) | T_j)^2 \cdot \frac{Pr(T_j)}{Pr(T_j(I, \Sigma_j))}$$
$$= Pr(T_j(I, \Sigma_j) | T_j)^2 \cdot \frac{|T_j|}{|T_j(I, \Sigma_j)|}.$$

As building blocks of Σ_j, we use the sets $\Sigma_{j,i}$ containing only one candidate rule $\alpha_{j,i} T_j(D, X) \leftarrow S_i(D, X)$:

$$\Sigma_{1,1} = \{\texttt{creator(D, V))} \leftarrow \texttt{author(D, V))}\} \qquad \Sigma_{2,1} = \{\texttt{date(D, V))} \leftarrow \texttt{author(D, V))}\}$$
$$\Sigma_{1,2} = \{\texttt{creator(D, V))} \leftarrow \texttt{editor(D, V))}\} \qquad \Sigma_{2,2} = \{\texttt{date(D, V))} \leftarrow \texttt{editor(D, V))}\}$$
$$\Sigma_{1,3} = \{\texttt{creator(D, V))} \leftarrow \texttt{date(D, V))}\} \qquad \Sigma_{2,3} = \{\texttt{date(D, V))} \leftarrow \texttt{date(D, V))}\}.$$

For s source relations and a fixed j, there are also s possible sets $\Sigma_{j,i}$, and $2^s - 1$ non-empty combinations (unions) of them, forming all possible non-trivial sets Σ_j. To simplify the notation, we set $S_i := T_j(I, \Sigma_{j,i})$ for the instance derived by applying a single rule. For computational simplification, we assume that S_{i_1} and S_{i_2} are disjoint for $i_1 \neq i_2$. If Σ_j is formed by the r single rule sets $\Sigma_{j,i_1}, \dots, \Sigma_{j,i_r}$, then we obtain:

$$Pr(T_j(I, \Sigma_j)|T_j) = \sum_{k=1}^{r} Pr(S_{i_k}|T_j) .$$

Thus, the probability $Pr(\Sigma, J, I)$ can be derived from the $O(s \cdot t)$ probabilities $Pr(S_i|T_j)$. Note, however, that this is only a trick for estimating the former probability. The final output, the rule weights, use the "inverse direction", i.e. $\alpha = Pr(T_j|S_i)$. Section 3.4 shows how this rule probability is computed.

3.2   Estimating the Probability That a Mapping Rule Is Plausible

Similar to LSD [3], the probability $Pr(S_i|T_j)$ is estimated by combining different classifiers $CL_1, \dots CL_n$. Each classifier CL_k computes a weight $w(S_i, T_j, CL_k)$, which has to be normalized and transformed into $Pr(S_i|T_j, CL_k) = f(w(S_i, T_j, CL_k))$, the classifier's approximation of $Pr(S_i|T_j)$. We employ different normalization functions f:

$$w(S_i, T_j, CL_k) \mapsto Pr(S_i|T_j) ,$$
$$f_{id}(x) := x ,$$
$$f_{sum}(x) := \frac{x}{\sum_{i'} w(S_{i'}, T_j, C_k)} ,$$
$$f_{lin}(x) := c_0 + c_1 \cdot x ,$$
$$f_{log}(x) := \frac{\exp(b_0 + b_1 \cdot x)}{1 + \exp(b_0 + b_1 \cdot x)} .$$

The functions f_{id}, f_{sum} and the logistic function f_{log} return values in $[0, 1]$. For the linear function, results below zero have to mapped onto zero, and results above one have to be mapped onto one. The function f_{sum} ensures that each value is in $[0, 1]$, and that the sum equals 1. Its biggest advantage is that is does not use external parameters. In contrast, the parameters of the linear and logistic function have to be learned by regression in a system-training phase. This phase is only required once, and their results can be used for learning arbitrary many schema mappings. Of course, normalization functions can be combined. Often it is useful to bring the classifier weights in the same range (using f_{sum}), and then to apply another normalization function with parameters (e.g. the logistic function).

For the final probability $Pr(S_i|T_j, CL_k)$, we have the constraint

$$0 \leq Pr(S_i|T_j, CL_k) \leq \frac{\min(|S_i|, |T_j|)}{|T_j|} = \min(\frac{|S_i|}{|T_j|}, 1) . \qquad (1)$$

Thus, the normalized value (which is in $[0, 1]$) is multiplied with $\min(|S_i|/|T_j|, 1)$ in a second normalization step.

The final predictions $Pr(S_i|T_j, CL_k)$ are then combined using the Total Probability Theorem, which results in a weighted sum:

$$Pr(S_i|T_j) \approx \sum_{k=1}^{n} Pr(S_i|T_j, CL_k) \cdot Pr(CL_k) . \qquad (2)$$

The probability $Pr(CL_k)$ describes the probability that we rely on the judgment of classifier CL_k, which can for example be expressed by the confidence we have in that classifier. We simply use $Pr(CL_k) = \frac{1}{n}$ for $1 \leq k \leq n$, i.e. the predictions are averaged.

3.3   Classifiers

Most classifiers require instances of both schemas. However, these instances do not need to describe the same objects. The instances should either be a complete collection, or a representative sample of it, e.g. acquired by query-based sampling [1]. Below, see a list of classifiers we considered.

Same Attribute Names. This binary classifier CL_N returns a weight of 1 if and only if the two attributes have the same name, and 0 otherwise:

$$w(S_i, T_j, CL_N) := \begin{cases} 1 & , \quad S_i = T_j, \\ 0 & , \quad \text{otherwise} \end{cases}$$

Exact Tuples. This classifier CL_E (for testing and evaluation) measures the fraction of the tuples in T_j which also occur in $S_i = T_j(I, \Sigma_{j,i})$:

$$w(S_i, T_j, CL_E) := \frac{|S_i \cap T_j|}{|T_j|} .$$

Correct Literals. This classifier CL_L (suitable in particular for numbers, URLs and other facts) measures the fraction of the tuples in T_j where the data value (the second argument, without the document id) also occurs in any tuple in S_i:

$$w(S_i, T_j, CL_L) := \frac{|\{T_j(t_1, t_2): T_j(t_1, t_2) \in T_j, \exists T_j(s_1, s_2) \in S_i = T_j(I, \Sigma_{j,i}).s_2 = t_2\}|}{|T_j|} .$$

kNN Classifier. A popular classifier for text and facts is kNN [15]. For CL_{kNN}, each attribute acts as a category, and training sets are formed for every tuple in S_l:

$$Train = \bigcup_{l=1}^{s} \{(S_l, t'): t' \in S_l\} .$$

A probabilistic variant of the scalar product is used for computing the similarity values. The values t and t' are considered as bags of words, and $Pr(w|S_i)$ and $Pr(w|T_j)$ are computed as the normalized frequencies of the words in the instances:

$$RSV(t, t') = \sum_{w \in t \cap t'} Pr(w|S_i) \cdot Pr(w|T_j) .$$

Naive Bayes Text Classifier. The classifier CL_B uses a naive Bayes text classifier [15] for text content. Again, each attribute acts as a category, and attribute values are considered as bags of words (with normalized word frequencies as probability estimations). The final formula is:

$$w(S_i, T_j, CL_B) = Pr(S_i) \cdot \sum_{x \in T_j} \prod_{w \in x} Pr(w|S_i) .$$

3.4   Estimating the Weight of a Rule

After a schema mapping (a set of rules) is learned, the weights $Pr(T_j|S_i)$ for these rules have to be computed. The probability $Pr(S_i|T_j)$ has already been computed for the quality estimation and, thus, can easily be transformed in the rule weight using Bayes theory:

$$Pr(T_j|S_i) = Pr(S_i|T_j) \cdot \frac{Pr(T_j)}{Pr(S_i)} = Pr(S_i|T_j) \cdot \frac{|T_j|}{|S_i|} . \qquad (3)$$

As the final normalization step in section 3.2 ensures that $Pr(S_i|T_j) \leq \min(|S_i|/|T_j|, 1)$ (see equation (1)), the resulting value $Pr(T_j|S_i)$ is always in $[0, 1]$.

This completes the schema mapping learning process.

4   Experiments for Learning Schema Mappings

This chapter describes the experiments conducted so far for evaluating sPLMap.

4.1   Evaluation Setup

This section describes the test sets (source and target instances) and the classifiers used for the experiments. It also introduces different effectiveness measurements for evaluating the learned schema mappings (error, precision, recall). Experiments were performed on two different test beds[1]:

- BIBDB contains over 3,000 BibTeX entries about information retrieval and related areas. The documents are available both in BibTeX (source schema) and in a manually created standard schema (from the MIND project), derived from BibTeX via simple rules. Both schemas share a large amount of common attribute names.
- LOC is an Open Archive collection of the Library of Congress with about 1,700 documents, available in MARC 21 (source schema) and in Dublin Core (target schema). MARC 21 has a higher granularity as DC, thus a lot of DC attribute values are the concatenation of several MARC 21 attributes. Both schemas use a completely different name scheme, thus they do not have attribute names in common.

Each collection is split randomly into four sub-collections of approximately the same size. The first sub-collection is always used for learning the parameters of the normalization functions (same documents in both schemas). The second sub-collection

---

[1] http://faure.isti.cnr.it/~straccia/download/TestBeds/ecir05-exp.tar.gz

is used as source instance for learning the rules, and the third sub-collection is used as the target instance. Finally, the fourth sub-collection is employed for evaluating the learned rules (for both instances, i.e. we evaluate on parallel corpora).

Each of classifiers introduced in section 3.3 are used alone, plus the combinations $CL_{kNN} + CL_B + CL_L$ and $CL_{kNN} + CL_B + CL_L + CL_N$. The three normalization functions from section 3.2 (f_{sum}, f_{minmax} and f_{id}) are used; in every experiment, every classifier used the same normalization function.

The probability of a tuple t in the given target instance $\mathbf{T}_j^J$ is denoted by $Pr(T_j(d,v) \in T_j^J)$. Often the target instance only contains deterministic data, then we have $Pr(T_j(d,v) \in T_j^J) \in \{0,1\}$. Similarly, $Pr(T_j(d,v) \in T_j(I,\Sigma_j)) \in [0,1]$ denotes the probability of tuple t w.r.t. the minimal solution of the given source instance and the learned schema mapping, i.e. by applying the schema mapping on the source instance. Rule application includes mapping the resulting tuple weights onto 0 or 1, respectively, in the case where a rule weight α outside $[0,1]$ (due to a wrong estimation) leads to a tuple weight which is less than zero or higher than one.

The error of the mapping is defined by:

$$E(\mathcal{M}) = \frac{1}{\Sigma_j |U_j|} \sum_j \sum_{T_j(d,v) \in U_j} (Pr(T_j(d,v) \in T_j^J) - Pr(T_j(d,v) \in T_j(I,\Sigma_j)))^2 ,$$

$$U_j = T_j \cup T_j(I,\Sigma_j) .$$

Here, the set U_j contains the union of the given target instance tuples and the tuples created by applying the mapping rules. For each of these tuples, the squared difference of the given weight $Pr(t|T_j)$ in the target instance and the computed weight $Pr(t|T_j(I,\Sigma_j))$ is computed. Furthermore, we evaluated if the learning approach computes the correct rules (neglecting the corresponding rule weights). Similar to the area of document retrieval, precision defines how many learned rules are correct, and recall defines how many correct rules are learned. Finally, the F-measure denotes the harmonic mean of precision and recall. So, let R_L denote the set of rules (without weights) returned by the learning algorithm, and R_A the set of rules (again without weights) which are the actual ones. Then

$$precision := \frac{|R_L \cap R_A|}{|R_L|}, \quad recall := \frac{|R_L \cap R_A|}{|R_A|}, \quad F = \frac{2}{\frac{1}{precision} + \frac{1}{recall}} .$$

4.2   Results

In the experiments presented in this section, the learning steps are as follows:

1. Find the best schema mapping
   (a) Estimate the plausibility probabilities $Pr(S_i|T_j)$ for every $S_I \in \mathbf{S}$, $T_j \in \mathbf{T}$ using the classifiers.
   (b) For every target relation T_j and for every non-empty subset of the 10 best[2] schema mapping rules having T_j as head, estimate the probability $Pr(\Sigma_j, J, I)$.
   (c) Select the rule set Σ_j which maximizes the probability $Pr(\Sigma_j, J, I)$.

---

[2] These are the rules with the highest prediction $Pr(S_i|T_j)$.

2. Estimate the weights $Pr(T_j|S_i)$ for the learned rules by converting $Pr(S_i|T_j)$, using equation (3).
3. Compute the error, precision and recall as described above.

Table 1. Experimental results – BIBDB

	f_{id}	f_{sum}	$f_{lin} \circ f_{sum}$	$f_{log} \circ f_{sum}$
CL_E	0.8615	0.3689	0.3689	0.3689
CL_L	0.4042	0.0855	0.0854	0.0548
CL_N	0.2639	0.2639	0.2639	0.2639
CL_{kNN}	0.1696	0.0578	0.0535	0.0382
CL_B	0.7024	0.1607	0.1621	0.1629
$CL_{kNN}+CL_B+CL_L$	0.3287	0.0694	0.0686	0.0555
$CL_{kNN}+CL_B+CL_L+CL_N$	0.3225	0.0920	0.0916	0.0806

(a) Error

	f_{id}	f_{sum}	$f_{lin} \circ f_{sum}$	$f_{log} \circ f_{sum}$
CL_E	1.0000	1.0000	1.0000	1.0000
CL_L	0.8750	0.8750	0.8750	0.8750
CL_N	1.0000	1.0000	1.0000	1.0000
CL_{kNN}	0.7692	0.7692	0.7692	0.7500
CL_B	0.5000	0.5000	0.5000	0.4667
$CL_{kNN}+CL_B+CL_L$	0.7692	0.5882	0.5882	0.5263
$CL_{kNN}+CL_B+CL_L+CL_N$	1.0000	0.7692	0.7692	0.7692

(b) Precision

	f_{id}	f_{sum}	$f_{lin} \circ f_{sum}$	$f_{log} \circ f_{sum}$
CL_E	0.3636	0.3636	0.3636	0.3636
CL_L	0.6364	0.6364	0.6364	0.6364
CL_N	0.6364	0.6364	0.6364	0.6364
CL_{kNN}	0.9091	0.9091	0.9091	0.8182
CL_B	0.5455	0.5455	0.5455	0.6364
$CL_{kNN}+CL_B+CL_L$	0.9091	0.9091	0.9091	0.9091
$CL_{kNN}+CL_B+CL_L+CL_N$	1.0000	0.9091	0.9091	0.9091

(c) Recall

	f_{id}	f_{sum}	$f_{lin} \circ f_{sum}$	$f_{log} \circ f_{sum}$
CL_E	0.5333	0.5333	0.5333	0.5333
CL_L	0.7368	0.7368	0.7368	0.7368
CL_N	0.7778	0.7778	0.7778	0.7778
CL_{kNN}	0.8333	0.8333	0.8333	0.7826
CL_B	0.5217	0.5217	0.5217	0.5385
$CL_{kNN}+CL_B+CL_L$	0.8333	0.7143	0.7143	0.6667
$CL_{kNN}+CL_B+CL_L+CL_N$	1.0000	0.8333	0.8333	0.8333

(d) F-measure

The results depicted in the tables 1 and 2 show that the LOC collection is much harder, as the schemas have different granularities, and both schemas do not have any attribute

Table 2. Experimental results – LOC

	f_{id}	f_{sum}	$f_{lin} \circ f_{sum}$	$f_{log} \circ f_{sum}$
CL_E	0.7655	0.7602	0.7602	0.7613
CL_L	0.6754	0.7207	0.7110	0.6266
CL_N	1.0000	1.0000	1.0000	1.0000
CL_{kNN}	0.5948	0.5874	0.5763	0.2140
CL_B	0.6273	0.6315	0.5708	0.2760
$CL_{kNN}+CL_B+CL_L$	0.6250	0.5561	0.5527	0.3837
$CL_{kNN}+CL_B+CL_L+CL_N$	0.6421	0.5427	0.5545	0.3771

(a) Error

	f_{id}	f_{sum}	$f_{lin} \circ f_{sum}$	$f_{log} \circ f_{sum}$
CL_E	0.8889	0.8889	0.8889	0.7333
CL_L	0.8000	0.8000	0.8000	0.4737
CL_N	N/A	N/A	N/A	N/A
CL_{kNN}	0.7059	0.7059	0.7059	0.1688
CL_B	0.4375	0.4375	0.4375	0.1731
$CL_{kNN}+CL_B+CL_L$	0.7692	0.6429	0.6923	0.3000
$CL_{kNN}+CL_B+CL_L+CL_N$	0.7692	0.6429	0.6923	0.3000

(b) Precision

	f_{id}	f_{sum}	$f_{lin} \circ f_{sum}$	$f_{log} \circ f_{sum}$
CL_E	0.1951	0.1951	0.1951	0.2683
CL_L	0.1951	0.1951	0.1951	0.2195
CL_N	0.0000	0.0000	0.0000	0.0000
CL_{kNN}	0.2927	0.2927	0.2927	0.3171
CL_B	0.1707	0.1707	0.1707	0.2195
$CL_{kNN}+CL_B+CL_L$	0.2439	0.2195	0.2195	0.2195
$CL_{kNN}+CL_B+CL_L+CL_N$	0.2439	0.2195	0.2195	0.2195

(c) Recall

	f_{id}	f_{sum}	$f_{lin} \circ f_{sum}$	$f_{log} \circ f_{sum}$
CL_E	0.3200	0.3200	0.3200	0.3929
CL_L	0.3137	0.3137	0.3137	0.3000
CL_N	N/A	N/A	N/A	N/A
CL_{kNN}	0.4138	0.4138	0.4138	0.2203
CL_B	0.2456	0.2456	0.2456	0.1935
$CL_{kNN}+CL_B+CL_L$	0.3704	0.3273	0.3333	0.2535
$CL_{kNN}+CL_B+CL_L+CL_N$	0.3704	0.3273	0.3333	0.2535

(d) F-measure

name in common. The error for the BIBDB collection can be quite low (below 0.1 for CL_L), while the error is in all but two cases above 0.5 for LOC. Precision is high for both collections, but higher for BIBDB. As the learner CL_N cannot learn any rule for LOC (as both schemas use completely different attribute names), the precision is not defined. For the BIBDB collection, recall can be quite high (over 0.9 for CL_{kNN} and the combined classifiers). For LOC, however, the best recall achieved is 0.3171

Averaged on both collections and all normalization functions, the error is minimized by CL_{kNN} with an error of 0.2864, followed by the two combinations with an error of 0.4334, followed by $CL_{kNN} + CL_B + CL_L$ and and $CL_{kNN} + CL_B + CL_L + CL_N$ (each 15-18% worse). Not surprisingly, CL_N and CL_E performed worst (more than 100% worse than CL_{kNN}). These results are replicated considering recall. Interestingly, CL_E yields the highest precision with 0.9250, followed by CL_L (about 14% worse) and $CL_{kNN} + CL_B + CL_L + CL_N$ (about 23% worse). The worst precision (<=0.5 on average) is obtained by CL_N and CL_B. This last result is due to the fact that CL_N does not work on the LOC collection (with no attribute names in common), but perfectly works on the BIBDB collection; while CL_B performs worst for both collection. Overall, combining classifiers can reduce the error and increase recall and precision.

Averaged on both collections and all classifiers, the best normalization functions w. r. t. the error are $f_{log} \circ f_{sum}$ (0.3331) and $f_{lin} \circ f_{sum}$ (about 25% worse). Precision is maximized for f_{id} (0.7346), while recall is maximized for $f_{log} \circ f_{sum}$ and f_{id} (both about 0.45). The experiments show that using the trivial normalization function f_{id} dramatically increases the error (70%), but performs best w. r. t. precision and recall. In other words, the trivial normalization function helps in finding the correct rules, but fails in finding good rule weights (for which a different normalization function has to be applied).

The best classifier/normalization function combination is CL_{kNN} with $f_{log} \circ f_{sum}$ with an error of 0.1261. Best precision is obtained for using CL_E with any normalization function (virtually no difference on average). Recall is maximized for $CL_{kNN} + CL_B + CL_L + CL_N$ with f_{id} (surprisingly), followed by the other normalization functions for CL_{kNN}.

As an illustrative example, in one of BIBDB runs, these two rules are returns for the target attribute booktitle:

$$0.51 \; \texttt{standard\_booktitle(D,X)} \leftarrow \texttt{BIBDB\_booktitle(D,X}'),$$
$$\texttt{conv}(\texttt{id}_{\texttt{Text}}, \texttt{X}, \texttt{X}, \texttt{id}_{\texttt{Text}}, \texttt{X}', \texttt{X}')$$
$$0.98 \; \texttt{standard\_booktitle(D,X)} \leftarrow \texttt{BIBDB\_journal(D,X}'),$$
$$\texttt{conv}(\texttt{id}_{\texttt{Text}}, \texttt{X}, \texttt{X}, \texttt{id}_{\texttt{Text}}, \texttt{X}', \texttt{X}')$$

Notice that, for instance, a query for booktitle is then converted into the source schema, using the above rules, by unfolding the query into two source queries (one for booktitle, the other for journal).

5   Related Work

In the field of federated databases, two approaches are distinguished (see [11, 14]). In "local as view" (LaV), the source schemas are defined as views (mappings) over a fixed global schema. This makes it easy to add a new source, but query transformation has exponential time complexity. In contrast, the global schema is defined as a view over local schemas in the "global as view" (GaV) approach. Here, query transformation can be reduced to rule unfolding, but adding new sources might require to modify the global view. The GLaV approach [6] combines the advantages of both worlds. The global schema is specified ontologically and independent from the sources, the source schema models the documents returned by the source, and mappings are defined by logical rules between query expressions. We adopt the main GLaV idea of independent schemas, but use probabilistic GaV rules, and restrict the schema structure to binary relations (for attributes).

Automatically learning rules is an important problem in machine learning, e.g. for learning relationships between taxonomies or document classifications. A general approach to this pronlem (not only for schema mapping) is described in [12]. ILP (Inductive Logic Programming) is employed for learning rules, while PAC learning algorithm is used for learning the rule weights. The approach requires the same documents in both schemas ("parallel corpora"), which is infeasible in most environments. A second drawback is that it is based on exact match only.

Similar to sPLMap, the heuristic system LSD [3] for finding 1:1 matchings in XML documents uses a linear combination of the predictions of multiple base learners (classifiers). The combination weights are learned via regression on manually specified mappings bctween a small number of learning schemas. LSD has several extensions, e.g. iMAP [2] for complex matchings in relational databases and GLUE [4] for matching ontologies on the semantic web (which relies on joint probability distributions).

Information theory measures and graph matching is used in [10]. Graphs are constructed from the schemas, where the attributes form the nodes, labelled with the entropy of the attribute. All nodes are connected, the edges are labelled with the mutual information (correlation between two distributions). Both measures do not require any interpretation of the data, i.e. data type do not have to be considered. A distance measure is defined, and optimum graph matchings is applied for finding schema mappings.

A completely different approach is taken in MGS [9]. It aims at finding a "hidden model", a schema that probabilistically generates the observed schemas. A hidden model is a partition of the attribute space with a probability function of the partitions and their attributes. The first step finds cliques in the graph where two nodes (attributes) are connected if they are not occurring in the same schema. These cliques do not contradict the schemas. The problem of selecting those cliques which form a partitions is then reduced to a set-cover problem, and the probability functions are computed by maximum-likelihood. In a final step, χ^2 statistical testing is employed for finding sufficiently consistent models.

6   Conclusion and Outlook

Learning rules automatically is an important problem in machine learning, and a large amount of work has been devoted to it. Schema matching is one instantiation of this task, where correspondences ("rules") between two heterogeneous schemas have to be found. In this paper we introduced sPLMap, a formal GLaV-like framework for schema matching, where the mappings are defined as uncertain rules in probabilistic Datalog. These schema mapping rules do not only cover transforming data from one attribute into another, but can also be used for transforming query conditions (potentially also modifying the operator or the comparison value). Although the framework is based on logics, real-world documents and queries with a linear schema can easily be converted into the logical formalism.

The framework sPLMap also covers learning of schema mappings. Different classifiers are used for predicting the probability that tuples in a target relation are plausible for a source relation. Similar to LSD, these predictions are combined to an overall approximation of rule probability. From these probabilities, a probability that a set of such schema mapping rules is plausible is derived. Finally, the rule weights have to be computed. The evaluation shows good performance in error, precision and recall, depending on the chosen classifier(s) and normalization function(s). In particular, instance-based classifiers perform surprisingly well.

The results in this paper can be employed in different ways:

1. Specific schema mapping services can be built automatically. Each schema mapping service has associated two schemas, and it is responsible for mapping between these two schemas. The mapping should be learned automatically instead of being defined manually.
2. Peer-to-peer networks are dynamic scenarios where services can dynamically join and leave, so the system can–for each query–only consider the services which are currently available. Using a decision-theoretic model as for the narrower task of resource selection, we have to find a quality measurement for a schema mapping service.

We mainly target at the information exchange problem: Two schemas are given, and an object instance in one schema is transformed into an instance of the other schema. Our mechanism could also be used for the problem of information integration: Given two source schemas, a mediated schema of them has to be created. A solution would be to build the union of both schemas, learn mapping rules, and remove useless attributes.

In future, more variants should be developed and evaluated to improve the quality of the learning mechanism. Additional classifiers could consider the data types of two attributes, could use a thesaurus for finding synonym attribute names, or could use other measures like KL-distance or mutual information. Instead of averaging the classifier predictions, the weights could be learned via regression. Odds or statistical significance tests could be employed for determining the best schema mapping.

In this work, the conv predicate is given. In environments with large numbers of data types, or a dynamically changing set of data types, learning the conversion predicate would be desirable, e.g. the conversion from centimeter to inch.

A more basic extension is the application onto ontologies. Instead of linear schemas, classification hierarchies are given. The task then is to map instances from one class onto classes in the other hierarchy. We are currently developing a variant oPLMap which is able to infer mapping rules between ontologies.

Acknowledgements

This work is supported in part by ISTI-CNR (project "Distributed Search in the Semantic Web") and in part by the DFG (grant BIB47 DOuv 02-01, project "Pepper").

References

[1] J. Callan and M. Connell. Query-based sampling of text databases. *ACM Transactions on Information Systems*, 19(2):97–130, 2001.

[2] R. Dhamankar, Y. Lee, A. Doan, A. Halevy, and P. Domingos. iMAP: Discovering complex semantic matches between database schemas. In *SIGMOD 2004*, 2004.

[3] A. Doan, P. Domingos, and A. Y. Halevy. Reconciling schemas of disparate data sources: A machine-learning approach. In *SIGMOD Conference*, 2001.

[4] A. Doan, J. Madhavan, R. Dhamankar, P. Domingos, and A. Halevy. Learning to match ontologies on the semantic web. *VLDB Journal*, 2004.

[5] R. Fagin, P. G. Kolaitis, W.-C. Tan, and L. Popa. Composing schema mappings: Second-order dependencies to the rescue. In *Proceedings PODS*, 2004.

[6] M. Friedman, A. Y. Levy, and T. D. Millstein. Navigational plans for data integration. In *Proceedings of 16th Natl Conf on Artificial Intelligence*, pages 67–73, 1999.

[7] N. Fuhr. Towards data abstraction in networked information retrieval systems. *Information Processing and Management*, 35(2):101–119, 1999.

[8] N. Fuhr. Probabilistic Datalog: Implementing logical information retrieval for advanced applications. *Journal of the American Society for Information Science*, 51(2):95–110, 2000.

[9] B. He and K. C.-C. Chang. Statistical schema matching across web query interfaces. In Papakonstantinou et al. [13].

[10] J. Kang and J. F. Naughton. On schema matching with opaque column names and data values. In Papakonstantinou et al. [13].

[11] M. Lenzerini. Data integration: a theoretical perspective. In *Proceedings of the 21st ACM SIGMOD-SIGACT-SIGART symposium on Principles of database systems (PODS-02)*, pages 233–246. ACM Press, 2002.

[12] H. Nottelmann and N. Fuhr. Learning probabilistic Datalog rules for information classification and transformation. In H. Paques, L. Liu, and D. Grossman, editors, *Proceedings of the 10th International Conference on Information and Knowledge Management*, pages 387–394, New York, 2001. ACM.

[13] Y. Papakonstantinou, A. Halevy, and Z. Ives, editors. *Proceedings SIGMOD 2003*, 2003.

[14] E. Rahm and P. A. Bernstein. A survey of approaches to automatic schema matching. *The VLDB Journal*, 10(4):334–350, 2001.

[15] F. Sebastiani. Machine learning in automated text categorization. *ACM Computing Surveys*, 34(1):1–47, 2002.

Encoding XML in Vector Spaces

Vinay Kakade[1,*] and Prabhakar Raghavan[2]

[1] A9.com, Inc., USA
vkakade@a9.com
[2] Verity, Inc., USA
pragh@verity.com

Abstract. We develop a framework for representing XML documents and queries in vector spaces and build indexes for processing text-centric semi-structured queries that support a proximity measure between XML documents. The idea of using vector spaces for XML retrieval is not new. In this paper we (i) unify prior approaches into a single framework; (ii) develop techniques to eliminate special purpose auxiliary computations (outside the vector space) used previously; (iii) give experimental evidence on benchmark queries that our approach is competitive in its retrieval quality and (iv) as an immediate consequence of the framework, are able to classify and cluster XML documents.

1 Overview

1.1 Background and Motivation

We begin with three motivating examples. Consider a product search across multiple heterogeneous catalogs: *find red sweters* [sic] *and return their IDs ranked by price*; we seek matches even if a catalog entry uses *scarlet* instead of red and *pullover* instead of sweater. Text retrieval engines handle thesauri (e.g., for colors), stemming and misspelling, but cannot return specific elements within an XML document that best match the query.

Our second example comes from clustering semi-structured auto service records from multiple dealerships. There is value in discovering a cluster in which the free text contains words such as *blowout* and *rollover*, the `Make` field contains *Ford* or *Mercury* while the (child) `Model` node respectively contains *Explorer* or *Mountaineer*, while the `Parts Replaced` field includes terms such as *Firestone* and *tyre* – clearly this cannot be addressed by standard text clustering.

Our final example is of classification: consider an organization processing job applications. As each resume[3] comes in, we wish to route it to the job requisition best suited for that resume. For instance, computer science students take a wide variety of courses but few of the specialties survive into their work experience;

---

* Work done while the author was a graduate student at Stanford University, USA.
[3] We cannot expect these resumes to conform to any single DTD.

D.E. Losada and J.M. Fernández-Luna (Eds.): ECIR 2005, LNCS 3408, pp. 96–111, 2005.

thus the word *networking* under the element `Work Experience` is likely to be a stronger feature than under `Education`, for resume routing.

Text retrieval systems use proximity metrics between documents while databases *select* using rigid range criteria; can we combine these ideas to provide semi-rigid proximity measures between semi-structured documents?

1.2   Main Contributions and Guided Tour

(1) We develop a framework for vector space XML indexing (Section 2) through the notion of *tree filters*. The choice of these filters governs the index size as well as its retrieval effectiveness. We measure index sizes for a class of tree filters derived from paths in a document (Section 2.2). (2) We benchmark our indexes on INEX *Content Only* queries (Section 3)[4]. We thus show that structure encoded in the vector space helps retrieval quality (Section 3.5), but at the expense of significantly larger indexes (Section 2.2). (3) We introduce *randomized indexes* (Section 2.2). Vector space encodings for XML are challenging in the absence of reliable DTD's. Whereas previous work handled this through additional calculations outside the vector space, randomized indexing lets us preserve the vector space framework. (4) We apply our framework to the classification and clustering of XML documents (Section 4) using standard vector space algorithms.

1.3   Some Technical Underpinnings

Vector spaces: The vector space paradigm has been a standard in text retrieval [28]. The research community has responded with a slew of techniques for improved vector space retrieval such as dimensionality reduction. The vector space paradigm gives us the full power of linear algebra and geometry. Given this background of effective and efficient vector space retrieval, a natural question arises: to what extent can XML retrieval exploit vector spaces?

Content-Centric Queries: We begin with an example:

Example 1. Consider a search for books whose title includes *mystery* and author includes *Agatha* and *Christie*. We should get results from different catalogs, one of which encodes books with the `author` element further split into `first_name` and `last_name` sub-elements, while the other does not. In Figure 1 we seek a partial match even though the path from `author` to each leaf is not strictly a match in the document tree.

A user with a semi-structured information need cannot be expected to conform to a rigid schema or query syntax for two reasons: (1) As argued in [22], end users (unlike applications) avoid detailed structure specification in their queries. (2) The majority of public XML documents have no DTD and only a minuscule

---

[4] The INEX data was made available to us by Tarragon Consulting Corp., USA as consultants to Tarragon and in accordance with all the Terms and Conditions of Tarragon's INEX data handling agreement.

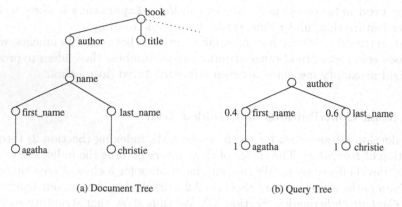

(a) Document Tree   (b) Query Tree

Fig. 1. Tree views of a document and a query

fraction have XML schema [24]. We view an XML document as a tree whose leaves are terms in the lexicon[5] (Figure 1).

Definition 1. *A query tree is a rooted tree in which each internal node is an element and each leaf is a term in the lexicon. Nodes of the query tree may have positive real weights associated with them, to assign a relative weight to the different elements in the query.*

This is the query abstraction used in much previous research on INEX queries [4, 22, 30]. In Figure 1, the query seeks an element with a weight of 0.6 on the match in the last_name element and a weight of 0.4 in the first_name element. Query processing assigns to a (query, document component) pair a real-valued score in [0, 1]. The system may return a book, or another element that appears to match the query (that could be a descendant or ancestor of a book element). In INEX the onus is on the engine to return the matching document component at the right level of specificity. Accordingly, each result for each INEX query is evaluated not only for the relevance of the match but also for the specificity (was the element returned too specific, too general or just right for the query).

1.4   Related Prior Work

Schlieder and Meuss [30] were among the earliest to adopt a vector space model for XML retrieval. The experimental results in [30] are modest in scale (22 documents) and there is no report of retrieval quality. The JuruXml engine [4, 5, 22] is perhaps the furthest developed vector space XML engine; our framework generalizes their work. They supplement their vector space with post-processing to handle cases such as the subpath match in Figure 1. Besides slowing down retrieval this makes the similarity computation unwieldy for classification/clustering. More significantly, post-processing robs us of a crucial tool:

---

[5] Henceforth *lexicon terms*. Our indexes will in general contain terms/axes that need not be terms in the lexicon.

linear algebra. This means that we lose access to linear algebraic techniques such as support vector machines and latent semantic indexing.

Grabs and Schek [14] index only certain *basic* elements into a vector space; the remainder are materialized depending on the query. The XIRQL language and HyREX engine [10, 12] represent the most substantial efforts at providing capabilities for XML motivated by information retrieval, such as relevance ranking and fuzzy matching. A drawback of XIRQL is that it requires a DTD/Schema. XQuery [6] is the W3C's draft specification for a query language for XML. While still evolving, it has favored a data-centric view focusing on highly structured queries. More recently TexQuery [2] addresses this gap by proposing a framework for adding scoring primitives based on a data model called a *fullmatch*. XRANK [16] extends link analysis to a method they call ElemRank, for hyperlinked XML corpora. XRANK works for keyword search rather than for the more general tree queries. The tutorial by Amer-Yahia et al. [1] provides a comprehensive review of XML query languages.

Doucet and Ahonen-Myka [8] initiate a study of XML document clustering. Treating text terms and element tags as separate feature sets in the INEX collection (Section 3.1), they run clustering algorithms and compare the results to a known partition of the documents.

2   The General Framework

We next argue that prior work relating XML to vector spaces falls within a framework in which four components specify an index.

1. **Index units $\mathcal{IU}$** : Which document elements are indexable as vectors? In a vector space text retrieval system, the index represents each document as a vector; what are the corresponding vectors here?
2. **Index terms $\mathcal{IT}$** : What are the axes of the vector space? In a text retrieval system, each lexicon term (possibly after stemming) becomes an axis.
3. **Retrievable units $\mathcal{RU}$** : What nodes in the documents can be returned as answers in a results list?
4. **Composition function $\mathcal{CF}$** : For a document d, let $v \in \mathcal{IU}$ be an index unit and $t \in \mathcal{IT}$ an index term. What is the weight of t in v? A composition function $\mathcal{CF}$ maps the triplet (d, v, t) to a non-negative real weight.

Note that composition functions capture two natural forms of weighting considered in prior literature. First, the notion of *inverse document frequency* (IDF) from text retrieval has been used by virtually all previous vector space formulations. Second, Fuhr *et al.* [10, 12] suggest a positive real *downgrade factor* $\gamma < 1$ as follows. For $v \in \mathcal{IU}$ and $t \in \mathcal{IT}$, let $\mathcal{CF}(v, t)$ be the weight of t in v. Then for $h > 0$, an index unit $a_h(v)$ that is the ancestor at height h above v, $\mathcal{CF}(a_h(v), t) = \gamma^h$. Intuitively, a lexicon term contributes a small but non-zero index entry even for an ancestor far above.

Schlieder and Meuss [30] use all nodes of each document for $\mathcal{IU}$ and $\mathcal{RU}$; they use all subtrees of each document for $\mathcal{IT}$. The elegance of this: the query-to-document score computation reduces to a form of tree pattern matching [18].

This has the disadvantage that the (possibly exponentially many) index terms cannot be pre-compiled into an index structure. This necessitates query-time index materialization that cannot exploit the many preprocessing techniques available in multidimensional retrieval.

While JuruXML [22] similarly uses all nodes as $\mathcal{IU}$ and $\mathcal{RU}$, it uses all root-to-leaf paths as $\mathcal{IT}$; this ensures a more tractable index size. Two additional ideas in JuruXML depart from a vector space formulation: (1) Dynamic programming for longest-common subsequence matching so that we have a match on the example in Figure 1. We invoke randomization in Section 2.2 to reduce this match problem to vector space retrieval. (2) A post-filtering step to enforce hard query constraints (+ and - operators to include/exclude specific content).

2.1   Tree Filters

In our indexes, $\mathcal{IU}$ and $\mathcal{RU}$ are as in [22, 30]: all nodes of all document trees are indexed and retrievable. For $\mathcal{IT}$ we introduce a notion of a *tree filters:* a graph property $\mathcal{P}$ that selects a subset of all subtrees of a document that satisfy $\mathcal{P}$. For instance [30] uses no tree filter at all, thus allowing all possible subtrees as index terms. In contrast JuruXML [22] uses $\mathcal{P}$ to select root-to-leaf paths. As another example, we could use a tree filter that selects all triplets of nodes (as vector space axes), one of which is the parent of the other two.

For query processing, the query tree is likewise expressed as a vector in the space of filtered index terms, normalized and scored using cosine similarity as in classic information retrieval. The class of tree filters used in a particular implementation determines (a) index space and retrieval time and (b) the quality of retrieved results. Below we study a particular class of simple tree filters.

2.2 ℓ-Path Filters and $VeXML_{\gamma,\ell}$

For a non-negative integer ℓ, consider all paths of exactly ℓ nodes of the document tree D *not* including the lexicon term nodes. Our index terms $\mathcal{IT}$ are as follows: to each such path $v_1, \ldots, v_\ell$, append each lexicon term t that appears in any sub-tree of D rooted at v_ℓ. Thus we would have one index term (which we call a *qualified term*) of the form $v_1, \ldots, v_\ell, t$ for each t and each path of the form $v_1, \ldots, v_\ell$. The notion of the appropriate set of document components for computing *inverse document frequencies (IDF)* is discussed in the prior work on vector space XML retrieval [4, 22, 30]; their ideas can easily be folded into our indexes so we do not discuss IDF further.

The case $\ell = 0$ and $\gamma = 1$ corresponds to using the lexicon terms as $\mathcal{IT}$. For convenience, we use $\ell = \infty$ to denote the case when $\mathcal{IT}$ consists of all root-to-leaf paths [22]. Below, we report empirical findings for index size as a function of ℓ, on the INEX 2002 corpus. For a real $\gamma \in [0, 1]$, denote by $VeXML_{\gamma,\ell}$ an index in our framework with the ℓ-path filter for selecting $\mathcal{IT}$, and downgrade factor γ [10, 12] in $\mathcal{CF}$. An algorithm to build $VeXML_{\gamma,\ell}$ is given in Algorithm 1. In this algorithm, $P = v_1, \ldots, v_k, v$ is a root-to-leaf path from the root of document D to v; tag_j is the tag of the node v_j, $1 \leq j \leq k$.

Algorithm 1 Construction of $VeXML_{\gamma,\ell}$

---

for each text node v in D **do**
  $m = min(k, \ell)$
  if $m = 0$ **then** $numberOfTerms = k$
  else $numberOfTerms = k - m + 1$
  endif
  for each lexicon term t in v **do**
    for $i = 1$ to $numberOfTerms$ in steps of 1 **do**
      if $m = 0$ **then**
        $qualified\_term = \{t\}$
      else
        $qualified\_term = \{tag_i, \ldots, tag_{i+m-1}, t\}$
      end if
      $L = $ (possibly empty) postings list of $qualified\_term$ in $VeXML_{\gamma,\ell}$
      for $j = k$ to 1 in steps of -1 **do**
        $weight = \gamma^{k-j}$
        if $\exists w$ such that $\langle v_j, w \rangle \epsilon L$ **then**
          $w = w + weight$
        else
          $L = L \cup \langle v_j, weight \rangle$
        end if
      end for
    end for
  end for
end for
Normalize $VeXML_{\gamma,\ell}$ so that each vector in it is a unit vector

---

Index Sizes: We study two size metrics for our $VeXML_{\gamma,\ell}$ indexes: *dictionary size* and *postings size*. The former, $|\mathcal{IT}|$, corresponds to the dimensionality of the vector space; this in turn affects the cost of elementary operations such as the inner product of two vectors. Postings size on the other hand depends on $|\mathcal{IU}|$. We study these as a function of the number of documents in the input.

The results are shown in Figures 2(a) and 2(b); for clarity we only show the representative cases $\ell = 0, 1, 4, 6, \infty$. Thus, we have a roughly linear increase in dictionary size, for all ℓ. (Note that the parameter γ does not affect the *number* of dictionary and postings entries, only the associated weights.)

A $VeXML_{\gamma,\ell}$ index does not address an important requirement for unreliable DTD's: subpath matching between query and document subtrees. In [22] this is addressed by computing a score based on substring matching *outside* of the vector space. To avoid such "outside" computation, we provide a randomized solution that approximately solves this substring matching problem.

Randomized Index Construction: We augment the deterministically constructed $VeXML_{\gamma,\ell}$ index with index terms of path length L, randomly generated from the documents. We give an intuitive description for the case $L = 2$ in the running text and a precise description in Algorithm 2. Let $v_1, \ldots, v_k, v$ be a root-to-leaf path (v being a lexicon term) in the document being indexed. For i, j

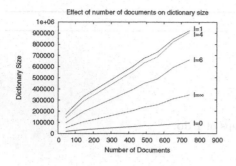
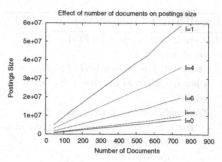

(a) Dictionary size vs. number of documents

(b) Postings size vs. number of documents

Fig. 2. Effect of number of documents on the dictionary size and postings size

---

Algorithm 2 Construction of randomized index

Let $VeXML_{\gamma,\ell}$ be constructed for D as per Algorithm 1.
for each root-to-leaf path $v_1, v_2, \ldots, v_k, v$ in D **do**
    Randomly select subsequences of length L of $v_1, \ldots, v_k$
    for each lexicon term t in v **do**
        for each randomly selected subsequence $s_1, \ldots, s_L$ of $v_1, \ldots, v_k$ **do**
            Let $tag_1, \ldots, tag_L$ be the corresponding tags.
            Add a qualified term $qualified\_term = \{tag_1, \ldots, tag_L, t\}$ to $VeXML_{\gamma,\ell}$, if it
            is not already there. The postings list of $qualified\_term$ is as in Algorithm 1.
        end for
    end for
end for

---

chosen randomly such that $1 \le i < j \le k$, we add index terms of the form $v_i v_j w$ for all lexicon terms w in v. The simplest such random choice would be uniformly from all $1 \le i < j \le k$; we could in fact weigh the distribution towards small values of i, j, to capture an effect suggested in [22]: matching structure close to the root is more important than structure deeper in the tree. This is repeated with independent random choices i, j.

Query Processing: Given a query tree we generate (in addition to the "deterministic" index terms corresponding to $VeXML_{\gamma,\ell}$) index terms for random ordered L-sequences of nodes in root-to-leaf paths. We then compute cosine similarity in this augmented vector space that includes $VeXML_{\gamma,\ell}$ together with random index terms. The net similarity score is the sum of two components: (a) an exact path match score from the axes of $VeXML_{\gamma,\ell}$ index as in Section 2.2 and (b) a subsequence match score resulting from the random sample.

Notes: In this method the index has random *terms*. Consequently, there is no absolute guarantee of identifying a specific subsequence match using our scheme, only a likelihood that increases as more randomized index terms are used. This is defensible on several grounds: (1) our analysis below suggests that the scheme should perform reasonably well at modest index size increase, while eliminating the need for subsequence matching outside the vector space. (2) The entire vector space approach is predicated on several layers of approximation – how well the user's information need is expressed as a vector, how document semantics are expressed as a vector in a feature space, how well cosine similarity approximates the end-user's perception of quality, etc. Over a large sample of documents and queries, a well-designed vector space does well on many queries but could be mediocre on some. Our randomized approach is similar: document/query representations and match criteria are still approximate and (over an ensemble of documents and queries) will do well in the sense of the *expectation* of the match score. (3) Our method will never falsely assign a positive score when there is no subsequence match.

Analysis of Randomized Indexing. We sketch an analysis for $L = 2$; it can easily be extended for longer paths. Let d denote the length of a document path and q the length of a query path. Consider the case where the query and document path have a common subsequence of m elements. The probability that a sampled pair from the document and a sampled pair from the query are both in the common subsequence is $\binom{m}{2}/\binom{d}{2} \times \binom{m}{2}/\binom{q}{2}$. Consider such pair-sampling in conjunction with a base index $VeXML_{\gamma,2}$. Letting λ denote the number of lexicon terms in the document path, the number of index terms in $VeXML_{\gamma,2}$ from this document path is $\leq \lambda d$. A single sample in the randomized index will result in $\leq \lambda$ additional index terms. With S sample pairs, the increase in index size is $\leq \lambda S$. The probability of failing to detect a match is

$$\left[1 - \binom{m}{2}^2 / \binom{d}{2}\binom{q}{2}\right]^S \approx e^{-S\binom{m}{2}^2 / \binom{d}{2}\binom{q}{2}}.$$

For $S \approx \Theta(d)$, we have on the one hand only a constant factor increase in index size over the underlying $VeXML_{\gamma,2}$ index, but a failure probability $\approx e^{-\binom{m}{2}^2 / d\binom{q}{2}}$ that diminishes rapidly as the length m of the matching subsequence increases — as desired. Note that in practice q and m are likely to be very small (probably no more than 3 or 4) while d may be a little larger; the average for the INEX corpus is about 7. By suitably weighting the contribution of these randomized index terms to those from the underlying $VeXML_{\gamma,2}$ index, we can balance the contribution of subsequence matches to more strict path matches; this would depend on the application and its reliability of DTD's.

3 INEX Content-Only Queries

What is the tradeoff between index complexity and the quality of results retrieved? In Section 2 we examined the impact of ℓ on index size. Here we study the the impact of ℓ on the quality of the results. We begin (Section 3.2) by explaining our query formulation methodology. In Section 3.3 we review the INEX

2002 methodology for going from query results (furnished by an engine) to scores and precision-recall curves. Next (Section 3.4) we note some issues in applying this methodology to any engine (such as ours) that did not participate in INEX 2002, and our remedies. Finally in Section 3.5 we detail our results for varying γ and for $\ell = 0, 1$. Encouragingly, even for these cases we find that our quality is competitive; this suggests further experiments with $\ell > 1$.

3.1   INEX 2002 and Our Test Suite

The INEX 2002 corpus consisted of approximately 12000 articles from 12 magazines and 6 transactions published by the IEEE, for a total of approximately 500MB of data. On average a document contained over 1500 XML nodes at an average depth of nearly 7. The retrieval benchmark consists of 60 retrieval tasks, with 30 each of so-called *content-only* (CO) and *content-and-structure* (CAS) queries (see Figure 3 for an example). For each query, an engine had to return a ranked list of document components, each of which was then assessed by the INEX participants manually under two independent criteria: *relevance* and *coverage*. Based on the pair of scores assigned to each document component retrieved by an engine, the engine was assigned accuracy scores and precision-recall curves using ideas described in [13].

3.2   CO Topics Translation Methodology

The CO topics translation methodology we used is a slightly modified version of the one suggested by [22]. We apply the following translation rules for automatically constructing queries for $\ell = 0$:

- If there is only one word in the $\langle cw \rangle$ tag, we add it to the query with a weight of 1.0, along with all the terms in the $\langle Keywords \rangle$ tag with a weight of 0.3.
- If there are only two words in the $\langle cw \rangle$ tag, we add them to the query as a phrase with a weight of 1.0, along with all the terms in the $\langle Keywords \rangle$ tag with a weight of 0.3.
- If there are more than two words in the $\langle cw \rangle$ tag, we add them to the query with a weight of 0.3, and ignore the words in the $\langle Keywords \rangle$ tag (as they likely add noise).

For example, the query for $\ell = 0$ corresponding to Figure 3 is **1.0 "computational biology" 0.3 bioinformatics 0.3 genome 0.3 genomics 0.3 proteomics 0.3 sequencing 0.3 "protein folding"**.

The queries corresponding to $\ell = 1$ are constructed from those for $\ell = 0$. For each term t with weight w in a query for $\ell = 0$, we add three terms bdy/t, fm/t, bm/t with weight w to the query for $\ell = 1$. The reason is that most of the answers to the INEX queries lie in the subtrees of $\langle bdy \rangle$, $\langle fm \rangle$ and $\langle bm \rangle$ nodes.

3.3   INEX Evaluation Methodology

The reader should consult [13] for a detailed description of the INEX process; here we touch upon the salient points. We focus on the 30 content-focused in-

```
<INEX-Topic topic-id="31" query-type="CO" ct-no="003">
    <Title>
      <cw>computational biology</cw>
    </Title>
    <Keywords>
      computational biology, bioinformatics, genome, genomics, proteomics,
      sequencing, protein folding
    </Keywords>
    <Description>
      Challenges that arise, and approaches being explored, in the
      interdisciplinary field of computational biology.
    </Description>
    <Narrative>
      To be relevant, a document/component must either talk in general
      terms about the opportunities at the intersection of computer
      science and biology, or describe a particular problem and the ways
      it is being attacked.
    </Narrative>
</INEX-Topic>
```

Fig. 3. INEX Topic 31: Computational Biology

formation needs in the benchmark, referred to in INEX 2002 as the "CO query suite". Figure 3 gives an example, with only the relevant tags included. As in the TREC benchmark (http://trec.nist.gov/), each topic description is then turned into a query by the participant team, for its query engine. Next, the engine retrieves the top 100 results for each query, where a result is a document component from the collection (e.g., the abstract of a paper).

All components retrieved by any engine for a query are then put in a results pool; the typical such pool has about 2000 document components from 1000 articles [13]. Each result is evaluated by two criteria — its *relevance* and its *coverage*. The latter is motivated by the fact that an XML engine may retrieve a document component at any level — e.g., a whole paper, its abstract, a section within it or perhaps a definition. The evaluators assessed the relevance and coverage of each result, to determine whether it was too broad (say a whole book when a definition was sought) or too narrow. Relevance was assessed on a scale from Irrelevant (scoring 0) to Highly Relevant (scoring 3). Coverage was assessed on a scale with four levels: No Coverage (N: the query topic does not match anything in the document component retrieved), Too Large (L: the topic is only a minor theme of the component retrieved), Too Small (S: the component is too small to provide the information required) or Exact (E). At this point, every result returned by each engine has a pair of ratings from $\{0, 1, 2, 3\} \times \{N, S, L, E\}$ (although clearly some of these combinations would never arise).

3.4   Adapting the INEX Evaluations

To adapt the INEX 2002 assessments we first review the manner in which INEX combined the relevance/coverage assessments into scores. Define two f values

$$f_{strict}(rel, cov) = \begin{cases} 1 \text{ if } rel = 3 \text{ and } cov = E \\ 0 \text{ otherwise} \end{cases}$$

and

$$f_{generalised}(rel, cov) = \begin{cases} 1.00 \text{ if } rel, cov = 3E \\ 0.75 \text{ if } rel, cov \in \{2E, 3L\} \\ 0.50 \text{ if } rel, cov \in \{1E, 2L, 2S\} \\ 0.25 \text{ if } rel, cov \in \{1S, 1L\} \\ 0.00 \text{ if } rel, cov = 0N. \end{cases}$$

These f values allow us to combine the pair of assessments for a result into a single number in two ways — referred to respectively in INEX as *strict* and *generalised* quantization.

There is a difficulty in adopting this methodology: our engine could return some document components for which no assessments are available from the INEX pool. It is then impossible to average, over all query topics, our f value as a function of rank. Further, this makes it impossible for us to generate precision-recall curves as the INEX participants were able to. We circumvent this as follows: for each rank $r \in \{1, 2, \ldots, 100\}$ we average our f value over all results that we report at rank r, on any query, *for which INEX assessments are available*. Of the 30 INEX CO queries, six had no assessments at all; our results below are on the remaining 24 queries.

3.5   Results Quality for $VeXML_{\gamma, \ell}$

We give here the results for $VeXML_{\gamma, 0}$ and $VeXML_{\gamma, 1}$ for varying γ. Figure 4 shows the average f values for both strict and generalized quantization. For both, the best value of γ is about 0.9, for both $\ell = 0$ and $\ell = 1$. As noted above we could not generate precision-recall curves (the only published metrics for the INEX participants). However, we were able to obtain the actual retrieved document components from Tarragon, a team that was ranked 10th (out of 49) in strict quantization and 17th in generalized quantization for CO queries. We

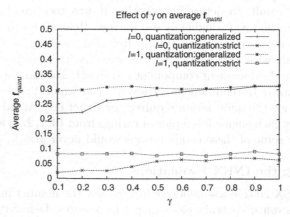

Fig. 4. Average f vs. γ

were thus able to average Tarragon's f values; they had an average of 0.0636 for f_{strict} and 0.243 for $f_{generalised}$. We clearly compare favorably on generalized quantization as well as on strict quantization. More interestingly, our f values are consistently higher for $\ell = 1$ than for $\ell = 0$, establishing that encoding XML structure in the vector space actually yields better retrieval quality.

4   Classification and Clustering

4.1   Classification

Because of our pure vector space approach, we can directly invoke any classification method that uses vector spaces. We demonstrate this with two classification methods – NN and CENTROID. We only classify the root of each document, for varying values of ℓ and γ. We ran our experiments on two datasets: INEX, and the CSLOG dataset [33] used in earlier work on XML classification.

For the INEX dataset we used as training documents articles four journals from the years 1996-98: IEEE Annals of the History of Computing, IEEE Computer Graphics and Applications, IEEE Computational Science & Engineering and IEEE Design & Test of Computers. As test documents, we used articles from the years 1999, 2000 and 2001 from the same four journals. NN and CENTROID were used to predict, for each test article, which journal it came from.

The CSLOG dataset contains documents that describe log reports at the CS department website of the Rensselaer Polytechnic Institute. Each document is in the Log Markup Language (LOGML) [26], which expresses the contents of a log file in XML, by modelling each user session as a graph. Each user session is given one of the two class labels: *edu* for users visiting the CS department from the "edu" or "ac" domains, and *other* for users from all other domains. We used the log reports of the first week as our training documents and used them to predict the class of each of the second week logs. Table 1 shows the number of features (i.e., $\mathcal{IT}$:) in our vector spaces for both these datasets. The column "Training features" shows the number of features in the training set, while the column "Total features" shows the number of features in the training as well as test sets.

Classification results for varying values of ℓ and γ are given in Table 2. They suggest that structure helps in classification for the CSLOG dataset, but does not help for the INEX dataset. In fact for $\ell = \infty$, the classifier fails to classify

Table 1. The number of features

	INEX		CSLOG	
ℓ	Training features	Total features	Training features	Total features
0	112434	189994	54953	71173
1	941264	1542911	219134	282537
2	910469	1608216	165490	213071
∞	371935	638416	73387	97986

Table 2. Classification accuracy (%) for the INEX and CSLOG dataset

γ	INEX Accuracy (1-NN)				INEX Accuracy (CENTROID)			
	$\ell=0$	$\ell=1$	$\ell=2$	$\ell=\infty$	$\ell=0$	$\ell=1$	$\ell=2$	$\ell=\infty$
0.1	69.04	71.81	70.00	0	44.68	38.29	40.00	0.11
0.5	68.33	67.02	62.34	0	72.55	76.38	60.74	0.11
0.9	72.65	66.17	60.01	0	74.04	72.58	52.44	0.11
1.0	72.76	64.78	58.90	0	74.14	73.08	50.74	0.11

γ	CSLOG Accuracy (1-NN)				CSLOG Accuracy (CENTROID)			
	$\ell=0$	$\ell=1$	$\ell=2$	$\ell=\infty$	$\ell=0$	$\ell=1$	$\ell=2$	$\ell=\infty$
0.1	96.77	96.81	97.11	98.61	96.86	97.30	96.93	97.84
0.5	78.90	78.61	78.59	79.71	71.80	71.97	71.96	75.65
0.9	77.78	77.64	77.42	77.80	72.15	73.95	73.41	73.08
1.0	77.72	77.54	77.24	77.54	73.06	74.22	73.22	72.80

the INEX documents, while it achieves near-perfect classification for CSLOG. The reason: the INEX corpus is richer in textual content than the LOGML server logs in the CSLOG dataset and likely demands more from the content for classification accuracy. So, we get good classification results for the INEX dataset for $\ell = 0$ and a high value of γ. The classifier fails to classify the documents for $\ell = \infty$, as the lexicon terms in the test collection become a lot more "qualified", and do not appear anywhere in the training collection.

On the other hand, the CSLOG dataset demands more from the structure than from the content. The class of each document in the CSLOG dataset turns out to be derived solely from the contents of the *name* attribute of the $\langle graph \rangle$ element — if the name attribute contains the token "edu" or "ac" in it, then the document is of type *edu*, otherwise it is of type *other*. A low γ effectively minimizes the contribution of all the descendants of the $\langle graph \rangle$ node; a high value of ℓ qualifies the lexicon terms occurring in the *name* attribute so that they will not match with the same lexicon terms occurring elsewhere in the document. Thus a low γ with high values of ℓ gives near-perfect classification results for the CSLOG dataset, somewhat better than the ones in [33]. Simple vector space classification thus gives near-perfect results here, without apparent need for tree mining [33].

4.2   Clustering

We evaluated our approach on the k-means clustering of XML documents. We clustered on the same subsets of the INEX and CSLOG datasets as the test documents used in classification (Section 4.1). The goal was to confirm our understanding of ℓ and γ in $VeXML_{\gamma,\ell}$. For the INEX dataset, we set the number of clusters (k) to 4, corresponding to the 4 journals. For the CSLOG dataset, we set the number of clusters to 2, corresponding to whether or not the documents are from the "edu"/"ac" domains. We compared our clusterings obtained with the ground truth using the *Variation of Information* (VI) measure [23]. The results are given in Table 3. These results confirm our intuition in Section 4.1

Table 3. k-means clustering quality (VI measure) for the INEX and CSLOG dataset

γ	INEX VI measure				CSLOG VI measure			
	$\ell = 0$	$\ell = 1$	$\ell = 2$	$\ell = \infty$	$\ell = 0$	$\ell = 1$	$\ell = 2$	$\ell = \infty$
0.1	3.703	3.592	3.603	3.860	1.142	1.209	1.289	1.216
0.5	2.590	2.960	3.541	3.633	1.364	1.525	1.770	1.737
0.9	2.569	3.192	3.495	3.536	1.545	1.770	1.764	1.761
1.0	2.570	3.202	3.497	3.542	1.772	1.769	1.763	1.759

regarding the parameters γ and ℓ. A high value of γ with small ℓ gives good clustering results for INEX, while a low value of γ with a high ℓ gives good clustering results for CSLOG dataset, for the reasons outlined in Section 4.1.

5   Conclusion and Future Work

Our work validates that encoding XML in vector spaces can tap the wealth of techniques in vector space information retrieval. Several interesting directions open up as a result. First, there is the detailed empirical study of randomized indexing, as well as its potential application to other settings. Second, it would be interesting to understand the power of spectral techniques such as LSI for retrieval and support vector machines for classification. Third, our classification and clustering results show that index parameters are influenced by the nature of the XML content; what guidelines can we develop for these choices?

Acknowledgement

We thank Dr. Richard Tong of Tarragon Consulting Corp. for his suggestions and his help with the INEX dataset and the authors of [33] for their help with the CSLOG dataset.

References

1. S. Amer-Yahia, N. Koudas and D. Srivastava. Approximate matching in XML. http://www.research.att.com/ sihem/publications/PART1.pdf
2. S. Amer-Yahia, C. Botev and J. Shanmugasundaram. TeXQuery: A Full-Text Search Extension to XQuery. *WWW* 2004.
3. S. Amer-Yahia, L. V. S. Lakshmanan and S. Pandit. FleXPath: Flexible Structure and Full-Text Querying for XML *SIGMOD* 2004.
4. D. Carmel, N. Afraty, G. Landau, Y. Maarek and Y. Mass. An extension of the vector space model for querying XML documents via XML fragments. *XML and Information Retrieval Workshop at SIGIR*, 2002.
5. D. Carmel, Y. Maarek, M. Mandelbrod, Y. Mass, A. Soffer. Searching XML documents via XML fragments. *SIGIR* 2003.
6. D. Chamberlin, D. Florescu, J. Robie, J Siméon, M. Stefanescu. XQuery: A query language for XML. W3C Technical Report.

7. C.J. Crouch, S. Apte and H. Bapat. Using the extended vector model for XML retrieval. In [9], 95–98, 2002.
8. A. Doucet and H. Ahonen-Myka. Naive clustering of a large XML document collection. In [9], 81–88, 2002.
9. N. Fuhr, N. Gövert, G. Kazai and M. Lalmas. Proceedings of the First Workshop of the INitiative for the Evaluation of XML Retrieval (INEX), 2002.
10. N. Fuhr and K. Großjohann. XIRQL: A Query Language for Information Retrieval in XML Documents. In *Research and Development in Information Retrieval*, 172–180, 2001.
11. N. Fuhr and G. Weikum. Classification and Intelligent Search on Information in XML. *IEEE Data Engineering Bulletin* **25**(1), 2002.
12. N. Gövert, M. Abolhassani, N. Fuhr and K. Großjohann. Content-oriented XML retrieval with HyRex. In [9], 26–32, 2002.
13. N. Gövert and G. Kazai. Overview of INEX 2002. In [9], 1–17, 2002.
14. T. Grabs and H-J Schek. Generating vector spaces on-the-fly for flexible XML retrieval. Second SIGIR XML workshop, 2002.
15. D. Guillaume and F. Murtagh. Clustering of XML documents, *Computer Physics Communications*, **127**:215–227 (2000).
16. L. Guo, F. Shao, C. Botev and J. Shanmugasundaram. XRANK: Ranked Keyword Search over XML Documents. *SIGMOD* 2003.
17. Initiative for the evaluation of XML retrieval. http://qmir.dcs.qmul.ac.uk/INEX/
18. P. Kilpeläinen. Tree Matching Problems with Applications to Structured Text Databases. PhD thesis, Dept. of Computer Science, University of Helsinki, 1992.
19. G. Kazai, M. Lalmas, N. Fuhr and N. Gövert. A report on the first year of the INitiative for the Evaluation of XML Retrieval (INEX 02). *Journal of the American Society for Information Science and Technology* **54**, 2003.
20. R. Luk, H. Leong, T. Dillon, A. Chan, W. Bruce Croft, J. Allan. A survey in indexing and searching XML documents. *JASIST 53(6)* 415-437 (2002).
21. G. Kazai, S. Masood, M. Lalmas. A Study of the Assessment of Relevance for the INEX'02 Test Collection. *ECIR* 2004.
22. Y. Mass, M. Mandelbrod, E. Amitay, D. Carmel, Y. Maarek and A. Soffer. JuruXML – an XML retrieval system at INEX'02. In [9],73–80, 2002.
23. M. Meila. Comparing Clusterings. Technical Report 418, University of Washington Statistics Dept., 2002.
24. L. Mignet, D. Barbosa and P. Veltri. The XML Web: a First Study. *Proceedings of the 12th International World Wide Web Conference*, 2003. Evaluating Structural Similarity in XML Documents. *Proceedings of the Fifth International Workshop on the Web and Databases (WebDB 2002)*.
25. N. Polyzotis, M. Garofalakis, Y. Ioannidis. Approximate XML Query Answers. *SIGMOD 2004.*
26. J. Punin, M. Krishnamoorthy, M. Zaki. LOGML: Log markup language for web usage mining. *In WEBKDD Workshop (with SIGKDD)*, 2001.
27. F. Rizzolo and A. Mendelzon. Indexing XML Data with ToXin. *Proceedings of Fourth International Workshop on the Web and Databases*, 2001.
28. G. Salton. The SMART Retrieval System – Experiments in automatic document processing. Prentice Hall Inc., Englewood Cliffs, 1971.
29. T. Schlieder. Similarity search in XML data using cost-based query transformations. *Proc. 4th WebDB*, 19–24, 2001.
30. T. Schlieder and H. Meuss. Querying and Ranking XML Documents. *Journal of the American Society for Information Science and Technology* **53**(6):489-503, 2002.

31. J. Shanmugasundaram, K. Tufte, G. He, C. Zhang. D. DeWitt and J. Naughton. Relational Databases for Querying XML Documents: Limitations and Opportunities. *Proc. VLDB* 1999.

32. M. Zaki. Efficiently Mining Frequent Trees in a Forest. *Proceedings of ACM KDD*, 2002.

33. M. Zaki and C. Aggarwal. XRULES: An Effective Structural Classifier for XML Data. *Proceedings of ACM KDD*, 2003.

Features Combination for Extracting
Gene Functions from MEDLINE

Patrick Ruch[1], Laura Perret[2], and Jacques Savoy[2]

[1] University Hospital of Geneva
Patrick.Ruch@sim.hcuge.ch
[2] University of Neuchâtel
{Laura.Perret, Jacques.Savoy}@unine.ch

Abstract. This paper describes and evaluates a summarization system that extracts the gene function textual descriptions (called GeneRIF) based on a MedLine record. Inputs for this task include both a locus (a gene in the LocusLink database), and a pointer to a MedLine record supporting the GeneRIF. In the suggested approach we merge two independent phrase extraction strategies. The first proposed strategy (LASt) uses argumentative, positional and structural features in order to suggest a GeneRIF. The second extraction scheme (LogReg) incorporates statistical properties to select the most appropriate sentence as the GeneRIF. Based on the TREC-2003 genomic collection, the basic extraction strategies are already competitive (52.78% for LASt and 52.28% for LogReg, respectively). When used in a combined approach, the extraction task clearly shows improvement, achieving a Dice score of over 55%.

1 Introduction

As an increasing amount of information becomes available in the form of electronic documents, the increasing need for intelligent text processing makes shallow text understanding methods such as the Information Extraction (IE) particularly useful [19]. Until now, IE has been defined in a restricted manner by DARPA's MUC (Message Understanding Conference) program [4], as a task involving the extraction of specific, well-defined types of information from natural language texts in restricted domains, with the specific objective of filling pre-defined template slots and databases. Examples of such classical information extraction tasks are given by the Bio-Creative[1] named-entity recognition task or the JNLPBA shared task (e.g., [14]). Recently, the TREC-2003 Genomics Track proposed that the IE task be extended by extracting entities that were less strictly defined. As such, the 2003 Genomics Track suggested extracting gene functions as defined in the LocusLink database. In this repository, records (called *locus*, which refer to a gene or a protein) are provided with a short fragment of text to explain their biological function together with a link to the corresponding scientific article. These so-called Gene Reference Into Functions (GeneRIFs) are usually short extracts taken from MedLine articles. As with classical Named-Entities (NE) such as the names of persons, locations or genes, GeneRIFs are

---

[1] www.pdg.cnb.uam.es/BioLINK/workshop_BioCreative_04

D.E. Losada and J.M. Fernández-Luna (Eds.): ECIR 2005, LNCS 3408, pp. 112–126, 2005.
© Springer-Verlag Berlin Heidelberg 2005

too extensive to be comprehensively listed, but their major difference is that gene functions are usually expressed by a sentence rather than a single word, an expression or a short phrase. GeneRIF variations thus contrast with those of other related tasks. Just as in the context of the BioCreative challenge, the automatic text categorization task also attempts to predict the function of proteomic entities (based on the SwissProt repository) using literature excepts [7]. In that task however, the set of available functions is strictly defined in the Gene Ontology[2]. Moreover, the application of machine learning techniques [22] to filter relevant fragments has received little attention in IE ([5] is an exception) compared to other tasks such as named entity recognition. This lack of interest is due to the type of texts that are generally handled by IE, which are those proposed in the MUC competition. These texts are often short newswires and the information to be extracted is generally dense, so there is much less if any need for prefiltering. For example, the type of information to be extracted may be company names or seminar starting times, often only requiring a shallow analysis. The computational cost is thus fairly low and prefiltering can be avoided. This is clearly not the case in other IE tasks such as those for identifying gene functions in genomics, the application that we describe here.

The remainder of the paper is organized as follows: Section 2 provides an overview of the state of the art. Section 3 describes the different methods and their combinations, as well as the metrics defined for the task. Section 4 reports on the results.

2 Background and Applications

Historically, seminal studies dedicated to the selection of textual fragments were done for automatic summarization purposes, but recently, due to developments in life sciences, more attention has been focused on sentence filtering.

2.1 Summarization

In automatic summarization, the sentence is the most common type of text-span[3] used because in most general cases, it is too difficult to understand, interpret, abstract, and generate a new document or a short summary. By choosing sentences as generation units, many co-reference issues [28] are partially avoided. Although more knowledge intensive approaches have been investigated, it seems simpler and more effective to view the summarization problem as a sentence extraction problem.

In this vein, Goldstein *et al.* [8] distinguish between two summary types: generic and query-driven. This distinction is useful relative to our information extraction task, since it involves question answering (with the query-driven type) or summarization (generic). In our study, other summarization criteria such as the length and style of the generated abstract can be ignored. Feature selection and their weighting, often based on term frequency and inverse document frequency factors (*tf idf*) have been reported. Conclusions reached are however not always consistent [25] about *tf idf*. Among other

---

[2] www.geneontology.org/

[3] Berger & Mittal [1] define a summarization task, called *gisting* which aims at reducing the sentences by modeling content-bearing words. The suggested strategy seems effective for summarizing non-argumentatively structured documents such as Web pages.

interesting features, both sentence location as well as sentence length seem important [15]. In addition these authors rely on a set of frequent phrases and keywords. Finally, to extract important sentences from documents, a document's titles and uppercase words such as named-entities are reported to be good predictors. Of particular interest for our approach, Teufel & Moens [31] define a large list of manually weighted triggers (using both words and expressions such as *we argued, in this article, the paper is an attempt to, etc.*) to automatically structure scientific articles into seven argumentative moves, namely: BACKGROUND, TOPIC, RELATED WORK, PURPOSE, METHOD, RESULT, and CONCLUSION.

2.2 A Genomics Perspective on Information Extraction

To date and as with gene functions, descriptions of most of the biological knowledge about these interactions cannot be found in databanks, but only in the form of scientific summaries and articles. Making use of these represents a major milestone towards building models of the various interactions between entities in molecular biology; and sentence filtering has therefore been greatly studied for its potential in mining literature on functional genomics. For example, sentence filtering for protein interactions was previously described in [23] and [3]. In these studies, sentence filtering is viewed as a prerequisite step towards deeper understanding of texts.

Input

Locus - ABCA1: ATP-binding cassette, sub-family A (ABC1), member 1

MedLine record - PMID - 12804586

TI - Dynamic regulation of alternative ATP-binding cassette transporter A1 transcripts.

AB – [...] The longest (class 1) transcripts were abundant in adult brain and fetal tissues. Class 2 transcripts predominated in most other tissues. The shortest (class 3) transcripts were present mainly in adult liver and lung. To study the biochemical significance of changes in transcript distribution, two cell models were compared. In primary human fibroblasts, upregulation of mRNA levels by oxysterols and retinoic acid increased the relative proportion of class 2 transcript compared to class 1. Phorbol ester stimulated human macrophage-derived THP-1 cells increased the abundance of class 1 transcripts relative to class 2. In both cell lines class 3 transcript levels were minimal and unchanged. It is shown here for the first time that the **regulation of ABCA1 mRNA levels exploits the use of alternative transcription start sites**.

Output

GeneRIF - **regulation of ABCA1 mRNA levels exploits the use of alterntive transcription start sites**

Fig. 1. Example of a LocusLink record and the corresponding GeneRIF (bold added)

2.3 TREC-2003 Corpus

To provide a general view of the problems underlying the generation of the most appropriate GeneRIF during the TREC-2003 Genomics Track [10], a simple example is provided in Fig. 1. In this figure we can see the locus ("ABCA1") and the MedLine record identifier ("PMID – 12804586"). Under the label "TI" is found the article's title and under "AB" its abstract (from which the GeneRIF is extracted).

A preliminary study [21] showed that around 95% of the GeneRIF snippets were extracted from the title or from the abstract of the corresponding scientific paper. Moreover, from this set, around 42% were a direct "cut & paste" from either the title or the abstract (Fig. 1 is such an example) while another 25% contained significant portions of the title or abstract.

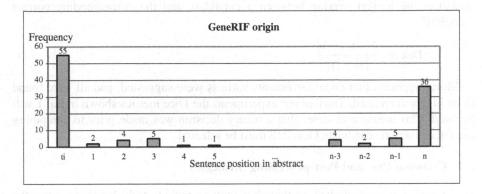

Fig. 2. GeneRIF distribution in titles ("ti") and in abstracts (from 1 to n)

In the TREC evaluation data, we analyzed the sentence location distribution used to produce the GeneRIF. In this case, we considered the title (see Fig. 2, the first column labeled "ti") and the abstract's sentence sequence. From the 139 GeneRIFs used in our experiments, 55 were mainly extracted from the article's title, as depicted in Fig. 2. The second most frequent source of GeneRIF was the abstract's last sentence (see the last column in Fig. 2, following the label "n"), showing the source of 36 GeneRIFs. Between these two extreme positions, the GeneRIF location distribution is rather flat.

3 Methods

As for automatic abstracting, evaluating sentence classifiers is difficult. First of all establishing the benchmark notion is clearly a more complex task. Secondly it is less universally defined, as compared to other automatic text classification tasks such as spelling correction, document routing or in information retrieval systems evaluation.

3.1 Metrics

In general, for each input text the classification techniques yield a ranked list of candidates. Thus, sentence filtering like information extraction and text categorization may be formally evaluated by the usual recall and precision measures. However, we must recognize that it is hard to obtain complete agreement regarding the appropriate measure that should be used. It has been argued [18] that in evaluating a binary classification system, one should use effectiveness measures based on estimates of class membership rather than measures based on rankings. On the other hand, a precision oriented-metric such as 11-point average precision has been suggested [17]. In the TREC-2003 genomic evaluation campaign, a third type of measure was used to evaluate information extraction: the Dice coefficient as shown in Eq. 1. In this formula, the numerator indicates the number of common words between the candidate sentence and the exact GeneRIF, while the denominator represents the total number of words in the GeneRIF and in the candidate. Thus, this similarity coefficient measures the lexical overlap between a candidate and the corresponding correct GeneRIF.

$$\text{Dice} = \frac{2 \cdot |X \cap Y|}{|X| + |Y|} \tag{1}$$

More precisely, four Dice coefficients variants were suggested, and all were found to be highly correlated. Thus, in our experiments the Dice metrics shown in Eq. 1 will be used. This measure assumes that a binary decision was made prior to computing the Dice: a unique candidate GeneRIF must be selected.

3.2   Common Pre- and Post-processing Strategies

We started designing the task as though a form of ranking task. Sentences were the entities to be classified, so we assumed that GeneRIFs were sentences or significant sentence fragments. This has its limitations since some examples in the training and test data showed the opposite effect: GeneRIFs were sometimes the synthesis of more than one sentence. Such examples were however not the norm and also the generation of a well-formed sentence required the resolution of complex linguistic phenomena (e.g., anaphora, pronoun generations), and this was beyond the scope of our study. For sentence splitting, we developed a robust tool based on manually crafted regular expressions. This served to detect sentence boundaries with more than 97% precision on MedLine abstracts, and was deemed competitive with more elaborate methods [26]. In order to avoid applying our classifiers on erroneously segmented sentences, segments with less than 20 characters were simply removed from the list of candidate sentences.

Next, both strategies ranked the candidate sentences separately. From these two rankings, our aim was to identify a confidence estimator and then choose the final candidate when both our schemes disagreed on the best choice. This last step transformed the two ranking tools into a binary classifier, thus finally deciding whether a candidate sentence was relevant or not. The relevant sentence (the one that was unique in each [locus, abstract] pair) is post-processed by a syntactic module, in an attempt to eliminate irrelevant phrases from the selected sentence.

This sentence reduction step used a part-of-speech tagger [27] and a standard list of 369 stopwords (e.g., *so, therefore, however, then,* etc.) together with a set of stop phrases (e.g., *in contrast to other studies, in this paper,* etc.). When these stop phrases occurred they were removed from the beginning of the selected GeneRIF candidate. Part-of-speech information was used to augment the list of stopwords, thus any adverb (e.g., *finally*, *surprisingly*, etc.) located at the beginning of a sentence was removed. In the same manner, this procedure removed non-content bearing introductory syntagms when they were located at the beginning of the sentence: any fragment of text containing a verb and ending with *that*, as in *we show that*, *the paper provides the first evidence that*, were deleted. The stopword and stop phrase removal steps were applied sequentially, but we arbitrarily limited the length of the deleted segment at a maximum of 60 characters. Moreover, text removal was blocked when clauses contained gene and protein names (GPN). Our GPN tagger is based on a very simple heuristic: any non-recognized token was considered as a GPN. We used the UMLS SPECIALIST Lexicon and a frequency list of English words (totaling more than 400,000 items) to separate between known and unknown words.

INTRODUCTION: Chromophobe renal cell carcinoma (CCRC) comprises 5% of neoplasms of renal tubular epithelium. CCRC may have a slightly better prognosis than clear cell carcinoma, but outcome data are limited. *PURPOSE:* In this study, we analyzed 250 renal cell carcinomas to a) determine frequency of CCRC at our Hospital and b) analyze clinical and pathologic features of CCRCs. *METHODS:* A total of 250 renal carcinomas were analyzed between March 1990 and March 1999. Tumors were classified according to well-established histologic criteria to determine stage of disease; the system proposed by Robson was used. *RESULTS:* Of 250 renal cell carcinomas analyzed, 36 were classified as chromophobe renal cell carcinoma, representing 14% of the group studied. The tumors had an average diameter of 14 cm. Robson staging was possible in all cases, and 10 patients were stage 1) 11 stage II; 10 stage III, and five stage IV. The average follow-up period was 4 years and 18 (53%) patients were alive without disease. *CONCLUSION:* The highly favorable pathologic stage (RI-RII, 58%) and the fact that the majority of patients were alive and disease-free suggested a more favorable prognosis for this type of renal cell carcinoma.

Fig. 3. Example of an explicitly structured abstract in MedLine

3.3 Latent Argumentative Structuring

The first classifier (called LASt) started ranking abstract sentences as to their argumentative classes (as proposed in [20, 30]). Four argumentative categories defined four moves: PURPOSE, METHODS, RESULTS and CONCLUSION. These moves were chosen because in scientific literature they have been found to be quite stable [24], [29] and were also recommended by ANSI/ISO guidelines for professionals. We obtained 19,555 explicitly structured abstracts from MedLine in order to train our Latent[4] Argumentative Structuring classifier (LASt) (this set does not contain the MedLine records used during the evaluation). A conjunctive query was used to combine the four following strings: "PURPOSE," "METHODS," "RESULTS," "CONCLUSION". From the original set, we retained 12,000 abstracts (an example is given in Fig. 3) used for training our LASt system, and 1,200 were used for fine-tuning and evaluating the tool, following removal of explicit argumentative markers.

---

[4] We assume that documents to be classified contain at least a *latent* argumentative structure.

> CONCLUSION |00160116| The highly favorable pathologic stage (RI-RII, 58%) and the fact that the majority of patients were alive and disease-free suggested a more favorable prognosis for this type of renal cell carcinoma.

> PURPOSE |00156456| In this study, we analyzed 250 renal cell carcinomas to a) determine frequency of CCRC at our Hospital and b) analyze clinical and pathologic features of CCRCs.

> PURPOSE |00167817| Chromophobe renal cell carcinoma (CCRC) comprises 5% of neoplasms of renal tubular epithelium. CCRC may have a slightly better prognosis than clear cell carcinoma, but outcome data are limited.

> METHODS |00160119| Tumors were classified according to well-established histologic criteria to determine stage of disease; the system proposed by Robson was used.

> METHODS |00162303| Of 250 renal cell carcinomas analyzed, 36 were classified as chromophobe renal cell carcinoma, representing 14% of the group studied.

> RESULTS |00155338| Robson staging was possible in all cases, and 10 patients were stage 1) 11 stage II; 10 stage III, and five stage IV.

Fig. 4. Classification example for abstract shown in Fig. 3. The attributed class comes first, then the score obtained by the class, and finally the text segment

3.3.1 Features and Heuristics

Our system relied on four Bayesian classifiers [16], one binary classifier for each argumentative category. Each binary classifier combined three types of features: words, word bigrams and trigrams. The log of the class frequency represented the weight of each feature, but for every category, DF thresholding [33] was applied so that rare features were not selected. Finally, the class estimate provided by each binary classifier was used to attribute the final class (an example is shown in Fig. 3 and 4): for each sentence the classifier with the highest score assigns the argumentative category. Optionally, we also investigated the sentence position's impact on classification effectiveness through assigning a relative position to each sentence. Thus, if there were ten sentences in an abstract: the first sentence had a relative position of 0.1, while the sentence in position 5 received a relative position of 0.5, and the last sentence has a relative position of 1. The following heuristics were then applied: 1) if a sentence has a relative score strictly inferior to 0.4 and is classified as CONCLUSION, then its class becomes PURPOSE; 2) if a sentence has a relative score strictly superior to 0.6 and is classified as PURPOSE, then its class is rewritten as CONCLUSION.

Table 1 shows the results of argumentative classification system based on the evaluation set. This table indicates the confusion matrices between the four classes, with and without the use of relative position heuristics. When the sentence position was not taken into account, 80.65% of PURPOSE sentences were correctly classified, while 16% were wrongly classified as CONCLUSION, and 3.23% as RESULTS. On the other hand, when the sentence position was taken into account, 93.55% of PURPOSE sentences were correctly classified. The data depicted in this table demonstrates that position can be useful for separating between the PURPOSE and CONCLUSION classes. However, the percentages of correct classified sentences in the METHODS or RESULTS classes did not vary when the sentence position was taken into account. In both cases, the percentage of correct answers was similar, 78% and around 50% respectively, for the METHODS and RESULTS classes.

Table 1. Confusion matrices for the argumentative classifier: the columns denote the manual classification and the rows indicate the automatic ones; percentages on the diagonal give the proportion of sentences, which are appropriately categorized by the argumentative classifier (evaluation done on 17,612 sentences)

Without sentence positions				
	PURP	METH	RESU	CONC
PURP	80.65%	0%	3.23%	16%
METH	8%	78%	8%	6%
RESU	18.58%	5.31%	52.21%	23.89%
CONC	18.18%	0%	2.27%	79.55%
With sentence positions				
	PURP	METH	RESU	CONC
PURP	93.55%	0%	3.23%	3%
METH	8%	78%	8%	6%
RESU	12.43%	5.31%	74.25%	13.01%
CONC	2.27%	0%	2.27%	95.45%

3.3.2 Argumentation and GeneRIF

In another preliminary experiment we tried to establish a relation between GeneRIF and argumentative moves. We selected two sets of 1000 GeneRIFs from our training data and submitted them to the argumentative classifier. Set A was a random set and set B was also a random set, but we imposed the condition that the extract describing the GeneRIF had to be found in the abstract (as exemplified in Fig. 1). We wanted to verify if the argumentative distribution of GeneRIF originating from sentences is similar to the distribution of GeneRIF originating from both titles and abstracts. Results of the argumentative classification are given in Table 2 for these two sets. These proportions indicate that GeneRIFs are mainly classified as PURPOSE and CONCLUSION sentences (respectively 41% and 55% in Set A). The significance of these observations was accentuated for the GeneRIFs coming from the abstract sentences (see Set B in Table 2). In this case, two thirds of the sentence-based GeneRIFs came from the CONCLUSION, and around a quarter from the PURPOSE section. Together, these two moves concentrated between 88% (Set B) and 96% (Set A) for the GeneRIFs in LocusLink. Fortunately, as shown in Table 1, the discriminative power of the argumentative classifier was better for these two classes than for the RESULTS and METHODS classes.

Based on these findings, the sentence ranking order would be: CONCLUSION, PURPOSE, RESULTS, METHODS, and thus our classifier would return to the first position, when available, a sentence classified as CONCLUSION. However, selecting the best conclusion sentence is not sufficient (such a strategy exhibits a Dice performance of 35.2%), due to the fact that 45% of GeneRIFs in the TREC evaluation set were strictly "cut & paste" from the article's title. In our argumentation-based ranking we clearly needed to take the title into account. To do so, we simply computed the Dice distance between each candidate and the title, so that among sentences classified as CONCLUSION and PURPOSES, those lexically similar to the title would move to the top of the list. In a complementary manner, a negative filter was also used; meaning sentences without GPNs were simply eliminated. Finally, to select between the title and the best-ranked sentence from the abstract, the Dice score was again used. If the sentence score was above a given threshold, then the sentence was selected, otherwise the title was returned. From our training data, the best threshold was 0.5. This threshold value gives the best results on the test set: the classifier choses 14 sentences from the abstract vs. 125 from the title, from a total of 139 queries (see Table 6).

Table 2. Class distribution in 1000 GeneRIFs after argumentative classification. Sets A and B are samples of GeneRIFs as in LocusLink, but Set B contains only GeneRIFs originating from the abstract

	Set A (%)	Set B (%)
PURPOSE	41%	22%
METHODS	2%	4%
RESULTS	2%	8%
CONCLUSION	55%	66%

3.4 Logistic Regression

The second suggested extraction strategy (called LogReg) is based on logistic regression and works in two stages. During the first step, the system computes a score for each sentence in order to define the best possible candidate sentence. During the second step and as was done is our LASt scheme, the selected candidate was compared to the paper's title in order to define whether the title or the candidate should be returned as the suggested GeneRIF. In the first step, we removed all stopwords (we used the SMART stopword list) appearing in the title or in the abstract sentences. We then applied the S stemmer [9] in an attempt to remove the English plural form (mainly the final « -s »). After removing stopwords and applying the S stemmer, we computed a score for each sentence and for the title, using the following formula:

$$\text{score} = \frac{1}{\text{len}} \sum_{j=1}^{\text{len}} w(tf_j) \qquad (2)$$

where tf_j was the term frequency in GeneRIF vocabulary, len was the sentence length measured by word count and $w(tf_j)$ was a weight function as defined in Table 3, returning an integer that depended on the term frequency tf_j. To define each term frequency in the GeneRIFs vocabulary, we simply counted the number of occurrences of the corresponding term in all GeneRIFs. For example, we were able to observe that the term "cell" appeared 36 times, "role" 25 or "protein" 21.

Table 3. Ad hoc weight according to term frequency in GeneRIF

tf_j	$w(tf_j)$
$9 < tf_j$	4
$4 < tf_j \leq 9$	3
$2 < tf_j \leq 4$	2
$1 < tf_j \leq 2$	1
$tf_j \leq 1$	0

Finally, we ranked the sentences (including the title) according to their scores in decreasing order and then selected the desired candidate: the sentence with the highest score (this candidate could be the title). Such a weighting scheme thus promoted the sentence having the most terms in common with the vocabulary found in the GeneRIFs. Moreover, if these common terms were also frequent words (e.g., like "cell" or "protein"), the underlying score would increase.

Table 4. Title and candidate sentence for Query #30

Original title	Comparative surface accessibility of a pore-lining threonine residue (T6') in the glycine and GABA(A) receptors.
After stopword removal and stemming	Comparative surface accessibility pore-lining threonine residue (T6') glycine GABA(A) receptor
Original candidate	This action was not induced by oxidizing agents in either receptor.
After stopword removal and stemming	action induced oxidizing agent either receptor

Just as in the LASt approach, knowing that the title is often an appropriate GeneRIF source we wanted to account for this by suggesting a selection model. This selection scheme had to choose between either the paper's title or the best candidate sentence. The following example illustrates how this selection scheme worked. As shown in Table 4, for Query #30 we reported the paper's title and the best candidate sentence. Note that the table shows both the original form and the resulting expression once stopwords were removed and the stemming procedure applied.

For each candidate sentence, we computed statistics such as length (denoted "Len"), number of indexed terms (or number of words appearing in GeneRIF vocabulary, denoted "Terms"). We also added statistics related to the *idf* value, based on the work of Cronen-Townsend *et al.* [6], who demonstrated that the *idf* could be, under certain conditions, a good estimator for predicting query performance.

Table 5. Variables used in our logistic model

Variable	Estimate	Meaning
Len	0.4512	candidate sentence length
Un-known	0.2823	number of unknown terms in WordNet
Terms	-0.5538	number of indexed terms
Max2Idf	-0.3638	2nd max idf of candidate sentence
MinIdf	-0.5611	min idf of candidate sentence
d.Len	-0.3560	length difference between candidate and title
d.Terms	0.4465	indexed term number difference between candidate and title
d.Max2Idf	0.4084	2nd max idf difference between candidate and title
d.MinIdf	1.0351	min idf difference between candidate and title

Moreover, since we compared the title and a given sentence, we were able to compute statistics on the differences between this sentence and the paper's title. For example, we included the length difference (d.Len) or idf minimum difference (d.MinIdf), between the candidate and the title. Once a set of potential useful explanatory variables was obtained, we selected the most important ones using the stepAIC procedure [32]. Table 5 describes all retained variables used in our selection model.

To implement this selection procedure we chose the logistic regression model [11] in order to predict the probability of a binary outcome variable according to a set of explanatory variables. In this case, our logistic regression model returned a probability estimate that the candidate sentence was a good GeneRIF, based on the explanatory variables depicted in Table 5. For example, if the candidate sentence length was greater than the title length (variable "d.Len" would be positive), then the probability that the candidate sentence was a good GeneRIF would decrease (because, as shown in Table 5, the estimate for "d.Len" is negative). Finally, if the estimated probability was greater than 0.5, then the sentence was returned as the proposed GeneRIF, otherwise the article title was returned as the GeneRIF. Using this method, we returned the paper's title 97 times and the candidate sentence 42 times (see Table 6).

3.5   Fusion of Extraction Strategies

This last step attempts to combine our two extraction schemes. To achieve this goal, we used the following rules: 1) Agreement - if the sentence selected by LASt is also chosen by the logistic regression strategy (LogReg), then we keep it; 2) Disagreement - if both strategies do not agree, then we look at the probability estimate returned by LogReg: if this probability is below a given threshold (0.5), then the candidate sentence provided by LASt is selected, otherwise the LogReg candidate is returned. Finally, if a unique candidate GeneRIF is selected and if this segment does not come from the title, then the sentence is processed by the reduction procedure (see Section 3.2). The output segment is used for comparison to the correct GeneRIF provided by LocusLink's annotators, as explained in the next section.

4 Results and Related Works

In this section, we first evaluated each isolated extraction strategy. Second, we evaluated our suggested combined approach. Table 6 depicts the overall performance measure using the Dice coefficient (last column). The table's middle column shows how the proposed GeneRIF may have originated from the article's title or from an abstract sentence. Our baseline approach was very simple. For each of the 139 queries (composed of a locus and a MedLine article), we returned the article's title. Such a naïve selection procedure achieved a relatively high performance of 50.47%, due to the fact that 45% of GeneRIFs were extracted from the article's title. On the other hand, if for each query we had an oracle that always selected the title or the sentence achieving the highest Dice score, we could obtain a performance of 70.96%, one that represents our upper bound. In this optimal run, we had to extract 59 titles and 80 sentences from the abstract. We could not however obtain a better performance level due to the fact that LocusLink's annotators may have used words that did not appear in the article's title or in the abstract. Moreover, correct GeneRIFs may paraphrase a sentence or the article's title, revealing the same gene function with different words or expressions. Finally, GeneRIFs may be expressed using more than one sentence. In this case, the human annotator chose to combine different segments, taken from various sentences or in part from the article's title.

Table 6. Performance of each basic strategy and their combination

	Origin of proposed GeneRIF		
	Title	**Abstract**	**Dice**
Baseline	139	0	50.47%
LASt	125	14	51.98%
LogReg	97	42	52.28%
Combination	106	33	54.44%
Combination & shortening	106	33	55.08%

As shown in Table 6, the LASt extraction approach produced an overall performance of 51.98%, and in this case, 125 GeneRIFs came from the article's title and 14 from the article's abstract. Our second extraction scheme (run labeled "LogReg") performed at similar levels (52.28%). However, in this case, it was seen that a greater number of proposed GeneRIFs came from the abstract (42 vs. 14 in the LASt scheme). The last two rows of Table 6 indicate the performance of our combined approach (54.44%), clearly showing better overall results than those for each extraction scheme run separately. When we applied our sentence reduction procedure, the Dice score increased slightly (55.08% vs. 54.44%). When analyzing the origin of each proposed GeneRIF in this combined approach, we could see that 106 come from the title and 33 from the abstract. Moreover, when applying another point of view, we found that 48 suggested GeneRIFs were provided by LASt, 22 came from LogReg, and the two extraction strategies agreed 69 times.

While these results reveal attractive performance levels when compared to other runs in the TREC-2003 genomic evaluation campaign [10], several teams were faced with the same extraction problem yet suggested other interesting approaches. For example, Bhalotia *et al.* [2], ranked second at TREC (Dice = 53%) suggested a scheme that selected between the article's title and the last sentence of the article's abstract (as shown in Fig. 2, 91 out of the 139 GeneRIFs were extracted from either the title or the abstract's last sentence). These authors suggested basing this selection on a Naive Bayes [22] machine learning approach. The relevant variables were the verbs, the MeSH and the genes, all weighted by *tf idf*, as well as a Boolean value representing the presence of the target gene in the abstract. Although we were not able to reproduce their results based on their TREC report, Jelier *et al.* [12] report a Dice score close to 57%, using similar classifiers, but trained on the sentence position in the abstract. Another interesting approach proposed by Kayaalp *et al.* [13] separates the articles, abstracts and titles into sentences in order to combine their various characteristics, such as the number of words, number of figures and number of uppercase letters. The first model applied a linear combination on a set of characteristics so as to extract the best candidate sentence, whereas the second model was based on the predicate calculus, using another set of characteristics.

5   Conclusion

This research focuses on the extraction of gene functions (a GeneRIF) from a MedLine record given a gene name, as was proposed in the TREC Genomics Track in 2003 [10]. Because almost half of the human-provided GeneRIFs were simply "cut & paste" from the title, the method focused on deciding whether a sentence from the abstract would likely express the GeneRIF or if the title would be a better choice. The investigated method combines two independent extraction strategies. The first relies on argumentative criteria and considers that apart from the title, the best GeneRIF candidate should appear in the article's conclusion or purpose sections. The second extraction approach is based on logistic regression which returns a probability estimate that the selected sentence provides a better GeneRIF than does the title. The probabilistic estimates are based on the lexical usage in the sentence and on various statistical properties (together with their differences) shared between the candidate sentence and the title (e.g., the length difference, the minimal *idf* value, etc.). Each extraction strategy operates on the same basic unit: the sentences and/or the article's title. Moreover, each suggested approach shows a preference for the sentences in which genes and protein names occur.

When examined separately, each method (argumentative filtering and logistic regression) yielded effective results during the TREC-2003 challenge [10]. However combining achieved a highly competitive score: the lexical overlap – measured by Dice metrics – was improved by about 9% compared to the baseline (55.08% vs. 50.47%). In conclusion, the methods used in these experiments provide a general view of the gene function extraction task within the TREC genomic evaluation campaign. As with summarization and sentence selection, these methods clearly show that a variety of feature sets must be considered when performing such information extraction tasks.

Acknowledgments

This research was supported in part by the SNSF (Grants 21-66 742.01 and 3200-065228) and in part by the EU/OFES (Grant 507505/03.0399).

References

[1] Berger, A.L., Mittal, V.O.: OCELOT: A System for Summarizing Web Pages. In Proceedings ACM-SIGIR'2000, ACM Press, New York, 144-151

[2] Bhalotia, G., Nakov, P.I., Schwartz, A.S., Hearst, M.A.: BioText Team Report for the TREC 2003 Genomics Track. In Proceedings TREC-2003, NIST, 612-621

[3] Blaschke, C., Andrade, M.A., Ouzounis, C.A., Valencia, A.: Automatic Extraction of Biological Information from Scientific Text: Protein-Protein Interactions. In Proceedings Intelligent Systems for Molecular Biology, 1999, 60-67

[4] Chinchor, N., Hirschman, L.: MUC-7 Named-Entity Task Definition. In MUC-7 Proceedings, 1998.

[5] Chuang W.T., Yang, J.: Extracting Sentence Segments for Text Summarization. In Proceedings ACM-SIGIR'2000, ACM Press, New York, 152-159

[6] Cronen-Townsend, S., Zhou, Y., Croft, W.B.: Predicting Query Performance. In Proceedings ACM-SIGIR'2002, ACM Press, New York, 299-306

[7] Ehrler F., Jimeno Yepes A., Ruch P.: Data-Poor Categorization and Passage Retrieval for Gene Ontology Annotation in Swiss-Prot. BMC Bioinformatics, 2005, to appear

[8] Goldstein, J., Kantrowitz, M., Mittal, V., Carbonell, J.: Summarizing Text Documents. In Proceedings ACM-SIGIR'99, ACM Press, New York, 121-128

[9] Harman, D.: How Effective is Suffixing? J Am Soc Infor Scien. 42 (1991) 7-15

[10] Hersh, W., Bhupatiraju, R.T.: TREC Genomics Track Overview. In Proceedings TREC-2003, NIST, 14-23

[11] Hosmer, D.W., Lemeshow, S.: Applied Logistic Regression. 2nd edn. John Wiley & Sons, New York (2000)

[12] Jelier, R., Schuemie, M., van der Eijk, C., Weeber, M., van Mulligen, E., Schijvenaars, B., Mons, B., Kors, J.: Searching for GeneRIFs: Concept-Based Query Expansion and Bayes Classification. In Proceedings TREC-2003, NIST, 225-233

[13] Kayaalp, M., Aronson, A.R., Humphrey, S.M., Ide, N.C., Tanabe, L.K., Smith, L.H., Demner, D., Loane, R.R., Mork, J.G., Bodenreider, O.: Methods for Accurate Retrieval of MEDLINE Citations in Functional Genomics. In Proceedings TREC-2003, 441-450

[14] Kirsch, H., Rebholz-Schuhmann D.: Distributed Modules for Text Annotation and IE applied to the Biomedical Domain. COLING Workshop on Natural Language Processing in Biomedicine and its Applications (NLPBA/BioNLP), 2004, 50-53

[15] Kupiec, J., Pedersen, J., Chen, F.: A Trainable Document Summarizer. In Proceedings ACM-SIGIR'95, ACM Press, New York, 68-73

[16] Langley, P., Iba, W., Thompson, K.: An Analysis of Bayesian Classifiers. In Proceedings AAAI, Menlo Park, 1992, 223-228

[17] Larkey, L.S., Croft, W.B.: Combining Classifiers in Text Categorization. In Proceedings ACM-SIGIR'96, ACM Press, New York, 289-297

[18] Lewis, D.D.: Evaluating and Optimizing Autonomous Text Classification Systems. In Proceedings ACM-SIGIR'95, ACM Press, New York, 246-254

[19] Mani, I., Maybury, M.T.: Advances in Automatic Text Summarization. The MIT Press, Cambridge (1999)

P. Ruch, L. Perret, and J. Savoy

[20] McKnight, L. Srinivasan, P.: Categorization of Sentence Types in Medical Abstracts. In Proceedings AMIA 2003, 440-444

[20] McKnight, L. Srinivasan, P.: Categorization of Sentence Types in Medical Abstracts. In Proceedings AMIA 2003, 440-444
[21] Mitchell, J.A., Aronson, A.R., Mork, J.G., Folk, L.C., Humphrey, S.M., Ward, J.M.: Gene Indexing: Characterization and Analysis of NLM's GeneRIFs. In Proceedings AMIA 2003, 460-464
[22] Mitchell, T.: Machine Learning. McGraw Hill, New York (1997)
[23] Nédellec, C., Vetah, M., Bessières, P.: Sentence Filtering for Information Extraction in Genomics. In Proceedings PKDD, Springer-Verlag, Berlin, 2001, 326-237
[24] Orasan, C.: Patterns in Scientific Abstracts. In Proceedings Corpus Linguistics, 2001, 433-445
[25] Paice, C.D.: Constructing Literature Abstracts by Computer: Techniques and Prospects. Inform Proc & Manag. 26 (1990) 171-86
[26] Reynar, J.C., Ratnaparkhi, A.: A Maximum Entropy Approach to Identifying Sentence Boundaries. In Proceedings Applied NLP, 1997, 16-19
[27] Ruch, P., Baud, R., Bouillon, P., Robert, G.: Minimal Commitment and Full Lexical Disambiguation. In Proceedings of CoNLL, 2000, 111-116
[28] Strube, M., Hahn, U.: Functional Centering. In Proceedings of ACL, Morgan Kaufmann, 1996, 270-277
[29] Swales, J.: Genre Analysis: English in Academic and Research Settings. Cambridge University Press, Cambridge (1990)
[30] Tbahriti, I., Chichester, C., Lisacek, F., Ruch P.: Using Argumention to Retrieve Articles with Similar Citations from MEDLINE. COLING Workshop on Natural Language Processing in Biomedicine and its Applications (NLPBA/BioNLP), 2004, 8-14
[31] Teufel S., Moens, M.: Argumentative Classification of Extracted Sentences as a First Step Towards Flexible Abstracting. In: I. Mani, M. Maybury (eds.): Advances in Automatic Text Summarization. MIT Press, Cambridge (1999) 155-171
[32] Venables, W.N., Ripley, B.D.: Modern Applied Statistics with S-Plus. 3rd edn. Spinger-Verlag, New York (2000)
[33] Yang, Y., Pedersen, J.O.: A Comparative Study on Feature Selection in Text Categorization. In Proceedings Machine Learning, Morgan Kaufmann, 1997, 412-420

Filtering for Profile-Biased Multi-document Summarization

Sana Leila Châar, Olivier Ferret, and Christian Fluhr

CEA-LIST/LIC2M,
18, route du Panorama - BP6,
92265 Fontenay-aux-Roses Cedex
{chaars, ferreto, fluhrc}@zoe.cea.fr

Abstract. In this article, we present an information filtering method that selects from a set of documents their most significant excerpts in relation to a user profile. This method relies on both structured profiles and a topical analysis of documents. The topical analysis is also used for expanding a profile in relation to a particular document by selecting the terms of the document that are closely linked to those of the profile. This expansion is a way for selecting in a more reliable way excerpts that are linked to profiles but also for selecting excerpts that may bring new and interesting information about their topics. This method was implemented by the REDUIT system, which was successfully evaluated for document filtering and passage extraction.

1 Introduction

The need for tools that enable users to face the large amount of documents that are now available in digital form has led the Information Retrieval field to go further than document retrieval. The recent success of the Question/Answering field is representative of this trend. When the query of a user is a factoid question, it is possible to find a short excerpt that contains the expected answer. But when the query is about a topic rather than a fact, an answer can be obtained most of the time only by gathering and putting together several pieces of information coming from several documents. The work we present in this article takes place in this second perspective.

This perspective is also the one of multi-document summarization, which has received great interest during the last years, especially through the DUC (Document Understanding Conference) evaluation [1]. Although query-biased summarization is generally not the focus of the work achieved in this field, this subject was already tackled by work such as [2], [3] or [4]. More recently, a convergence of Question/Answering and multi-document summarization has led to answer-focused summarization ([5], [6]), which was introduced as a task of DUC in 2003.

Our approach, that can be named profile-biased multi-document summarization, is closer to query-biased summarization than to answer-focused one. As we

D.E. Losada and J.M. Fernández-Luna (Eds.): ECIR 2005, LNCS 3408, pp. 127–141, 2005.
© Springer-Verlag Berlin Heidelberg 2005

will see in section 3.1, the user profiles we use are not very different from the TREC topics used in SUMMAC [7] for the evaluation of query-biased summarization. However, our work focuses more specifically on two important points in relation to profiles. First, a profile generally corresponds to a configuration of topics and not only to one large topic. Hence, selecting only the excerpts of documents that refer to all the subtopics of a profile instead of taking the profile as a whole should improve the precision of filtering. Second, profiles are only partial descriptions of the topics they represent. These descriptions can be enriched from the processed documents and adapted to them, which should improve the recall of filtering.

2   Overview

The method we present in this article aims at extracting from a set of documents, for instance the result of a search engine, the text excerpts that match with the information need of a user, expressed in our case by a profile that is structured from a topical viewpoint. This method, which is implemented by the REDUIT system, can be split up into four main steps. First, the input documents are preprocessed, both for selecting and normalizing their content words and segmenting them into topically coherent units that can be compared to the topical units of the profile. The second step, which is a filtering step, is based on the matching between the profile and the topical segments of documents. The result of this matching is first used for discarding the documents without any relation with the profile. Then, it supports the selection of the segments of the remaining documents that match the profile. This selection is also based on the detection of the vocabulary of documents that is closely linked to the profile's one, which is a kind of adaptation of the profile to the documents. Segments whose the selection relies on this extended vocabulary are more likely to contain new information in relation to the profile. Hence, they have a specific status for information filtering: in the following steps, they are processed as the other segments but they are kept separate from them. The third step performs information fusion by detecting and removing redundancies among the selected segments. This operation is first achieved among the segments of a document and then, among the segments coming from all the selected documents. Finally, the fourth step is turned towards users: the selected segments are ranked according to their significance, both from the viewpoint of the profile and the viewpoint of the documents, and they are pruned for limiting the amount of text to read.

3   Profiles

3.1   Structure

In the REDUIT system, users express their needs through profiles. Unlike queries sent to search engines, profiles are used during a long period, which is a reason for asking users to take some time for building them not only as bags of words. More precisely, we chose to structure user profiles according to a topical criterion:

Table 1. The most significant terms of a profile about the role of radios during war

war subtopic	radio subtopic
guerre (war)	radio (radio)
arme (weapon)	réception (reception)
conflit (conflict)	auditeur (listener)
champ_bataille (battlefield)	capter (to pick up)
cesser_feu (ceasefire)	spot (commercial)
paix (peace)	récepteur (receiver)
agression (aggression)	émetteur (transmitter)
combattant (combatant)	onde_hertzien (Hertzian wave)

a profile is a set of terms that are grouped into topically homogeneous subsets. This structure aims at improving the precision of filtering by giving a higher score to the documents in which all the topics of a profile are represented. For instance, for a profile about the role of radio during wars (see Table 1), the most relevant documents are those that contain both terms related to war and terms related to radio. A document that only contains terms about war, even if they are numerous, is not likely to be relevant. Only the distinction between the two topics and the dividing of the profile terms according to them can give to a filtering system the ability to discard documents that mainly refer to one of the two topics and to select documents that contain fewer profile terms but terms that are spread in a more balanced way among the two topics. Having such a structure for profiles can improve the precision of filtering but also corresponds to a large part of requests for information coming from users. Those requests are often defined by a configuration of several topics rather by giving only one big topic. The profile of Table 1 is a typical example of this phenomenon.

As illustrated by Table 1, a topic of a profile is represented by a set of terms. These terms can be mono-terms or compounds. They are normalized by applying the same kind of linguistic preprocessing as the one applied to documents (see section 4.1).

3.2   Topical Structuring of Profiles

For facilitating the use of the REDUIT system by a user, especially for a new user, we do not impose to him to structure the profiles he defines. In such a case, the user can only give a list of terms and a specific algorithm is applied to structure automatically the profile in a topical way. This algorithm performs the unsupervised clustering of a set of words by relying on a network of lexical co-occurrences. The nodes of this network are the words of the vocabulary of a corpus and the edges between them stand for the co-occurrences found in the corpus between these words. The network we used for this work was built from a 39 million word corpus made of 24 months from the *Le Monde* newspaper. After a filtering procedure was applied [8] to select the co-occurrences that are likely to be supported by a topical relation, we got a network of 7,200 lemmas and 183,000 co-occurrences.

The clustering algorithm applied to profiles is based on the idea that in such a network, the density of links between the words referring to the same topic is much higher than the density of links between words that are not part of the same topic. Hence, a subtopic in a profile can be identified by the fact that its words form a strongly connected subgraph in the network. The detection of such a subgraph is performed by the following iterative algorithm[1]:

1. selection of the profile words to cluster and building of a topical representation of each of them;
2. building of a similarity matrix for all the selected words of the profile;
3. identification of the most significant subtopic;
4. return to the first step after discarding from the words to cluster those that are part of the new subtopic. The algorithm stops when the number of remaining words is too low (less than 3 words) for building a new subtopic.

The first step exploits the network of lexical co-occurrences for associating to each profile word the words of the network that are the most strongly linked to it in the context of the profile. It also discards the profile words that are not considered as topically significant. As the global algorithm, this step is iterative:

1.1 selection of the words in the network $\{nw_i\}$ that have a minimal number of links, in our case fixed to 4, with profile words;
1.2 selection of the profile words that have supported the selection of a minimal number, fixed to 3, of the $\{nw_i\}$;
1.3 return to step 1.1 with the profile words selected in step 1.2. The process stops when the sets of selected words, both for the profile and the network, are stabilized.

The topical representation associated to each selected word of the profile after this first step is used for evaluating their similarity in step 2. The similarity value of two profile words is the size of the intersection of their topical representations. The similarity vector of a profile word is then filtered for making clustering less sensitive to noise: all values lower than 30% of the maximal value of the vector are set to zero.

The third step is two-fold. First, the seed of a new subtopic is selected. This is the profile word whose the sum of its similarity values with the other profile words is the highest one, that is to say, the word that can be considered as the most central one for the new subtopic. Second, the subtopic is built by aggregating to the initial seed its closest profile words. More precisely, a profile word is associated to the seed if its similarity value with it is the highest of its non-null similarity values with profile words. For extending the new topic, the aggregation step is redone with all the words of the topic as possible targets and not only its seed. For not introducing noise, the new word must also have a

---

[1] The various thresholds hereafter were set experimentally from the CLEF 2003 topics.

non-null similarity value with a minimal number, fixed to 3 in our case, of words already tied to the new subtopic.

In the more global perspective of the evaluation of the REDUIT system (see section 7), the algorithm for structuring profiles we have presented above was tested on the French version of 200 topics of the CLEF evaluations from 2000 to 2003. Each topic was transformed into a list of content words by applying the same linguistic preprocessing as the one applied to documents (see section 4.1). Only the removal of some "meta-words" (such as *trouver* (to find), *document*, *information* ...) related to the Information Retrieval field was specifically done for CLEF topics [9]. Among these 200 topics, the structuring algorithm found 145 of them with only one topic, 48 with two subtopics and 7 with three subtopics.

4   Filtering

4.1   Preprocessing of Documents

The first step of the filtering process is a linguistic and topical preprocessing of the input documents. The goal of this preprocessing step is to represent documents in a same way as profiles to make their comparison easier. The linguistic preprocessing of documents mainly consists in normalizing words of documents and selecting those that are considered as significant from a topical viewpoint. These two tasks are achieved by the LIMA (LIc2m Multilingual Analyzer) tool [9], which performs more precisely the tokenization, the morphological analysis and the Part-of-Speech (POS) tagging of documents. The selection of the topically significant words is based on their POS category: only nouns, verbs and adjectives are kept. The LIMA tool also achieves named entity recognition, that is to say, identifies persons, locations, organizations, dates, numerical values, companies and events.

The topical preprocessing of documents relies on the result of their linguistic preprocessing and aims at segmenting them into topically homogeneous segments. These segments are delimited in our case by the means of the C99 algorithm [10], which is a state-of-the-art linear text segmentation algorithm that only exploits word reiteration. Classically, each segment is represented as a vector of normalized terms according to the Vector Space Model.

4.2   Selection of Documents

Principles. As the REDUIT system does not go on the assumption that all its input documents are relevant for its current profile, its first task is to discard documents without relation with it. More precisely, the REDUIT system distinguishes three cases for a document and a profile:

- the document globally matches with the profile, even if some of its parts are about topics not in the profile;
- only a part of the document matches with the profile. This one is only a secondary topic of the document;
- the document has no relation with the profile, even locally.

132   S.L. Châar, O. Ferret, and C. Fluhr

The REDUIT system aims at selecting the documents that come under the first two cases. As we assume that a global match between a document and a profile implies that at least a part of it matches with the profile (see 4.3), the main criterion for selecting a document comes from the second case: a document is selected if at least one of its segments matches with the profile.

Similarity Between a Profile and a Segment. As mentioned in section 3.1, the profiles in the REDUIT system are structured from a topical viewpoint to avoid selecting a document or a part of it while it only refers to a part of a profile. Following this principle, a segment of a document can match with a profile only if each subtopic of the profile is represented in the segment. As the size of a document segment is generally equal to the average size of a paragraph, that is not too large, we consider that a subtopic of a profile is represented in a segment when at least one of the terms that defines the subtopic is present in the segment. This criterion may seem not very strict for one topic but it is more significant for a multi-topic profile.

Although compounds are generally less ambiguous than mono-terms, we do not place conditions on the presence of compounds for the identification of topics in segments as we do not want to impose too strict constraints on the way profiles are defined by users. Nevertheless, one can observe that manually built profiles often contain a large number of compounds, which has led us to pay attention to their identification. In order to favor robustness, this identification is not performed in our case by a general terminology extractor but by the set of the following heuristics:

- the words MT_i that are part of a compound CT must occur in a segment in the same order as in CT^2. The identification of the MT_i directly relies on the linguistic preprocessing of documents;
- an occurrence of CT can not be larger than $1.5 * N$ content words, where N is the number of words in CT. This heuristic takes into syntactical variations such as insertions;
- if CT contains prepositions, they must also be present in its occurrences and their position in relation to the MT_i must be the same as in CT. Moreover, a possible occurrence of CT must not contain any punctuation mark.

A compound CT can also be recognized when only one of its sub-terms ST is identified, which is called *approximate recognition*. Three conditions must be fulfilled for such a recognition:

- ST must contain at least half of the content words of CT;
- ST is recognized by fulfilling the three conditions mentioned above for the *strict recognition* of a compound;
- CT must be recognized in a strict way in the document at least one time.

For the identification of a topic in a segment, one of its terms can be recognized in a strict or approximate way.

---

[2] Of course, this kind of heuristics is less effective for languages where the order of words in compounds is very flexible.

4.3   Selection of Segments

Core Segments and Extension Segments. As defined in section 4.2, the selection of a document results from two situations: the document globally matches with the considered profile or only a part of this document matches with the profile. In the second case, as the profile does not correspond to the main topic of the document, there is no reason for selecting other segments than those matching the profile according to the criteria of section 4.2. These segments, whose the matching with the profile is strictly based on the terms of that profile, are called *core segments* and can be viewed as direct instances of the profile in a document.

On the contrary, segments can be selected in the first case according to less reliable criteria because of the global similarity between the document and the profile. More precisely, the selection of a segment can rely on the presence of terms of the document that are considered as linked to those of the profile and not only on terms of the profile. These terms are called *inferred terms*. This is a way to specialize a profile in relation to a document and also a way to detect new trends in relation to the topics of the profile. Hence, when a document globally matches a profile, the criterion for selecting one of its segment is slightly modified: a segment is selected if a term or an inferred term of each subtopic of the profile occurs in the segment. A segment whose the selection is based, at least partly, on inferred terms is called an *extension segment*, as it is more likely to bring new information in relation to the profile.

Selection of Inferred Terms. The detection of a a link between a term of a profile and a term of a document is based on co-occurrences in the document. More precisely, let $\{tp_{Ti}\}$ be the set of terms defining the topic T that are present in the document. $\{td_{Tj}\}$ is the set of terms of the document such that td_{Tj} co-occurs with a term tp_{Ti} in a segment (tp_{Ti} is not necessarily the same term in all these segments). td_{Tj} is considered as an inferred term when this co-occurrence is observed among a significant proportion (1/3 in our experiments) of the segments of the document.

The inferred terms represent a kind of adaptation of profiles in relation to the documents to which they are compared. When a profile is defined manually, the description of its topics tends to be somewhat general. The terms of this description are found in documents but the topics they characterized are also expressed through more specific terms that are not present in the profile and that are useful to identify for improving the results of the filtering process. The detection of inferred terms is quite similar to the blind relevance feedback used in Information Retrieval.

Table 2 shows the inferred terms extracted from documents of the CLEF 2003 corpus (see section 7) for the profile of Table 1 about the role of radio during wars. Some of these terms, such as *extrémiste, massacrer or défense*, are linked to the topic of war whereas terms such as *station, studio or communiqué* are rather linked to the topic of radio. With the REDUIT system, a user can validate or discard the inferred terms extracted from documents. Moreover, he can dispatch these terms among the topics of the profile or let the system to do it by applying the algorithm described in section 3.2.

Table 2. Example of inferred terms for the profile of Table 1

war subtopic	radio subtopic
extrémiste (extremist)	station (station)
massacrer (to slaughter)	studio (studio)
défense (defense)	appel (call)
exode (exodus)	communiqué (communiqué)
ONU (UN)	programme (program)
génocide (genocide)	BBC (BBC)

Matching of a Profile and a Document. We assume that the global matching of a document with a profile implies that the main topic of the document fits with the topic represented by the profile. Although the problem of identifying the topical structure of texts is far from being solved, the work in the field of automatic summarization exploits an empirical definition of the notion of main topic: the main topic of a text is the topic that is found at the beginning or the end of the text and that covers a significant part of it.

If we transpose this definition in our context, the main topic of a document matches with a profile if the two following conditions are fulfilled:

- the profile must match with the first or the last segment of the document;
- more globally, the segments that match with the profile must represent a significant part of all the segments of the document (1/3 in our experiments).

The first condition relies on the evaluation of the similarity between a segment and a profile presented in section 4.2. The second one is based the extended version of this similarity evaluation (see section 4.3) that takes into account inferred terms.

5   Information Fusion

The information filtering performed by the REDUIT system aims at selecting the parts of the filtered documents that are relevant in relation to a profile but also to detect and to discard redundancies among these selected segments. Hence, the selection stage described in the previous section must be followed by a fusion stage. This fusion, which is first achieved among the segments of a document, then among the segments from several documents, is performed by selecting the segment that conveys in the more representative way the information brought by a set of similar segments.

5.1   Intra-document Fusion

As the two types of segments we have distinguished in section 4.3 are complementary, we do not try to detect redundancies between core segments and extension segments. For each kind of segments, the detection of redundancies relies on a the computation of a similarity measure between segments and the comparison of the resulting value to a fixed threshold, T_{fusion}. Classically, we used the cosine measure, which was applied to the segment vectors coming the preprocessing of a document (see section 4.1):

$$sim(S_1, S_2) = \frac{\sum_i freq(t_i, S_1) \cdot freq(t_i, S_2)}{\sqrt{\sum_i freq(t_i, S_1)^2 \cdot \sum_i freq(t_i, S_2)^2}} \qquad (1)$$

where $freq(t_i, S_{\{1,2\}})$ is the frequency of the term t_i in the segment $S_{\{1,2\}}$. If the similarity value between two segments is higher than T_{fusion}, they are considered as similar and are supposed to contain roughly the same information. Hence, only one of them can represent the twos for a document. In the opposite case, the two segments are kept.

More globally for a document, the similarity measure (1) is computed for each pair of its core segments and its extension segments respectively. Its segments are then grouped according to their similarity value: each segment is associated to its nearest segment, provided that their similarity value is higher than T_{fusion}. The result of this process is a set of non-overlapping groups of similar segments. If all the selected segments of a document are closely linked to each others, only one group may be formed for one kind of segments.

Then, a representative is selected for each group of similar segments: it is the segment that conveys the largest part of the information that characterizes the group. More specifically, this representative is the segment that contains the largest part of the vocabulary of the group, i.e. those of the lemmas of its segments that are shared by at least two segments. This last condition ensures that a segment is selected because its content actually characterizes the group of segments it belongs to and not only because it conveys a large amount of information.

5.2   Inter-document Fusion

After the intra-document fusion, each document is represented by two sets (one for core segments and the second one for the extension segments) of segments that are not similar to each others according to (1). The first step of the inter-document fusion consists in merging all the sets containing the same kind of segments. Two large sets are obtained and in each of them, the algorithm described in section 5.1 for intra-document fusion is applied for detecting redundancies between segments coming from different documents and choosing a representative for each group of similar segments. Finally, the fusion process produces a set of core segments and a set of extension segments.

6   Towards Summaries

6.1   Ranking of Segments

The REDUIT system is not a fine-grained summarization system which aims at producing short or very short summaries as in the DUC evaluation for instance.

Our main objective is rather to design a tool to help users to focus quickly on the document excerpts that are likely to match with their needs. Hence, putting to the front the most relevant of these excerpts is necessary.

As for the fusion step, we chose for this ranking to keep separate the core segments and the extension segments because they represent two complementary aspects of filtering. Each segment is given a relevance score based on its vocabulary. This score takes into account both how well it matches with the profile and how well it is the representative of its group of segments:

$$score(S) = \alpha \cdot \sum_i freq(tps_i, S) + \beta \cdot \sum_i freq(tpa_i, S) + \gamma \cdot \sum_i freq(tcg_i, S) \quad (2)$$

where tps_i is a term of the profile that is recognized in a strict way, tpa_i is a term of the profile that is recognized in an approximate way and tcg_i is one the shared terms of the group of segments whose S is the representative. α, β and γ are modulators which are set in our case[3] in such a way that the stress is put on the similarity with the profile but with a significant place given to the terms linked to it (terms tcg_i). As the size of segments is quite homogeneous, none normalization in relation to this factor was applied to (2).

Finally, segments are ranked in the decreasing order of (2) so that a user can inspect first the segments at top of the list as in a search engine or more radically choose to see only a subset of them by applying a compression ratio.

6.2   Pruning of Segments

Although our attention is not focused on the size of summaries, it is quite obvious that the more text a user has to read, the more time he spends for having a view of what could interest him in a set of documents. Hence, the REDUIT system performs a kind of filtering at the segment level. In this case, the basic units are the sentences of the segment. For selecting coherent units, a sentence always comes with a minimal context made of its N preceding sentences and its N following sentences[4]. Hence, if a segment is not larger than $2N + 1$ sentences, it is selected as a whole. Otherwise, the REDUIT system delimits and selects the groups of adjacent sentences that contain terms of the profile. Two such groups in a segment must be separated by at least $2N + 1$ sentences for not being joined. Moreover, as named entities are considered as especially significant elements, each sentence of a segment that contains at least one of the named entities of the profile is selected with its context.

7   Evaluation

7.1   Methodology

For evaluating the REDUIT system, we adopted an intrinsic method based on the content of documents. This method is an adaptation of the existing evaluations

---

[3] $\alpha = 1.0$, $\beta = 0.75$ and $\gamma = 0, 5$.

[4] In our experiments, N is equal to 1, which means that an excerpt from a segment cannot be smaller than 3 sentences.

in the summarization field, SUMMAC [7] and DUC [1] for English and NTCIR
[11] for Japanese, to the characteristics of the REDUIT system, that is to say,
a multi-document summarization system for French that is guided by a profile
and produces passage-based summaries.

For our evaluation, profiles were, as in the *Ad-Hoc* task of SUMMAC, topics
such as those used in the Ad-Hoc task of the TREC evaluation. TREC topics
were replaced in our case by topics coming from the CLEF evaluation, which
exist for French and many other languages. 14 CLEF topics, that were considered
as multi-topic ones, were selected and converted into profiles for the REDUIT
system. The profile of Table 1 is an example of these transformed topics. For
each one, the CLEF judgment data (*qrels*) give a set of documents from the
CLEF collection that were judged as relevant or non-relevant for this topic. For
French, the documents are articles from the *Le Monde* newspaper and the *SDA*
news agency. Each relevant document (around 20 on average for a topic) was
preprocessed to delimit sentences, which are our basic units for summarization,
and a manual annotation of the units that fit with the topic of the document
was performed to build a "gold standard" for the evaluation of the filtering and
the pruning of segments.

The filtering of documents and the filtering of segments were evaluated separately but in both cases, the main objective of our evaluation was to show the
interest of taking into account the topical heterogeneousness of profiles. Hence,
we compared the results of the filtering with topically structured profiles and its
results with the same profiles but without any topical structuring. In this last
case, all the terms of each profile were gathered into one topic. In order to make
this comparison as objective as possible, the structuring of the 14 test profiles
was performed automatically by the structuring algorithm of section 3.2.

Work about summarization evaluation has given rise to several metrics such
as the relative utility proposed by [12] or more recently, the ROUGE measure
developed in the context of the last DUC conferences [13]. For evaluating RE-
DUIT, we adopted the classical recall/precision measures used in Information
Retrieval, as metrics that are more specific to summarization are rather adapted
to short summaries. In our context, precision and recall are defined by:

$$precision = \frac{P}{NP + P} \qquad recall = \frac{P}{P + R} \qquad (3)$$

where NP is the number of non-relevant units selected by the system, P, the
number of relevant units selected by the system and R, the number of relevant
units missed by the system. For the filtering of documents, units are documents.
For the filtering of segments, they are sentences. Classically, the $F_1 measure$ was
used for combining recall and precision. The results presented in the next section
are average values of these metrics for the 14 test topics.

7.2   Experimental Results

Document Filtering. Our first evaluation was focused on the ability of the
REDUIT system to select documents in relation to a profile. The corpus we

Table 3. Results of the evaluation of document filtering

Filtering method	Recall	Precision	$F_1 measure$
REDUIT (v0)	0.89	0.11	0.21
REDUIT (v1)	0.82	0.44	0.57

relied on was made of the 3780 documents from the CLEF collection for which a relevance judgment against the 14 selected topics was available. It should be note that this corpus can be considered as especially difficult as, according to the pooling procedure used in TREC-like evaluations, it gathers the documents that were considered as the most relevant ones by the search engines that participated to CLEF. Among these 3780 documents, only 320 of them were relevant for the 14 selected topics.

In Table 3, REDUIT (v0) is a version of the REDUIT system in which the whole profile is taken as one topic, while REDUIT (v1) is a version that exploits the topical structure of profiles but not the inferred terms. As expected, taking into account the topical heterogeneousness of profiles leads to a significant improvement of precision while recall only decreases slightly. Nevertheless, the global improvement is clear. Precision values are low, which is not surprising: as mentioned above, our corpus is quite difficult and moreover, the filtering of documents with a profile that was defined manually, as TREC-like topics for instance, is known as a difficult task which was given up by the filtering track of TREC [14].

Segment Filtering. Our second evaluation was dedicated to the ability of the REDUIT system to select the parts of a document that match with a profile. Three versions of the REDUIT system (see Table 4) were tested on the subset of 320 documents that were manually annotated (see section 7.1). REDUIT (v0) and REDUIT (v1) refer to the same versions as in the previous section. Hence, the summaries produced by REDUIT (v0) are made of all the segments of a document that contain terms of the profile, without any constraint on which topic they belong to. Nevertheless, for having comparable results between REDUIT (v0) and REDUIT (v1), the number of profile terms that determines the selection of a segment is the same in the two cases[5]. Table 4 also shows the results of three baseline systems that implement basic strategies that are well-known in the summarization field:

- *baseline 1* always selects the first segment of each document;
- *baseline 2* always selects the first and the last segment of each document;
- *baseline 3* always selects the last segment of each document.

These strategies, that are also used as baselines in the DUC evaluations, rely on the observation that the introduction or the conclusion of a text is frequently comparable to a summary or at least, gather an important part of its content.

---

[5] According to section 4.3, a segment could be selected when one term of the profile is found if this profile has only one topic, which is always the case for REDUIT (v0).

Table 4. Results of the evaluation of segment filtering

Filtering method	Recall	Precision	$F_1 measure$
baseline 1	0.56	0.36	0.44
baseline 2	0.68	0.34	0.45
baseline 3	0.11	0.23	0.14
REDUIT (v0)	0.68	0.53	0.6
REDUIT (v1)	0.67	0.65	0.65
REDUIT (v2)	0.82	0.60	0.70

As for document filtering, Table 4 shows the interest of the topical structuring of profiles for segment filtering. The impact on results is the same: precision increases in a significant way while recall decreases slightly, which leads to a clear improvement of global results. Moreover, the results all the versions of the REDUIT system exceed those of all the baseline systems: only the recall of *baseline 2* is comparable to the recall of REDUIT (v0) and REDUIT (v1). This fact can be viewed as an *a posteriori* justification of the criteria defined in section 4.3 for detecting the matching between a profile and a document. The last line of Table 4 corresponds to the most complete version of the REDUIT system, that is to say, a version that also exploits inferred terms. For this evaluation, the dispatching of the inferred terms among the subtopics of the profile was performed manually. In comparison with REDUIT (v1), REDUIT (v2) gets a far better recall with a stable precision, which shows that the kind of adaptation of profiles performed for document filtering is also useful for the selection of segments and more generally, for summarization.

8   Related Work

The way we perform query-biased summarization is not radically different from the way it is achieved by Sanderson in [2] for SUMMAC, but we differ from his work by heavily relying on the notion of topic, both for structuring profiles and for delimiting and selecting document excerpts. Sanderson tested a kind of relevance feedback called Local Context Analysis but did not find a positive impact on results, contrary to what we got. One important difference with our inferred words can explain these findings: the topical constraints applied to the selection of inferred words turn out to be quite restrictive, which avoids to introduce too much noise.

The importance of taking into account the topical heterogeneousness of documents was also illustrated for mono-document summarization in [15]. In this case, summarization is not guided by a profile or a query and the topics of a document must be found in an unsupervised way. But this work shows that summaries are less redundant when the selection of sentences is based on their topic as the first criterion than when it relies on a non-topical weighting scheme.

Finally, our work is also related to several evaluations. SUMMAC is the most evident of them as mentioned above but DUC also tested a similar task in 2003: a set of documents had to be summarized given a TDT topic. However, as TDT topics refer to events and not to themes, they are not heterogeneous from a topical viewpoint and the systems developed for this task were mainly focused on taking into account named entities or the semantic links between the topic and the sentences of documents. The HARD track of TREC [16] is also a recent evaluation that pays special attention to profiles. But the focus in this case is put on data related to the context of the query, as the purposes of the user or the kind of documents he is interested in, more than on its topical content.

9   Conclusion and Future Work

We have presented in this article a method for selecting the most relevant excerpts of a set of documents in relation to a profile. This method puts the stress on two points: taking into account the topical heterogeneousness of profiles can improve the precision of selection; the adaptation of the profile to the input documents can improve its recall. This method was implemented by the REDUIT system and its evaluation showed positive results in favor of its two specificities.

However, several aspects of this work may be improved or extended. For instance, the definition of profiles in REDUIT is done only by giving a set of terms. We are interested in enabling users to define a profile by giving a set of example documents. In this case, a profile would be built by performing the topical segmentation of the documents and clustering in an unsupervised way the resulting segments for discovering its subtopics. Expanding profiles is also a possible way of improving REDUIT's results. The network of co-occurrences used for structuring profiles was used in [9] for the topical expansion of queries. Such an expansion could be easily adapted to profiles. Finally, a module could be added to REDUIT for detecting more specifically redundancies among the sentences of the pruned segments to produce short or very short summaries.

References

1. Over, P., Yen, J.: An introduction to DUC 2003: Intrinsic evaluation of generic new text summarization systems. In: Document Understanding Conference 2003. (2003)
2. Sanderson, M.: Accurate user directed summarization from existing tools. In: CIKM'98. (1998) 45–51
3. Okumura, M., Mochizuki, H.: Query-biased summarization based on lexical chaining. Computational Intelligence 16 (2000) 578–585
4. Berger, A., Mittal, V.O.: Query-relevant summarization using faqs. In: ACL 2000. (2000) 294–301
5. Wu, H., Radev, D.R., Fan, W.: Towards answer-focused summarization. In: 1st International Conference on Information Technology and Applications. (2002)
6. Mori, T., Nozawa, M., Asada, Y.: Multi-answer-focused multi-document summarization using a question-answering engine. In: COLING 2004. (2004) 439–445

7. Mani, I., House, D., Klein, G., Hirshman, L., Orbst, L., Firmin, T., Chrzanowski, M., Sundheim, B.: The TIPSTER SUMMAC text summarization evaluation. Technical Report MTR 98W0000138, The Mitre Corporation (1998)
8. Ferret, O.: Filtrage thématique d'un réseau de collocations. In: TALN 2003, Batz sur mer, France (2003) 347–352
9. Besançon, R., de Chalendar, G., Ferret, O., Fluhr, C., Mesnard, O., Naets, H.: Concept-based Searching and Merging for Multilingual Information Retrieval: First Experiments at CLEF 2003. In: 4th Workshop of the Cross-Language Evaluation Forum, CLEF 2003. (2004)
10. Choi, F.Y.Y.: Advances in domain independent linear text segmentation. In: NAACL'00. (2000) 26–33
11. Fukusima, T., Okumura, M.: Text summarization challenge: Text summarization evaluation in japan. In: NAACL 2001 Workshop on Automatic Summarization. (2001) 51–59
12. Radev, D.R., Jing, H., Budzikowska, M.: Centroid-based summarization of multiple documents: Sentence extraction, utility-based evaluation, and user studies. In: ANLP/NAACL 2000 Workshop on Automatic Summarization, Seattle, WA (2000)
13. Lin, C.Y., Hovy, E.H.: Automatic evaluation of summaries using n-gram co-occurrence statistics. In: HLT/NAACL 2003, Edmonton, Canada (2003)
14. Hull, D., Robertson, S.: The TREC-8 filtering track final report. In: 8th Text Retrieval Conference (TREC-8). (2000) 35–55
15. Hu, P., He, T., Ji, D.: Chinese text summarization based on thematic area detection. In: ACL-04 Workshop: Text Summarization Branches Out, Barcelona, Spain, Association for Computational Linguistics (2004) 112–119
16. Allan, J.: HARD track overview in trec 2003 - High accuracy retrieval from documents. In: 12th Text Retrieval Conference (TREC-2003). (2004)

Automatic Text Summarization Based on Word-Clusters and Ranking Algorithms

Massih R. Amini, Nicolas Usunier, and Patrick Gallinari

Computer Science Laboratory of Paris 6,
8 Rue du Capitaine Scott,
75015 Paris, France
{amini, usunier, gallinari}@poleia.lip6.fr

Abstract. This paper investigates a new approach for Single Document Summarization based on a Machine Learning ranking algorithm. The use of machine learning techniques for this task allows one to adapt summaries to the user needs and to the corpus characteristics. These desirable properties have motivated an increasing amount of work in this field over the last few years. Most approaches attempt to generate summaries by extracting text-spans (sentences in our case) and adopt the classification framework which consists to train a classifier in order to discriminate between relevant and irrelevant spans of a document. A set of features is first used to produce a vector of scores for each sentence in a given document and a classifier is trained in order to make a global combination of these scores. We believe that the classification criterion for training a classifier is not adapted for SDS and propose an original framework based on ranking for this task. A ranking algorithm also combines the scores of different features but its criterion tends to reduce the relative misordering of sentences within a document. Features we use here are either based on the state-of-the-art or built upon word-clusters. These clusters are groups of words which often co-occur with each other, and can serve to expand a query or to enrich the representation of the sentences of the documents. We analyze the performance of our ranking algorithm on two data sets - the Computation and Language (cmp_lg) collection of TIPSTER SUMMAC and the WIPO collection. We perform comparisons with different baseline - non learning - systems, and a reference trainable summarizer system based on the classification framework. The experiments show that the learning algorithms perform better than the non-learning systems while the ranking algorithm outperforms the classifier. The difference of performance between the two learning algorithms depends on the nature of datasets. We give an explanation of this fact by the different separability hypothesis of the data made by the two learning algorithms.

1 Introduction

With the actual huge and continuously growing online text resources, it becomes necessary to help users get quick answers to their queries. Single document text summarization (SDS) can be coupled with conventional search engines, and help users to quickly evaluate the relevance of documents or to navigate through a corpus.

Automated text summarization dates back to the end of the fifties [14]. Two main ideas have emerged to deal with this task; the first was how a summarizer has to treat a

D.E. Losada and J.M. Fernández-Luna (Eds.): ECIR 2005, LNCS 3408, pp. 142–156, 2005.
© Springer-Verlag Berlin Heidelberg 2005

huge quantity of data and the second, how it may be possible to produce a human quality summary. Different attempts on the latter have shown that a professional summarization system has to encompass discourse understanding, abstraction and language generation [19]. These processes make the summarization very complex and often intractable for on-line textual documents. To deal with the first point, simpler approaches were explored which consist in extracting representative text-spans, using statistical techniques or techniques based on superficial domain-independent linguistic analyses [9, 29]. For these approaches, SDS can be defined as the selection of a subset of the document sentences which is representative of its content. This is typically done by ranking document text-spans with respect to the similarity measure with a relevant source. Most of the recent work in SDS uses this paradigm. Summarization systems can operate in two modes: generic summarization, which consists in extracting text-spans relevant to the main *topics* of a whole document and query-based summarization, which aims at abstracting the information relevant to a given query. For both approaches, it has been shown that in SDS, extracted text-span units do not always retain their precedence orders in the summary [10]. Usually, sentences are used as text-span units but paragraphs have also been considered [17, 20].

In this paper we present a statistical text summarizer based on Machine Learning (ML) and the text-span extraction paradigm. Our approach allows both generic and query-based summaries. However for evaluation purposes, we present here results for a generic SDS. For a given document, the system provides a set of unordered extracts which are supposed to be the most relevant to its topics. Previous work on the application of machine learning techniques for SDS used the classification framework. Such approaches usually train a classifier, using a training set of documents and their associated summaries, to distinguish between summary and non-summary sentences [13, 26, 5, 1]. After training, these systems operate on unlabeled text by ranking sentences of a new document according to the output of the classifier. The classifier is learned by comparing its output to a desired output reflecting a global class information. Under this framework one assumes that all sentences from different documents are comparable with respect to this class information. This hypothesis holds for scientific articles [13, 26] but for a large variety of collections, documents are heterogeneous and their summaries depend much more on the content of their texts than on a global class information.

We explore a new ML approach for SDS based on *ranking*. The latter has been successfully used in other domain-specific tasks such as Named-entity extraction [4] or metasearch [7]. We also believe that this framework is more adapted to SDS than the usual classification approach. It allows to learn a system with a weaker hypothesis on document sentences than the one assumed in classification. This makes the approach more efficient on other types of collections than scientific articles. The aim here is to combine automatically different features, giving each a relative ranking of sentences in a document, in order to achieve a high accurate ranking for summary sentences. For this combination, we propose generic and word cluster queries. The latter are new for SDS. To this aim, we group words occuring in the same sentences into a much smaller number of word-clusters than the initial vocabulary and use these clusters as features.

The paper is organized as follows, in section 2, we describe the features associated to each sentence, and in section 3 we show that ranking is more adapted to SDS than the classification framework. We then detail the proposed ranking method for SDS in section 4 and show empirically in section 5 that the latter approach outperforms a state-of-art classifier on SUMMAC Cmp_lg and WIPO datasets.

2   Features for Text Summarization

A generic summary of a document has to reflect its key points. We need here statistical features which give different information about the relevance of sentences for the summary. If these features are sufficiently relevant for the SDS task, one can expect that they assign high scores to summary sentences in a document but rank them differently. We argue that there exists an optimal combination of these features which gives better results than the performance of the best feature. These Features constitute the input of the ML algorithms we developed here.

[18] defined different sentence features he considered important for a generic summary and grouped them into seven categories: *Indicator phrases* (such as cue-words or acronyms), *Frequency and title keywords, location* as well as *sentence length cuttoff* heuristics and the number of *semantic links* between a sentence and its neighbours. These features have partially or completely been used in the state of the art since then [13, 15, 9].

We also build from his work taking the *Indicator phrases* and *title keywords* features. As a feature gives a score to sentences in a document, we represent a ranking feature as a couple $(q, sim(q, s))$ where q is a generic query and $sim(q, s)$ is the similarity between q and a sentence s. In the following, we present different generic queries and similarity measures we used in this work.

2.1   Generic Queries

We start from two baseline generic queries constituted of the most frequent terms in the collection, **MFT** and no-stop words in the title of a document **title keyword**. These queries represent two sources of evidence we use to find relevant sentences in a document. Since **title keywords** may be very short, we have employed query-expansion techniques such as Local Context Analysis (LCA) [28] or thesaurus expansion methods (i.e. WordNet [6]) as well as a learning based expansion technique.

Expansion via WordNet and LCA: From the **title keyword** query, we formed two other queries, reflecting local links between the title keywords and other words in the corresponding document:

- **title keyword and LCA**, constituted by keywords in the title of a document and the most frequent words in most similar sentences to the **title keyword** query according to the cosine measure.
- **title keyword and most frequent terms**, constituted by high frequency document words and the keywords in the title of a document,

We also obtained an expanded query from the title keywords of a document and their first order synonyms using WordNet, **title keyword and WordNet**.

We propose next an unsupervised learning approach to expand the **title keyword** query. Such a technique allows one to find global links between words in a title of a document and words in the document collection.

Expansion with Word-Clusters: We first form different word-clusters based on words co-occurring in sentences of all documents in the corpus [3]. For discovering these word-clusters, each word w in the vocabulary V is first characterized as an p-dimensional vector $\mathbf{w} = < n(w, i) >_{i \in \{1, \ldots, p\}}$ representing the number of occurrences of w in each sentence i. Under this representation, word clustering is then performed using the `Naive-Bayes` clustering algorithm maximizing the Classification Maximum Likelihood criterion [23]. We have arbitrary fixed the number of clusters to be found to $\frac{|V|}{100}$.

From these clusters we obtained two other expanded queries by first adding to title keywords, words in their respective clusters, **title keyword and term-clusters**. And secondly by projecting each sentence of a document and the **title keyword** query in the space of these word-clusters, **Projected title keyword**. For the latter we characterize each sentence in a document and the **title keyword** query by a vector where each characteristic represents the number of occurrences of words from a cluster in that sentence or in the **title keyword** query. The characteristics in this representation are related to the degree of representation of each word-cluster in a given sentence or in the **title keyword** query.

2.2 Similarity Measures

Following [12], we use the *tf-idf* representation and compute the cosine similarity measure between sentence x and query q as :

$$Sim_1(q, s) = \frac{\sum_{w \in s, q} tf(w, q) tf(w, s) idf^2(w)}{\|w\| \|s\|}$$

Where, $tf(w, x)$ is the frequency of word w in x (q or s), $idf(w)$ is the inverse document frequency of word w and $\|x\| = \sqrt{\sum_{w \in x} (tf(w, x) idf(w))^2}$.

We also expected to reweight sentences containing acronyms e.g. HMM (Hidden Markov Models), NLP (Natural Language Processing), ... The resulting feature computes similarity between the **title keywords** and sentences using the same similarity measure than Sim_1 except that acronyms are given a higher weight. The resulting similarity measure writes

$$Sim_2(q, s) = \frac{\sum_{w \in s, q} tf(w, q) tf^*(w, s) idf^2(w)}{\|w\| \|s\|}$$

Hence, we have counted as twice the term frequency of acronyms e.g. $tf^*(w, s) = 2 * tf(w, s)$ if w is an acronym. In our experiments, acronyms are extracted using the *Acronym Finding Program* described in [24].

We have conducted experiments on scientific articles. For these documents, sentences containing any of a list of fixed phrases like "in this paper", "in conclusion", ... are more likely to be in summaries. We counted as twice the similarity of sentences containing such cue-words : $Sim_3(q, s) = 2 Sim_1(q, s)$ if s contains cue-terms and $Sim_3(q, s) = Sim_1(q, s)$ if s does not contain cue-terms.

Table 1. Ranking features

#	Ranking features	(q, sim)
1	Title	(**title keywords,** Sim_1)
2	Title+LCA	(**title keywords and LCA,** Sim_1)
3	Title+WN	(**title keywords and WordNet,** Sim_1)
4	Title+MFT	(**title keywords and most frequent terms,** Sim_1)
5	Title+Term-clusters	(**title keywords and term-clusters,** Sim_1)
6	Title+Acronyms	(**title keywords,** Sim_2)
7	Title+Cue words	(**title keywords,** Sim_3)
8	CommonTerms	(**title keywords,** Sim_4)
9	SumOfIdfs	(**title keywords,** Sim_5)
10	Projected title	(**Projected title keywords,** Sim_6)
11	GenericMFT	(**MFT,** Sim_1)

Based on the first similarity measure we have also introduced three other similarities; $Sim_4(q, s) = \sum_{w \in s,q} 1$ computing the number of common words in the query q and a sentence s, $Sim_5(q, s) = \sum_{w \in s,q} idf(w)$ the sum of idf's of words in common in q and s and $Sim_6(q, s) = q.s$ the dot product between q and s.

The ranking features we considered are then constituted of 11 couples, (query, similarity), shown in table 1.

3   Ranking for Text Summarization

In order to combine sentence features, ML approaches for SDS adopt a classification framework, either using the Naive Bayes model [13] or a logistic regression classifier [1]. The motivation for such approaches is that a classification training error of 0 implies that scores assigned to relevant/irrelevant sentences from a classifier are all greater/lower than a constant c, resulting in an appropriate rankings of sentences.

However, on real life applications, this classification error is never zero. In this case, for a given document, we cannot predict about the ranking of a misclassified sentence relatively to the other ones. The reason is that the classification error is computed by comparing sentence scores with respect to a constant, and not relatively to each other. It can then happen that a misclassified irrelevant sentence gets higher score than relevant ones. In other terms, minimizing the classification error does not necessary leads to the optimization of the ranks of relevant sentences in the same document.

We believe that algorithms relying on the ML *ranking* framework will be more effective in practice for the SDS task. In this case, instead of classifying sentences as relevant/irrelevant, a ranking algorithm classifies pairs of sentences. More specifically, it considers the pair of sentences $(\mathbf{s}, \mathbf{s}')$ coming from a same document, such that just one of the two sentences is relevant. The goal is then to learn a scoring function H from the following assumption: a pair is correctly classified if and only if the score of the relevant sentence is greater than the score of the irrelevant one. The error on the pairs of sentences, called the *Ranking loss* of H [7], is equal to:

$$Rloss(\mathcal{D}, H) = \frac{1}{|\mathcal{D}|} \sum_{d \in \mathcal{D}} \frac{1}{|\mathcal{S}_1^d||\mathcal{S}_{-1}^d|} \sum_{s \in \mathcal{S}_1^d} \sum_{s' \in \mathcal{S}_{-1}^d} [[H(s') \geq H(s)]] \qquad (1)$$

where $\mathcal{D}$ is the training document collection, $\mathcal{S}_1^d$ the set of relevant sentences for document d, and $\mathcal{S}_{-1}^d$ the set of the irrelevant ones of the same document and $[[\pi \geq 0]]$ is equal to 1 if $\pi \geq 0$ holds and 0 in the contrary case.

It is straightforward that minimizing *Ranking loss* is equivalent to minimize the number of irrelevant sentences scored higher than the relevant ones of the same document. *Ranking loss* results then in a direct optimization of the ranks of the relevant sentences. This fact motivates the use of a ranking algorithm instead of a classification algorithm for the SDS task.

3.1 Logistic Regression Classifier for SDS

The logistic regression has already been used for SDS [1]. It has shown good empirical results in terms of Precision/Recall for the combination of features. We will see in the next section that an efficient ranking algorithm can be naturally derived from the logistic regression.

As input of the logistic classifier, we represent each sentence s by a vector of scores $(s_1, ..., s_n)$, where the score s_i is given by the feature i (Table 1).

The logistic classifier makes the following assumption on the form of the posterior probability of the class *relevant* given a sentence s:

$$P(relevant|\mathbf{s}) = \frac{1}{1 + e^{-2\sum_{i=1}^{n} \lambda_i s_i}}$$

And learns the parameters $\Lambda = (\lambda_1, ..., \lambda_n)$ by maximizing the binomial log-likelihood [8], which writes:

$$\mathcal{L}(\mathcal{D}; \Lambda) = -\frac{1}{2} \sum_{y=-1,1} \frac{1}{|\mathcal{S}^y|} \sum_{\mathbf{s} \in \mathcal{S}^y} \log(1 + e^{-2y\sum_{i=1}^{n} \lambda_i s_i}) \qquad (2)$$

where $\mathcal{D}$ is the set of training documents, and $\mathcal{S}^{-1}$ and $\mathcal{S}^1$ are respectively the set of relevant and irrelevant sentences in the training set and $y \in \{-1, 1\}$ (1 represents the class of the relevant sentences).

3.2 Adaptation to Ranking for SDS

There exist several ranking algorithms in the ML literature, based on the perceptron [4, 21] or *AdaBoost* - called *RankBoost* [7]. For the SDS task, as the total number of sentences in the collection may be very high we need a simple and efficient ranking algorithm. Perceptron-based ranking algorithms would lead to quadratic complexity in the number of examples, while the *RankBoost* algorithm in its standard setting does not search a linear combination of the input features. For the sake of simplicity, we compare in this paper a linear classifier with a linear ranker - called LinearRank in the following - which combines both efficiency (complexity linear in the number of examples) and simplicity.

We represent the pair $(\mathbf{s}, \mathbf{s}')$ by the difference of their representative vectors, $(s_1 - s'_1, ..., s_n - s'_n)$. We want to learn a scoring function $H(s) = \sum_{i=1}^{n} \theta_i s_i$, for any sentence s in the collection. The *Ranking loss* (1) can be written as the following:

$$Rloss(\mathcal{D}, H) = \frac{1}{|\mathcal{D}|} \sum_{d \in \mathcal{D}} \frac{1}{|\mathcal{S}_1^d||\mathcal{S}_{-1}^d|} \sum_{\mathbf{s} \in \mathcal{S}_1^d} \sum_{\mathbf{s}' \in \mathcal{S}_{-1}^d} [[\sum_{i=1}^{n} \theta_i(s'_i - s_i) \geq 0]]$$

This expression is a standard linear classification error, on the pairs of sentences represented by the difference of the sentence vectors. We can then adapt any linear classification algorithm to ranking (logistic regression in our case) in order to optimize the previous criterion.

The logistic assumption, adapted to ranking, becomes:

$$P(1|\,\mathbf{s}, \mathbf{s}') = \frac{1}{1 + e^{-2 \sum_{i=1}^{n} \theta_i(s_i - s'_i)}}$$

where $\mathbf{s}$ is a relevant sentence for a given document, and $\mathbf{s}'$ an irrelevant sentence for the same document. $P(1|\,\mathbf{s}, \mathbf{s}')$ denotes the posterior probability that the considered pair is well classified.

The parameters $\Theta = (\theta_1, ..., \theta_n)$ are learned by maximizing the corresponding binomial log-likelihood:

$$\mathcal{L}(\mathcal{D}; \Theta) = -\frac{1}{|\mathcal{D}|} \sum_{d \in \mathcal{D}} \frac{1}{|\mathcal{S}_d^{-1}||\mathcal{S}_d^1|} \sum_{(\mathbf{s}, \mathbf{s}') \in \mathcal{S}_d^1 \times \mathcal{S}_d^{-1}} \log(1 + e^{-2 \sum_{i=1}^{n} \theta_i(s_i - s'_i)}) \qquad (3)$$

where $\mathcal{D}$ is the set of training documents, and, for $d \in \mathcal{D}$, $\mathcal{S}_d^1$ is the set of relevant sentences in d and $\mathcal{S}_d^{-1}$ the set of irrelevant ones.

[8] have shown that the optimization of (3) leads to the same parameters as minimizing the exponential loss[1]:

$$\mathbf{ELoss}(\mathcal{D}; \Theta) = \frac{1}{|\mathcal{D}|} \sum_{d \in \mathcal{D}} \frac{1}{|\mathcal{S}_d^{-1}||\mathcal{S}_d^1|} \sum_{(\mathbf{s}, \mathbf{s}') \in \mathcal{S}_d^1 \times \mathcal{S}_d^{-1}} e^{\sum_{i=1}^{n} \theta_i(s'_i - s_i)} \qquad (4)$$

This latter function is convex, so standard optimization algorithms can be used to minimize it. In our case, we used an iterative scaling algorithm to learn the parameters, which is an adaptation for ranking of an algorithm developed for classification described in [11]. The interesting property of the exponential loss is that in our case, it can be computed in time linear in the number of examples, simply by rewriting (4) as follows:

$$\mathbf{ELoss}(\mathcal{D}; \Theta) = \frac{1}{|\mathcal{D}|} \sum_{d \in \mathcal{D}} \frac{1}{|\mathcal{S}_d^{-1}||\mathcal{S}_d^1|} (\sum_{\mathbf{s}' \in \mathcal{S}_d^{-1}} e^{\sum_{i=1}^{n} \theta_i s'_i})(\sum_{\mathbf{s} \in \mathcal{S}_d^1} e^{- \sum_{i=1}^{n} \theta_i s_i}) \qquad (5)$$

---

[1] It is interesting to note that this exponential loss is the one minimized by the *RankBoost* algorithm [7] and is intuitively related to the ranking problem, because the following inequality holds: $\mathbf{ELoss}(\mathcal{D}; \Theta) \geq \mathbf{Rloss}(\mathcal{D}; \Theta)$. No such inequality can be found between the ranking loss and the binomial likelihood.

On the opposite, the computation of the maximum likelihood of equation (3) requires to consider all the pairs of sentences, and leads to a complexity quadratic in the number of examples. Thus, although ranking algorithms consider the pairs of examples, in the special case of SDS, the proposed algorithm is of complexity linear in the number of examples through the use of the exponential loss.

In order to compare equitably between classification and ranking for SDS, we employed in both cases the same logistic model but trained it differently depending on the framework in use. Hence, we trained the model in a classification framework by maximizing the binomial likelihood criterion (2). While the model parameters are learned by minimizing the **ELoss** criterion (5) in the case of ranking.

4 Experiments

4.1 Data Sets: Properties

A good extractive summarizer has to find the relevant information for which the user is looking as well as to eliminate the irrelevant one. It is then crucial to evaluate the system on the way it is able to identify how well it can extract the pieces of articles that are relevant to a user. To this end we used two datasets from the SUMMAC cmp_lg evaluations sets [22] and the WIPO collection [27].

The SUMMAC corpus is constituted of 183 articles. Documents in this collection are scientific papers which appeared in ACL sponsored conferences. The collection has been marked up in xml by converting automatically the latex version of the papers to xml. The second data set, WIPO, is an automated categorization collection which contains over 75000 patent documents in English. Documents in this collection are also marked up in xml. In our experiments, we have chosen 1000 documents in random from this corpus. In both datasets markup include tags covering information such as title, authors or inventors, etc., as well as basic structure such as abstract, body, sections, lists, etc.

In order to find the relevant information in documents, we have used the text-span alignment method descried by [16] to generate extract-based summaries from the abstract of each document. In this method, summaries required for training and evaluation are automatically generated as follows: from a pool of all sentences in a document, Marcu's algorithm discard those which removal increases the similarity between the rest of the pool and the abstract. And this until that any removal decreases the similarity measure.

For learning systems, an advantage of the Marcu's algorithm is that, in the case of huge datasets, *gold* summaries are not available. The human extraction of such reference summaries is infeasible. Moreover in [16] Marcu has proven empirically that the performance of his alignment algorithm is close to that of humans by means.

Contrarily to the SUMMAC corpus, WIPO collection is constituted from heterogeneous documents in which a relevant sentence from a document may have a completely different feature representation than another relevant sentence from another document. It is then interesting to see the behaviour of the ranking and the classification algorithms in such a corpus where relevant sentences in different documents are mapped into different parts of the feature space.

Table 2. Data Set properties

Data set comparison		
source	SUMMAC	WIPO
Number of docs	173(183)	854(1000)
Average # of sent. per doc.	156.57	179.63
Maximum # of sent. per doc.	928	1507
Minimum # of sent. per doc.	15	21
Number of doc. in (training-test) sets	73-100	360-494
Average # of words per sent.	11.73	14.22
Size of the vocabulary	15621	56856
Summary as % of doc. length	10	10
Average summary size (in # of sent)	11.44	6.07
Maximum # of sent. per summary	27	19
Minimum # of sent. per summary	3	2

Documents are tokenized by removing *xml* tags as well as words in a stop list and sentence boundaries within each document are found using the morpho-syntactic tree-tagger program [25]. In each data collection, low collection frequency words (occurring in less than two documents) are also removed. A compression ratio must be specified or computed for extractive summaries. For both datasets we followed the SUMMAC evaluation by using a 10% compression ratio [22].

From each dataset, we removed documents having summaries (found by Marcu's algorithm) composed of 1 sentence arguing that a sentence is not sufficient to summarize a scientific or a patent article. From the WIPO data collection, we have also removed documents having less than 2 words in their title. In total we have removed respectively 10 documents from SUMMAC and 146 from WIPO collections. Table 2 gives the characteristics of both datasets.

4.2   Results

Evaluation issues of summarization systems have been the object of several attempts, many of them being carried within the tipster program and the summac competition. This is a complex issue and many different aspects have to be considered simultaneously in order to evaluate and compare different summaries. For the extraction task we are dealing here, things are a bit easier. We compared the extract of a system with the desired summary at 10% compression ratio and used the following Precision and Recall measures to plot the curves:

$$\text{Precision} = \frac{\text{\# of sentences extracted by the system which are in the target summaries}}{\text{total \# of sentences extracted by the system}}$$

$$\text{Recall} = \frac{\text{\# of sentences extracted by the system which are in the target summaries}}{\text{total \# of sentences in the target summaries}}$$

For each dataset, we ran the ranking algorithm (LinearRank), the logistic classifier and statistical features giving scores to sentences. First we sought to show the ability of query expansion techniques (without learning effects). Expansion using LCA and WordNet thesaurus were found to be effective for summarization; we went further by introducing the expansion based on word-clusters. The benefits of query expansion for summarization consisted of comparing the **Title** feature to **Title+LCA**, **Title+WN**, **Title+MFT**, **Projected Title** and **Title+Term-clusters** features. The results of this experiment are shown in Figure 1.

These results show that the three best features are **Title+LCA**, **Projected Title** and **Title+Term-clusters**. It comes that local and global query expansions improve the performance of the baseline **title keywords** query for SDS. However we note that the performance of LCA varies between the two datasets: on the SUMMAC corpus, **Title+LCA** has 70% precision for 50% recall while the **Title** feature gives a 40% precision. On the WIPO corpus the difference between the precisions of these two features is reduced to approximately 6% for the same recall. This may be due to the fact that there are fewer relevant sentences in documents from the WIPO dataset (see table 2). Thus, it is possible that more irrelevant sentences are used in the computation of co-occurences of words for LCA. The difference between the two features **Title+Term-clusters** and **Projected Title** is that the first one does not take into account all the words from the word-clusters, while the second one considers sentences and the title in the cluster space. This consideration leads to a different computation of *idf* weights for the second query, which is highly affected by the number of clusters. In our experiments, **Title+Term-clusters** performs better in both datasets. This may be due to the fact that the clusters contain too much irrelevant words, which makes the feature **Projected Title** give high scores to some irrelevant sentences. Consequently, some future work is needed to study the effect of the optimal number of word-clusters and to fully understand the effect of representing sentences in the cluster space instead of adding words into the query.

The performance of the learning algorithms are plotted in figure 2. In both datasets, these algorithms perform better than statistical features while the ranking algorithm outperforms the logistic classifier. This means basically that the two learning frameworks lead to a good combination of statistical features, but the ranking framework is more adapted to SDS than the classification framework.

On the SUMMAC corpus, the difference in terms of precision between classification and ranking vary from 2% to 5% at different levels of recall. On the WIPO corpus, it varies between 5% and 9%. The difference between the classification algorithm and the best feature varies from 3% to 9% on the SUMMAC corpus, and from 0% to 5% on the WIPO corpus at different levels of recall. This shows that the performance of the combination of features found by the classifier, compared to the best feature, vary a lot depending on the corpus, while the ranking algorithm finds an accurate combination of features on both datasets.

An analysis of the weights given by both learning algorithms to different features shows that the most important features in the combination are **Title**, **Title+LCA**, **Title+Term-clusters**, **Projected Title** and **generic query**. It comes that learning algorithms give importance to features upon two criteria: firstly, their ability to give high scores to relevant sentences and, secondly, their independence with other features. Thus, the **generic query** which gives the worst performance in our experiments, is given a higher weight by the ranking algorithm than features such as **Title+WN** or **Title+Cue Words** which are highly correlated to the **Title** feature.

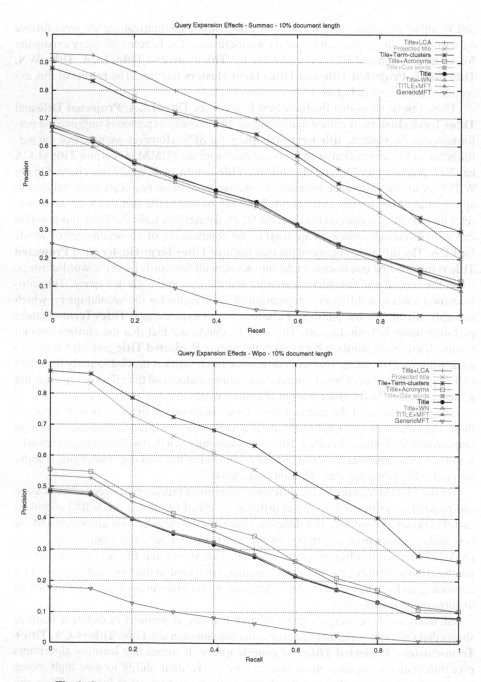

Fig. 1. Query expansion effects on SUMMAC (top) and WIPO (down) datasets

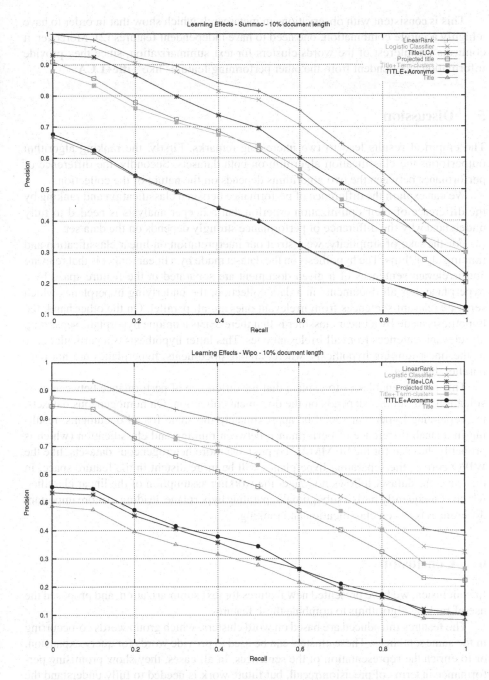

Fig. 2. Learning effects on SUMMAC (top) and WIPO (down) datasets

This is consistent with observations in metasearch which show that in order to have a highly accurate combination, one need to have independent features [2]. Moreover, it confirms the interest of the words clusters for text summarization, since they provide information independent from the other performing features like **Title+LCA**.

5   Discussion

The empirical results lead to two interesting remarks. Firstly, the ranking algorithm outperforms the classification algorithm on both datasets. Secondly, the difference of performance between the two algorithms depends on the nature of the collection.

We can explain the difference of performance between classification and ranking by the difference of their optimization criterion, but a deeper analysis is needed to fully understand why the difference of performance strongly depends on the data set.

For the sake of simplicity, we restrict our interpretation on linear classification and ranking algorithms. The hypothesis on the dataset made by a linear ranker is that relevant and irrelevant sentences of a given document are separated in the feature space by a hyperplane. For all documents in a data collection, the underlying hyperplanes which separate relevant sentences from irrelevant ones are all parallel. On the other hand, the hypothesis made by a linear classifier is that there exists a unique hyperplane separating all relevant sentences from all irrelevant ones. This latter hypothesis is a particular case of the linear ranking hypothesis, where, among documents, hyperplanes are not only parallel, but equal.

This remark enables us to explain that the difference of performance between classification and ranking depends on the document collection. On homogeneous datasets, the separating hyperplanes will be approximately the same for all documents, resulting in a small difference of performance between ranking and classification (which is probably the case for the SUMMAC corpus). On more heterogeneous datasets, like the WIPO corpus, the separating hyperplanes will be more distant in the feature space. In this case, the dataset follows no longer the working assumption of the linear classifier, which consequently finds a suboptimal separating hyperplane, leading to more important differences between classification and ranking.

6   Conclusion

In conclusion, we have presented new features for text summarization, and proposed the use of ranking algorithms to combine these features.

The features introduced are based on word clusters, which group words co-occurring in the same sentences. These clusters can be used to provide words for query expansion, or to enrich the representation of the sentences. In all cases, they show promising performance in terms of precision/recall, but future work is needed to fully understand the difference between the two techniques as well as studying the effect of the number of clusters and their size on the performance of the features. Moreover, they bring additional and independent information to standard features used in SDS, and are therefore of great interest in the case where we want to build an accurate combination of features.

To the best of our knowledge, this paper is the first one to propose the use of a ML ranking algorithm for SDS. We have shown empirically that ranking algorithms outperform classification algorithms. Ranking algorithms have a weaker working hypothesis than classification algorithms, and seem more appropriate to the SDS, although the difference of performance between the two depends on the dataset we are studying. However, important gains can be expected on specific datasets, while it is probable that classification algorithms can do worse.

This understanding of the behavior of ranking algorithms can lead to its use on other tasks of passage level extraction, where the optimization criterion as well as the working hypothesis of ranking algorithms may be more suited than classification algorithms.

Acknowledgments

This work was supported in part by the IST Programme of the European Community, under the PASCAL Network of Excellence, IST-2002-506778. This publication only reflects the authors views.

References

1. Amini M.-R., Gallinari P.: The Use of unlabeled data to improve supervised learning for text summarization. Proceedings of the 25th ACM SIGIR, 105–112, (2002).
2. Aslam, J.A., Montague, M.: Models for metasearch. In Proceedings of the 24th annual international ACM SIGIR conference on Research and development in information retrieval, (2001)
3. Caillet M., Pessiot J.-F., Amini M.-R., Gallinari P.: Unsupervised Learning with Term Clustering for Thematic Segmentation of Texts. Proceedings of RIAO, (2004).
4. Collins, M. Ranking algorithms for named-entity extraction: Boosting and the voted perceptron. In Proceedings of the 40th Annual Meeting of the Association for Computational Linguistics (ACL-2002)
5. Chuang W.T., Yang J.: Extracting sentence segments for text summarization: a machine learning approach. Proceedings of the 23th ACM SIGIR, 152–159, (2000).
6. Fellbaum C.: WordNet, an Electronic Lexical Database. MIT Press, Cambridge MA (1998)
7. Freund, Y., Iyer, R., Schapire, R.E., Singer, Y.: An efficient boosting algorithm for combining preferences. Journal of Machine Learning Research, **4** (2003) 933–969
8. Friedman J., Hastie T., Tibshirani R.: Additive Logistic Regression: a Statistical View of Boosting. Technical Report Stanford University, (1998).
9. Goldstein J., Kantrowitz M., Mittal V., Carbonell J.: Summarizing Text Documents: Sentence Selection and Evaluation Metrics. Proceedings of the 22th ACM SIGIR, 121–127, (1999).
10. Jing H.: Summary generation through intelligent cutting and pasting of the input document. Technical Report Columbia University, (1998).
11. Lebanon, G., Lafferty J.: Boosting and maximum likelihood for exponential models. Technical Report CMU-CS-01-144, School of Computer Science, CMU (2001).
12. Knaus D., Mittendorf E., Shauble P., Sheridan P.: Highlighting Relevant Passages for Users of the Interactive SPIDER Retrieval System. In TREC-4 Proceedings (1994).
13. Kupiec J., Pederson J., Chen F.A.: Trainable Document Summarizer. Proceedings of the 18th ACM SIGIR, 68–73, (1995).
14. Luhn P.H.: Automatic creation of litterature abstracts. IBM Journal, pp. 159–165 (1958).

15. Mani I., Bloedorn E.: Machine Learning of Generic and User-Focused Summarization. Proceedings of hte Fifteenth National Conferences on AI pp. 821–826 (1998).
16. Marcu D.: The Automatic Construction of Large-Scale corpora for Summarization Research. Proceedings of the 22th ACM SIGIR, (1999).
17. Mitra M., Singhal A., Buckley C.: Automatic Text Summarization by Paragraph Extraction. Proceedings of the ACL'97/EACL'97 Workshop on Intelligent Scalable Text Summarization, pp. 31–36 (1997).
18. Paice C.D., Jones P.A.: The identification of important concepts in highly structured technical papers. Proceedings of the 16th ACM SIGIR, 69–78, (1993).
19. Sparck-Jones K.: Discourse modeling for automatic summarizing. Technical Report 29D, Computer Laboratory, university of Cambridge, (1993).
20. Strzalkowski T., Wang J., Wise B.: A Robust practical text summarization system. Proceedings of hte Fifteenth National Conferences on AI pp. 26–30 (1998).
21. Shen, L., Joshi, A.K.: Ranking and Reranking with Perceptron. Machine Learning, Special Issue on Learning in Speech and Language Technologies (2004)
22. http://www.itl.nist.gov/iaui/894.02/related_projects/tipster_summac/cmp_lg.html
23. Symons M.J.: Clustering Criteria and Multivariate Normal Mixture. Biometrics Vol. 37. 35–43 (1981).
24. Taghva K., Gilbreth J.: Recognizing acronyms and their definitions. IJDAR Vol. 1. 191–198 (1999).
25. http://www.ims.uni-stuttgart.de/projekte/corplex/TreeTagger/DecisionTreeTagger.html
26. Teufel S., Moens M.: Sentence Extraction as a Classification Task. Proceedings of the ACL'97/EACL'97 Workshop on Intelligent Scalable Text Summarization, pp. 58–65 (1997).
27. http://www.wipo.int/ibis/datasets/index.html
28. Xu, J., Croft, W.B.: Query expansion using local and global document analysis. Proceedings of the 19th annual international ACM SIGIR conference on Research and development in information retrieval (1996).
29. Zechner K.: Fast Generation of Abstracts from General Domain Text Corpora by Extracting Relevant Sentences. COLING, 986–989, (1996).

Comparing Topiary-Style Approaches to Headline Generation

Ruichao Wang, Nicola Stokes, William P. Doran, Eamonn Newman,
Joe Carthy, and John Dunnion

Intelligent Information Retrieval Group, Department of Computer Science,
University College Dublin, Ireland
{rachel, nicola.stokes, william.doran, eamonn.newman,
joe.carthy, john.dunnion}@ucd.ie

Abstract. In this paper we compare a number of Topiary-style headline generation systems. The Topiary system, developed at the University of Maryland
with BBN, was the top performing headline generation system at DUC 2004.
Topiary-style headlines consist of a number of general topic labels followed by
a compressed version of the lead sentence of a news story. The Topiary system
uses a statistical learning approach to finding topic labels for headlines, while
our approach, the LexTrim system, identifies key summary words by analysing
the lexical cohesive structure of a text. The performance of these systems is
evaluated using the ROUGE evaluation suite on the DUC 2004 news stories
collection. The results of these experiments show that a baseline system that
identifies topic descriptors for headlines using term frequency counts outperforms the LexTrim and Topiary systems. A manual evaluation of the headlines
also confirms this result.

1   Introduction

A headline is a very short summary (usually less than 10 words) describing the essential message of a piece of text. Like other types of summaries, news story headlines
are used to help a reader to quickly identify information that is of interest to them in a
presentation format such as a newspaper or a website. Although newspaper articles
are always accompanied by headlines, there are other types of news text sources, such
as transcripts of radio and television broadcasts, where this type of summary information is missing. In 2003 the Document Understanding Conference (DUC) [1] added
the headline generation task to their annual summarisation evaluation. This task was
also included in the 2004 evaluation plan, where summary quality was automatically
judged using a set of n-gram word overlap metrics called ROUGE [2]. The best performing system at this workshop was the Topiary approach [3] which generated headlines by combining a set of topic descriptors extracted from the DUC 2004 corpus
with a compressed version of the lead sentence of the news story, e.g. **COCHETEL
CHECHNYA: French United Nations official kidnapped** As can be seen these
topic descriptors provide the reader with a general event description while the lead
compressed sentence provides a more focussed summary of the news story.

D.E. Losada and J.M. Fernández-Luna (Eds.): ECIR 2005, LNCS 3408, pp. 157–168, 2005.

Topiary-style summaries performed well in the ROUGE-based 2004 evaluation for a number of reasons. Firstly, summarisation researchers have observed that the lead sentence of a news story is in itself often an adequate summary of the text. However, it has also been observed that additional important information about a topic may be spread across other sentences in the news story. The success of the Topiary-style summaries at DUC 2004 can be attributed to fact that this technique takes both of these observations into consideration when generating titles.

In this paper, we compare three distinct methods of identifying topic labels and observe their effect on summary quality when combined with a compressed lead sentence. The Topiary system generates topic descriptors using a statistical approach called Unsupervised Topic Discovery (UTD) [3]. This technique creates topic models with corresponding topic descriptors for different news story events in the DUC 2004 corpus. One of the problems with this approach is that it requires additional on-topic documents related to the news story being summarised to facilitate the generation of relevant topic models and descriptors, i.e. Topiary used the DUC 2004 corpus when generating summaries for the DUC 2004 evaluation.

In this paper, we investigate the use of lexical cohesion analysis as a means of determining these event labels. The advantage of this approach is that the descriptors are gleaned from the source text being summarised, so no auxiliary training corpus or additional on-topic news story documents from the DUC corpus are needed to determine appropriate topic labels for a particular story headline. In Section 3 and 4, we describe the Topiary, and LexTrim (lexical cohesion-based approach) in more detail. The performance of these systems is compared with a baseline system called TFTrim (term frequency-based approach). These systems were evaluated using the ROUGE evaluation metrics on the DUC 2004 collection, and a manual evaluation performed by four human evaluators. The results of these experiments and our overall conclusions are discussed in Section 5 and 6 respectively. In the following section, we provide an overview of recent approaches to automatic headline generation described in the summarisation literature.

2 Related Work

The aim of this paper is to improve Zajic, Dorr and Schwartz's Topiary-style parse-and-trim approach to headline summarisation [3]. This approach falls into the extractive category of headline generation techniques, where a compressed sentence or series of compressed sentences are concatenated to produce a readable headline. Extractive approaches differ mainly in how they determine which textual units to included in the summary. Some common sentence weighting approaches include Kraaij et al.'s [4] probabilistic approach, Alfonseca et al.'s [5] genetic algorithmic approach, and Copeck et al.'s [6] approach based on the occurrence of features that denote appropriate summary sentences. These lexical, syntactic and semantic features include the occurrence of discourse cues, the position of the sentence in the text, and the occurrence of content phrases and proper nouns. Biasing the extraction process with additional textual information such as these features is a standard approach to headline generation that has proved to be highly effective in most cases [4-7, 27].

At the DUC 2004 evaluation, a number of other parse-and-trim style headline techniques were presented [8-11]. However, all of these techniques were outperformed by the Topiary title generation system. More recently Zhou and Hovy [12] have proposed a template-based title generation approach, where part-of-speech tagged templates (automatically determined from a training corpus) are filled with content words selected using a keyword clustering technique. These templates help preserve the readability of the headlines by guiding the most suitable combination of keywords using grammatical constraints.

An alternative to extractive gisting approaches is to view the title generation process as being analogous to statistical machine translation. Wittbrock and Mittal's paper on 'ultra-summarisation' [13], was one of the first attempts to generate headlines based on statistical learning methods that make use of large amounts of training data. More specifically, during title generation a news story is 'translated' into a more concise version using the Noisy Channel model. The Viterbi algorithm is then used to search for the most likely sequence of tokens in the text that would make a readable and informative headline. This is the approach adopted by Banko et al. [14], Jin and Hauptmann [15], Berger and Mittal [16], and Zajic and Dorr's DUC 2002 title generation system [17].

These researchers state two advantages of a generative technique over an extractive one. Firstly, a generative approach can create compact representations of text at any compression rate, and secondly they can combine information that is spread across different sentences in the text. However, researchers are now favouring an extractive approach that compresses text using linguistically rich methods because of the difficulty of integrating grammaticality into a generative model of title generation [18]. Nevertheless, generative approaches still have an important role to play in title generation, especially where syntactic information such as punctuation and capitalisation (a prerequisite for most NLP-based techniques) is either missing or unreliable as in the case of automatic speech recognised (ASR) news transcripts.

3 The Topiary Headline Generation System

In this section, we describe the Topiary system developed at the University of Maryland with BBN. As already stated, this system was the top performing headline generation system at DUC 2004. A Topiary-style headline consists of a set of topic labels followed by a compressed version of the lead sentence. Hence, the Topiary system views headline generation as a two-step process: first, create a compressed version of the lead sentence of the source text, and second, find a set of topic descriptors that adequately describe the general topic of the news story. We will now look at each of these steps in more detail.

In [18] Dorr, Zajic and Schwartz stated that when human subjects were asked to write titles by selecting words in order of occurrence in the source text, 86.8% of these headline words occurred in the first sentence of the news story. Based on this result Dorr, Zajic and Schwartz, concluded that compressing the lead sentence was sufficient when generating titles for news stories. Consequently, their DUC 2003 system HedgeTrimmer used linguistically motivated heuristics to remove constituents that could be eliminated from a parse tree representation of the lead sentence without affecting the factual correctness or grammaticality of the sentence. These linguistically motivated trimming rules [3, 18] iteratively remove constituents until a desired sentence compression rate is reached. The compression algorithm begins by removing determiners, time expressions and other low content words. More drastic compression rules are then applied to remove larger constituents of the parse tree until the required headline length is achieved. For the DUC 2004 headline generation task systems were required to produce headlines no longer than 75 bytes i.e. about 10 words. The following worked example helps to illustrate the sentence compression process[1].

Lead Sentence: The U.S. space shuttle Discovery returned home this morning after astronauts successfully ended their 10-day Hubble Space telescope service mission.

Parse: (S (S (NP (NP The U.S. space shuttle) Discovery) (VP returned (NP home) (NP this morning)) (SBAR after (S (NP astronauts) (VP (ADVP successfully) ended (NP their 10-day Hubble Space telescope service mission))))))

1. Choose leftmost S of parse tree and remove all determiners, time expressions and low content units such as quantifiers (e.g. each, many, some), possessive pronouns (e.g. their, ours, hers) and deictics (e.g. this, these, those):

Before: (S *(S (NP (NP **The** U.S. space shuttle) Discovery) (VP returned (NP home) (NP **this morning**)) (SBAR after (S (NP astronauts) (VP (ADVP successfully) ended (NP **their** 10-day Hubble Space telescope service mission)))))*)

After: (S (S (NP (NP U.S. space shuttle) Discovery) (VP returned (NP home)) (SBAR after (S (NP astronauts) (VP (ADVP successfully) ended (NP 10-day Hubble Space telescope service mission))))))

2. The next step iteratively removes constituents until the desired length is reached. In this instance the algorithm will remove the trailing SBAR.

Before: (S (S (NP (NP U.S. space shuttle) Discovery) (VP returned (NP home)) *(SBAR after (S (NP astronauts) (VP (ADVP successfully) ended (NP 10-day Hubble Space telescope service mission))))*))

After: U.S. space shuttle Discovery returned home

Like the 'trailing SBAR' rule, the other iterative rules identify and remove non-essential relative clauses and subordinate clauses from the lead sentence. A more detailed description of these rules can be found in [3, 18]. In this example, we can see that after compression the lead sentence reads more like a headline. The readability of the sentence in this case could be further improved by replacing the past tense verb 're-turned' with its present tense form; however, this refinement is not currently implemented by the Topiary system or by our implementation of this compression algorithm.

As stated earlier, a list of relevant topic words is also concatenated with this compressed sentence resulting in the final headline. The topic labels are generated by the

---

[1] The part of speech tags in the following example are explained as follows: **S** represents a simple declarative clause; **SBAR** represents a clause introduced by a (possibly empty) subordinating conjunction; **NP** is a noun phrase; **VP** is a verb phrase; **ADVP** is an adverb.

UTD (Unsupervised Topic Discovery) algorithm [3]. This unsupervised information extraction algorithm, creates a short list of useful topic labels by identifying commonly occurring words and phrases in the DUC corpus. So for each document in the corpus it identifies an initial set of important topic names for the document using a modified version of the *tf.idf* metric. Topic models are then created from these topic names using the OnTopic™ software package. The list of topic labels associated with the topic models closest in content to the source document are then added to the beginning of the compressed lead sentence produced in the previous step, resulting in a Topiary-style summary.

One of the problems with this approach is that it will only produce meaningful topic models and labels if they are generated from a corpus containing additional on-topic documents on the news story being summarised. In the next section, we explore two alternative techniques for identifying topic labels, where useful summary words are identified 'locally' by analysing the source document rather than 'globally' using the entire DUC corpus i.e. the UTD method.

4 LexTrim and TFTrim Headline Generation Systems

In this section, we describe two Topiary-style headline generation systems that use our implementation of the Topiary sentence compression algorithm[2], but identify pertinent topic labels by analysing the lexical cohesion structure of a news story in the case of the LexTrim system, and term frequency scores in the case of the TFTrim system.

Lexical cohesion is the textual characteristic responsible for making the sentences of a text appear coherent [19]. One method of exploring lexical cohesive relationships between words in a text is to build a set of lexical chains for that text. In this context a lexical chain is a cluster of semantically related proper noun and noun phrases e.g. {boat, ship, vessel, rudder, hull, gallery, Titanic}. These semantic relationships can be identified using a machine-readable thesaurus, in our case the WordNet taxonomy [20]. Here are some examples of these semantic relationships:

- **Synonymy:** *ship* and *vessel* are synonyms because they share the same meaning and can be used interchangeable in text.
- **Holonymy:** ship *has part* rudder, therefore ship is a holonym of rudder.
- **Meronymy:** the gallery is *part of* a ship, therefore gallery is a meronym of ship.
- **Hypernymy:** Ship *is a generalisation* of a Titanic, therefore ship is a hypernym of Titanic.
- **Hyponymy:** boat *is a specialisation of* a vessel, therefore boat is a hyponym of vessel.

By clustering semantically related nouns into lexical chains, a more accurate picture of the semantic content of a document can be determined. In particular, lexical

---

[2] The only significant difference between our compression algorithm and the University of Maryland/BBN approach is that we use Collins' parser [21], while they use the BBN parser [22].

cohesion analysis, unlike a term frequency analysis approach, can differentiate between low frequency terms that are 'genuinely' unimportant, and low frequency terms
that are important topic words because of their strong semantic association with other
high content words in the text. For example, in a particular news story, although the
noun 'murder' occurs only twice in the text, it will be considered an important topic
descriptor because of its strong association with terms in a 'dominant' lexical chain
containing the nouns {homicide, manslaughter, shooting}.

There are three main steps to our technique for identifying topic labels using lexical cohesion analysis. First, the text is processed by a part-of-speech tagger [23], and
all proper noun and noun phrases are extracted. These phrases and their location information in the text are then passed as input to the lexical chaining algorithm. The
aim of the Chainer is to find relationships between these phrases using the WordNet
thesaurus. The Chainer uses a single-pass word clustering algorithm, where the first
noun phrase in the news story forms the first lexical chain, and each subsequent
phrase is then added to an existing chain if it is semantically related to at least one
other noun phrase in that chain. One of the problems with generating lexical chains
for news stories is that many of important proper noun phrases will not be present in
WordNet since keeping an up-to-date repository of such phrases is a substantial and
never ending problem. However, these proper nouns are still useful to the chaining
process since they provide an additional means of capturing lexical cohesion in the
text though repetition relationships. So our chaining algorithm uses a fuzzy string
matching   technique   to   identify   full   syntactic   match   (*U.S_President*   ⇔
U.S_President), partial full-word match (U.S_*President* ⇔ *President*_Bush) and a
'constrained' form of partial word match between two proper noun phrases
(*cave*_dwellers ⇔ *cave*rs). This chaining procedure results in the creation of two
distinct sets of lexical chains: WordNet-based noun and proper noun chains, and non-
WordNet proper noun chains. A more detailed explanation of our lexical chaining
algorithm is given in [24].

The final step, once all lexical chains have been created for a text, is to decide
which chain words are the best topic descriptors for the news story. In this way, we
can view lexical chaining as a feature extraction method that identifies promising
topic labels by virtue of their strength of association with other important noun/proper
noun phrases in the text. Noun/proper noun phrase importance, in this context, is
calculated with respect to the strength of the lexical chain in which the phrase occurred. More specifically, as shown in Equation 1, the chain strength score is the sum
of each strength score assigned to each word pair in the chain.

$$Score(chain) = \sum((reps_i + reps_j) * rel(i, j)) \tag{1}$$

where $reps_i$ is the frequency of word i in the text, and $rel(i,j)$ is a score assigned based
on the strength of the relationship between word i and j. Relationship strengths between chain words are defined as follows: a repetition relationship is assigned a value
of 1.0, a synonym relationship a value of 0.9, hypernymy/hyponymy and mero-
nymy/holonymy a value of 0.7. Proper noun chain word scores are assigned depending on the type of match, 1.0 for an exact match, 0.8 for a partial match and 0.7 for a
fuzzy match. The lexical cohesion score of a chained word is then the strength score
assigned to the chain where the word occurred. These lexical chain words are then

concatenated with the compressed lead sentence in order of their lexical cohesion strength, where the number of chain words added depends on the shortfall between the length of the compressed lead sentence and the maximum allowable length of the headline. We have also used this lexical chaining technique to weight the importance of sentence content in an extractive approach to headline generation for closed-caption broadcast news transcripts with segmentation errors; however, no parse-and-trim style sentence compression was employed in that experiment [25].

The third headline generation system examined in this paper, the TFTrim system, employs a much simpler topic labelling strategy, where high frequency words (excluding stopwords) in the news story are added to the topiary-style headline in the order of frequency. In both cases, the LexTrim and TFTrim systems will only assign topic labels that are not included in the compressed sentence part of the headline.

5 Evaluation Methodology and Results

In this section we present the results of our headline generation experiments on the DUC 2004 corpus[3]. The aim of these experiments was two-fold: to build a linguistically motivated heuristic approach to title generation, and to look at alternative techniques for padding Topiary-style headlines with content words. There are two parts to our evaluation methodology. Firstly, we used the ROUGE evaluation metrics as an automatic means of evaluating headlines, and secondly a randomly selected subset of titles was manually evaluated by a set of human judges. For the DUC 2004 evaluation, participants were asked to generate headlines consisting of no more than 75 bytes for documents on TDT-defined events. The DUC 2004 corpus consists of 625 Associated Press and New York Times newswire documents. The headline-style summaries created by each system were evaluated against a set of human generated (or model) summaries using the ROUGE (Recall-Oriented Understudy for Gisting Evaluation) metrics: ROUGE-1, ROUGE-2, ROUGE-3, ROUGE-4, ROUGE-LCS and ROUGE-W. The first four metrics are based on the average n-gram match between a set of model summaries and the system-generated summary for each document in the corpus. ROUGE-LCS calculated the longest common sub-string between the system summaries and the models, and ROUGE-W is a weighted version of the LCS measure. So for all ROUGE metrics, the higher the ROUGE value the better the performance of the summarisation system, since high ROUGE scores indicate greater overlap between the system summaries and their respective models. Lin and Hovy [2] have shown that these metrics correlated well with human judgements of summary quality, and the summarisation community is now accepting these metrics as a credible and less time-consuming alternative to manual summary evaluation. In the offical DUC 2004 evaluation all summary words were stemmed before the ROUGE metrics were calculated; however, stopwords were not removed. No manual evaluation of headlines was performed.

---

[3] Details of our official DUC 2004 headline generation system can be found in [27]. This system returned a list of keywords rather than a 'sentence + keywords' as a headline. It used a decision tree classifier to identify appropriate summary terms in the news story based on a number of linguistic and statistical word features.

5.1 ROUGE Evaluation Results

Table 1 and Figure 1 show the results of our headline **generation** experiments on the DUC 2004 collection. Seven systems in total took part in this evaluation, three Topiary-style headline generation systems and four baselines:

- The **LexTrim** system, as explained in Section 4, augments condensed lead sentences with high scoring noun phrases that exhibit strong lexical cohesive relationships with other terms in a news story. The **Lex** system is a baseline version of this system, where headlines consist of lexical chain phrases only.
- The **Topiary** system is the University of Maryland/BBN DUC 2004 headline generation system. The **UTD** system, like the Lex system, returns a set of topic descriptors. The UTD algorithm is explained in Section 3. The **Trim** system is another baseline system that only returns the compressed lead sentence as a headline.
- The **TFTrim** system, as explained in Section 4, pads the compressed sentence with high frequency terms found in the original source text when generating a headline. The baseline version of this system is **TF** which returns a sequence of high frequency keywords as the headline.

Table 1. ROUGE scores for headline generation systems on the DUC 2004 collection

	System	ROUGE-1	ROUGE-L	ROUGE-W
Topi-ary-style systems	TFTrim	0.27933	0.21336	0.12600
	LexTrim	0.25370	0.20099	0.11951
	Topiary	0.24914	0.19951	0.11970
Baseline systems	TF	0.24428	0.17074	0.09805
	Trim	0.20061	0.18248	0.10996
	Lex	0.18224	0.14679	0.08738
	UTD	0.15913	0.13041	0.07797

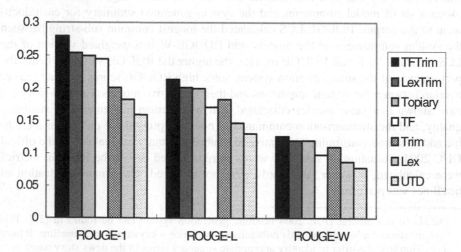

Fig. 1. ROUGE scores for headline generation systems on the DUC 2004 collection

Since the DUC 2004 evaluation, Lin [26] has concluded that certain ROUGE metrics correlate better with human judgements than others depending on the summarisation task being evaluated i.e. single document, headline, or multi-document summarisation. In the case of headline generation, Lin found that ROUGE-1, ROUGE-L and ROUGE-W scores worked best and so only these scores are included in Table 1 and Figure 1. Looking at these scores we can see that the best of the Topiary-style headline systems is the TFTrim system, while the ROUGE scores for the LexTrim and Topiary systems indicate that their performance is very similar. On the other hand, the TF system is the best of the baseline systems where headlines either consisted of a list of keywords (i.e. Lex and UTD) or a compressed sentence (i.e. Trim). Both of these conclusions, suggest that although our lexical chaining method appears to produce better topic descriptors than the UTD method, the best approach is actually the simplest. In other words, the TF technique that uses source document term frequency statistics to identify salient topic labels can outperform both a knowledge-based NLP approach (using WordNet), and a statistical-based approach requiring additional word frequency and cooccurrence information from the entire DUC 2004 corpus.[4]

5.2 Manual Evaluation Results

In this section, we report on the results of our manual headline evaluation of the TFTrim and Topiary systems. One of the main criticisms of automatic metrics, such as the ROUGE scores presented in the previous section, is that they do not directly evaluate important summary attributes like readability and grammatical correctness. They also fail to recognise cases where synonymous or semantically similar words are used in the system and reference titles for a news story (e.g. the noun phrase 'Israeli capital' is equivalent to the proper noun 'Jerusalem'), which could result in a system title appearing less relevant than it actually is. It is also unclear whether these ROUGE metrics are sensitive enough to be able to correctly determine the quality of similar style-summaries. To address this problem, we asked four human judges to evaluate the quality of 100 randomly selected headlines generated from the DUC 2004 corpus. These judges were asked to decide, given the human generated titles and the Topiary and TFTrim titles for each document, which system headline was better. In some cases, the system titles were too similar to decide between, so judges were also given a third 'undecided' option.

Overall, each of the four judges ranked the TFTrim titles higher than the Topiary titles; however, this result was close with an average of 32.5% of TFTrim headlines and 27.5% of Topiary headlines considered better than the alternative system title. The judges also concluded that 40.0% of titles were too similar to decide between. The average Kappa statistic between each set of human judgements was 0.385 (standard deviation 0.055) which indicates low agreement between judges for this task. One of the factors contributing to this low Kappa score may have been the inclusion

---

[4] In previous headline generation experiments using lexical chains (and no sentence compression), we found that the TF system was outperformed by our gisting system [25]. However, in those experiments we compared sentence extraction rather than word extraction based summarisation. In addition, these experiments were conducted on a broadcast news corpus with segmentation errors, i.e. the end of one news story may be merged with the beginning of the next. We believe that this noise attributed to the poor performance of TF system.

of the 'undecided' option, as it is obvious from the judgements that judges disagreed most with respect to this aspect of the evaluation. However, even though there is very little difference between the performance of these systems, the aim of these experiments was to determine if Topiary-style summaries require topic descriptors generated from the entire DUC corpus in order to be effective news story headlines. As already stated, one of the problems with the UTD method of topic labelling is that it relies on the existence of a news corpus with similar on-topic documents to the news story being summarised. In many summarisation scenarios such a collection is not readily available, in which case the results of these experiments suggest that keywords identified in the source text are as good as, if not better, than UTD topic descriptors in Topiary-style summaries.

6 Conclusions

In this paper, we have compared the performance of three Topiary-style headline generation systems that use three distinct techniques for 'padding out' compressed lead sentences in the automatic generation of news story headlines. The results of our experiment using the ROUGE evaluation suite and a manual evaluation of the system titles, indicate that topic descriptors identified by simple term frequency counts in the source document outperform either keywords identified by a lexical cohesion analysis of the source text, or statistically derived topic labels from the DUC 2004 corpus using the UTD algorithm.

Following a manual inspection of these system headlines by the authors, it is clear that the strength of the term frequency-based topic labelling method is that it is more consistent in its assignment of quality descriptors to Topiary-style headlines than either of the other labelling techniques. More specifically, the UTD and lexical chaining techniques suffer from the following weaknesses:

- During lexical cohesion analysis, weak descriptors are sometimes chosen from cohesively strong lexical chains. For example, in the case of the following chain {country, Palestine, Israel}, 'country' was chosen as an appropriate topic word by virtue of its strong relationship with the other two frequently occurring chain members generated for a particular news story. It is hoped that the inclusion of an *idf* statistic in the lexical cohesion weighting function, described in Section 4, will help to lower the cohesion score of these low content words and improve the performance of the LexTrim system.

- One of the potential strengths of the UTD algorithm is that it can assign topic words to headlines that didn't occur in the original news story, but are frequently occurring in related on-topic news stories. However, this also commonly leads to the assignment of inappropriate topic labels; for example, in the DUC 2004 corpus there are two prominent topics that frequently mention the country 'Portugal', i.e. a topic relating to the former Portuguese colony, East Timor, and a topic discussing the Portuguese Nobel prize winner for Literature, José Saramago. The assignment of the topic label 'East Timor' to a headline generated for a news story discussing José Saramago indicates both the dependence of the UTD method on a related corpus of news documents, and the problems associated with the occurrence of related, yet distinct topics in that corpus.

In future work, we intend to proceed by improving both the lexical cohesion score in the LexTrim system, and the sentence compression procedure described in this paper. In addition, we intend to investigate the use of lexical cohesion information as a means of improving the performance of the compression algorithm by helping to limit the elimination of 'cohesively strong' parse tree components during sentence compression.

Acknowledgements

The funding support of the Enterprise Ireland is gratefully acknowledged.

References

1. Document Understanding Conference (DUC) http://duc.nist.gov/
2. Lin C-Y, Hovy E. Automatic Evaluation of Summaries using n-gram Co-occurrence Statistics. In the Proceedings of HLT/NACCL, 2003.
3. Zajic D., Dorr, B., Schwartz, R. BBN/UMD at DUC-2004: Topiary. In the Proceedings of the Document Understanding Conference (DUC), 2004.
4. Kraaij W., M. Spitters, A. Hulth. Headline extraction based on a combination of uni- and multi-document summarization techniques. In the Proceedings of the ACL workshop on Automatic Summarization/Document Understanding Conference (DUC 2002), 2002.
5. Alfonseca E., P. Rodriguez. Description of the UAM system for generating very short summaries at DUC 2003. In the Proceedings of the HLT/NAACL workshop on Automatic Summarization/Document Understanding Conference (DUC 2003), 2003.
6. Copeck T., S. Szpakowicz. Picking phrases, picking sentences. In the Proceedings of the HLT/NAACL workshop on Automatic Summarization/Document Understanding Conference (DUC 2003), 2003.
7. Zhou L., E. Hovy. Headline Summarization at ISI. In the Proceedings of the HLT/NAACL workshop on Automatic Summarization/Document Understanding Conference (DUC 2003), 2003.
8. Lacatusu F., A. Hickl, S. Harabagiu, L. Nezda. Lite-GISTexter at DUC2004. In the Proceedings of the HLT/NAACL workshop on Automatic Summarization/Document Understanding Conference (DUC 2004), 2004.
9. Angheluta R., R. Mitra, X. Jing, M.-F. Moens. K.U. Leuven Summarization System at DUC 2004. In the Proceedings of the HLT/NAACL workshop on Automatic Summarization/Document Understanding Conference (DUC 2004), 2004.
10. Alfonseca E., A. Moreno-Sandoval, J. M. Guirao. Description of the UAM System for Generation Very Short Summaries at DUC 2004. In the Proceedings of the HLT/NAACL workshop on Automatic Summarization/Document Understanding Conference (DUC 2004), 2004.
11. Kolluru B., H. Christensen, Y. Gotoh. Decremental Feature-based Compaction. In the Proceedings of the HLT/NAACL workshop on Automatic Summarization/Document Understanding Conference (DUC 2004), 2004.
12. Zhou L., E. Hovy. Template-filtered Headline Summarization. In the Proceedings of the ACL workshop, Text Summarization Branches Out, pp. 56-60, 2004.

13. Witbrock M., V. Mittal, Ultra-Summarisation: A Statistical approach to generating highly condensed non-extractive summaries. In the Proceedings of the ACM-SIGIR, pp. 315-316, 1999.
14. Banko M., V. Mittal, M. Witbrock. Generating Headline-Style Summaries. In the Proceedings of the Association for Computational Linguistics, 2000.
15. Jin R., A.G. Hauptmann. A new probabilistic model for title generation. In the Proceedings of the International Conference on Computational Linguistics, 2002.
16. Berger, A.L., V.O. Mittal: OCELOT: a system for summarizing Web pages. In the Proceedings of the ACM-SIGIR, pp.144-151, 2000.
17. Zajic, D., B. Dorr. Automatic headline generation for newspaper stories. In the Proceedings of the ACL workshop on Automatic Summarization/Document Understanding Conference (DUC 2002), 2002.
18. Dorr B., Zajic D., Schwartz, R. Hedge Trimmer: A Parse-and-Trim Approach to Headline Generation. In the Proceedings of the Document Understanding Conference (DUC), 2003.
19. Morris J., G. Hirst, *Lexical Cohesion by Thesaural Relations as an Indicator of the Structure of Text*, Computational Linguistics 17(1), 1991.
20. Miller G.A., R. Beckwith, C. Fellbaum, D. Gross, K. Miller, Five Papers on WordNet. CSL Report 43, Cognitive Science Laboratory, Princeton University, July 1990.
21. Collins M. Three generative lexicalised models for statistical parsing. In the Proceedings of ACL, 1997.
22. Miller, S., M. Crystal, H. Fox, L. Ramshaw, R. Schwartz, R. Stones, R. Weischedel. BBN: Description of the SIFT system as used for MUC-7. In the Proceedings of MUC-7, 1998.
23. Xu J., J. Broglio, and W. B. Croft. The design and implementation of a part of speech tagger for English. Technical Report IR-52, University of Massachusetts, Amherst, Center for Intelligent Information Retrieval, 1994.
24. Stokes N. Applications of Lexical Cohesion Analysis in the Topic Detection and Tracking domain. Ph.D. thesis. Department of Computer Science, University College Dublin, 2004.
25. Stokes N., E. Newman, J. Carthy, A. F. Smeaton. Broadcast News Gisting using Lexical Cohesion Analysis. In the Proceedings of the 26th European Conference on Information Retrieval (ECIR-04), pp. 209-222, Sunderland, U.K., 2004.
26. Lin C-Y. ROUGE: A Package for Automatic Evaluation of Summaries. In the Proceedings of the ACL workshop, Text Summarization Branches Out, pp. 56-60, 2004.
27. Doran W. P., N. Stokes, E. Newman, J. Dunnion, J. Carthy, F. Toolan. News Story Gisting at University College Dublin. In the Proceedings of the Document Understanding Conference (DUC), 2004.

Improving Retrieval Effectiveness
by Using Key Terms in Top Retrieved Documents

Yang Lingpeng, Ji Donghong, Zhou Guodong, and Nie Yu

Institute for Infocomm Research,
21 Heng Mui Keng Terrace,
Singapore 119613
{lpyang, dhji, zhougd, ynie}@i2r.a-star.edu.sg

Abstract. In this paper, we propose a method to improve the precision of top retrieved documents in Chinese information retrieval where the query is a short description by re-ordering retrieved documents in the initial retrieval. To re-order the documents, we firstly find out terms in query and their importance scales by making use of the information derived from top N ($N<=30$) retrieved documents in the initial retrieval; secondly, we re-order retrieved K ($N<<K$) documents by what kinds of terms of query they contain. That is, we first automatically extract key terms from top N retrieved documents, then we collect key terms that occur in query and their document frequencies in the N retrieved documents, finally we use these collected terms to re-order the initially retrieved documents. Each collected term is assigned a weight by its length and its document frequency in top N retrieved documents. Each document is re-ranked by the sum of weights of collected terms it contains. In our experiments on 42 query topics in NTCIR3 Cross Lingual Information Retrieval (CLIR) dataset, an average 17.8%-27.5% improvement can be made for top 10 documents and an average 6.6%-26.9% improvement can be made for top 100 documents at relax/rigid relevance judgment and different parameter setting.

1 Introduction

For Chinese Information Retrieval where query is a short description by natural language (please see appendix for some examples), many retrieval models, indexing strategies, query expansion strategies and document re-ordering methods have been proposed. Different from most of the western languages, Chinese sentence is a contiguous Chinese character sequence without white space between Chinese words. Chinese Character, bi-gram, n-gram (n>2) and word are the most widely used indexing units. The effectiveness of single Chinese Characters as indexing units has been reported in [9]. The comparison between the three kinds of indexing units (single Characters, bi-grams and short-words) is given in [7]. It shows that single character indexing is good but not sufficiently competitive, while bi-gram indexing works surprisingly well and it's as good as short-word indexing in precision. [11] suggests that word indexing and bi-gram indexing can achieve comparable performance but if we consider the time and space factors, it is preferable to use words (and characters)

D.E. Losada and J.M. Fernández-Luna (Eds.): ECIR 2005, LNCS 3408, pp. 169–184, 2005.

as indexes. It also suggests that a combination of the longest-matching algorithm with single characters is a good method for Chinese IR and if there is a module for unknown word detection, the performance can be further improved. Some other researches give similar conclusions. Bi-gram and word are considered as the top two indexing units in Chinese IR and they are also used in many reported Chinese IR systems.

Regarding retrieval models, two models are most widely used in Chinese Information Retrieval, i.e., Vector Space Model [15] and Probabilistic Retrieval Model [3].

For query expansion, most strategies make use of global analysis or local analysis [2, 10, 13, 17]. For global analysis, the expansion terms are acquired by analyzing the whole document collection. For local analysis, the top N retrieved documents in initial retrieval will be used. Generally, it selects M indexing units from the top N documents according to some criteria and adds these M indexing units to original query to form a new query. In such a process of query expansion, it's supposed that the top N documents are related with original query. However in practice, such an assumption is not always true. Although many literatures report that query expansion can improve the recall in many situation, they also suggest that the actual relevance quality of top retrieved documents affects the effectiveness of query expansion.

While query expansion tries to improve the recall of top retrieved documents, document re-ordering is used to improve the precision of top retrieved documents.

Lee, K. et.al. propose a document re-ranking method which uses document clusters [8]. Firstly, they build a hierarchical cluster structure for the whole document set; secondly, they divide top retrieved documents into some clusters, that is, they find sub-trees in hierarchical cluster structure which contain some retrieved documents by some criteria; finally, they calculate similarity between each cluster and each query topic, and use the similarity to adjust the similarity between query and each document in this document cluster. It's reported their method achieves significant improvements on their experiments on Korean corpus. One difficulty of this method is it needs to build hierarchical cluster structure for document set.

Kamps, J. [6] proposes a method to re-order retrieved documents by making use of manually assigned controlled vocabularies in documents. By building a controlled vocabulary - controlled vocabulary matrix on co-occurrences, each document can be represented as a vector by controlled vocabularies which occur in and each query can be represented as a vector by the vectors of top N retrieved documents. Finally, each document is re-ordered by the distances between the document vector and query vector. It's reported this re-ranking strategy significantly improves retrieved effectiveness on their experiments on German GIRT and French Amaryllis collections. This method depends on the controlled vocabularies assigned to document, but in most case, no controlled vocabulary is assigned to documents.

Qu, Y. L. [12] uses manually built thesaurus to re-rank retrieved documents. Each term in query topic is expanded with a group of terms in thesaurus. It's a hard job to manually build a large thesaurus for unexpected query topics.

Bear J. el al. [1] use manually constructed or automatically learned small grammars for topics to re-order documents by matching grammar rules in some segment in articles. But grammar construction itself is a difficult problem in Chinese language.

Yang, L.P., et. al [18,19] use extracted long terms in query and document to re-order retrieved documents in Chinese IR. Firstly, they cluster the whole document set into some clusters; secondly, they automatically extract global key terms from these clusters; thirdly, they make use of these global terms and their frequencies to find local terms in a query or a document; finally, they use long local terms to re-calculate the similarity between query and document, and use the new similarity value to re-order retrieved documents. Their experiments show that long terms play an important role in document re-ordering, since they tend to be more significant for the retrieval precision than short terms. It's reported their experiments based on NTCIR3 CLIR dataset can achieve an average 10%-11% improvement for top 10 documents and an average 2%-5% improvement for top 100 documents. One difficulty of this method is how to identify local key terms in query and document because there are a few parameters needed to set.

In this paper, we propose an approach to re-order retrieved documents. We first find out terms in query and their importance scales by making use of the information derived from top N ($N<=30$) retrieved documents in the initial retrieval; secondly, we re-order retrieved K ($N<<K$) documents by what kinds of terms of query they contain.

The rest of this paper is organized as following. In section 2, we describe how to automatically extract key terms from document. In section 3, we describe how to re-rank retrieved documents. In section 4, we evaluate the performance of our proposed method on NTCIR3 CLIR dataset and give out some result analysis. In section 5, we present the conclusion and some future work.

2 Key Term Extraction

Key term extraction concerns the problem of what is a key term. Intuitively, key terms in a documents are some conceptual terms that are prominent in document and play main roles in discriminating itself from other documents. In other words, key terms in a document can represent the main content of the document. Generally, in the viewpoint of conventional linguistic studies, key terms maybe are some NPs, NP-phrases or some kind of VPs, adjectives that can represent some specific concepts in document content representation.

We use a seeding-and-expansion mechanism to extract key terms from documents [4, 5]. The procedure of key term extraction consists of two phases, seed positioning and term determination. Intuitively, a seed for a candidate term is an individual Chinese Character within the term, seed positioning is to locate the rough position of a term in the text, while term determination is to figure out which string covering the seed in the position forms a term.

To determine a seed needs to weigh the individual Chinese Characters to reflect their significance in the text in some way. To do so, we make use of a very large corpus r (2GB data from NTCIR3 dataset, LDC's Mandarin Chinese News Text and news articles from www.sina.com.cn) as a *reference*. Suppose s is a document, w is an individual Chinese Character in the text, let $P_r(w)$ and $P_s(w)$ be the probability of w occurring in r and s respectively, we adopt *relative probability* or *salience* of w in s with respect to r [16], as the criteria for evaluation of seed words.

$$P_s(w) / P_r(w) \tag{1}$$

We call w a *seed* if $P_s(w) / P_r(w) \geq \delta$ (δ=1). That is, its probability in document must be equal or great than its average probability in large corpus.

Although it is difficult to give out the definition of key term, we try to give some assumptions about a key term. We have the following assumptions about a key term in a document.

  i) A key term contains at least one seed.
  ii) A key term occurs at least L $(L>1)$ times in the document.
  iii) A *maximal word string* meeting i) and ii) is a key term.
  iv) For a key term, a *real maximal substring* meeting i) and ii) without considering their occurrence in all those terms containing it is also a key term.

Here a *maximal word string* meeting i) and ii) refers to a word string meeting i) and ii) while no other longer word strings containing it meet i) and ii). A *real maximal substring* meeting i) and ii) refer to a real substring meeting i) and ii) while no other longer real substrings containing it meet i) and ii).

The above assumptions tell us a key term is an independent maximal string which must occur at least 2 times in a document and contain a seed. For example, given document d, suppose Chinese Character 博 (bo3) is a seed in d, 故宫博物院 (National Palace Museum) occurs 3 times in d, 博物院 (Museum) occurs 5 times in d, if we set the parameter L in ii) as 2, then both string 故宫博物院 (National Palace Museum) and 博物院 (Museum) are terms in d; but if we set the parameter L in ii) as 3, then 故宫博物院 (National Palace Museum) is term in d, but 博物院 (Museum) is not a term in d because its independent occurrence is 2 (excluding 3 occurrences as substring in 故宫博物院 (National Palace Museum)).

Fig. 1 describes the procedure to extract key terms from document d.

Given threshold δ ($\delta>=1$) and L $(L>1)$;
Let $F_d(t)$ represents the frequency of term t in document d;
$T = \{\}$;
Collect every *Seed* w in d into E by $P_d(w) / P_r(w) \geq \delta$;
For all $c \in E$ {
  Let $Q = \{t: t$ contains c and $F_d(t) \geq L\}$;
  While $Q \neq NIL$ {
    max-t ← the longest string in Q;
    $T \leftarrow T + \{$ *max-t* $\}$;
    Remove *max-t* from Q;
    For all other t in Q {
      If t is a substring of *max-t* {
        $F_d(t) \leftarrow F_d(t) - F_d(max\text{-}t)$;
        If $F_d(t) < L$ {
          Remove t from Q; }
        }
      }
    }
  }
Return T as key terms in document d;

Fig. 1. Term Extraction from Document d

3 Document Re-ordering

For Chinese information retrieval where query is a short description by natural language, we argue that different terms in query may play different roles. While many terms in query are descriptive or functional, some terms in query are important and may represent the main point of query. The difficulty is that we cannot find out if a term is important or not directly from the query itself. One alternative is we may make use of some information derived from top retrieved documents in initial retrieval. Firstly, we assume, like most pseudo feedback methods, that the top N ($N<=30$) retrieved documents are relevant with query q; secondly, we extract separately key terms from these documents by using our term extraction algorithm introduced at section 2; thirdly, for each key term t, we collect its document frequency DF_t in top N retrieved documents, that is, we collect how many documents of top N retrieved

---

Given q is a query, N is the number of top pseudo relevant documents, and K is the number of returned documents to be re-ordered in initial retrieval.

Step 1: Find out terms in q and their weight by information in top N documents;

Step 1.1 Extract key terms from each document d in top N retrieved documents by using term extraction algorithm in Fig. 1;

Step 1.2 For each key term t, collect its document frequency, that is, how many documents of top N retrieved document it occurs in;

Step 1.3 Collect key terms that occur at query q and their document frequencies;

Let $T=\{T_1, T_2, ..., T_n\}$ is the set of collected key terms;

Let $D=\{DF_1, DF_2, ..., DF_n\}$ is the set of document frequencies of terms in T;

Step 1.4 Assign each term T_i in T a weight W_i by:

$$W(T_i) = \mathtt{sqrt}(|T_i|) \ \mathtt{X} \ \mathtt{sqrt}(DF_i) \qquad (2)$$

where $|T_i|$ is the length of term T_i, i.e., the number of Chinese characters in term T_i. The weight reflects the scale of importance of T_i in query q.

Step 2: Re-order top K retrieved documents by terms in q and their weight;

Step 2.1 For each document d_i in top K retrieved documents, calculate its re-ordered similarity value S_i by its initial similarity value R_i in the initial retrieval;

$$w = \sum_{t_j \in q, d_i} W(t_j) \qquad (3)$$

$$S_i = \begin{cases} w \times R_i & (w>0) \\ R_i & (w=0) \end{cases} \qquad (4)$$

Step 2.2: Re-order top K retrieved documents by their new re-ordered similarity values $S=\{S_1, S_2, ..., S_i, ..., S_K\}$.

Fig. 2. The Procedure of Document Re-ordering

documents term *t* occurs in; fourthly, we pick up these key terms which occur in query topic as terms of query *q* and regard their document frequencies (in practise, we use square root of document frequencies to smooth them) as their weight in query; these weight reflect their importance in query, that is, more important term has more document frequency, descriptive or functional term has less document frequency; furthermore, for each term of query *q*, we also use their length (number of Chinese characters in term) as weight to reflect an observation that long term may contain more information.

After having valued each term in query *q*, we can use the information to re-order retrieved documents. Firstly, for each document *d* in returned documents, we find out what query terms occur in it; secondly, we sum the weight of these query terms in *q* and use the accumulated value to re-calculate the similarity between document *d* and query *q*; finally, we use the new similarity value (it is not a real similarity value but a value which is used to rank documents) to order retrieved documents.

Figure 2 gives out the pseudo code of the procedure of document re-ordering for query *q* and top *K* retrieved documents.

4 Experiments and Evaluation

We use NTCIR3 CLIR dataset as our test dataset. The dataset contains Chinese document set CIRB011 (132,173 documents from China Times, China Times Express, Commercial Times, China Daily News and Central, Daily News) and CIRB20 (249,508 documents from United Daily News). We also use the Chinese-Chinese D-run query topics in NTCIR3 CLIR as query topics. There are 50 query topics released in NTCIR3, but only 42 topics are finally used to evaluate. Each query is a simple description of a topic by Chinese language. (Appendix lists the top 10 query topics. You may also find more information about NTCIR3 CLIR task from http://research.nii.ac.jp/ntcir-ws3/work-en.html).

For initial retrieval, we use bi-gram as index unit and we separately use vector space model and probabilistic retrieval model as our retrieval models. The initial retrieval result is used as 1st baseline to evaluate our proposed method.

Our experiments re-rank the top 1000 initial retrieved documents and evaluate the effectiveness by precisions at different document levels. We use NTCIR3's relax relevance judgment and rigid relevance judgment to measure the precision of retrieved documents. Relax Relevance Judgment considers highly relevant documents, relevant documents and partially relevant documents, while Rigid Relevance Judgment only considers highly relevant documents and relevant documents. We use PreAt10 and PreAt100 to separately represent the precision of top 10 retrieved documents and top 100 retrieved documents.

Our experiments focus on two parts: Which kind of key terms in documents will be used to re-order retrieved documents? How many top retrieved documents should we use to extract key terms from? For the first part, we extract different key terms by using different parameters in our term extraction method. There are two parameters in our term extraction method. One parameter is δ - the minimum saliency of seed in term, the other parameter is *L* - the minimum occurrence of term in document. For the second part, we only test parameter *N* - the number of top retrieved documents that are used to extract terms from. Following is the parameter setting in our experiments:

δ=1, 10: We consider terms which contain at least a seed whose salience is 1 or 10;
L=2, 3, 4: We consider terms which occur at least 2 times, 3 times or 4 times in document;
N=20, 25, 30: We consider top 20, 25 or 30 retrieved documents as related documents and extract key terms from them to re-order retrieved documents.

4.1 Vector Space Model

In our first group experiments, we use vector space model to represent documents and queries. We also use Yang L.P et.al. [18]'s result on NTCIR3 CLIR dataset as 2nd baseline. Each document or query is represented as a vector in vector space where each dimension of vector is a bi-gram. The weight of bi-gram t in document d is given by the following $tf \cdot idf$ weighting scheme:

$$w(t, d)=\log(T(t, d)+1) * \log(N/D(t)+1) \qquad (5)$$

where, $w(t, d)$ is the weigh given to t in d, $T(t, d)$ is the frequency of t in d, N is the number of documents in document set, $D(t)$ is the number of documents in document set which contain t.

The weight of bi-gram t in query q, $w(t, q)$, is given by the following weight scheme:

$$w(t, q) = T(t, q) \qquad (6)$$

where $T(t, q)$ is the frequency of t in q.

The similarity (distance) between a document d and a query q is calculated by the cosine of the document vector and the query vector.

The comparison of precisions at different parameters setting is given at table 1-6. In table 1-6, column [PreAt10(relax)] represents the average precision of 42 topics on PreAt10 relax relevance judgment; Column [PreAt10(rigid)] represents the average precision of 42 topics on PreAt10 rigid relevance judgment; Column [PreAt100(relax)] represents the average precision of 42 topics on PreAt100 relax relevance judgment; Column [PreAt100(rigid)] represents the average precision of 42 topics on PreAt100 rigid relevance judgment. Row [BaseLine1] represents the initial retrieved result; Row [BaseLine2] represents experiment result reported on Yang et. al [14]; Row [N=20] represents the re-ordered result which make use of key terms in top 20 retrieved documents; Row [N=25] represents the re-ordered result which make use of key terms in top 25 retrieved documents; Row [N=30] represents the re-ordered result which make use of key terms in top 30 retrieved documents. Each item in table represents the precision and its improvement over [BaseLine1] at the conditions expressed by Column and Row.

Table 1. Statistics on (δ=1, L=2)

	PreAt10(relax)	PreAt10(rigid)	PreAt100(relax)	PreAt100(rigid)
BaseLine1	0.3619	0.2595	0.1886	0.1279
BaseLine2	0.4052 (12%)	0.2871 (10.6%)	0.1926 (2.1%)	0.133 (4%)
N=20	0.4143 (14.5%)	0.3024 (16.5%)	**0.2055 (9%)**	**0.1376 (7.6%)**
N=25	**0.4262 (17.8%)**	**0.3143 (21.1%)**	0.2052 (8.8%)	0.1371 (7.2%)
N=30	0.4167 (15.1%)	0.3119 (20.2%)	0.2048 (8.6%)	0.1369 (7%

Table 2. Statistics on (δ=1, L=3)

	PreAt10(relax)	PreAt10(rigid)	PreAt100(relax)	PreAt100(rigid)
BaseLine1	0.3619	0.2595	0.1886	0.1279
BaseLine2	0.4052 (12%)	0.2871 (10.6%)	0.1926 (2.1%)	0.133 (4%)
N=20	0.4119 (13.8%)	0.3001 (15.6%)	0.205 (8.7%)	0.1376 (7.6%)
N=25	**0.4333 (19.7%)**	**0.3167 (22%)**	0.2079 (10.2%)	0.1381 (8%)
N=30	**0.4333 (19.7%)**	**0.3167 (22%)**	**0.2083 (10.4%)**	**0.1388 (8.5%)**

Table 3. Statistics on (δ=1, L=4)

	PreAt10(relax)	PreAt10(rigid)	PreAt100(relax)	PreAt100(rigid)
BaseLine1	0.3619	0.2595	0.1886	0.1279
BaseLine2	0.4052 (12%)	0.2871 (10.6%)	0.1926 (2.1%)	0.133 (4%)
N=20	0.4262 (17.8%)	0.3143 (21.1%)	**0.2117 (12.2%)**	**0.14 (9.5%)**
N=25	**0.4357 (20.4%)**	0.319 (22.9%)	0.2098 (11.2%)	0.1393 (8.9%)
N=30	0.4333 (19.7%)	**0.3214 (23.9%)**	0.2105 (11.6%)	0.1395 (9.1%)

Table 4. Statistics on (δ=10, L=2)

	PreAt10(relax)	PreAt10(rigid)	PreAt100(relax)	PreAt100(rigid)
BaseLine1	0.3619	0.2595	0.1886	0.1279
BaseLine2	0.4052 (12%)	0.2871 (10.6%)	0.1926 (2.1%)	0.133 (4%)
N=20	0.4262 (17.8%)	0.3119 (20.2%)	**0.2043 (8.3%)**	**0.1369 (7%)**
N=25	**0.4381(21.1%)**	**0.3214 (23.9%)**	0.2038 (8.1%)	0.1364 (6.6%)
N=30	0.4357(20.4%)	**0.3214 (23.9%)**	0.2038 (8.1%)	0.1362 (6.5%)

Table 5. Statistics on (δ=10, L=3)

	PreAt10(relax)	PreAt10(rigid)	PreAt100(relax)	PreAt100(rigid)
BaseLine1	0.3619	0.2595	0.1886	0.1279
BaseLine2	0.4052 (12%)	0.2871 (10.6%)	0.1926 (2.1%)	0.133 (4%)
N=20	0.4286 (18.4%)	0.3119 (20.2%)	0.2076 (10.1%)	0.1379 (7.8%)
N=25	**0.4476 (23.7%)**	**0.331(27.5%)**	0.2064 (9.4%)	0.1383 (8.1%)
N=30	0.4405 (21.7%)	0.319 (22.9%)	**0.2086 (10.6%)**	**0.14 (9.5%)**

From table 1-6, our proposed method gets better result than [BaseLine1] and [BaseLine2] in every parameter setting. If only considering PreAt100, it seems we may get better result by using terms in top 20 retrieved documents; but if only considering PreAt10, it seems we may get better result by using terms in top 25 or top 30 retrieved documents. If considering PreAt10 and PreAt100 together, we regard that we may get better and stable result by using terms in top 25 retrieved documents. Table 7-8 gives the comparison of precisions on different term extraction parameter settings using terms in top 25 retrieved documents.

Table 6. Statistics on (δ=10, L=4)

	PreAt10(relax)	PreAt10(rigid)	PreAt100(relax)	PreAt100(rigid)
BaseLine1	0.3619	0.2595	0.1886	0.1279
BaseLine2	0.4052 (12%)	0.2871 (10.6%)	0.1926 (2.1%)	0.133 (4%)
N=20	**0.4405 (21.7%)**	**0.3262 (25.7%)**	**0.2129 (12.9%)**	**0.141 (10.2%)**
N=25	**0.4405 (21.7%)**	0.3238 (24.8%)	0.2112 (12%)	0.1402 (9.6%)
N=30	0.4381(21.1%)	0.3238 (24.8%)	0.21 (11.3%)	0.139 (8.7%)

Table 7. Statistics on (δ=1, N=25)

	PreAt10(relax)	PreAt10(rigid)	PreAt100(relax)	PreAt100(rigid)
BaseLine1	0.3619	0.2595	0.1886	0.1279
BaseLine2	0.4052 (12%)	0.2871 (10.6%)	0.1926 (2.1%)	0.133 (4%)
L=2	0.4262 (17.8%)	0.3143 (21.1%)	0.2052 (8.8%)	0.1371 (7.2%)
L=3	0.4333 (19.7%)	0.3167 (22%)	0.2079 (10.2%)	0.1381 (8%)
L=4	**0.4357 (20.4%)**	**0.319 (22.9%)**	**0.2098 (11.2%)**	**0.1393 (8.9%)**

Table 8. Statistics on (δ=10, N=25)

	PreAt10(relax)	PreAt10(rigid)	PreAt100(relax)	PreAt100(rigid)
BaseLine1	0.3619	0.2595	0.1886	0.1279
BaseLine2	0.4052 (12%)	0.2871 (10.6%)	0.1926 (2.1%)	0.133 (4%)
L=2	0.4381(21.1%)	0.3214 (23.9%)	0.2038 (8.1%)	0.1364 (6.6%)
L=3	**0.4476 (23.7%)**	**0.331(27.5%)**	0.2064 (9.4%)	0.1383 (8.1%)
L=4	0.4405 (21.7%)	0.3238 (24.8%)	**0.2112 (12%)**	**0.1402 (9.6%)**

From table 7 and table 8, our proposed method can improve PreAt10 by 17.8%-23.7% from 0.3619 to 0.4262-0.4476 in relax relevance judgment and improve PreAt10 by 21.1%-27.5% from 0.2595 to 0.3143-0.331 in rigid relevance judgment. In PreAt100 level, our method can improve 8.1%-12% and 6.6%-9.6% in relax relevance judgment and rigid relevance judgment. Even in worst case, our proposed method get better result than [BaseLine2] with 18.8%, 21.1%, 8.1% and 6.6% improvement at PreAt10(relax), PreAt10(rigid), PreAt100(relax) and PreAt100(rigid) level compared with 12%, 10.6%, 2.1% and 4% improvement in [BaseLine2].

From table 7 and table 8, we may conclude that using key terms that occur at least 3 times or 4 times in documents may get better results.

The above experiments on NTCIR3 dataset show our method can achieve significant improvements on PreAt10 and PreAt100 results.

The comparison of the precisions of 42 query topics before and after document re-ordering at parameter setting (δ =1, N=25, L=4) is given at Fig. 3-4. From Fig. 3-4, for 42 topics in NTCIR3, there are only 2 query topics (topic 9 and 43) whose precisions are slightly decreased after document re-ordering, the other 40 topics are all improved after document re-ordering.

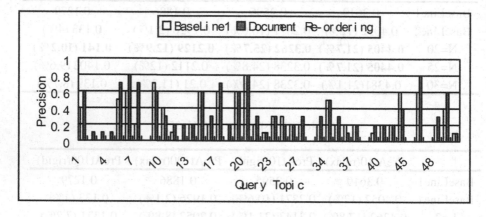

Fig. 3. PreAt10 at rigid relevance judgment (δ =1, N=25, L=4)

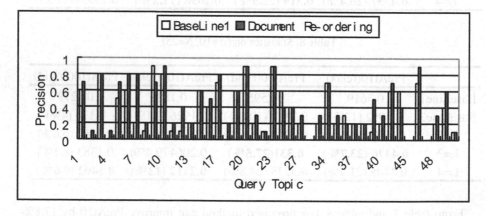

Fig. 4. PreAt10 at relax relevance judgment (δ =1, N=25, L=4)

4.2 Probabilistic Retrieval Model

In our second group experiments, we use the famous OKAPI BM11 [14] model as retrieval model. The other parameter settings are the same as that in our first group experiments except no [BaseLine2] is used.

OKAPI BM11 is a kind of probabilistic retrieval model based on 2-Possion model. We use the following BM11 weighting function:

$$BM11(q, d_i) = \sum_j q_j \, \log\left(\frac{N - n_j + 0.5}{n_j + 0.5}\right)\left(\frac{t_{i,j}}{t_{i,j} + \dfrac{len_i}{len}}\right)$$

where q is the query, d_i is the i-th document, q_j is the j-th query term weight, N is the number of documents in the document collection, n_j is the number of documents which contain the j-th term, $t_{i,j}$ is the number of occurrence of j-th term in i-th document, len_i is the Euclidean document length of the i-th document and len is the average Euclidean document length.

The comparison of precisions at different parameters setting is given at table 9-14.

Table 9. Statistics on (δ=1, L=2)

	PreAt10(relax)	PreAt10(rigid)	PreAt100(relax)	PreAt100(rigid)
BaseLine1	0.3333	0.2452	0.1529	0.1026
N=20	0.3595 (7.9%)	0.2571 (4.9%)	0.1681 (9.9%)	0.1117 (8.9%)
N=25	**0.3667 (10%)**	**0.2595 (5.8%)**	**0.1688 (10.4%)**	**0.1129 (10%)**
N=30	0.3595 (7.7%)	0.2576 (5.1%)	0.1671 (9.3%)	0.1114 (8.6%)

Table 10. Statistics on (δ=1, L=3)

	PreAt10(relax)	PreAt10(rigid)	PreAt100(relax)	PreAt100(rigid)
BaseLine1	0.3333	0.2452	0.1529	0.1026
N=20	**0.3762 (12.9%)**	**0.269 (9.7%)**	0.1721 (12.6%)	0.116 (13.1%)
N=25	0.369 (10.7%)	0.2667 (8.8%)	**0.1729 (13.1%)**	**0.1162 (13.3%)**
N=30	0.3571 (7.1%)	0.2571 (4.9%)	0.1719 (12.4%)	0.1145 (11.6%)

Table 11. Statistics on (δ=1, L=4)

	PreAt10(relax)	PreAt10(rigid)	PreAt100(relax)	PreAt100(rigid)
BaseLine1	0.3333	0.2452	0.1529	0.1026
N=20	**0.3738 (12.2%)**	0.2713 (10.6%)	**0.1798 (17.6%)**	**0.1212 (18.1%)**
N=25	**0.3738 (12.2%)**	**0.2738 (11.7%)**	0.1771 (15.8%)	0.1198 (16.8%)
N=30	0.369 (10.7%)	0.2667 (8.8%)	0.1733 (13.3%)	0.1164 (13.5%)

Table 12. Statistics on (δ=10, L=2)

	PreAt10(relax)	PreAt10(rigid)	PreAt100(relax)	PreAt100(rigid)
BaseLine1	0.3333	0.2452	0.1529	0.1026
N=20	0.4 (20%)	0.2881 (17.5%)	0.1836 (20%)	0.1248 (21.6%)
N=25	**0.4048 (21.5%)**	**0.2952 (20.4%)**	**0.185 (21%)**	**0.1264 (23.2%)**
N=30	0.3929 (17.9%)	0.2857 (16.5%)	0.1807 (18.2%)	0.1229 (19.8%)

Table 13. Statistics on (δ=10, L=3)

	PreAt10(relax)	PreAt10(rigid)	PreAt100(relax)	PreAt100(rigid)
BaseLine1	0.3333	0.2452	0.1529	0.1026
N=20	0.3952 (18.6%)	**0.2929 (19.5%)**	0.1883 (23.2%)	**0.1293 (26%)**
N=25	0.3952 (18.6%)	0.2881 (17.5%)	**0.189 (23.6%)**	0.1288 (25.5%)
N=30	**0.3976 (19.3%)**	0.2905 (18.5%)	0.1881 (23%)	0.1283 (25%)

Table 14. Statistics on (δ=10, L=4)

	PreAt10(relax)	PreAt10(rigid)	PreAt100(relax)	PreAt100(rigid)
BaseLine1	0.3333	0.2452	0.1529	0.1026
N=20	0.3786 (13.6%)	0.2762 (12.6%)	**0.1912 (25%)**	**0.1314 (28.1%)**
N=25	**0.3952 (18.6%)**	0.2857 (16.5%)	**0.1905 (25%)**	0.1302 (26.9%)
N=30	**0.3952 (18.6%)**	0.2857 (16.5%)	0.1893 (23.8%)	0.1295 (26.2%)

From table 9-14, our proposed method gets better result than [BaseLine1] in every parameter setting. If only considering PreAt100, it seems we may get better result by using terms in top 20 or 25 retrieved documents; but if only considering PreAt10, it seems we may get better result by using terms in top 25 retrieved documents. If considering PreAt10 and PreAt100 together, we regard that we may get better and stable result by using terms in top 25 retrieved documents.   Table 15-16 gives the comparison of precisions on different term extraction parameter settings using terms in top 25 retrieved documents.

Table 15. Statistics on (δ=1, N=25)

	PreAt10(relax)	PreAt10(rigid)	PreAt100(relax)	PreAt100(rigid)
BaseLine1	0.3333	0.2452	0.1529	0.1026
L=2	0.3667 (10%)	0.2595 (5.8%)	0.1688 (10.4%)	0.1129 (10%)
L=3	0.369 (10.7%)	0.2667 (8.8%)	0.1729 (13.1%)	0.1162 (13.3%)
L=4	**0.3738 (12.2%)**	**0.2738 (11.7%)**	**0.1771 (15.8%)**	**0.1198 (16.8%)**

Table 16. Statistics on (δ=10, N=25)

	PreAt10(relax)	PreAt10(rigid)	PreAt100(relax)	PreAt100(rigid)
BaseLine1	0.3333	0.2452	0.1529	0.1026
L=2	**0.4048 (21.5%)**	**0.2952 (20.4%)**	0.185 (21%)	0.1264 (23.2%)
L=3	0.3952 (18.6%)	0.2881 (17.5%)	0.189 (23.6%)	0.1288 (25.5%)
L=4	0.3952 (18.6%)	0.2857 (16.5%)	**0.1905 (25%)**	**0.1302 (26.9%)**

From table 15 and table 16, our proposed method can improve precision at every parameter setting. We also see that the respectively results in table 16 is better than these in table 15. Since the only difference between table 15 (δ=1, where almost all terms are considered equally) and table 16 (δ=10, where more prominent terms are considered) is the setting of parameter δ, we may come to a conclusion: important key terms (more prominent terms) in topic play key roles and it can be used to improve precision.

From table 16, our proposed method can improve PreAt10 by 18.6%-21.5% from 0.3333 to 0.3952-0.4048 in relax relevance judgment and improve PreAt10 by 16.5%-20.4% from 0.2452 to 0.2881-0.2952 in rigid relevance judgment. In PreAt100 level, our method can improve 21%-25% and 23.2%-26.9% in relax relevance judgment and rigid relevance judgment.

The comparison of the precisions of 42 query topics before and after document re-ordering at parameter setting (δ=1, N=25, L=4) is given at Fig 5-6. From Fig. 5-6, for 42 topics in NTCIR3, there are only 3 query topics (topic 21, 24 and 38) whose precisions are slightly decreased after document re-ordering, the other 39 topics are all improved after document re-ordering.

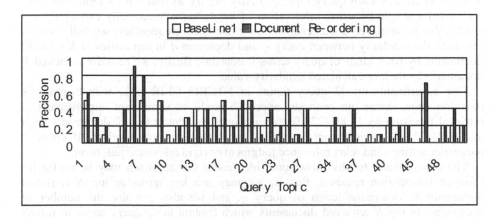

Fig. 5. PreAt10 at rigid relevance judgment (δ=1, N=25, L=4)

From our two group experiments based on bi-gram as index unit and vector space model and probabilistic retrieval model as retrieval models, our proposed method can improve precision at every parameter setting. From table 6 and table 16(δ =10, N=25), our method can improve 18.6%-23.7% and 16.5%-27.5% in relax relevance judgment and rigid relevance judgment; in PreAt100 level, our method can improve 8.1%-25% and 6.6.2%-26.9% in relax relevance judgment and rigid relevance judgment.

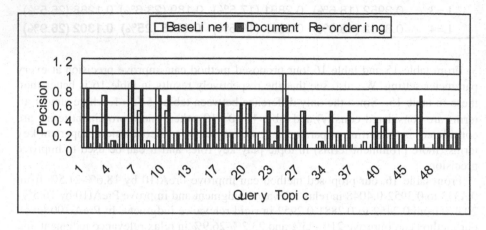

Fig. 6. PreAt10 at relax relevance judgment (δ=1, N=25, L=4)

5   Conclusion and Future Work

Document re-ordering is very important for improving the precision of retrieved documents. In this paper, we introduce our approach to re-order retrieved documents in Chinese IR. For each query topic q, firstly, we try to find out its terms and give each term a weight by using information of key terms automatically extracted from top N (N<=30) retrieved documents and their document frequencies; secondly, we re-calculate the similarity between query q and document d in top retrieved K (N<<K) documents by what kinds of query terms it contains; finally, we re-order retrieved K documents by their re-calculated similarity value.

Our experiments on 42 query topics in NTCIR3 CLIR task, with bi-gram as indexing units, shows our proposed approach produced significant improvement in retrieval precision by 17.8%-27.5% average improvement at top 10 documents level and 6.6%-26.9% average improvement at top 100 documents level at all kinds of parameter settings and relax relevance judgment or rigid relevance judgment.

The experimental results show some idea under our approach may be useful for Chinese information retrieval, that is, we may use key terms in top N retrieved documents to determine terms of query q, and we also can use the number of documents in top N retrieved documents which contain these query terms to reflect the importance of query terms in query q; moreover, long query term may contain more precise information and can be used to improve precision.

Our experiments are all based on Chinese information retrieval. In the future, we'll do some experiments on other languages. We also want to try other term extraction approaches to analyse what kind of role each part plays in our approach.

References

[1] Bear J., Israel, D., Petit J., Martin D.: Using Information Extraction to Improve Document Retrieval. Proceedings of the Sixth Text Retrieval Conference, 1997.

[2] Carpineto, C., Romano, G., Giannini, V.: Improving Retrieval Feedback with Multiple Term-Ranking Function Combination. In ACM Transactions on Information Systems, Vol. 20, n. 3, pp. 259-290. 2002.

[3] Fuhr. N.: Probabilistic Models in Information Retrieval. The Computer Journal. 35(3):243-254, 1992.

[4] Ji D.H., Yang L.P., Nie Y.: Chinese Language IR Based on Term Extraction. In The Third NTCIR Workshop, 2002.

[5] Ji D.H., Yang L.P., Nie Y., Tang L.: Online Discovery of Relevant Terms from Internet. IEEE International Conference on Natural Language Processing and Knowledge Engineering (NLPKE2003), Beijing, China, Oct, 2003.

[6] Kamps, J.: Improving Retrieval Effectiveness by Reranking Documents Based on Controlled Vocabulary. The 21th European Conference on Information Retrieval, 2004.

[7] Kwok K.L.: Comparing Representation in Chinese Information Retrieval. In Proceedings of the ACM SIGIR-97, pp. 34-41.1997

[8] Lee K., Park Y., Choi, K.S.: Document Re-ranking Model Using Clusters. Information Processing and Management. V. 37 n.1, p1-14, 2001.

[9] Li. P. Research on Improvement of Single Chinese Character Indexing Method, Journal of the China Society for Scientific and Technical Information, Vol. 18 No. 5. 1999.

[10] M. Mitra., A. Singhal. and C. Buckley. Improving Automatic Query Expansion. In Proc. ACM SIGIR'98, Aug. 1998.

[11] Nie J.Y., Gao J., Zhang J., Zhou M.: On the Use of Words and N-grams for Chinese Information Retrieval. In Proceedings of the Fifth International Workshop on Information Retrieval with Asian Languages, IRAL-2000, pp. 141-148, 2000

[12] Qu, Y.L., Xu, G.W.,Wang J.: Rerank Method Based on Individual Thesaurus. Proceedings of NTCIR2 Workshop. 2000.

[13] Robertson S.E., Walker, S.: Microsoft Cambridge at TREC-9: Filtering track: In NIST Special Pub. 500-264: The Eight Text Retrieval Conference (TREC-8), pages 151-161, Gaithersburg, MD, 2001.

[14] Robertson S.E., Walker, S., Jones S.: Okapi at TREC-2. In The Second Text Retrieval Conference (TREC-2). 1994.

[15] SALTON, G., MCGILL, M.: Introduction to Modern Information Retrieval, McGraw-Hill.1983

[16] Schutze, H.: The Hypertext Concordance: A Better Back-of-the-Book Index. Proceedings of First Workshop on Computational Terminology. 101-104, 1998.

[17] Vechtomova O., Robertson S.E., Jones S. Query Expansion With Long-Span Collocates. Information Retrieval, 6(2), 2003, pp. 251-273.

[18] Yang L.P., Ji D.H., Tang L.: Document Re-ranking Based on Automatically Acquired Key Terms in Chinese Information Retrieval. Proceedings of 20th International Conference on Computational Linguistics (COLING). 2004.

[19] Yang L.P., Ji D.H., Tang L.: Chinese Information Retrieval Based on Terms and Ontology. Proceedings of NTCIR4 Workshop. 2004.

Appendix: 10 Query Topics in NTCIR3 (Part of 42 Query Topics)

001:查询故宫博物院所举办之千禧汉代文物大展相关内容(Find information of the exhibition "Art and Culture of the Han Dynasty" in the National Palace Museum)

002:查询台湾加入WTO後各产业可能面对的问题(Find possible problems that industries will meet after Taiwan's joining WTO.)

003:查询大学学术追求卓越计划的相关内容(Find the content of Program for Promoting Academic Excellence of Universities.)

004:查询何谓电子商务及电子商务之内容(Find what E-Commerce is and its contents)

005:查询朱熔基担任中国总理後所提出的经济改革计划。(Find Zhu Rong ji's economic reform after his serving as the premier)

006:查询有关一九九八年诺贝尔物理学奖的相关报导(Retrieve reports relating to 1998 Nobel Prizes in Physics)

007:查询有关华航於桃园中正机场失事的相关报导(Retrieve reports about China Airlines' crash while trying to land at Taoyan international airport.)

008:查询一九九八年电影「铁达尼号」获得奥斯卡奖之相关报导(Retrieve reports of Oscar winners, Titanic, in 1998)

009:查询有中新一号卫星相关报导及评论(Find reports and comments related to satellite ST1)

010:查询何谓反圣婴现象及其与圣婴现象的比较与影响(Find what the anti-El Nino is and the comparison with El Nino)

Evaluating Relevance Feedback Algorithms for Searching on Small Displays

Vishwa Vinay[1], Ingemar J. Cox[1],
Natasa Milic-Frayling[2], and Ken Wood[2]

[1] Department of Computer Science,
University College London, UK
v.vinay@cs.ucl.ac.uk, ingemar@ieee.org
[2] Microsoft Research Ltd,
7 J.J.Thomson Avenue, Cambridge, UK
{natasamf, krw}@microsoft.com

Abstract. Searching online information resources using mobile devices is affected by displays on which only a small fraction of the set of ranked documents can be displayed. In this paper, we ask whether the search effort can be reduced, on average, by user feedback indicating a single most relevant document in each display. For small display sizes and limited user actions, we are able to construct a tree representing all possible outcomes. Examination of the tree permits us to compute an upper limit on relevance feedback performance. Three standard feedback algorithms are considered - Rocchio, Robertson/Sparck-Jones and a Bayesian algorithm. Two display strategies are considered, one based on maximizing the immediate information gain and the other on most likely documents. Our results bring out the strengths and weaknesses of the algorithms, and the need for exploratory display strategies with conservative feedback algorithms.

1 Introduction

The continuing evolution of portable computing and communications devices (cell phones, PDAs, etc.) means that more and more people are accessing information and services on the Internet with devices that have small displays. This small display size presents challenges. The need for extensive scrolling makes viewing of standard pages very difficult. Also, devices like mobile phones still lack the resources needed to perform sophisticated processing on the client side.

We are particularly concerned with implications that small display devices have on searching online information resources. Generally, it has been observed that users engage in a variety of information seeking tasks, from "finding" a specific, well defined piece of information, to "gathering information" as a more open ended, research oriented activity ([21]). Adoption of Internet enabled mobile phones is still in its infancy and no general patterns of use have been established. Anticipating that mobile users will search for specific, well defined information, we study the methods which will enable the users to perform the operations of searching for a target.

D.E. Losada and J.M. Fernández-Luna (Eds.): ECIR 2005, LNCS 3408, pp. 185–199, 2005.
© Springer-Verlag Berlin Heidelberg 2005

In this study we explore the effectiveness of relevance feedback methods in assisting the user to access a predefined target document through searching or browsing. We devise an innovative approach to study this problem by exploiting the fact that the display size and thus the user's choices are limited. It is then feasible to generate and study the complete space of a user's interactions and obtain the upper bound on the effectiveness of relevance feedback. This bound represents the actions of an "ideal user" who at every step makes choices that enable the system to reach the target in the minimum number of iterations.

We believe that analysis of the complete search space is a novel experimental paradigm and can lead to interesting insights into the behavior of relevance feedback algorithms. This approach has the further advantage of permitting the study of relevance feedback and display strategies without the need for time-consuming user studies. This, in turn, allows a far greater number of experiments to be performed and we are optimistic that the statistical evidence gathered in this way can be used to predict actual user performance. This will be verified in future work.

In Section 2 we give an overview of the related research for mobile devices and relevance feedback and describe the particular algorithms we use here. In Section 3 we describe the display strategies that we consider - (i) one that maximizes the likelihood that the target is in the display (Top-K) and (ii) one that maximizes the immediate information gain. Experimental results characterize these two strategies. In Section 4 we describe the experimental procedure. In Section 5 we present the results and conclude with a summary of the presented work and an outline of the future research directions.

2   Background

A considerable body of research has been dedicated to the issues related to user interaction ([10][11]), browsing ([1][2]), searching ([21][23]), and reading ([4]) on mobile devices, and the idea of using relevance feedback or other adaptive measures to aid searching on small devices is not new. Most directly relevant to our study is Toogle [22], a front end application that post-processes Google results based on the user's actions, i.e., the user's clicks on documents in the ranked list. Toogle collects evidence, i.e., relevant and non-relevant documents from a single or multiple screens of search results, and applies machine learning techniques to re-rank the remaining documents.

In contrast, our approach focuses on searching using mobile devices and constrains the user feedback model to selection of a single relevant document at each iteration. Under these conditions, we take advantage of the small display size and limited space of user actions to study the full interaction space and all possible outcomes determined by the relevance feedback and display strategies. We are therefore able to provide an upper bound on the performance of relevance feedback systems for small displays.

2.1   Relevance Feedback

Conceptually, a system that involves user relevance feedback can be described by a three-phase iterative process as depicted in Figure 1. This three phase process can represent most, if not all, relevance feedback algorithms.

During the display phase, typically manifested as a list, the user is presented with a number of documents and given an opportunity to indicate which documents are relevant and which are not. This information is then used by the relevance feedback algorithm to induce a new ranking of documents in the database. The new ranking is the basis of the system's next display of a new set of documents to the user. And the process repeats. The process may begin with an initial query to the ranking engine, as depicted, or by a display of some selection of documents generated by the system itself. A good overview of relevance feedback techniques can be found in [8].

In our case, the display phase is the presentation of four documents from the ranked list. The user feedback phase is a single action where the user nominates one of the four displayed documents as most relevant to his or her information need. The document ranking phase applies one of three relevance feedback algorithms, described below, to create a new query based on a weighted combination of the previous query and terms from document selected by the user, and this new query is then used to compute the next ranking of the document collection.

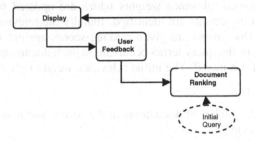

Fig. 1. Relevance Feedback

2.2 The Rocchio Algorithm

The Rocchio relevance feedback scheme [17] is used in conjunction with the term-frequency inverse-document-frequency (tf-idf) representation where documents and queries are represented as vectors of term weights and similarity is measured by the cosine distance between these vectors.

A document is a vector $d_i=(d_{i,1},d_{i,2},...,d_{iT})$ where T is the number of words across the collection, excluding a predefined set of stopwords, and $d_{i,j}= t(i,j)\cdot s_j$. Here $t(i,j)$ corresponds to the number of occurrences of term j in document i and s_j is the inverse document frequency of term j across the whole collection. A query $q= (q_1,q_2,...,q_T)$ is defined similarly, though their values are typically 0 or 1. Both documents and queries are normalized for length by setting

$$d'=\frac{d}{\|d\|} \text{ and } q'=\frac{q}{\|q\|} \text{ where } \|x\|=\sqrt{\sum_{j=1}^{t}x_j^2}$$

and the similarity score between document d and query q is then given by the dot product of the normalized vectors, i.e., $score_{rocchio}(d_i,q) = d_i \cdot q'$. The Rocchio algorithm takes a set **R** of relevant documents and a set **N** of non-relevant documents (as selected in the user feedback phase) and updates the query weights according to the following equation:

$$w'_j = \alpha \, w_j + \beta \, \frac{\sum_{i \in R} d_{i,j}}{n_R} + \gamma \, \frac{\sum_{i \in N} d_{i,j}}{n_N}$$

where

n_R and n_N are the number of relevant and non-relevant documents respectively.

The parameters α, β, and γ control the relative effect of the original weights, the relevant documents, and the non-relevant documents. We do not have non-relevant documents and we use $\alpha = \beta = 1$.

2.3   The Robertson/Sparck-Jones Algorithm

In the Robertson/Sparck Jones model of information retrieval [19], the terms in a corpus are all assigned relevance weights which are updated for a particular query whenever relevant documents are identified. Initially the relevance weights are given idf-based values. Documents are given ranking scores against a query based on the relevance weights of the query terms occurring in each document. We use the following formulation of this model. The initial relevance weight for term j is given by

$$w_j = log \, (C \, / \, n_j)$$

where C is the total number of documents in the corpus and n_j is the number of documents containing term j.

A document d_i is assigned a score against query q as follows:

$$score_{rsj}(d_i, q) = \sum_{j \in Q} \frac{(K+1)*t(i, j)}{K(1-b) + \frac{b*|d_i|}{l} + t(i, j)}$$

where

$t(i,j)$ is the number of occurrences of term j in document d_i
K and b are parameters typically set to 2.0 and 0.75 respectively
$|d_i|$ is the length of document d_i
l is the average length of all documents in the corpus

Documents are then ranked in descending score order. If certain documents are flagged as relevant, the relevance weights are updated as follows:

$$w_j = log\left(\left(\frac{(r_j + 0.5)}{(n_j - r_j + 0.5)} \right) \left(\frac{(C - n_j - n_R + r_j + 0.5)}{(n_R - r_j + 0.5)} \right) \right)$$

where

R is the number of relevant documents
r_j is the number of relevant documents containing term j
C and n_j are defined as before

In addition to updating the relevance weights, the relevant documents are used to select new (or additional) query terms according to the offer weights, o_j, where $o_j = r * w_j$

Terms are ranked in decreasing order of offer weight, and the top terms are used as part of the subsequent query. How many such terms are to be chosen per iteration is another parameter of the system.

2.4 The Bayesian Algorithm

The Bayesian relevance feedback algorithm [5], first proposed for a Content-Based Image Retrieval System – PicHunter – is a recursive probabilistic formulation in which, at each iteration, k, the probability, P_k of document d_i, being the target document, d_T, is computed. This probability is conditioned on all current and past user actions and the history of displayed documents, which collectively is denoted by H_k. The concept of a current query, q, is not explicitly present in this formulation. Thus, at each iteration, the document rankings are given by

$$score_{bayesian}(d_i) = P_k(d_i = d_T \mid H_k)$$

$$= P_{k-1}(d_i = d_T \mid H_{k-1}) * G(d_i, R))$$

where

P_{k-1} is the document's probability in the previous iteration

R is the set of documents marked relevant in this iteration

$G(d_i, R)$ is given by

$$G(d_i, R) = \prod_{j \in R} \left(\frac{\exp\left(\frac{sim(d_i, d_j)}{\sigma}\right)}{\left(\sum_{((k \in D) and\ (k \notin R))} \exp\left(\frac{sim(d_i, d_k)}{\sigma}\right)\right) + \exp\left(\frac{sim(d_i, d_j)}{\sigma}\right)} \right)$$

The term $sim(x,y)$ computes the similarity of document x with document y, which for textual documents can be taken as the cosine dot product of tf-idf vectors normalized for length. σ is a tuning noise parameter which is set according to the specific dataset.

3 Display Strategies

At each search iteration, it is necessary to display K documents to the user. The most obvious strategy is to display the K documents with the highest rank. This *Top-K display* is likely to result in a set of documents all very similar to one another. If these documents are close to the target (or even include it), then this may well be optimum. However, if the target is not similar to any of the documents in the currently displayed set, then it is very difficult for a user to direct the search away from the displayed documents and towards the target. This problem has been previously discussed in the context of content-based image retrieval [5] and observed in the current experiments (see Section 6.1.1 – on Convergence). An alternative approach is to display documents for which a user's response would be most informative to the system and help minimize the number of search iterations. This was proposed in [5] and formulated as finding a selection of K documents that maximizes the *immediate information gain* from the user's response in each iteration. Unfortunately, determining such a document selection is computationally expensive. However, it can be approximated by sampling K documents from the underlying similarity score distribution. There are computationally efficient methods for performing this sampling - usually, this is done by simulating a roulette wheel with the size of each item's field proportional to its score with respect to the current query.

Within such *sampled displays* both documents with high and low ranking have a non-zero probability of being included, thus exhibiting more variability and enabling the user to direct the search away from a local maximum. We expect that a sampled display strategy will be useful in situations where the initial query is imprecise, i.e., when the target document is ranked very low in the search result list.

The situation of using small display sizes for search makes the problem similar to the task of Adaptive Information Filtering where the importance of the interplay between *exploitation* and *exploration* has been recognized. It is to be expected that other more optimal sampling strategies exist which provide a better balance between exploitation and exploration. Providing these *preliminary* results we illustrate both the need and effectiveness of such strategies.

4   Experimental Procedure

In order to quantify the effect of relevance feedback and alternative display strategies, we need to define (i) the search task, (ii) the evaluation methodology and (iii) the initial conditions. These issues are discussed in Sections 4.1-4.3.

In the experiments we use the Reuters-21578 collection of textual documents. From the documents we extract the contents of the two fields, the "Body" and the "Title" and after removing the stop words we create vector representation of documents with *tf-idf* weights. Since some of the documents in the collection have empty "Body" fields, we removed them from the collection and arrived at a data set of 19,043 documents.

4.1   Task Model

In the context of retrieval, at least three classes of search may be identified [5]:

- Target document search – the user's information need is satisfied by a particular document. For example, a researcher may be looking for a particular paper on a research topic.
- Category search - the user seeks one or more items from a general category or a topic. This task places more emphasis on the semantic content of the data and often requires subjective judgements.
- Open ended browsing – the user has some vague idea of what to look for but is open to exploration and may repeatedly change topic during search.

Of these three scenarios, the target document search (or known-item search) is most amenable to evaluation for there are several clear measures of effectiveness including the total time or the total number of documents examined before the target is found.

We chose to compare different systems based on the total number of documents examined before the target is found. For comparison purposes, this number is compared with the rank of the document after the initial query, i.e. before any relevance feedback is applied. This rank is the number of documents that a user must examine when scrolling and no feedback is provided.

In the context of target search, we restrict a user's actions to selecting one of the K documents currently being displayed. Thus, there are K possible user actions in each iteration.

While target document search is typically equated with the 'known item search', the former encompasses a wider spectrum of search scenarios. It can include any information search that is satisfied with a specific document, regardless of whether or not the user is familiar with the target document. So long as the user can recognize that his or her information need is satisfied when the specific document is displayed, we can model this as target document search.

4.2 Evaluation Methodology

The experimental procedure to examine the effect of relevance feedback and alternative display strategies is designed to include the complete space of possible user's interactions with the system within the particular scenario. This is possible because of the small number of documents K that are displayed at each iteration. Thus, we can examine all user's strategies, including the optimal performance of an 'ideal user' whose selections minimize the number of documents that must be examined before identifying the target.

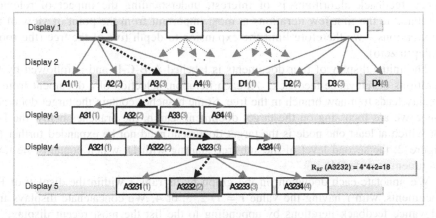

Fig. 2. Decision tree for iterative relevance feedback, showing nodes in which the target document is reached, the rank of a document within each display, and the calculation of RF-rank for the target. Expansion of this branch has stopped at depth five because the target has been found

At each iteration, the tree expands by a factor of K (See Figure 2). For practical purposes, we limit the depth of the tree to depth five, i.e., an initial display of K documents followed by five iterations of relevance feedback. For K=4, the maximum number of nodes in the tree is $1+4+4^2+4^3+4^4+4^5=1365$, where a node represents a display of K documents. The tree may be smaller if the target is located earlier since branches of the tree are not expanded once the target has been displayed. The choice of using a display size of four is made keeping in mind the display size of a typical mobile device. To account for a variety and range of such devices, a range of display size could be investigated using the same methodology

The *minimum rank* for a given target document corresponds to the best case scenario where the user always provides the system with the optimal document for relevance feedback. It is important to note that 'optimal' may not always mean the document most similar to the target.

We can also examine the *number of target document occurrences* in a tree. This provides a measure of the likelihood of a non-ideal user locating the target document. For example, if the target document appears in only one path of the tree, then any deviation by a real user from the "ideal" would result in a failed search. Conversely, if the target document appears in many paths, then deviations from the "ideal" are still likely to yield successful searches, albeit that these searches require further effort. Examining the set of documents displayed after each iteration can also reveal properties of the relevance feedback and/or display strategy.

Finally, since the trees are generated automatically with no user interaction, it is possible to generate a very large number of trees, thereby facilitating statistical analysis.

4.2.1 Construction of the User Decision Trees

Figure 2 illustrates a tree that represents the space of all user decisions. At each iteration, the tree expands by a factor of four. While the general behaviour of relevance feedback algorithms is of interest, understanding the impact of relevance feedback to the first few iterations is most important from the point of view of real applications – we therefore limit the expansion to depth five of the tree (the root is at depth zero).

The initial display of four documents is labelled A-B-C-D and is followed by five iterations of relevance feedback. At each iteration, selection of a document from the display leads to a new branch in the tree. Some branches contain the target document. Since we are focussing on the target document search, the branches below the level for which at least one node is the target document need not be expanded further (see Figure 2; the second level of the sub-tree starting with D, which contains the target document at node D4).

We annotate each document in the graph by its rank r within the display of K=4 documents, with r having the value r = 1, 2, 3, or 4. We concatenate displays from relevance feedback iterations by appending to the list the most recent display. The resulting list shows documents in the order in which the user would view them. For each document in the graph, we can identify the corresponding ranked list and calculate the *relevance feedback rank* $R_{RF}=d \cdot K+r$, where d is the number of previous displays, d = 0, 1, 2, 3, 4 or 5. R_{RF} essentially corresponds to the number of documents that the user has viewed before locating the document. In our evaluations we compare R_{RF} of the document with its rank in the baseline ranked list obtained from the initial query. We refer to this baseline rank as the *scroll rank*, R_{Scroll}, since this is the number of documents that the user would have to examine by scrolling down the original search result in order to reach the target document.

The task is therefore similar to the Ostensive Retrieval Model [3], except that we use standard relevance feedback algorithms between two displays. Very recently, [26] dealt with the question of measuring the performance of implicit feedback models by conducting a simulation-based evaluation.

4.3 Initialisation

We begin experiments by randomly selecting a target document from the database. An initial query is then automatically generated by randomly selecting M terms from the target document. In our experiments M=4. These M terms are used in two ways: as a search query to obtain the baseline search results and as input to the relevance feedback procedure which will further refine the query based on the user's responses. Using four query terms is higher than the average even in internet search engines - the development of predictive texting features in these devices makes this number reasonable. The query vector is simply a vector of equally weighted terms, reflecting our assumption that the user may have some expectations of finding certain terms in the document but is otherwise unaware of the characteristics of the target document or the document corpus in general. The user's relevance feedback iterations start with an initial display of K documents that are chosen based on which display strategy is being used.

The user's response is used by the relevance feedback algorithm to modify the query. The documents in the collection are then scored against the new query and a new display of K documents is presented to the user, based on the search ranking and display strategy. Previously viewed documents are not included in the subsequent search iterations.

5 Results

In our experiments we generated 100 trees, corresponding to 100 distinct target documents, randomly selected from the subset of 19,043 documents from the Reuters collection. The initial query was composed of four random terms present in the target document and the scroll rank of each target document was recorded.

For each target document we generated a complete search tree based on iterative feedback, with two types of displays: (1) the Top-K display always showing the top 4 ranked documents from the search iteration and (2) the Sampled display that probabilistically selects the documents based on the current ranking of documents in the database. Trees and paths within the trees that contain the target documents are referred to as *successful searches* for the relevance feedback scheme. Tables 1-4 summarize the statistics of the tree displays and successful searches.

Table 1. Statistics about search tree results for three feedback algorithms and the two display strategies

	Rocchio Feedback Algorithm		RSJ Feedback Algorithm		Bayesian Feedback Algorithm	
	Top-K Display Scheme	Sampled Display Scheme	Top-K Display Scheme	Sampled Display Scheme	Top-K Display Scheme	Sampled Display Scheme
Percentage of trees with target	52	97	39	33	52	90
Percentage of paths containing the target	46.67	4.5	27.99	0.087	46.80	4.30
Average R_{Scroll} of targets found in trees	13.79	98.54	37.28	312.03	7.92	64.23
Average min R_{RF} of targets found in trees	6.5	11.25	7.20	17.76	6.13	10.61
Average R_{RF} for the 'average user'	20.53	20.2	20.22	18.26	21.27	19.94

Table 2. Performance of the Rocchio RF Algorithm based on the Initial Query

Scroll Rank Range	Number of Targets	Number of Targets Found		Avg. No. of Documents viewed without RF		Avg. No. of Documents viewed by the 'ideal user' using RF		No. of Documents viewed with RF averaged over all successful users	
		Top-K	Sampled	Top-K	Sampled	Top-K	Sampled	Top-K	Sampled
1 – 20	45	45(100%)	45(100%)	4.38	4.38	4.31	5.33	16.54	19.13
21 – 40	14	6(42.8%)	14(100%)	25.5	29.79	20.67	13.07	21.62	21.92
41 – 60	5	0(0%)	5(100%)	-	54.2	-	16.6	-	21.99
61 – 80	4	0(0%)	4(100%)	-	66.5	-	16.5	-	21.80
81 – 100	6	0(0%)	6(100%)	-	92.83	-	15.33	-	21.49
101 – Last Rank	26	1(3.84%)	23(89%)	367	341.3	20	18.56	20.78	22.14

Table 3. Performance of the RSJ RF Algorithm based on the Initial Query

Scroll Rank Range	Number of Targets	Number of Targets Found		Avg. No. of Documents viewed without RF		Avg. No. of Documents viewed by the 'ideal user' using RF		No. of Documents viewed with RF averaged over all successful users	
		Top-K	Sampled	Top-K	Sampled	Top-K	Sampled	Top-K	Sampled
1 – 20	27	27(100%)	7(25.93%)	5.67	4.72	4.26	17	19.21	18.67
21 – 40	6	2(33.33%)	2(33.33%)	34	31	7.5	17	12.46	17
41 – 60	5	3(60%)	3(60%)	47.33	41.67	6.33	17.33	7.4	17.33
61 – 80	8	1(12.5%)	3(37.5%)	74	68.33	17	21	18.15	21
81 – 100	2	1(50%)	2(100%)	81	88	24	17	24	17
101 – Last Rank	52	5(9.61%)	16(30.77%)	187.2	606	18.2	17.5	21.72	17.94

Table 4. Performance of the Bayesian RF Algorithm based on the Initial Query

Scroll Rank Range	Number of Targets	Number of Targets Found		Avg. No. of Documents viewed without RF		Avg. No. of Documents viewed by the 'ideal user' using RF		No. of Documents viewed with RF averaged over all successful users	
		Top-K	Sampled	Top-K	Sampled	Top-K	Sampled	Top-K	Sampled
1 – 20	45	45(100%)	45(100%)	4.38	4.38	4.31	5.02	16.54	18.75
21 – 40	14	6(42.8%)	14(100%)	25.17	29.78	17.67	13.07	22.21	21.35
41 – 60	5	0(0%)	5(100%)	-	54.2	-	13.4	-	21.52
61 – 80	4	1(25%)	4(100%)	64	66.5	17	18.5	18.05	21.98
81 – 100	6	0(0%)	6(100%)	-	92.83	-	18.33	-	22.18
101 – Last Rank	26	0(0%)	16(61.53%)	-	254.56	-	18.44	-	21.92

6 Discussion

6.1 Top-K Display Scheme

The number of documents *seen* without relevance feedback(RF) is the scroll rank of the target in the initial ranked list. The RF rank of an *ideal user* is the minimum path length from the root of the tree to a node with the target, whereas the mean length of all paths leading to the target represents the average performance of a successful user. The first row in Table 1 is the probability that a search (using a given display scheme) will be successful, and row two is the probability that a non-ideal user will find the target. For the Top-K display strategy, about 50% of the trees contain the target (lower for RSJ). In the remaining cases, the target was not found within five rounds of relevance feedback. This percentage is clearly a function of the accuracy of the initial query, which can be judged by examining the scroll rank of the target document.

For the Rocchio and Bayesian algorithms, we see that for a scroll rank of less than 20, relevance feedback with Top-K display is successful 100% of the time. For higher values of the initial scroll ranks, i.e.; poor queries, we observe a fall off in the percentage of successful searches. However, the sampled display scheme offers performance that is more or less constant. For the case of RSJ, which explicitly incorporates a term expansion strategy, the Top-K display strategy performed better.

The ideal user represents the best possible performance achievable. Real users are unlikely to perform as well. However, the average number of paths in the tree that contain the target suggests that deviations from the ideal still have a reasonable chance of locating the target document. The average rank of target documents in the tree was obtained by calculating first the average rank for the target document within its particular tree and then averaged over the set of all the trees that contain target documents.

6.1.1 Convergence

It was observed that sub-trees below a node at depth 4 were identical. That is, the set of four documents displayed to the user at depth 5 was the same, irrespective of the choice of relevant document at the preceding level. Note that the relative *order* of displayed four documents may be affected by the relevance feedback, but the *same* documents appeared in all four sub-trees. It is important to note that the convergence was observed for all three algorithms: even though the sets to which they converged were different.

Since the phenomenon was not symptomatic of any one particular algorithm, we suspect that this *convergence* is due to the greedy nature of the display updating strategy – that of picking the K most probable items (based on the score with respect to the current query). Since the aim of the RF algorithm is to extract *similar* documents from the collection, it results in a situation where successive displays offer no diversity. The small variation across the documents in the display is also due to the small number of documents, 4, in the display. However, similar convergence properties were observed for larger displays.

6.2 Sampled Display Scheme

For the alternative display, a higher percentage of the trees contained the target document with the *conservative* Rocchio and Bayesian schemes. More importantly, we do not observe a performance degradation as the quality of the initially query degrades. And for very poor initial queries, the alternative display strategy is superior. Since the RSJ algorithm itself considers exploring different regions of the search space by query expansion, use of the Sampled display strategy led to an over-adventurous approach, resulting in a smaller number of successful searches and fewer paths leading to the target in a given tree. This illustrates the classical dilemma between exploration and exploitation.

Analysis of the trees containing the target revealed that the average scroll rank was much higher than the rank for an ideal user using relevance feedback and the alternative display, representing a very significant reduction in the number of documents examined. However, once more, we need to recognize that real users are unlikely to perform as well as the ideal user. For the sampled display, the average number of paths in the tree that contain the target is low, which suggests that deviations from the ideal may have a significant detrimental effect on performance.

Finally, we note that the convergence phenomenon observed with the Top-K display was not exhibited using the Sampled display.

6.3 Comparing the Feedback Algorithms

When comparing the 3 feedback algorithms, we find that the following points stand out:

1) The performance of the Rocchio algorithm and the Bayesian one are very similar. We hypothesize that this is mainly because of the fact that in this implementation, they both use the Cosine similarity metric.
2) Even with the same queries (the same terms chosen from the same targets), the RSJ algorithm produces a very different initial ranking because it uses the BM25 ranking algorithm.
3) RSJ uses a specifically constructed term expansion strategy, which results in the feedback process itself working – shown by the fact that even with the cases where the initial scroll rank is low and the Top-K display update is used, RSJ still man-

ages to find the target in a few cases. The sensitivity to feedback in this case is reflected in the smaller number of paths with the target, as compared to similar runs for Rocchio and the Bayesian algorithm.

4) The default values of parameters were used in all three algorithms. While the 'K' and 'b' values for RSJ are more or less generally accepted values for similar situations, the α and β values in Rocchio (which control the relative effect of past and present feedback provided) and the σ in the Bayesian algorithm (which loosely controls the noise associated with the current feedback) can be tuned to alter the results.

7 Conclusions

We examined whether relevance feedback and alternative display strategies can be used to reduce the number of documents that a user of a mobile device with limited display capabilities has to examine before locating a target document. In this scenario, it is possible to construct a tree representing all possible user actions for a small number of feedback iterations. This allows us to determine the performance of an "ideal" user, i.e. no real user can perform better. We are therefore able to establish an upper limit on the performance improvement such systems can deliver. To the best of our knowledge, this has not previously been done. The experimental paradigm has the further advantages of (i) not requiring a real user study, which can be time consuming, and (ii) the ability to simulate very many searches, thereby facilitating statistical analysis.

Using each of three relevance feedback algorithms with a display size of four documents, we constructed 100 trees. With a greedy display strategy, analysis of the trees containing the target(i.e; the successful searches) revealed that relevance feedback with a greedy display strategy resulted in close to 50% reduction in the number of documents that a user needed to examine compared with simply performing a linear search of a ranked list calculated from the initial query. It should however be noted that this number is exaggerated because of the presence of outliers.

It is unclear as to why the improvement is so low. This may be due to the experimental procedure which required a user to always select one document as relevant, even if none of the displayed documents actually was relevant. Future work is needed to examine whether performance can be improved by:

1. alternative values for the algorithm parameters
2. the identification of non-relevant as well as relevant documents
3. alternative distance metrics

Similarly, the formation of the initial query by selection of random terms from the target document should also be examined. Experiments in which the query is created by selecting terms which occur most or more frequently are obvious directions for investigation. The observation of convergence of the relevance feedback algorithm using a greedy display also needs investigation. More positively, it was observed that relevance feedback almost never led to worse performance for an ideal user.

We also examined how the performance of the system was affected by an alternative display strategy in which the displayed documents were drawn with the same underlying distribution as the current scores of documents in the database. This sampling strategy crudely approximates a strategy in which we attempt to maximize the immediate information gain.

Using this display strategy, the Rocchio algorithm (with no explicit feature selection) and the Bayesian algorithm (which implicitly uses all the features incorporated into the distance metric) had a larger number of successful searches. However, this large improvement may be misleading. Firstly, the target is present in an extremely small fraction of the 1024 paths of the tree. Thus, while the "ideal" user is guaranteed to find the target, any deviation by real users from the "ideal" is likely to result in a failed search. RSJ's offer weight selection mechanism is known to be unstable, and coupling this with an exploratory display update strategy led to worse performance.

Generalizing, it is clear that if the user's query is sufficiently accurate, then the initial rank of the target document is likely to be high and scrolling or relevance feedback with a greedy display performs almost equally well. However, if the user's initial query is poor, then scrolling is futile and relevance feedback is required – either with a display strategy that explores larger regions of the search space or a feedback algorithm that does the same.

The end result of our investigations is that inclusion of Relevance Feedback into the retrieval process is not, on average, likely to drastically improve the retrieval effectiveness. It would however by interesting to measure how the utilization of more complicated inter-document properties (apart from the simple cosine distance metric) affects the performance gain. Other future work includes the examination of other display strategies, including hybrid strategies that attempt to optimally combine the exploratory properties of maximizing information gain with the exploitative properties of greedy displays.

References

[1] Buyukkokten, O., Garcia-Molina, H., Paepcke, A. and T. Winograd. Power Browser: Efficient Web Browsing for PDAs. In the Proceedings of the ACM Conference on Computers and Human Interaction (CHI'00), 2000.

[2] Buyukkokten, O., Garcia-Molina, H., and Paepcke, A. Seeing the Whole in Parts: Text Summarization for Web Browsing on Handheld Devices. In the Proceedings of the Tenths International World Wide Web Conference (WWW 10), 2001.

[3] Campbell, I. & van Rijsbergen, C.J. (1996). The Ostensive model of developing information needs. In: Ingwersen, P. & Pors, N.O. (eds.). Information Science: Integration in Perspective. Proceedings of CoLIS 2, p. 251-268

[4] Chen, Y., Ma, W-Y., and Zhang, H-J. Detecting Web Page Structure for Adaptive Viewing on Small Form Factor Devices. In the Proceedings of the Twelfth World Wide Web Conference, Budapest, May 2003 (to appear).

[5] Cox, I. J., Miller, M.L., Minka, T.P., Papathomas, T.V., and Yianilos, P.N. The Bayesian Image Retrieval System, PicHunter: Theory, Implementation and Psychophysical Experiments. IEEE Transactions on Image Processing, 9(1):20-37, 2000.

[6] Evans, D.A. and Lefferts, R.G. CLARIT-TREC experiments. Information Processing and Management, 31(3):494-501, 1995.

[7] Grossman, D.A., Frieder, O., Holmes, D.O., and Roberts, D.C. Integrating Structured Data and Text: A Relational Approach. Journal of the American Society of Information Science, 48(2), February 1997.

[8] Harman, D. Relevance feedback and other query modification techniques. In W. Frakes and R. Baeza-Yates, editors. Information Retrieval. Data Structures and Algorithms. Pages 131-160. Prentice Hall, 1992.

[9] Harman, D. Relevance feedback revisited. Proceedings of 15th annual international ACM SIGIR conference on research and development in information retrieval, Copenhagen, 1.10, 1992.

[10] Jones, M., Marsden, G., Mohd-Nasir, N., and Boone, K., and Buchanan, G. Improving Web Interaction on Small Displays. In the Proceedings of the 8th World Wide Web Conference, Toronto, Canada, May 1999.

[11] Jones, M. and Marsden, G., From the Large Screen to the Small Screen. Retaining the Designer's Design for Effective user Interaction. In IEEE Colloquium on Issues for Networked Interpersonal Communicators. 239(3), pp 1-4., 1997.

[12] Lewis and Ringuette, 1994   David Lewis and Marc Ringuette. A comparison of two learning algorithms for text categorization. In Symposium on Document Analysis and Information Retrieval, 1994.

[13] Magennis, Mark, and van Rijsbergen, Cornelis J. The potential and actual effectiveness of interactive query expansion.   Proceedings of 20th annual international ACM SIGIR conference on research and development in information retrieval, Philadelphia, 1997.

[14] Milic-Frayling, N. and R. Sommerer, R., SmartView: Enhanced document viewer for mobile devices. Microsoft Technical Report MSR-TR-2002-114, November 2002.

[15] Over, P. TREC-5 interactive track report. In Proceedings of the Fifth Text REtrieval Conference (TREC-5), 1996.

[16] Overview of the Fifth Text REtrieval Conference (TREC-5). Edited by D.K. Harman. Gaithersburg, MD: NIST, 1997.

[17] Rocchio, J. Relevance feedback information retrieval. In Gerard Salton (ed.): The Smart Retrieval System — Experiments in Automatic Document Processing, pp. 313–323. Prentice-Hall, Englewood Cliffs, N.J., 1971.

[18] Robertson, S.E., Sparck Jones, K. Relevance weighting of search terms. Journal of the American Society for Information Science 27, 1976, pp. 129-146.

[19] Robertson, S.E. at al. Okapi at TREC-3. In Overview of the Third Text Retrieval Conference (TREC-3). Edited by D.K. Harman. Gaithersburg, MD: NIST, 1995 (NIST Special Publication 500-225).

[20] Robertson, Stephen and Hull, David A. The TREC-9 Filtering Track Final Report. In NIST Special Publication 500-249: The Ninth Text Retrieval Conference (TREC-9). Edited by E.M. Voorhees and D.K. Harman, Gaithersburg, MD, 2000.

[21] Rodden, K., Milic-Frayling, N., Sommerer, R., & Blackwell, A., Effective Web Searching on Mobile Devices. In the *Proceedings of the HCI Conference*, Bath, September 2003.

[22] Ruvini, J-D. Adapting to the User's Internet Search Strategy. IUI'03, Miami, Florida, January 12-15, 2003.

[23] Sellen, A.J., Murphy, R., and Shaw, K.L., How knowledge workers use the web, in D. Wixon (ed.), Proceedings of CHI 2002, ACM, pp 227-234, 2002.

[24] Sparck Jones, K., Walker, S., and Robertson, S.E. A probabilistic model of information retrieval: development and comparative experiments. Information Processing and Management 36 (2000) 779-808, 809-840.

[25] Vinay, V, Cox, I J, Milic-Frayling, N, Wood, K. Evaluating Relevance Feedback and Display Strategies for Searching on Small Displays. SPIRE 2004

[26] White, R.W, Jose, J.M, van Rijsbergen, Cornelis J and Ruthven I, A Simulated Study of Implicit Feedback Models, ECIR 2004

Term Frequency Normalisation Tuning for BM25 and DFR Models

Ben He and Iadh Ounis

Department of Computing Science,
University of Glasgow,
United Kingdom

Abstract. The term frequency normalisation parameter tuning is a crucial issue in information retrieval (IR), which has an important impact on the retrieval performance. The classical pivoted normalisation approach suffers from the collection-dependence problem. As a consequence, it requires relevance assessment for each given collection to obtain the optimal parameter setting. In this paper, we tackle the collection-dependence problem by proposing a new tuning method by measuring the normalisation effect. The proposed method refines and extends our methodology described in [7]. In our experiments, we evaluate our proposed tuning method on various TREC collections, for both the normalisation 2 of the Divergence From Randomness (DFR) models and the BM25's normalisation method. Results show that for both normalisation methods, our tuning method significantly outperforms the robust empirically-obtained baselines over diverse TREC collections, while having a marginal computational cost.

1 Introduction

An Information Retrieval (IR) system receives a query from the user and returns the supposedly relevant documents [8]. A crucial issue underlying an IR system is to rank the returned documents by decreasing order of relevance. For example, recent surveys on the Web show that users rarely look beyond the top returned documents [10]. Usually, ranking is based on a weighting model.

Almost all weighting models take the within document term frequency (tf), the number of occurrences of the given query term in the given document, into consideration as a basic factor for weighting documents. For example, the classical $tf \cdot idf$ weighting formula is the following:

$$w(t, d) = tf \cdot \log \frac{N}{df} \tag{1}$$

where $w(t, d)$ is the weight of document d for term t, N is the number of documents in the collection and df is the document frequency, which is the number of documents containing the term t.

D.E. Losada and J.M. Fernández-Luna (Eds.): ECIR 2005, LNCS 3408, pp. 200–214, 2005.
© Springer-Verlag Berlin Heidelberg 2005

The above $tf \cdot idf$ formula is based on two basic principles of weighting:

- For a given term, the higher its frequency in the collection the less likely it is that it reflects much content.
- For a given term in a given document, the higher the within document term frequency (tf) is, the more information the term carries within the document.

However, the term frequency is dependent on the document length, i.e. the number of tokens in a document, and needs to be normalised by using a technique called *term frequency normalisation*.

In [11], Singhal et. al. gave the following two reasons for the need of the tf normalisation:

- The same term usually occurs repeatedly in long documents.
- A long document has usually a large size of vocabulary.

The two reasons above are based on the observation of term occurrences in the documents. As a consequence, a weighting model without employing a normalisation method, such as $tf \cdot idf$, could produce biased weights with respect to the document length, favouring long documents.

A classical method of the tf normalisation tuning is the *pivoted normalisation* approach proposed by Singhal et. al. [11]. The idea of the pivoted normalisation is to fit the document length distribution to the length distribution of relevant documents. However, since the document length distribution is collection-dependent, the optimal parameter settings on different collections are different. Therefore, it requires relevance assessment on each given collection. This refers to the so-called *collection-dependence problem*. According to the study in [4], there is indeed a need to re-calibrate the tf normalisation parameter for different collections.

For the collection-dependence problem, we have proposed a tuning method by measuring the normalisation effect [7]. The idea is to use a collection-independence measure, namely the normalisation effect, to indicate the optimal parameter settings on diverse collections. In [7], the method has been applied to the *normalisation 2* with the PL2 model. PL2 is one of the divergence from randomness (DFR) document weighting models [2]. Using the PL2 model, the relevance score of a document d for query Q is given by:

$$score(d, Q) = \sum_{t \in Q} w(t, d)$$

$$= \sum_{t \in Q} \frac{1}{tfn + 1} \left(tfn \cdot \log_2 \frac{tfn}{\lambda} + (\lambda + \frac{1}{12 \cdot tfn} - tfn) \cdot \right.$$

$$\left. \log_2 e + 0.5 \cdot \log_2(2\pi \cdot tfn) \right) \qquad (2)$$

where λ is the mean and variance of a Poisson distribution. $w(t, d)$ is the weight of document d for query term t.

The normalised term frequency tfn is given by the *normalisation 2*:

$$tfn = tf \cdot \log_2(1 + c \cdot \frac{avg\_l}{l}), (c > 0) \qquad (3)$$

where l is the document length and avg_l is the average document length in the whole collection. tf is the original term frequency. c is the free parameter of the normalisation method. The experiments in [7] have shown that applying the tuning method by measuring the normalisation effect to the normalisation 2 achieves a robust performance across collections.

However, the tuning method of measuring the normalisation effect also suffers from the following two problems:

1. The tuning method can not be systematically applied to BM25's normalisation method. As one of the most well-established IR systems, Okapi uses BM25 to perform the document ranking, where the *idf* factor $w^{(1)}$ is normalised as follows [9]:

$$w(t,d) = w^{(1)} \frac{(k_1 + 1)tf}{K + tf} \frac{(k_3 + 1)qtf}{k_3 + qtf} \tag{4}$$

   where $w(t,d)$ is the weight of document d for query term t. The sum of $w(t,d)$ of the query terms gives the final weight of document d. K is given by $k_1((1-b)+b\frac{l}{avg\_l})$, where l and avg_l are the document length and the average document length in the collection, respectively. For the parameters k_1 and k_3, the standard setting recommended in [12] are $k_1 = 1.2$ and $k_3 = 1000$. qtf is the number of occurrences of a given term in the query and tf is the within document term frequency of the given term. b is the free parameter of the BM25's term frequency normalisation method, which can be seen as:

$$tfn = \frac{tf}{(1 - b) + b \cdot \frac{l}{avg\_l}} \tag{5}$$

   where tfn is the normalised term frequency.
   As mention in [7], the function defining the normalisation effect is not systematically applicable to BM25 because the parameter b is only valid within $[0, 1]$. However, it was also suggested that it is possible to tackle the problem by proposing an alternative normalisation effect function.
2. For each given collection, the tuning involves the use of real user queries, which is not very practical, especially when such real user queries are not readily available.

In this paper, we aim to tackle the above two problems by improving the tuning method of [7]. First, we propose a new function defining the notion of normalisation effect, which is applicable to the Okapi's BM25 weighting model. We also show that this new function still applies to the normalisation 2. Second, we employ a novel query simulation method that is inspired by the query-based sampling approach described in [3]. Thus, the queries, which are used for document length sampling in a given collection, are created by this simulation method.

In the remainder of this paper, we briefly introduce the tuning method by measuring the normalisation effect in Section 2. By refining and extending this method, we propose a new tuning method in Section 3. In Sections 4 and 5, we provide our experimental setting and evaluation results. Finally, we conclude our work and suggest future work in Section 6.

2   Term Frequency Normalisation Tuning by Measuring Normalisation Effect

The tuning method proposed in [7] is based on measuring the *normalisation effect*, whose optimal value was experimentally shown as a collection-independent constant. The underlying idea of the method is that the effect of a normalisation method, with respect to a specific parameter value, on the term frequency is correlated with the document length distribution in a collection. Since the document length distribution is collection-dependent, the constant optimal normalisation effect corresponds to different parameter values. Thus, the tuning method assumes a constant optimal normalisation effect across collections. For a given collection, it applies the parameter setting such that it gives this constant. The approach has two steps, namely the training step and the tuning step.

In the training step, it obtains the optimal normalisation effect, which was shown experimentally to be a collection-independent constant in [7], on a training collection (e.g. disk1&2 of the TREC collections) with a set of real user queries (e.g. TREC topics 51-200) and their relevance assessment.

In the tuning step, for a given new collection, it samples the document length distribution using a set of real user queries, and then applies the parameter value such that it gives the optimal normalisation effect with respect to the sampled document length.

Then, the normalisation effect (NE) is defined as:

$$NE = \tau \frac{NE_D(\alpha)}{NE_{D,max}(\alpha)} \tag{6}$$

where α is the parameter of the applied tf normalisation method, e.g. the parameter c of the normalisation 2 in Equation (3). τ is 1 if $NE'_D(\alpha) \geq 0$, and -1 if $NE'_D(\alpha) < 0$. $NE_{D,max}(\alpha)$ is the maximum $NE_D(\alpha)$ value with respect to all possible settings of α[1]. The relation $NE_D(\alpha)$ is given by:

$$NE_D(\alpha) = \frac{Var(T_d)}{\mu}, d \in D \tag{7}$$

where D is the set of documents containing at least one of the query terms. Thus, NE_D can be interpreted as the normalisation effect on the document set D. To restrict the size of the set D to a fixed number so that the variance $Var(T_d)$ is not biased by the size of data, similar to the pivoted normalisation approach [11], we divide D into 1000 bins by document length. Each bin contains an equal number of documents, and is represented as a document that has the length of the average document length within the bin. Thus, d represents a bin in D, i.e. it can be seen as a document representing a bin.

For example, assuming that there are 2000 documents in D. If these 2000 documents are divided into 1000 bins by document length, then, each bin contains two documents, and documents with similar length are in the same bin. In

---

[1] In [7], it has been proved that with the use of the normalisation 2, a unique maximum $NE_D(\alpha)$ value does exist.

this case, the first and second shortest documents are in the same bin, the third and fourth shortest ones are in the same bin and so forth.

Moreover, in Equation (7), Var stands for variance. μ is the mean of T_d for all bins in D, where T_d is defined by:

$$T_d = \frac{tfn}{tf} \tag{8}$$

In Equation (8), the normalised term frequency tfn is given by the applied normalisation method, e.g. the normalisation 2 introduced in Section 1. Note that T_d depends only on the applied method's parameter setting and the mean document length within the bin. In the rest of this paper, the notion of bin length refers to the mean document length of the bin.

Having defined the notion of normalisation effect, on a training collection, the approach measures the optimal NE value that is assumed to be a constant. For a new collection, it applies the parameter giving this constant.

The approach has been applied for the normalisation 2 and clearly outperformed the robust empirically-based default setting. However, as introduced in the previous section, it also suffers from the following two problems:

1. The approach can not be systematically applied for BM25 because with the use of BM25, the maximum $NE_D(\alpha)$ value does not exist. This refers to the so-called "out-of-range" problem.
2. The tuning step involves the use of real user queries, which is not practical when not enough real user queries are available.

In the next section, we tackle the first problem by replacing the definition of $NE_D(\alpha)$ in Equation (7) with a new definition, and tackle the second problem by proposing a novel and efficient query simulation method.

3   The New Tuning Approach

In this section, we tackle the two above mentioned problems. In Section 3.1, we tackle the "out-of-range" problem by proposing a new definition for the relation $NE_D(\alpha)$ in Equation (7). In our derivation, we show that this new definition can be applied to both the normalisation 2 and BM25's normalisation method. In Section 3.2, we propose a novel query simulation method. Using this query simulation method, we sample the document length distribution by the simulated queries. Thus, our approach does not involve the need of real user queries in the tuning process.

3.1   Tackling the "Out-of-Range" Problem

The "out-of-range" problem is due to the fact that the parameter b of BM25 ranges only within [0,1]. As a consequence, using the original function of relation $NE_D(\alpha)$ in Equation (7), the b value, giving the maximum $NE_D(b)$, can be out of the range of [0,1]. In this section, we propose a new normalisation effect function by replacing the definition of relation $NE_D(\alpha)$ in Equation (7) with a new one, which can solve the "out-of-range" problem. Our new proposed definition for the relation $NE_D(\alpha)$ is the following:

$$NE_D(\alpha) = Var\left(\frac{T_d}{T_{d,max}}\right), d \in D \qquad (9)$$

where D is the set of documents containing at least one of the query terms. d is a bin in D. $T_{d,max}$ is the maximum T_d among all the bins in D, which is the T_d of the bin with the smallest average document length (the smallest bin length), since $T_d = \frac{tfn}{tf}$ is a decreasing function of document length.

Next, we approximate $NE'_D(\alpha)$, the derivative of function $NE_D(\alpha)$. If this derivative is a monotonic decreasing function of both parameter c of the normalisation 2 and parameter b of BM25, then the unique maximum $NE_D(\alpha)$ value exists, and the new definition can be applied to both normalisation methods. However, according to the definition in Equation (9), it is cumbersome to derive $NE'_D(\alpha)$ directly. To simplify the derivation, we assume a continuous and uniform distribution of T_d from $T_{d,min}$ to 1. $T_{d,min}$ is the minimum T_d in D, which is the T_d of the bin with the largest bin length in D. Although this assumption might not stand in real applications, because we just want to approximate $NE'_D(\alpha)$ to see if it is a monotonic decreasing function of α, this assumption is still applicable. Using the above mentioned assumption, we obtain:

$$NE_D(\alpha) = \sum_D \left(\frac{T_d}{T_{d,max}}\right)^2 - \frac{(\sum_D \frac{T_d}{T_{d,max}})^2}{n}$$

$$\approx \int_{T_{d,min}}^1 \frac{T_d}{T_{d,max}} d(T_d) - \frac{(\int_{T_{d,min}}^1 \frac{T_d}{T_{d,max}} d(T_d))^2}{n}$$

$$\approx \frac{1 - T_{d,min}^3}{3n} - \frac{(1 - T_{d,min})^2}{4n^2} \qquad (10)$$

and the derivative is:

$$NE'_D(\alpha) \approx \left(\frac{1 - T_{d,min}^3}{3n} - \frac{(1 - T_{d,min})^2}{4n^2}\right)'$$

$$= -\frac{T_{d,min}^2}{n} \cdot T'_{d,min} + \frac{(1 - T_{d,min})}{2n^2} \cdot T'_{d,min}$$

$$= \frac{-nT_{d,min}^2 - T_{d,min} + 1}{2n^2} \cdot T'_{d,min} \qquad (11)$$

Using BM25's normalisation method, $T_{d,min}(\alpha)$ becomes

$$T_{d,min}(b) = \frac{1}{(1 - b) + b \cdot \frac{l_{max}}{avg\_l}}, (0 \le b \le 1)$$

and

$$T'_{d,min}(b) < 0$$

Using the normalisation 2, $T_{d,min}(\alpha)$ becomes

$$T_{d,min}(c) = \log_2(1 + c \cdot \frac{avg\_l}{l_{max}}), (c > 0)$$

and

$$T'_{d,min}(c) > 0$$

where l_{max} is the maximum bin length in D.

We can see that using both the normalisation 2 and BM25's normalisation method, $NE'_D(\alpha)$ is a monotonic decreasing function of the parameter of the applied normalisation method. Therefore, the curve of the function $NE_D(\alpha)$ has a bell shape. When $NE'_D(\alpha) = 0$ is satisfied, $NE_D(\alpha)$ is at the peak point of the bell and has its unique maximum value. This demonstrates that our definition for relation $NE_D(\alpha)$ in Equation (9) is applicable to both normalisation methods, i.e. BM25's normalisation method and the DFR normalisation 2.

3.2   Query Simulation for Document Length Sampling

The computation of the normalisation effect needs a set of queries to sample the document length in a given new collection. A possible solution is to use real user queries to obtain the optimal parameter setting for each given collection, which is not practical. Instead, in this paper, we employ a novel query simulation method to sample the document length.

The idea of the proposed query simulation method is to formulate a query with the informative terms from documents that are related to a particular topic. In this way, the simulated queries can be meaningful rather than consisting of stop-words, or unrelated terms. This method is similar to the query-based sampling approach described in [3]. The difference between the two approaches is that our method adopts a term weighting model to extract the most informative terms from the top-ranked documents to formulate a query, while the query-based sampling approach uses the top-ranked documents to get various collection samples.

To simulate a query consisting of exp_term query terms, our query simulation method follows the steps listed below:

1. Randomly choose a seed-term from the vocabulary.
2. Rank the documents containing the seed-term using a specific document weighting function, e.g. PL2 or BM25 introduced in Section 1.
3. Extract the $exp\_term - 1$ most informative terms from the exp_doc top-ranked documents using a specific term weighting model. exp_doc is a parameter of the query simulation method. At this stage, we can use any term weighting model from the literature. In this paper, we apply a particular divergence from randomness (DFR) term weighting model, i.e. Bo1. The reason for using Bo1 is that it is one of the best-performing and stable DFR term weighting models [1]. Using this model, the weight of a term t in the exp_doc top-ranked documents is given by:

$$w(t) = tf_x \cdot \log_2 \frac{1 + P_n}{P_n} + \log_2(1 + P_n) \tag{12}$$

where tf_x is the frequency of the query term in the *exp_doc* top-ranked documents. P_n is given by $\frac{F}{N}$, where F is the term frequency of the query term in the collection and N is the number of documents in the collection.

4. To avoid selecting a junk term as the seed-term, we consider the most informative one of the extracted terms in step 3 as the new seed-term. Note that the original seed-term is discarded at this stage.
5. Repeat steps 2 and 3 to extract the *exp_term* $- 1$ most informative terms from the *exp_doc* top-ranked documents, which are ranked according to the new seed-term.
6. The simulated query consists of the new seed-term and the *exp_term* $- 1$ terms extracted in Step 5.

Adopting the above query simulation method, our new tuning method does not involve the use of real queries.

3.3   The New Tuning Method

Replacing the relation $NE_D(\alpha)$ in Equation (7) with our definition in Equation (9), and adopting the query simulation method proposed in Section 3.2, the new tuning method for the tf normalisation parameter is summarised below:

1. In the training step, on a training collection with a set of training queries, we obtain the optimal parameter setting using relevance assessment, and compute the corresponding optimal NE value that is assumed to be a constant across collections.
2. In the tuning step, on a given new collection, we apply the parameter setting such that it gives the constant optimal NE value obtained in the training step. In this step, the normalisation effect NE is computed over the document length sampled by a set of queries, which are created using the query simulation method proposed in Section 3.2.

In the above algorithm, the NE value is computed using our new normalisation effect function proposed in Section 3.1. Moreover, for a given collection, the tuning process is performed prior to the retrieval process. There is no additional overhead in the retrieval process.

In the following two sections, we introduce our experimental setting and evaluate our new tuning method.

4   Experimental Setting

Our experiments of evaluating the proposed approach are done within the Terrier Information Retrieval (IR) framework developed at the University of Glasgow. Terrier is a modular platform for the rapid development of large-scale IR applications, providing indexing and retrieval functionalities. Terrier is based on the DFR framework. It can index various document collections, including the

Table 1. Details of the four TREC collections used in our experiments. The second row gives the number of topics associated to each collection. N is the number of documents in the given collection. σ_l is the standard deviation of document length in the collection

	disk1&2	disk4&5	WT2G	WT10G
TREC topics	51 - 200	301 - 450 and 601 - 700	401 - 450	451 - 500
N	741860	528155	247491	1692044
σ_l	862.4977	558.1173	2009.3760	2303.4063

standard TREC collections. It also provides a wide range of parameter-free weighting approaches and full-text search algorithms, aiming to offer a public test-bed for performing IR experiments. Further information about Terrier can be found at http://ir.dcs.gla.ac.uk/terrier.

In our experiments, we evaluate our new term frequency (tf) normalisation tuning method on diverse collections. The training collection is the disk1&2 of the classical TREC collections. The reason for using this training collection is that it has a relatively large number of training queries available, which are the TREC topics numbered from 51 to 200. Having obtained the optimal NE value on the training collection using the corresponding relevance assessment, we evaluate our approach on three diverse TREC collections, including the disk4&5 (minus the Congressional Record on disk4) of the classical TREC collection[2], and two TREC Web collections, i.e. the WT2G [6] and the WT10G [5] collections. The test queries are TREC topics that are numbered from 301 to 450 and from 601-700 for the disk4&5, from 401 to 450 for the WT2G, and from 451 to 550 for the WT10G, respectively. Although these collections come with a set of test queries, such real user queries may not be readily available in an operational environment of a search engine. Therefore, it is more practical to employ the query simulation method in the tuning step.

Table 1 lists the test TREC topics, the number of documents, and the standard deviation of document length in each collection. As expected, the document length distribution of the four collections is quite different. In particular, the two Web collections clearly have large standard deviation values of document length compared to the two classical collections. This indicates that the document length distribution of the Web and the classical collections are widely diverse. Therefore, the default parameter setting for the classical collections might not be appropriate for the Web collections. This suggestion is confirmed later in our experiments.

Each TREC topic consists of three fields, i.e. title, description and narrative. In this paper, we experiment with three types of queries with respect to the use of different topic fields, in order to check the impact of query length on the effectiveness of our new tuning method. The three types of queries are:

---

[2] Related information of disk1&2 and disk4&5 of the TREC collections can be found from the following URL: http://trec.nist.gov/data/docs_eng.html

- **Short queries**: Only the title field is used.
- **Normal queries**: Only the description field is used.
- **Long queries**: All the three fields (title, description and narrative) are used.

Our evaluation is done with the use of PL2 and BM25 (see Equations (2) and (4)), respectively. Therefore, we test our new tuning method on both the normalisation 2 and BM25's normalisation method (see Equations (3) and (5)).

Our baselines are the empirical default settings of the two applied normalisation methods. For BM25's normalisation method, we use $b = 0.75$ for the three types of queries, which is the empirically recommended default setting [12]. For the normalisation 2, we use the default setting applied in [1], which is $c = 1$ for short queries and $c = 7$ for long queries. Since [1] does not report experiments using normal queries, we use the optimal parameter setting on the training collection as the baseline, i.e. $c = 1.40$ for normal queries.

For each type of queries, on the training collection, we retrieve documents for the training queries using a particular weighting model, and obtain the optimal parameter setting of the normalisation method of the applied weighting model, using relevance assessment.

In all our experiments, standard stop-words removal and the Porter's stemming algorithm are applied. We used one AMD Athlon 1600 processor, running at 1.4GHz.

For the query simulation approach in the tuning step (Section 3.2), we apply the PL2 DFR model (see Equation (2)) for document ranking and the Bo1 DFR model for term weighting (see Equation (12)). Both models were proposed in [1].

On each collection, we simulate 200 queries to sample the document length. The parameter exp_doc is set to 10. For each query type, exp_term, the number of composing query terms, is randomly chosen between $avql$ and $avql + 1$, where $avql$ stands for the integer part of the average query length of the TREC queries associated to the training collection. For example, the average query length of the long queries associated to the training collection, i.e. disk1&2, is 35.64. Thus, $avql$ is 35. On each collection, the length of a simulated long query is either 35 or 36. In the next section, we report our obtained results.

5   Description of Results

In the training step, on the training collection, we obtain the optimal parameter setting and the corresponding optimal normalisation effect NE using relevance assessment. The obtained results in the training step are listed in table 2.

Moreover, the experiments on the four collections confirm that for both the normalisation 2 and BM25's normalisation method, the corresponding unique maximum $NE_D(\alpha)$ value does exist. Our new normalisation effect function in Equation (9) is indeed applicable to both normalisation methods. The parameter values giving the maximum $NE_D(\alpha)$ value are listed in table 3.

Tables 4, 5 and 6 provide the evaluation results for short, normal and long queries, respectively. In the three tables, the values of the parameter b of BM25's normalisation method and parameter c of the normalisation 2 are obtained using our tuning approach. MAP_d and MAP_t are the mean average precision obtained

Table 2. The optimal NE values and the corresponding parameter values for the training collection with respect to the three types of queries

	Short	Normal	Long
	BM25		
NE	+0.8571	-0.9878	-0.9307
b	0.35	0.65	0.75
	PL2		
NE	-0.9595	+0.9792	-0.9874
c	7	1.40	1

Table 3. The parameter value that gives the unique maximum $NE_D(\alpha)$ with respect to the three types of queries for the four collections used in our experiments

	Short Queries	Normal Queries	Long Queries
	disk1&2		
b	0.55	0.60	0.63
c	2.55	2.14	1.85
	disk4&5		
b	0.59	0.61	0.65
c	1.70	1.53	1.27
	WT2G		
b	0.49	0.57	0.67
c	2.95	2.05	1.29
	WT10G		
b	0.49	0.60	0.69
c	2.71	1.60	0.99

Table 4. Evaluation results for short queries on the three collections

Collection	parameter	MAP_d	MAP_t	Δ (%)	Wilc.
		BM25			
disk4&5	0.40	0.2418	0.2534	+4.80	5.271e-09*
WT2G	0.30	0.2601	0.3161	+21.53	3.598e-06*
WT10G	0.27	0.1868	0.2110	+12.96	2.995e-06*
		PL2			
disk4&5	3.63	0.2570	0.2533	-1.44	2.115e-06*
WT2G	10.99	0.3099	0.3164	+2.10	0.0008*
WT10G	13.13	0.2092	0.2095	≈ 0	0.5746

using the default setting and our tuning method, respectively. Δ (%) is the improvement obtained by our tuning method in percentage. Wilc. stands for the significance values according to the Wilcoxon test. A significance value marked

Table 5. Evaluation results for normal queries on the three collections

Collection	parameter	MAP_d	MAP_t	Δ (%)	Wilc.
BM25					
disk4&5	0.66	0.2461	0.2478	+0.69	0.0005*
WT2G	0.59	0.2527	0.2630	+4.08	0.0104*
WT10G	0.58	0.1776	0.1872	+5.29	0.0004*
PL2					
disk4&5	1.06	0.2361	0.2337	-1.02	0.9676
WT2G	2.33	0.2406	0.2490	+3.49	0.0072*
WT10G	2.65	0.1779	0.1875	+5.40	0.0116*

Table 6. Evaluation results for long queries on the three collections

Collection	parameter	MAP_d	MAP_t	Δ (%)	Wilc.
BM25					
disk4&5	0.76	0.2857	0.2858	≈ 0	0.4652
WT2G	0.73	0.2805	0.2802	≈ 0	0.1402
WT10G	0.70	0.2311	0.2338	+1.17	0.0042*
PL2					
disk4&5	2.23	0.2703	0.2769	+2.44	0.0150*
WT2G	4.80	0.2523	0.2679	+6.18	0.2507
WT10G	5.58	0.2235	0.2288	+2.37	0.6702

Table 7. The computational cost of the tuning process on the three collections for evaluation. The cost is measured in seconds

	Short	Normal	Long
disk4&5			
BM25	182.079s	249.994s	412.694s
PL2	222.955s	266.397s	478.540s
WT2G			
BM25	114.103s	138.249s	215.423s
PL2	240.584s	209.395s	275.028s
WT10G			
BM25	360.879s	672.493s	934.130s
PL2	542.648s	597.100s	981.056s

with a star indicates a statistically significant difference at the 0.05 level. From the results, we have the following observations:

- The tuning method significantly outperforms our baselines in most cases, apart from the 7th row in table 4, where there is a 1.44 percent negative improvement.

Table 8. Results on the WT2G collection obtained by using the query simulation method and the real queries, respectively

Query Type	Real	Sim.	MAP_r	MAP_s
BM25				
Short	0.27	0.30	0.3181	0.3159
Normal	0.59	0.59	0.3161	0.3161
Long	0.75	0.73	0.2805	0.2802
PL2				
Short	10.91	10.99	0.3166	0.3164
Normal	2.19	2.33	0.2483	0.2490
Long	4.28	4.80	0.2698	0.2679

Table 9. Results on the WT10G collection obtained by using the query simulation method and the real queries, respectively

Query Type	Real	Sim.	MAP_r	MAP_s
BM25				
Short	0.24	0.27	0.2112	0.2110
Normal	0.58	0.58	0.1872	0.1872
Long	0.73	0.70	0.2320	0.2338
PL2				
Short	13.29	13.13	0.2095	0.2095
Normal	2.42	2.65	0.1879	0.1875
Long	4.35	5.58	0.2336	0.2288

- Our tuning method works better for the two Web collections than for the disk4&5 of the TREC collection. This confirms our suggestion in the previous section, i.e. the baseline parameter settings for the classical collections might not be appropriate for the Web collections. Consequently, our tuning approach outperforms our baselines on the Web collections.
- For the normalisation 2, it seems that our tuning method works the best for long queries, while it achieves comparable performance with the baseline for short and normal queries.
- On the contrary, for BM25's normalisation method, our tuning method works better for short queries, although its performance with normal and long queries is at least as good as the baseline.

We report also the efficiency of our tuning method. Table 7 provides the computational cost of our tuning process for the three types of queries. As shown in the table, the cost of the tuning process is insignificant. Note that on a particular collection and for a particular type of queries, we only need to run the tuning process once during the indexing process.

To test our query simulation method of Section 3.2, we compared the results obtained by using two different sampling methods, i.e. query simulation and the real provided TREC queries, on the three test collections. Because of the space limitation, we only report the results on the WT2G and WT10G collections. In tables 8 and 9, the second and the fourth columns correspond to the parameter values and mean average precision obtained using the real queries, respectively; the third and fifth columns correspond to the results obtained by the query simulation method. As shown in the tables, we find almost no difference between the obtained results, excepting the result for long queries using PL2 on WT10G. In this case, the simulated queries perform slightly less compared to the real queries. Note that both sampling methods result in a better retrieval performance than our robust baselines (see tables 4, 5 and 6).

In summary, our new normalisation effect function (see Equation (9)) is applicable to both PL2 and BM25. Moreover, adopting our query simulation method of Section 3.2, the tuning step does not involve the use of real user queries. This simulation method successfully samples the document length leading to an optimised tuning of the tf normalisation parameter as shown in the obtained results. According to the experiments, the new tuning method achieves robust and effective retrieval performance over the three diverse TREC collections with a marginal computational cost.

6   Conclusions and Future Directions

In this paper, we have proposed a term frequency (tf) normalisation tuning method, which refines and extends our methodology proposed in [7]. We have applied a new normalisation effect function by changing the definition of relation $NE_D(\alpha)$, i.e. the normalisation effect on the set of documents with at least one query term, such that the application of the tuning method can be extended to BM25. We have also proposed a novel query simulation method to avoid the use of real user queries in the tuning step.

Using various and diverse TREC collections, we have evaluated our new tuning method using both the normalisation 2 and BM25's normalisation method. In particular, by extending the application of the tuning method to BM25, the flexibility of the methodology in [7] has been significantly enhanced.

Compared to the used robust baselines, which are the empirically-based recommended parameter settings of the two applied normalisation methods, our new tuning method achieves robust and effective retrieval performance. Indeed, the results show that our method is at least as good as the baselines, and significantly outperforms them in most cases. Moreover, the computational cost of our tuning process is marginal.

In the future, we will investigate further applications of the tuning method by measuring the normalisation effect. In particular, we are currently investigating the application of our tuning method in the context of XML retrieval and intranet search. Moreover, so far, the tuning method has only been evaluated for ad-hoc tasks. We plan to apply the tuning method to other tasks, such as topic-distillation and named-page finding tasks.

Acknowledgments

This work is funded by the Leverhulme Trust, grant number F/00179/S. The project funds the development of the Smooth project, which investigates the term frequency normalisation (URL: http://ir.dcs.gla.ac.uk/smooth). The experimental part of this paper has been conducted using the Terrier framework (EPSRC, grant GR/R90543/01, URL: http://ir.dcs.gla.ac.uk/terrier).

References

1. G. Amati. *Probabilistic Models for Information Retrieval based on Divergence from Randomness*. PhD thesis, Department of Computing Science, University of Glasgow, 2003.
2. G. Amati and C. J. van Rijsbergen. Probabilistic models of information retrieval based on measuring the divergence from randomness. In *ACM Transactions on Information Systems (TOIS)*, volume 20(4), pages 357 – 389, 2002.
3. J. Callan and M. Connell. Query-based sampling of text databases. In *ACM Transactions on Information Systems (TOIS)*, pages 97 – 130, Volume 19, Issue 2, April, 2001.
4. A. Chowdhury, M. C. McCabe, D. Grossman, and O. Frieder. Document normalization revisited. In *Proceedings of the 25th Annual International ACM SIGIR Conference on Research and Development in Information Retrieval*, pages 381–382, Tampere, Finland, 2002.
5. D. Hawking. Overview of the TREC-9 Web Track. In *Proceedings of the Nineth Text REtrieval Conference (TREC-9)*, pages 87 – 94, Gaithersburg, MD, 2000.
6. D. Hawking, E. Voorhees, N. Craswell, and P. Bailey. Overview of the TREC-8 Web Track. In *Proceedings of the Eighth Text REtrieval Conference (TREC-8)*, pages 131 – 150, Gaithersburg, MD, 1999.
7. B. He and I. Ounis. A study of parameter tuning for term frequency normalization. In *Proceedings of the Twelveth ACM CIKM International Conference on Information and Knowledge Management*, pages 10 – 16, New Orleans, LA, 2003.
8. C. J. van Rijsbergen. *Information Retrieval, 2nd edition*. Department of Computer Science, University of Glasgow, 1979.
9. S. Robertson, S. Walker, M. M. Beaulieu, M. Gatford, and A. Payne. Okapi at TREC-4. In *NIST Special Publication 500-236: The Fourth Text REtrieval Conference (TREC-4)*, pages 73 – 96, Gaithersburg, MD, 1995.
10. C. Silverstein, M. R. Henzinger, H. Marais, and M. Moricz. Analysis of a very large web search engine query log. *SIGIR Forum*, 33(1):6–12, 1999.
11. A. Singhal, C. Buckley, and M. Mitra. Pivoted document length normalization. In *Proceedings of the 19th Annual International ACM SIGIR Conference on Research and Development in Information Retrieval*, pages 21–29, 1996.
12. K. Sparck-Jones, S. Walker, and S. E. Robertson. A probabilistic model of information retrieval: Development and comparative experiments. *Information Processing and Management*, 36(2000):779 – 840, 2000.

Improving the Context-Based Influence Diagram Model for Structured Document Retrieval: Removing Topological Restrictions and Adding New Evaluation Methods

Luis M. de Campos, Juan M. Fernández-Luna, and Juan F. Huete

Departamento de Ciencias de la Computación e Inteligencia Artificial,
E.T.S.I. Informática, Universidad de Granada, 18071 – Granada, Spain
{lci, jmfluna, jhg}@decsai.ugr.es

Abstract. In this paper we present the theoretical developments necessary to extend the existing Context-based Influence Diagram Model for Structured Documents (CID model), in order to improve its retrieval performance and expressiveness. Firstly, we make it more flexible and general by removing the original restrictions on the type of structured documents that CID represents. This extension requires the design of a new algorithm to compute the posterior probabilities of relevance. Another contribution is related to the evaluation of the influence diagram. The computation of the expected utilities in the original CID model was approximated by applying an independence criterion. We present another approximation that does not assume independence, as well as an exact evaluation method.

1 Introduction

Document collections in the Information Retrieval (IR) field have been considered as composed of only textual information for a long time [1]. Information Retrieval Systems (IRS) represented their contents by means of index terms, and they were mostly the only tool to retrieve the relevant documents given the users' information needs. Nowadays, the internal structure of these documents is taking more and more importance, basically due to the development of new formalisms, like SGML and XML, that contribute with features to easily represent a well defined structure, in order to organize the document contents comprehensibly and also to facilitate the reading to the user. Therefore, the aim of new IRSs has changed: by also using the document organization, instead of returning a relevant document as a whole, these applications will retrieve the set of document components (structural units) more relevant to a query (chapters, sections, or paragraphs in a book, for example), giving as a result a new research subarea on structured documents [2].

Classical probabilistic IRSs [4] rank the documents by considering their probability of relevance to a given query. In these systems, the action of retrieving (or not) a document is independent on the action of retrieving (or not) any other

D.E. Losada and J.M. Fernández-Luna (Eds.): ECIR 2005, LNCS 3408, pp. 215–229, 2005.

216 L.M. de Campos, J.M. Fernández-Luna, and J.F. Huete

document. However, this is no longer true when dealing with structured documents, where the decision about retrieving a document component clearly may affect the retrieval of other components (for example, it makes no sense to retrieve two sections of a chapter and also the complete chapter itself). Therefore, it is clear that not only the probability of relevance has to be used to retrieve the document components, but we could also use the *usefulness* of these components for the user, taking into account the context where they are placed and what has been previously retrieved.

Following this direction, the Context-based Influence Diagram model for Structured Documents (CID model) [6] was born with the capability of making decisions about which document components should be retrieved, not only depending on their probability of relevance, but also on their *utility* for the user and the influences provided by the context in which each structural component is located. This is carried out by means of an *Influence Diagram* (ID) [11], a generalization of the well founded Bayesian network formalism [13] in the context of Decision Theory [8]. Examples in the specialised literature about the application of Bayesian networks to Structured Information Retrieval are [3, 9, 12, 14], although the CID model is the only one, as far as we know, that applies IDs.

However, the CID model presents an important restriction on the structure of the documents that it can represent: the documents have to be composed of a strict set of structural layers. So, the structural units from the j-th layer (all of them being of the same type) must be included in broader units from the $(j-1)$-th layer and so on (except for the units from the first layer). The last layer would contain the smallest structural units, composed only of text and not of other units. The CID model was endowed with an efficient propagation algorithm to compute the posterior probability of relevance of each unit given a query, which was specifically designed to deal with this strict structure. In this paper we extend this model to work with a general document organization, where the rule of strict layers is broken and textual units can be placed anywhere as well, reformulating the original propagation algorithm.

A second contribution is the development of two new mechanisms to evaluate the underlying influence diagram of the CID model. Solving an ID means to determine the expected utility of each one of the possible decisions, for those situations of interest, with the aim of making decisions which maximize the expected utility [15]. The expected utility in the CID model depends on the bi-dimensional posterior probabilities, corresponding to each structural unit and the unit where it is contained. In [6], and in order to simplify the computations, it was assumed that the two involved units were independent given the query, so the bi-dimensional distributions could be approximated just multiplying the unidimensional posterior probabilities of each unit given the query. In this paper we present, on the one hand, an exact evaluation method that computes the bi-dimensional distributions and, on the other hand, another efficient and more precise approximated evaluation method.

In order to describe precisely these ideas and formalize them, this paper is organised in the following way: In Section 2 we briefly introduce some preliminary concepts: we assume a basic knowledge about Bayesian networks to the reader and only provide some background about influence diagrams. Section 3 describes the type of structured documents being considered. The next two sections introduce the model: Section 4 presents the Bayesian network that graphically represents the structure of the documents, and the corresponding influence diagram is described in Section 5. Section 6 explains how to use the model for retrieval purposes by computing the expected utilities of the document components. Formulas for the posterior probabilities which are necessary to carry out this computation are described in Section 7. Section 8 gives an illustrative example. Finally, Section 9 contains the concluding remarks.

2   Background: Influence Diagrams

Influence Diagrams [11, 16] are probabilistic graphical models that provide a simple notation for designing decision models by clarifying the qualitative issues of what factors need to be considered and how they are related, i.e. an intuitive representation of the model. They have also associated an underlying quantitative representation in order to measure the strength of the relationships: we can quantify uncertain interactions among random variables and also the decision maker's options and preferences. The model is used to determine the optimal decision policy. IDs contain three types of nodes: (a) *Decision nodes* (drawn as rectangles) represent variables that the decision maker controls directly, and model the decision alternatives available for the decision maker. (b) *Chance nodes* (drawn as circles) represent random variables, i.e. uncertain quantities that are relevant to the decision problem and can not be controlled directly, quantified by means of conditional probability distributions. (c) *Utility nodes* (drawn as diamonds) represent utility, i.e. express the profit or the preference degree of the consequences derived of the decision process, and are quantified by the utility of each of the possible combinations of outcomes of their parent nodes.

There are also different types of arcs in an influence diagram: arcs between chance nodes represent probabilistic dependences (note that the subgraph containing only chance nodes and the related arcs is a Bayesian network). Arcs from a decision node to a chance node or to a utility node establish that the future decision will influence the value of the chance node or in the profit obtained, respectively. Finally, arcs from a chance node to a utility node will express that the profit will depend on the value that this chance node takes.

3   Type of Structured Documents

We start with a document collection containing M *documents*, $\mathcal{D}=\{D_1,\ldots,D_M\}$, and the set of the *terms* used to index these documents (the glossary of the collection). We assume that each document D_i is organized hierarchically, representing structural associations of elements in D_i, which will be called *structural units*. Each structural unit is composed of other smaller structural units, except some

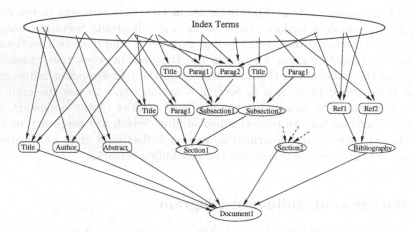

Fig. 1. Example of the structure of a scientific article

'terminal' or 'minimal' units which are indivisible, they do not contain any other unit. Instead, these are composed of terms: each term used to index the complete document D_i will be assigned to all the terminal units containing it. Conversely, each structural unit, except the one corresponding to the complete document, is included in only one structural unit. Therefore, the structural units associated to a document D_i form a (inverted) tree. There is not any restriction about this tree structure, which contrasts with the rigid structure considered in [6], where all the paths from the root to the leaves have the same length.

For instance, a scientific article may contain a title, authors, abstract, sections and bibliography; sections may contain a title, subsections and paragraphs; in turn subsections contain paragraphs and perhaps also a title; the bibliography contains references; titles, authors, paragraphs, abstract and references would be in this case the terminal structural units (see Figure 1).

4   The Underlying Bayesian Network

The Bayesian network will contain two kinds of nodes, representing the terms and the structural units. The former will be represented by the set $\mathcal{T} = \{T_1, T_2, \ldots, T_l\}$. There are two types of structural units: *basic structural units*, those which only contain terms, and *complex structural units*, that are composed of other basic or complex units. The notation for these nodes is $\mathcal{U}_b = \{B_1, B_2, \ldots, B_m\}$ and $\mathcal{U}_c = \{S_1, S_2, \ldots, S_n\}$, respectively. Therefore, the set of all structural units is $\mathcal{U} = \mathcal{U}_b \cup \mathcal{U}_c$. In this paper, T or T_k will represent a term; B or B_i a basic structural unit, and S or S_j a complex structural unit. Generic structural units (either basic or complex) will be denoted as U_i or U. Each node T, B or S has associated a binary random variable[1], which can take its values from the

---

[1] In this paper, the random variable and its associated node in the graph will be noted identically.

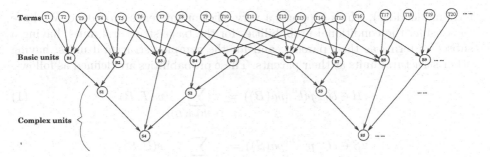

Fig. 2. Bayesian network representing a structured document collection

sets $\{t^-, t^+\}$, $\{b^-, b^+\}$ or $\{s^-, s^+\}$ (the term/unit is not relevant or is relevant), respectively. A unit is relevant for a given query if it satisfies the user's information need expressed by this query. A term is relevant in the sense that the user believes that it will appear in relevant units/documents.

Regarding the arcs of the model, there is an arc from a given node (either term or structural unit) to the particular structural unit node it belongs to, expressing the fact that the relevance of a given structural unit to the user will depend on the relevance values of the different elements (units or terms) that comprise it. It should be noted that with this criteria, terms nodes have no parents. Formally, the network is characterized by the following parent sets, $Pa(.)$:

- $\forall T \in \mathcal{T}$, $Pa(T) = \emptyset$.
- $\forall B \in \mathcal{U}_b$, $\emptyset \neq Pa(B) \subseteq \mathcal{T}$.
- $\forall S \in \mathcal{U}_c$, $\emptyset \neq Pa(S) \subseteq \mathcal{U}_b \cup \mathcal{U}_c$, with $Pa(S_1) \cap Pa(S_2) = \emptyset$, $\forall S_1 \neq S_2 \in \mathcal{U}_c$.

It should be noticed that the hierarchical structure of the model determines that each structural unit $U \in \mathcal{U}$ has only one structural unit as its child, the unique structural unit containing U (except for the leaf nodes, i.e. the complete documents, which have no child). We shall denote indistinctly by $Hi(U)$ or $U_{hi(U)}$ the single child node associated with node U (with $Hi(U) = null$ if U is a leaf node). Figure 2 displays an example of the proposed network topology.

The numerical values for the conditional probabilities have also to be assessed: $p(t^+)$, $p(b^+|pa(B))$, $p(s^+|pa(S))$, for every node in $\mathcal{T}$, $\mathcal{U}_b$ and $\mathcal{U}_c$, respectively, and every configuration of the corresponding parent sets ($pa(X)$ denotes a configuration or instantiation of the parent set of X, $Pa(X)$). Once specified, the network may be used to compute the posterior probabilities of relevance of all the structural units $U \in \mathcal{U}$ for a given query.

In our case, the number of terms and structural units considered may be quite large (thousands or even hundreds of thousands). Moreover, the topology of the Bayesian network contains multiple pathways connecting nodes (because the terms may be associated to different basic structural units) and possibly nodes with a great number of parents (so that it can be quite difficult to assess and store the required conditional probability tables). For these reasons we shall use the canonical model to represent the conditional probabilities proposed in [5] (as the

CID model does), which supports a very efficient inference procedure. We have to consider the conditional probabilities for the basic structural units, having a subset of terms as their parents, and for the complex structural units, having other structural units as their parents. These probabilities are defined as follows:

$$\forall B \in \mathcal{U}_b,\, p(b^+|pa(B)) = \sum_{T \in R(pa(B))} w(T, B),\tag{1}$$

$$\forall S \in \mathcal{U}_c,\, p(s^+|pa(S)) = \sum_{U \in R(pa(S))} w(U, S),\tag{2}$$

where $w(T, B)$ is a weight associated to each term T belonging to the basic unit B, $w(U, S)$ is a weight measuring the importance of the unit U within S. In any case $R(pa(U))$ is the subset of parents of U (terms for B, and either basic or complex units for S) relevant in the configuration $pa(U)$, i.e., $R(pa(B)) = \{T \in Pa(B)\,|\,t^+ \in pa(B)\}$ and $R(pa(S)) = \{U \in Pa(S)\,|\,u^+ \in pa(S)\}$. So, the more parents of U are relevant the greater the probability of relevance of U. These weights can be defined in any way, the only restrictions are that $w(T, B) \geq 0$, $w(U, S) \geq 0$, $\sum_{T \in Pa(B)} w(T, B) \leq 1$, and $\sum_{U \in Pa(S)} w(U, S) \leq 1$. For example, they can be defined using a normalized tf-idf scheme, as in [6], or we could also consider the relative importance of each type of unit (for example, the title or the abstract could be more representative of the content of a document than a section).

With respect to the prior probabilities of relevance of the terms, $p(t^+)$, they can also be defined in any reasonable way, for example an identical probability for all the terms, $p(t^+) = p_0,\, \forall T \in \mathcal{T}$, as proposed in [6].

5   The Influence Diagram Model

Once the Bayesian network has been constructed, it is enlarged by including decision and utility nodes, thus transforming it into an influence diagram. We use the same topology proposed in [6] for the CID model: a) *Decision nodes*: One decision node, R_i, for each structural unit $U_i \in \mathcal{U}$. R_i represents the decision variable related to whether or not to return the structural unit U_i to the user. The two different values for R_i are r_i^+ and r_i^-, meaning 'retrieve U_i' and 'do not retrieve U_i', respectively. b) *Utility nodes*: One of these, V_i, for each structural unit $U_i \in \mathcal{U}$, will measure the value of utility of the corresponding decision.

In addition to the arcs between chance nodes (already present in the Bayesian network), a set of arcs pointing to utility nodes are also included, employed to indicate which variables have a direct influence on the desirability of a given decision, i.e. the profit obtained will depend on the value of these variables. In order to represent that the utility function of V_i obviously depends on the decision made and the relevance value of the structural unit considered, we use arcs from each chance node U_i and decision node R_i to the utility node V_i. Another important set of arcs are those going from $Hi(U_i)$ to V_i, which represent that the utility of the decision about retrieving the unit U_i also depends on the relevance of the unit which contains it (obviously, for the units which are

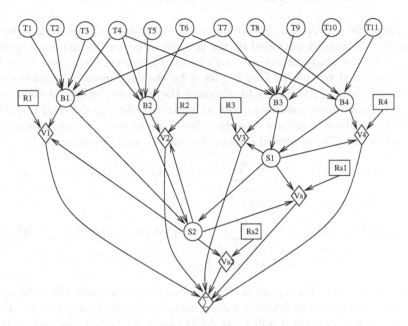

Fig. 3. Topology of the influence diagram

not contained in any other unit these arcs do not exist). This last kind of arc allows us to represent the context-based information and can avoid redundant information being shown to the user. For instance, we could express the fact that on the one hand, if U_i is relevant and $Hi(U_i)$ is not, then the utility of retrieving U_i should be large (and the one of not retrieving it almost null). On the other hand, if $Hi(U_i)$ is relevant, even if U_i were also relevant the utility of retrieving U_i should be small because, in this case, it would be preferable to retrieve the largest unit as a whole, instead of each of its components separately.

Another utility node, denoted by Σ, that represents the joint utility of the whole model is also considered. It has all the utility nodes V_j as its parents. These arcs represent the fact that the joint utility of the model will depend (additively) on the values of the individual utilities of each structural unit. Figure 3 displays an example of the topology of the influence diagram being considered.

Moreover, the influence diagram requires numerical values for the utilities. For each utility node V_i we need eight numbers, one for each combination of values of the decision node R_i and the chance nodes U_i and $Hi(U_i)$ (except for the leaf nodes, which only require four values). These values are represented by $v(r_i, u_i, u_{hi(U_i)})$, with $r_i \in \{r_i^-, r_i^+\}$, $u_i \in \{u_i^-, u_i^+\}$, and $u_{hi(U_i)} \in \{u_{hi(U_i)}^-, u_{hi(U_i)}^+\}$.

6   Solving the Influence Diagram

To solve an influence diagram, the expected utility of each possible decision (for those situations of interest) has to be computed, thus making decisions which maximize the expected utility. In our case, the situation of interest corresponds with the information provided by the user when he/she formulates a query. Let $\mathcal{Q} \subseteq \mathcal{T}$ be the set of terms used to express the query. Each term $T_i \in \mathcal{Q}$ will be instantiated to either t_i^+ or t_i^-; let q be the corresponding configuration of the variables in $\mathcal{Q}$. We wish to compute the expected utility of each decision given q. As we have assumed a global additive utility model, and the different decision variables R_i are not directly linked to each other, we can process each one independently. The expected utilities for each U_i can be computed by means of

$$EU(r_i^+ \mid q) = \sum_{\substack{u_i \in \{u_i^-, u_i^+\} \\ u_{hi(U_i)} \in \{u_{hi(U_i)}^-, u_{hi(U_i)}^+\}}} v(r_i^+, u_i, u_{hi(U_i)}) \, p(u_i, u_{hi(U_i)} \mid q). \quad (3)$$

$$EU(r_i^- \mid q) = \sum_{\substack{u_i \in \{u_i^-, u_i^+\} \\ u_{hi(U_i)} \in \{u_{hi(U_i)}^-, u_{hi(U_i)}^+\}}} v(r_i^-, u_i, u_{hi(U_i)}) \, p(u_i, u_{hi(U_i)} \mid q). \quad (4)$$

In the context of a typical decision making problem, once the expected utilities are computed, the decision with greatest utility is chosen: this would mean to retrieve the structural unit U_i if $EU(r_i^+|q) \geq EU(r_i^-|q)$, and not to retrieve it otherwise. However, our purpose is not only to make decisions about what to retrieve but also to give a ranking of those units. The simplest way to do it is to show them in decreasing order of the utility of retrieving U_i, $EU(r_i^+|q)^2$. In this case only four utility values have to be assessed, and only eq. (3) is required.

7   Computing Probabilities

In order to provide to the user an ordered list of structural units, we have to be able to compute the posterior probabilities of relevance of all the structural units $U \in \mathcal{U}$, $p(u^+|q)$, and also the bi-dimensional posterior probabilities, $p(u^+, u_{hi(U)}^+|q)^3$. The specific characteristics of the canonical model used to define the conditional probabilities will allow us to efficiently compute the posterior probabilities[4].

7.1   Calculus of Unidimensional Posterior Probabilities

Proposition 1

$$\forall B \in \mathcal{U}_b, \;\; p(b^+|q) = \sum_{T \in Pa(B) \setminus \mathcal{Q}} w(T, B) \, p(t^+) + \sum_{T \in Pa(B) \cap R(q)} w(T, B). \quad (5)$$

---

[2] Other options would also be possible to generate a ranking, as for example to use the difference between both expected utilities, $EU(r_i^+|q) - EU(r_i^-|q)$.

[3] Notice that the other required bi-dimensional probabilities, $p(u^+, u_{hi(U)}^-|q)$, $p(u^-, u_{hi(U)}^+|q)$ and $p(u^-, u_{hi(U)}^-|q)$, can be easily computed from $p(u^+, u_{hi(U)}^+|q)$, $p(u^+|q)$ and $p(u_{hi(U)}^+|q)$.

[4] Proofs of the results stated in the paper are not included due to space limitations. They can be found in [7].

$$\forall S \in \mathcal{U}_c, \ p(s^+|q) = \sum_{U \in Pa(S)} w(U,S) \, p(u^+|q) \,. \tag{6}$$

As we can see, the posterior probabilities of the basic units can be computed directly. The posterior probabilities of the complex units can be calculated in a top-down manner, starting from those for the basic units. However, it is possible to design a more direct inference method. We need some additional notation: $\forall S \in \mathcal{U}_c$, let $A_b(S) = \{B \in \mathcal{U}_b \,|\, B$ is an ancestor of $S\}$, $A_c(S) = \{S' \in \mathcal{U}_c \,|\, S'$ is an ancestor of $S\}$, and $\forall B \in \mathcal{U}_b$, let $D_c(B) = \{S \in \mathcal{U}_c \,|\, S$ is a descendant of $B\}$. Notice that, for each basic unit B in $A_b(S)$, there is only one path going from B to S. Let us define the weight $w(B,S)$ as the product of the weights of the arcs in the path from B to S, i.e. $w(B,S) = w(B, Hi(B)) \prod_{S' \in A_c(S) \cap D_c(B)} w(S', Hi(S'))$. Then, we get the following result:

Proposition 2

$$\forall S \in \mathcal{U}_c, \ p(s^+|q) = \sum_{B \in A_b(S)} w(B,S) \, p(b^+|q) \,. \tag{7}$$

Proposition 2 states that we can compute the posterior probability of a complex structural unit S by calculating the average of the posterior probabilities of all the basic structural units B contained in S, each probability being weighted by the product of the weights of the arcs in the (single) path going from B to S. This result is the basis to develop an inference process able to compute all the posterior probabilities of the structural units in a single traversal of the graph, starting only from the instantiated terms in $\mathcal{Q}$, provided that the prior probabilities of relevance have been calculated and stored within the structure:

Proposition 3

$$\forall B \in \mathcal{U}_b, \ p(b^+|q) = p(b^+) + \sum_{T \in Pa(B) \cap R(q)} w(T,B) \, (1 - p(t^+)) - \sum_{T \in Pa(B) \cap (Q \setminus R(q))} w(T,B) \, p(t^+) \tag{8}$$

$$\forall S \in \mathcal{U}_c, \ p(s^+|q) = p(s^+) + \sum_{\substack{B \in A_b(S) \\ Pa(B) \cap Q \neq \emptyset}} w(B,S) \, (p(b^+|q) - p(b^+)) \,. \tag{9}$$

This result indicates how we can compute the posterior probabilities from the prior probabilities traversing the nodes in the graph that will require updating. An algorithm that computes all the posterior probabilities $p(b^+|q)$ and $p(s^+|q)$, based on Proposition 3, starts from the terms in $\mathcal{Q}$ and carries out a width graph traversal until it reaches the basic units that require updating, computing $p(b^+|q)$ using eq. (8). Starting from these modified basic units, it carries out a depth graph traversal to compute $p(s^+|q)$, only for those complex units that require updating, using eq. (9). This algorithm needs the previous computation and storage of the nodes' prior probabilities. This can be done easily using Propositions 1 and 2 (with $q = \emptyset$).

7.2   Calculus of Bi-dimensional Posterior Probabilities

Now, the required probabilities are the posterior bi-dimensional probabilities $p(u^+, u^+_{hi(U)}|q)$, for any structural unit $U \in \mathcal{U}$ and its unique child $U_{hi(U)}$, provided that $U_{hi(U)} \neq null$. We have to distinguish two cases, depending on whether U is a basic unit ($U \in \mathcal{U}_b$) or a complex unit ($U \in \mathcal{U}_c$). The following two propositions provide formulas to compute these bi-dimensional probabilities.

Proposition 4. $\forall S \in \mathcal{U}_c$, $\forall B \in \mathcal{U}_b$ such that $B \in Pa(S)$,

$$p(s^+, b^+|q) = \sum_{\substack{B_i \in A_b(S) \\ B_i \neq B}} w(B_i, S)\, p(b^+_i, b^+|q) \;+\; w(B, S) p(b^+|q). \tag{10}$$

Proposition 5. $\forall S_1, S_2 \in \mathcal{U}_c$ such that $S_1 \in Pa(S_2)$,

$$p(s^+_1, s^+_2|q) = \sum_{B_1 \in A_b(S_1)} \sum_{B_2 \in A_b(S_2) \backslash A_b(S_1)} w(B_1, S_1) w(B_2, S_2)\, p(b^+_1, b^+_2|q) + w(S_1, S_2) p(s^+_1|q).$$

$$\tag{11}$$

These results, which are analogous to Proposition 2 in the unidimensional case, show that we can compute the required bi-dimensional probabilities as soon as we compute the bi-dimensional probabilities for pairs of basic structural units in $\mathcal{U}_b$ and the unidimensional probabilities of all the structural units in $\mathcal{U}_b \cup \mathcal{U}_c$. The following proposition shows how these bi-dimensional probabilities for pairs of basic structural units can be computed.

Proposition 6. $\forall B_1, B_2 \in \mathcal{U}_b$, let us define

$$\delta(B_1, B_2|q) = \sum_{T \in (Pa(B_1) \cap Pa(B_2)) \backslash \mathcal{Q}} w(T, B_1) w(T, B_2)\, p(t^+)(1 - p(t^+)). \tag{12}$$

Then
$$
\begin{aligned}
p(b^+_1, b^+_2|q) &= p(b^+_1|q)\, p(b^+_2|q) + \delta(B_1, B_2|q) \\
p(b^+_1, b^-_2|q) &= p(b^+_1|q)\, p(b^-_2|q) - \delta(B_1, B_2|q) \\
p(b^-_1, b^+_2|q) &= p(b^-_1|q)\, p(b^+_2|q) - \delta(B_1, B_2|q) \\
p(b^-_1, b^-_2|q) &= p(b^-_1|q)\, p(b^-_2|q) + \delta(B_1, B_2|q)
\end{aligned}
\tag{13}
$$

The results in Proposition 6 state that the bi-dimensional probabilities can be expressed as the product of the unidimensional probabilities, plus a factor that outweighs the common relevance or irrelevance of the units and penalizes relevance of one unit and irrelevance of the other. This factor, $\delta(B_1, B_2|q)$, depends essentially of the number of common terms for B_1 and B_2 which are not instantiated. So, if two basic units do not share any term, or all the shared terms are instantiated, $\delta(B_1, B_2|q) = 0$ and the units are independent. On the other hand, the more uninstantiated terms share B_1 and B_2, the greater $\delta(B_1, B_2|q)$ and the more degree of dependence between these units exists.

This way of expressing the bi-dimensional probabilities of the basic units as a product of marginals plus an interaction factor, can be extended to the other cases, as the following two propositions show.

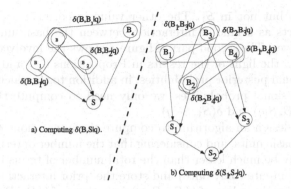

Fig. 4. Graphical representations of some δ interactions

Proposition 7. $\forall S \in \mathcal{U}_c$, $\forall B \in \mathcal{U}_b$ such that $B \in Pa(S)$, let us define

$$\delta(B, S|q) = \sum_{\substack{B_i \in A_b(S) \\ B_i \neq B}} w(B_i, S)\, \delta(B, B_i|q). \tag{14}$$

Then

$$p(s^+, b^+|q) = p(s^+|q)\, p(b^+|q) + \delta(B, S|q) + w(B, S)\, p(b^+|q)\, (1 - p(b^+|q)) \tag{15}$$
$$p(s^+, b^-|q) = p(s^+|q)\, p(b^-|q) - \delta(B, S|q) - w(B, S)\, p(b^+|q)\, (1 - p(b^+|q))$$
$$p(s^-, b^+|q) = p(s^-|q)\, p(b^+|q) - \delta(B, S|q) - w(B, S)\, p(b^+|q)\, (1 - p(b^+|q))$$
$$p(s^-, b^-|q) = p(s^-|q)\, p(b^-|q) + \delta(B, S|q) + w(B, S)\, p(b^+|q)\, (1 - p(b^+|q))$$

The interaction factor between a complex unit S and a basic unit B, $\delta(B, S|q)$, is a weighted average of the interaction factors between B and the basic units (different from B) included in S. The other value in eq. (15), $w(B, S)p(b^+|q)(1 - p(b^+|q))$, can be considered as a kind of interaction of B with itself. The first part of figure 4 shows the interactions computed according to eq. (15).

Proposition 8. $\forall S_1, S_2 \in \mathcal{U}_c$ such that $S_1 \in Pa(S_2)$, let us define

$$\delta(S_1, S_2|q) = \sum_{B_1 \in A_b(S_1)} \sum_{B_2 \in A_b(S_2) \backslash A_b(S_1)} w(B_1, S_1) w(B_2, S_2)\, \delta(B_1, B_2|q). \tag{16}$$

Then

$$p(s_1^+, s_2^+|q) = p(s_1^+|q)\, p(s_2^+|q) + \delta(S_1, S_2|q) + w(S_1, S_2)\, p(s_1^+|q)\, (1 - p(s_1^+|q)) \tag{17}$$
$$p(s_1^+, s_2^-|q) = p(s_1^+|q)\, p(s_2^-|q) - \delta(S_1, S_2|q) - w(S_1, S_2)\, p(s_1^+|q)\, (1 - p(s_1^+|q))$$
$$p(s_1^-, s_2^+|q) = p(s_1^-|q)\, p(s_2^+|q) - \delta(S_1, S_2|q) - w(S_1, S_2)\, p(s_1^+|q)\, (1 - p(s_1^+|q))$$
$$p(s_1^-, s_2^-|q) = p(s_1^-|q)\, p(s_2^-|q) + \delta(S_1, S_2|q) + w(S_1, S_2)\, p(s_1^+|q)\, (1 - p(s_1^+|q))$$

The interaction factor between two complex units S_1 ans S_2 is also a weighted average of the interaction factors between the basic units included in S_1 and those included in S_2 but not in S_1. The other value in eq. (17), $w(S_1, S_2)p(s_1^+|q)$ $(1-p(s_1^+|q))$, acts as a kind of interaction between the basic units included in S_1 with themselves. The second part of figure 4 shows the involved interactions.

Therefore, in the light of the results in Propositions 6, 7 and 8, to compute the bi-dimensional posterior probabilities, in addition to the calculus of the posterior unidimensional probabilities, we only need to compute the interactions $\delta(B_1, B_2|q)$, $\delta(B, S|q)$ and $\delta(S_1, S_2|q)$.

In order to design an algorithm to compute the interactions $\delta(B_1, B_2|q)$ between pairs of basic units, and considering that the number of terms instantiated in $\mathcal{Q}$ will usually be much lesser than the total number of terms in $\mathcal{T}$, it may be interesting to compute (only once) and store the 'prior interactions' $\delta(B_1, B_2|\emptyset)$ and then to derive the values of $\delta(B_1, B_2|q)$ from those of $\delta(B_1, B_2|\emptyset)$, by traversing the graph starting only from the terms in $\mathcal{Q}$. This can be done easily because from eq. (12) we obtain:

$$\delta(B_1, B_2|q) = \delta(B_1, B_2|\emptyset) - \sum_{T \in Pa(B_1) \cap Pa(B_2) \cap \mathcal{Q}} w(T, B_1)w(T, B_2)\, p(t^+)(1 - p(t^+)). \quad (18)$$

In order to design an algorithm to compute $\delta(B, S|q)$ and $\delta(S_1, S_2|q)$, it is important to notice that we need these values only when $B \in Pa(S)$ and $S_1 \in Pa(S_2)$; as each unit has only one child, the required values are $\delta(B, Hi(B)|q)$ and $\delta(S, Hi(S)|q)$, which only depend on B and S respectively. Therefore, we shall use a variable delta[U] to store the value $\delta(U, Hi(U)|q)$ for each unit $U \in \mathcal{U}_b \cup \mathcal{U}_c$ such that $Hi(U) \neq null$. As in the case of $\delta(B_1, B_2|q)$, it is also convenient to compute (only once) and store the values $\delta(U, Hi(U)|\emptyset)$. This will allow us to compute all the values $\delta(U, Hi(U)|q)$ by only traversing the nodes in the graph that require updating, starting from the terms instantiated in $\mathcal{Q}$. This is possible because from of eqs. (14) and (16), we easily obtain:

$$\delta(B, Hi(B)|q) = \delta(B, Hi(B)|\emptyset) + \sum_{\substack{B_i \in A_b(Hi(B)) \\ B_i \neq B}} w(B_i, Hi(B))\,(\delta(B, B_i|q) - \delta(B, B_i|\emptyset))\,.$$

$$\delta(S, Hi(S)|q) = \delta(S, Hi(S)|\emptyset) + \sum_{B \in A_b(S)} \sum_{B' \in A_b(Hi(S)) \setminus A_b(S)} w(B, S)w(B', Hi(S))\,(\delta(B, B'|q) - \delta(B, B'|\emptyset))\,.$$

From eq. (14) and (16), it can also be noticed that $\delta(U, Hi(U)|q)$ is the weighted sum, over all the pairs of basic units B_1 and B_2, B_1 included in U and B_2 included in $Hi(U)$ but not in U, of the values $\delta(B_1, B_2|q)$, the weighting values being the products of the weights of the arcs in the single path joining B_1 and B_2 and passing through U and $Hi(U)$, except the weight $w(U, Hi(U))$ of the arc from U to $Hi(U)$. This simple observation is the basis of the algorithm to compute all the values $\delta(U, Hi(U)|q)$. Starting from each pair of basic units that had required updating (i.e. $\delta(B_1, B_2|q) \neq \delta(B_1, B_2|\emptyset)$), we traverse the graph from parents to children (and computing the product of the weights of the arcs we encounter), until we identify the single node S (if it exists) where the two paths that started at B_1 and B_2 converge. If U_1 and U_2 are the nodes in these two paths nearest to S (i.e. arcs $U_1 \rightarrow S \leftarrow U_2$ exist in the graph), then we can update the values $\delta(U_1, S|q)$ and $\delta(U_2, S|q)$ by adding to delta[U_1] the computed product of weights of arcs times the difference between $\delta(B_1, B_2|q)$ and $\delta(B_1, B_2|\emptyset)$, divided by the weight $w(U_1, Hi(U_1))$ (and performing the same kind of updating for delta[U_2]).

7.3   Approximating the Bi-dimensional Posterior Probabilities

The previous results show how we can compute exactly the bi-dimensional probabilities involved in the computation of the expected utilities. But this process could be expensive in terms of memory and time for very large document collections. This reason leads us to propose another approximation, finer than the one presented in [6], which assumed the independence between each structural unit and the one which contains it, i.e. $p(u^+, u^+_{hi(U)}|q) = p(u^+|q)p(u^+_{hi(U)}|q)$. In the light of the results in the previous section, this approximation assumes that $\delta(U, U_{hi(U)}|q) \approx 0$ and $w(U, U_{hi(U)})p(u^+|q)(1 - p(u^+|q)) \approx 0$. While the first equality may be justified at some extend, the second one clearly can not. The proposed approximation is therefore

$$p(u^+, u^+_{hi(U)}|q) = p(u^+|q)p(u^+_{hi(U)}|q) + w(U, U_{hi(U)})\, p(u^+|q)\,(1 - p(u^+|q)) \quad (19)$$

which can be computed as efficiently as the previous one.

8   Example

To illustrate the behaviour of the generalized CID model, let us consider a simple example, where there is a single document, composed of the Sections 6 and 7 of this paper. Moreover, we use as indexing terms only the words appearing in the titles of these sections and the corresponding subsections. The Bayesian network representing this document is displayed in Figure 5. This 'collection' contains ten terms, five basic and two complex structural units. We shall use the same normalized tf-idf weighting scheme proposed in [6] (the resulting weights of the arcs are also displayed in Figure 5), and the prior probability of all the terms has been set to 0.1. The utility values are $v(r^+_i, u^+_i, u^+_{hi(U_i)}) = 0.5$, $v(r^+_i, u^+_i, u^-_{hi(U_i)}) = 1$, $v(r^+_i, u^-_i, u^+_{hi(U_i)}) = -1$, $v(r^+_i, u^-_i, u^-_{hi(U_i)}) = 0$ for all the structural units, except for the complete document, where $v(r^+_i, u^+_i) = 1$ and $v(r^+_i, u^-_i) = -0.5$.

Let us study the output provided by the model for two queries Q_1 and Q_2, where Q_1 is "posterior probabilities" and Q_2 is "approximating posterior probabilities". After instantiating to relevant these terms, we propagate this evidence through the network. The posterior probabilities of the structural units are displayed in Table 1. For Q_1, all the three subsections of section 7 appear more relevant than the section itself, whereas for Q_2 subsection 7.3 is clearly the most relevant structural unit and section 7 is the second one. However, for Q_1, it seems us that retrieving section 7 would be better for the user than retrieving its subsections (section 7 speaks about posterior probabilities as a whole). If we

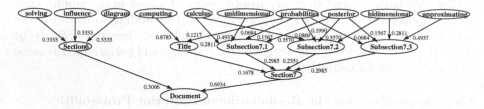

Fig. 5. The Bayesian network representing part of this document

Table 1. Posterior probabilities and expected utilities for queries Q_1 and Q_2. EU_{ex}, EU_{ap} and EU_{in} represent the utilities computed using the exact method, the approximation proposed in eq. (19) and the approximation using independence, respectively

	section 6	section 7	title (sect.7)	subsect. 7.1	subsect. 7.2	subsect. 7.3	document
$p(.|Q_1)$	0.100	0.300	0.210	0.303	**0.357**	0.303	0.239
$EU_{ex}(.|Q_1)$	-0.113	**0.170**	-0.045	0.081	0.141	0.081	-0.142
$EU_{ap}(.|Q_1)$	-0.113	**0.170**	-0.045	0.080	0.138	0.080	-0.142
$EU_{in}(.|Q_1)$	-0.127	0.097	-0.059	0.048	**0.111**	0.048	-0.142
$p(.|Q_2)$	0.100	0.432	0.210	0.303	0.357	**0.747**	0.331
$EU_{ex}(.|Q_2)$	-0.180	0.258	-0.164	-0.032	0.032	**0.505**	-0.004
$EU_{ap}(.|Q_2)$	-0.180	0.258	-0.164	-0.033	0.029	**0.504**	-0.004
$EU_{in}(.|Q_2)$	-0.214	0.173	-0.178	-0.064	0.002	**0.476**	-0.004

compute the expected utilities (Table 1 also displays all the utility values) using either the exact method or the proposed approximation, we can see that section 7 gets the highest value for Q_1 (and subsection 7.3 maintains the highest value for Q_2), as desired. Notice also that the approximation that assumes independence behaves differently.

9   Concluding Remarks

In this paper we have presented the theoretical developments concerning two extensions of the CID model for structured document retrieval. First, we have generalised the type of structure of documents that the CID model can deal with. In the new approach, the structural units containing text can be placed anywhere, and the organization of document components is general, in the sense that they do not have to be included in homogeneous layers. The change of structure has required the design of a new propagation algorithm that supports it.

We have also proposed two new methods of computing the bi-dimensional probability distributions needed for the calculus of the expected utilities of retrieving document components. The CID model assumed independence between each structural unit and the unit containing it, given the query. This is a very strong assumption, reason by which we have designed a method to compute exactly these distributions, based on interactions among units. We have also developed a new approximation in order to alleviate the possible computational cost of the exact method in very large collections, which also considers interactions but approximates them without complex calculations.

At present, we are in the implementation stage. We intend to test our model with the INEX structured collection [10], in order to determine the quality and efficiency of each evaluation method. Also, as future work, we want to perform some experiments oriented towards the detection of best entry points, since this structured IRS has been specifically designed to find them.

Acknowledgments. This work has been supported by the Spanish Fondo de Investigación Sanitaria, under Project PI021147.

References

1. R. Baeza-Yates and B. Ribeiro-Nieto. *Modern Information Retrieval.* Addison-Wesley, Harlow, UK, 1999.
2. Y. Chiaramella. Information retrieval and structured documents. *Lectures Notes in Computer Science*, 1980:291–314, 2001.
3. F. Crestani, L.M. de Campos, J.M. Fernández-Luna, and J.F. Huete. A multi-layered Bayesian network model for structured document retrieval. *Lectures Notes in Artificial Intelligence*, 2711:74–86, 2003.
4. F. Crestani, M. Lalmas, C.J. van Rijsbergen, and L. Campbell. Is this document relevant?... probably. A survey of probabilistic models in information retrieval. *ACM Computing Survey*, 30(4):528–552, 1998.
5. L.M. de Campos, J.M Fernández-Luna, and J.F. Huete. The BNR model: foundations and performance of a Bayesian network-based retrieval model. *International Journal of Approximate Reasoning*, 34:265–285, 2003.
6. L.M. de Campos, J.M. Fernández-Luna, and J.F. Huete. Using context information in structured document retrieval: An approach using influence diagrams. *Information Processing & Management*, 40(5):829–847, 2004.
7. L.M. de Campos, J.M. Fernández-Luna, and J.F. Huete. Bayesian networks and influence diagrams: Models and algorithms useful for structured retrieval. *DECSAI Technical Report*, 2004. Available at ftp://decsai.ugr.es/pub/utai/tech_rep/lci
8. S. French. *Decision Theory. An introduction to the Mathematics of Rationality.* Ellis Horwood Limited, Wiley, 1986.
9. A. Graves and M. Lalmas. Video retricval using an MPEG-7 based inference network. In *Proc. of the 25th ACM–SIGIR Conference*, 339–346, 2002.
10. INitiative for the Evaluation of XML Retrieval. http://inex.is.informatik.uni-duisburg.de:2004/
11. F.V. Jensen. *Bayesian Networks and Decision Graphs.* Springer Verlag, 2001.
12. S.H. Myaeng, D.H. Jang, M.S. Kim, and Z.C. Zhoo. A flexible model for retrieval of SGML documents. In *Proc. of the 21th ACM–SIGIR Conference*, 138–145, 1998.
13. J. Pearl. *Probabilistic Reasoning in Intelligent Systems: Networks of Plausible Inference.* Morgan and Kaufmann, San Mateo, 1988.
14. B. Piwowarski, G.E. Faure, and P. Gallinari. Bayesian networks and INEX. In *Proc. of the INEX Workshop*, 7–12, 2002.
15. R. Shachter. Evaluating influence diagrams. *Operations Research*, 34:871–882, 1986.
16. R. Shachter. Probabilistic inference and influence diagrams. *Operations Research*, 36(5):527–550, 1988.

Knowing-Aboutness: Question-Answering Using a Logic-Based Framework

Terence Clifton and William Teahan

School of Informatics,
University of Wales, Bangor

Abstract. We describe the background and motivation for a logic-based framework, based on the theory of "Knowing-Aboutness", and its specific application to Question-Answering. We present the salient features of our system, and outline the benefits of our framework in terms of a more integrated architecture that is more easily evaluated. Favourable results are presented in the TREC 2004 Question-Answering evaluation.

1   Background and Motivation

We are in the process of designing and developing a novel logic-based framework based on the concept of "Knowing-aboutness" that will become the core component for our multi-agent information retrieval systems. This paper provides the background and motivation for this framework, and then describes a prototype Question Answering system based on it.

The logic of Aboutness is a framework devised for Information Retrieval by Bruza and Huibers [2][3][4]. The key idea behind Aboutness is the use of propositions, either true or false, that state whether a document is about a certain topic or not. Our approach, in contrast, is about the person producing the document (we use the term agent), and whether that agent has knowledge about the topic or topics discussed by the document. Our idea has inspiration in the approach that epistemic logic-based multi-agent systems adopt, which is about the logic of knowing, and which are usually formulated as normal modal logics using the semantics of Kripke [24].

Our approach diverges substantially from these systems. We feel that the traditional propositional truth-based approach (which is the basis for both the epistemic logic and Aboutness approaches mentioned above) is not expressive enough for our purposes. Although we can readily use propositions to state what a document may be about or what an agent may know per se, it does not help us find out whether the agent producing the document knows an answer to a question and just as importantly, what answers that agent knows to a question. Neither does it help us find out what that agent knows about (where knowing about a topic implies that you know something about the topic, but it does not imply that you know everything about the topic). We also wish to know

D.E. Losada and J.M. Fernández-Luna (Eds.): ECIR 2005, LNCS 3408, pp. 230–244, 2005.

whether the agent producing a document is knowledgeable, and would like to rank the documents for a specific topic or topics in terms the knowledgeability of the agents[1].

1.1   Knowing-Aboutness

In [20], we describe a framework for designing and implementing knowledgeable agents and Knowledge Grids based on the concept of Knowing-aboutness. Space precludes a full description of this framework in this paper. However, we hope that the examples listed later can provide a flavour for how it works. The framework is based on three types of knowledge relations: **Knows**, **KnowsAbout**, and **KnowledgeableAbout**. These are used to define what an agent knows, what it knows about, and whether an agent has been judged to be knowledgeable by other agents. Essentially, the Knowledge Grid based architecture is founded on using knowledgeable agents as a middle layer between the user and the information resources. A key aspect of the overall design is the use of information extraction coupled with compression-based language modelling technology [21] and the use at some future time of a conversational agent that the user asks questions of and receives answers from the system.

In this architecture, there are three types of objects: users, knowledgeable agents and information resources. The users do not interface directly with the information resources. Instead, they must go through a knowledgeable agent who effectively acts as a knowledge broker in determining which of the information resources are likely to contain an answer to the user's questions. Notice that knowledgeable agents may need to go though other knowledgeable agents in the hunt to find the most relevant answer to the user's questions.

In the next two sub-sections, we highlight the differences between the notions of Aboutness and Knowing-aboutness, and then we motivate our use of an agent-based approach for Question Answering.

1.2   Aboutness Versus Knowing-Aboutness

Aboutness and knowing-aboutness describe different logics for four reasons. Firstly, aboutness concerns documents; knowing-aboutness concerns agents (i.e. the entities producing the documents). Secondly, aboutness is based on the logical implication that documents are about topics; knowing-aboutness is based on the epistemic logic of the answers that agents know about to questions. Thirdly, aboutness does not explicitly address relevance, whereas relevance is explicit in knowing-aboutness. And finally, the concepts of aboutness and knowing-aboutness are subtly different, for the following reasons:

---

[1] We assume that each document in a collection is produced by a separate agent, even if separate documents have been produced by the same person(s), as the state of mind of the person(s) and time of production of the document will differ in any case.

- A document may be about a topic, but at the same time the agent who produced[2] it may not know about that topic.
- Similarly, passages in a document may indicate that the agent knows about a topic, but the document itself may be about something else altogether.

1.3   Why an Agent-Based Approach to Question Answering?

Our definition of knowledge is what motivates our use of agents for Question-Answering. In our definition, knowledge must be associated with some agent. If we define information as being data (e.g. numbers or text) that is potentially useful in answering a question in a particular context, then in our definition, an agent has knowledge if it knows how to use that information to help answer a question.

We also have a more pragmatic reason for using agents. The traditional approach to Question-Answering is based on an Information Retrieval (IR) engine being a core component. Here, a question is translated into a query which is then sent to the IR system, and a number of documents are returned, which are then individually processed using an Information Extraction (IE) engine to produce a list of candidate passages of answer texts that in likelihood match the original question. For a number of reasons, this hybrid approach seems unsatisfactory to us. There are many difficult research issues, such as how to translate the question to the query, which IR system to use, how many documents to process, how this affects the response time, how the IE is affected by the decisions made, and how this subsequently affects the overall system's performance. The evaluation of solutions to each of these problems is hindered by the fact that the system's components are not integrated, i.e., the IR system does not retrieve answers - it retrieves documents; and the query sent to the IR system is not a question.

Our approach to Question-Answering is to remove the IR engine completely from the system. We do this by performing IE on the entire collection in a one-off step offline. The output of the IE process is a database consisting of a set of questions and answers linked back to the documents. Then the retrieval simply requires matching the user's question directly to the questions in the database (in other words, like is being matched with like).

The offline processing is potentially an expensive process. However, we stress that this is a one-off step, and a price we are willing to pay to produce a more integrated system that is more easily evaluated. Hence the pragmatic reason for our use of agents: experimental results described in [7] show that it is possible to tag a large collection (10^6 documents) with our IE engine using a distributed agent-based approach with a small number of processors (8) with limited resources in reasonable time.

This paper details the practical implementation of our logic-based framework in the form of a question answering system (QITEKAT - Question Inference Tools Employing Knowledgeable Agent Technologies), and is organised as follows. In section 2 we give a brief overview of previous work in the field of question

---

[2] By "producing" we refer to the actions of the person(s) involved in the production of that document (e.g. author, editor, and so on).

answering. Section 3 describes the architecture of the system, and in sections 4, 5, 6 and 7 we present the novel elements of our system, and the developments which best illustrate the benefits of our logic-based framework. We conclude with a discussion of the performance of our system in a suitable question answering evaluation.

2   Previous Work

Much research has been carried out in the field of question answering (Q&A), predominantly fuelled by the Text Retrieval Conference (TREC), organised by NIST [23]. Prager *et al* [16][17] introduced the technique of predictive annotation, a methodology whereby document contents are annotated with labels which anticipate their use as targets for certain question types. Hovy developed a Q&A system called Webclopedia based on established IR and Natural Language Processing (NLP) techniques [10]. Questions are parsed, and a query created, which is passed to their IR system to retrieve the top-ranked documents. Potential answers are then extracted and ranked according to their correspondence to the question type.Abney *et al.* [1] described a method based on named entity identification. For each question, a set of relevant passages containing the answers are identified, and a set of candidate entities are returned. Named entity classification is performed to categorise both the type required by the question, and the type of the answer. Matches are retained and ranked using frequency and positional information. Clarke *et al.* [5] applied a passage retrieval techniques for initial preprocessing. These passages are then ranked, and WordNet[14] is used to determine the question category. Top ranked passages were then scanned for patterns matching the desired answer category and potential answers are extracted and ranked using various heuristics. A technique called 'boosting', is presented in [9], which combines syntactic and semantic techniques, and again makes use of WordNet[14] to ensure high quality passage retrieval. Candidate answers are further justified by using abductive reasoning and only those that pass the test are returned. Harabagiu also employed an abductive reasoning approach in [8], combined with information extraction, which performed well in the 2003 Text Retrieval Conference [23].

The approach used for the QITEKAT system, in contrast is completely different. The QITEKAT system has been evaluated in the last two TREC Q&A tracks, and we provide detail in the following sections of the overall system architecture that has emerged as a result of our participation. The focus is on the information extraction engine, rather than on an information retrieval system, as we have stated in section 1.3.

3   QITEKAT System Architecture

The knowledge framework proposed here essentially relies on a reverse approach to standard Q&A techniques. Rather than using the question text to retrieve a

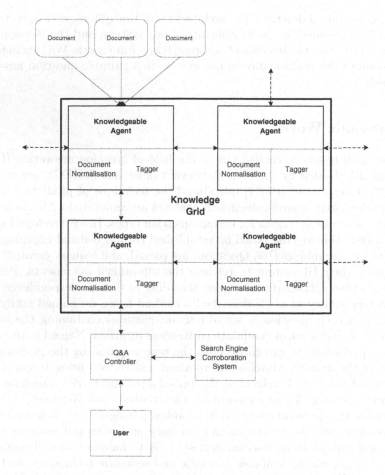

Fig. 1. System architecture (simplified)

subset of documents from the test collection, which are then analysed to find an answer, the QITEKAT Q&A system parses an entire document collection, forming a number of question/answer relations before any actual questions are posed. The TREC Q&A Track, which we have used to experimentally test our system, uses the AQUAINT document collection as its source corpus, which consists of over 1 million documents, totalling 375 million words. The system was developed based around three main stages:

- Documents are normalised;
- Agents tag and extract Question/Answer pairs;
- Input questions are analysed, and answers are retrieved and ranked.

Figure 1 shows the component make up, and how each of the individual modules interacts with the rest of the system. Space precludes a full description from appearing here, where we focus on the novel aspects of our system, and the elements directly related to the proposed framework. We refer the reader to [7] for a more complete system description.

4   Regular Expressions

Regular expressions were developed to pattern match sentence construction for common question types. This approach is similar to that used by Ravichandran and Hovy in [18]. It was important to make the best use of the previously tagged documents, and to ensure that regular expressions used by the system were not too specific as to require multiple expressions for a single question construct. This led us to develop a dynamic substitution system, whereby a generic regular expression was populated at runtime using the tagged contents of the sentence it was being applied to. We maintained a data store of basic regular expression formats, suitable substitution types, an allowable answer type, and a generic question format for the particular relation.

By using the named entities already tagged in the document (see [7] for a description of our tagging system), the system can create a number of actual regular expressions, substituting suitable types into the *ANSWER* and *OBJECT* locations. For example, given the sentence:

"John Lennon died on December 8th, 1980 during a public dramatic interpretation of J.D. Salinger's Catcher in the Rye"

the system would tag one *DATE* entity (December 8th, 1980) and two *PERSON* entities (John Lennon and J.D. Salinger). The system would then dynamically produce two regular expressions:

1. (John Lennon)\sdied\s((on—in—around)\s(December 8th, 1980)
2. (J.D.Salinger)\sdied\s((on—in—around)\s(December 8th, 1980)

These would then be applied to the document to extract any matches which would be transformed into **Knows** relations. In this case, option 1 would match, resulting in the following relation (given that the agent who produced the document text referred to as Doc-XXX-Agent).

K_a = Knows(Doc-001-Agent, "Domain: John Lennon",
"When did John Lennon die?", "December 8th, 1980", 1.0).

Further examples of extracted **Knows** relations:

K_1 = Knows(Doc-004-Agent, "Domain: George W. Bush",
"Who is George W. Bush?", "United States President", 1.0).

K_2 = Knows(Doc-004-Agent, "Domain: George W. Bush",
"When was George W. Bush born?", "July 6th 1946", 1.0).

These Knows relations are then used to populate suitable **KnowsAbout** relations such as the following:

KnowsAbout(Doc-004-Agent, "Domain: PEOPLE",
"George W. Bush", $\{K_1, K_2\}$, 1.0).

KnowsAbout(Doc-001-Agent, "Domain: PEOPLE",
"John Lennon", K_a, 1.0).

Details regarding the classification of domains can be found in Section 7.

Our initial regular expressions were hand-crafted, but it became quickly evident that this would not be efficient, either in terms of the time taken, or the required generality of the expressions. Using previous Question-Answering data as a source, we were able to implement an automated system to generate regular expressions, based on a combination of entity type tagging and proximity matching. Given a source document, a question, and an answer (that exists in the document), the following procedure is followed:

1. Extract the 'subject' of the question using traditional speech tagging techniques, and PPM compression based language modeling (see [7] for further details).
2. Analyse the source document for the proximity of the known answer to the subject.
   (a) Partial matching is applied here to ensure that subjects are recognised in the answer document.
3. If the answer falls within a given proximity threshold to the subject (i.e. is within a certain number of characters either side of the subject), we retrieve the surrounding subtext.

Table 1. Effect of proximity level on regular expression generation

Proximity	No. of Regular Expressions	No. of Questions
10	152	1.4 million
20	263	2.8 million
50	393	3.2 million
100	469	3.6 million
150	532	3.7 million
200	566	3.8 million
500	579	3.9 million

Table 2. Example source information for regular expression induction

Source Document	NYT19980601.0001
Known Question	When did Kenneth Lenihan die?
Known Answer	May 25
Source Excerpt	Kenneth Joseph Lenihan, a New York research sociologist who helped refine the scientific methods used in criminology, died May 25 at his home in Manhattan. He was 69.

```
<domain>PEOPLE</domain>
<answer>DATE</answer>
<object1>PERSON</object1>
<object2>LOCATION</object2>
<object3>PROFESSION</object3>
<regexp>
  (OBJECT1)\s.*\s((OBJECT2)\s)?▷
  ((OBJECT3)\s)?.*\sdied\s(ANSWER)
</regexp>
<format>Who is OBJECT1 married to?</format>
```

Fig. 2. Generated regular expression

4. This subtext is then parsed and a regular expression generated.

   (a) Stopwords are ignored.

   (b) Named Entity tags are inserted where possible to generalise the expression.

Our experiments with different proximity limits (number of characters) on the AQUAINT corpus led us to adopt a proximity level of 150 characters, which offered the best compromise between performance and the quality of expressions. (Larger proximity expressions lose generality, and thus effectiveness).

4.1 Example

Given the information in figure 2, the system would extract a question subject of 'Kenneth Lenihan', and parse the source text to find a suitable match. Through the use of our partial matching algorithm [7] we are able to recognise a match between 'Kenneth Joseph Lenihan' in the source text and 'Kenneth Lenihan' as our subject, resulting in a matching string:

"Kenneth Joseph Lenihan, a New York research sociologist who helped refine the scientific methods used in criminology, died May 25"

From this string we apply our proximity check to determine if the match is within our distance threshold. In this example, the subject is 101 characters from the answer, and thus the match is accepted. We then generalise the string to a suitable regular expression, by removing stopwords and inserting named entity classes where appropriate. Part-of-speech groups in close proximity to the answer, which correlate to the question text are kept to ensure the meaning is retained:

"PERSON\s.*\s(LOCATION\s)?(PROFESSION\s)?.*\sdied\sDATE"

This would provide us with the regular expression construct shown in figure 2:

5   Question Matching

Matching of question text in our *Knows* relations to questions posed to the system is a key factor in good overall performance levels. We implemented a vector matching system, whereby entered and known questions were compared based on their non-stopword content. In addition to simple positional matching, we added two extra factors that influenced match-weight:

– Subject - Matching the subject explicitly (i.e. not a partial match, see below) boosted a question's match-weight.
– Word frequency - Using the same dictionary we adopted for tagging, we tested matched words for frequency, boosting weights for less frequent words, as a match was likely to have more significance.

The 2004 TREC evaluation brought in a major change to question specifications by explicitly providing topics for a series of questions in advance of the question text. To handle this change, we only needed to implemented a minor alteration to substitute the subject for occurrences of personal pronouns in the question text. For example, given the topic for a question series "Fred Durst" and the question "What record company is he with?" the system would generate the actual question "What record company is Fred Durst with?"

6   Confidence Ranking

In the specific area of question-answering, it is often the case that systems are able to generate a number of candidate answers for a particular query. In fact, recent measure of Q&A performance have begun to include multiple-result questions (so called 'List' and 'Other' questions - see Section 7) [22].

This poses the problem of determining the best result for a particular query, which is often achieved through a confidence ranking for an answer, reflecting the degree of certainty the system places on the answer returned being correct. The confidence ranking is often returned as a decimal value in the range 0.0 (zero confidence that the answer is correct) to 1.0 (completely confident that the answer is correct), which is how our knowledge-based framework defines the value (in the framework, the confidence ranking is considered to be the 'relevance' of the answer for a particular question).

Past Q&A systems have used various means for determining a confidence measure from answers. Weighting based on matching named entity types from the answer to that expected by a specific question type is popular(see [12] for example). i.e. A 'where' type question expects a 'LOCATION' type answer, and so a corresponding answer gets a higher weighting. Other popular measures include keyword densities in the answer document, and vector matching of question and answer pairs [11][19].

We adopted an approach based on corroboration with external data sources (popular search engines), inspired by [6][13]. Search engines provide a large document base - Google for example currently claims to index over 4.3 billion Web

pages. As a result, they are likely to contain many examples of the correct answer to any query likely to be posed to a Q&A system. This offers scope to use
Web search results as a source corpus for practical Q&A applications, which is
a direction we are hoping to take as our framework develops. Currently, we use
Web search results to aid in the Q&A process by generating a confidence ranking
of answers, based on the results of an appropriate Web search query.

The fact that a suitable query to a search engine, based on the original
question, is likely to result in many examples of the correct answer means that
we can use the proportion of each possible answer within these search results to
determine a relevance rank for that answer.

Noun and verb phrase chunks from the question text are used to form a
suitable search query, and the abstracts of the first 1000 results are retrieved from
the search engine. These results are then scanned to determine the frequency of
each of the possible results as produced by the Q&A system. The proportion of
these frequencies are then used to calculate a relevance ranking.

6.1 Example

Given the question:

> When did John Lennon die?

We extract the noun and verb phrases

> John Lennon, Die

These are then passed as a query to a search engine, and the first 1000 abstracts
retrieved

> John Lennon + die

The Knowledgeable Agents have returned three possible answers

- 8th December
- 15th August
- 19th July

We find frequency counts for each of these answers in the search abstracts,
and calculate a relevance ranking (table 3)

Table 3. Relevance ranking calculation

Answer	Frequency	Calculation	Relevance
19th July	43	43/533	*0.87*
15th August	28	28/533	0.05
8th December	462	468/533	0.08

This gives us a corroborated relevance for each of the answers, and the Q&A system is able to return the answer 8th December as the most favourable. This has the benefit of eliminating the problem of conflicting data (i.e. when one agent returns one answer, and another something completely different), as the most relevant answer at a specific time is returned, rather than what may have been ranked the best answer when first generated.

In a sense, our search engine corroboration system is an external way of generating relevance measures for our questions and answers that we have extracted from the documents. This external evidence is one means by which we can test the knowledgeability of the agents producing the documents. We also wish to explore the knowledgeability of the Q&A system as a whole, but work in this area goes beyond the scope of this paper, and we have set this aside for future work.

7   Other and List Questions

The knowledge framework which forms the basis of the QITEKAT system was designed to incorporate the notion of context, and this was practically implemented through the use of domain specification both at the **Knows** and **Knows-About** level of our architecture. This put us in an excellent position when addressing 'list' and 'other' question types. List questions asked for multiple answers to a single question, whereas other questions were defined as:

> The final question in each series is an explicit 'other' question that should be interpreted as "tell me other interesting things about this target I didn't know enough to ask directly" [23].

Our system determines specific domain types for **Knows** relations using the following procedure:

1. Determine the most likely question/answer subject. This was done using traditional speech tagging techniques, and PPM compression based language modeling (see [7] for further details) to extract named entities from the question.
   (a) When required, selection was made based on frequency of occurrence in the parent document, with the assumption that more frequent occurrences were likely to be the focus of information.

These specific domains were then grouped into KnowsAbout relations stored at each agent and generalised where possible using our partial matching algorithm. For example:

- *Bush*;
- *George Bush*; and
- *George W. Bush*

occurring in three different **Knows** relations in the same document would be grouped into a single **KnowsAbout** relation. In this case, the more explicit domain - George W. Bush - would be used, to allow for improved matching at later stages in the process. The specific domain classifications were used as topic elements within the **KnowsAbout** relations, and the named entity tagger was applied to them to determine a broad domain category (PERSON entity type yields PEOPLE domain, etc.). A small number of broad domain types were used (*PEOPLE, GEOGRAPHY, BUSINESS, MISC*).

Once we had our **KnowsAbout** information, answering 'list' queries was a matter of retrieving all corresponding relations for a particular question subject, applying our improved question-matching algorithm, as detailed previously, to find answers that correspond to those required by the list, and returning the results. In generating answers to the 'other' questions we would have ideally liked to reconstruct useful 'nuggets' from the question/answer pairs our system extracted, but time did not permit this element of the system to be completed, and it has been scheduled for a future revision. As a result we were only able to return our known answers, and provide no context from the question, which made the information of little use[3].

7.1   Example

Given the following question/answer pairs extracted from a document:

- When was John Lennon born? *October 9, 1940*
- When did Lennon die? *December 8, 1980*
- How did John Lennon die? *Assassinated*

The system would first extract the named entities from each of the questions to determine their subjects

- John Lennon
- Lennon
- John Lennon

And produce the **Knows** relations:

K_1= Knows(Doc-001-Agent, "Domain: John Lennon",
"When was John Lennon born?", "October 9, 1940", 1.0).

K_2 = Knows(Doc-001-Agent, "Domain: Lennon",
"When did Lennon die?", "December 8, 1980", 1.0).

K_3 = Knows(Doc-001-Agent, "Domain: John Lennon",
"How did John Lennon die?", "Assassinated", 1.0).

Using partial matching, the system would recognise 'Lennon' and 'John Lennon' as the same subject class, and produce the following **KnowsAbout** relation (using the more explicit subject as the topic, and the general entity type as the domain):

---

[3] In fact, technical difficulties in the evaluation meant that NIL results were returned for all 'other' question types.

KnowsAbout(Doc-001-Agent, "Domain: PEOPLE",
"John Lennon", $\{K_1, K_2, K_3\}$, 1.0).

In other words this would indicate that Doc-001-Agent (the agent who produced
the document numbered 001) knows about the topic "John Lennon" in the context "Domain: PEOPLE" because it knows the answers to questions specified in
the three relations denoted by K_1, K_2, K_3.

8   Evaluation and Discussion

In order to evaluate both our framework, and its implementation as a practical question answering system, we entered QITEKAT into the TREC Q&A
evaluation for 2003 and 2004. The results for the TREC 2003 evaluation were
promising [7], although time constraints prevented use from providing a complete entry. The recent performance in the 2004 evaluation, however, shows that
the fully operational system is approaching the state-of-the-art, particularly in
the case of Factoid question types. Table 4 shows the relative comparison of
the QITEKAT performance with the minimum, maximum and average scores
for the 2004 evaluation[4]. These figures demonstrate that factoid performance
on the 2004 evaluation was very good - well above average, and placed the
QITEKAT system second overall in this section of the evaluation. The 'list'
performance was also well above the recorded mean, and third in the overall
evaluation. Technical issues with 'other' questions meant that the system failed
to return any responses, resulting in a zero ranking, which pulled down the overall score. This was still above average, however, and place the system in third
place overall.

Table 4. Relative comparison of 2004 evaluation results

	QITEKAT	MIN	MAX	AVE
Factoid	0.643	0.009	0.770	0.170
List	0.258	0.000	0.622	0.094
Other	0.000	0.000	0.460	0.184
Overall	0.386	0.005	0.656	0.155

Table 5. TREC 2004 factoid results (positive responses only)

Result	No. of responses
Correct	129
Inexact	5
Unsupported	6
Wrong	12

---

[4] Overall minimum, maximum and average scores are based on the winning entry in
the TREC 2004 evaluation [15].

One major benefit evident with the QITEKAT system and the knowledgeable framework approach is the ability of the system to return NIL responses if it is unable to find an answer. As the system preprocesses all documents in the test collection, we are able to say for certain that no answer is matched in our *Knows* relations (i.e. all vector matching falls below an empirically determined threshold), then we can state that no answer could be found by the system. This provides far less scope for incorrect answers, and is a key-factor in any real-world question answering system. By not responding incorrectly, the user has higher confidence in the responses of the system, allowing them to search elsewhere when no answer is returned, ensuring a better chance of a correct result. Table 5 shows the 2004 factoid results for those questions where a positive response was provided, and demonstrates the high level of confidence the system promotes.

These results are promising, and imply that our Q&A system based on the framework is approaching the state-of-the art, and provides a solid foundation to build on the work in Knowledgeable Agents and the concepts of Knowing-Aboutness.

References

[1] Abney S., Collins., Singhal A. "Answer extraction". In *Proceedings of 6th Conference on Applied Natural Language Processing*, 2000. Washington, USA. pp 296-301.

[2] Bruza P. D., Huibers T. W. C. "A Study of Aboutness in Information Retrieval". In *Artificial Intelligence Review*, 1996. 10:5-6. pp 381-407.

[3] Bruza P.D., Song D.W., Wong K.F. "Fundamental Properties of Aboutness". In *Proceedings of SIGIR*, 1999. California, USA. pp 277-278.

[4] Bruza P.D., Song D.W., Wong K.F. "Aboutness From a Commonsense Perspective". In *Journal of American Society for Information Science*, 2000. 51:12. pp 1090-1105.

[5] Clarke C. L. A., Cormack G. V., Kisman D. I .E., Lynam T. R. "Question Answering by Passage Selection (Multitext Experiments for TREC9)". In *Proceedings of the Ninth Text Retrieval Conference*, 2000. Washington, USA. pp 673-683.

[6] Clark C. L. A., Cormack G. V., Lynam T. R. "Exploiting Redundancy in Question Answering". In *Proceedings of SIGIR*, 2001. Louisiana, USA. pp 358-365.

[7] Clifton T., Colquhoun A., Teahan, W. "Bangor at TREC 2003: Q&A and Genomics Tracks". In *Proceedings of the Twelfth Text Retrieval Conference*, 2003. Washington, USA. pp 600-611.

[8] Harabagiu S., Moldovan D., Clark C., Bowden M., Williams J., Bensley J. "Answer Mining by Combining Extraction Techniques with Abductive Reasoning". In *Proceedings of the Twelfth Text Retrieval Conference*, 2003. Washington, USA. pp 375-382.

[9] Harabagiu S., Moldovan D., Mihalcea R., Pasca M., Bunescu R., Surdeanu M., Gîrju R., Rus V., Morarescu P. "Falcon: Boosting Knowledge for Answer Engines". In *Proceedings of the Ninth Text Retrieval Conference*, 2000. Washington, USA. pp 479-488.

[10] Hovy E., Gerber L., Hermjakob U., Junk M., Lin C-Y. "Question Answering in Webclopedia". In *Proceedings of the Ninth Text Retrieval Conference*, 2000. Washington, USA. pp 655-664.

[11] Kwok C., Etzioni O., Weld D. "Scaling Question Answering to the Web". In *Proceedings of the Tenth World Wide Web Conference*, 2001. Hong Kong, China. pp 150-161.

[12] Lita L., Rogati M., Carbonell J. "Cross Lingual QA: A Modular Baseline". In *Lecture Notes in Computer Science*, 2004. 3273/2004. pp 535-538.

[13] Magnini B., Negri M., Prevete R., Tanev H. "Is it the Right Answer? Exploiting Web Redundancy for Answer Validation". In *Proceedings of ACL*, 2002. Philadelphia, USA. pp 41-47.

[14] Miller G. "WordNet: An On-Line Lexical Database". In *International Journal of Lexicography*. 1990. 3:4. pp 235-312.

[15] Moldovan D., Harabagiu S., Clark C., Bowden M., Lehmann J., Williams J. "Experiments and Analysis of LCC's two QA Systems Over TREC 2004". In *Thirteenth Text Retrieval Conference Notebook*, 2004, Washington, USA. pp 21-33.

[16] Prager J., Radev D., Brown E., Coden A. "The Use of Predictive Annotation for Question Answering in TREC8". In *Proceedings of the Eighth Text Retrieval Conference*, 1999. Washington, USA. pp 399-411.

[17] Radev D., Prager J., Samn V. "Ranking Suspected Answers to Natural Language Questions using Predictive Annotation". In *Proceedings of 6th Conference on Applied Natural Language Processing*, 2000. Washington, USA. pp 150-157.

[18] Ravichandran D., Hovy E. "Learning Surface Text Patterns for a Question Answering System". In *Proceedings of ACL* 2002, Philadelphia, USA. pp 41-47.

[19] Tanev, H. "Socrates - A Question Answering Prototype for Bulgarian". In *Proceedings of RANLP*, 2003. Borovets, Bulgaria.

[20] Teahan W. 2003. "Knowing About Knowledge: Towards a Framework for Knowledgeable Agents and Knowledge Grids". *Artificial Intelligence Tech Report AIIA03.2*. 2003. School of Informatics, University of Wales, Bangor.

[21] Teahan W., Harper D. "Using Compression-Based Language Models for Text Categorization". In *Language Modelling for Information Retrieval*, 2003. Kluwer Academic Publishers. pp 141-165.

[22] Vorhees E. "Q&A Track Guidelines". In *Proceedings Thirteenth Text Retrieval Conference*, 2004, Washington, USA.

[23] Vorhees E. "Overview of the TREC 2003 Question Answering Track". In *Proceedings of the Twelfth Text Retrieval Conference*, 2003. Washington, USA. pp 54-68.

[24] Wooldridge M., "An Introduction to MultiAgent Systems", 2002. Wiley.

Modified LSI Model for Efficient Search by Metric Access Methods

Tomáš Skopal[1] and Pavel Moravec[2]

[1]Charles University in Prague, FMP, Department of Software Engineering,
Malostranské nám. 25, 118 00 Prague, Czech Republic
`tomas@skopal.net`
[2]Technical University of Ostrava, FEECS, Department of Computer Science,
17. listopadu 15, 708 33 Ostrava, Czech Republic
`pavel.moravec@vsb.cz`

Abstract. Text collections represented in LSI model are hard to search
efficiently (i.e. quickly), since there exists no indexing method for the LSI
matrices. The inverted file, often used in both boolean and classic vector
model, cannot be effectively utilized, because query vectors in LSI model
are dense. A possible way for efficient search in LSI matrices could be
the usage of metric access methods (MAMs). Instead of cosine measure,
the MAMs can utilize the deviation metric for query processing as an
equivalent dissimilarity measure. However, the intrinsic dimensionality
of collections represented by LSI matrices is often large, which decreases
MAMs' performance in searching. In this paper we introduce σ-LSI, a
modification of LSI in which we artificially decrease the intrinsic dimensionality of LSI matrices. This is achieved by an adjustment of singular
values produced by SVD. We show that suitable adjustments could dramatically improve the efficiency when searching by MAMs, while the
precision/recall values remain preserved or get only slightly worse.

1 Introduction

Text collections represented in the classic vector model (CVM) can be efficiently
(i.e. quickly) searched using the inverted file. More precisely, the inverted file
provides a way for very efficient processing of queries, the vectors of which are
sparse (such a query contains only several terms). However, in case of LSI model
the query vectors are dense, and the usage of inverted file becomes useless, since
processing of any query deteriorates to sequential search over the entire concept-
by-document matrix.

In this paper we utilize a method of searching in LSI collections by metric
access methods (MAMs). The metric access methods are, however, sensitive to
the curse of dimensionality, i.e. they become inefficient for high dimensionalities.
Therefore, in this paper we propose σ-LSI, a modified LSI model in which we
artificially reduce the intrinsic dimensionality of the indexed collection. This is
achieved by an adjustment of singular values produced by SVD. We show that
suitable adjustments could dramatically improve the efficiency when searching

D.E. Losada and J.M. Fernández-Luna (Eds.): ECIR 2005, LNCS 3408, pp. 245–259, 2005.

by MAMs, while the precision/recall values remain preserved or get only slightly worse.

The paper is organized as follows: In the rest of this section we briefly overview CVM, the LSI model, and formulate the problem of searching in LSI model. In Section 3 we show how the classic similarity search in CVM (LSI model respectively) can be turned into metric search. We also mention the principles of metric access methods and the problem of high intrinsic dimensionality. In Section 4 we propose σ-LSI model allowing a more efficient search by MAMs. The *effectiveness* (the quality) and *efficiency* (the response time) of retrieval in the σ-LSI model are evaluated in Section 5.

1.1   Classic Vector Model

In CVM, a given text collection (containing n documents consisting of m unique terms) is represented by an $m \times n$ *term-by-document matrix A*, where each column vector d_j in A represents a single document D_j. Thus, the documents are represented as points in m-dimensional vector space (the *document-space*). Each dimension of the document-space is associated with a single term, while each coordinate in a *document vector* d_j represents a weight of the respective term in the document. There are many ways how to compute the term weights A_{ij} – a popular weight construction is computed as $tf \cdot idf$ (see e.g. [3]).

The most important part of CVM is the query semantics for searching the matrix A with respect to a query Q, and returning only the relevant document vectors (appropriate documents respectively). The query Q is represented by a vector q in the document space the same way as a document D_j is represented by d_j. The goal is to return the most similar documents to the query. For this purpose a similarity measure must be defined, assessing a similarity score for each pair of query and document vectors (q, d_j). In many cases, the *cosine measure*

$$\text{SIM}_{cos}(q, d_j) = \frac{\sum_{i=1}^{m} q_i d_{ji}}{\sqrt{\sum_{i=1}^{m} q_i^2 \cdot \sum_{i=1}^{m} d_{ji}^2}}$$

is widely used. Besides the simple ranking to q (used for *ranked lists*), we also distinguish bounded queries, in particular *range queries* and *k-nearest neighbors (k-NN) queries*. A range query returns documents with similarity to the query

term \ doc.	D$_1$	D$_2$	D$_3$	D$_4$	D$_5$
database	0	0.48	0.05	0	0.70
vector	0.23	0	0.23	0	0
index	0.43	0	0	0	0
image	0	0	0.10	0	0.54
compression	0	0	0	0	0.21
multimedia	0.12	0.52	0.62	0	0

Fig. 1. Term-by-document matrix A

higher than a given similarity threshold t. A k-NN query returns the k most similar documents[1].

2 Latent Semantic Indexing

Latent semantic indexing (LSI) [3,4] is an algebraic extension of CVM. Its benefits rely on discovering *latent semantics* hidden in the term-by-document matrix A. Informally, LSI discovers significant groups of terms (called *concepts*) and represents the documents as linear combinations of the concepts. Moreover, the concepts are ordered according to their significance in the collection, which allows us to consider only the first k concepts important (the remaining ones are interpreted as "noise" and discarded). To name the advantages, LSI helps solve problems with synonymy and homonymy. Furthermore, LSI is often referred to as more successful in recall when compared to CVM [4], which was proved for pure (only one topic per document) and style-free collections [17].

Formally, we decompose the term-by-document matrix A by *singular value decomposition (SVD)*, calculating singular values and singular vectors of A. SVD is especially suitable in its variant for sparse matrices (Lanczos [13]). Several approximate methods for faster SVD calculation were offered recently, such as using random projection of document vectors into suitable subspace before LSI calculation [17] or application of Monte-Carlo method [11].

There are several other methods for latent semantic indexing, such as ULV-decomposition [5], random indexing [16] (and some other approaches achieving similar goals, e.g. language modeling [19]), which we do not discuss in this paper.

Theorem 1 (Singular Value Decomposition [4]). *Let A is an $m \times n$ rank-r matrix. Be values $\sigma_1, \ldots, \sigma_r$ calculated from eigenvalues of matrix AA^T as $\sigma_i = \sqrt{\lambda_i}$. Then there exist column-orthonormal matrices $U = (u_1, \ldots, u_r)$ and $V = (v_1, \ldots, v_r)$, where $U^T U = I_m$ a $V^T V = I_n$, and a diagonal matrix $\Sigma = diag(\sigma_1, \ldots, \sigma_r)$, where $\sigma_i > 0, \sigma_i \geq \sigma_{i+1}$. The decomposition*

$$A = U\Sigma V^T$$

is called singular decomposition *of matrix A and the numbers $\sigma_1, \ldots, \sigma_r$ are* singular values *of the matrix A. Columns of U (or V) are called* left (or right) singular vectors *of matrix A.*

Now we have a decomposition of the original term-by-document matrix A. The left and right singular vectors (i.e. U and V matrices) are not sparse. We get r nonzero singular numbers, where r is the rank of the original matrix A. Because the singular values usually fall quickly, we can take only k greatest singular values with the corresponding singular vector coordinates and create a *k-reduced singular decomposition* of A.

---

[1] In the next section we independently use k for another parameter (rank-k SVD), but in either case the respective meaning of k is obvious from the actual context.

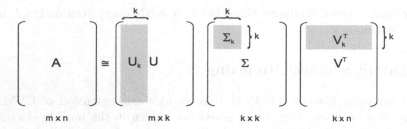

Fig. 2. k-reduced singular value decomposition

Definition 1. *Let us have* k $(0 < k < r)$ *and singular value decomposition of* A

$$A = U\Sigma V^T \approx A_k = (U_k U_0) \begin{pmatrix} \Sigma_k & 0 \\ 0 & \Sigma_0 \end{pmatrix} \begin{pmatrix} V_k^T \\ V_0^T \end{pmatrix}$$

We call $A_k = U_k \Sigma_k V_k^T$ *a* k-*reduced singular value decomposition (rank-k SVD).*

Instead of the A_k matrix, a *concept-by-document matrix* $D_k = \Sigma_k V_k^T$ is used in LSI as the representation of document collection. The document vectors (columns in D_k) are now represented as points in k-dimensional space (the *pseudodocument-space*). For an illustration of rank-k SVD see Figure 2.

The value of k was experimentally determined as several tens or hundreds (e.g. 50–250), however, the optimal[2] value of k is hard to choose; it is dependent on the number of topics in collection. Rank-k SVD is the best rank-k approximation of the original matrix A, regarding to Frobenius norm (see e.g. [12]). This means, that any other decomposition will increase the sum of squares of matrix $A - A_k$. However, this does not tell us that we could not obtain better precision and recall values with a different approximation.

To execute a query Q in the pseudodocument-space, we create a reduced query vector $q_k = U_k^T q$ (another approach is to simply use a matrix $D'_k = V_k^T$ instead of D_k, and $q'_k = \Sigma_k^{-1} U_k^T q$). Instead of A against q, the matrix D_k against q_k (or q'_k) is evaluated using the cosine measure. The crucial property is that, due to the projection by dense matrix U_k^T, q_k is dense as well (even if q is sparse).

2.1   LSI Model and Inverted Files

In CVM, searching the term-by-document matrix A according to a query Q can be provided using *inverted file* [15, 18, 1], which can be viewed as the matrix A stored by rows. For a given matrix A the inverted file consists of m lists, each list is associated with a single term. Each list stores entries, which are pairs consisting of a document id and weight of the term in corresponding document (obviously, entries with zero weights are not stored). When a query is processed, only the lists representing terms from the query are sequentially searched.

---

[2] optimal in sense of best achieved precision/recall values.

The inverted file is very efficient for processing of sparse query vectors (few-term queries respectively), because only several lists have to be processed. Unfortunately, in case of LSI the pseudo-query vector is dense and usage of inverted file for indexing D_k would deteriorate to sequential search over the entire file and thus, over the entire matrix D_k.

3   Metric Indexing

Recently, there has been introduced an approach to searching in LSI model, based on *metric indexing* [20]. Instead of inverted file, the *M-tree* [9] was used for indexing the matrix D_k. Before we discuss benefits of the metric approach, we must turn the cosine measure (similarity) into metric (distance).

3.1   Turning Vector Model into Metric Model

The cosine measure $\text{SIM}_{cos}(d_i, d_j)$ itself is not a metric, since it does not satisfy three metric properties (reflexivity, positivity and triangular inequality). Even $1 - \text{SIM}_{cos}(d_i, d_j)$ is not a metric, since it does not satisfy the triangular inequality. As an appropriate metric, we use the *deviation metric* (or angular distance) $d_{dev}(d_i, d_j)$, defined as

$$d_{dev}(d_i, d_j) = arccos(\text{SIM}_{cos}(d_i, d_j))$$

Instead of cosine, the deviation metric measures directly the angle between two vectors[3]. Since *arccos* is strictly decreasing on $\langle -1, 1 \rangle$, the deviation metric preserves the semantic meaning of cosine measure. There is only a difference in terminology – cosine measure is *similarity function* (similar documents have a high score), while the deviation metric is *dissimilarity function* (similar documents have a lower score, i.e. they are close). Hence, the k-dimensional pseudodocument-space $\mathbb{R}^k$ together with the deviation metric d_{dev} can be regarded as a metric space $\mathcal{M} = (\mathbb{R}^k, d_{dev})$.

The queries in metric model are evaluated in similar way as in CVM; the difference is that range queries select objects within a *query radius* r_Q (which equals to *arccos* of the desired similarity threshold t), while k-NN queries select the k closest objects.

3.2   Metric Access Methods

The *metric access methods* [8] organize (or index) a given metric dataset $\mathbb{S} \subset \mathcal{M}$ in a way that metric queries (e.g. range or k-NN queries) can be processed efficiently – without a need of processing the entire dataset $\mathbb{S}$. The main principle behind all MAMs is the triangular inequality property satisfied by every metric. Due to the triangular inequality, MAMs can organize the objects in equivalence

---

[3] Actually, we can view the deviation metric d_{dev} as a kind of Euclidean (L_2) distance, defined just on the surface of unitary hyper-sphere.

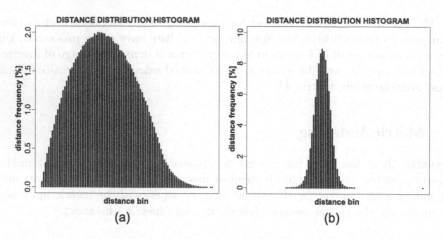

Fig. 3. DDHs indicating (a) low (b) high intrinsic dimensionality

classes (the classes are some regions in the metric space). When a query is processed, many irrelevant equivalence classes are filtered (those with metric regions not overlapping the query region), and so the searching becomes more efficient. Another advantage is that MAMs use solely the metric function for indexing, no information about the indexed objects representation is necessary. This feature allows to index/search non-vectorial datasets, too.

There has been developed a plenty of MAMs, varying in applicability to different problems. Besides others, we name *M-tree* [9], *vp-tree* [22], *LAESA* [14], *D-index* [10], etc.

3.3   Intrinsic Dimensionality

The metric indexing itself (as was presented in [20]) could be quite beneficial for searching in the LSI model. However, searching in a collection of high-dimensional document vectors is negatively affected by a phenomenon called the *curse of dimensionality* [6,7]. For MAMs the curse of dimensionality causes almost all equivalence classes to be overlapped by nearly every "reasonable" query region, so that searching deteriorates to sequential scan over all the classes.

In the context of metric indexing, the curse of dimensionality can be generalized for general metric spaces. The major condition determining the efficiency limits of any metric access method is the *intrinsic dimensionality* of the indexed dataset, defined as (proposed in [7]):

$$\rho(\mathbb{S}, d) = \frac{\mu^2}{2\sigma^2}$$

where μ and σ^2 are the mean and the variance of the dataset's *distance distribution* (according to a metric d). In other words, the intrinsic dimensionality is low if there exist tight clusters of objects. Conversely, if all pairs of the indexed objects are almost equally distant, the intrinsic dimensionality is high

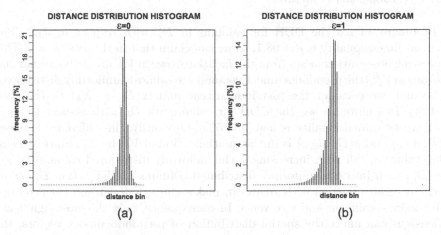

Fig. 4. (a) DDH for D'_k (b) DDH for D_k

(i.e. the mean is high and/or the variance is low), which means the dataset is poorly intrinsically structured. In Figure 3 see an example of distance distribution histograms (DDHs) indicating lower ($\rho \approx 2$) and higher ($\rho \approx 30$) intrinsic dimensionalities.

In case of vector datasets, the intrinsic dimensionality can reach up to (or even beyond) the value of the classic (embedding) dimensionality. For example, for uniformly distributed n-dimensional vectors (i.e. not clustered) $\rho \approx n$.

So far, for datasets of high intrinsic dimensionality there still does not exist an efficient MAM for exact[4] metric search.

4   The σ-LSI Model

In case of LSI, we are concerned by intrinsic dimensionality of the pseudodocument vectors (columns in D_k), with respect to the deviation metric d_{dev}. The smaller ρ, the greater search efficiency can be achieved for the MAMs.

In this section we propose the σ-LSI model, a modification of LSI in which we are able to artificially decrease the intrinsic dimensionality of D_k.

4.1   Motivation

In order to understand the intrinsic dimensionality of D_k, we first consider the simpler approach of LSI, where the pseudodocument matrix is just $D'_k = V_k^T$ (instead of $D_k = \Sigma_k V_k^T$). This is equivalent to $D'_k = \Sigma_k^0 V_k^T$, where Σ_k^0 is unitary matrix (the singular values σ_i are powered by 0). To illustrate the situation on an example, we use a term-by-document matrix A (closely described in Section 5) decomposed using rank-k SVD, $k = 100$.

---

[4] Nevertheless, efficient searching in high-dimensional datasets can be realized by approximate or probabilistic MAMs, but such methods often suffer from lower precision/recall values [23, 7].

In Figure 4a see the DDH for columns in D'_k with respect to d_{dev}. The intrinsic dimensionality is $\rho = 98.1$, so we can claim that in this case $k \approx \rho$. This interesting observation arises from the fact that rows in V_k^T are orthonormal and columns in V_k^T (the pseudodocument vectors) are (almost) uniformly distributed.

Second, we consider the pseudodocument matrix $D_k = \Sigma_k V_k^T$ (the classic LSI). In Figure 4b see the DDH for columns in D_k with respect to d_{dev}, the intrinsic dimensionality is now $\rho = 52.6$. Obviously, the difference between $\rho(D'_k, d_{dev})$ and $\rho(D_k, d_{dev})$ is in the multiplication of V_k^T by Σ_k. Since the singular values σ_i fall with increasing i, the uniformly distributed columns of V_k^T (i.e. D'_k) turn into non-uniformly distributed columns of $\Sigma_k V_k^T$ (i.e. D_k). Furthermore, multiplication with greater σ_i makes the i-th dimension (i-th concept resp.) more significant and vice versa. In consequence, only the most significant dimensions can affect the spatial distribution of pseudodocument vectors; the small values in insignificant dimensions can "shift" the vectors only fractionally. Hence, the quicker falling of σ_i, the smaller number of significant dimensions and, in turn, the smaller intrinsic dimensionality of D_k.

4.2   Singular Values Modification

To decrease the intrinsic dimensionality of D_k, we can adjust the singular values σ_i such that they fall more quickly (with increasing i). This can be achieved by a suitable modifying function f.

$$\Sigma_k = diag(\sigma_1, \ldots, \sigma_k) \quad \Longrightarrow \quad \Sigma_k^f = diag(f(\sigma_1), \ldots, f(\sigma_k))$$

The function f must be increasing in order to preserve the ordering of singular values (they are ordered by values). Moreover, f must be convex, because we need to make the falling of σ_i faster (concave functions do the opposite).

Finally, we apply the modified values in Σ_k^f instead of the original Σ_k, i.e. we use $D_k^f = \Sigma_k^f V_k^T$ instead of D_k and $q_k^f = \Sigma_k^f \Sigma_k^{-1} U_k^T q$ instead of q_k.

In the following we have chosen functions $f(x) = x^\varepsilon$ ($\varepsilon \geq 1$), so we will denote Σ_k^f as Σ_k^ε, D_k^f as D_k^ε, and q_k^f as $q_k^\varepsilon = \Sigma_k^{\varepsilon-1} U_k^T q$. Note the notation is consistent with the simple LSI (i.e. usage of Σ_k^0). In Figure 5 see a normed visualization of the singular values modified by several functions $f(x) = x^\varepsilon$. The greater ε, the more quick falling of σ_i^ε.

From the semantic point of view, a convex modification of singular values means that we even more emphasize the significant concepts and even more inhibit the less significant ones. It seems that we perform a kind of an additional dimensionality reduction.

On the other side, any modification of singular values surely must increase the approximation error mentioned in Section 2. However, this kind of error is algebraical; the human-dependent effectiveness measures (e.g. the precision and the recall) are something else. We present an experimental evaluation of the σ-LSI model effectiveness in Section 5.1.

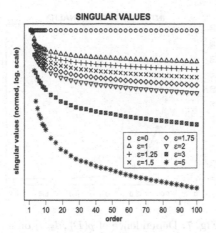

Fig. 5. Visualization of modified singular numbers σ_i^ε (for different ε)

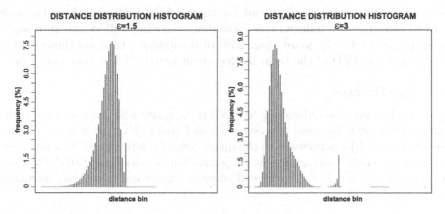

Fig. 6. DDHs for $D_k^{1.5}$ and D_k^3 DDHs for $D_k^{1.5}$ and D_k^3

4.3 Intrinsic Dimensionality Reduction

In Figure 6 see distance distribution histograms for D_k^ε, $\varepsilon = 1.5$ and $\varepsilon = 3$. The intrinsic dimensionality for $D_k^{1.5}$ (or D_k^3) is $\rho = 21.22$ ($\rho = 1.72$ respectively).

In Figure 7 the intrinsic dimensionality ρ of D_k^ε is presented in dependence on ε. As we have assumed, ρ is decreasing with growing ε, which should be reflected by a more efficient searching by MAMs. The search efficiency achieved by the M-tree is presented in Section 5.2.

5   Experimental Query Evaluation

For testing of our approach, we used a subset of TREC collection [21], consisting of 30,000 Los Angeles Times articles (years 1989 and 1990), from which 16,889 articles were assessed in TREC-8 ad-hoc queries (see below). The remaining arti-

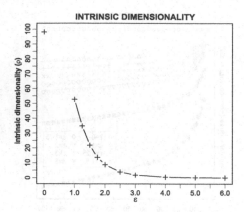

Fig. 7. Dependence of $\rho(D_k^\varepsilon, d_{dev})$ on ε

cles were added chronologically (from January to April 1989) and should provide finer LSI concepts. We indexed this collection, removing well-known stop-words and terms appearing in more than 25% of documents, thus obtaining 49,689 terms. Rank-100 SVD of the term-by-document matrix A was then calculated.

5.1   Effectiveness

For the evaluation of σ-LSI model, we need some qualitative measures for evaluating query results. We used *precision* (P) and *recall* (R), which are calculated from set Rel of objects relevant to the query (usually determined by manual annotation of the collection, giving us subjective human assessment of documents' relevance) and a set Ret of retrieved objects. Based on these sets, we define precision and recall as:

$$P = \frac{|Rel \cap Ret|}{|Ret|}, \quad R = \frac{|Rel \cap Ret|}{|Rel|}$$

For the overall comparison of precision and recall across different methods, we can use rank lists and evaluate precision on 11 standard recall levels (0.0, 0.1, 0.2, ..., 0.9, 1.0). Since the queries may have different number of relevant documents, we can use interpolated values for each query. For complete description of this method, see e.g. [2].

Unfortunately, it was observed that with the increase of recall, the precision usually decreases. This means that when it is necessary to retrieve more relevant objects, a higher percentage of irrelevant will be probably retrieved, too. To obtain a single ratio for evaluation of the retrieval performance, we can employ a measure called F-score – harmonic mean of recall and precision. Determination of the maximum value for F can be interpreted as an attempt to find the best possible compromise between recall and precision.

The universal version of F-score employs a coefficient β, by which can be the precision-recall ratio tuned. We will use the basic form of F score with $\beta = 1$:

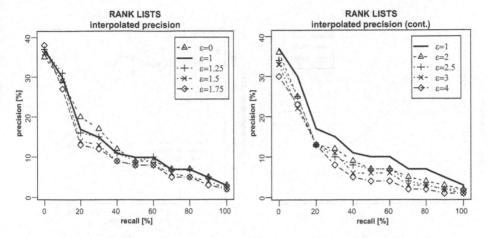

Fig. 8. Precision for 11 standard recall levels calculated from rank lists

$$F_\beta = \frac{(1+\beta^2) \cdot P \cdot R}{\beta^2 P + R}, \quad F = F_1 = \frac{2 \cdot P \cdot R}{P + R}$$

To measure the effectiveness of σ-LSI, we must know the values of precision and recall for both the original method (LSI) and the modification (σ-LSI). Since we use a subset of TREC collection, we have a baseline for the effectiveness measurement via a set of predefined topics and assessed documents, called TREC Queries. TREC topics (written in SGML) contain at least the following tags:

```
<top>
   <num> Number: 401
   <title> foreign minorities, Germany
   <desc> Description:
      What language and cultural differences impede the
      integration of foreign minorities in Germany?
   <narr> Narrative:
      A relevant document will focus on ...
</top>
```

For every topic, there is a set of relevance assessments for selected documents, which indicates, whether the particular assessed document was relevant or irrelevant. The remaining unassessed documents were *assumed* irrelevant.

We used TREC-8 Ad-hoc topics 401-450 with their relevance assessments for Los Angeles Times subcollection for our task. Term weights in query vectors were calculated from term frequency (tf) component, the query vectors were then projected to pseudodocument space for given ε. The values of ε have been chosen from $\{0\} \cup <1, 9>$[5]. The cosine measure SIM_{cos} (deviation metric d_{dev} respectively) values were calculated for both k-NN queries and rank lists for each TREC Query in the pseudodocument spaces.

---

[5] For $\varepsilon = 1$, we obtain classic LSI model with $D_k = \Sigma_k V_k^T$, which we used as a baseline; for $\varepsilon = 0$ we get simple LSI with $D_k' = V_k^T$.

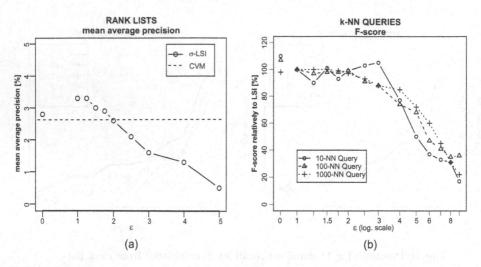

Fig. 9. (a) Mean average precision of σ-LSI for all relevant documents for different values of ε with CVM baseline (b) F-score of k-NN queries for different values of ε

Firstly, we used rank lists and measured interpolated average precision of the above mentioned TREC Queries for 11 standard recall levels. The comparison for different values of ε and original LSI ($\varepsilon = 1$) is addressed in Figure 8. The precision-recall curves for reasonably small values of ε are very similar to classic LSI, thus the method yields similar results even with much smaller intrinsic dimensionality, which is suitable for MAMs.

Additionally, we calculated the mean average precision for all relevant documents in rank lists. The results for σ-LSI are shown in Figure 9a together with the mean average precision of corresponding CVM representation.

Secondly, we executed TREC Queries as k-NN queries for several values of k, ranging from 10 to 1000 and compared the F-score for different values of ε. Some of the results are shown in Figure 9b. We can observe, for the values of $\varepsilon < 3$ the precision and F-score seem to be well-preserved.

5.2   Efficiency

The motivation and main reason for introduction of the σ-LSI model is an improvement of query evaluation efficiency, when using MAMs. Among the many metric access methods, we have chosen the M-tree [9] as a "database-friendly" MAM (M-tree is a balanced, paged and dynamic structure), which we employed to index several D_k^ε matrices. The matrices were stored externally (the M-tree index contained just pointers to the respective vectors in D_k^ε) and size of each matrix was about 12 MB. The size of each M-tree index was quite small, about 600 kB.

As search costs of k-NN queries, we measured the I/O costs (disk accesses) and also the realtimes. Each k-NN query was executed 1000 times, every time for a (new) randomly selected vector from D_k^ε (i.e. as query vectors we have reused

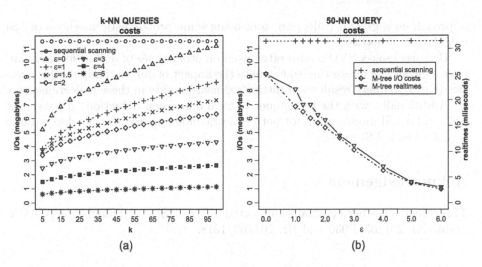

Fig. 10. (a) k-NN queries costs (b) 50-NN query costs, depending on ε

the pseudodocument vectors). The results were averaged. To have an efficiency baseline, we also present results for searching by simple sequential scanning of the entire matrix D_k^ε.

In Figure 10a see the costs of k-NN queries evaluation for several values of ε. With growing ε the query evaluation is more efficient, up to 8 times for $\varepsilon = 6$ and $k = 100$, when related to $\varepsilon = 1$ (the classic LSI). Even in case when $\varepsilon = 3$ (for which the F-score is still well-preserved) the efficiency is improved more than twice, when compared to $\varepsilon = 1$.

The dependence of efficiency on ε is presented in Figure 10b. For 50-NN queries, both I/O costs and realtimes decrease with growing ε. However, had we compared Figures 10b and 7, the intrinsic dimensionality drops much faster than the costs needed for processing a 50-NN query by the M-tree. This observation indicates that an "ideal" MAM should perform even better than the M-tree.

6   Conclusions

In this paper we have proposed σ-LSI – a novel modification of LSI model for efficient searching in document collections by metric access methods. To battle high intrinsic dimensionality, a convex modification of singular values σ_i by calculating σ_i^ε, $\varepsilon \geq 1$ was proposed. We have shown that for reasonable values of ε the intrinsic dimensionality drops quickly, while the similarity of documents is still well-preserved. In fact, we have observed that our collection seemed to yield almost the same results for $\varepsilon \leq 2.5$, while the search efficiency was doubled.

In future, we would like to apply other convex functions on singular values, testing whether they yield better global results for precision, recall and intrinsic dimensionality than the currently proposed approach. We would like test the approach on a greater collection, too, using some probabilistic methods of LSI calculation, if needed.

Because rank-k SVD is also often used on other types of data, especially images, it would be interesting to evaluate the impact of our method on other metrics (e.g. L_2), query results and intrinsic dimensionality in these collections, too.

Additionally, with the techniques of local dimension reduction, approximate LSI, and σ-LSI modification for better metric indexing, we may be able to build a really viable LSI index.

Acknowledgement

This research has been partially supported by Czech Science Foundation (GAČR) grants Nr. 201/05/P036 and Nr. 201/03/1318.

References

1. V. N. Anh, O. de Kretser, and A. Moffat. Vector-space ranking with effective early termination. In *Proceedings of the 24th annual international ACM SIGIR conference on Research and development in information retrieval*, pages 35–42. ACM Press, 2001.
2. R. Baeza-Yates and B. Ribeiro-Neto. *Modern Information Retrieval*. Addison Wesley, New York, 1999.
3. M. Berry and M. Browne. *Understanding Search Engines, Mathematical Modeling and Text Retrieval*. Siam, 1999.
4. M. Berry, S. Dumais, and T. Letsche. Computation Methods for Intelligent Information Access. In *Proceedings of the 1995 ACM/IEEE Supercomputing Conference*, 1995.
5. M. W. Berry and R. D. Fierro. Low-Rank Orthogonal Decomposition for Information Retrieval Applications. *Numerical Algebra with Applications*, 1(1):1–27, 1996.
6. C. Böhm, S. Berchtold, and D. Keim. Searching in High-Dimensional Spaces – Index Structures for Improving the Performance of Multimedia Databases. *ACM Computing Surveys*, 33(3):322–373, 2001.
7. E. Chávez and G. Navarro. A probabilistic spell for the curse of dimensionality. In *Proc. 3rd Workshop on Algorithm Engineering and Experiments (ALENEX'01)*, *LNCS 2153*. Springer-Verlag, 2001.
8. E. Chávez, G. Navarro, R. Baeza-Yates, and J. L. Marroquín. Searching in metric spaces. *ACM Compututing Surveys*, 33(3):273–321, 2001.
9. P. Ciaccia, M. Patella, and P. Zezula. M-tree: An Efficient Access Method for Similarity Search in Metric Spaces. In *Proceedings of the 23rd Athens Intern. Conf. on VLDB*, pages 426–435. Morgan Kaufmann, 1997.
10. V. Dohnal, C. Gennaro, P. Savino, and P. Zezula. D-index: Distance searching index for metric data sets. *Multimedia Tools Applications*, 21(1):9–33, 2003.
11. A. Frieze, R. Kannan, and S. Vempala. Fast Monte-Carlo Algorithms for Finding Low Rank Approximations. In *Proceedings of 1998 FOCS*, pages 370–378, 1998.
12. G. H. Golub and C. F. V. Loan. *Matrix computations (3rd ed.)*. Johns Hopkins University Press, 1996.

13. R. M. Larsen. Lanczos bidiagonalization with partial reorthogonalization. Technical report, University of Aarhus, 1998.
14. M. L. Micó, J. Oncina, and E. Vidal. An algorithm for finding nearest neighbour in constant average time with a linear space complexity. In *International Conference on Pattern Recognition*, pages 557–560, 1992.
15. A. Moffat and J. Zobel. Fast ranking in limited space. In *Proceedings of the Tenth International Conference on Data Engineering*, pages 428–437. IEEE Computer Society, 1994.
16. J. K. P. Kanerva and A. Holst. Random Indexing of Text Samples for Latent Semantic Analysis. In *Proceedings of the 22nd Annual Conference of the Cognitive Science Society*, page 1036, 2000.
17. C. H. Papadimitriou, H. Tamaki, P. Raghavan, and S. Vempala. Latent semantic indexing: A probabilistic analysis. In *Proocedings of the ACM Conference on Principles of Database Systems (PODS)*, pages 159–168, 1998.
18. M. Persin. Document filtering for fast ranking. In *Proceedings of the 17th annual international ACM SIGIR conference on Research and development in information retrieval*, pages 339–348. Springer-Verlag New York, Inc., 1994.
19. J. Ponte and W. Croft. A language modelling approach to IR. In *Proceedings of the 21 st ACM SIGIR Conference*, pages 275–281, 1998.
20. T. Skopal, P. Moravec, J. Pokorný, and V. Snášel. Metric Indexing for the Vector Model in Text Retrieval. In *Proceedings of the 11th Symposium on String Processing and Information Retrieval (SPIRE), Padova, Italy, LNCS 3246, Springer-Verlag*, pages 183–195, 2004.
21. E. M. Voorhees and D. Harman. Overview of the sixth text REtrieval conference (TREC-6). *Information Processing and Management*, 36(1):3–35, 2000.
22. P. N. Yanilos. Data Structures and Algorithms for Nearest Neighbor Search in General Metric Spaces. In *Proceedings of Fourth Annual ACM/SIGACT-SIAM Symposium on Discrete Algorithms - SODA*, pages 311–321, 1993.
23. P. Zezula, P. Savino, G. Amato, and F. Rabitti. Approximate Similarity Retrieval with M-Trees. *VLDB Journal*, 7(4):275–293, 1998.

PIRE: An Extensible IR Engine Based on Probabilistic Datalog

Henrik Nottelmann

Institute of Informatics and Interactive Systems, University of Duisburg-Essen,
47048 Duisburg, Germany
nottelmann@uni-duisburg.de

Abstract. This paper introduces PIRE, a probabilistic IR engine. For both document indexing and retrieval, PIRE makes heavy use of probabilistic Datalog, a probabilistic extension of predicate Horn logics. Using such a logical framework together with probability theory allows for defining and using data types (e.g. text, names, numbers), different weighting schemes (e.g. normalised tf, tf.idf or BM25) and retrieval functions (e.g. uncertain inference, language models). Extending the system thus is reduced to adding new rules. Furthermore, this logical framework provide a powerful tool for including additional background knowledge into the retrieval process.

1 Introduction

Information Retrieval has been investigated intensively within the last decades. Through all the years, researchers did not only aim at finding new techniques, one major focus always was on implementing the techniques and evaluating them with standard test collections, for example within the Text REtrieval Conference (TREC) or, more recently, the INEX evaluation initiative for XML retrieval.

Many IR techniques have been proposed. Besides heuristic approaches like the vector-space model, probabilistic IR can be justified theoretically following the Probability Ranking Principle (PRP) [14]. Thus, probabilistic IR approaches have become more and more popular, including the Binary Independence Retrieval (BIR) approach, the Darmstadt Indexing Approach (DIA), Language Models [13] or Uncertain Inference [18]. In combination with logics (e.g. probabilistic Datalog [6], a probabilistic extension of predicate Horn logics), probabilistic IR provides a powerful tool on a solid theoretical basis, which is extensible via additional rules, and which can take additional background knowledge into account.

The software presented in this paper, PIRE, is an extensible, general-purpose IR engine on the basis of probabilistic Datalog. Due to this logical foundation, PIRE has several advantages compared to common IR engines: The set of weighting schemes and retrieval functions is not fixed, but defined by logical rules. Using predicate logic increases the expressiveness, and enables to incorporate external knowledge, e.g. term associations from a thesaurus, into the retrieval process in a natural way.

PIRE uses the concept of data types. Each data type provides a number of operators which can be used for comparing document content with a query. As vagueness of query

D.E. Losada and J.M. Fernández-Luna (Eds.): ECIR 2005, LNCS 3408, pp. 260–274, 2005.
© Springer-Verlag Berlin Heidelberg 2005

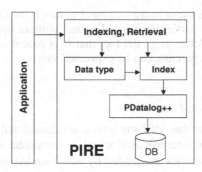

Fig. 1. PIRE architecture

formulations is an important concepts of Information Retrieval (e.g. when a user is uncertain about the exact publication year of a document), these operators have a probabilistic interpretation (as proposed in [4]). Vagueness is required when a user is uncertain about the exact publication year of a document or the spelling of an author's name.

PIRE is implemented in Java and consists of five different components (see figure 1). The top component provides basic indexing and retrieval functions. It uses several indexes, each of them storing a specific part (called attributes) of the documents. In addition, operations that are specific for the data type like computing indexing weights are controlled by data type classes (e.g. for text, for names, for numbers). Probabilistic Datalog is employed for communication among the components, for defining the IR technique, and for storing the actual index (using a relational database system).

This paper is organised as follows. The next section summarises probabilistic Datalog and describes two major extensions which are required for Information Retrieval. Sections 3 and 4 explains how indexing and retrieval can be performed with probabilistic Datalog. Implementation details are presented in section 5, and further extensions are contained in section 6. The last section of this paper contains concluding remarks and an outlook into future work.

2   Probabilistic Predicate Logics

This section describes (probabilistic) Datalog and presents its extension, called pDatalog++.

2.1   Probabilistic Datalog

Datalog [16] is a variant of predicate logic based on function-free Horn clauses. An atom $p(t_1,\ldots,t_n) = p(\bar{t})$ is formed by a n-ary predicate p and terms $\bar{t}$ (constants or variables for constants). A literal is either an atom $p(\bar{t})$ (positive literal) or its negation $\neg p(\bar{t})$ (negative literal). A clause $\{\neg p_1(\bar{t}), \neg q(\bar{t}), r(\bar{t})\}$ is a set of literals with one positive literal. It can be seen as a disjunction $\neg p(\bar{t}) \wedge \neg q(\bar{t}) \wedge r(\bar{t})$ or the equivalent rule $r(\bar{t}) \leftarrow p(\bar{t}), q(\bar{t})$. Here, the positive literal r denotes the head of the rule, the negative literals p and q form the rule body. Facts are rules with empty body.

In the remainder, we use a more technical notation for Datalog rules, which also PIRE uses internally. In particular, variables start with an upper-case letter, and constants with a lowercase letter. E.g., the fact that Jo is parent of Mary, that Jo is a man, and that fathers are male parents, can be expressed by:

```
parent(jo,mary).
male(jo).
father(X,Y) :- parent(X,Y) & male(X).
```

An interpretation contains all facts which are considered to be true. A model of a Datalog program is an interpretation which is consistent with the given facts and rules. As the Datalog semantics are defined by well-founded models [17], every Datalog program has at most one model.

In probabilistic Datalog [6], every fact or rule has attached a probabilistic weight α, prefixed to the fact or rule (weights $\alpha = 1$ can be omitted):

```
0.5 male(X) :- person(X).
0.8 person(ed).
```

The intended meaning of a rule αr is that "the probability that any instantiation of rule r is true is α". Thus, the preceding example pDatalog program expresses the fact a person is male with a probability of 50%, and that Ed is a person with probability of 0.8. Thus, $Pr(\text{male(ed)}) = 0.8 \cdot 0.5 = 0.4$.

The probabilities, and thus the semantics, are formally defined as follows: The pDatalog program is modelled as a probability distribution over the set of all "possible worlds". A possible world is the well-founded model of a possible deterministic program, which is formed by the deterministic part of the program and a subset of the indeterministic part. As for deterministic Datalog, only modularly stratified programs are allowed [15]. The formal definition of modular stratification is rather complicated, basically it states that no ground fact is allowed to depend negatively on itself.

By default, facts are assumed to be independent; so the probability that two facts are true equals the product of the probabilities of the two facts. In addition, computing the probability of a disjunction requires to use the incluse-exclusion formula.

As a consequence, the possible worlds in the example are:

$$Pr(W_1) = 0.2 \quad W_1 := \{\},$$
$$Pr(W_2) = 0.4 \quad W_2 := \{\text{person(ed)}\},$$
$$Pr(W_3) = 0.4 \quad W_3 := \{\text{person(ed)},\text{male(ed)}\}.$$

The probability of a fact is then computed by summing up the probabilities of all worlds in which the fact is true. Thus, we obtain $Pr(\text{male(ed)}) = 0.4$, and $Pr(\text{person(ed)}) = 0.4 + 0.4 = 0.8$ as stated as a fact.

Alternatively, sets of facts (e.g. all tuples in one relation) can be defined to be disjoint, which means that the probability of the conjunction equals zero. In this case, the probability of a disjunction equals the sum of the underlying probabilities. This feature will be heavily used throughout this paper.

2.2   Probabilistic Datalog++

We will show that probabilistic Datalog is not sufficient for PIRE. Thus, we introduce its extension pDatalog++, with the following differences:

- Constants are now numbers (integers or decimals) or strings, and are optionally enclosed in "..." or in '...' (for constants which contain e.g. whitespace).
- Variables that are never used in another argument of the same rule can be replaced by _ (the underscore). This is syntactic sugar which prevents to introduce variables which are only used once.
- SQL-like aggregation operators are introduced.
- The independence assumption can be replaced by arbitrary functions for computing the probabilities for a rule.

Aggregation Operators. Aggregation operators like sum have proven to be useful in SQL, and are thus introduced into pDatalog++. An aggregation function $f : 2^D \mapsto D$ takes a bag of values in the domain D as input, and returns a single value in D. Currently, the functions sum, count, avg, min and max (with the typical meaning) are supported. Aggregation functions can be embedded in pDatalog++ by aggregation operators, which have the prototypical form:

$$op(A, Y_1, \ldots, Y_y, \{p(X_1, \ldots, X_x)\}) \,.$$

Here, op denotes the aggregation function and the variable A the aggregation result. Furthermore, the Y_i are variables, p is a predicate, and each variable X_j either equals one of the Y_i, the placeholder _, or #, which denotes the argument containing the values from the domain D which have to be aggregated (thus, the # appears exactly once). Such a literal defines the following (nameless) relation:

$$\{(a, \bar{y}) | \exists \bar{t} : S = \{v | (\bar{y}, \bar{t}, v) \in p\}, S \neq \emptyset, a = op(S).\}$$

Here, $\bar{y} = (y_1, \ldots, y_y)$ is bound to the variables Y_i; one aggregation value $a = a(\bar{y})$ is computed for each of these tuples $\bar{y}$. In addition, $\bar{t}$ stands for the occurrences of the underscore (the free variables), and v denotes the values which are aggregated. Obviously, this approach ignores any probabilities, and just considers any tuple with a non-zero probability.

This is equivalent to group by in SQL, here:

$$\text{select } A, Y_1, \ldots, Y_y \text{ from } p \text{ group by } Y_1, \ldots, Y_y$$

The following real-world examples compute the document length as the sum of the corresponding term frequencies, count all documents containing the term, and compute the average document length:

```
dl(D,DL)  :- sum(DL,D,{tf(D,_,#)}).
df(T,DF)  :- count(DF,T,{tf(#,T,_)}).
rd('avgdl',AVGDL) :- avg(AVGDL,{dl(_,#)}).
```

Computing Probabilities. Probabilistic Datalog is based on an independence assumption. In some cases, for example for most retrieval methods, arbitrary functions for computing the probability of facts derived by a single rule are required. These functions can use the probabilities of facts bound by literals, their product, and any variable occurring in the rule.

A probabilistic version of normalised tf.idf can be computed by these rules:

```
tmp_tf(D,T) :- tf(D,T,TF) & dl(D,DL) | TF/DL.
tmp_idf(T) :- df(T,DF) & numdocs(N) | log(N/DF)/log(N).
weight(D,T) :- tmp_tf(D,T) & tmp_idf(T) | PROB1*PROB2.
```

The part after the pipe symbol | denotes the function used for computing the probabilities of derived facts. The first rule computes the TF part, where the variables TF and DL (bound by the two subgoals) are used for computing the TF-based probability. Similarly, the second rule computes the IDF part.

The last rule combines the two probabilities; where PROB1 refers to the probability of the first literal, and PROB2 refers to the probability of a ground atom bound by the second literal. For simplicity, PROB1*PROB2 is equivalent to PROB (always the product, following an independence assumption). As this is the default, it can be omitted.

3   Indexing Documents with pDatalog++

This section describes the indexing part of PIRE. First, the document model is introduced (which is very similar to the one proposed in [5]). Then, indexing weights are defined for several operators. Finally, pDatalog++ relations and rules for computing indexing weights are presented.

3.1   Data Types and Operators

We first assume a finite set $\mathbf{D}$ of elementary data types, where each data type $d \in \mathbf{D}$ has a domain (set of values) $dom(d)$. Furthermore, we consider a set $\mathbf{O}$ of operators[1]. Given an interpretation I, an operator $o \in \mathbf{O}$ defines a binary relation (instantiation) $o^I \subseteq dom(d_1(o)) \times dom(d_2(o))$ with respect to two data types $d_1(o), d_2(o) \in \mathbf{D}$. In the remainder, $\mathbf{D}$ contains the data type DOCID which denotes the set of all document ids. There is no operator defined for DOCID, i.e. $\forall o \in \mathbf{O} : d_1(o), d_2(o) \neq$ DOCID.

Vagueness of query formulations is supported by probabilistic interpretations of operators, i.e. each fact $o(v_1, v_2)$ has attached a probabilistic weight which describes the probability that v_1 is a match for v_2. Sometimes, we use an operator as a function and refer to this probability as $o(v_1, v_2) \in [0, 1]$. Similar to [10], PIRE supports these data types:

"Text": For Text, one textual value (called d here, as it refers to the document content) is compared with a single term t. The operator stemen uses stemming (Porter stemmer for the English language) and stop-word removal, while nostem does not apply stemming. Both share the same modified BM25 weighting scheme (using the term frequency $tf(d,t)$, the document length $dl(d)$ and its average value $avgdl$, the number of documents N and the document frequency $df(t)$):

$$\text{stemen}(d,t) := \frac{tf(d,t)}{tf(d,t) + 0.5 + 1.5 \cdot \frac{dl(d)}{avgdl}} \cdot \frac{\log \frac{N+0.5}{df(t)}}{\log N + 0.5}. \tag{1}$$

---

[1] Also called "data type predicates" in the Digital Library field. We use the term "operator" here to avoid confusion with predicates in logics.

"Name": This data type for person names supports two Boolean operators plainname and soundex, i.e.

$$\texttt{plainname}(v_1,v_2),\texttt{soundex}(v_1,v_2) \in \{0,1\}.$$

As an example, we have $\texttt{soundex}(\texttt{"Jones","Johnson"}) = 1$.

"Number", "Year": The data type Number has the Boolean operators =, <, >, <= and >=, i.e. the indexing weight is in $\{0,1\}$. The data type Year is equivalent to Number, but intended for years and not for numbers.

When a user is uncertain about the exact publication year of a document and requests documents from the year 1999, a document from the year 2000 might also be relevant (although the probability is lower). Thus, vague operators $\sim=$, $\sim<$ and $\sim>$ are introduced:

$$\sim>(v_1,v_2) := \begin{cases} 1 - \frac{v_2-v_1}{v_1} & , \quad v_1 < v_2 \\ 1 & , \quad else \end{cases},$$

$$\sim=(v_1,v_2) := 1 - \left(\frac{v_1-v_2}{v_2}\right)^2.$$

3.2 Schemas and Indexing Weights

Each document in PIRE adheres to a schema, which defines a list of (potentially multi-valued) attributes A_i. This document model is mapped onto our logical framework: Each attribute A_i is modelled as a binary relation symbol with a data type $d_{A_i} \in \mathbf{D}$. The relations A_i can be uncertain, too, for modelling uncertain knowledge. For an interpretation I, each relation symbol A_i is mapped onto a relation instance $A_i^I \subseteq \texttt{DOCID} \times dom(d_{A_i})$ with the correct data types. The value (second argument) of a relation A_i for a specific document d is denoted by $A_i^I(d)$, abbreviated by $A_i(d)$.

Closely related to attributes and operators are indexing weights. They are the result of applying an operator $o \in \mathbf{O}$ to the content of a document attribute $A_i(d) \in dom(d_1(o))$ and a second value $v \in dom(d_2(o))$. The notion of "indexing weight" typically appears in the area of text retrieval, where a document/term pair in the index has assigned a weight (derived from the index). This weight is typically stored in the index for performance reasons. We generalise this idea and call the result of an operator also an indexing weight (even in cases where it is not stored explicitly, e.g. for a data type "Year" and a less-than operator).

3.3 PDatalog++ Rules for Indexing

This section describes how PIRE indexes documents via pDatalog++ relations and rules. For each attribute and each their possible operators, a separate "index" is created. An index is a set of pDatalog++ relations which belong to the same attribute/operator pair. Indexing is performed locally in an index; retrieval requires the combination of several indexes.

Every index has a ternary relation tf (this name, like all others, is local to the index) which stores the token frequencies $tf(d,t)$, where the definition of a "token" depends on the operator (e.g. terms for Text, a first name or a last name for Name, and the complete number for Year). This relation is created first, by splitting the document content (using program code which depends on the data type). The deterministic unary relation docid contains all document ids. The final indexing weights are stored in a binary relation weight, where the indexing weight is the probability of the corresponding fact. Furthermore, each index has a binary relation rd for the "resource description". A resource description contains parameters which can be used in all stages of the IR process. Numerical data, e.g. parameters for the mapping functions, which are identified via textual keys. Some data types and operators use additional temporary relations for computing the indexing weights.

The following example shows how BM25 indexing weights (see equation 1) are computed for the operator stemen. In a preprocessing step, document frequency, document length, average document length and the number of documents are determined:

```
df(T,DF) :- count(DF,T,{tf(#,T,_)}).
dl(D,DL) :- sum(DL,D,{tf(D,_,#)}).
rd('avgdl',AVGDL) :- avg(AVGDL,{dl(_,#)}).
rd('numdocs',NUMDOCS) :- count(NUMDOCS,{tf(#,_,_)}).
```

Then, BM25 indexing weights can be computed. For simplicity, the computation is split into two parts (TF and IDF):

```
tmp_tf(D,T) :- tf(D,T,TF) & dl(D,DL) &_rd('avgdl',A) | TF/(TF+0.5+1.5*DL/A).
tmp_idf(T) :- df(T,DF) & rd('numdocs',N) | log((N+0.5)/DF)/log(N+0.5).
weight(D,T) :- tmp_tf(D,T) & tmp_idf(T) | PROB1*PROB2.
```

4   Retrieval with PDatalog++

This section describes the retrieval part of PIRE. First, query syntax and semantics as well as mapping functions are defined. Then, pDatalog++ rules for actually performing retrieval are presented.

4.1   Queries

An abstract syntax is used for expressing queries, which will later be translated into sets of pDatalog++ rules. Each query refers to one schema **R**, and returns document ids.

A query condition c consists of a schema attribute $A(c) \in \mathbf{R}$, an operator $o(c)$ and a comparison value $v(c)$ with matching data types, i.e. $d_{A(c)} = d_1(o(c))$ and $v(c) \in d_2(o(c))$. An example is:

author soundex "nottelmann".

Queries are formed by conditions. Two different types of queries are supported: weighted sums and Boolean-style queries.

Weighted sums have the form $\mathrm{wsum}(w(c_1)\ c_1,\ldots,w(c_n)\ c_n)$, where the c_i are conditions, and the $w(c_i) \in [0,1]$ are probabilistic weights representing the importance of the conditions. The idea is that the comparison weight for a document w.r.t. the query is the sum of the comparison weights w.r.t. the conditions c_i, weighted by the $w(c_i)$; the precise semantics are described in section 4.2.

Boolean-style queries use the Boolean operators and (conjunction) and or (disjunction) as connectors of conditions. This example query will return documents published in 2003 by a person whose name sounds like "Doe":

$$(\texttt{year} >= 2003) \text{ and } (\texttt{author soundex "doe"}).$$

By abuse of notation, $c \in q$ denotes that condition c occurs in query q.

4.2   Uncertain Inference and Probabilities of Relevance

Probabilistic Datalog adopts Rijsbergen's view of information retrieval as uncertain inference, a variant of the logical view on databases, where queries and document contents are treated as logical formulae, and a database only returns those documents d which logically imply the query q, i.e. it proves $q \leftarrow d$. For considering the intrinsic uncertainty of information retrieval, Rijsbergen interprets probabilistic IR as estimating the probability $Pr(q \leftarrow d) = Pr(q|d)$ that the document logically implies the query, and used this probability as the retrieval status value (RSV).

First, the probability that a document implies a single condition is considered:

$$Pr(c_i \leftarrow d) := o(c_i)(A(c_i)(d), v(c_i)).$$

Weighted sum queries consist of a set of conditions c_i with associated weights $Pr(q \leftarrow c_i) = w(c_i) \in [0,1]$. The underlying facts are defined to be disjoint, and the widely used linear retrieval function [20] is employed for computing the probability of inference:

$$Pr(q \leftarrow d) = \sum_{c \in q} Pr(q \leftarrow c) \cdot Pr(c \leftarrow d).$$

For Boolean-style queries, the inclusion-exclusion formula has to be applied for disjunctions, and the probabilities have to be multiplied for conjunctions (independence assumption):

$$Pr((c_1 \wedge c_2) \leftarrow d) = Pr(c_1 \leftarrow d) \cdot Pr(c_2 \leftarrow d).$$

For advanced applications like combining different operators, the RSVs have to be transformed (using a mapping function) into the probability $Pr(\text{rel}|d, q)$ that document d is relevant to a user query q ("probability of relevance") [12]:

$$f : \mathbb{R} \mapsto [0,1], \quad f(Pr(q \leftarrow d)) \approx Pr(\text{rel}|q, d).$$

Each operator has its own mapping function. Thus, we split the query q into sub-queries $q_{A,o}$ which only refer to one attribute A and operator o combination.[2] The retrieval status values $Pr(q_{A,o} \leftarrow d)$ for this sub-query are then converted into probabilities of relevance using an attribute- and operator-specific mapping function $f_{A,o}$. The overall probability of relevance is derived by combining the probabilities of relevance for the sub-queries according to the original query structure.

---

[2] When a Boolean-style query is split, several sub-queries can refer to the same attribute/operator pair, depending on the overall query structure.

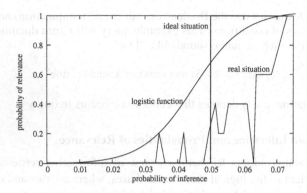

Fig. 2. Ideal and real case

In this paper, we consider linear and logistic mapping functions:

$$f_{lin}(x) := c_1 \cdot x,$$
$$f_{alin}(x) := c_0 + c_1 \cdot x,$$
$$f_{log}(x) := \frac{\exp(b_0 + b_1 \cdot x)}{1 + \exp(b_0 + b_1 \cdot x)},$$
$$f_{max}(x) := \frac{x}{\max x'}.$$

Both linear functions have the same drawback. They do not ensure that the results are between 0 and 1 in the general case of $c_0, c_1 \in I\!\!R$. In other words, the result cannot necessarily be regarded as a probability. However, linear mapping functions can be justified in the context of uncertain inference [19].

A better alternative is the logistic function [2, 3], which has been used in different application areas within IR for quite some time [7, 1, 9]. It can be seen as a continuous approximation of the step function in the ideal situation, where exactly the documents in the ranks $1, \dots, l$ are relevant, and the documents in the remaining ranks $l + 1, \dots$ are irrelevant (see figure 2).

In PIRE, the operators of the data type Text use a combination of f_{max} (applied first, so that the top-ranked document has a weight of one) and the logistic mapping function (with default parameters $b_0 = -4$ and $b_1 = 12$, other parameters can be set as well in the resource description). The same mapping functions are defined for the operators $\sim<$, $\sim>$ and $\sim=$ for the data type Year. The operators of the other data types return values in $\{0, 1\}$, and thus employ the identity mapping function $f_{id}(x) = x$.

4.3   PDatalog++ Rules for Retrieval

For each sub-query q_i (with the sub-query id $i \geq 0$), a temporary predicate rsv[query id]_[i] stores the RSV $Pr(q_i \leftarrow d)$. The corresponding temporary predicate prob[query id]_[i] is used for computing $Pr(\text{rel}|q_i, d)$ from $Pr(q_i \leftarrow d)$. In a final step, the probabilities from the relations prob[query id]_[i] are combined in a relation prob[query id].

For weighted sum queries, each sub-query contains all conditions for one combination of an attribute and an operator. The condition weights in the sub-query are normalised so that their sum equals one. Thus, the query

```
q := wsum(0.1 ti stemen ''hello'',0.3 ti stemen ''world'',
          0.6 ab stemen ''java'')
```

with the attributes `ti` and `ab` is split into two sub-queries

```
q1 := wsum(0.25 ti stemen ''hello'',0.75 ti stemen ''world'')
q2 := wsum(1,ab stemen ''java'')
```

The probabilities of relevance $Pr(\text{rel}|q_i,d)$ are computed by these rules. For simplicity, we use f_{max} as a mapping function, where 0.25 and 0.33 are arbitrarily chosen maximum RSV just for illustrating the retrieval process:

```
rsv42_0(D) :- weight(D,'hello') | (0.1/0.4)*PROB.
rsv42_0(D) :- weight(D,'world') | (0.3/0.4)*PROB.
prob42_0(D) :- rsv42_0(D) | PROB/0.25.

rsv42_1(D) :- weight(D,'java') | (0.6/0.6)*PROB.
prob42_1(D) :- rsv42_1(D) | PROB/0.33.
```

The resulting probabilities of relevance for the sub-queries are then combined by a weighted sum:

$$Pr(\text{rel}|q,d) = \sum_i \left(\sum_{c \in q_i} Pr(q_i \leftarrow c) \right) \cdot Pr(\text{rel}|q_i,d).$$

This can easily be converted into two pDatalog++ rules, assuming disjointness of the facts in `prob42_0` and those in `prob42_1`:

```
prob42(D) :- prob42_0(D) | 0.4*PROB.
prob42(D) :- prob42_1(D) | 0.6*PROB.
```

Boolean-style queries are transformed into disjunctive form (a disjunction of conjunctions of conditions). Each single condition forms a sub-query, and their results are combined straight-forward. Thus, the query

```
q := (ti stemen ''hello'' and ti stemen ''world'') or ab stemen ''java''
```

is transformed into these rules:

```
rsv42_0(D) :- weight(D,'hello').
prob42_0(D) :- rsv42_0(D) | PROB/0.2.

rsv42_1(D) :- weight(D,'world').
prob42_1(D) :- rsv42_1(D) | PROB/0.4.

rsv42_2(D) :- weight(D,'java').
prob42_2(D) :- rsv42_2(D) | PROB/0.1.

prob42(D) :- prob42_0(D) & prob42_1(D).
prob42(D) :- prob42_2(D).
```

Here, no disjointness is assumed for the facts of the relations `prob42_0`, `prob42_1` and `prob42_2`.

5 Implementation

PIRE itself is fully implemented in Java, but in its current state heavily uses a relational database. PIRE is available as Open Source.[3]

A specialised index class is used for managing the IR indexes (one for every attribute/operator combination, as mentioned before). In addition, each data type has its own class so that operations which depend on the data type can easily be separated from general code. A third, thin component (named "Indexing, Retrieval" in figure 1) glues together index and data type classes and can be called from outside with high-level methods. E.g., indexing documents (for simplicity, only with one attribute and operator) requires these few lines of pseudo code (each line corresponds to exactly one Java call):

```
create new PIRE instance
for all attributes:
  register attribute with operators
init all indexes
for all document:
  add document id to index
  for all attributes in document:
    add attribute content to index
compute indexing weights
```

PDatalog++ rules as described in this paper are used for communication between these classes, e.g. for the rules for computing indexing weights.

The architecture is flexible so that this index class can easily be exchanged by a new implementation (see below for a concrete implementation). The current implementation passes facts and rules to a pDatalog++ layer. This component stores facts (e.g. the weight facts) in relational tables. The arguments of a pDatalog++ predicate correspond to the columns $arg0,...,argn$ in the table; an additional column prob stores the probability of the tuples. Rules are converted into SQL statements. As an example, the rule

```
rsv42_0(D) :- weight(D,'hello') | (0.1/0.4)*PROB.
```

will be transformed into

```
insert into rsv42_0 select arg0,0.1/0.4*prob from weight where arg1='hello'
```

The details of this mapping procedure are beyond the scope of this paper. Different relational database management systems can be used via JDBC. In particular, HSQLDB[4] provides in-memory tables, so that no I/O effort is required. This is particularly useful where indexing and retrieval has to be done on the fly, e.g. for ranking the final results in distributed IR.

For efficiency reasons, PIRE currently uses extensional semantics [6], which means that probabilities are derived directly from the probabilities of the underlying facts. In some cases (not with the rules used so far), the probability of the same fact is considered twice. This problem can be solved by switching to intensional semantics which keeps tracks of all underlying facts. The drawback of intensional semantics is their exponential time complexity.

---

[3] http://www.is.informatik.uni-duisburg.de/projects/pire/
[4] http://hsqldb.sourceforge.net

6   Possible Extensions

As PIRE is based on logical rules, it can easily be extended towards other retrieval models (e.g. BIR or language models). It is also easy to incorporate external knowledge like a thesaurus, or to include hyper links in the retrieval process.

6.1   Language Models

So far, we only investigated weight sums and Boolean-style queries. The flexibility of pDatalog++ allows for further retrieval models, e.g. language models. Here, the probabilities $Pr(t|d) = Pr(t \leftarrow d)$ (the normalised frequency of term t in document d) and $Pr(t|G)$ (normalised frequency of t in the background knowledge, e.g. the complete collections) are combined with parameter λ; queries are sets of words:

$$Pr(q|d) = \prod_{t \in q}(\lambda Pr(t|d) + (1-\lambda)Pr(t|C)) .$$

This can easily be modelled in pDatalog++. First the probabilities $Pr(t|d)$ (stored in the relation weight) and the collection-specific probabilities $Pr(t|C)$ (stored in the relation cweight) have to be computed (the latter could also be specified manually through facts):

```
df(T,DF)    :- count(DF,T,{tf(#,T,_)}).
dl(D,DL)    :- sum(DL,D,{tf(D,_,#)}).
numdocs(N)  :- count(N,{docid(#)}).
tfc(T,TF)   :- sum(TF,T,{tf(_,T,#)}).
cl(DL)      :- sum(DL,{dl(_,#)}).
weight(D,T) :- tf(D,T,TF) & dl(D,DL) | TF/DL.
cweight(T)  :- tfc(T,TFC) & cl(DLC) | TFC/DLC.
```

Then, for each query term, retrieval status values have to be computed, and combined in the final result (if required, also probabilities of relevance could be computed):

```
rsv42_i(D) :- weight(D,'hello') | 0.3*PROB.
rsv42_i(D) :- cweight('hello') | 0.7*PROB.
...
rsv42(D) :- rsv42_0(D) & rsv42_1(D) & ... & rsv42_n(D).
```

6.2   External Knowledge

One of the major advantages of logical frameworks in IR is that external knowledge can easily be incorporated into the retrieval process. For example, term associations from a thesaurus like WordNet[5] can be used for query expansion.

WordNet already contains a set of facts which can be directly be used in pDatalog. E.g. "synsets" group synonyms together:

```
s(100012748,1,'animal',n,1,67).
s(100012748,2,'animate_being',n,1,0).
s(100012748,3,'beast',n,1,4).
```

---

[5] http://www.cogsci.princeton.edu/~wn/

```
s(100012748,4,'brute',n,2,0).
s(100012748,5,'creature',n,1,16).
s(100012748,6,'fauna',n,2,0).
```

The first argument is the synset id, the third one the term. Thus, among other terms, "animal", "beast" and "fauna" are seen as synonyms. These synsets can be exploited for retrieval, by searching for documents which contain a synonym of a search term:

```
rsv42_0(D) :- weight(D,'hello').
rsv42_0(D) :- weight(D,T) & s(N,_,T,_,_,_) & s(N,_,'hello',_,_,_).
```

Of course, more complex situations can be incorporated as well.

7 Conclusion and Outlook

This paper introduced PIRE, a probabilistic IR engine. PIRE is based on probabilistic Datalog, provides a theoretically founded basis for information retrieval. PIRE is simple to use in applications, and is already integrated in the federated Digital Library system Daffodil[6] for retrieval on locally available collections as well as for ranking the merged result list. For indexing and retrieval of documents, probabilistic Datalog has been extended by aggregation operators and by arbitrary functions for computing probabilities. This extension is called pDatalog++.

PIRE can be easily extended towards new application areas. Besides some glue code and a small amount of document preprocessing like splitting a document value into tokens (for which a variety of existing classes can be used), everything is captured in rules. This makes it easy to integrate new data types, operators, weighting schemes and retrieval functions.

We did not mention an additional feature of PIRE, namely computing moments (expectation and variance) of indexing weights, that allows for using the PIRE infrastructure also for the decision-theoretic framework of resource selection [11].

With logics, it is straight-forward to integrate additional background knowledge into account, e.g. a thesaurus, or to include hyper links between documents (or parts of them), annotations or contextual information into the retrieval process. In the near future, we will add this feature to PIRE.

We also plan to tune the pDatalog++ processing component to enhance speed, by improving the transformation of pDatalog++ rules into SQL statements.

PIRE can also be extended towards other directions. E.g., we did not use negation throughout this paper, but the limited usage of negation in pDatalog can quite easily be integrated into the system. Documents could also be described by logical expressions, allowing for a richer document model. Partial representations of documents are possible when switching to four-valued probabilistic Datalog [8] (with additional probabilities for the truth values "unknown" and "inconsistent").

Finally, XML retrieval should be supported. A primitive approach which is already implemented is to map sub-trees of the XML document (defined e.g. by XPath expressions) onto attributes. We plan to turn PIRE into a fully-fledged XML retrieval engine

---

[6] http://www.daffodil.de

which explicitly takes the hierarchical structure of the documents into account. Logics seem to be an excellent starting point for this.

Acknowledgements

This work is supported in part by the DFG (grant BIB47 DOuv 02-01, PEPPER).

References

[1] W. S. Cooper, F. C. Gey, and D. P. Dabney. Probabilistic retrieval based on staged logistic regression. In N. J. Belkin, P. Ingwersen, and A. M. Pejtersen, editors, *Proceedings of the 15th Annual International ACM SIGIR Conference on Research and Development in Information Retrieval. Copenhagen, Denmark, June 21-24, 1992*, pages 198–210, New York, 1992. ACM.

[2] S. Fienberg. *The Analysis of Cross-Classified Categorical Data*. MIT Press, Cambridge, Mass., 2. edition, 1980.

[3] D. H. Freeman. *Applied Categorical Data Analysis*. Dekker, New York, 1987.

[4] N. Fuhr. A probabilistic framework for vague queries and imprecise information in databases. In *Proceedings of the 16th International Conference on Very Large Databases*, pages 696–707, Los Altos, California, 1990. Morgan Kaufman.

[5] N. Fuhr. Towards data abstraction in networked information retrieval systems. *Information Processing and Management*, 35(2):101–119, 1999.

[6] N. Fuhr. Probabilistic Datalog: Implementing logical information retrieval for advanced applications. *Journal of the American Society for Information Science*, 51(2):95–110, 2000.

[7] N. Fuhr and U. Pfeifer. Combining model-oriented and description-oriented approaches for probabilistic indexing. In *Proceedings of the Fourteenth Annual International ACM SIGIR Conference on Research and Development in Information Retrieval*, pages 46–56, New York, 1991. ACM.

[8] N. Fuhr and T. Rölleke. HySpirit – a probabilistic inference engine for hypermedia retrieval in large databases. In *Proceedings of the 6th International Conference on Extending Database Technology (EDBT)*, pages 24–38, Heidelberg et al., 1998. Springer.

[9] F. C. Gey. Inferring probability of relevance using the method of logistic regression. In B. W. Croft and C. J. van Rijsbergen, editors, *Proceedings of the Seventeenth Annual International ACM SIGIR Conference on Research and Development in Information Retrieval*, pages 222–231, London, et al., 1994. Springer-Verlag.

[10] H. Nottelmann and N. Fuhr. Decision-theoretic resource selection for different data types in MIND. In J. Callan, F. Crestani, and M. Sanderson, editors, *Recent research in multimedia distributed information retrieval. Proceedings of the ACM SIGIR 2003 Workshop on Distributed Information Retrieval, Toronto, Canada. (Lecture Notes in Computer Science, 2924).*, Heidelberg et al., 2003. Springer.

[11] H. Nottelmann and N. Fuhr. Evaluating different methods of estimating retrieval quality for resource selection. In J. Callan, G. Cormack, C. Clarke, D. Hawking, and A. Smeaton, editors, *Proceedings of the 26st Annual International ACM SIGIR Conference on Research and Development in Information Retrieval*, New York, 2003. ACM.

[12] H. Nottelmann and N. Fuhr. From retrieval status values to probabilities of relevance for advanced IR applications. *Information Retrieval*, 6(4), 2003.

[13] J. M. Ponte and W. B. Croft. A language modeling approach to information retrieval. In W. B. Croft, A. Moffat, C. J. van Rijsbergen, R. Wilkinson, and J. Zobel, editors, *Proceedings of the 21st Annual International ACM SIGIR Conference on Research and Development in Information Retrieval*, pages 275–281, New York, 1998. ACM.

[14] S. E. Robertson. The probability ranking principle in IR. *Journal of Documentation*, 33:294–304, 1977.

[15] K. Ross. Modular stratification and magic sets for Datalog programs with negation. *Journal of the ACM*, 41(6):1216–1266, Nov. 1994.

[16] J. D. Ullman. *Principles of Database and Knowledge-Base Systems*, volume I. Computer Science Press, Rockville (Md.), 1988.

[17] A. van Gelder, K. Ross, and J. Schlipf. The well-founded semantics for general logic programs. *Journal of the ACM*, 38(3):620–650, July 1991.

[18] C. J. van Rijsbergen. A non-classical logic for information retrieval. *The Computer Journal*, 29(6):481–485, 1986.

[19] C. J. van Rijsbergen. Probabilistic retrieval revisited. *The Computer Journal*, 35(3):291–298, 1992.

[20] S. K. M. Wong and Y. Y. Yao. On modeling information retrieval with probabilistic inference. *ACM Transactions on Information Systems*, 13(1):38–68, 1995.

Data Fusion with Correlation Weights

Shengli Wu and Sally McClean

School of Computing and Mathematics,
University of Ulster, Northern Ireland, UK
{s.wu1, si.mcclean}@ulster.ac.uk

Abstract. This paper is focused on the effect of correlation on data fusion for multiple retrieval results. If some of the retrieval results involved in data fusion correlate more strongly than the others, their common opinion will dominate the voting process in data fusion. This may degrade the effectiveness of data fusion in many cases, especially when very good results appear to be a minority. For solving this problem, we assign each result a weight, which is derived from the correlation coefficient of that result to the other results, then the linear combination method can be used for data fusion. The evaluation of the effectiveness of the proposed method with TREC 5 (ad hoc track) results is reported. Furthermore, we explore the relationship between results correlation and data fusion by some experiments, and demonstrate that a relationship between them does exists.

1 Introduction

In the last couple of years the data fusion issue has been investigated by many researchers in the information retrieval field. The starting point is: for the same information need, different information retrieval systems retrieve different sets of documents (usually some overlap does exist) from the same document collection. The difference between these information retrieval systems could be diversified: different query representations, different document representations, different retrieval strategies; difference may also include factors such as parsing rules, stemming, phrase processing, relevance feedback techniques, etc. Researchers try to merge these results from multiple systems for better retrieval effectiveness. This provides an alternative method for implementing an effective information retrieval system by taking advantage of data fusion technique (e.g., in [7, 11]). On the other hand, meta-search engines in the context of WWW appear to be a relevant application for data fusion, and some results for data fusion may be useful here as well.

In this paper, we aim to investigate data fusion from the perspective of results correlation. To our knowledge, the effect of results correlation to data fusion has not been investigated previously. Correlation among component results for data fusion may vary from quite low to very high depending on the similarity of the component information retrieval systems involved. There are quite a few possibilities. If many or all systems involved are very similar to each other and the

D.E. Losada and J.M. Fernández-Luna (Eds.): ECIR 2005, LNCS 3408, pp. 275–286, 2005.
© Springer-Verlag Berlin Heidelberg 2005

retrieved results are strongly correlated, then it is not very likely that data fusion can improve the result. Another situation is that if some of the results correlate strongly with each other, while some others do not, then the common opinion among those strongly correlated results will dominate the voting process in data fusion. Such a phenomena is harmful to the performance of data fusion in many cases, especially when all component results are quite good. How to eliminate the effect of some strongly correlated results in data fusion is the major concern of this paper. Probably the most relevant work to this was done by Beitzel and his colleagues [2]: they observed very high Spearman rank correlation (0.5-0.9) existing in results from three effective strategies in the same information retrieval system of their own; and they observed medium Spearman rank correlation (0.4-0.6) in results from top three systems submitted to TREC 6, 7, 8, 9, and 2001. Different from that, we present a data fusion method, in which results correlation is used for determining a result's weight, then the linear combination method is used for data fusion. Furthermore, we carry out some experiments to demonstrate the relationship between results correlation and data fusion.

The rest of this paper is organized as follows: in Section 2 we briefly review some related work. In Section 3 we describe the methodology of the data fusion method which considers results correlation, and then in Section 4 we present the experimental results for the evaluation of the proposed method. Section 5 describes some other experiments which demonstrate the relationship between results correlation and data fusion. Section 6 concludes the paper.

2   Related Work

There has been quite a large body of research on data fusion in the field of information retrieval. We only review a few of them here, while quite a detailed survey about data fusion in the field of information retrieval can be found in [2].

Some early research such as [3, 12, 4] discussed fusing results from different query representations or retrieval strategies. Fox and his colleagues [5, 6] introduced a group of result merging methods such as CombSum and CombMNZ. CombSum sets the score of each document in the combination to the sum of the scores obtained by the individual resource, while in CombMNZ the score of each document is obtained by multiplying this sum by the number of resources which have non-zero scores. More recently CombMNZ has become the standard method in data fusion experiments.

Lee [8] did some initial work by conducting an experiment to support the hypothesis: different retrieval processes might retrieve similar sets of relevant documents but retrieve different sets of non-relevant documents. Furthermore, Lee stated that as long as the component results being used for fusion had greater relevant overlap than non-relevant overlap, improvement would be observed. That can explain why the multiple evidence fusion methods such as CombMNZ are very effective data fusion methods. In addition, a linear [0,1] normalization method for document scores in all component results has been proposed.

Vogt and Cottrell [14] carried out extensive experiment with linear combination method–weighted CombSum, and their results seemed to agree with Lee's hypothesis.

Wu and Crestani [15] proposed a method of estimating the weights of systems by "reference count", in which each document in the result returned by the evaluated system is scored according to the number of its references in the results of all other participants. The final score for the system is the sum of all document scores in its result. The estimated weights were used for the linear combination method.

Aslam and Montague proposed several data fusion methods using Bayesian inference, Borda fusion, and Condorcet fusion [1, 10]. These methods are close to CombMNZ in performance.

Score distribution models for relevant and non-relevant documents were proposed in [9]. These models can be useful for score normalization which is needed in all data fusion methods.

Very recently, Beitzel and his colleagues [2] did some experiments to compare the performances of CombMNZ using several different groups of systems. They observed no improvement when fusing results from three different retrieval strategies in the same information retrieval system, while the merged result was better than the best system when choosing top three systems submitted to TREC 6, 7, 8, 9, and 2001. In all these cases, relevant overlap was greater than non-relevant overlap. Therefore, they argued that Lee's hypotheses did not hold in such a situation when results were from different retrieval strategies in the same information retrieval system, and the difference between relevant overlap and non-relevant overlap of component results was a poor indicator of the effectiveness of fusion.

3   The Methodology of Data Fusion with Correlation Weights

We assume that all component results for data fusion are reasonably good, which is a similar assumption to [2]. This is because if all the results are reasonably good and their performance difference are not big, then it is possible to obtain better result than that of any individual result by data fusion; if some of the results are very poor while some others are very good, then it is not possible to achieve that goal. We should therefore be able to avoid the latter situation from happening by excluding poor results from the fusion.

We hypothesize that the correlation among component results affects their fusion: the less the component results correlate, the more advantageous it is for data fusion. Conversely, high correlation among component results hurts data fusion. Suppose we have two groups of component results ($g_1=\{r_{11}, r_{12}, ..., r_{1n}\}$, $g_2=\{r_{21}, r_{22}, ..., r_{2n}\}$), and for all i, r_{1i} and r_{2i} have equal performance, but the correlation among component results in the first group is much stronger than that in the second group. Then it is very likely that data fusion will obtain better result for the second group than for the first group. Furthermore, we hypothesize that a few component results having higher correlation than the others is harmful to data fusion in many cases, especially when all component results are quite good. Because in such a situation, the common opinion among highly correlating results may dominate the voting process, and the common non-relevant documents included in these highly correlating results will be over-promoted, while the relevant documents in the less correlating results cannot be properly promoted.

Certainly, the performance of all the component results affects the performance of the fused result, but correlation among component results is another aspect which may affect the performance of data fusion. How to eliminate the effect of some high result correlations is the major concern of this paper. The idea is to analyze the correlation for different results, then calculate a weight for each component: if a component result correlates more closely to all other results on average, then a lighter weight is assigned to it; otherwise, a heaver weight is assigned to it.

Suppose we have n $(n > 2)$ results $r_1, r_2, ..., r_n$ for fusion, first we calculate correlation coefficient for every pair of results r_i and r_j $(1 \leq i \leq n, 1 \leq j \leq n, i \neq j)$. In the experiments, two methods are used to calculate the correlation coefficient between two results. The first one is:

$$v_{ij} = \frac{2 * |o_{ij}|}{|r_i| + |r_j|} \tag{1}$$

where $|o_{ij}|$ is the number of overlapping documents in component results r_i and r_j. $|r_i|$ and $|r_j|$ are the number of documents in result i and j, respectively. The second one is to use Spearman rank correlation coefficient:

$$s_{ij} = 1 - \frac{6}{n^3 - n} \sum d_k^2 \tag{2}$$

where d_k is the rank difference of common document k, and n is the number of documents in both results. Two rankings are identical when the coefficient is 1, and in reverse order when the coefficient is -1. Otherwise the coefficient lies between -1 and 1.

For every result r_i, we obtain its average correlation coefficient with all other results $c_i = \frac{1}{n-1} \sum_{j=1,2,...,n,j \neq i} v_{ij}$ or $c_i = \frac{1}{n-1} \sum_{j=1,2,...,n,j \neq i} s_{ij}$ respectively. A weight $w_i = 1 - c_i$ can be set for every result. Another option is to include the performance p_i of result r_i, we let $w_i = (1 - c_i) * p_i$. Having w_i for every result r_i, we use the linear combination method to achieve data fusion:

$$s(w, d, q) = \sum_{i=1}^{n} w_i s_i(d, q)$$

where $s = (s_1(d, q), s_2(d, q), ..., s_n(d, q))$ are the scores of document d in the fused result for a given query q.

It is interesting to compare the method presented in the above with the method proposed in [15]. Two methods are similar to some extent, since they both estimate the weights of all participants by "reference count" for the linear combination method. However, in [15], a heavier weight is assigned to a popular system; while a lighter weight is assigned to a "popular" system in this paper. The totally opposite solution works without contradiction because they have been used in different situations. Different settings have been used in the experiments with TREC collections and queries. For the former, we only choose results submitted by different organizations so as to avoid highly correlating results coming together; while for the latter, we only choose quite good results.

4   Evaluation of the Data Fusion Method

In this section we present the experimental results for the evaluation of the data fusion method proposed in last section.

We used a group of results submitted to ad hoc track (category A) in TREC 5 [13]. Out of 61 results, we chose 41, which met the following requirements:

- 1000 documents were retrieved for each of the 50 queries;
- the mean average precision was 0.15 or over.

With these requirements, it provided us a homogeneous environment for the evaluation. Poor results were discarded since they did not represent the normal situation for information retrieval, and they were harmful to data fusion.

We used 3 results for each data fusion run. With total 41 results, there were 10660 different combinations. In each run, different results were assigned different weights using $w_i = 1 - c_i$. If the weights assigned to all component systems are very similar, then the performance of the linear combination is very close to that of CombSum; if the weights assigned to all component systems are quite different, we may observe bigger difference between combSum and the linear combination method. Therefore, we calculated simple standard deviation for the weights in every run ($s = \sqrt{\frac{\sum_{i=1}^{n}(w_i - \bar{w})^2}{n-1}}$), then we divided these runs into two groups ($s > t$ and $s \leq t$), where t is a threshold chosen by experimentation.

Table 1-4 show the experimental results with $t = 0.1$ for both overlap count (see Equation 1) and Spearman rank correlation (see Equation 2). However, the experimental results for these two methods were very similar. Several different measures were used as in TREC [13]: average precision at different document levels (5, 10, 15, 20, 30, and 100), average precision over all relevant documents, and R-precision (precision after R documents retrieved where R is the number of relevant documents for the given query). Table 1 and Table 2 show the results when the standard deviation value $s \leq 0.1$, in which CombSum, CombMNZ, and the linear combination method are very close in performance, especially combSum and the linear combination method are almost the same since in the latter method, similar weights are assigned to component results. Table 3 and 4 show the results with standard deviation value $s > 0.1$, in which the linear combination method performs slightly better (varies from 0.8% to 4.7%) than CombSum on all measures. Especially, the difference between the linear combination method and CombSum is bigger when considering average precision at

280   S. Wu and S. McClean

Table 1. Performance of merging methods with correlation weights (overlap count, $w_i = 1 - c_i$, deviation ≤ 0.1, 10015 runs)

Measure	CombSum	CombMNZ	Linear combination
ave_5	0.5039	0.5064	0.5035
ave_10	0.4492	0.4526	0.4491
ave_15	0.4108	0.4144	0.4107
ave_20	0.3833	0.3867	0.3833
ave_30	0.3438	0.3474	0.3438
ave_100	0.2283	0.2302	0.2283
ave_precision	0.2577	0.2599	0.2574
R_precision	0.2872	0.2885	0.2872

Table 2. Performance of merging methods with correlation weights (Spearman rank, $w_i = 1 - c_i$, deviation ≤ 0.1, 10145 runs)

Measure	CombSum	CombMNZ	Linear combination
ave_5	0.5038	0.5064	0.5038
ave_10	0.4491	0.4525	0.4492
ave_15	0.4107	0.4143	0.4108
ave_20	0.3833	0.3867	0.3833
ave_30	0.3437	0.3473	0.3438
ave_100	0.2283	0.2301	0.2283
ave_precision	0.2577	0.2599	0.2576
R_precision	0.2872	0.2885	0.2871

Table 3. Performance of merging methods with correlation weights (overlap count, $w_i = 1 - c_i$, deviation > 0.1, 645 runs, * indicates a significant difference)

Measure	CombSum	CombMNZ	Linear combination
ave_5	0.4435	0.4533*(+2.2%)	0.4643*(+4.7%)
ave_10	0.4032	0.4098*(+1.6%)	0.4164*(+3.3%)
ave_15	0.3720	0.3766*(+1.2%)	0.3820*(+2.7%)
ave_20	0.3486	0.3525*(+1.1%)	0.3567*(+2.3%)
ave_30	0.3148	0.3175*(+0.9%)	0.3206*(+1.8%)
ave_100	0.2140	0.2136(-0.2%)	0.2154*(+1.1%)
ave_precision	0.2389	0.2394(+0.2%)	0.2415*(+1.1%)
R_precision	0.2726	0.2713*(-0.5%)	0.2745*(+0.7%)

the 5-20 document levels. The linear combination method and CombMNZ are close in performance.

In the above, $t = 0.1$ has been set arbitrarily. Some other values can be chosen as well. When a value t greater than 0.1 is chosen, we observe bigger improvement than that shown in Table 3 and 4 for the linear combination method in the group $(s > t)$, and vice versa.

Table 4. Performance of merging methods with correlation weights (Spearman rank, $w_i = 1 - c_i$, deviation > 0.1, 515 runs, * indicates a significant difference)

Measure	CombSum	CombMNZ	Linear combination
ave_5	0.4294	0.4408*(+2.7%)	0.4497*(+4.7%)
ave_10	0.3926	0.4010*(+2.1%)	0.4061*(+3.4%)
ave_15	0.3636	0.3694*(+1.6%)	0.3739*(+2.8%)
ave_20	0.3415	0.3463*(+1.4%)	0.3501*(+2.5%)
ave_30	0.3092	0.3123*(+1.0%)	0.3153*(+2.0%)
ave_100	0.2107	0.2103(-0.2%)	0.2124*(+0.8%)
ave_precision	0.2334	0.2341*(+0.7%)	0.2364*(+1.3%)
R_precision	0.2689	0.2676*(-0.5%)	0.2713*(+0.9%)

Next we used $w_i = (1 - c_i) * p_i$ to do the experiment, and all other aspects were kept the same. For every result r_i we used the mean average precision value of that result over 50 queries as the value of p_i. The experimental results are shown in Table 5-8. As before we divide them into two groups, one with ($s \leq 0.05$) and the other with ($s > 0.05$). Table 5 and 6 show the result of group ($s \leq 0.05$), in which the combination method is slightly better than CombSum

Table 5. Performance of merging methods with correlation weights (overlap count, $w_i = (1 - c_i) * p_i$, deviation ≤ 0.05, 10233 runs, * indicates a significant difference)

Measure	CombSum	CombMNZ	Linear combination
ave_5	0.5015	0.5041*(+0.5%)	0.5162*(+2.9%)
ave_10	0.4474	0.4509*(+0.8%)	0.4591*(+2.6%)
ave_15	0.4093	0.4129*(+0.9%)	0.4200*(+2.6%)
ave_20	0.3820	0.3855*(+0.9%)	0.3920*(+2.6%)
ave_30	0.3426	0.3462*(+1.1%)	0.3512*(+2.5%)
ave_100	0.2277	0.2295*(+0.8%)	0.2322*(+2.0%)
ave_precision	0.2567	0.2590*(+0.9%)	0.2629*(+2.4%)
R_precision	0.2863	0.2876*(+0.5%)	0.2914*(+1.8%)

Table 6. Performance of merging methods with correlation weights (Spearman rank, $w_i = (1 - c_i) * p_i$, deviation ≤ 0.05, 9003 runs, , * indicates a significant difference)

Measure	CombSum	CombMNZ	Linear combination
ave_5	0.4981	0.5009*(+0.6%)	0.5092*(+2.3%)
ave_10	0.4451	0.4486*(+0.8%)	0.4544*(+2.1%)
ave_15	0.4076	0.4112*(+0.9%)	0.4161*(+2.1%)
ave_20	0.3805	0.3841*(+0.9%)	0.3886*(+2.1%)
ave_30	0.3414	0.3450*(+1.1%)	0.3484*(+2.1%)
ave_100	0.2271	0.2289*(+0.8%)	0.2309*(+1.7%)
ave_precision	0.2552	0.2575*(+1.3%)	0.2603*(+2.0%)
R_precision	0.2846	0.2861*(+0.5%)	0.2889*(+1.5%)

Table 7. Performance of merging methods with correlation weights (overlap count, $w_i = (1 - c_i) * p_i$, deviation > 0.05, 427 runs, , * indicates a significant difference)

Measure	CombSum	CombMNZ	Linear combination
ave_5	0.4701	0.4810*(+2.3%)	0.5516*(+17.3%)
ave_10	0.4219	0.4288*(+1.6%)	0.4818*(+14.5%)
ave_15	0.3884	0.3930*(+1.2%)	0.4373*(+12.6%)
ave_20	0.3638	0.3670*(+0.9%)	0.4072*(+11.9%)
ave_30	0.3292	0.3310*(+0.5%)	0.3631*(+10.3%)
ave_100	0.2226	0.2204*(-1.0%)	0.2378*(+10.0%)
ave_precision	0.2522	0.2520(± 0.0%)	0.2745*(+8.8%)
R_precision	0.2877	0.2848*(-1.0%)	0.3027*(+5.2%)

Table 8. Performance of merging methods with correlation weights (Spearman rank, $w_i = (1 - c_i) * p_i$, deviation > 0.05, 1657 runs)

Measure	CombSum	CombMNZ	Linear combination
ave_5	0.5118	0.5157*(+0.8%)	0.5569*(+8.8%)
ave_10	0.4532	0.4575*(+0.9%)	0.4866*(+7.4%)
ave_15	0.4131	0.4170*(+0.9%)	0.4419*(+7.0%)
ave_20	0.3853	0.3885*(+0.8%)	0.4110*(+6.7%)
ave_30	0.3458	0.3490*(+0.9%)	0.3671*(+6.2%)
ave_100	0.2296	0.2307*(+0.5%)	0.2401*(+4.6%)
ave_precision	0.2640	0.2651*(+0.4%)	0.2799*(+6.0%)
R_precision	0.2958	0.2953*(-0.2%)	0.3073*(+3.9%)

and CombMNZ by 1% to 2%. Table 7 and 8 show the result of group ($s > 0.05$), in which the combination method outperforms CombSum by 4% to 17%, and outperforms combMNZ by 4% to 15%.

Paired-samples T test was done for two pairs (CombMNZ, CombSum) and (the linear combination method, CombSum). In Table 3-8, a figure with a "*" indicates that it is significantly different from the one in CombSum at 95% significance level.

5   The Relationship Between Results Correlation and Data Fusion

The experimental results in Section 4 suggest that results correlation coefficients are useful for data fusion, thus it is very likely that there is certain relationship between results correlation and data fusion. In this section we aim to find out more about this.

First let us analyze all possible pair of 41 results. We have $41 * 40/2 = 820$ different combinations from 41 results. For every combination (r_1, r_2) and every query, we count the number of overlapping documents, the number of non-overlapping documents, the number of relevant documents in the overlapping

Table 9. Component document analysis for all pairs of results

Overlap rate	Total runs	Overlaps	O_rel	O_rel/ overlaps	Unique_rel	Total_rel
(0%-10%)	0	-	-	-	-	-
(10%-20%)	26	172.88	28.00	16.2%	37.99	65.99
(20%-30%)	270	253.31	33.00	13.03%	34.58	67.58
(30%-40%)	265	347.42	40.17	11.56%	28.99	69.16
(40%-50%)	178	446.19	43.58	9.77%	23.47	67.05
(50%-60%)	56	538.40	47.37	8.80%	19.38	66.75
(60%-70%)	9	654.98	51.15	7.92%	13.98	65.13
(70%-80%)	1	710.56	43.36	6.10%	7.06	50.42
(80%-90%)	5	836.24	54.15	6.48%	6.38	60.53
(90%-100%)	10	950.35	44.90	4.72%	0.04	44.94

Table 10. Component document analysis for all triples of results

Group	Overlap rate	Total runs	O3	O2	O3_rel	O2_rel	Uni_rel	Total_ rel	Average precision
1	(0%-20%)	0	-	-	-	-	-	-	-
2	(20%-30%)	80	8.5%	19.9%	20.46	21.78	31.48	73.72	0.1757
3	(30%-40%)	1515	12.8%	23.9%	25.13	23.73	28.52	77.38	0.2002
4	(40%-50%)	4111	17.9%	27.5%	29.89	22.40	23.90	75.19	0.2132
5	(50%-60%)	3337	25.4%	29.0%	35.13	19.10	20.27	74.50	0.2217
6	(60%-70%)	1149	33.0%	31.0%	38.95	16.20	16.79	71.94	0.2264
7	(70%-80%)	436	32.0%	41.9%	37.02	13.61	17.66	68.29	0.2124
8	(80%-90%)	28	49.6%	32.4%	45.49	9.48	10.91	65.88	0.2124
9	(90%-100%)	4	90.8%	6.2%	37.02	1.64	1.64	40.30	0.2179

part, and the number of relevant documents in the non-overlapping part (in either r_1 or r_2), and we average these numbers over 50 queries for every combination. Then we divide these combinations into 10 groups according to their overlap rates. Table 9 shows the result. In Table 9, item "Overlaps" stands for the average number of total overlapping documents of that group, "O_rel" stands for the average number of relevant documents in the overlapping part, "Unique_rel" stands for the average number of relevant documents in the non-overlapping part, "O_rel/Overlaps" stands for the ratio of "O_rel" to "Overlaps", while "Total_rel" stands for the total number of relevant documents in all component results. "Overlaps", "O_rel", "Unique_rel", and "Total_rel" are the average of that group over 50 queries.

For most groups, the total number of relevant documents in both the overlapping part and the non-overlapping part (Total_rel) are close, between 60-70. Only two groups (with a overlap rate of 70%-80% and 90%-100%, respectively) have fewer relevant documents. When the overlap rate increases, both "Overlaps" and "O_rel" increase accordingly. However, if we consider the percentage of the latter to the former (O_rel/Overlaps), it decreases when the overlap rate increases.

"Total runs" are very different among groups. About $(270+265+178)/820 =$ 87% of the total pairs has a overlap rate between 20% and 50%. All pairs of results have at least 10% of overlapping documents. Only 26 pairs of results have below 20% of overlapping documents, and only 26 pairs of results have over 60% of overlapping documents. All 16 pairs of results having over 70% of overlapping documents are retrieved by the same information retrieval system with small difference in one way or another. For example, one result is retrieved by automatically generated queries and another is retrieved by manually generated queries. This indicates that fairly good information retrieval systems have certain similar behavior, in that they tend to retrieve considerable number of identical documents (including relevant documents) for the same information need. On the other hand, each of these information retrieval systems is able to retrieve some relevant documents of its own, which are not retrieved by some other systems.

Next let us reconsider the experiment in the previous section by grouping all 10660 runs using another measure-total overlap rate among three results, which will be referred as overlap rate in the remainder of this paper. Total overlap rate among three results is defined as follow:

$$o\_rate_{123} = \frac{2 * (|o_{12}| + |o_{13}| + |o_{23}|) + 3 * |o_{123}|}{|r_1| + |r_2| + |r_3|}$$

where $|o_{ij}|$ stands for the number of overlapping documents in results r_i and r_j $(1 \le i \le 3, 1 \le j \le 3, i \ne j)$, and $|o_{123}|$ stand for the number of overlapping documents occurring in results r_1 and r_2 and r_3.

We divide all 10660 runs into 9 groups according to their overlap rate, which is shown in Table 10. In Table 10, "O3" stands for the percentage of overlapping documents occurring in all three results to the total documents in all three results, "O2" stands for the percentage of overlapping documents in any two of the results to the total documents in three results, "O3_rel" stands for the number of relevant documents occurring in all three results, "O2_rel" stands for the number of relevant documents occurring in any two of the three results, "Uni_rel" stands for the number of relevant documents occurring in only one result (anyone of the three), "Total_rel" stands for the total number of relevant documents in all three results (Uni_rel+O2_rel+O3_rel), while "Average precision" stands for the mean average precision of all results in that group. We observe that triples of results with an overlap rate between 30% and 70% take up as much as 95% of all runs. when "Overlap rate" increases, both "O3" and "O3_rel" increase, and "Uni_rel" decreases with a few exceptions. When "Overlap rate" increases, there is no obvious variation tendency for "O2", but "O2_rel" decreases. Finally, "Total_rel" decreases when "Overlap rate" increases.

For Group 2 and 3 whose overlap rate are (20%-30%) and (30%-40%) respectively, the mean average precision of the results are lower than that of the other groups. It suggests that not very good results (they are still good results, please note that all results chosen in the experiment are quite good results.) weakly correlate with each other while the correlation between very good results are quite strong (with an overlap rate of 40% or above), We cannot observe any co-variation between "Total_rel" and "Average precision", however, we can observe one interesting thing by compare group 6-10 and group 2-3. Though the value of "Average precision" of group 6-9 is higher than that of group 2 and 3, the value of "Total_rel" of group 6-10 is not as high as that of group 2-3. This suggests that very high overlap rate and therefore, strong correlation among component results is harmful to data fusion since they are very likely not to provide as many relevant documents as in the low overlap rate situation, even when very good results are involved.

6   Conclusions and Future Work

In this paper we have presented a data fusion method which takes account of the effect of results correlation. Each result in data fusion is assigned a weight, which is determined by its average correlation measure to all other results, then the linear combination method is used for data fusion. Experiments have been conducted with a group of results submitted to TREC5 (ad hoc track), which show that an improvement can be obtained over CombSum when some of the component results correlate with each other more closely than with the others. Also if combined with estimated performance measure, the proposed method can be further improved.

Furthermore, we have investigated why results correlation has an effect on data fusion by analyzing the distribution of overlapping documents with all different combinations of component results. The experimental results indicate that the total number of relevant documents involved in all these results decreases when overlapping rate increases, which is harmful to data fusion. This suggests that ideally, results that are being combined for data fusion should be satisfied:

- all component results should be close in performance; very poor results should be avoided;
- all component results should not not strongly correlate with each other ;
- considering all pairs of component results, the closeness of these correlations should be similar. That means no pair should have a much strong correlation than any other pairs.

The effect of result correlation on data fusion can be furthered by experimenting with more data collections/queries and building a model to describe their relationship more precisely. This remains as our future work.

References

1. J. A. Aslam and M. Montague. Models for metasearch. In *Proceedings of the 24th Annual International ACM SIGIR Conference*, pages 276–284, New Orleans, Lousiana, USA, September 2001.
2. S. Beitzel, E. Jensen, A. Chowdhury, D. Grossman, O. Frieder, and N. Goharian. On fusion of effective retrieval strategies in the same information retrieval system. *Journal of the American Society of Information Science and Technology*, 55(10):859–868, 2004.

3. N. J. Belkin, C. Cool, W. B. Croft, and J. P. Callan. The effect of multiple query representations on information retrieval performance. In *Proceedings of ACM SIGIR'93. Pittsburgh, USA.*, pages 339–346, Pittsburgh, USA, June-July 1993.

4. P. W. Foltz and S. T. Dumais. Personalized infromation delivery: an analysis of information-filtering methods. *Communications of the ACM*, 35(12):51–60, 1992.

5. E. A. Fox, M. P. Koushik, J. Shaw, R. Modlin, and D. Rao. Combining evidence from multiple searchs. In *The First Text REtrieval Conference (TREC-1)*, pages 319–328, Gaitherburg, MD, USA, March 1993.

6. E. A. Fox and J. Shaw. Combination of multiple searchs. In *The Second Text REtrieval Conference (TREC-2)*, pages 243–252, Gaitherburg, MD, USA, August 1994.

7. D. K. Harman, editor. *Proceedings of 3rd Text Retrieval Conference (TREC-3)*, Gaithersburg, Maryland, USA, April 1995. National Technical Information Service of USA.

8. J. H. Lee. Analysis of multiple evidence combination. In *Proceedings of the 20th Annual International ACM SIGIR Conference*, pages 267–275, Philadelphia, Pennsylvania, USA, July 1997.

9. R. Manmatha, T. Rath, and F. Feng. Modeling score dsitributions for combining the outputs of search engines. In *Proceedings of the 24th Annual International ACM SIGIR Conference*, pages 267–275, New Orleans, USA, September 2001.

10. M. Montague and J. A. Aslam. Condorcet fusion for improved retrieval. In *Proceedings of ACM CIKM Conference*, pages 538–548, McLean, VA, USA, November 2002.

11. K. B. Ng, D. Loewenstern, C. Basu, H. Hirsh, and P. B. Kantor. Data fusion of machine-learning methods for the trec5 routing task. In E. M. Voorhees and D. K. Harman, editors, *Proceedings of the 5th Text REtrieval Conference*, Gaithersburg, Maryland, USA, November 20-22 1996. National Technical Information Service of USA.

12. H. Turtle and W. B. Croft. Evaluation of an inference network-based retrieval model. *ACM Transaction on Information Systems*, 9(3):187–222, 1991.

13. E. M. Voorhees and D. K. Harman, editors. *Proceedings of the 5th Text Retrieval Conference*, Gaithersburg, Maryland, USA, November 20-22 1996. National Technical Information Service of USA.

14. C. C. Vort and G. A. Cotterell. A fusion via a linear combination of scores. *Information Retrieval*, 1(3):151–173, October 1999.

15. S. Wu and F. Crestani. Data fusion with estimated weights. In *Proceedings of the 2002 ACM CIKM International Conference on Information and Knowledge Management*, pages 648–651, McLean, VA, USA, November 2002.

Using Restrictive Classification and Meta Classification for Junk Elimination

Stefan Siersdorfer and Gerhard Weikum

Max-Planck-Institute for Computer Science, Germany
{stesi, weikum}@mpi-sb.mpg.de

Abstract. This paper addresses the problem of performing supervised classification on document collections containing also *junk documents*. With "junk documents" we mean documents that do *not* belong to the topic categories (classes) we are interested in. This type of documents can typically not be covered by the training set; nevertheless in many real world applications (e.g. classification of web or intranet content, focused crawling etc.) such documents occur quite often and a classifier has to make a decision about them. We tackle this problem by using restrictive methods and ensemble-based meta methods that may decide to leave out some documents rather than assigning them to inappropriate classes with low confidence. Our experiments with four different data sets show that the proposed techniques can eliminate a relatively large fraction of junk documents while dismissing only a significantly smaller fraction of potentially interesting documents.

1 Introduction

1.1 Motivation

Automatic document classification is useful for a wide range of applications such as organizing web, intranet, or portal pages into topic directories, filtering news feeds or mail, focused crawling on the web or in intranets, and many more. In the classical scenario it is often assumed that all topic categories (classes) are known and that the training corpus provides example documents for all these categories. However in many real world applications these assumptions do not hold. As an example consider a focused crawler where we are interested just in a limited number of topics and, as the case may be, subtopics. Here we have to deal with the problem that the web covers such a phletora (and growing number) of other topics that it is impossible to build a training set that comprises all these topics. However a focused crawler will very likely see such "junk documents", although the underlying classifier has never seen (and never had a chance to see) any training data for the "junk" class, and will have to make a decision about them. It is not clear how a classifier trained to discriminate topics based on training data about "computer sciene","mathematics" and "physics" will behave on documents about, say, "esoterism"; there is a significant difference between negative examples and "junk" documents.

D.E. Losada and J.M. Fernández-Luna (Eds.): ECIR 2005, LNCS 3408, pp. 287–299, 2005.

In this paper we propose restrictive classification methods to tackle the "junk problem". In restrictive classification, we consider classifiers for a given topic that make a ternary decision on a newly seen document: they can accept the document for the topic, reject it for the topic, or abstain if there is neither sufficiently evidence for acceptance nor for rejection. With the abstention option we aim to achieve a lower error on the remaining documents and to eliminate the junk documents that would be spuriously assigned to one of the classes of interest.

1.2   Contribution

In [17] a framework for restrictive classification and meta methods with ternary decisions was introduced. It was assumed that all underlying classifiers had sufficient training data: both positive and negative samples of every thematic that might occur among the test documents. In the current paper we drop this assumption and make a major step forward to cope with corpora that are not necessarily "in tune" with the thematic classes that were defined a priori. This is a very significant case with "open" corpora like the web with a huge amount of topics and documents for which comprehensive training is absolutely impossible.

The current paper makes the following technical contributions:

1. It develops decision procedures for junk elimination based on restrictive classifiers and meta classifiers.
2. It develops a probabilistic explanation model and analytically shows that the elimination ratio of junk documents is larger than the loss of potentially interesting documents.
3. It presents comprehensive experiments, using four different data sets, including a web document collection, that demonstrate the benefits of the proposed methods.

1.3   Related Work

There is a considerable prior of work on text document classification using all kinds of probabilistic and discriminative models [6]. The machine learning literature has studied a variety of meta methods such as bagging, stacking, or boosting [4, 20, 12, 9], and also combinations of heterogeneous learners (e.g., [22]).

In [17] restrictive meta methods based on training set splitting and a probabilistic model are developed for automatic handling of the tradeoffs between different aspects of the classifier quality (loss, classification error, and efficiency). In [16] a similar probabilistic model is applied to meta clustering.

However, to our knowledge, these techniques were, up to now, not considered in the context of junk reduction.

1.4   Outline

The rest of the paper is organized as follows. In Section 2 we briefly review the technical basics of classification methods. Section 3 presents our notion of restrictive methods: we describe simple restrictive methods and the restrictive combination of different classification methods, and we provide a probabilistic model for junk reduction. Section 4 provides experiments on different real-world data sets.

2   Technical Basics

Classifying text documents into thematic categories usually follows a supervised learning paradigm and is based on training documents that need to be provided for each topic. Moreover, the best classification methods, most notably, SVMs, need both positive and negative samples for training. This prerequisite is not satisfied in the presence of "junk documents" for which no training samples are available.

Both training documents and test documents, which are later given to the classifier, are represented as multidimensional feature vectors. In the prevalent bag-of-words model the features are derived from word occurrence frequencies, e.g. based on tf*idf feature weights [3, 13]. Often feature selection algorithms are applied to reduce the dimensionality of the feature space and eliminate "noisy", non-characteristic features, based on information-theoretic measures for feature ordering (e.g., relative entropy or information gain).

Feature vectors of topic labeled text documents (e.g., capturing $tf \cdot idf$ weights of terms) are used to train a classification model for each topic, using probabilistic (e.g., Naive Bayes) or discriminative models (e.g., SVM). Linear support vector machines (SVMs) construct a hyperplane $w \cdot x + b = 0$ that separates the set of positive training examples from a set of negative examples with maximum margin. This training requires solving a quadratic optimization problem whose empirical performance is somewhere between quadratic and cubic in the number of training documents [5]. For a new, previously unseen, document d the SVM merely needs to test whether the document lies on the "positive" side or the "negative" side of the separating hyperplane. The decision simply requires computing a scalar product of the vectors w and d. SVMs have been shown to perform very well for text classification (see, e.g., [7, 10]).

Multiple classifiers can be combined using a meta classifier approach [4, 20, 9], for example, by voting on the final decision (including weighted voting, see, e.g., [19]). Such a setup is interesting not only to combine different algorithmic techniques, but mostly for combining classifiers that have been trained with different training sets or for different feature spaces.

In this paper we consider only binary classifiers that make a decision for a single topic, based on positive and negative training examples.

3   Elimination of Junk by Restrictive Classification

3.1   Tradeoffs in Restrictive Classification

In this paragraph we describe the tradeoffs that occur in restrictive classification. Consider a training set T consisting of documents from two classes *pos* and *neg*,

		classification		
		+	-	0
real class	pos	P+	P-	P0
	neg	N+	N-	N0
	junk	J+	J-	J0

Fig. 1. Contingency Table for Restrictive Classification with Junk Reduction

and a set of unlabeled documents U containing documents from *pos* and *neg* and *junk* documents, that are not in these classes. (The scenario can be easily generalized to a set of l classes $C = \{c_1, \ldots, c_l\}$ instead of two classes.) Given a document $d \in U$, a restrictive classifier gives us the result $+1$ if it classifies the document into *pos*, -1 if it classifies the document into *neg*, 0 if the classifier abstains. The possible combinations between the real classes and the result of a classifier are shown in the contingency table in figure 1. In this notation e.g. $N+$ is the set of documents in *neg* which are assigned to class *pos* by the classifier, $J0$ is the set of junk documents from U where the classifier abstains, etc.

An appropriate restrictive classifier should optimize the following quality measures:

1. Maximize $junk - reduction$ (fraction of junk documents dismissed by the classifier):

$$junkRed := \frac{|J0|}{|J+| + |J-| + |J0|} \quad (1)$$

2. Minimize *loss* (fraction of dismissed documents from the classes of interest *pos* and *neg*):

$$loss := \frac{|P0| + |N0|}{|P+| + |P-| + |P0| + |N0|} \quad (2)$$

3. Minimize *error* (fraction of non-dismissed documents classified into the wrong class):

$$error := \frac{|P-| + |N+| + |J+| + |J-|}{|P+| + |P-| + |N+| + |N-| + |J+| + |J-|} \quad (3)$$

As document reduction (not to confuse with the loss), we define the fraction of documents in U, where the classifier abstains:

$$docRed := \frac{|P0| + |N0| + |J0|}{|U|} \quad (4)$$

The document reduction can observed directly from the classifier output without knowing the real class labels of the documents in U. The document reduction has an implicit influence on $junkRed$, *loss* and *error*.

In practice we observe a tradeoff between the loss at the one hand and junk-decimation and error on the other hand.

3.2   Making Simple Methods Restrictive

We can use confidence measures to make simple methods restrictive. For SVMs or the Centroid method a natural confidence measure is the distance of a test document vector from the separating hyperplane. So we can tune these methods by requiring that accepted or rejected documents have a distance above some threshold, and abstain otherwise. The threshold is our tuning parameter.

Given a document reduction of R percent, we can make a classifier restrictive by dismissing the R percent of the test documents with the lowest confidence values.

3.3   Restrictive Meta Methods

For meta classification we are given a set $V = \{v_1, \ldots, v_k\}$ of k binary classifiers with results $R(v_i, d)$ in $\{+1, -1, 0\}$ for a document d, namely, $+1$ if d is accepted for the given topic by v_i, -1 if d is rejected, and 0 if v_i abstains. We can combine these results into a meta result: $Meta(d) = Meta(R(v_1, d), \ldots, R(v_k, d))$ in $\{+1, -1, 0\}$ where 0 means abstention. A family of such meta methods is the linear classifier combination with thresholding [15]. Given thresholds t_1 and t_2, with $t_1 > t_2$, and weights $w(v_i)$ for the k underlying classifiers we compute $Meta(d)$ as follows:

$$Meta(d) = \begin{cases} +1 \text{ if } \sum_{i=1}^{n} R(v_i, d) \cdot w(v_i) > t_1 \\ -1 \text{ if } \sum_{i=1}^{n} R(v_i, d) \cdot w(v_i) < t_2 \\ 0 \quad \text{otherwise} \end{cases} \qquad (5)$$

This meta classifier family has some important special cases, depending on the choice of the weights and thresholds:

1) voting [4]: Meta returns the result of the majority of the classifiers.
2) unanimous decision: if all classifiers give us the same result (either $+1$ or -1), Meta returns this result, 0 otherwise.
3) weighted averaging [19]: Meta weighs the classifiers by using some predetermined quality estimator, e.g., a leave-one-out estimator for each v_i.

The restrictive and tunable behavior is achieved by the choice of the thresholds: we dismiss the documents where the linear result combination lies between t_1 and t_2. In the rest of the paper we will consider only the unanimous-decision meta classifier as the simplest and most conservative of the above cases in order to demonstrate the feasibility of our approach. Of course other meta options might be worthwile. The tuning of the thresholds t_1 and t_2 is beyond the scope of this paper.

3.4   A Probabilistic Model for Restrictive Meta Methods

In this subsection we develop a simplified probabilistic model to a better understanding of why meta classification works and provide approximations for *loss*, *error* and *junkRed*. Consider the unanimous-decision meta method described above.

We associate a Bernoulli random variable X_i with each classification method v_i, where $X_i = 1$ if v_i classifies a document into class *pos* and $X_i = 0$ if v_i classifies a document into class *neg*. We want to compute the probability $P(X_1 = \ldots = X_k | junk)$ that the classifiers v_i provide a unanimous decision if they are presented a junk document. From basic probability theory it follows that

$$P(X_1 = 1 \wedge X_2 = 1 | Junk)$$
$$= cov(X_1, X_2 | Junk) + P(X_1 = 1 | Junk) \cdot P(X_2 = 1 | Junk) \qquad (6)$$

Where

$$cov(X_1, X_2 | Junk) = \frac{1}{n-1} \sum_j (x_1 - \overline{x_1})(x_2 - \overline{x_2}) \qquad (7)$$

is the covariance for the data points (x_1, x_2) of the joint distribution of (X_1, X_2) on the set of junk documents.

To model the case of $l > 2$ classification methods we use a tree dependence model, which is a well known approximation method in probabilistic IR ([14]). We define a *Dependence Graph* $G = (V, E)$ where V consists of the Bernoulli variables X_i and which contains for all X_i, X_j ($i \neq j$) an undirected edge $e(X_i, X_j)$ with weight $w(e(X_i, X_j))) = cov(X_i, X_j)$. We approximate the Dependence Graph by a maximum spanning tree $G' = (V, E')$ which maximizes the sum of the edge weights. The nodes in G' with no edges in between are considered as independent. So we obtain:

$$P(X_1 = x_1, \ldots, X_k = x_k | Junk) =$$
$$P(X_{root} = 1 | Junk) \prod_{(i,j) \in E'} \frac{P(X_i = x_i, X_j = x_j | Junk)}{P(X_i = x_j | Junk)} \qquad (8)$$

where X_{root} is the root node of the tree G' and $x_i \in \{0, 1\}$. Now we introduce the following special case: For any two classification methods v_i, v_j the covariance has approximately the same value *cov*. With $w(e(X_i, X_j)) = cov$ we can (without loss of generality) choose X_1 as the root node and the edges (X_i, X_{i+1}) as tree edges.

Now we have:

$$P(X_1 = 1, \ldots, X_k = 1 | Junk) =$$
$$P(X_1 = 1 | Junk) \prod_{i=1}^{k-1} P(X_{i+1} = 1 | X_i = 1 | Junk) =$$
$$P(X_1 = 1 | Junk) \prod_{i=1}^{k-1} \frac{P(X_i = 1, X_{i+1} = 1 | Junk)}{P(X_i = 1 | Junk)} \qquad (9)$$

By considering equation 6 and the above assumption about the covariance we obtain

$$P(X_1 = 1, \ldots, X_k = 1 | Junk) =$$
$$P(X_1 = 1 | Junk) \prod_{i=1}^{k-1} \frac{P(X_i = 1 | Junk) P(X_{i+1} = 1 | Junk) + cov}{P(X_i = 1 | Junk)} \qquad (10)$$

Analogously we obtain $P(X_1 = 0 \wedge \ldots \wedge X_k = 0 | Junk)$.

If we assume that for *junk* documents the classes *pos* and *neg* are equally likely, we can substitute in the above formulas:

$$P(X_i = 1 | Junk) = P(X_i = 0 | Junk) = \frac{1}{2} \tag{11}$$

For the junk reduction we substitute the above formulas into:

$$junkRed = 1 - P(X_1 = \ldots = X_k | Junk) =$$
$$1 - (P(X_1 = 0 \wedge \ldots \wedge X_k = 0 | Junk) + P(X_1 = 1 \wedge \ldots \wedge X_k = 1 | Junk)) \tag{12}$$

To compute the probabilities that all classifiers v_i classify a document into the same class, if the document belongs to one of the classes in $C = \{pos, neg\}$, we associate a Bernoulli variable X_i' with each classification method v_i, where $X_i = 1$ if v_i classifies a document correctly, 0 otherwise. We want to compute the probabilities $P(X_1' = 1 \wedge \ldots \wedge X_k' = 1 | C)$ and $P(X_1' = 0 \wedge \ldots \wedge X_k' = 0 | C)$ that all classifiers classify a document correctly / incorrectly if the document belongs to one of the classes in C.

With analog arguments as above we obtain the following approximation:

$$P(X_1' = 1, \ldots, X_k' = 1 | C) =$$
$$P(X_1' = 1 | C) \prod_{i=1}^{k-1} \frac{P(X_i' = 1 | C) P(X_{i+1}' = 1 | C) + cov'}{P(X_i' = 1 | C)} \tag{13}$$

where cov' is the covariance on the documents in C. Analogously we obtain $P(X_1' = 0, \ldots, X_k' = 0 | C)$.

Let $P(C)$ be the probability that a document belongs to a class in C and $P(Junk)$ be the probability that a document is a junk document. Then we obtain approximations for *docRed*, *loss* and *error* by inserting the above expressions into:

$$loss =$$
$$1 - (P(X_1' = 1, \ldots, X_k' = 1 | C) + P(X_1' = 0, \ldots, X_k' = 0 | C)) \tag{14}$$

$$error =$$
$$\frac{P(C)P(X_1' = 0, \ldots, X_k' = 0 | C) + P(Junk)P(X_1 = 0, \ldots, X_k = 0 | Junk)}{1 - junkRed - loss} \tag{15}$$

$$docRed = junkRed + loss \tag{16}$$

As an illustrative example we consider the case that the k classification methods have the same probabilitiy $p < 0.5$ (i.e. the classification methods perform better than random) to misassign a document from C, that in the case of a junk document the assignment of the classes *pos* or *neg* are equally likely and that we have in all cases a covariance $c < 1.0$ (i.e. the classification methods are not perfectly correlated.) and that our document corpus contains 50 percent junk documents. In this case we would obtain for *junkRed*, *loss* and *error*:

$$junkRed = 1 - \left(\frac{c + 1/4}{1/2}\right)^{k-1} \tag{17}$$

$$loss = 1 - \left((1-p)\left(\frac{c + (1-p)^2}{1-p}\right)^{k-1} + p\left(\frac{c + p^2}{p}\right)^{k-1}\right) \tag{18}$$

$$error = \frac{1}{2}\frac{p\left(\frac{c+p^2}{p}\right)^{k-1} + 1/2\left(\frac{c+1/4}{1/2}\right)^{k-1}}{\left(\frac{c+1/4}{1/2}\right)^{k-1} + (1-p)\left(\frac{c+(1-p)^2}{1-p}\right)^{k-1} + p\left(\frac{c+p^2}{p}\right)^{k-1}} \tag{19}$$

It is easy to show that for $k \to \infty$ the loss converges monotonically to 1, and the error to 0 (i.e. with more classification methods we can obtain a lower error but pay the price of a higher loss). Furthermore also *junkRed* converges to 1 and the salient invariant *loss* > *junkRed* holds. Even $\frac{1-loss}{1-junkRed}$ converges to 1; this means, that with increasing k we dismiss much more junk documents than documents of interest. The covariance plays the role of a "smoothing constant": with higher correlated classification methods the convergence of both loss and error is slowed down.

4   Experiments

4.1   Setup

We performed a series of experiments with real-life data from

1. Newsgroups collection at [1]. This collection contains 17847 postings collected from 20 Usenet newsgroups. Particular topics ('rec.autos', 'sci.space', etc.) contain between 600 and 1000 documents.
2. The Reuters articles [11]. This is the most widely used test collection for text categorization research. The collection contains 21578 Reuters newswire stories, subdivided into multiple categories ('earn', 'grain', 'trade', etc.).
3. The Internet Movie Database (imdb) at [2]. Documents of this collection are short and impressive movie descriptions that include the storyboard, cast overview, and user comments. This collection contains 20 topics according to particular movie genres ('drama', 'horror' etc.).

For each data set we identified all topics with sufficiently many documents. These were 20 topics for newsgroups, 7 for reuters and 9 from imdb. Among these topics we randomly chose 100 topic pairs from newsgroups, 30 from imdb and 20 from reuters. For each topic pair we choose randomly 25,50 or 100 trainining documents per class and kept 500 documents per class for newsgroups, 200 documents per class for imdb and 400 documents per class from reuters (distinct form the training set and also randomly chosen) for the validation of the classifiers for each pair. Additionally we "spoiled" the validation set for each pair by increasing this set by 50 percent by adding randomly chosen "junk documents" from different topics. Finally, we computed macro-averaged results for these topic pairs.

4.2   Results

In all discussed experiments, the standard bag-of-words model (using term frequencies to build L1-normalized feature vectors) with different feature selection methods was used for document representation and we used SVM as learning algorithm.

In our experiments we considered the following base methods:

- *base1*: Feature selection by Mutual Information (top 200 terms); learning by SVM
- *base2*: Feature selection by Information Gain(top 200 terms); learning by SVM
- *base3*: Feature selection by Chi Squared Statistics (top 200 terms); learning by SVM

There are many alternative ways to build the base classifiers, e.g. using Naive Bayes, Decision Trees, etc. Here we chose SVM because it has been shown to often outperform other methods in text classification tasks - see e.g. [8]. Furthermore it has been shown that the above feature selection methods are highly correlated [21]. We accepted this here because we wanted to obtain base classifiers with comparable performance. To find the optimal number of features for the different feature selection methods is beyond the scope of this paper.

In the first experimental serial we compared the meta results with the results of the underlying base methods and the restrictive base methods (inducing the same document reduction as the meta method). (Figures 2 and 3)

In the second experimental serial we compared each base method for different degrees of restrictivity [1] (inducing different document reductions). (Figure 4).

The main observations are:

- The average error of the meta method was for all experiments lower or at least equal to the error of the *best* underlying base method.
- The junk reduction is (for restrictive base methods as well as for meta methods) always significantly higher than the loss (i.e. we dismiss a higher percentage of junk than of documents of interest).
- For the imdb data set the ratio *junkRed : loss* is best for the best base method, for the reuters and newsgroups data sets this ratio is best for the meta method.
- We can clearly observe the tradeoffs between *loss* on the one hand and *error* and *junkRed* on the other hand described and analyzed in chapter 3.

---

[1] We randomly chose the training and test documents once more for these experiments, causing minimal differences in the results for $docRed = 0$ compared to the base methods of the first experimental serial.

# TrainDocs	Meta		restrictive Base			Base			Dataset
	avg(docRed)	avg(error)	base1 avg(error)	base2 avg(error)	base3 avg(error)	base1 avg(error)	base2 avg(error)	base3 avg(error)	
25	0.159	0.489	0.493	0.489	0.489	0.52	0.515	0.518	
50	0.208	0.457	0.463	0.457	0.457	0.506	0.499	0.499	IMDB
100	0.188	0.432	0.439	0.433	0.433	0.483	0.475	0.479	
25	0.165	0.344	0.358	0.358	0.358	0.419	0.416	0.417	
50	0.166	0.316	0.327	0.328	0.329	0.398	0.396	0.397	Newsg.
100	0.143	0.31	0.318	0.315	0.315	0.385	0.381	0.381	
25	0.099	0.326	0.335	0.334	0.331	0.378	0.374	0.375	
50	0.086	0.318	0.323	0.319	0.318	0.366	0.362	0.362	Reuters
100	0.078	0.314	0.321	0.316	0.315	0.360	0.357	0.356	
79	0.074	0.301	0.282	0.319	0.327	0.323	0.348	0.351	Web

Fig. 2. Error of Meta Classification on Reuters, Newsgroups and IMDB

# TrainDocs	Meta			restrictive Base						Dataset
	avg(docRed)	avg(loss)	avg(jRed)	base1 avg(loss)	base2 avg(loss)	base3 avg(loss)	base1 avg(jRed)	base2 avg(jRed)	base3 avg(jRed)	
25	0.159	0.147	0.183	0.149	0.146	0.148	0.181	0.186	0.182	
50	0.208	0.192	0.239	0.188	0.186	0.187	0.246	0.252	0.248	IMDB
100	0.188	0.167	0.231	0.165	0.162	0.163	0.234	0.24	0.238	
25	0.165	0.109	0.276	0.118	0.122	0.12	0.259	0.251	0.254	
50	0.166	0.098	0.301	0.103	0.108	0.108	0.29	0.281	0.282	Newsg.
100	0.143	0.077	0.275	0.078	0.079	0.078	0.272	0.271	0.273	
25	0.099	0.047	0.202	0.055	0.057	0.055	0.186	0.184	0.187	
50	0.086	0.034	0.188	0.038	0.037	0.037	0.181	0.182	0.184	Reuters
100	0.078	0.024	0.186	0.034	0.029	0.028	0.167	0.178	0.179	
79	0.074	0.044	0.144	0.032	0.055	0.06	0.173	0.118	0.143	Web

Fig. 3. Loss and JunkReduction of Meta Classification on Reuters, Newsgroups and IMDB

As an application example we tested junk reduction for a web crawl. We obtained our training set from a bookmark file containing 79 documents of the categories "Movies" and "Computer Science" and started the crawl on the portals shown in figure 5. By this crawl we obtained an overall number of 1061 documents consisting of 400 documents about computer science, 348 about movies, and 313 junk documents. We evaluated the techniques described above on this data set. The results are shown in figures 2 through 4 (data set "web"). As in the previous experiments, the junk reduction was much higher than the loss for all restrictive methods. In terms of loss, error and junkReduction the meta method performed better than two of the 3 underlying base methods but the best restrictive base method outperformed the meta method in this experiment.

4.3   Discussion

The experiments show that all restrictive methods (i.e. meta methods as well as restrictive base methods) dismiss a significantly higher percentage of junk than of documents of interest, and additionally decrease the classification error on all data sets.

docRed	base1 avg(error)	base2 avg(error)	base3 avg(error)	base1 avg(loss)	base2 avg(loss)	base3 avg(loss)	base1 avg(jRed)	base2 avg(jRed)	base3 avg(jRed)	Dataset
0	0.517	0.509	0.509	0	0	0	0	0	0	
0.1	0.498	0.492	0.489	0.094	0.091	0.092	0.111	0.117	0.116	
0.2	0.48	0.472	0.47	0.183	0.182	0.183	0.234	0.237	0.233	
0.3	0.461	0.449	0.451	0.278	0.273	0.277	0.345	0.354	0.346	
0.4	0.441	0.431	0.433	0.372	0.369	0.374	0.456	0.462	0.452	IMDB
0.5	0.416	0.407	0.412	0.466	0.464	0.47	0.568	0.572	0.561	
0.6	0.397	0.389	0.391	0.567	0.565	0.567	0.666	0.669	0.666	
0.7	0.375	0.369	0.372	0.67	0.667	0.67	0.76	0.765	0.759	
0.8	0.351	0.345	0.348	0.777	0.776	0.777	0.847	0.849	0.847	
0.9	0.309	0.313	0.307	0.884	0.885	0.885	0.932	0.93	0.93	
0	0.42	0.417	0.417	0	0	0	0	0	0	
0.1	0.386	0.384	0.383	0.073	0.075	0.074	0.154	0.15	0.153	
0.2	0.348	0.346	0.345	0.145	0.147	0.146	0.31	0.307	0.309	
0.3	0.307	0.305	0.304	0.218	0.22	0.219	0.463	0.461	0.462	
0.4	0.261	0.259	0.26	0.297	0.298	0.298	0.605	0.605	0.604	Newsg.
0.5	0.216	0.215	0.216	0.385	0.387	0.387	0.729	0.727	0.726	
0.6	0.176	0.172	0.173	0.488	0.487	0.487	0.825	0.827	0.825	
0.7	0.139	0.135	0.137	0.602	0.6	0.601	0.897	0.899	0.897	
0.8	0.108	0.102	0.105	0.727	0.725	0.726	0.947	0.95	0.948	
0.9	0.081	0.076	0.078	0.86	0.859	0.859	0.98	0.982	0.981	
0	0.38	0.377	0.377	0	0	0	0	0	0	
0.1	0.336	0.336	0.334	0.057	0.06	0.058	0.185	0.181	0.183	
0.2	0.291	0.292	0.29	0.119	0.121	0.119	0.362	0.359	0.361	
0.3	0.247	0.247	0.245	0.188	0.19	0.189	0.523	0.52	0.522	
0.4	0.209	0.209	0.208	0.272	0.274	0.275	0.656	0.652	0.65	Reuters
0.5	0.174	0.172	0.172	0.369	0.369	0.37	0.763	0.762	0.761	
0.6	0.142	0.144	0.144	0.477	0.479	0.48	0.847	0.842	0.841	
0.7	0.113	0.111	0.109	0.596	0.595	0.595	0.908	0.909	0.91	
0.8	0.087	0.083	0.085	0.724	0.723	0.723	0.952	0.955	0.954	
0.9	0.068	0.064	0.068	0.86	0.859	0.859	0.981	0.983	0.981	
0	0.323	0.348	0.351	0	0	0	0	0	0	
0.1	0.266	0.311	0.316	0.041	0.074	0.079	0.24	0.163	0.15	
0.2	0.214	0.265	0.284	0.095	0.143	0.164	0.45	0.335	0.284	
0.3	0.168	0.215	0.229	0.166	0.214	0.225	0.62	0.505	0.479	
0.4	0.152	0.198	0.206	0.27	0.31	0.317	0.709	0.613	0.597	Web
0.5	0.134	0.162	0.177	0.377	0.4	0.409	0.792	0.738	0.716	
0.6	0.127	0.146	0.167	0.497	0.509	0.521	0.843	0.815	0.786	
0.7	0.116	0.119	0.15	0.62	0.62	0.634	0.888	0.888	0.856	
0.8	0.113	0.117	0.122	0.745	0.746	0.747	0.93	0.927	0.923	
0.9	0.131	0.056	0.093	0.873	0.862	0.868	0.962	0.987	0.974	

Fig. 4. Error, Loss and Junk Reduction for Restrictive Base Methods on Reuters, Newsgroups and IMDB and T = 25 TrainDocs per Class and for Web Documents with T = 79 TrainDocs per Class

Comparing meta classifiers and restrictive base classifiers there is no clear winner: For the imdb and web data, the best base classifier outperformed the meta classifier; for newsgroups and reuters, the meta classifier outperformed the base classifiers.

5   Conclusion and Future Work

In this paper we have shown, by a probabilistic model as well as by experiments on various data sets, that restrictive classification methods can be used to eliminate junk documents. Theory and experiments show that the junk reduction is

Computer Science:

```
http://dir.yahoo.com/Science/Computer_Science/
http://www.developer.com/
http://www.techweb.com/
http://directory.google.com/Top/Computers/Computer_Science/
http://library.albany.edu/subject/csci.htm
```

Movies:

```
http://www.allmovieportal.com/
http://www.galatta.com/
http://adutopia.subportal.com/cgi-bin/apollo/apollo.cgi
http://dir.yahoo.com/Entertainment/Movies_and_Film/Genres/
http://www.badmovies.org/
```

Fig. 5. Starting Points for the Web Crawl

significantly higher than the loss, and the classification error is decreased. This holds for restrictive base methods as well as meta methods.

Possible topics for future work are:

– The improvement of restrictive meta methods and their parameter tuning.
– A theory that enables us to build a probabilistic model for restrictive base models (and not just for restrictive meta methods).
– Application of clustering methods to a data set, adjusted by our junk elimination method, to identify subtopics among the topics of interest.
– Application of clustering methods to the dismissed documents to identify distinct subtopics among the junk documents. This could be used to find new topics of interest or to build refined junk filters.
– Application of semisupervised learning to train on junk documents and to further improve classification quality in terms of error, loss and junk reduction, e.g., by first applying our junk reduction methods as an initial step and then performing some iterative, EM(Estimation Maximization)-like algorithm.

The work presented here is embedded in the BINGO! project [18], a toolsuite for building information portals and specialized search engines. Our long-term objective is to better understand the engineering of how to incorporate, adapt, and tune machine learning methods into more intelligent next-generation systems for information organization and search.

References

1. The 20 newsgroups data set. *http://www.ai.mit.edu/ jrennie/20Newsgroups/*.
2. Internet movie database. *http://www.imdb.com*.
3. R. Baeza-Yates and B. Ribeiro-Neto. *Modern Information Retrieval*. Addison Wesley, 1999.
4. L. Breiman. Bagging predictors. *Machine Learning*, 24(2):123–140, 1996.
5. C. Burges. A tutorial on Support Vector Machines for pattern recognition. *Data Mining and Knowledge Discovery*, 2(2), 1998.

6. S. Chakrabarti. *Mining the Web*. Morgan Kaufmann, 2003.
7. S. Dumais and H. Chen. Hierarchical classification of Web content. *SIGIR*, 2000.
8. S. Dumais, J. Platt, D. Heckerman, and M. Sahami. Inductive learning algorithms and representations for text categorization. In *Proceedings of ACM-CIKM 98, pp. 148-155.*, 1998.
9. Y. Freund. An adaptive version of the boost by majority algorithm. *Workshop on Computational Learning Theory*, 1999.
10. T. Joachims. Text categorization with Support Vector Machines: Learning with many relevant features. *ECML*, 1998.
11. D. D. Lewis. Evaluating text categorization. In *Proceedings of Speech and Natural Language Workshop*, pages 312–318. Defense Advanced Research Projects Agency, Morgan Kaufmann, Feb. 1991.
12. N. Littlestone and M. Warmuth. The weighted majority algorithm. *FOCS*, 1989.
13. C. Manning and H. Schuetze. *Foundations of Statistical Natural Language Processing*. MIT Press, 1999.
14. C. V. Rijsbergen. A theoretical basis for the use of co-occurence data in information retrieval. *Journal of Documentation, 33:2, pp. 106-119*, 1977.
15. S. Siersdorfer and S. Sizov. Construction of feature spaces and meta methods for classification of Web documents (in german). *Conference on Database Systems for Business, Technology and Web (BTW)*, 2003.
16. S. Siersdorfer and S. Sizov. Restrictive clustering and metaclustering for self-organizing document collections. In *Proceedings of the 27th annual international conference on Research and developement in information retrieval (SIGIR 04)*, 2004.
17. S. Siersdorfer, S. Sizov, and G. Weikum. Goal-oriented methods and meta methods for document classification and their parameter tuning. In *ACM Conference on Information and Knowledge Management (CIKM 04), Washington*, 2004.
18. S. Sizov, M. Biwer, J. Graupmann, S. Siersdorfer, M. Theobald, G. Weikum, and P. Zimmer. The BINGO! system for information portal generation and expert Web search. *Conference on Innovative Systems Research (CIDR)*, 2003.
19. H. Wang, W. Fan, P. Yu, and J. Han. Mining concept-drifting data streams using ensemble classifiers. *SIGKDD*, 2003.
20. D. Wolpert. Stacked generalization. *Neural Networks, Vol. 5, pp. 241-259*, 1992.
21. Y. Yang and O. Pedersen. A comparative study on feature selection in text categorization. *ICML*, 1997.
22. H. Yu, K. Chang, and J. Han. Heterogeneous learner for Web page classification. *ICDM*, 2002.

On Compression-Based Text Classification

Yuval Marton[1,*], Ning Wu[2], and Lisa Hellerstein[2,**]

[1] University of Maryland, Department of Linguistics,
1401 Marie Mount Hall, College Park, MD 20742-7505
ymarton@umiacs.umd.edu

[2] Polytechnic University, Department of Computer and Information Science,
5 Metrotech Center, Brooklyn, NY, 11201
{wning, hstein}@cis.poly.edu

Abstract. Compression-based text classification methods are easy to apply, requiring virtually no preprocessing of the data. Most such methods are character-based, and thus have the potential to automatically capture non-word features of a document, such as punctuation, word-stems, and features spanning more than one word. However, compression-based classification methods have drawbacks (such as slow running time), and not all such methods are equally effective. We present the results of a number of experiments designed to evaluate the effectiveness and behavior of different compression-based text classification methods on English text. Among our experiments are some specifically designed to test whether the ability to capture non-word (including super-word) features causes character-based text compression methods to achieve more accurate classification.

1   Introduction

Text classification is the task of taking a set of input documents that are labeled according to some classification (e.g. by topic, author, or style) and using that information to classify other, unlabeled documents. Many different methods have been used for text classification, including support vector machines (SVM), logistic regression, boosting, Naive Bayes, nearest neighbor (kNN), and language modeling (cf.[30, 39, 38, 23]).

Compression-based classification is a non-standard approach to classification. It was discovered independently by different researchers, and has been explored by proponents as well as opponents [16, 34, 1, 13, 8, 33, 11, 19]. Compression programs build a model or dictionary of the files they process. Thus compression

---

* Part of this research was performed while Y. Marton was studying at Polytechnic University.

** Research of L. Hellerstein and her coauthors partially supported by NSF Grants CCR-9877122 and ITR-0205647 and by the Othmer Institute for Interdisciplinary Studies at Polytechnic University.

D.E. Losada and J.M. Fernández-Luna (Eds.): ECIR 2005, LNCS 3408, pp. 300–314, 2005.

can be used to "train" classifiers on the labeled documents for each class. Classification of a new document is done by compressing it multiple times, each time using a different class model or dictionary obtained during "training". The new document is assigned to the class that yielded the highest compression rate. This procedure can be viewed from an information-theoretic perspective: the compression rate measures the cross-entropy between the training text and the new document, and the new document is assigned to the class whose training text minimizes that cross-entropy (see e.g. [33]).

A main attraction of compression-based methods for classification is that they are extremely easy to apply. They require virtually no preprocessing of the input documents. Moreover, the compression-based classification procedures used by Khmelev, in [16], and by Benedetto et al. [1] enable average computer users with access to off-the-shelf compression programs to easily perform classification. These procedures run quite slowly, however, and thus are not suitable when speed is important.

Most text classification methods are word-based; they treat a text document as a collection of words (or stems). In contrast, nearly all research on compression-based classification has been done using byte/character-based compression methods ([34] is an exception). Researchers have noted that character-based classification methods have a potential advantage over word-based methods, in that they are able to automatically capture document features other than words (cf. [24, 8]). Such non-word features include subword features such as stems, superword features that span more than one word, and punctuation.

In this paper, we present a variety of experiments using compression-based classification methods on English text. For simplicity, we restrict our experiments to problems in which each document belongs to exactly one class. We measure performance in terms of micro-averaged accuracy (total number of correct classifications over total number of tests), which is a useful measure for problems with single-class labels, and classifiers with no tuning parameters [38]. We perform our experiments using three standard off-the-shelf compression methods, RAR, gzip, and LZW, on topic classification and authorship attribution tasks. We compare the procedure of Kukushkina et al. [16] (which builds one model or dictionary per class) to the procedure of Benedetto et al. [1] (which is a nearest neighbor approach). We present novel experiments designed to address the question of whether compression methods do, in fact, benefit from their potential to capture non-word features. We believe these experiments are also relevant to the study of other character-based classification methods. We also examine the change in classification accuracy as the amount of training data increases, and explore the effect of imbalanced class size.

We begin with the history of compression-based text classification in Section 2; we then discuss three classification procedures (SMDL, AMDL, and BCN) in Section 3 , the compression programs used here for classification in Section 4, and the corpora they were tested on in Section 5; we present our experiments in Section 6, and our conclusions in Section 7.

2   Related Work

It is difficult to determine who first suggested using compression for classification (cf. [8, 11, 19]). Here we review previous experimental work on the approach. Khmelev [16] performed experiments using a large variety of compression methods to classify a large corpus of Russian literary works by author. Thaper used LZ78, character-based PPM, and word-based PPM to classify English literary works by author [34]. Frank et al. applied PPM to topic classification [8]. They concluded that compression methods are handicapped by their inability to exploit a handful of highly informative terms. Subsequently, Teahan and Harper [33] applied variants of PPM to topic classification. They concluded that compression could, in fact, be an effective method of classification.

Benedetto et al. used gzip and a nearest neighbor procedure for authorship classification [1]. Their paper received media attention (e.g., [28]), and generated some controversy [14, 3, 11, 2]. In this paper we examine one question raised by a critic of the paper, and contested by the authors – whether gzip and the nearest neighbor procedure do, in fact, perform accurate classification [2, 11].

Recently, Khmelev and Teahan tested a number of classification methods on the Reuters corpus, including both SVM and compression-based classification (with gzip and RAR) [13]. RAR outperformed all other methods, including SVM. (However, the authors noted that their method of using SVM for multiclass problems might not be optimal). Khmelev and Teahan hypothesized that SVM and other methods using "bag-of-words" models are handicapped by their inability to capture word sequences.

Peng et al. proposed the use of character-based language modeling methods for text classification and achieved excellent results [23, 24]. As they noted, their work is related to Teahan's work on classification with PPM compression [32, 33]. Both PPM compression and language modeling work by building n-gram Markov models of the text. Both calculate the degree of match between the learned model and the test document via a cross-entropy calculation.

Other previous approaches to character-based text classification include the work of Damashek [6], Cavnar and Trenkle [4], and Khmelev and Tweedie [15].

3   Classification Procedures

We discuss three different compression-based classification procedures from the literature. We refer to them as the *standard MDL* (minimum description length), the *approximate MDL*, and the *best-compression neighbor* procedures.

The standard MDL procedure (SMDL) was used in [8, 34, 33]. It is analogous to the procedures used in Multinomial Naive Bayes text classification (e.g., [18]) and language-modeling methods [23], but typically does not allow the use of off-the-shelf compression methods. Given training documents for categories $C_1, \ldots, C_n$ SMDL forms for each C_i a single file A_i consisting of all documents in that category. It then runs the compression algorithm on each A_i to obtain a model (or dictionary) M_i. Then, for each M_i, it runs the compression algorithm "statically" on a test file T, i.e., it uses model M_i as input and doesn't update it as T is processed. Finally, it assigns test document T to the class i whose model M_i achieves the best compression of T. We define SMDL here for completeness, but in this paper we do not present any experimental results using SMDL.

In most of our experiments, we use the approximate MDL procedure (AMDL) proposed by Khmelev [16] and used by Khmelev and Teahan [13]. Suppose the input documents are from categories $C_1, \ldots, C_n$. AMDL, like SMDL, forms for each C_i a single training file A_i consisting of all training documents in C_i. It then runs the compression program on each A_i to produce a compressed file $\mathcal{A}_i$ of length $|\mathcal{A}_i|$. Given a test file T, AMDL appends T to each A_i, producing A_iT. It then runs the compression program on each A_iT to produce a compressed file $\mathcal{A}_i\mathcal{T}$. Finally, it assigns T to the class C_i that minimizes the compressed size difference $v_i = |\mathcal{A}_i\mathcal{T}| - |\mathcal{A}_i|$. The value v_i can be viewed as an estimate of the cross-entropy of text T with respect to text A_i. AMDL can be viewed as an attempt to approximate SMDL with off-the-shelf compression methods, which are "adaptive" with regard to test documents, rather than "static" as above.

The best-compression neighbor (BCN) procedure was developed by Benedetto et al. [1]. They use a similar approach to AMDL, but instead of concatenating all the training documents in a class into a single input file, they keep each training document D in a separate file. They concatenate test document T to each D, forming DT, and calculate $v_{DT} = |\mathcal{D}\mathcal{T}| - |\mathcal{D}|$, the difference between the sizes of the compressed versions of DT and D. Then they assign T to the class containing the document D that minimizes v_{DT}. Their procedure is thus a nearest-neighbor approach, using v_{DT} as the distance measure. As we discuss in Section 6.2 the BCN procedure can require significantly more running time than AMDL.

SMDL will typically be faster than both AMDL and BCN in classifying a new file, because it uses *saved* models or dictionaries for each class. In AMDL and BCN, the new file is concatenated to the training files, causing models or dictionaries for the training files to be recomputed. Note that if one can alter the compression program's source code, runtime can be dramatically decreased by not actually writing compressed files to disk. One can instead just calculate the number of bytes that would be written into in each compressed file.

4   Classification Methods

Gzip [12] is a compression program available on most UNIX systems. It uses Lempel-Ziv compression (LZ77), a dictionary-based scheme. We used the command line option "-9fc", for best compression. Its efficacy in classification is limited by its use of a sliding window. Although we were not able to definitely ascertain the size of our gzip version's window, we assume it is of size 32K; this is a typical size of a gzip sliding window, and our experimental results are consistent with that size.

LZW is a well-known, dictionary-based compression method. We used a straightforward implementation of LZW, based on published source code [21], which we modified slightly, to increase the dictionary size from 14 to 16 bits. On large datasets, even the increased 16-bit dictionary becomes full, usually after processing approximately 300KB of text.

RAR is a proprietary shareware program [25]. In the reported experiments, we used the default mode (no command line options). Current versions of RAR, such as the one we experimented with, can use either LZ (Lempel-Ziv) based or PPM based compression, and chooses between them based on the input data (early versions of RAR used only LZ compression) [27]. For text, it usually uses PPM based compression, in particular, a version of the PPMII algorithm due to Shkarin [29]. In classification experiments performed by Khmelev and Teahan, the performance of RAR was similar to the performance of PPMC [13].

5   Corpora

As mentioned in the introduction, for simplicity we restricted our experiments to problems in which each document belongs to exactly one class. We used the following corpora.

20 Newsgroups (20news)[1] – This widely-used corpus consists of approximately 20,000 postings that are labeled by the Usenet discussion groups to which they were posted (around 1000 postings in each of the corpus' 20 newsgroups). We used J. Rennie's version of the corpus [2], in which duplicate postings to more than one newsgroup were removed, and in each posting most headers were removed, while Subject and From fields were retained. This subset contains 18828 documents. We used 5 random splits of 80/20 training/testing. We also used **10 Newsgroups (10news)**, a subset of the 20news corpus, consisting of the 10 categories containing the most documents (and also the most bytes), as in [33]. This subset contains 8998 documents, many of which are 2-6K bytes long, although some are as short as 100 bytes or as long as 51K bytes. No class has fewer than 700KB of training data. We used one random split: 80% training, 20% testing.

Industry Sector[3] – This dataset consists of approximately 6000 company web pages classified by industry sector. Many of the web pages are 10-20K long, although some are as small as 370 bytes, and others as long as 128K. Training data per sector varies from about 100KB to over 700KB. The 105 sectors are arranged in a 2-level hierarchy, which we ignored. This corpus has been used previously in other text classification experiments (cf. [18, 38, 9, 26]). According to [9], 15 of the web pages in this corpus appear in more than one category. We did not remove these. We used one random 80% training, 20% testing split, and excluded the 0.3% of the test documents that were empty.

---

[1] Some researchers use this corpus for what they call "genre classification" - a coarser resolution than the usual topic classification problem [18, 32].

[2] http://people.csail.mit.edu/people/jrennie/20Newsgroups/20news-18828.tar.gz

[3] http://www-2.cs.cmu.edu/afs/cs.cmu.edu/project/theo-4/text-learning/www/ sector-data.tar.gz, made available by Market Guide Inc. (www.marketguide.com)

Reuters-10 (R10) – This corpus is a subset of the popular Reuters-21578 corpus[4]. We used the ModApte split for dividing the documents into training and test sets. We removed any articles appearing in more than one class. We then removed all articles from classes that lacked either training or testing articles. Finally, we selected the 10 classes containing the most documents (and bytes). The resulting corpus has 5444 training documents (4MB), and 2150 tests (1.4MB). Document size ranges from 84 bytes to 6.4K. Training data per class varies from 91KB to 1.27MB.

Reuters-Author (R9) – This is another subset of the Reuters-21578 corpus, but with articles labeled by author, rather than topic. We chose the 9 authors who contributed at least 12 articles, and then included the first 12 articles from each author. We used 6-fold cross-validation, with 10 training and 2 testing documents per class in each fold. Training data per author varies from 24KB to 40KB.

Gutenberg-10 (Gu-10) – This dataset, used in experiments by [34] consists of 4 works of each of 10 well known authors (40 works in total), all taken from the Gutenberg Project[5]. We used 4-fold cross-validation, with 3 training and 1 test document per class in each fold. Some works are as short as 123KB, and some as long as 1.1MB (many are novels). Training data per class ranges from 416KB to 2.5MB.

Federalist Papers (Fed.) – This is a classic corpus in authorship identification literature (cf. [20, 33]), and is also available at the Gutenberg Project. We arbitrarily removed the first of two slightly different versions of Paper 70. We trained on six Hamilton papers (#65-70), six of Madison's (#40-45), and tested on twelve disputed papers (#49-58, 62-63) and on three undisputed papers of each (#46-48, and #59-61, respectively). Each Paper is 7-21KB long. The training data sizes for the two classes are 82KB and 109KB.

6   Experiments

6.1   A Comparison of RAR, gzip, and LZW on Full Corpora

We compared RAR, gzip, and LZW on a variety of corpora, using AMDL (described in Section 3). Our experimental results are presented in Table 1.

RAR is the best performing method on all but the small Reuters-9 corpus, in which it correctly classified only 2 test documents fewer than gzip (out of 108). RAR's superiority confirms results obtained by Khmelev and Teahan [13].

The poor performance of gzip on Gutenberg-10 is due both to its 32K sliding window, and to how that window interacts with AMDL. Under AMDL, the training file for each Gutenberg-10 author consists of the concatenation of three of the author's works. After processing the training file, gzip's sliding window has

---

[4] At http://www.daviddlewis.com/resources/testcollections/reuters21578
[5] http://gutenberg.net

Table 1. RAR, LZW, and gzip using AMDL

Corpus	RAR	LZW	GZIP
Federalist	0.94	0.83	0.67
Gutenberg-10	0.82	0.65	0.62
Reuters-9	0.78	0.66	0.79
Reuters-10	0.87	0.84	0.83
10news (20news)	0.96 (0.90)	0.66	0.56 (0.47)
Sector	0.90	0.61	0.19

information only from the last 32K bytes of the file. Since works in Gutenberg-10 are longer than 32K bytes, gzip is effectively trained on only 32K bytes from each author, and those 32K bytes are drawn from only one of the author's three training works. We discuss the effect of gzip's window on its accuracy again in Sections 6.2 and 6.6.

LZW performs only slightly better than gzip on Gutenberg-10. Like gzip, it is unable to use all three training documents in each class. Since LZW's dictionary becomes full after reading approximately 300KB of text, and no changes to the dictionary are made after that point, LZW uses information from only the first 300KB of each class training file in doing classification. The shortest documents in Gutenberg-10 are about 150KB, and many are over 500KB, so for most classes LZW benefits only from the first (and sometimes the second) document in each class training file. Note that gzip and LZW effectively use different training documents, since gzip's information comes from the *third* document in each class training file. In Section 6.6 we present results suggesting that the limited dictionary size may not be the only reason for LZW's mediocre performance.

We are not sure what the proprietary RAR does, but as mentioned in Section 4, it usually defaults to PPMII when run on text. PPM methods typically use data to compute estimates for the transition probabilities of the relevant Markov chains. In contrast to gzip and LZW, RAR has the potential to benefit from *all three* training documents in each Gutenberg-10 class.

Despite its 32K window, gzip does perform almost as well as RAR on the Reuters-9 corpus. One reason may be Reuter-9's small class sizes; gzip can use all the class training data for about half the classes, and most of the training data for the rest. But in fact, as can be seen in gzip's results for Reuters-10, gzip doesn't need a high percentage of the data to perform well in all tasks. It seems that on some corpora, a 32K window is a limitation for gzip (e.g., Sector; see Section 6.6), but on others, a 32K window is enough (e.g., Reuters-10). Note that the particular documents that end up in gzip's sliding window may happen to be especially "good" or "bad" ones, potentially making its accuracy unstable.

Our 90.5% result for RAR on 20news is competitive with some of the best results reported in the literature, such as the 89.23% accuracy reported by Peng et al. using language modeling techniques [23], the 82.1% obtained by Teahan and Harper [33], and the 86.2% reported by Rennie et al. using an extended version of Nave Bayes [26]. The 94.8% accuracy figure reported by Zhang and

Table 2. RAR, LZW and gzip in AMDL and BCN procedures

Corpus	RAR		LZW		gzip	
	AMDL	BCN	AMDL	BCN	AMDL	BCN
Federalist	0.94	0.78	0.83	0.83	0.67	0.78
Gu-10	0.82	0.75	0.65	0.53	0.62	0.72
R-9	0.78	0.77	0.66	0.49	0.79	0.77

Oles [38] should not be compared to the above results, because "Newsgroup:" headers were not removed in their experiment [37].

Our 89.6% result for RAR on Sector can be compared with the 64.5% obtained by Ghani using Multinomial Nave Bayes [9], but is not as high as the 93.6% reported by Zhang and Oles using SVM [38], or the 92.3% by Rennie et al. using their extended version of Nave Bayes [26].

6.2   A Comparison of AMDL and BCN Procedures

In Table 2 we present the results of experiments with gzip and RAR comparing the AMDL procedure to the BCN procedure.

On Gutenberg-10 and on the small Federalist Papers corpus, gzip performs better under BCN than it does under AMDL. It performs only slightly worse on the small Reuters-9 corpus. We also applied gzip to 10news (not shown in the table), and its accuracy increased dramatically from 0.56 to 0.89 when we used BCN instead of AMDL. On Gutenberg-10, BCN allows gzip to make use of 32KB from *each* of an author's three works, as opposed to 32KB from *one* of those works. Similarly, on 10news, gzip can use up to 32KB of each training document, rather than just a handful of them. On Reuters-9, gzip was already competitive with RAR in AMDL, and remains competitive with RAR in BCN. From these results, it seems that gzip's sliding window size is *not* a severe handicap under BCN (as opposed to what is suggested in [13]). In fact, the performance of RAR and gzip are very similar across these corpora under BCN.

BCN is a 1-nearest-neighbor method. It is well known that 1NN is highly sensitive to noise. BCN might be improved by using a k-nearest-neighbor approach, for some $k > 1$ (see e.g. [30, 35] for uses of k-NN in text categorization).

In our experiments, BCN ran much more slowly than AMDL. This is not surprising, because in BCN, each byte of a test file is compressed as many times as there are training *documents*, because the test file is concatenated to each training file before compression. In contrast, in AMDL, each byte of a test file is compressed as many times as there are training *classes*. Thus, for example, if a Reuters-10 experiment takes several hours using AMDL, it can easily take over a month using BCN. All remaining experiments reported in this paper use AMDL.

6.3   Testing Effect of Punctuation

To test whether compression-based classification methods successfully exploit patterns of punctuation usage, we devised the following experiment. For each

Table 3. Sensitivity to Punctuation Information (Raw files vs. NOP files)

corpus	gzip		LZW		RAR	
	Raw	NOP	Raw	NOP	Raw	NOP
Fed.	0.67	0.39	0.83	0.83	0.94	0.83
Gu-10	0.62	0.65	0.65	0.70	0.82	0.82
R-9	0.79	0.81	0.66	0.62	0.78	0.81
R-10	0.83	0.83	0.84	0.85	0.87	0.87
10news	0.56	0.54	0.66	0.73	0.96	0.96
Sector	0.19	0.22	0.61	0.69	0.90	0.90

training file, we created a modified version of the file by removing all punctuation and replacing all white spaces (tab, line, paragraph, and page breaks) with spaces; we call this preprocessing procedure NOP. This kind of preprocessing is typically done for word-based methods, but not for character-based methods. We compared the performance of the compression methods on the original files to their performance on files processed with NOP.

We show the results of our experiments in Table 3.The first three lines of the table correspond to authorship classification tasks, and the last three to topic classification tasks. Intuitively, punctuation usage seems an important factor in writing style, and therefore one might expect removal of punctuation to adversely affect authorship classification accuracy. Although this did happen in some of our authorship experiments, accuracy remained the same, or even increased, in many cases.

It is interesting to note that removal of punctuation had a relatively small effect on the performance of RAR, the best algorithm overall. The only two corpora in which its performance changed, Federalist and Reuters-9, contain relatively a small amount of data.

6.4   Exploitation of Sub-words in Character-Based Methods

We devised two related experiments to test whether compression-based methods exploit sub-word features. Because we wanted to avoid interaction with punctuation effects, we began both experiments using files preprocessed with NOP, rather than with the original files.

In the first experiment, for each word w in the input corpus, we generated a random string s containing between 3 and 5 characters, and then replaced each occurence of w in the documents with s. The purpose of this procedure was to destroy subword features. For example, "walk" and "walked" might be replaced by "sxq" and "zvro", thus eliminating their common stem "walk," and the suffix "ed." We call this procedure Random-String Words (RSW).

We were concerned, however, that such a radical transformation might affect the compression algorithms in unexpected ways. Therefore, we performed a second experiment, in which We generated a random permutation of the words in the corpus, thus defining a mapping from each word w in the corpus vocabulary

Table 4. Exploitation of subword and superword information

corpus	gzip				LZW				RAR			
	NOP	WP	RSW	WOS	NOP	WP	RSW	WOS	NOP	WP	RSW	WOS
Fed.	0.39	0.61	0.39	0.56	0.83	0.83	0.83	0.83	0.83	0.89	0.89	0.83
Gu-10	0.65	0.50	0.45	0.68	0.70	0.78	0.78	0.72	0.82	0.75	0.72	0.72
R-9	0.81	0.76	0.80	0.70	0.62	0.53	0.64	0.66	0.81	0.78	0.81	0.71
R-10	0.83	0.81	0.81	0.78	0.85	0.84	0.84	0.83	0.87	0.87	0.87	0.85
10news	0.54	0.48	0.51	0.56	0.73	0.54	0.64	0.72	0.96	0.96	0.95	0.90
Sector	0.22	0.20	0.24	0.21	0.69	0.58	0.69	0.66	0.90	0.89	0.84	0.77

to a unique word w' also in the vocabulary. We then replaced each occurence of w in the input with w'. Thus, for example, the words "walk" and "walked" might be replaced by the words "the" and "met." We call this procedure Word Permutation (WP).

The results of our experiments are shown in Table 4. [6] Note first that in many experiments, the accuracy obtained with RSW is close to the accuracy obtained with NOP. This suggests that the compression algorithms often behave much like word-based methods, and have relatively little regard for what's *in* a word. Also, contrary to what one might expect, WP does not consistently achieve higher accuracy than RSW.

In some experiments, accuracy was higher with NOP than with RSW and PW, suggesting that the compression methods may exploit subword features to achieve more accurate classification. However, in other experiments, accuracy in RSW or PW equaled, or even exceeded, accuracy in NOP. Character-based compression methods may indeed benefit from exploiting subword features, but our experiments provide mixed evidence for this phenomenon, and the benefit may depend both on corpus and on compression method.

The experiments in which RSW or WP accuracy exceeded NOP accuracy suggest that exploitation of (some) subword features may sometimes have a negative effect on classification accuracy. This is plausible, since subword relationships can be misleading. For example, "of" is a subword of "offer" and "office". Both RSW and WP reduce such misleading relationships. In RSW, one random word is unlikely to be a a subword of another. In WP, shorter words, which are typically function words or stop-words, tend to appear more frequently, and will likely be replaced by longer words. Hence fewer words in a document will accidentally be substrings of other words.

---

[6] We also performed additional experiments in which we limited the amount of training data per class to 80K. The pattern of results was similar, although not identical, to the results shown in Table 4, with one exception. On 10-news, RAR performed dramatically worse with RSW than with NOP. This result was especially surprising because in our other experiments, we found RAR's performance to be relatively stable under changes to the training data size.

6.5   Exploitation of Superwords in Character-Based Methods

To test the effect of capturing superword information in character-based methods, we devised the following preprocessing procedure: First we preprocessed all documents with NOP, and then we randomly reordered the words in each document. We call this procedure Word Order Scrambling (WOS).

WOS leaves subword and word information intact, while destroying superword relations. If character-based compression methods rely on superword information such as word-based n-gram information, word order scrambling should result in decreased accuracy. Results for our WOS experiments are presented in Table 4. Comparing WOS and NOP results reveals that RAR's accuracy did decline in all but one corpus after scrambling (the exception is Fed.). Additional experiments in which we limited the amount of training data to 80K per class (not shown), show RAR's accuracy declining in all but one corpus (R-9), but but the results for LZW and gzip do not show a consistent decline.

6.6   Effects of Variable and Unbalanced Training Data Size

Methodology. There are different ways to artificially vary the amount of training data available to a class. One option is to concatenate all training documents in a class into a single file, and then to truncate the concatenated file at different points. In preliminary experiments using this procedure, we found that the learning curves exhibited strange behavior. We then realized that for small data sizes, the truncated training file contains only a small number of available training documents. In addition, increasing the amount of training data adds new documents to the end of the training file, resulting in jagged learning curves (especially for gzip, with its sliding window). This was especially problematic for Gutenberg-10, in which documents are long, and different documents by the same author can be diverse.

We decided instead, for each desired amount of training data, to use small chunks from as many class training files as possible, within reason. There are many ways to do this; we used the following procedure. Let t be the original number of training documents in a given class. Let $b = max(\lceil s/t \rceil, 0.5K)$. Truncate each training document D_i (i=1..t) in the class to $b_i = min(b, |D_i|)$ bytes. If $\sum b_i < s$, compensate by restarting this process with the value of b increased by 1. Concatenate the truncated D_1 with a (file containing a) single space followed by the truncated D_2, space, D_3, space, and so on. This procedure results in a single mega-document for the class. Truncate the mega-document after s bytes.

To get meaningful results using this approach, one should not use too small a chunk size b. E.g., one shouldn't take a single byte from each document. The 0.5K parameter was our choice for a minimum chunk size. (We assumed that no document was smaller than .5K.)

We used this procedure to obtain the results shown in Figures 6.6- 6.6. Note that, because of the minimum chunk size, not every training document from a class is necessarily in the mega-document used for a given training size s. More importantly, it is also possible that length(mega-document) $< s$, if the total amount of training data in a class is less than s bytes. The larger s gets,

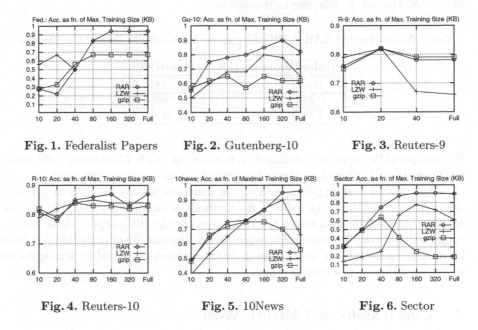

Fig. 1. Federalist Papers   Fig. 2. Gutenberg-10   Fig. 3. Reuters-9

Fig. 4. Reuters-10   Fig. 5. 10News   Fig. 6. Sector

the more imbalance in the amount of training data per class. For $s = 40K$, all corpora except Reuters-9 do get 40K bytes of training data. For $s = 80K$, all corpora except Reuters-9 and Reuters-10 have 80K bytes of training data (Reuters-10 has slightly less).

Discussion of Experiments Varying Amount of Training Data. As seen in Figures 6.6- 6.6, more training data does not always lead to higher accuracy. Gzip's increase in accuracy is constrained by the size of its sliding window, and it does not exhibit much increase in accuracy beyond 40K, The curves for LZW flatten out somewhere between 300K and 500K, depending on how soon its dictionary fills up (which varies between corpora). Notice that at 40K (and to some extent at 80K), LZW's accuracy is often low compared to RAR's. Thus LZW's poor performance cannot be attributed solely to its small dictionary size, nor to an inability to handle imbalanced training data.

RAR, on the other hand, seems to improve consistently as the amount of training data increases. This reflects RAR's ability to exploit additional data to obtain more exact probability estimates. At the 20K point, RAR's results are similar to gzip's, but then RAR's results climb up, while gzip's do not.

The Importance of Balanced Training Data. The problem of imbalanced training data is well-known, and classification methods are often adversely affected by this imbalance (see e.g. [26]). To test how much training data imbalance affects the accuracy of compression-based classification methods, we performed the following small experiment on Gutenberg-10. We first created a skewed version of the Gutenberg-10 corpus, as follows: we gave classes 1-5 the first 40K of their training data each, and classes 6-10 the first 70K of their training data each.

Table 5. Accuracy of RAR, LZW and gzip on balanced and skewed Gu-10 subset

Method	Skewed-40K/70K	40K	70K
RAR	0.50	.78	.80
GZIP	0.55	.65	.57
LZW	0.53	.65	.72

We compared the accuracy obtained on this corpus (with 4-fold cross-validation) to the accuracy obtained on two other versions of the corpus – one in which each class has 40K of training data, and one in which each class has 70K of training data. Results are shown in Table 5. All methods perform worse with the skewed corpus than they do with either the 70K corpus or the 40K corpus. These results suggest that it may be desirable to equalize the amount of training data per class by discarding data from larger classes. Such an approach would be analogous to under-sampling in machine learning.

7   Conclusions and Future Work

We tested three compression methods (RAR, gzip and LZW) under two procedures (AMDL and BCN) on English language topic/genre categorization and authorship attribution problems. RAR almost always produced more accurate classification than LZW and gzip, sometimes by a wide margin. LZW often performed poorly, not always because of its limited size dictionary, and gzip was handicapped by its sliding window on some corpora. We found AMDL to be superior to BCN for RAR, both in runtime and accuracy, We found BCN to be superior to AMDL for gzip's accuracy, although it runs even more slowly than AMDL. Overall, RAR under AMDL seems to give best results.

There remains a need for careful experiments comparing the current best compression-based classification methods to state-of-the-art classification methods, and to methods similar to the ones explored here, namely PPMC with SMDL (as used by [33]) and the related n-gram language modeling methods of [22, 23]. Further experiments are also needed to determine when artificially balancing class sizes (by throwing away data) is desirable.

We presented a new approach to test whether character-based methods can actually benefit from their ability to capture subword, superword, and other non-word (punctuation) features. Our approach consisted of applying different preprocessing procedures to the corpora, and comparing results between the original corpora and the preprocessed versions. Our subword experiments indicated that in some cases, compression algorithms may benefit from subword information in performing classification. Our superword experiments provided evidence that RAR (PPM) benefits from information contained in word sequences, and thus successfully exploits an ability not shared by more traditional bag-of-words methods.

References

1. Benedetto, B., Caglioti, E., Loreto, V.: Language trees and zipping. Physical Review Letters **88**(048702) (2002).
2. Benedetto, B., Caglioti, E., Loreto, V.: On J. Goodman's comment, to "Language trees and zipping". http://arxiv.org/abs/cond-mat/0203275 July 2004.
3. Benedetto, D. and Caglioti, E.: Benedetto, Caglioti, and Loreto reply. Physical Review Letters, **90**(089804) (2003)
4. Cavnar, W. B., Tenkle, J. M.: N-gram-based text categorization. Proc. of the 3rd Annual Symposium on Document Analysis and Information Retrieval (SDAIR 94) (1994) 161–175
5. Chen, Stanley F., and Goodman, Joshua: An Empirical Study of smoothing techniques for language modeling. Proc. of the Thirty-Fourth Annual Meeting of the Association for Computational Linguistics. 1998
6. Damashek, M.: Gauging similarity with n-grams: Language-independent categorization of text. Science **267**(5199) (1995):843–848
7. Eyheramendy, S., Lewis, D. D., Madigan, D.: On the naive Bayes model for text categorization. Proc. of the Ninth International Workshop on Artificial Intelligence and Statistics (2003)
8. Frank, E., Chui, C., Witten, I.H.: Text Categorization Using Compression Models. Proc. of DCC-00, IEEE Data Compression Conference (2000) 200–209.
9. Ghani, Rayid: Using Error Correcting Codes for Efficient Text Classification with a Large Number of Categories. KDD project report. Masters Thesis. Center for Automated Learning and Discovery, Carnegie Mellon University (2001)
10. Goodman, Joshua T.: A Bit of Progress in Language Modeling, Extended Version. Computer Speech and Language, October 2001, pages 403-434.
11. Goodman, J.: Extended comment on language trees and zipping. http://arxiv.org/abs/cond-mat/0202383
12. gzip, a GNU license compression tool, version 1.3.3 (2002-03-08). Copyright 2002 Free Software Foundation Copyright 1992-1993 Jean-loup Gailly
13. Khmelev D., Teahan W.: A repetition based measure for verification of text collections and for text categorization. Proc. of the 26th annual international ACM SIGIR conference on Research and development in informaion retrieval (2003):104–110
14. Khmelev, D. V., Teahan, W. J.: Comment: "Language trees and zipping". Physical Review Letters, **90** (2003):089803.
15. Khmelev D., Tweedie F.: Using Markov Chains for Identification of Writers. Literary and Linguistic Computing **16**(4) (2001):299–307
16. Kukushkina O. V., Polikarpov A. A., Khmelev D. V.: Using literal and grammatical statistics for authorship attribution. Problems of Information Transmission **37** (2001):172–184.
17. Lowenstern D., Hirsh H., Noordiwier M., Yianilos P.: DNA Sequence Classification Using Compression-Based Induction. DIMACS Technical Report 95-04 (1995)
18. McCallum, A., Nigam, K.: A Comparison of Event Models for Naive Bayes Text Classification. Proc. of the AAAI-98 Workshop on "Learning for Text Categorization" (1998)
19. Mitchell, T.: Tutorial on machine Learning over natural language documents. http://www.cs.cmu.edu/ tom/text-learning.ps
20. Mosteller, F., Wallace, D. L.: Inference and Disputed Authorship: The Federalist. Springer-Verlag, New York, (1964) (Second edition: Applied Bayesian and Classical Inference. (1984)).

21. Nelson, Mark R.: LZW source code. Dr. Dobb's Journal, October, 1989 (Also available at http://www.dogma.net/markn/articles/lzw/lzw.htm).
22. Peng, F., Schuurmans, D.: Combining Naive Bayes and n-gram language models for text classification. Proc. of The 25th European Conference on Information Retrieval Research (ECIR03)LNCS 2633 (2003):335-350
23. Peng, F., Schuurmans, D., Wang, S.: Augmenting Naive Bayes classifiers with statistical language models. Information Retrieval 7 (2004):317-345.
24. Peng, F., Schuurmans, D., Wang, S.: Language and task independent text categorization with simple language models. Proc. Human Language Technology Conference of the North American Chapter of the ACL (2003) 189–196
25. RAR compression tool by RAR Labs, Inc. (www.rarlab.com). Version 3.30 (22 Jan 2004). Copyright (c) 1993-2004 Eugene Roshal.
26. Rennie, J. D. M., Shih, L., Teevan, J., Karger, D. R. Tackling the poor assumptions of Naive Bayes text classifiers. Proc. of the Twentieth International Conference on Machine Learning (2003)
27. Rorshal, Eugene (RAR Labs Inc.): Personal communication (2004)
28. Schechter, B.: Fun with your zip program: Sort through texts, and more. New York Times, April 30, 2002.
29. Shkarin, D.: Improving the efficiency of PPM algorithm. Problems of information transmission 34(3) (2001):44–54 (In Russian. English description available at http://www.dogma.net/DataCompression/Miscellaneous/PPMII_DCC02.pdf).
30. Sebastiani, F.: Machine learning in automated text categorization, ACM Computing Surveys 34(1) (2002):1–47
31. Teahan, W.J.: Modelling English Text. PhD thesis, University of Waikato (1998)
32. Teahan, W.J.: Text classification and segmentation using minimum cross-entropy Proc. RIAO-00, 6th International Conference Recherche d'Information Assistee par Ordinateur (2000)
33. Teahan, W. J., Harper, D. J.: Using compression-based language models for text categorization. Proc. of the Workshop on Language Modeling and Information Retrieval (2001)
34. Thaper, N.: Using Compression For Source Based Classification Of Text. Master's Thesis, Massachusetts Institute of Technology (2001).
35. Yang, Yiming: An Evaluation of Statistical Approaches to Text Categorization. Information Retrieval, 1(1/2):67-88. (1999).
36. Yang, Yiming, Pederson, Jan O.: A Comparative Study on Feature Selection in Text Categorization. Proc. of 14th International Conference on Machine Learning (ICML-97).
37. Zhang, Tong: Personal communication (2004).
38. Zhang, Tong, Oles, J. Frank.: Text Categorization Based on Regularized Linear Classification Methods. Information retrieval 4 (2001):5–31.
39. Zhang, J., Jin, R., Yang, Y., Hauptmann, A.G.: Modified Logistic Regression: An Approximation to SVM and Its Applications in Large-Scale Text Categorization. Proc. of the 20th International Conference on Machine Learning (2003):888–895

Ontology as a Search-Tool: A Study of Real Users' Query Formulation With and Without Conceptual Support

Sari Suomela and Jaana Kekäläinen

University of Tampere, Department of Information Studies,
FI-33014 University of Tampere, Finland
Sari.Suomela@uta.fi, Jaana.Kekalainen@uta.fi

Abstract. This study examines 16 real users' use of an ontology as a search tool. The users' queries constructed with the help of a Concept-based Information Retrieval Interface (CIRI) were compared to queries created independently based on the same search task description. Also the effectiveness of the CIRI queries was compared to the users' unaided queries. The simulated search task method was used to make the searching situations as close to real as possible. Due to CIRI's query expansion feature the number of search terms was remarkably higher in ontology queries than in Direct interface queries. The search results were evaluated with generalised precision and generalised relative recall as well as precision based on personal assessments. The Direct interface queries performed better in all methods of comparison.

1 Introduction

This study examines the usability and effectiveness of an ontology as a search tool. With emergence of the semantic web, ontologies have become popular. Although there are different kinds of ontologies, they all can be described as specifications of a conceptualisation, or models showing concepts and their relations. They are used as a unifying framework or shared understanding for communication between people, systems, or people and systems. [6, 7]. In our test real users interact with a conceptual model representing the subject area of search tasks.

The ontology of the study is based on three abstraction levels: It includes concepts, expressions representing concepts, and matching models representing expressions as search keys [12]. Semantic relations typical of thesauri are also represented in the ontology. The idea thus is that from the ontology a searcher selects concepts that best represent her information need, and queries are constructed for the searcher by the system managing the ontology. The system (Concept-based IR interface, CIRI) can facilitate searchers by showing the concepts and their relations of an area of interest; by giving search keys for the search concepts; and by expanding a query with synonyms and narrower and associated concepts. [11]

The ontology is a product of the ongoing *Finnish semantic web ontologies* project, and was constructed for searching a digital newspaper archive. The archive includes full texts of newspaper articles that are not indexed with the ontology. CIRI thus supports free text searching, and performs automatic query expansion. Our aim was to

D.E. Losada and J.M. Fernández-Luna (Eds.): ECIR 2005, LNCS 3408, pp. 315–329, 2005.

test how real users interact with CIRI. As a comparison for CIRI we used a similar interface without an ontology support. We state the following research questions:

- What kind are the queries constructed through the ontology compared to the searchers' unaided queries?
- What is the effectiveness of the ontology queries compared to the searchers' unaided queries?

Next, we shall review related studies. In Section 3 we shall introduce the test setting and in Section 4 the results. Discussion and conclusions are in Section 5.

2 Related Studies

Query expansion and reformulation have been studied intensively, also in interactive information retrieval (IIR for short). The sources for expansion are typically results of the initial search (relevance feedback) or some external knowledge structure [5]. A thesaurus is an external expansion source in several studies on real users' searching. Jones and others [10] give a good overview of the – somewhat – older literature. They themselves tested query expansion with INSPEC thesaurus in INSPEC database with the best match system OKAPI. Genuine users with own information needs ran first their own query. The query was mapped to the thesaurus, and a list of terms partly or completely mapping the original search key was presented to the users. They then selected any number of terms to be added as expansion keys to the queries. Based on results at document cut-off value (DCV) 20 no significant difference in effectiveness of original and expanded queries was detected, whether run against full text or index terms. The expansion had a reordering effect on the result sets, however [10] .

Sihvonen and Vakkari [16] studied subject novices' and experts' query formulation and expansion. The source of expansion was a thesaurus. They found out that the number of search terms in initial or expanded queries did not vary much between the two groups, yet the experts' selection of expansion keys was more accurate with relation to effectiveness. Sutcliffe, Ennis and Watkinson [18] studied users' searching behaviour including query formulation and reformulation. They emphasise the effects of search task, but found no simple correlation between behaviour and performance.

Within TREC interactive track relevance feedback methods for query reformulation have been examined by several researchers [15]. Belkin and others [3] conducted a series of IIR experiments in TREC instance finding task. Negative and positive feedback as well as automatic and interactive feedback were tested with different interfaces. The article explains the system and interface development experiment by experiment. Joho, Sanderson and Beaulieu [9] studied interactive query expansion using conceptual hierarchies as expansion source using TREC topics and measures for the instance finding task. The hierarchies were kind of summaries of the retrieved result set. They conclude that hierarchies could help improve precision at higher DCVs (in instance finding task 5-30).

To summarise, there are several studies on real users' query formulation and reformulation, and on interaction with thesauri at searching phase in intellectually indexed environments. Query formulation is crucial for the initial results yet not a trivial effort. Relevance feedback is generally found performance enhancing, but the results of the effectiveness of thesaurus expansion are mixed. Our test environment is not intellectually indexed, and the initial query formulation starts within the ontology, which is thus not solely used as an expansion source.

3 Test Setting

3.1 Ontology

The experiment was a pilot study of the *Finnish web ontologies* project. Food industry was chosen as the theme of the ontology, as the research team assessed the topic area large enough but easily outlined. Also the document collection contained sufficiently documents on food industry for meaningful search tasks. The user group of the study was food industry professionals, so the terms included professional as well as general food industry terms.

The information of the ontology is organised according to the model of three abstraction levels: conceptual level, where the concepts and their relationships are found; linguistic level that contains expressions corresponding to the concepts; and occurrence level that consists of matching models of the expressions. The relationships between the concepts are generic, partitive, instance and associative relationships. At linguistic level the principle name of a concept (term) and its synonyms are defined. At occurrence level matching models corresponding to the expressions represent search keys suitable for different database indices. [12, 11]

The test ontology was created with Protégé ontology editor. It is an open source Java tool developed by Stanford Medical Informatics at the Stanford University School of Medicine (http://protege.stanford.edu/index.html). [1]

The ontology consists of 479 food industry concepts represented by 689 expressions, which again are represented by 2087 matching models. Between the concepts 603 relationships have been defined. The top level of the ontology consists of 11 concepts and there are up to six lower levels of concepts for the top level concepts.

3.2 Database, Search System and Interfaces

The test database consists of Finnish newspaper articles published in Aamulehti in years 2000-2004. Aamulehti is the second largest daily newspaper in Finland. There are 396 255 articles in the test collection and the average length of an article is 255 words. The index terms of the database have been lemmatised. The test database is managed under the InQuery retrieval system which is a best match IR system. (For details see [2,19].) Two tasks were searched with CIRI, and two tasks with a regular IR interface (Direct) by all users. CIRI acts between the user, the relational database containing the ontology information, the search engine and the document database. It is based on applet-servlet architecture, where the applet submits the queries through a Java Database Connectivity (JDBC) interface in a PostgreSQL relational database.

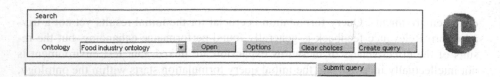

Ciri search

Instructions

1. Press *Options* button and choose the database you want.

2. Choose a terminology from *Ontology* drop-down menu and press *Open*.
   Navigation tree will open into its own window.

3. Choose the terms and number of expansion levels you want. As you are choosing
   the terms, query is being built in *Search* window.

4. Do not close Ontology window after choosing your search terms. Press *Create query*
   and CIRI expands the chosen concepts up to the desired level and transforms the result
   of the expansion into corresponding matching models. This expanded query will appear
   in the text field below the search applet. You may still modify the created query and add
   your own search terms into it. Complete the search by pressing *Submit query*
   Pressing *Clear choices* will erase all choices made.

Fig. 1. Concept-based Information Retrieval Interface CIRI

CIRI is used via a web browser. It allows the user to open an ontology, select concepts from it, select a search engine, a database and the number of query expansion levels, create a query from the ontology concepts and submit the query to the search engine [1]. In query expansion, narrower concepts and directly associated concepts of the search concept are collected, and the terms and all synonyms denoting these concepts are put into the query. If no expansion level is selected (i.e. expansion level is 1), only the term and synonyms are utilized in query formulation. [12,13.] The default expansion level of CIRI is three. The user can also add her own query terms or remove terms from the query. CIRI has been constructed as a part of a long-term cooperation between the media house Alma Media and the Department of Information Studies of University of Tampere.

CIRI web interface is shown in Figure 1. The user first presses the *Options* button and chooses the database and a search system in the opening applet window. She then selects the ontology from the dropdown menu and opens the ontology with the *Open* button. In our experiment these two first steps were done on behalf of the user. The ontology navigation tree opens up into a new window, which is shown in Figure 2. The user selects her choice of concepts, which appear in the Search text field on the top of the CIRI window in Figure 1. After selecting her query concepts and possibly choosing the number of expansion levels, the user presses *Create query* button on CIRI window. CIRI then constructs the query from the selected concepts according to the syntax of the selected search system. The query is displayed in the lower Search text field. At this stage the user may remove search terms from the query as well as add her own search keys. Pressing *Submit query* button sends the query to InQuery.

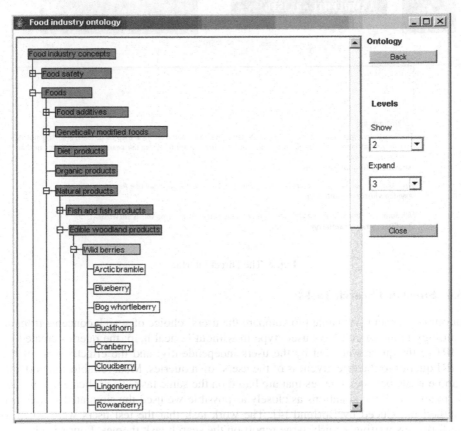

Fig. 2. The ontology navigation tree partly opened

A part of the ontology navigation tree is shown in Figure 2. The ontology navigation tree is presented as a standard tree structure. One chooses a concept to the query
by clicking the concept box. Chosen concept boxes are highlighted like the concept
'*Wild berries*' in Figure 2. Expansion concepts that come with a chosen concept are
highlighted in a different shade like berry names are in Figure 2. By clicking the concept box again one can remove the concept from the query.

The Direct interface of the study is a straightforward web IR interface, where one
types in search keys in a text field and submits the query with a button (see Figure 3).

3.3 Test Users

Food manufacturing companies, catering businesses, food industry related companies,
organisations and authorities in Western, Eastern and Southern Finland were ap-
proached to recruit 16 test users. Due to the specificity of the ontology and the tasks
the test users needed to have a food industry education at least at secondary level,
work within food industry and follow the food industry news in the media.

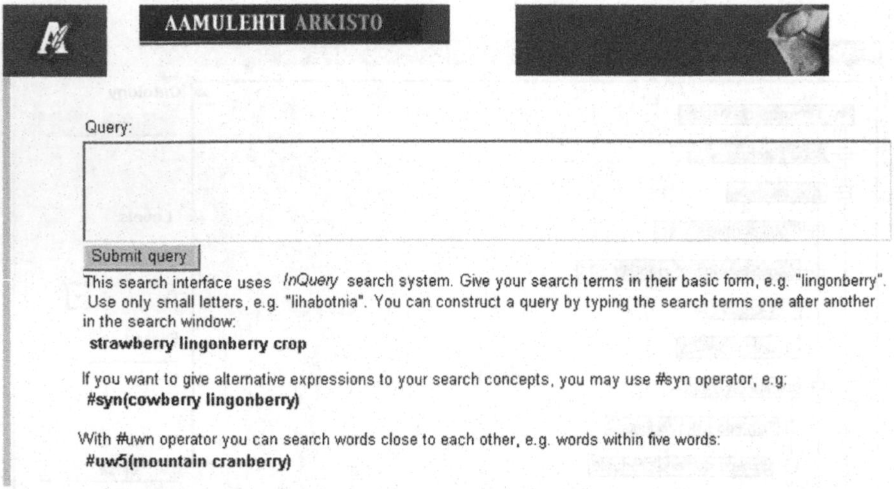

Fig. 3. The Direct interface

3.4 Simulated Search Tasks

In our experiment we wanted to compare the users' choice of search concepts from an ontology to the search keys users type in without lexical help; the queries created by CIRI to the queries created by the users independently; and the effectiveness of the CIRI queries to the effectiveness of the users' own queries. Most reliable comparisons can be made between queries that are based on the same task. To replicate real life information retrieval situations as closely as possible we used the simulated search task method introduced by Borlund [4]. The work task that the test users were asked to perform was writing a fairly large report on the search task themes. Four search tasks were created. The test was run in Finnish so the search tasks were in Finnish, too. Here are the tasks translated into English:

Fat: Which cholesterol lowering edible fats exist on the market and how has their market situation developed worldwide?

Gene: How has the import controversy over transgenic food products between the United States and Europe progressed?

Ice cream: How has manufacture of ice cream been concentrated and reduced in Finnish milk processing companies?

Organic: ow has the demand of organic products developed in Finland within the past few years? What is restraining the sale of organic products?

The tasks were tested by the researchers to make sure that the database contained sufficiently relevant documents on each topic for a meaningful search. The wording of the tasks was planned a rather straightforward match with the ontology concepts in two tasks: *Ice cream* and *Organic*. In the wording of two tasks, *Fat* and *Gene*, synonyms of the ontology concepts were used instead of the ontology concepts to make the use of the ontology slightly less automatic.

Each task was searched by all test users. The users performed two searches with one interface and then two searches with the other. The order of the task sequence - interface combinations were permuted based on basic 2x2 Latin squares: no task sequence –interface combination pair was repeated in the matrix of eight users. The matrix was run twice, so each task sequence – interface combination was searched by two searchers.

3.5   Test Procedure and Questionnaires

The experiment session was begun with some general information on the study. Then the user filled a background information questionnaire mapping e.g. her education, computer use and information retrieval experience and frequency and food industry news following. After that the first test interface was introduced to the user and the first search task description sheet was handed to her and the user performed the first search. The relevance of 15 documents from the top of the result list was assessed using a four point scale (see Section 3.6). If the user chose to modify the query, the last search result was evaluated as well. A questionnaire reflecting the search experience was filled in after the task, see Table 1. Then the task-related steps were repeated with the second interface. A post-system questionnaire was filled in after the two tasks on the first interface, see Tables 2 and 3. Then the second interface was introduced and the search task and interface related steps were repeated for the second interface. In the end of the experiment a post-experiment questionnaire presented in Table 4 was filled in and the experimenter and the test user discussed freely.

Table 1. Post-task questionnaire

Statement	Answer type
I was familiar with the topic of the task	5 = fully agree to 1 = totally disagree
Carrying out the search was easy	5 = fully agree to 1 = totally disagree
I'm satisfied with the search result	5 = fully agree to 1 = totally disagree
I had enough time to complete the task	5 = fully agree to 1 = totally disagree

Table 2. Post-CIRI questionnaire

Statement or question	Answer type
The system was easy to use	5 = fully agree to 1 = totally disagree
Finding search concepts needed in the tasks in the ontology was easy	5 = fully agree to 1 = totally disagree
Terms found in the ontology were same as those I use for the same concepts	5 = fully agree to 1 = totally disagree
Structure of the ontology was logical	5 = fully agree to 1 = totally disagree
What was good about the system?	Unstructured text
What was bad about the system?	Unstructured text

Table 3. Post Direct interface questionnaire

Statement or question	Answer type
The system was easy to use	5 = fully agree to 1 = totally disagree
What was good about the system?	Unstructured text
What was bad about the system?	Unstructured text

Table 4. Post-experiment questionnaire

Statement or question	Answer type
The tasks I performed were similar to the searches I typically carry out.	5 = fully agree to 1 = totally disagree
The tested systems were similar to each other	5 = fully agree to 1 = totally disagree
Ontology helped with coming up with search terms.	5 = fully agree to 1 = totally disagree
Ontology helped to analysing the topic.	5 = fully agree to 1 = totally disagree
Using the ontology was laborious.	5 = fully agree to 1 = totally disagree
Which system did you find easier to use?	The first one / the second one / can't say
Which system did you like better? Why?	The fist one / the second one / can't say
Do you have additional comments on the systems?	Unstructured text
Do you have additional comments on the ontology?	Unstructured text
Do you have additional comments on the test arrangements?	Unstructured text

3.6 Relevance Assessments

The users were asked to assess the relevance of the search results of their first and, when the user chose to modify the query, final queries. From the top of the result list fifteen documents were evaluated. Relevance in real life is not a bi-dimensional quality, therefore relevance assessments were made with a four-point scale:

- Very relevant
- Rather relevant
- Marginally relevant
- Non-relevant.

The liberal recall base consists of documents that at least one user assessed at least marginally relevant in at least one of her searches. Thus it contains all relevant documents of all of the searches performed in the study. The numbers of documents and their relevance assessments per topic in liberal recall base are shown in Table 5. The assessments were quantified for calculation of precision and recall. Documents assessed very relevant got value 3, rather relevant documents were given value 2 and marginally relevant documents value 1. Non-relevant documents got value 0.

Table 5. Documents in liberal recall base

	Fat	Gene	Ice cream	Or-ganic	Sum
Documents	74	57	54	49	234
Assessments	239	255	278	252	1024
Very relevant	106	156	161	152	575
Rather relevant	46	33	41	49	169
Marginally relevant	55	46	36	38	175
Non-relevant	32	20	40	13	105

3.7 Measures

The users' own view of their search success was studied by adding a sum of the quantified relevance assessments of each search result. DCV being at 15, when the user assessed the whole set very relevant, the result set is worth 45 points. If there is not a single relevant document in the set, the value of the result set is 0. When the user had performed two searches of the same task, the better result was chosen for the comparison. This gives us a user's point of view of the results.

To get a more general view, we measured the effectiveness of search results with generalised precision and generalised relative recall [14]. For this, an average relevance score was calculated for all documents in the liberal recall base. A document's final score is an average of all given scores. In this comparison the result of the first search of cach user in each task is used. Relative recall calculation was based on the number of relevant documents in the recall base. Generalised precision and recall are defined as follows:

$$gP = \sum_{d \in R} r(d) / n \qquad gR = \sum_{d \in R} r(d) / \sum_{d \in D} r(d) \qquad (1)$$

where D = set of N documents, database; R = set of n retrieved documents, $R \subseteq D$; $r(d)$ = score of the document.

4 Results

4.1 Analysis of the Questionnaires

The first questionnaire inquired the test users' background information. Our test users worked e.g. within product development, communications, consumer service, restaurant management, information systems development, food safety and quality control. All test users either had or were acquiring an education within food industry (see Table 6). There were two students in the test user group, but they both worked within food industry at the same time. Test users were predominantly female, only one was male. No test user was under age 25 years nor over 55 years (see Table 7).

Test users were rather experienced computer users and information searchers, but information retrieval was not the main task of any of them (see Table 8). All test users used computers both at work and at free time. All but one performed searches both at home and at work, one performed searches only at work. Online searching is performed weekly by nine test users while three users reported to search online daily and three monthly. Online searching is carried out less often than monthly by one user.

Table 6. Education levels of test users

Education levels	Test users
Academic	10
Polytechnic	3
other	3

Table 7. Age distribution of test users

Age groups	Test users
25-35	6
35-45	4
45-55	6

Table 8. Information searching experience

Years	Test users
less than 3	3
3-5	4
6-10	7
over 10	2

Internet is the most familiar digital information source to the users: All users have used Internet information resources. Half of them have used library online catalogues, and also a half professional databases. A large majority of the test users reported to follow up food industry news regularly. One test user follows the news seldom and two users very closely.

The results of the post-task questionnaires are presented in Table 9. Assessments 4-5 were summed under 'agree' and 1-2 under 'disagree'. A large majority of the users were familiar with all the task topics. Also a majority of the users found carrying out a search easy in all topics. In all other tasks but *Fat* the users were predominantly satisfied with the results. In task *Fat* nearly half of the users were satisfied with the results.

The post system questionnaires mapped the users' experience with the interfaces. Since our primary interest is in the experiences of using CIRI, we present the results of the post-CIRI questionnaire in Table 10. The ontology was easy to use to 13 of the users. Finding the concepts in the ontology was easy to 9 users. The ontology was apparently well built, since 14 users found the terms representing concepts in the ontology the same they use for the same concepts and 12 users found the structure of the ontology logical. In their written comments several users pointed out, that the CIRI interface is not very user-friendly. For a novice CIRI user it is hard to figure out whether and where a certain concept exists in the ontology tree. Several users pointed out, that practice would enhance user satisfaction, as one would become familiar with the structure of the ontology. A search window to help locate a concept within the ontology was suggested by one user.

The results of the post-experiment questionnaire are shown in Table 11. The search tasks were a rather good match with the target group: The tasks were found at least fairly similar to their own search tasks by 9 users. The system was found helpful in creating search terms by 10 users and in analysing the search task by 11 users. Using the interface was easy to 13 users while only 8 users didn't find using it laborious.

Table 9. Results of the post-task questionnaire (N=16)

	Topic was familiar			Searching easy			Satisfied w/ result		
	Agree	Dis-agr	Can't say	Agree	Dis-agr	Can't say	Agree	Dis-agr	Can't say
Fat	12	3	1	9	4	3	7	8	1
Gene	11	5	0	11	5	0	13	3	0
Ice cream	14	1	1	13	3	0	13	2	1
Organic	15	0	1	13	3	0	14	1	1

The Direct interface was clearly found easier to use than CIRI, by 11 users (see Table 12). Almost the same number of users (10) also liked the Direct interface better. There was a user who found the Direct interface easier to use but liked CIRI better. Users that were less familiar with the search task terminology pointed out that the ontology was a great help for coming up with search keys while users familiar with both the topic and information retrieval stated that it was both quicker and less frustrating just to type in the search keys than browse the ontology looking for the concepts. One user thought that given a chance she would use both interfaces to the same search to make the best possible search. Another user thought she might use CIRI for searches that have a highly specific specialized vocabulary, e.g. legal text databases.

Table 10. Results of the post-CIRI questionnaire (N=16)

Statement or question	Agree	Disagree	Can't say
Ontology interface easy to use	13	2	1
Finding search concepts needed in the tasks in the ontology was easy	9	7	0
Terms found in the ontology were same as those I use for the same concepts	14	2	0
Structure of the ontology was logical	12	4	0

Table 11. Results of the post-experiment questionnaire (N=16)

Statement or question	Agree	Disagree	Can't say
Search tasks similar to own searches	9	4	3
Ontology helped to create search terms	10	3	3
Ontology helped to analyse search task	11	2	3
Using ontology was laborious	6	8	2

Table 12. Easier and preferred system (N=16)

Question	Ontology	Direct	Can't say
Easier system	3	11	2
Preferred system	4	10	2

4.2 Analysis of Search Keys and Search Concepts

The following analysis is based on the test users' first queries and results, because most of the users did not reformulate their queries. Table 13 gives the average numbers of search keys and Table 14 the average numbers of search concepts per query. The average numbers of both keys and concepts are lower for the Direct search interface because of the expansion feature in the CIRI interface. All users had the default expansion level (3) in CIRI. However, the number of search keys in Direct search mode is high compared to Internet searches. The test users of CIRI were able to add their own search keys into queries, for example such keys that did not exist in the ontology, yet the average figure is rather low (see column # *own keys* in Table 13).

The overlap between Direct searchers' keys / concepts and ontology terms / concepts is given in Tables 13-14 (see column # *keys / concepts also in ontology*). It seems that in some search tasks the concepts are shared between the test users leading also to a higher overlap (tasks *Ice cream, Organic* in Tables 13-14). In general, the number of search keys and concepts does not vary much within each interface group, except the task *Organic* searched in CIRI has lower number of keys and concepts.

The idea of expansion in CIRI was not very intuitive or clear to the test users. They tended to select very general concepts, i.e. concepts high up in the hierarchies, which caused quite intense query expansion. The test users did not actually select more concepts in CIRI than in Direct interface, but the automatic expansion makes the difference. Some users deleted expansion keys they found inappropriate.

Table 13. Average number of search keys per query (16 queries per search task – interface combination)

Search tasks	CIRI			Direct		
	# ontology keys	# own keys	# all keys	# keys also in ontology	# own keys	# all keys
Fat	22.6	0.5	23.1	0	7.5	7.5
Gene	51.0	0.4	51.4	0.8	5.7	6.5
Ice cream	39.3	0	39.3	1.9	3.5	5.4
Organic	11.9	0.1	12.0	1.5	4.8	6.3
Mean	31.2	0.3	31.5	1.1	5.4	6.4

Table 14. Average number of search concepts per query (16 queries per search task – interface combination)

Search tasks	CIRI			Direct		
	# ontology concepts	# own concepts	# all concepts	# concepts also in ontology	# own concepts	# all concepts
Fat	17.5	0.5	18.0	1.4	5.4	6.8
Gene	18.9	0.4	19.3	0.8	4.8	5.6
Ice cream	16.5	0	16.5	2.3	2.7	5.0
Organic	9.3	0	9.3	2.0	3.9	5.9
Mean	15.6	0.2	15.8	1.6	4.2	5.8

4.3 Precision by Personal Relevance Assessments

The users' own view of their search success was measured by summing the relevance scores of each search result. The results are shown in Table 15. In average the users who had performed the search with the Direct interface assessed their results with higher grades than the users who had searched the same topic with CIRI. The difference varies between 23 and 61 points. The Direct interface results are 9-32 percent better than the CIRI results. The difference between average scores of a set varies between three and seven points being largest in Gene and smallest in Ice cream. Comparison between CIRI and Direct interface reveals that Direct interface performs significantly ($p<0.05$) better than CIRI. Test used in comparison was Mann-Whitney U.

Table 15. Precisions by users' own relevance assessments (16 queries per search task – interface combination, DCV 15)

	Sums		Averages		Points per document	
	CIRI	Direct	CIRI	Direct	CIRI	Direct
Fat	167	214	21	27	1.4	1.8
Gene	188	249	24	31	1.6	2.1
Ice cream	249	272	31	34	2.1	2.3
Organic	245	292	31	37	2.0	2.4
Mean	212	257	27	32	1.8	2.1

4.4 Generalised Precision and Relative Recall

Generalised precision and recall are given in Table 16. In all search tasks the direct interface searches outperform the CIRI searches. When CIRI and Direct interfaces are compared on the basis of generalised precision and recall, there is no statistically significant difference between the interfaces (test was Mann-Whitney U).

Table 16. Averages of generalised precision and recall by search task and interface types (16 queries per search task – interface combination, DCV 15)

	gPrecision			gRecall		
	CIRI	Direct	Direct – CIRI	CIRI	Direct	Direct – CIRI
Fat	0.08	0.11	0.03	0.12	0.16	0.04
Gene	0.10	0.14	0.05	0.14	0.21	0.07
Ice cream	0.15	0.19	0.04	0.20	0.26	0.06
Organic	0.21	0.25	0.04	0.28	0.32	0.04
Mean	0.13	0.17	0.04	0.19	0.24	0.05

5 Discussion and Conclusions

We tested the usefulness and effectiveness of an ontology search tool for real users. Altogether 16 food industry professionals searched two simulated search tasks with an ontology interface (CIRI) and two tasks with an interface without vocabulary support (Direct interface). The results indicate that the effectiveness of the Direct interface was slightly better. The numbers of both search concepts and keys were clearly higher in CIRI queries but that was largely due to the expansion feature of CIRI.

The ontology was shown to the users as a tree structure. Difficulty of locating the desired concepts in the ontology frustrated several users. Particularly the more experienced searchers with solid conceptual knowledge strongly preferred using the Direct interface. Users with less conceptual knowledge found CIRI's lexical help useful.

The expansion feature of the CIRI was not very well understood. The users tended to choose concepts high in the hierarchies, which led to intensive expansion especially since it was not possible to choose a general term without the expansion terms. Other features in the users' behaviour were that they did not use proper names as much as expected in their unaided searches although it would have been helpful in at least two of the tasks. In this experiment ontology and users were specialised but article collection general. Ontology was built with specific professional terms while the articles contained several colloquialisms, e.g. *geeniruoka ~gene food, geeniperuna ~gene potato*. Whether the expansion feature had been more useful in a more specialised text collection or less specialised users remains to be tested later on.

Further, many concepts were precoordinated, e.g. *genetically modified corn* instead of two concepts *genetic modification* and *corn*. This might not be a good solution for free text searching because modifiers of nouns may take many different positions, especially in newspaper language.

The test users' reactions were not totally negative. Many users found the ontology helpful in discovering search keys and they also praised the ontology's clear structure. Browsing the ontology helped several users to clarify the search topic to themselves. Some users thought they might use an ontology interface as an additional search tool. Further, they pointed out that for mastering CIRI more practise would be needed. In future experiments the hierarchies should be easier to navigate, e.g. by automatically mapping search keys to concept names, and the expansion feature more understandably presented.

Acknowledgements. This study was funded by Academy of Finland under the grant number 52894 and The National Technology Funding Agency Tekes under the grant number 20682. We are grateful to our test users and Eija Airio, Feza Baskaya, Kalervo Järvelin and Pirkko Saatsi for their help and co-operation.

References

1. Airio, E., Järvelin, K., Suomela, S., Saatsi, P., Kekäläinen, J.: CIRI - An Ontology-based Query Interface for Text Retrieval. The Web Intelligence –symposium, Helsinki, Finland (2004). Available at: <URL: http://www.cs.helsinki.fi/group/seco/conference /step2004/material.html> [Cited October 26, 2004]
2. Allan, J., Callan, J., Croft, B., Ballesteros, L., Byrd, D., Swan, R., Xu, J.: INQUERY does battle with TREC-6. (1997) Available at: <URL: http://trec.nist.gov/pubs/trec6/papers/ umass-trec97.ps> [Cited 26.10.2004]

3. Belkin, N.J., Cool, C., Kelly, D., Lin, S.J., Park, S.Y., Perez-Carballo, J., Sikora, C.: Iterative exploration, design and evaluation of support for query formulation in interactive information retrieval. Information Processing & Management 37 (2001) 403-434
4. Borlund, P.: Evaluation of interactive information retrieval systems. Doctoral dissertation. Åbo: Åbo Akademi University Press (2000)
5. Efthimiadis, E.N.: Query expansion. In: Williams, M.E. (ed.): Annual Review of Information Science and Technology, vol. 31. Information Today, Medford, NJ (1996) 121–187
6. Guarino, N.: Formal ontology, conceptual analysis and knowledge representation. International Journal of Human and Computer Studies 43 (1995) 625–640
7. Guarino, N., Masolo, C., Vetere, G.: OntoSeek: Using large linguistic ontologies for gathering information resources from the Web. LADSEB-CNR Technical Report 01/98 (1998)
8. ISO International Standard 2788. Documentation - Guidelines for the establishment and development of monolingual thesauri. International Organization for Standardization (1986)
9. Joho, H., Sanderson, M., Beaulieu, M.: A study of user interaction with a concept-based interactive query expansion support tool. In Advances in Information Retrieval, Proceedings of 26th European Conference on IR Research, ECIR 2004. Lecture Notes in Computer Science, Vol. 2997. Springer-Verlag, Berlin (2004) 42-56
10. Jones, S., Gatford, M., Robertson, S., Hancock-Beaulieu, M., Secker, J.: Interactive thesaurus navigation: Intelligence rules ok? Journal of the American Society for Information Science 46 (1995) 52–59
11. Järvelin, K., Kekäläinen, J., Niemi, T.: ExpansionTool: Concept-based query expansion and construction. Information Retrieval 4 (2001) 231-255
12. Järvelin, K., Kristensen, J., Niemi, T., Sormunen, E., Keskustalo, H.: A deductive data model for query expansion. In: Frei, H.-P., Harman, D., Schäuble, P., Wilkinson, R. (eds.): Proceedings of the 19th Annual International ACM–SIGIR Conference on Research and Development in Information Retrieval. ACM press New York NY (1996) 235–249
13. Kekäläinen, J.: The effects of query complexity, expansion and structure on retrieval performance in probabilistic text retrieval. PhD dissertation, Department of Information Studies, University of Tampere. Acta Universitatis Tamperensis 678 (1999)
14. Kekäläinen, J., Järvelin, K.: Using graded relevance assessments in IR evaluation. Journal of the American Society for Information Science and Technology 53 (2002) 1120-1129
15. Over, P.: The TREC interactive track: an annotated bibliography. Information Processing & Management 37 (2001) 369-381
16. Sihvonen, A., Vakkari, P.: Subject knowledge improves interactive query expansion assisted by a thesaurus. To appear in Journal of Documentation (2004)
17. Sparck Jones, K.: Automatic indexing. Journal of Documentation 30 (1974) 393–432
18. Sutcliffe, A.G., Ennis, M., Watkinson, S.J.: Empirical studies of end-user information searching. Journal of the American Society for Information Science 51 (2000) 1211-1231
19. Turtle, H.R.: Inference networks for document retrieval. Ph.D. dissertation. COINS Technical Report 90–92. Computer and information Science Department, University of Massachusetts (1990)

An Analysis of Query Similarity in Collaborative Web Search

Evelyn Balfe and Barry Smyth

Smart Media Institute, Department of Computer Science,
University College Dublin, Belfield, Dublin 4, Ireland
{Evelyn.Balfe, Barry.Smyth}@ucd.ie*

Abstract. Web search logs provide an invaluable source of information regarding the search behaviour of users. This information can be reused to aid future searches, especially when these logs contain the searching histories of specific communities of users. To date this information is rarely exploited as most Web search techniques continue to rely on the more traditional term-based IR approaches. In contrast, the I-SPY system attempts to reuse past search behaviours as a means to re-rank result-lists according to the implied preferences of like-minded communities of users. It relies on the ability to recognise previous search sessions that are related to the current target search by looking for similarities between past and current queries. We have previously shown how a simple model of query similarity can significantly improve search performance by implementing this reuse approach. In this paper we build on previous work by evaluating alternative query similarity models.

1   Introduction

Web search is dominated by a small number of commercial search engines such as Google, MSN, Yahoo etc. For the most part, these search engines provide searchers with access to a *generic* search facility paying little or no attention to a user's search context. Nevertheless it is clear that many searches are initiated within a certain context and may even be conducted within the scope of a community of like-minded fellow searchers. For example, many search engines allow third-parties to provide search boxes as part of their own web sites, in order to provide visitors with easy access to site search and standard Web search facilities; a motoring Web site might add a Google search box to its pages for instance. The point is that searches that are initiated from such search boxes are likely to share a certain context within a community of users, even though such searches are processed by a generic search engine.

By monitoring and profiling the search histories of communities of like-minded searchers, the I-SPY system aims to deliver significant improvements

---

* The support of the Informatics Research Initiative of Enterprise Ireland is gratefully acknowledged.

D.E. Losada and J.M. Fernández-Luna (Eds.): ECIR 2005, LNCS 3408, pp. 330–344, 2005.
© Springer-Verlag Berlin Heidelberg 2005

in search performance. For instance, the query "jaguar" originating from the motoring Web site is more likely to relate to cars than cats. In collaborative search the past search behaviours (queries and result selections) of searches that have originated from this motoring Web site are recorded and on receipt of a new query, such as "jaguar" those past queries that are *similar* to the new query are retrieved and those results that have been previously been selected in response to these similar queries are prioritised.

Query similarity plays a fundamental role in collaborative search because it governs the selection of related queries and influences the promotion and ranking of results. In the past a simple model of query similarity has been proposed based on term-overlaps between the terms in the current query and the terms in previous queries. We describe this standard model of query similarity in the context of the I-SPY search system in Section 3. In this paper we propose a number of alternative similarity models (Section 4) and evaluate their benefits in comparison to our benchmark term-overlap model using live-user search logs in Section 5.

2   Motivating Query Reuse

Two key ideas about Web search inform our research: *query repetition* and *selection regularity*. First, we assume that the world of Web search is a repetitive place: similar queries tend to recur. Second, we assume that the world of Web search is a regular place: searchers tend to select similar results for similar queries. If these assumptions hold, we believe that significant performance benefits can be realised by reusing past search histories.

In order to assess the degree of repetition among Web search queries we will make use of 5 sets of query logs for different types of search task [1, 2, 3] —general Web search using the Excite search engine (General), image search (Image), a more specialised topical search task (Nutrition), a focused fact-finding search task as part of a live-trial discussed in Section 5 (Live-Trial), and a second example of general Web search but this time from a small software development company of 50 people over a short (6 week) period of time (CW)— see Table 1.

In our query repetition study we use a simple measure of query similarity so that we can measure different degrees of duplication and repetition, from exact duplication to partial overlaps. Thus, to measure the similarity between two queries we compute the degree of overlap between their query terms; see

Table 1. Search log use during query repetition analysis

Name	Number of Queries	Search Scenario
General	65535	General search using Excite.com.
Image	33478	Image search.
Nutrition	16008	Specialised search in the Nutrition domain.
Live-Trial	1705	Fact-finding search task (see Section 5).
CW	7696	Local software company search log.

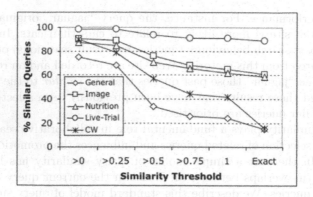

Fig. 1. The percentage of repeat queries

Equation 1. For example, the similarity between the query *"jaguar pictures"* and *"jaguar photos"* is 0.33.

$$Overlap(q, q') = \frac{|q \cap q'|}{|q \cup q'|} \tag{1}$$

Using this approach we can consider two queries to be duplicates if they are within a given similarity threshold; for example *"jaguar pictures"* and *"jaguar photos"* are considered to be duplicates above the 0.25 similarity threshold but not above the 0.5 threshold. Figure 1 shows the percentage of queries that have duplicates above a range of similarity thresholds for each of the query logs. Note that the values for exact duplicates are also shown and that a similarity threshold of 1 allows for duplication that involves permutations of the same query terms. The results indicate that there is a high level of overlap between queries even in the General search scenario. For example, 75% of general search queries share at least one term with other queries (that is similarity > 0) and approximately one third of these share 50% of their terms with other queries. In the more specialised search tasks the degree of overlap is even higher. In the Image, Nutrition and Live-Trial search logs, about 90% of queries share at least one search term, and more than 70% of queries share at least 50% of their terms. Interestingly the CW logs present with intermediate overlap statistics. Even though they refer to general searches, by virtue of the limited scope of the searches (50 employees of a small software company) it is likely that their searches will turn out to be fairly clustered, which is found to be the case. That said, the CW logs cover a relatively short period of time (6 weeks) so we might legitimately expect overlaps to increase further over a longer time period.

The above results provide us with high-level information about the prevalence of repetition in the query-space but they do not tell us about the degree of repetition. For example, 70% of Nutrition queries may share 50% of their terms with other Nutrition queries, but how many other Nutrition queries? This is partly answered in Figure 2 where we report the average number of similar queries that are available at the different similarity thresholds. We see, for example, that in

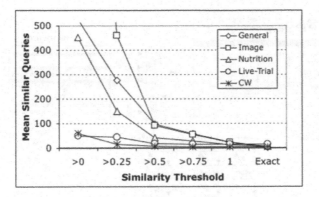

Fig. 2. The average number of similar queries available at different similarity thresholds

the General and Image search logs there are nearly 100 other similar queries, on average, for each duplicate query at the 0.5 similarity threshold. And even at the more stringent similarity thresholds the degree of repetition is surprisingly high. For instance, there are nearly 60 queries on average associated with every query that counts as a repeat at the 0.75 threshold in the Image search logs. In other words, Figure 1 tells us that nearly 70% of Image queries share at least 75% of their terms with other Image search queries, and Figure 2 tells us that, on average, for each of these 70% of the Image search queries there are nearly 60 such queries sharing more than 75% of their terms.

This analysis indicates two important things. First, similar queries do tend to recur frequently in Web search. Second, the degree of repetition varies from being especially high in very focused search tasks or at moderate overlap thresholds, although the degree of repetition does fall off for more general search tasks. This provides a firm foundation for any approach to Web search that attempts to exploit query-repetition—at least repetition occurs, and it is especially frequent in focused tasks.

3   Collaborative Web Search

Figure 3 outlines the basic I-SPY architecture which implements collaborative search. I-SPY is a meta-search engine, drawing on the results produced by a set of underlying search engines (in our implementation these include Google, HotBot, WiseNut, AllTheWeb among others). Thus, when I-SPY receives a new query, q_T, from some user, it submits this query to each of its underlying search engines $(S_1, ..., S_n)$ and combines the result-lists that are returned $(R_1, ..., R_n)$. To do this I-SPY must first adapt the new query so that it conforms to the query interface of the underlying search engine. In addition, the result-lists returned by each underlying search engine are transformed into a common result format, to produce a modified set of result-lists $(R'_1, ...R'_n)$.

I-SPY's key innovation stems from its ability to personalize search results by re-ranking results based on the selection history of previous searchers, effectively

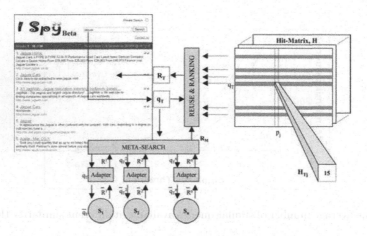

Fig. 3. The I-SPY system architecture

transforming the meta-search result-list R_m in to a modified result-list, R_T. Results that are more likely to be relevant to q_T, on the basis that they have been selected for this and similar queries in the past, are promoted within the combined result-list. In the following sections we will review how this is achieved; further detail is available in [4].

3.1   Profiling Search Histories

The *hit-matrix*, H, maintains a record of the results selected in past search sessions. Each time a searcher selects page (p_j) for some target query (q_T) the value of H_{Tj} is incremented. Thus, H_{Tj} is the number of times that p_j has been selected as a result for query q_T. The row of H that corresponds to q_T provides a complete account of the relative number of all page selections for this query over all search sessions that have used this query. Importantly, I-SPY maintains separate hit-matrices for separate communities of users; see Section 3.4.

3.2   Reusing Similar Queries

When a searcher submits a new target query (q_T) we use I-SPY to locate each row of the hit-matrix that relates to a similar *candidate* query; these are the rows that contain search behaviours that *may* be useful to guide the ranking of the new result-list. To do this we compute the overlap between the terms in q_T and the terms in each candidate query q_c recorded in the hit-matrix, as shown in Equation 1; see Section 4 for further discussion on query similarity. I-SPY then selects all queries that exceed a given similarity threshold to produce its list of related queries. If no similar queries exist in the hit-matrix or if the hit-matrix is empty then I-SPY performs at least as well as the underlying search engines.

3.3   Result Relevancy

The relevance of a result-page, p_j, to a query, q_T, can be estimated directly from the hit-matrix entries for q_T. Equation 2 calculates relevance as the number of page selections that have occurred for p_j in response to query q_T (that is, H_{Tj}) as a proportion of the total number of page selections that have occurred for all pages selected in response to q_T (that is, $\sum_{\forall i} H_{Ti}$). For example, a relevance of 0.25 for p_j and q_T, means that 25% of the page selections from result-lists for q_T have been for this page, p_j.

$$Relevance(p_j, q_T) = \frac{H_{Tj}}{\sum_{\forall i} H_{Ti}} \qquad (2)$$

Of course if multiple similar queries are available and selected for a target query, then there are potentially multiple search histories to inform the relevance of a given page. For example, the page $www.sun.com$ may have a high relevance value (let's say, 0.8) for a past query 'java language' but it may have a lower relevance for another past query 'java' (let's say 0.33). It is then a matter of combining these individual relevance values to produce a single relevance score for this page relative to the target query, say 'java inventor'.

We propose a normalised weighted relevance metric that combines the relevance scores for individual page-query combinations. This is achieved using the weighted-sum of the individual relevance scores, such that each score is weighted by the similarity of its corresponding query to the target query. Thus, in our example above, the relevance of the page $www.sun.com$ is 0.516: the sum of 0.264 (that is, 0.8 page relevance to query 'java language', multiplied by the 0.33 query similarity between this query and the target, 'java inventor') and 0.165 (0.33*0.5 for the past query, 'java'), divided by 0.83, the sum of the query similarities. Equation 3 provides the details of this weighted relevance metric with respect to a page, p_j, a target query, q_T, and a set of retrieved similar queries $q_1, ..., q_n$. $Exists(p_j, q_i)$ is simply a flag that is set to 1 when p_j is one of the result pages selected for query, q_i.

$$WRel(p_j, q_T, q_1, ..., q_n) = \frac{\sum_{i=1...n} Relevance(p_j, q_i) \bullet Sim(q_T, q_i))}{\sum_{i=1...n} Exists(p_j, q_i) \bullet Sim(q_T, q_i)} \qquad (3)$$

3.4   Communities and Collaboration

The above approach is likely to work as long as the query-space is limited to a relatively narrow and uniform context. One of the fundamental ideas in I-SPY, and the reason for the term 'collaborative search', is that a hit-matrix should be populated with queries and selections from a community of users operating within a specific domain of interest. As such I-SPY facilitates the creation of multiple hit-matrices. This affords different communities of users access to a search service that is adapted for their query-space and its preferred pages. For example, a motoring Web site might configure a hit-matrix for its users.

I-SPY facilitates this through a simple form-based Web interface and in doing so, provides the Web site with access to a search interface that is associated with this new hit-matrix. In this way the visitors to this motoring site form an *ad-hoc* community. As the community uses its search service, their queries and page selections will populate the hit-matrix and I-SPY's ranking metric will help to disambiguate vague queries by promoting previously preferred pages.

A large Web portal might create a range of different hit-matrices, and place corresponding search boxes in different parts of the portal (e.g. News, Sports, Business sections) on the grounds that searchers are more likely to submit queries that are related to the content that is found within this portal section. Alternatively, more formal communities of searchers can be formed by setting up private I-SPY groups that are only made accessible to individuals by invitation.

4   Query Similarity Metrics

In the previous section we outlined the basic approach to collaborative search as it is implemented in I-SPY. Our interest lies in the role of query similarity in this technique because it is used during the selection of related queries and the weighting of their relevant results. So far we have assumed a most basic model of query similarity, namely the term overlap metric as shown in Equation 1. Detailed experiments using this metric have been described in [5] and have demonstrated its value when it comes to improving search precision and recall in community-based search scenarios. In this paper we compare this basic technique to a number of alternative models that are detailed below.

These alternatives fall into two basic categories. First, *term-based* techniques estimate query similarity by examining the differences between the terms used in two queries. The standard overlap metric used previously is an example of a term-based technique and below we consider an alternative in the *edit-distance* metric and a hybrid metric that combines overlap and edit-distance. Our second category measures query similarity in a less direct fashion than the term-based approaches. Instead of looking for similarities between the queries themselves, similarity is estimated by examining the results of searches or, more accurately in our case, the behaviour of searchers. Specifically, we consider two metrics that compare queries by the results that are selected by searchers; this selection information is stored by I-SPY in its hit-matrix data structure.

4.1   Term-Based Query Similarity

The most obvious way to measure the similarity between two queries is to look at their terms. The overlap metric does this in a very crude way by measuring the proportion of shared terms between queries. However the overlap metric is far from satisfactory. For example, it makes no attempt to consider term-order during similarity assessment so that "River Phoenix Pictures" is deemed to be perfectly similar to "Phoenix Pictures River" even though the former is likely to indicate an interest in pictures of the late actor and the latter is likely to indicate an interest in pictures of rivers in the the area of Phoenix, Arizona. In addition, the simple overlap metric view individual terms as atomic units and as such cannot cope with minor term variations such as plurals; for example, "Internet inventor" is deemed to be only 50% similar to "Internet inventors".

To address this set of problems we propose the use of the *Levenshtein Distance* (LD) (also known as edit-distance) metric. The LD of two strings is the minimum number of edit operations needed to transform one string into the other where an operation is either a term insertion, deletion or substitution. For example, the LD between "River Phoenix Pictures" and "Phoenix Pictures River" is 18. We propose the use of a normalised version of LD, as shown in Equation 4, which measures the similarity between a target query, q_T, and a related query, q_i, relative to a set of possibly related queries, $q_1, ..., q_n$ which share at least one term in common with q_T.

$$EditDistance(q_T, q_i) = \frac{1 - LD(q_T, q_i)}{maxLD(q_T, (q_1, ..., q_n))} \tag{4}$$

Of course it is possible to combine the similarities produced by these two term-based metrics. For instance, we could simply compute the average of the overlap and EditDistance metrics. However, we propose to combine them using the harmonic mean so as to give preference to those queries that enjoy high overlap values and high edit-distance values – see Equation 5 – and penalising those queries that suffer from differing overlap and edit-distance scores.

$$HarmonicMean(q_T, q_i) \tag{5}$$
$$= \frac{Overlap(q_T, q_i) \bullet EditDistance(q_T, q_i)}{(Overlap(q_T, q_i) + EditDistance(q_T, q_i)/2}$$

4.2   Behaviour-Based Query Similarity

The data that I-SPY collects on the search behaviour of its communities permits an alternative type of query similarity approach. Instead of comparing queries directly, we can explore indirect measures of similarity. For instance, we might consider two queries to be similar if users tend to select the same results from their respective result-lists. Using I-SPY, we collect and store this selection data and compare queries based on user selection behaviours.

Accordingly we propose two metrics. The first metric is another simple overlap metric: the similarity of two queries is estimated by the percentage overlap between the sets of pages that have been selected for these queries during past search sesssions. We call this the *Page Overlap* metric and it is presented as Equation 6 between a target query, q_T, and a related query, q_i. Note that, $SelectionSet(q)$ refers to the set of pages that have been previously selected for query q; that is the set of pages that have hit values in the hit-matrix for q.

$$PageOverlap(q_T, q_i) = \frac{|SelectionSet(q_T) \cap SelectionSet(q_i)|}{|SelectionSet(q_T) \cup SelectionSet(q_i)|} \tag{6}$$

Of course this page overlap metric has its problems. In particular, it gives no credit to the relative number of times that individual result pages have been

338   E. Balfe and B. Smyth

selected for two queries. Hence, we propose an alternative behaviour-based metric that uses the correlation between the number of times that overlapping pages have been selected for two queries as a measure of query similarity. We call this the *Page Correlation* metric as shown in Equation 7. In this formula *Correl* refers to the standard Pearon's correlation formula, the set $p_1, ..., p_n$ refers to the set of result pages that have been selected for both q_T and q_i and $H_{i,k}$ refers to the number of hits that p_k has received for q_i.

$$PageCorrelation(q_T, q_i) = Correl(\{H_{T,1}, ..., H_{T,n}\}, \{H_{i,1}, ..., H_{i,n}\}) \qquad (7)$$

5   Evaluation

At this point we have 5 different similarity metrics, 3 that are term-based and 2 that are behaviour-based, and while many of these are designed to improve upon the standard term-based overlap benchmark, it is not yet clear to what extent they will deliver performance improvements. In this section we will consider this question in detail and we will evaluate each of these metrics using live-user data.

5.1   Live-User Data

The data used in this evaluation was collected during a live-user experiment that involved 92 computer science students from the Department of Computer Science at University College Dublin and took place in October 2003. The original experiment was designed to evaluate the benefits of the standard I-SPY system, relative to a standard meta-search engine, in the context of a fact-finding or question-answering exercise. To frame the search task, we developed a set of 25 general knowledge AI and computer science questions, each requiring the student to find out a particular fact (time, place, person's name, system name etc.).

The students were randomly divided into two groups. Group 1 contained 45 students and Group 2 contained the remaining 47. Group 1 served as the *training group* for I-SPY, in the sense that their search histories were used to populate the I-SPY hit-matrix but no re-ranking occurred for their search results. This group also served as a control against which to judge the search behaviour of the second group of users, who served as the *test group*. In total the Group 1 users produced 1049 individual queries and selected a combined total of 1046 pages, while the Group 2 users used 1705 queries and selected 1624 pages.

5.2   Methodology

The data from this earlier live-user experiment provides the following key information to form the basis of our current evaluation: the queries submitted by each user; the pages that they selected from the subsequent result-lists; the position of these pages within the result-list; the pages where they located a correct answer to a particular question; and the hit-matrix produced by the Group 1 users. We also have a set of test problems (the Group 2 queries), and a set of correct solutions to these problems (the pages that are known to contain the correct answer to a particular question).

Accordingly, we can "re-run" the live-user experiment by responding to Group 2 queries with the new result-lists that are recommended by I-SPY using the five query similarity metrics. In addition we also consider the result-lists that are produced prior to promotion. These result-lists correspond to the results of a standard meta-search engine and help us to understand the relative impact of I-SPY's result promotion and re-ranking.

We test our different metrics for 3 different query selection thresholds, in each case limiting I-SPY to the selection the top Q related queries, where Q is set to 5, 10 or 20. Note that this does not actually mean that this number of related queries will always be retrieved for every search session, rather it indicates the maximum number of related queries that are retrieved. This will allow us to understand the relative performance of each metric for different levels of query similarity. If $Q = 5$ then I-SPY will focus on only the most related queries but will have access to more limited result selection information. On the other hand if $Q = 20$ then many more queries can be considered but some of these may not be related at all and so may not contribute useful results to the final result-list.

Thus, each Group 2 user query is replayed and the results (for the different Q thresholds) are computed and compared against a ground-truth of known correct results for each query. This ground-truth is the solution set (the pages that are known to contain the correct answer to a particular question). It is a strong measure of relevance in the sense that we only consider a page to be relevant for a query if it contains the correct answer to the test question that the query was designed to satisfy. Obviously weaker notions of relevance might have been considered. Nevertheless, we believe that is appropriate to focus on this stronger measure of relevance, given the search task used in our evaluation.

5.3   Overall Accuracy

Perhaps the most basic measure of search engine accuracy concerns its ability to return a single relevant result in its result-list; we call this the *minimal accuracy* and we will look at more refined measures that focus on the actual number of relevant results in due course. To measure the minimal accuracy for each technique (Overlap, Edit Dist, Harmean, PgOverlap, PgCorrel and Meta), we compare each of the full result-lists returned for the 1705 test queries, to the list of known correct results associated for these queries. We compute the percentage of result-lists that contain at least one correct result among the top 30 returned.

The results are presented in Figure 4(a) as a graph of overall accuracy against each Q threshold. Each plot corresponds to a single query similarity metric. The plot for Meta remains flat at 65%; it is unaffected by variations in the number of similar queries retrieved.

Looking at the similarity-based query reuse techniques we see a general picture of improved accuracy. For example, Overlap returns a correct result in at least 90% of the sessions across all values of Q. The Edit Dist and Harmean metrics perform slightly worse but achieve a minimal accuracy of 88%. Clearly these 3 term-based techniques are managing to identify similar queries and these sim-

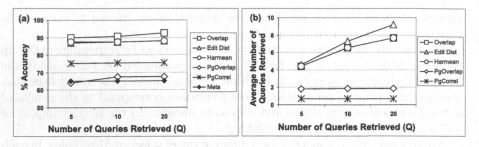

Fig. 4. (a) Minimal Accuracy (b) Average number of related queries

ilar queries are making useful result-list contributions above and beyond those made by the standard Meta search-engine.

The behaviour-based techniques do not perform quite so well. The PgCorrel metric achieves a minimal accuracy of approximately 75%, still a significant improvement on Meta, but the PgOverlap metric does little better than the Meta benchmark, except at the higher values of Q, and even then only marginally. This suggests that either the behaviour-based techniques are fundamentally less accurate measures of query similarity than the term-based methods or, alternatively, that the data they rely on is simply not rich enough to derive reliable similarity scores. To test this we also looked at the number of similar queries that were retrieved by each of the 5 metrics, averaged over the 1705 sessions, for each different Q threshold. The results (see Figure 4(b)) show that there is a big difference between the term-based methods and the behaviour-based methods. The former retrieve many more related queries than the latter, on average, and this suggests that the behaviour-based techniques suffer from a paucity of behavioural data on which to base their estimates. For instance, at $Q = 10$ the term-based metrics retrieve about 6-7 related queries on average, compared to less than 2 queries for the behaviour-based metrics.

5.4   Precision Versus Recall

The standard objective test of search engine accuracy is the precision and recall test: the former computes the percentage of returned results that are relevant while the latter computes the percentage of relevant results that are returned. We measure the percentage precision and recall values for each of the techniques under review for different result-list sizes (k=5 to 30).

The results are presented as precision vs. recall graphs, for each value of Q, in Figure 5(a, b & c). Each graph presents the plot of precision against recall for the 5 similarity metrics, along with Meta, for different sizes of result-lists, k. As expected we find that precision tends to fall-off with increasing result-list sizes; typically the number of relevant results is much less than k, and the majority of these relevant results should be positioned near the top of result-lists.

At Q=5, the performance of Edit Dist is significantly better than any of the other techniques and it is notable that the differences in performance are most pronounced for small result-list sizes. In 5(a) we see that Edit Distance precision

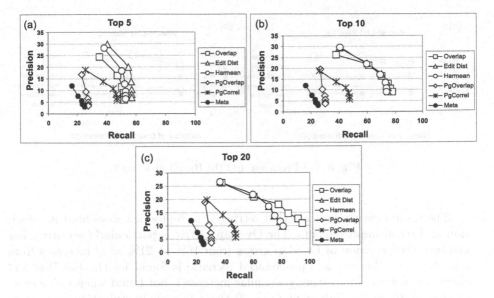

Fig. 5. Precision vs. Recall for (a) Q=5 (b) Q=10 (c) Q=20

varies between almost 30%(at k=5) to about 7% (at k=30). This is compared to precision values of between 24% and 6% for Overlap and values of between 12% and 3% for Meta. These results indicate that Edit Distance benefits from a precision improvement of between 25% and 16%, relative to Overlap and between 150% and 133%, relative to Meta. The recall results tell a similar story with a relative improvement in performance for Edit Distance to Overlap of between 17% and 9% and to Meta of between 156% and 128%.

As Q increases, the performance benefits of EditDist tends to diminish in comparison to the competing term-based methods and it is worth noting that when $Q = 20$ we see that the Overlap metric eventually outperforms the other contenders. For all values of Q we find that the term-based techniques continue to outperform the behaviour-based metrics highlighting the fact that these behaviour-based approaches lack the availability of sufficient data to inform reliable similarity estimations.

5.5   The Impact of Q

The above results indicate the term-based similarity metrics deliver far greater performance improvements for I-SPY than the behavioural approaches. However it is not immediately obvious how the setting of Q impacts on these improvements. If we set Q to be too low then we run the risk of missing related queries with relevant result selections. But if we set Q to be too high then too many unrelated queries may be retrieved and the final result-lists may become contaminated. For this reason, in Figure 6 we present separate graphs of precision and recall (at $k = 10$) for varying levels of Q.

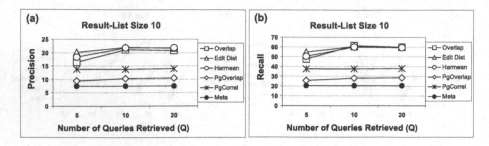

Fig. 6. (a) Precision and (b) Recall at $k = 10$

The results clearly indicate that setting Q to be too low does limit its precision and recall improvements. The Overlap metric is particularly sensitive. For instance the precision of Overlap grows from 16% to 21% as Q increases from 5 to 10. A similar but less pronounced increase is found for the EditDist and Harmean metrics. Interestingly a similar increase is not found when we increase Q beyond 10 to 20. Indeed at $Q = 20$ there is a slight reduction in average precision and recall for the term-based techniques. This suggests that relevant additional queries are being selected as Q is increased from 5 to 10 but that some irrelevant queries are being selected as Q increases to 20; although it must be said that these irrelevant queries are having a very limited impact on overall precision or recall. The behaviour-based techniques are far less sensitive to Q mainly because increasing Q beyond 5 has no real impact on the number of related queries retrieved because there simply aren't enough queries with behavioural overlaps.

6   Related Work

In recent times a number of researchers have begun to consider query reuse methods as a way to improve search-engine performance. For instance Cui et al [6] take advantage of the vast amount of information contained in Web logs as the basis for query expansion. Unlike the traditional query expansion technique, which extract terms from a subset of result documents, Cui et al. look for strong relationships between query terms and document terms based on past user actions (result selections) and use these relationships to aid in query expansion. Similarly, Wen et al. [7] mine query logs to aid query clustering rather than relying on term-overlap approaches alone; see also [8] for related work.

More traditional IR systems have also implemented forms of query similarity and reuse. Both [9] and [10] used query similarity metrics based on result-set overlaps. Raghavan et al. [9] proposed to either respond to new queries or to help formulate optimal queries. They highlight the importance of query-query similarity metrics and argue that existing query-document metrics are inappropriate in this context. Fitzpatrick et al. [10] used past queries as an additional source of evidence to improve automatic query expansion. They concluded that automatic past query feedback outperformed the more conventional automatic top document feedback and it delivered improved precision-recall performance. Interestingly in both cases result-overlap metrics were found to be better than term-overlap metrics as a measure of establishing query-query similarity. These result-overlap metrics are more in the spirit of our behaviour-based similarity metrics. In our experiments, our behaviour-based metrics performed poorly in comparison to the query-based techniques.

The common thread between our work in this paper and the work of others is that there are many different ways to estimate query similarity: term-based approaches compare queries according to their terms and term orderings; result-based methods compare queries by looking for similarities in the result-lists produced by a search engine when presented with these queries; behavioural methods look for similarities in the ways that users respond to these results. These different approaches highlight different types of query features. We have found term-based methods to work well, but behaviour-based methods have failed to deliver similar benefits, largely because of a lack of source data. As we have seen others have found result-based methods to work very well, especially when large result-lists can be used for comparison. It is likely that different approaches have different advantages in different settings and perhaps all of these different approaches will offer the best compromise in combination, a hypothesis that we leave as part of future work at this point.

7   Conclusions

The traditional term-based IR approach to document retrieval has held sway for much of the history of Web search. However, researchers have developed new approaches to Web search to solve problems with these term-based methods. Link analysis techniques and query reuse techniques are good examples. In our own work we have shown how a community-based approach to query reuse can result in significant performance improvements and in this paper we have extended our previous work into query reuse by developing and evaluating a number of alternative models of query similarity. In particular we have compared a set of term-based models to behaviour-based models to show that the former offer significant advantages, at least in our evaluation scenario. The behaviour-based methods were hampered by the lack of rich enough behavioural data, but this is likely to be repeated in other search scenarious too.

In summary the more sophisticated edit-distance distance metric appears to offer precision and recall advantages over the simpler overlap metric that we have been using in the past. This is especially true for small result-list sizes (<10 results) that are the norm when delivering search results to mobile devices.

References

1. Jansen, B.J., Spink, A., Bateman, J., Saracevic, T.: Real Life Information Retrieval: A Study of User Queries on the Web. SIGIR Forum **32** (1998) 5–17

2. Ozmutlu, S., Spink, A., Ozmutlu, H.C.: Multimedia web searching trends: 1997-2001. Inf. Process. Manage. **39** (2003) 611–621
3. Spink, A., Bateman, J., Jansen, B.: Searching Heterogeneous Collections of the Web: Behaviour of Excite Users. Information Research **4(2)** (1998)
4. Freyne, J., Smyth, B., Coyle, M., Balfe, E., Briggs, P.: Further Experiments on Collaborative Ranking in Community-Based Web Search. AI Review: An International Science and Engineering Journal **21(3-4)** (2004) 229–252
5. Balfe, E., Smyth, B.: Case Based Collaborative Web Search. In: Proceedings of the 7th European Conference on Cased Based Reasoning. (2004) 489–503
6. Cui, H., Wen, J.R., Nie, J.Y., Ma, W.Y.: Probabilistic Query Expansion Using Query Logs. In: Proceedings of the 11th International Conference on World Wide Web. (2002) 325–332
7. Wen, J.R., J.-Y., Zhang, H.J.: Query clustering using user logs. ACM Trans. Inf. Syst. **20** (2002) 59–81
8. Balfe, E., Smyth, B.: Improving Web Search Through Collaborative Query Recommendation. In: Proceedings of the 16th European Conference on Artificial Intelligence. (2004) 268–272
9. Raghavan, V.V., Sever, H.: On the reuse of past optimal queries. In: SIGIR'95, Proceedings of the 18th Annual International ACM SIGIR Conference on Research and Development in Information Retrieval), ACM Press (1995) 344–350
10. Fitzpatrick, L., Dent, M.: Automatic feedback using past queries: Social searching? In: SIGIR '97: Proceedings of the 20th Annual International ACM SIGIR Conference on Research and Development in Information Retrieval, July 27-31, 1997, Philadelphia, PA, USA, ACM (1997) 306–313

A Probabilistic Interpretation of Precision, Recall and *F*-Score, with Implication for Evaluation

Cyril Goutte and Eric Gaussier

Xerox Research Centre Europe,
6, chemin de Maupertuis,
F-38240 Meylan, France

Abstract. We address the problems of 1/ assessing the confidence of the standard point estimates, precision, recall and *F*-score, and 2/ comparing the results, in terms of precision, recall and *F*-score, obtained using two different methods. To do so, we use a probabilistic setting which allows us to obtain posterior distributions on these performance indicators, rather than point estimates. This framework is applied to the case where different methods are run on different datasets from the same source, as well as the standard situation where competing results are obtained on the same data.

1 Introduction

Empirical evaluation plays a central role in estimating the performance of natural language processing (NLP) or information retrieval (IR) systems. Performance is typically estimated on the basis of synthetic one-dimensional indicators such as the precision, recall or *F*-score. Even when multi-dimensional performance indicators are used, such as the recall-precision curve, synthetic indicators, such as the average precision at standard recall levels, are derived from it and used for comparison. One-dimensional performance measures, however, do not tell the full story, especially when they are estimated on the basis of little data, and are therefore intrinsically highly variable. This raises the following questions: Given a system and its results on a particular collection, how confident are we on the computed precision, recall and *F*-score? Do these measures tell us anything about the behavior of the system in general? The use of bootstrap [1, 2] allows one to partly answer these questions, by deriving approximate confidence intervals for the different point estimates. However, the summary statistics we consider here (precision, recall and *F*-score) do not always correspond to sample means or medians (as is the case for the summary statistics considered in [2]), and the bootstrap method may fail to give accurate confidence intervals. In this contribution, we adopt a different probabilistic point of view that allows us first to estimate the distribution of three indicators, precision, recall and *F*-score, and then to provide answers to the above questions.

D.E. Losada and J.M. Fernández-Luna (Eds.): ECIR 2005, LNCS 3408, pp. 345–359, 2005.

A related and crucial point is the comparison of experiments on the same dataset. Such a comparison is usually performed by resorting to paired statistical tests, as the paired t-test, the Wilcoxon test and the sign-test (see for example [3, 4]), or the bootstrap method or ANOVA. Some of these methods (e.g. the paired t and Wilcoxon tests) are not adapted to the three main indicators we retain, while others can be used (as the sign test or the bootstrap in some instances). The framework we rely on allows us to propose an additional tool for comparing two systems by providing an answer to the question: "What is the probability that sytem A outperforms (in terms of precision, recall and F-score) system B?"

In the following section, we introduce the probabilistic framework we retained, and show how we infer distributions for precision, recall and F-score, as well as how such distributions can be used to compare two different systems. We then proceed (section 3) to the case of paired comparison of experimental outcomes, which may be used when systems are tested on the same dataset. These models are tested in section 4 on the outcomes of text categorisation experiments. Finally, we discuss the implication and perspectives of this work and conclude.

2   Precision, Recall and F-Score

An arguably complete view of a system's performance is given by the precision-recall curve, which is commonly summarised in a single indicator using the average precision over various standard recall levels or number of documents. Other scores may be defined to reflect the performance, such as the break-even point, the scaled utility used at TREC[5], etc. Synthetic one-dimensional performance measures, however, do not allow to take into account the intrinsic variability in the scores, especially when calculated on little data. Note that this does not mean that evaluations performed on large collections are imune to this problem. At the 2002 TREC filtering track, for example, query 151 had only 22 relevant documents out of 723,141 test documents. This means that a variation in the assignment of one of the 22 relevant documents yields a variation of around 5% on recall. In the remainder of this paper, we focus on three standard performance indicators, namely precision, recall and F-score, and will first try to infer distributions that account for their intrisic variability.

For illustration purposes, we consider the following simple setting: each object is associated with a binary label ℓ which accounts for the correctness of the object with respect to the task at hand. In addition, the system produces an assignment z indicating whether it believes the object to be correct (or relevant) or not. The experimental outcome may be conveniently summarised in a confusion table:

		Assignment z	
		+	-
Label +	ℓ	TP	FN
	-	FP	TN

where $+$ and $-$ stand for relevant and non relevant, TP (resp. TN) stands for true positive (resp. negative) and FP (resp. FN) for false positive (resp. negative). From these counts, one can compute the precision (p) and recall (r):

$$p = \frac{TP}{TP + FP} \qquad r = \frac{TP}{TP + FN} \tag{1}$$

Taking the (weighted) harmonic average of precision and recall leads to the F-score ([6]):

$$F_\beta = (1 + \beta^2)\frac{p\,r}{r + \beta^2\,p} = \frac{(1 + \beta^2)TP}{(1 + \beta^2)TP + \beta^2 FN + FP} \tag{2}$$

Both precision and recall have a natural interpretation in terms of probability. Indeed, precision may be defined as the probability that an object is relevant given that it is returned by the system, while the recall is the probability that a relevant object is returned:

$$p = P(\ell = +|z = +) \qquad r = P(z = +|\ell = +) \tag{3}$$

This may seem like a trivial reformulation. However, there is a big semantic difference: in the original formulation, p and r are just formulas calculated from the observed data; in the probabilistic framework, the data $\mathcal{D} = (TP, FP, FN, TN)$ actually arises from p and r, which are parameters of a (primitive) generative model. Thus, the usual expressions (1) arise only as estimates of these unknown parameters.

2.1 Probabilistic Model

Each system divides a particular collection into four distinct sets, corresponding to the true and false positives and negatives. The actual counts TP, FP, FN and TN can thus be seen as the results of independently drawing elements from these four sets. This view justifies the following simple assumption:

Assumption 1. *Observed* TP, FP, FN *and* TN *counts follow a multinomial distribution with parameters* π_{TP}, π_{FP}, π_{FN}, π_{TN}:

$$P\left(\mathcal{D} = (TP,\ FP,\ FN,\ TN)\right) = \frac{n!}{TP!\ FP!\ FN!\ TN!}\pi_{TP}^{TP}\pi_{FP}^{FP}\pi_{FN}^{FN}\pi_{TN}^{TN} \tag{4}$$

This is denoted by $\mathcal{D}|\pi \sim \mathcal{M}(n; \pi)$, with the multinomial parameter $\pi \equiv (\pi_{TP}, \pi_{FP}, \pi_{FN}, \pi_{TN})$, and $\pi_{TP} + \pi_{FP} + \pi_{FN} + \pi_{TN} = 1$. Using the property that marginals and conditionals of a multinomial-distributed vector follow binomial distributions, it can be shown that (see Appendix A):

Property 1. *The distribution of* TP *given the number of returned objects* $M_+ = TP + FP$ *is a binomial with parameters* M_+ *and* p *(given by eq. 3).*

Property 2. *The distribution of* TP *given the number of relevant objects* $N_+ = TP + FN$ *is a binomial with parameters* N_+ *and* r.

From property 1, we can write the likelihood of p as:

$$L(p) = P(\mathcal{D}|p) \propto p^{TP}(1-p)^{FP} \qquad (5)$$

Inference on p can then be performed using Bayes' rule:

$$P(p|\mathcal{D}) \propto P(\mathcal{D}|p)P(p) \qquad (6)$$

where $P(p)$ is the prior distribution. A natural choice for the prior distribution of a binomial distribution is the conjugate Beta distribution ([7,8]). As there is no reason to favour high vs. low precision, we use a symmetric Beta prior:

$$p \sim Be(\lambda, \lambda) \quad : \qquad P(p) = \frac{\Gamma(2\lambda)}{\Gamma(\lambda)^2} p^{\lambda-1}(1-p)^{\lambda-1} \qquad (7)$$

where $\Gamma(\lambda) = \int_0^{+\infty} u^{\lambda-1} \exp(-u)\, du$ is the Gamma function. Combining equations 5, 6 and 7 we get:

$$P(p|\mathcal{D}) \propto p^{TP+\lambda-1}(1-p)^{FP+\lambda-1} \qquad (8)$$

that is, $p|\mathcal{D} \sim Be(TP+\lambda, FP+\lambda)$. The posterior distribution for the precision is therefore a Beta distribution that depends on TP, FP and the prior parameter λ. The expectation and mode for $P(p|\mathcal{D})$ are:

$$\overline{p} = \frac{TP+\lambda}{TP+FP+2\lambda}, \qquad mode(p) = \frac{TP+\lambda-1}{TP+FP+2\lambda-2} \qquad (9)$$

For $TP + FN < 2 - 2\lambda$ or $TP < 1 - \lambda$, the mode is either 0 or 1.

The Beta distribution offers a lot of flexibility on $[0;1]$, and subsumes two interesting cases: $\lambda = 1/2$, Jeffrey's non-informative prior, and $\lambda = 1$, the uniform prior. Jeffrey's non-informative prior has the nice theoretical property that it is invariant through re-parameterisation [8]. This means that the non-informative prior for an arbitrary transformation $p' = f(p)$ is the transformation of the non-informative prior for p using the usual change-of-variable rule (which is not the case for a uniform prior). For $\lambda = 1$, we get the maximum likelihood estimate $mode(p) = TP/(TP+FP)$. It turns out to be the usual formula for the precision (eq. 1). Note, however, that the expected value of p is a smoothed estimate $\overline{p} = (TP+1)/(TP+FP+2)$, aka Laplace smoothing. Obviously, using Property 2, a similar development yields the posterior distribution for the recall: $r|\mathcal{D} \sim Be(TP+\lambda, FN+\lambda)$, with the expectation and mode as in eq. 9 (replacing FP by FN).

Confidence intervals for p and r can easily be obtained from Beta tables, or through numerical approximations of (the integral of) the Beta distribution.[1] Estimating the probability that the precision/recall of a system is greater than the one of another system can be done through sampling strategies. We won't detail them here, as they are described for the F-score below.

---

[1] Standard mathematical packages usually provide such approximations.

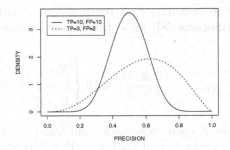

Fig. 1. Distribution of the precision for 2 systems with different outcomes (section 2.2). Although system 1 (solid) does worse on average, it is much less variable, and actually outperforms system 2 (dashed) in as much as 35% of cases

Two cases of particular practical interest are the situations where $TP + FP = 0$, that is, the system does not return anything, and $TP + FN = 0$, no objects are relevant in the test set. In such cases, the traditional expression (1) is not valid. On the other hand, with the probabilistic model, the posterior is equal to the prior and the expectation (9) gives an estimate of $\bar{p} = 1/2$. This seems intuitively reasonable as the fact that the system does not return any object does not mean it will never do so in the future. In addition, the evidence from our experiment does not allow to favour low or high precision, suggesting that 50% may be a reasonable guess for p.

2.2 Example

Let us consider an example where system 1 returns 10 true positives and 10 false positives, while system 2 returns 3 true positives and 2 false positives. Using only the traditional formula for precision (1), system 2 ($p = 3/5$) seems largely superior to system 1 ($p = 1/2$). The probabilistic view tells another story. Assuming Jeffrey's prior, system 2 seems better on average ($\bar{p} = 58\%$, mode = 63%) than system 1 (mode = $\bar{p} = 50\%$), but has a much larger variability, as shown in figure 1. As a consequence, the probability that system 2 outperforms system 1 with respect to precision is actually only around 65%, which implies that it is not significant at any reasonable level.

2.3 *F*-Score

In order to combine our results on precision and recall, we now consider the distribution of the F_1 score, given by eq. 2, with $\beta = 1$: $F_1 = \frac{2pr}{p+r}$. Given two variables with Gamma distributions $X \sim \Gamma(\alpha, h)$ and $Y \sim \Gamma(\beta, h)$, with identical shape parameter h, then three interesting properties hold:

(1) $\forall c > 0$, $c.X \sim \Gamma(\alpha, c.h)$; (2) $X + Y \sim \Gamma(\alpha + \beta, h)$; (3) $\frac{X}{X+Y} \sim Be(\alpha, \beta)$

Property 3 allows us to postulate that the posterior distributions of p and r, which are Beta distributions (8), arise from the combination of independent Gamma variates:

$$p = \frac{X}{X+Y}, \quad r = \frac{X}{X+Z} \quad \text{with} \begin{cases} X \sim \Gamma(TP+\lambda, h) \\ Y \sim \Gamma(FP+\lambda, h) \\ Z \sim \Gamma(FN+\lambda, h) \end{cases} \quad (10)$$

Combining these in the F-score expression, and using the fact that $U = 2X$ is a Gamma variate (Property 1) and that $V = Y + Z$ is also a Gamma variate (Property 2), we get:

$$F_1 = \frac{U}{U+V} \quad \text{with} \begin{cases} U \sim \Gamma(TP + \lambda, 2h) \text{ and} \\ V \sim \Gamma(FP + FN + 2\lambda, h). \end{cases} \quad (11)$$

In order to compare two systems with different experimental outcomes $D^{(1)} = \left(TP^{(1)}, FP^{(1)}, FN^{(1)}, TN^{(1)}\right)$ and $D^{(2)} = \left(TP^{(2)}, FP^{(2)}, FN^{(2)}, TN^{(2)}\right)$, we wish to evaluate the probability $P(F_1^{(1)} > F_1^{(2)})$, that is, since $F_1^{(1)}$ and $F_1^{(2)}$ are independent:

$$\int_0^1 \int_0^1 \mathrm{I}\left(F_1^{(1)} > F_1^{(2)}\right) P\left(F_1^{(1)}\right) P\left(F_1^{(2)}\right) \mathrm{d}F_1^{(1)} \mathrm{d}F_1^{(2)} \quad (12)$$

where $\mathrm{I}(\cdot)$ is the indicator function which has value 1 iff the enclosed condition is true, 0 otherwise. As the distributions of $F_1^{(1)}$ and $F_1^{(2)}$ are not known analytically, we cannot evaluate (12) exactly, but we can estimate whether $P(F_1^{(1)} > F_1^{(2)})$ is larger than any given significance level using Monte Carlo simulation. This is done by creating large samples from the distributions of $F_1^{(1)}$ and $F_1^{(2)}$, using Gamma variates as shown in equation 11. Let us write these samples $\left\{f_i^{(1)}\right\}_{i=1...L}$ and $\left\{f_i^{(2)}\right\}_{i=1...L}$. The probability $P(F_1^{(1)} > F_1^{(2)})$ is then estimated by the empirical proportion:

$$\widehat{P}(F_1^{(1)} > F_1^{(2)}) = \frac{1}{L} \sum_{i=1}^{L} \mathrm{I}\left(f_i^{(1)} > f_i^{(2)}\right) \quad (13)$$

Note that the reliability of the empirical proportion will depend on the sample size. We can use inference on the probability $P(F_1^{(1)} > F_1^{(2)})$, and obtain a Beta posterior from which we can assess the variability of our estimate. Lastly, the case $\beta \neq 1$ is similar, although the final expression for F_β is not as simple as (11), and involves three Gamma variates. Comparing two systems in terms of F_β is again done by Monte Carlo simulation, in a manner exactly equivalent to what we have described for F_1.

3   Paired Comparison

In the previous section, we have not made the specific assumption that the two competing systems were to be tested on the same dataset. Indeed, the inference that we presented is valid if two systems are tested on distinct datasets, as long as they are sampled from the same (unknown) distribution. When two systems are tested on the same collection, it may be interesting to consider the paired outcomes on each object. Typically, a small difference in performance may be highly consistent and therefore significant. This leads us to consider now the following situation: on a single collection of objects $\{d_j\}_{j=1...N}$, with relevance labels ℓ_j, we observe experimental outcomes for two systems: $\left\{z_j^{(1)}\right\}_{j=1...N}$ and $\left\{z_j^{(2)}\right\}_{j=1...N}$.

For each object, three cases have to be considered: 1. System 1 gives the correct assignment, system 2 fails; 2. System 2 gives the correct assignment, system 1 fails; 3. Both system yield the same assignment. Let us write π_1, π_2 and π_3 the probability that a given object falls in either of the three cases above. Given that the assignments are independent, both across systems and accross examples, and following the same reasoning as the one behind *assumption 1*, we assume that the experimental outcomes follow a multinomial distribution with parameters N and $\pi = (\pi_1, \pi_2, \pi_3)$. For a sequence of assignments $Z = \left\{z_j^{(1)}, z_j^{(2)}\right\}$, the likelihood of π is:

$$P(Z|\pi) \propto \pi_1^{N_1} \pi_2^{N_2} \pi_3^{N_3} \tag{14}$$

with N_1 (resp. N_2) the number of examples for which system 1 (resp. 2) outperforms system 2 (resp. 1), and $N_3 = N - N_1 - N_2$. The conjugate prior for π is the Dirichlet distribution, a multidimensional generalisation of the Beta distribution, $\pi|\alpha \sim D(\alpha_1, \alpha_2, \alpha_3)$:

$$P(\pi|\alpha) = \frac{\Gamma(\alpha_1 + \alpha_2 + \alpha_3)}{\Gamma(\alpha_1)\Gamma(\alpha_2)\Gamma(\alpha_3)} \pi^{\alpha_1-1} \pi_2^{\alpha_2-1} \pi_3^{\alpha_3-1} \tag{15}$$

with $\alpha = (\alpha_1, \alpha_2, \alpha_3)$ the vector of hyper-parameters. Again, the uniform prior is obtained for $\alpha = 1$ and the non-informative prior for $\alpha = 1/2$.[2] From equations 15 and 14, applying Bayes rule we obtain the posterior $P(\pi|Z, \alpha) \propto P(Z|\pi)P(\pi|\alpha)$:

$$P(\pi|Z, \alpha) = \frac{\Gamma(N + \sum_k \alpha_k)}{\prod_k \Gamma(N_k + \alpha_k)} \prod_k \pi_k^{N_k + \alpha_k - 1} \tag{16}$$

which is a Dirichlet $D(N_1 + \alpha_1, N_2 + \alpha_2, N_3 + \alpha_3)$.

---

[2] Although other choices are possible, it seems that if no prior information is available about which system is best, it is reasonable to impose $\alpha_1 = \alpha_2$. The choice of α_3 may be different, if the two competing systems are expected to agree more often than they disagree.

The probability that system 1 is superior to system 2 is

$$P(\pi_1 > \pi_2) = \mathrm{E}_{\pi|Z,\alpha} \left(\mathrm{I} \left(\pi_1 > \pi_2 \right) \right) \tag{17}$$

$$= \int_0^1 \left(\int_0^{min(\pi_1, 1-\pi_1)} P(\pi_1, \pi_2, 1 - \pi_1 - \pi_2 | Z, \alpha) d\pi_2 \right) d\pi_1 \tag{18}$$

which implies integrating over the incomplete Beta function. This can not be carried out analytically, but may be estimated by sampling from the Dirichlet distribution. Given a large sample $\left\{ \pi^j \right\}_{j=1...L}$ from the posterior (16), equation 17 is estimated by:

$$\widehat{P}(M1 > M2) = \frac{\# \left\{ j | \pi_1^j > \pi_2^j \right\}}{L} \tag{19}$$

Other ways of comparing both systems include considering the difference $\Delta = \pi_1 - \pi_2$ and the (log) odds ratio $\rho = \ln(\pi_1/\pi_2)$. Their expectations under the posterior are easily obtained:

$$\mathrm{E}_{\pi|Z,\alpha} \left(\Delta \right) = \frac{N_1 + \alpha_1 - N_2 - \alpha_2}{N + \alpha_1 + \alpha_2 + \alpha_3} \tag{20}$$

$$\mathrm{E}_{\pi|Z,\alpha} \left(\rho \right) = \Psi \left(N_1 + \alpha_1 \right) - \Psi \left(N_2 + \alpha_2 \right) \tag{21}$$

with $\Psi(x) = \Gamma'(x)/\Gamma(x)$ the Psi or Digamma function. In addition, the probability that either the difference or the log odds ratio is positive is $P(\Delta > 0) = P(\rho > 0) = P(\pi_1 > \pi_2)$.

Note: This illustrates the way this framework updates the existing information using new experimental results. Consider two collections $\mathcal{D}^1 = \left\{ d_j^1 \right\}_{1...N^1}$ and $\mathcal{D}^2 = \left\{ d_j^2 \right\}_{1..N^2}$. Before any observation, the prior for π is $D(\alpha)$. After testing on the first dataset, we obtain the posterior:

$$\pi|\mathcal{D}^1, \alpha \sim D \left(N_1^1 + \alpha_1, N_2^1 + \alpha_2, N_3^1 + \alpha_3 \right)$$

This may be used as a prior for the second collection, to reflect the information gained from the first collection. After observing all the data, the posterior becomes:

$$\pi|\mathcal{D}^2, \mathcal{D}^1, \alpha \sim D \left(N_1^2 + N_1^1 + \alpha_1, N_2^2 + N_2^1 + \alpha_2, N_3^2 + N_3^1 + \alpha_3 \right)$$

The final result is therefore equivalent to working with a single dataset containing the union of D^1 and D^2, or to evaluating first on D^2, then on D^1. This property illustrates the convenient way in which this framework updates our knowledge based on additional incoming data.

4   Experimental Results

In order to illustrate the use of the above probabilistic framework in comparing experimental outcomes of different systems, we use the text categorisation

Table 1. F-score comparison for 1/ 'ltc' versus 'nnn' weighting scheme (left), 2/ linear versus polynomial kernel on 'nnn' weighting (centre), and 3/ linear versus polynomial kernel on 'ltc' weighting (right)

Category	F_1 score ltc	nnn	Prob ltc>nnn	+/-	F_1 score (nnn) lin	poly	Prob lin>poly	+/-	F_1 score (ltc) lin	poly	Prob lin>poly	+/-
earn	98.66	98.07	93.71	0.24	98.07	96.36	99.96	0.02	98.66	98.80	34.68	0.48
acq	94.70	93.88	82.09	0.38	93.88	79.31	100.00	0.00	94.70	94.73	49.39	0.50
money-fx	76.40	75.12	63.31	0.48	75.12	64.40	99.64	0.06	76.40	73.90	75.45	0.43
crude	86.96	86.15	61.53	0.49	86.15	71.12	100.00	0.00	86.96	86.26	60.33	0.49
grain	89.61	88.22	69.55	0.46	88.22	73.99	99.99	0.01	89.61	86.57	85.66	0.35
trade	75.86	77.47	34.07	0.47	77.47	75.11	71.77	0.45	75.86	77.13	38.76	0.49
interest	73.98	77.93	17.03	0.38	77.93	68.24	98.83	0.11	73.98	72.27	64.72	0.48
wheat	79.10	80.79	36.81	0.48	80.79	77.27	75.14	0.43	79.10	80.92	36.45	0.48
ship	75.50	80.25	17.99	0.38	80.25	66.22	99.44	0.07	75.50	73.47	63.78	0.48
corn	83.17	83.64	46.73	0.50	83.64	65.35	99.76	0.05	83.17	82.00	58.15	0.49
dlr	78.05	74.23	69.34	0.46	74.23	25.17	100.00	0.00	78.05	72.97	74.18	0.44
oilseed	61.90	62.37	48.58	0.50	62.37	42.35	98.77	0.11	61.90	58.23	65.28	0.48
money-sup	70.77	67.57	64.53	0.48	67.57	70.13	38.19	0.49	70.77	74.19	36.06	0.48
Micro-avg	90.56	89.86	89.12	0.31	89.86	79.44	100.00	0.00	90.56	90.28	67.69	0.47

task defined on the Reuters21578 corpus with the ModApte split. We are here interested in evaluating the influence of two main factors: the term weighting scheme and the document similarity. To this end, we consider two term weighting schemes:

nnn (no weighting): term weight is the raw frequency of the term in the document, no inverse document frequency is used and no length normalisation is applied;

ltc (log-tf-idf-cosine): the term weight is obtained by taking the log of the frequency of the term in the document, multiplied by the inverse document frequency, and using cosine normalisation (which is equivalent to dividing by the euclidean norm of the unnormalised values).

For 13 categories with the largest numbers of relevant documents, we train a Support Vector Machine (SVM) categoriser ([9]) on the 9603 training document from the ModApte split, and test the models on the 3299 test documents. In SVM categorisers, the document similarity is used as the kernel. Here, we compare the linear and quadratic kernels. We wish to test whether 'ltc' is better than 'nnn' weighting, and whether the quadratic kernel *significantly* outperforms the linear kernel. Most published results on this collection show a small but consistent improvement with higher degree kernels.

We first compared the results we obtained by comparing the $F1$-score distributions, as is outlined in section 2 (using $\lambda = \frac{1}{2}$, Jeffrey's prior, and $h = 1$). This comparison is given in table 1. As one can note, with the linear kernel, the 'ltc' weighting scheme seems marginally better than 'nnn'. The most significant difference is observed on the largest category, 'earn', where the probability that 'ltc' is better almost reaches 94%. Note that despite the fact that the overall number of documents is the same for all categories, a half percent difference on 'earn' is more significant than a 5% difference on 'ship'. This is due to the fact that, as explained above, the variability is actually linked to the number of *relevant* and *returned* documents, rather than the overall number of documents in the collection.

The centre columns in table 1 show that the 'nnn' weighting scheme has devastating effects on the quadratic kernel. The micro-averaged F-score is about 10 points lower, and all but three categories are significantly worse (at the 98% level) using the quadratic kernel. This is because when no IDF is used, the similarity between documents is dominated by the frequent terms, which are typically believed to be less meaningful. This effect is much worse for the quadratic kernel, where the implicit feature space works with *products* of frequencies. Finally, the right columns of table 1 investigate the effect of the kernel, when using the 'ltc' weighting. In that case, both kernels yield similar results, which are not significant at any reasonable level. Thanks to IDF and normalisation, we do not observe the dramatic difference in performance that was apparent with 'nnn' weighting.

The results in table 1 do not take into account the fact that all models are run on the same data. Using the paired test detailed in section 3, we get more sensitive results (table 2; we have used here $\alpha_1 = \alpha_2 = \frac{1}{2}$, the value for α_3 being of no importance for our goal). The 'ltc' weighting seems significantly better than 'nnn' on the three biggest categories, and the performance improvement seems weakly significant on two additional categories: 'dlr' and 'money-sup'. Small but consistent differences (8 to 3 in favour of 'ltc' in 'money-sup') may actually yield better scores than large, but less consistent, disagreements (for example, 21 to 15 in 'crude'). The middle rows of table 2 confirm that, with 'nnn' weighting, the linear kernel is better than the quadratic kernel. 'trade', 'wheat' and 'money-sup' do not show a significant difference and, surprisingly, category 'money-fx' shows a weakly significant difference, whereas the F-score test (table 1) gave a highly significant difference (we will discuss this below). The rightmost rows in table 2 show that, with 'ltc' weighting, the polynomial kernel is significantly better than the linear kernel for three categories ('trade', 'wheat' and 'money-sup') and significantly worse for 'grain'. The polynomial kernel therefore significantly outperforms the linear kernel more often than the reverse, although the micro-averaged F-score given in table 1 is slightly in favour of the linear kernel.

5   Discussion

There has been a sizeable amount of work in the Information Retrieval community targetted towards proposing new performance measures for comparing the outcomes of IR experiments(two such recent atempts can be found in ([10, 11]). Here, we take a different standpoint. We focus on widely used measures (precision, recall, and F-score), and infer distributions for them that allow us to evaluate the variability of each measure, and assess the significance of an ob-

Table 2. Paired comparison of 1/ 'ltc' and 'nnn' weighting schemes (left), 2/ linear ('lin') and quadratic ('p2') kernel, on 'nnn' weighting, and 3/ linear and quadratic kernel on 'ltc' weighting

| Category | linear kernel | | Prob | | 'nnn' weighting | Prob | | | 'ltc' weighting | Prob | |
	ltc>	nnn>	ltc>nnn	+/-	lin>	p2>	lin>p2	+/-	lin>	p2>	lin>p2	+/-
earn	17	4	99.77	0.05	48	12	100.00	0.00	1	4	9.76	0.30
acq	43	28	96.41	0.19	282	14	100.00	0.00	6	7	39.68	0.49
money-fx	39	23	97.90	0.14	58	43	93.76	0.24	11	6	88.70	0.32
crude	21	15	84.32	0.36	62	21	100.00	0.00	4	2	78.66	0.41
grain	17	11	87.32	0.33	46	10	100.00	0.00	9	2	98.48	0.12
trade	23	22	55.75	0.50	28	28	49.19	0.50	2	7	4.36	0.20
interest	24	24	49.73	0.50	38	21	98.61	0.12	5	3	76.29	0.43
wheat	10	9	59.56	0.49	14	13	57.87	0.49	0	3	3.39	0.18
ship	6	11	11.38	0.32	22	4	99.97	0.02	3	1	83.71	0.37
corn	6	5	61.45	0.49	19	2	99.99	0.01	1	0	82.31	0.38
dlr	13	6	94.62	0.23	191	2	100.00	0.00	5	3	75.81	0.43
oilseed	12	9	74.31	0.44	24	10	99.23	0.09	3	2	66.66	0.47
money-sup	8	3	93.43	0.25	10	11	41.22	0.49	0	3	3.49	0.18

served difference. Although this framework may not be applicable to arbitrary performance measures, we believe that it can also apply to other ones, such as the TREC utility. In addition, using Monte-Carlo simulation, it is possible to sample from simple distributions, and combine the samples in non-trivial ways (cf the F-score comparison in section 2). The only alternative we are aware of to compute both confidence intervals for the three measures we retained and assess the significance of an observed difference is the bootstrap method. However, as we already mentioned, this method may fail for the statistics we retained. Note, nevertheless, that the bootstrap method is very general and may be used for other statistics than the ones considered here. It might also be the case that, based on the framework we developed, a parametric form of the bootstrap can be used for precision, recall and F-score. This is something we plan to investigate.

In the case where two systems are compared on the same collection, approaches to performance comparison typically rely on standard statistical tests such as the paired t-test, the Wilcoxon test or the sign test [4], or variants of them [12, 13]. Neither the t-test nor the Wilcoxon test directly apply to binary (relevant/not relevant) judgements (which are at the basis of the computation of precision, recall and F-score).[3] Both the sign test and, again, the bootstrap method seem to be applicable to binary judgements (the same objections as above hold for the bootstrap method). Our contribution in this framework is to have put at the disposal of experimenters an additional tool for system evaluation. A direct comparison with the aforementioned methods still has to be conducted.

---

[3] One possibility to use them would be to partition the test data into subsets, compute say precision on each subset and compare the distributions obtained with different systems. However, this may lead to poor estimates on each subset, hence to poor comparison (furthermore, the intrinsic variability of each estimate is not taken into account).

Experimental results provided in section 4 illustrate some differences between the two tests we propose. The F-score test assesses differences in F-score, and may be applied to results obtained on different collections (for example random splits from a large collection). On the other hand, the paired test must be applied to results obtained on the same dataset, and seems more sensitive to small, but consistent differences. In one instance ('money-fx', linear vs. quadratic on 'nnn', table 2), the F-score test was significant, while the paired test was not. This is because although a difference in F-score necessary implies a difference in disagreement counts (58 to 43 in that case), this disagreement may not be consistent, and therefore yield a larger variabliliy. In that case, an 8 to 3 difference would give the same F-score difference, and be significant for the paired test.

6   Conclusion

We have presented in this paper a new view on standard Information Retrieval measures, namely precision, recall, and F-score. This view, grounded on a probabilistic framework, allows one to take into account the intrinsic variability of performance estimation, and provides, we believe, more insights on system performance than traditional measures. In particular, it helps us answer questions like: "Given a system and its results on a particular collection, how confident are we on the computed precision, recall and F-score?", or "Can we compare (in terms of precision, recall and F-score) two systems evaluated on two different datasets from the same source?" and lastly "What is the probability that system A outperforms (in terms of precision, recall and F-score) system B when compared on the same dataset?".

To develop this view, we have first shown how precision and recall naturally lead to probabilistic interpretation, and how one can derive probabilistic distributions of them. We have then shown how the F-scores could be rewritten in terms of Gamma variates, and how to compare F-scores obtained by two systems based on Monte-Carlo simulation. In addition, we have presented an extension to paired comparison, which allows one to perform a deeper comparison between two systems run on the same data. Lastly, we have illustrated the new approach to performance evaluation we propose on a standard text categorisation task, with binary judgements (in class/not in class) for which several classic statistical tests are not well suited, and discussed the relations of our approach to existing ones.

References

1. Efron, B.E.: The Jacknife, the Bootstrap and Other Resampling plans. Volume 38 of CBMS-NSF Regional Conference Series in Applied Mathematics. SIAM (1982)
2. Savoy, J.: Statistical inference in retrieval effectiveness evaluation. Information Processing & Management **33** (1997) 495–512
3. Tague-Sutcliffe, J., Blustein, J.: A statistical analysis of the TREC-3 data. In Harman, D., ed.: Proceedings of the third Text Retrieval Conference (TREC). (1994) 385–398

4. Hull, D.: Using statistical testing in the evaluation of retrieval experiments. In: Proceedings of SIGIR'93, ACM, Pittsburg, PA (1993) 329–338
5. Robertson, S., Soboroff, I.: The TREC 2002 filtering track report. In: Proc. Text Retrieval Conference. (2002) 208–217
6. van Rijsbergen, C.J.: Information Retrieval. 2nd edition edn. Butterworth (1979)
7. Box, G.E.P., Tiao, G.C.: Bayesian Inference in Statistical Analysis. Wiley (1973)
8. Robert, C.: L'Analyse Statistique Bayesienne. Economica (1992)
9. Joachims, T.: Making large-scale svm learning practical. In Schölkopf, B., Burges, C., Smola, A., eds.: Advances in Kernel Methods — Support Vector Learning, MIT Press (1999)
10. Mizzaro, S.: A new measure of retrieval effectiveness (or: What's wrong with precision and recall). In: In T. Ojala editor, International Workshop on Information Retrieval (IR'2001). (2001)
11. Järvelin, K., Kekäläinen, J.: Cumulated gain-based evaluation of ir techniques. ACM Transactions on Information Systems **20** (2002)
12. Yeh, A.: More accurate tests for the statistical significance of result differences. In: Proceedings of COLING'00, Saarbrücken, Germany (2000)
13. Evert, S.: Significance tests for the evaluation of ranking methods. In: Proceedings of COLING'04, Geneva, Switzerland (2004)

A   Proof of Property 1 and 2

The available data is uniquely characterised by the true/false positive/negative counts TP, FP, TN, FN. Let us note $\mathcal{D} \equiv (TP, FP, FN, TN)$. Our basic modelling assumption is that for samples of fixed size n, these four counts follow a multinomial distribution. This assumption seems reasonable and arises for example if the collection is an independant identically distributed (i.i.d.) sample from the document population. If we denote by n_1, n_2, n_3 and n_4 (with $n_1 + n_2 + n_3 + n_4 = n$) the actual counts observed for variables TP, FP, FN and TN, then:

$$P\left(\mathcal{D} = (n_1, n_2, n_3, n_4)\right) = \frac{n!}{n_1!\, n_2!\, n_3!\, n_4!} \pi_1^{n_1} \pi_2^{n_2} \pi_3^{n_3} \pi_4^{n_4} \qquad (22)$$

With $\pi_1 + \pi_2 + \pi_3 + \pi_4 = 1$ and $\pi \equiv (\pi_1, \pi_2, \pi_3, \pi_4)$ is the parameter of the multinomial distribution: $\mathcal{D} \sim \mathcal{M}(n; \pi)$. We will use the following two properties of multinomial distributions:

Property 3 (Marginals). *Each component i of $\mathcal{D}$ follows a binomial distribution $\mathcal{B}(n; \pi_i)$, with parameters n and identical probability π_i.*

Property 4 (Conditionals). *Each component i of $\mathcal{D}$ conditionned on another component j follows a binomial distribution $\mathcal{B}\left(n - n_j; \frac{\pi_i}{1-\pi_j}\right)$, with parameters $n - n_j$ and probability $\frac{\pi_i}{1-\pi_j}$.*

It follows from these properties that:

$$(TP + FP) \sim \mathcal{B}(n; \pi_1 + \pi_2) \qquad \text{and} \qquad (TP + FN) \sim \mathcal{B}(n; \pi_1 + \pi_3) \qquad (23)$$

Proof. From the above properties, $TP \sim \mathcal{B}(n; \pi_1)$ and $FP|TP \sim \mathcal{B}\left(n - TP; \frac{\pi_2}{1-\pi_1}\right)$, hence:

$$P(TP + FP = k) = \sum_{x=0}^{k} P(TP = x)P(FP = k - x|TP = x)$$

$$= \sum_{x=0}^{k} \binom{n}{x} \pi_1^x (1 - \pi_1)^{n-x} \binom{n-x}{k-x} \left(\frac{\pi_2}{1 - \pi_1}\right)^{k-x}$$

$$\left(1 - \frac{\pi_2}{1 - \pi_1}\right)^{n-k}$$

$$= \binom{n}{k} (1 - (\pi_1 + \pi_2))^{n-k} \sum_{x=0}^{k} \binom{k}{x} \pi_1^x \pi_2^{k-x} \quad (24)$$

and as $\sum_{x=0}^{k} \binom{k}{x} \pi_1^x \pi_2^{k-x} = (\pi_1 + \pi_2)^k$ (the binomial theorem), the distribution of $TP + FP$ is indeed binomial with parameters n and $\pi_1 + \pi_2$ (and similarly for $TP + FN$). □

Using eq. 23 and the fact that $TP \sim \mathcal{B}(n; \pi_1)$, we obtain the conditional distribution of TP given $TP + FP$:

$$TP|(TP + FP) \sim \mathcal{B}\left(M_+; \frac{\pi_1}{\pi_1 + \pi_2}\right) \quad (25)$$

with $M_+ = TP + FP$.

Proof. The conditional probability of TP given $TP + FP$ is obtained as:

$$P(TP{=}k|TP + FP{=}M_+) = \frac{P(TP{=}k)P(FP{=}M_+{-}k|TP{=}k)}{P(TP + FP{=}M_+)}$$

As all probabilities involved are known binomials, we get:

$$P(TP = k|TP + FP = M_+) =$$

$$\frac{\binom{n}{k}\pi_1^k(1 - \pi_1)^{n-k} \cdot \binom{n-k}{M_+-k}\left(\frac{\pi_2}{\pi_1+\pi_2}\right)^{M_+-k}\left(1 - \frac{\pi_2}{\pi_1+\pi_2}\right)^{n-M_+}}{\binom{n}{M_+}(\pi_1 + \pi_2)^{M_+}(1 - \pi_1 - \pi_2)^{n-M_+}} \quad (26)$$

Using the fact that $\frac{\binom{n}{k}\binom{n-k}{M_+-k}}{\binom{n}{M_+}} = \binom{M_+}{k}$ and after some simple algebra, this simplifies to:

$$P(TP = k|TP + FP = M_+) = \binom{M_+}{k}\left(\frac{\pi_1}{\pi_1 + \pi_2}\right)^k \left(\frac{\pi_2}{\pi_1 + \pi_2}\right)^{M_+-k} \quad (27)$$

in other words, eq. 25. □

Now remember the definition of the precision:

$$p = P(z = +|l = +) = \frac{P(z = +, l = +)}{P(l = +)} \tag{28}$$

Notice that $P(z = +, l = +)$ is by definition π_1, the probability to get a "true positive", and $P(l = +)$ is $\pi_1 + \pi_2$, the probability to get a positive return (either false or true positive). This shows that $p = \pi_1/(\pi_1 + \pi_2)$, and that the distribution of TP given $TP + FP$ (eq. 25) is a binomial $\mathcal{B}(M_+, p)$. The justification for $TP|(TP + FN)$ goes the same way.

Exploring Cost-Effective Approaches to Human Evaluation of Search Engine Relevance

Kamal Ali, Chi-Chao Chang, and Yunfang Juan

Yahoo Search, 701 First Avenue, Sunnyvale, CA 94089, USA
{kamal, chichao, yunfang}@yahoo-inc.com

Abstract. In this paper, we examine novel and less expensive methods for search engine evaluation that do not rely on document relevance judgments. These methods, described within a proposed framework, are motivated by the increasing focus on search results presentation, by the growing diversity of documents and content sources, and by the need to measure effectiveness relative to other search engines. Correlation analysis of the data obtained from actual tests using a subset of the methods in the framework suggest that these methods measure different aspects of the search engine. In practice, we argue that the selection of the test method is a tradeoff between measurement intent and cost.

1 Introduction

In classical IR, the most common measures of the retrieval engine engine are based on human judgments of document relevance – is the document relevant to the query? The predominant methodology – the Cranfield [1] technique – compares IR systems over a set of topics, a set of documents for each topic, and a set of relevance judgments for each document. Researchers and business intelligence groups have adapted the Cranfield method to evaluate search engines (for example, topics become queries) with some success.

The task of a search engine is to accept a query and return a ranked list of references to documents that are relevant for that query to the user issuing the query. For an overall evaluation, one needs a representative sample of queries, which usually yields a representative sample of users across a representative set of documents. In addition, human judgments are idiosyncratic and vary depending on the judges. These are fundamental factors that were already present in classical IR evaluation studies and have been addressed extensively in the literature [4].

The main difficulty with the Cranfield-like approach is the cost of obtaining reliable and complete judgments. The average TREC collection contains about 800,000 documents spanning across 50 topics. Voorhes [4] estimates that nine person months are required to fully cover these documents. Pooling techniques—judging a subset of the documents rather than the entire set [5, 6]—and recent efforts in formulating robust metrics in the presence of incomplete judgments [5] and in term-based evaluation [2] are reasonable attempts to mitigate the cost factor.

D.E. Losada and J.M. Fernández-Luna (Eds.): ECIR 2005, LNCS 3408, pp. 360–374, 2005.

Besides the cost of collecting document relevance judgments, we are motivated by the following factors:

- **Advent of Domain-Specific Search Engines**. Domain-specific engines such as shopping, news and particularly image search pose specific evaluation challenges.
- **Improved Document Summarization**. Search engines typically return document abstracts that do a fairly good job of summarizing the underlying document. This opens the possibility of judging these summaries in lieu of judging the full document. We explore the relationship between document (landing-page) relevance and abstract relevance.
- **Diversity of Query Intent and Content.** The information needs of search engine users range from navigational, that is, users rely on search engines as a trampoline to specific documents and sites, to single-answer queries (simple question-answer sessions) such as "What is the capital of Afghanistan?" to research, that is, users searching for a set of documents for browsing. For many of these "types" of queries, it is unclear if the thorough perusal of the documents retrieved is preferred to simply looking for the right document or answer in the set of results. And more often than not, this can be accomplished by simply evaluating titles, abstracts, and URLs displayed.
- **Business Intelligence and Competitive Metrics.** Search engine evaluation serves two purposes: to improve the quality and relevance of the results as well as to gather data and metrics to understand the competitive landscape. Relative judgments, directly comparing two sets of results, can be more a more cost-effective approach than judging two sets of results separately.
- **Search Engine User Interface Features.** Engines such as Yahoo! and Google offer a multitude of features along with the search results, such as advertisements, spelling and related search suggestions, and opportunities for personalization and customization. We believe that the overall quality of the search experience is not the sum of its parts—a more holistic approach is needed.

In this paper, we detail our experiences with novel testing methodologies arranged along three axes of a methodology framework:

1. Judging the document summary (i.e. title, abstracts) versus the actual document. Perceived relevance versus 'actual' (landing-page) relevance.
2. Judging sets of results rather than each result individually. (We wil use the terms 'item' and 'result' interchangeably.)
3. Judging relative relevance (between two search engines) rather than absolute relevance.

We experimented with these methodologies in a practical setting, evaluating several domain-specific search engines, namely image search, news search, ads search, as well as web search. The results show that there is no "silver-bullet" methodology —correlation measures between two different evaluation methodologies for a given domain are not high— which means that each methodology is sensitive to certain aspects of relevance that others are oblivious to.

2 Related Work

In [10], Mizzaro et al. proposed a framework with three key dimensions of relevance evaluation: information needs (and their levels of expressiveness), information resources (which includes documents as well as their surrogates such as titles and abstracts), and information context (which is the context surrounding the search activity). Their framework illustrates that judgments within a cell in this 3-D space are not necessarily applicable to other cells, which is consistent with our results. Mizzaro's framework does not cover the dimension pertaining to absolute and relative judgments nor does it cover the effects of set-level versus item-level judgments.

Amento *et al.* [13] correlated editorial document relevance judgments from expert judges with automated evaluation metrics such as the in-degree, PageRank [15], page size, etc, of linked web documents. The results show that these metrics are good predictors of human relevance, although no particular metric stood out. Amento *et al.* reported that variations in human judgments are typically understated. Harter [14] had earlier warned that researchers take relevance judgments variations for granted and that judgments should be collected based on the specific needs and goals of an evaluation, which limited the ability to re-use judgments. Mizzaro [10] pointed out that high rate of disagreement can be attributed to poor testing set-up or to the inherent difficult in relevance evaluation. In our setting, we ensure that all tests are subject to QA and audit process. Nevertheless, disagreement between judges (regardless of the methodology) is measurable in our systems but is outside the scope of this paper [11].

3 Judgment Elicitation Methods

There appear to be at least broad classes of judgments:

1. **Implicit/Behavioral:** measurement of click-rates, dwell-times, patterns of clicking and returning to earlier results, etc.
2. **Explicit:** Ask a judge which engine is better. Such judgments are more expensive than click-rates but don't suffer the ambiguity of click-rates: higher click-rates don't necessarily mean the results were more relevant.

Furthermore, there are at least three sources of judgments:

1. **Live users:** Users who happen to come to the search engine. Survey data may be collected from such judges.
2. **Volunteer Panelists:** These are ideally random Internet users who have agreed to participate in tests where they may be given queries and asked to compare search engines. They are usually monitored by client-side software and given some monetary reward for their participation.
3. **Editors or domain experts:** These judges have extensive knowledge of web, offline and proprietary (e.g. Deep Web) resources in a particular domain. For our experiments we use domain-expert editors conforming to well-defined judgment guidelines. Internal work we have done has shown their judgments to be reliable with respect to click behavior of average Internet users [11].

Now we consider the advantages and disadvantages of each test type and judgments source. In an ideal scenario, we would like to elicit articulate, patient direct judgments from a perfectly random sample of live users such that that elicitation would not affect their subsequent use of the search engine. This ideal is unattainable for the reasons listed below. Since both implicit and explicit methods have disadvantages and since both measure different aspects of relevance, we need to use both methods.

- Elicitation of direct judgment involves asking the user; this may affect their subsequent searches. To avoid disturbing users, we can consider indirect measures of relevance such as click-through rates.
- The set of users that agree to give their judgments in an online survey is probably not random – it could easily be that busier people are unlikely to say yes to a survey. To avoid such a non-random sample we can again use indirect measures of relevance such as click-rates.
- Users are not perfectly articulate: their behavior may differ from their explanation of it. For this reason, one might again prefer measuring user behavior metrics such as click-rates rather than asking the user.
- Click-behavior is cheap and plentiful to obtain but it is ambiguous. A user may perform more clicks because she likes the results or simply because she is lost.

In practice, it is necessary to combine all these approximations to the ideal in order to build a better joint picture of relevance. In this first paper, we will concentrate on expert editors giving explicit judgments. Future papers will focus on explicit judgments from panelists, contrasting those with editors, and on assessing relevance using implicit (user-behavior) attributes such as click-rates, dwell-times and so on.

4 Framework of Methodologies

Having decided on the distribution of users, queries and documents, further experimental design questions need to be answered. Three of these dimensions form the basis of our framework for this paper:

1. Perceived Relevance Versus Landing-Page Relevance. The relevance of the web-site ("landing page") is mediated by the relevance of its presentation (abstract, title, URL) in the Search Engine Results Page (SERP). A site may well be very relevant, but if its presentation attributes are constructed carelessly, users may not click on the result. Judgment made of a landing-page using only its presentation is called *perceived* relevance. Search engines may differ in how well they summarize the underlying page so perceived relevance is a separate relevance metric from landing-page relevance. The following is a partial list of presentation factors, which we will refer to as the <T,A,U> triplet:

- **T: Title:** Sites may not have informative titles. Search engines that automatically construct better titles using the body of the document will get higher perceived relevance scores.

- **A: Abstract:** The abstract is the short paragraph describing the site that appears in the SERP. Abstracts fall into two categories: query-specific and query-independent. Query-specific abstracts (also called *dynamic*) are automatically generated and provide a summary of the site in the context of the user query. Abstract generation engines such as the ones found in Yahoo! and Google are generally of high quality. Static abstracts are often supplied by editors such as Yahoo! Directory or ODP; they tend to be carefully chosen short sentences that may not contain the user query.
- **U: URL:** A given web page may have several URLs as proxies. Search engines that select the URL that appears more relevant for a given query will receive higher perceived relevance scores. For example, for the query 'Disney', it would be better to display the alias 'www.disney.com' rather than the alias 'disney.go.com'.

2. Item-Level Versus Set-Level Relevance. In order to see the significance of this dimension, one only needs to ask whether ten repeats of an excellent result would constitute an excellent *set* of results. Since the answer is emphatically "No!", an excellent set should contain excellent individual results but should also have considerations about the diversity of the results or whether different senses of the query are addressed.

3. Absolute Relevance Versus Relative Relevance. This dimension refers to the method of measurement rather than to an entity whose relevance is being judged (by contrast, set-level, item-level and T,A,U are all entities whose relevance is being judged). Joachims [9] has postulated that it is easier to elicit comparative or relative judgments from users "Which engine is better: left or right?" rather than elicit an absolute measure of relevance on a fixed scale without reference to an alternative.

4.2 Advantages and Disadvantages

Each of the test types has its advantages and disadvantages as shown in Table 1. The main advantage of judging at the item level is that those judgments together with a "roll-up" function such as DCG (Jarvelin et al. [8]) that combines item scores into a set score, can be algorithmically re-applied when the ordering of the items is changed. So when a search engine needs to change its ranking function, we don't need to elicit a new set of judgments. In fact, one can hill-climb through the space of ranking functions to maximize rolled-up DCG score. A 'rolled-up' DCG score for a query is simply a position-weighted sum of item-level scores for all items for that query. This all assumes the existence of a good roll-up function. DCG is not an ideal roll-up function in that it does not penalize sets that have duplicates or lack of diversity.

There are also advantages and disadvantages of judging the presentation rather than the landing page. The presentation algorithm is an independent component of the search engine and should be judged separately. It is important to optimize presentation but this should be done relative to the relevance of the landing-page – the presentation should give a fair assessment of the relevance of the landing-page in response to the query. It should not over-sell or under-sell the landing page.

Table 1. Advantages and Disadvantages of different test types

	Set-level	Item-level
Advantages	Takes duplicates and diversity into account	Recomposable under ranking function changes
Disadvantages	Not recomposable	Doesn't take duplicates and diversity into account

There are also advantages and disadvantages of relative rather than absolute relevance measurements. Joachims [9] has stated that relative measurements are more reliable in the sense that given the task several times, judges would be more consistent than if they were asked to give absolute measurements. However, the advantage of absolute measurements is that (if they are reliable) they can be used for all kinds of unanticipated purposes. For instance, if a third search engine arises, absolute measurements need only be taken on the new engine and then can readily be compared to existing measurements for the existing engines. Alternatively, longitudinal analysis (trending over time) can be done and each engine's scores at one date can be compared to its performance one quarter later. Relative measurements also have the disadvantage that if A was judged to be better than B, and then later, A and B are judged to be the same, we do not know if A has gotten worse or if B has gotten better.

5   Experimental Setup

In Section 3 we listed different types of judgments and different sources of judgments. These are attributes of the test methodology. Conversely, the set of queries and results to be judged can also be characterized along several dimensions. The following is a partial list of these:

User Distribution. In order to measure the relevance of the engine, one must decide what population or distribution of users to use in the evaluation. Should the evaluation be done over random Internet users or some more specific class such as advanced users.

Query Distribution. Queries have changed in distribution since the early days of search engines [12]. Earlier queries tended to be shorter and contain prepositions; now users have realized that the engines are not paying attention to prepositions and so have adapted by accepting a less precise formulation of their need by constructing queries that are sets of keywords. At first glance, it may appear that the user factor is completely mediated by the query in that given the query, the engine can respond without knowing more about the user. This, however, ignores the fact that two users may construct the same query (e.g. 'jaguar') for completely different information needs. One user may intend the car, another the MAC operating-system and another the animal. For the experiments in this paper, we use random queries selected from our web server logs. Other sets we could consider include "Tail" queries, commercial queries and ambiguous queries. After the query set is selected, the judges are allowed to "self-select" queries from it. Thus the judge does not have to provide a judgment on an unfamiliar query.

Document Distribution. Search engines with different underlying indices retrieve different documents, which result in difference relevance scores. This dimension will be controlled for by selection of a random set of queries.

There are three kinds of tests we will explore in this paper. These correspond to three points out of the possible eight in the three-dimensional framework we presented in Section 4.

1. Per-set. These tests require the judge to give a single judgment for the entire set of results for the query. By 'entire set' we actually mean only the top 10 or 20 results. The ranking of the engine is preserved; judges see the <T,A,U> triplet per result.

2. Per-item. The second test type is the item-level or per-item (PI) test. Here, the judge gives a judgment on each result. The results are presented in a random order so the judge is truly judging the relevance of the result, not the ranking order. In a PI test, judges may or may not be presented the presentation attributes. Depending on the details of the test, they may be required to give a judgment using just the Title, just the Abstract or both. Afterwards, they may be required to click through to the landing page and then render a second judgment on the landing page.

3. Side-by-side (SBS). Judges see two sets of results: each result is presented using its <T,A,U> triplet and rank from its search engine is preserved. The URL is usually clickable to they can check out the landing page before giving their judgment. In addition to giving a score, they sometimes record free text reasons supporting their judgment and these have proved very useful. They don't know which side corresponds to which search engine. Sides are randomized so each engine gets 50% of the queries on the left side.

6   Set-Level Versus Item-Level Judgments

In this section, we explore the relationship between Set-level and Item-level Judgments for two domains: Image Search and News Search. For each domain, we look at the correlation between set-level and item-level judgments and characterize what kinds of result-sets receive high set-level but low rolled-up item-level scores.

6.1   Image Search

In the set-level test, the judges were shown 20 images in a 5-by-4 matrix with the 1st row being the images ranked highest by the search engine. 299 queries were judged by 2 or 3 judges each. The judgments were given on a scale of '1' being best and '3' being worst. The queries were self-selected by judges. 24 judges were involved in this test. In the item-level test, the images for a given query were presented one at a time, in randomized order. 282 queries were judged for a total of 6856 judgments. 198 queries were found in common between the tests (see grand total in bottom right cell of Table 2).

Table 2. Image Search: Contingency matrix for per-set versus rolled-up item-level judgments. For instance, there were 130 queries with SET=1 and DCG=1

	SET=1	SET=2	SET=3	Marginal
DCG=1	130	18	1	149; 75%
DCG=2	16	13	7	36; 18%
DCG=3	3	5	5	13; 7%
Marginal	149; 75%	36; 18%	13; 7%	198; r=0.54

To analyze the differences between set-level and item-level judgments, we only considered queries for which the search engine returned the full 20 images on page one. In order to do a query-level analysis between set-level and item-level scores, we had to, for each query, roll-up its 20 item-level scores to produce a single set-level score. To do this roll-up, we used the DCG position-weighted average. The rolled DCG score forms the *DCG* random variable in Table 2. For the set-level test, if the query was judged by several judges, we just used their average score to produce the *Set* random variable. We discretized the DCG scores so that the bucket boundaries would reflect the proportions seen in the three levels of the *Set* variable. In interpreting the table, recall that for *Set* and *DCG,* that '1' is the best score.

The Pearson correlation between Set-level judgments and rolled-up Item-level judgments is a middling 0.54. One can thus conclude that these two variables are measuring different kinds of image-relevance; judges are measuring different underlying factors in the Set-level test than they are in the Item-level test. To get a better idea of what kinds of search quality factors each measurement methods was sensitive to, we looked at a few outlier queries: queries which scored good scores on one axis and bad scores on the other. The query "hollow man" (after a movie) received a high set-level score but poor rolled-up DCG score. Looking at detail at the judgments for this query, we saw that most of the items were irrelevant but a couple of them were about the movie. At the set-level, the user only wants perhaps one icon or gif/jpeg to use; he does not much care if it is at a lower position. This is especially true for image search in which the images are scanned very quickly by the eye. At the item-level however, the judge saw that most of the items were irrelevant images so she gave poor item-level scores and a poor rolled-up DCG score. So we can conclude that for image searches *where just one or a few relevant items is sufficient to satisfy the user* that there will be a discordance between item-level and set-level scores.

Another effect occurring for this query was that the images with the highest individual scores were at the bottom of the set and thus the rolled-DCG score was low. So poor *ranking* can lead to a low rolled item-score but why did the set-level judge not penalize the set that had its best images as the bottom? We believe this is a idiosyncrasy of image search: all the images are scanned in parallel by the eye so ordering is not so important for image sets. Had this been web-search, the set-level judgment would have been a poor score.

At the other extreme we saw the query 'Slam Dunk' which had a poor set-level score but a good rolled-up item-level score. The set-level judge gave a poor score because about 90% of the images were about the video-game 'Slam Dunk' and only one was an actual photo of a slam dunk in a basketball game. The judge expected there to be many more real photos and judged the set as a whole to have essentially missed the most important sense of the phrase 'Slam Dunk'. The reason that this got good item-level scores was that the items are presented to the judge in a random order. The judge only needs to make individual judgments on each item and since each item was either about the video-game or a real photo, each item was scored well. The item-level judge did not maintain a memory of the *distribution* of real photos to video-game images.

6.2 News Search

For News Search, the set-level test involved 23 judges giving 150 judgments over 148 queries – only 2 queries were judged more than once. The item-level test involved 25 judges providing 1284 judgments over 128 queries for an average of about 10 judgments per query.

Table 3 shows results comparing news per-set and news PI. The correlation between news per-set and PI was 0.29, lower than it was for image search. Duplication of the same story from different sources seems to be a leading cause of the difference. Since the average number of results in News search is only 3 to 5, duplicates are more strongly penalized in News Search than in Image Search. Ranking also seems particularly important for news. A bad first result can mar the entire set. For example, for the query 'Mary Kate Olsen', the first result is actually about the debut of Jenna and Barbara Bush – Mary and Kate Olsen were tangentially mentioned in the article. This set got a terrible rating whereas the average PI score was high.

Table 3. News Search: Contingency table for per-set versus rolled-up item-level judgments

	SET=1	SET=2	SET=3	Marginal
DCG=3	9	3	11	23; 18%
DCG=2	17	12	4	33; 26%
DCG=1	45	19	7	71; 56%
Marginal	71; 56%	34; 27%	22; 17%	127, r=0.29

6.3 Cost Analysis

We use number of judgments as the primary metric of cost. The cost of a judgment is a function of the type of the judgment — PI or per-set — as well as the type of the result — image or text (news). To compute the relative cost of PI versus per-set in image search, let Rpi be the cost of one PI image judgment and Rps be the cost of one per-set judgment. There were 6856 item-level and 302 set-level judgments. The relative cost at the test level is (6856 * Rpi) / (302 * Rps). If we assume that each per-set judgment takes as much time as N PI judgments, then per-set will be less expensive than the PI as long as N is less than 22.7. Our experience indicates that N is on the order of 3 to 5 because it costs little to scan through the set and the judge need not scan through the entire set. This implies that per-set is about 5 to 7 times more cost-effective than PI. Similarly, for News search, we get 1784 * Rpi / (150 * Rps). With N being on the order of 4 to 6 (out of 10), we estimate that news per-set is about 2 to 3 times more efficient.

In summary, for image search, we identified two main sources of differences between set-level and item-level: poor rankings and missed important meanings. Item-level did not pick up these factors. However, as we pointed out in section 4.2, PI is still useful for computing tuning and ranking-function changes. For news search, we saw that duplication and poor first result were the main causes of differences between per-set and item-level evaluation.

7 Perceived Relevance Versus Landing-Page Relevance

In this section we compare perceived relevance versus landing-page relevance for item-level judgments for advertising results and news search results. That is, we hold constant the 'size' of the object being judged to be at the item-level. As in all PI tests, the results were presented in random order to the judges. The presentation of the item consisted of two parts: the title and the abstract (the URL was not presented). The judge had to render two Boolean judgments before clicking-through: one for whether the title was relevant (random variable *Title*) and another for whether the abstract was relevant (*Abstract*). After clicking-through, they could see the landing page behind the result and were asked to render another judgment (*LandingPage*).

7.1 Advertising Results Search

Since the advertising results section typically has four to six results, each judge had to judge fewer results per query than she had to for web results. The landing-page judgments ranged from '1' being perfect to '5' being poor. For our correlation analysis, we recoded this variable to Boolean by ignoring the neutral '3' score, by coding '1' and '2' to '1' and by recoding '4' and '5' to '-1'. The test was done over 470 random commercial queries by 32 judges yielding 2003 judgments. In this statistical formulation, we obtained a Pearson correlation of r = 0.63 (r^2 = 0.40) between the landing-page score and the title relevance. We obtained a lower r = 0.55 (r^2 = 0.30) correlation for abstract-relevance. We also wanted to create a compound variable that captured both aspects of perceived relevance (title and abstract). For this, we summed title-relevance and abstract-relevance and ignored the results with sum 0 (15% of all results). Combining these factors produced a higher correlation (r=0.77) but it may throw away the hard cases. If we re-include the '0's, we get a correlation of r=0.66. Tables 4 through 6 present these results; 'NR' stands for not-relevant, 'R' stands for relevant.

Table 4. Title (Presentation Factor) Relevance versus Landing-Page Relevance

	landingPg=NR	landingPg= R	marginal
title= NR	53	20	73; 15%
title= R	28	369	397; 85%
Marginal	81; 17%	389; 83%	470; r=0.63

Table 5. Abstract (Presentation Factor) Relevance versus Landing-Page Relevance

	landingPg=NR	landingPg= R	marginal
abstract=NR	64	58	122; 26%
abstract=relev.	17	331	348; 74%
Marginal	81; 17%	389; 83%	470; r=0.55

Table 6. Overall Perceived (Presentation Factor) Relevance versus Landing-Page Relevance

	landingPg=NR	landingPg=R	marginal
perceived=NR	53	9	62; 16%
perceived=R	17	320	337; 84%
Marginal	80; 20%	389; 80%	399; r=0.77

Looking in detail, we found a number of queries where the landing-pages were good but the title or abstract were not. In the first, the query was 'world war 2', the title was 'Perilous Fight on VHS and DVD: Save 15%' and the abstract was 'Publicvideostore.org offers a vast selection of offerings from the BBC...'. This is an example of the title/abstract essentially advertising the provider rather than being sensitive to the query. As the contingency matrices in Tables 4 through 6 imply, the converse was rarer: finding good titles and abstracts that led to poor landing pages. One class of these involves landing pages that generate HTTP Not-Found 404 errors. Another rare class involves over-advertising. For example, for the query 'DMV', the title was 'Access DMV Records' but the landing page did not lead to dmv.org; instead it directs users to an intermediary or broker: www.public-record-searches.com.

7.2 News Search

For news search, Tables 7 through 9 below summarize the results. We see higher correlations between perceived (title,abstract) and landing-page relevance than we did for advertisement search because news titles and abstracts are carefully written to describe the underlying documents, and not to advertise the provider.

Table 7. News Search: Title relevance versus landing page

	landingPg=NR	landingPg= R	marginal
title= NR	659	383	1042; 30%
title= R	23	2301	2324; 70%
marginal	682; 20%	2684; 80%	3366; r=0.72

Table 8. News Search: Abstract relevance versus Landing-Page relevance

	landingPg=NR	landingPg= R	Marginal
abstract=NR	512	80	592; 18%
abstract=relev.	170	2604	2774; 82%
marginal	682; 20%	2684; 80%	3366; r=0.76

Table 9. News Search: Perceived relevance versus Landing Page relevance

	landingPg=NR	landingPg=R	Marginal
perceived=NR	511	62	573; 20%
perceived=R	22	2283	2305; 80%
marginal	533; 19%	2345; 81%	2878; r=0.91

7.3 Cost Analysis

For perceived versus landing page relevance, we want to measure the cost of reading the title and abstract versus the cost of reading the landing page. One proxy for this is the number of words. In advertisement search, we estimate that the number of words in the title and abstract is less than 200. The average number of readable words in a advertisement landing page is about 500 words. This yields a 2 to 3 fold reduction in judgment cost. In news search, the reduction is more significant as the number of readable words in the landing-page is around 800.

8   Real-World Test: Absolute Versus Relative Judgments

In addition to the tests above that explore the effect of varying one factor at a time, we wanted to simulate the real-world condition where some users click-through and hence provide landing-page judgments whereas others provide perceived judgments. For this experiment we compared web results from two search engines and did two tests: Side-By-Side (Set-level, mixture of perceived and landing-page) and PI: Per-Item (Item-level, landing-page). For the set-level test we used 36 judges judging 887 randomly chosen queries. For the item-level test we used 40 judges judging 847 queries with up to 10 results each. Retaining only queries that were self-selected in both tests, and that yielded at least 10 results we ended up with 658 queries. For PI, the DCG rollup function was computed separately for each engine to yield two rolled-up scores: x, y. Then a relative DCG number was computed as $(x-y)/(x+y)$.

Figure 1 shows a weak correlation ($r^2 = 19\%$) between the SBS scores and the PI (relative DCG) scores. Outlying queries in the figure corresponded to queries that received a high rolled-up PI score, but low SBS score because the query had many duplicates or whose results were poorly ordered.

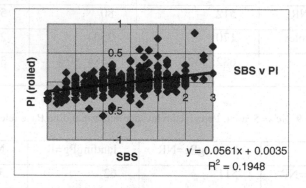

Fig. 1. Correlation between Set-level Relative and Item-level Absolute Judgments

There are other reasons for this low correlation. The SBS test allows some users to base judgments on perceived relevance, others on landing page relevance. Another reason is that, as previous sections showed, PI versus per-set correlation is already low so the correlation to SBS will be even lower. In related work [11] we have observed higher correlation by only considering queries with multiple judges and non-adult queries.

9   Conclusions

This paper presents a methodological framework for evaluating search engine relevance. We have experimented with a subset of methods that we found to be practical and cost-effective over four different types of search engines: image search, advertising results search, news search and web results search.

We have shown that set-level judgments are capable of measuring aspects (poor ranking, missed important senses) of relevance missed by item-level evaluation. We have presented results comparing perceived relevance versus "actual" (landing-page) relevance and shown that there is a moderate correlation between the two. The factors causing differences are poor title and abstract construction. We have also evaluated domain-specific search engines. For image search we found that ranking is less critical than it is for web search as long as the relevant image is somewhere in the first page. For advertising results, we found that query-insensitive titles and abstracts were under-selling the target web-sites. For news search we found a particularly high correlation between perceived relevance and landing page relevance. We conclude that overall our experiments suggest that there is no single method for comprehensively measuring search relevance. The methodology to be chosen depends on the search domain, the measurement intent (perceived or actual) and the cost of the available editorial resources.

Acknowledgments. Thank you to Jan Pedersen at Yahoo! and the editorial team for hundreds of hours of work on judging search results.

References

1. Cleverdon, C. The significance of the cranfield tests on index languages. Proceedings of the SIGIR Conference on Research and Development in Information Retrieval, pages 3-12, 1991.
2. Amitay, E., Carmel, D., Lempel, R., Soffer, A. Scaling IR-System Evaluatin using Term Relevance Sets. In Proceedings of SIGIR 2004, pages 10-17, Sheffield, UK.
3. Buckley, C., Voorhees, E., Retrieval Evaluation with Incomplete Information. In Proceedings of SIGIR 2004, pages 25-32, Sheffield, UK.
4. Voorhees, E., The philosophy of information retrieval evaluation. In Proceedings of the Second Workshop of the Cross-Language Evaluation Forum (CLEF 2001), pages 355-370, 2001.
5. Buckley, C., Voorhees, E., Evaluating evaluation measure stability. In Proceedings of SIGIR 2000, pages 33-40.
6. Zobel, J., How reliable are the results of large-scale information retrieval experiments? In Proceedings of SIGIR 1998, pages 307-314, Melbourne, Australia.
7. Gabrieli, S., and Mizzaro, S., Negotiating a Multidimensional Framework for Relevance Space. In Proceedings of MIRA Conference, 1999.
8. Jarvelin, K. and Kekalainen, J. Cumulated gain-based evaluation of IR techniques. ACM Transactions on Information Systems(ACM TOIS) 20(4), 422-446.
9. Joachims, T. Evaluating Retrieval Performance Using Clickthrough Data, Proceedings of the SIGIR Workshop on Mathematical/Formal Models in Information Retrieval, 2002.
10. Mizzaro, S. How Many Relevances in Information Retrieval? Interacting With Computers, 10(3):305–322, 1998.

374   K. Ali, C.-C. Chang, and Y. Juan

11. Chang, C. and Ali, K. How much correlation is there from one judge to another? Yahoo! Technical Report, 2004-12.
12. Silverstein, C., Henzinger, M., Marais, H. and Moricz, M. Analysis of a Very Large AltaVista Query Log, SRC Technical Note #1998-14.
13. Amento, B. Terveen L. and Hill W. D. "Does 'Authority' Mean Quailty? Predicting Expert Quality Ratings of Web Sites". Proceedings of SIGIR 2000(Athens, Greece).
14. Harter, S. Variations in Relevance Assessments and the Measurement of Retrieval Effectiveness." JASIS, 47(1):37-49, 1996.
15. Brin, S. and Page L. 1998. The anatomy of a large-scale hypertextual Web search engine. Computer Networks and ISDN Systems 30(1-7): 107-117.

Document Identifier Reassignment Through Dimensionality Reduction

Roi Blanco and Álvaro Barreiro

AILab. Computer Science Department, University of Corunna, Spain
roi@mail2.udc.es, barreiro@udc.es

Abstract. Most modern retrieval systems use compressed *Inverted Files* (IF) for indexing. Recent works demonstrated that it is possible to reduce IF sizes by reassigning the document identifiers of the original collection, as it lowers the average distance between documents related to a single term. Variable-bit encoding schemes can exploit the average gap reduction and decrease the total amount of bits per document pointer. However, approximations developed so far requires great amounts of time or use an uncontrolled memory size. This paper presents an efficient solution to the reassignment problem consisting in reducing the input data dimensionality using a SVD transformation. We tested this approximation with the Greedy-NN TSP algorithm and one more efficient variant based on dividing the original problem in sub-problems. We present experimental tests and performance results in two TREC collections, obtaining good compression ratios with low running times. We also show experimental results about the tradeoff between dimensionality reduction and compression, and time performance.

Keywords: Document identifier reassignment, SVD, indexing, compression.

1 Introduction

Large-scale Information Retrieval (IR) systems need an indexing mechanism for efficient retrieval. The most extended data structure used is the *inverted file* (IF). This IF is a traversed representation of the original document collection, organised in *posting lists*. Each entry in the inverted file contains information about a single term in the document collection. The format of the posting lists reflects the granularity of the inverted file, addressing in which documents and positions the term appears. In this work we suppose a document level granularity, therefore the posting list for term t_i is:

$$< t_i; f_{t_i}; d_1, d_2, \ldots, d_{f_{t_i}} >, d_i < d_j \forall i < j \qquad (1)$$

where f_{t_i} stands for the frequency of the term t_i (number of documents in which t_i appears), and d_i is the document identifier. As the notation implies, the document identifiers are ordered.

D.E. Losada and J.M. Fernández-Luna (Eds.): ECIR 2005, LNCS 3408, pp. 375–387, 2005.

Since this structure requires a large amount of storage space, posting lists usually are compressed. Several works aimed at efficiently encoding the document identifiers contained in each entry. Posting lists are stored as a sequence of differences between consecutive documents identifiers (*d-gaps*). This method improves compression, as variable-length encoding schemes represent small integers with less bits than large ones. Small *d*-gaps are more frequent than large ones, so inverted files can be compressed efficiently. Recent works have tried to increase the number of small d-gaps by reordering the document identifiers, hoping that the average d-gap is lowered. This process is done after the collection is traversed and the inverted file is built. These works are presented in [2] and [9], in the following of this paper, the *B&B* (Blandford and Blelloch) and the *TSP approach* (Travelling Salesman Problem) respectively. Results show that the document identifier reassignment technique is effective in lowering the average d-gap, and therefore allowing gains in compression ratios. Both solutions build a *weighted similarity graph* G where the nodes v_i, v_j represent the document identifiers i, j and an edge (v_i, v_j) represents the similarity between documents i and j.

The *B&B* algorithm recursively splits G into small subgraphs $G_{l,i} = (V_{l,i}, E_{l,i})$ representing smaller subsets of the collection until every subgraph becomes a singleton. After that, the technique performs a reordering of the document identifiers, by *depth-first* traversal. The TSP approaches the problem by considering it a *Travelling Salesman Problem* which can be solved by several ways pointed in graph literature. The objective is to find the traverse that minimizes the d-gaps by reassigning document identifiers according to the order in which they were visited.

Unfortunately these solutions lack of efficiency, and they turn nonviable for large collections in terms of space and time. In [10] the authors could only test the *B&B* algorithm in a collection of 60.000 documents, while the TSP implementation in [9] needs 2.17 GB of main memory and 23 hours to process a collection of 132.000 documents.

On the other hand, the work in [10] proposes a different approach by *assigning* the document identifiers *on the fly* during the inversion of the text collection. For this approach a *transactional* representation form of the documents is used, which stores for each document d_i a set of 4-byte integers representing the MD5 Message-Digest [8] of each term appearing in d_i. Using this representation, two families of algorithms were developed to compute an efficient document assignment: the *top-down assignment* and the *bottom-up assignment*. The top-down assignment schemes start with the whole collection and recursively split it into sub-collections, inserting similar documents into the same sub-collections. After this phase, the algorithm merges the sub-collections obtaining a single and ordered group of documents, which is used to compute the assigning order. Bottom-up schemes start from a set of documents, extracting disjoint sequences containing similar documents. Each sequence is ordered, and the final assignment is computed by considering an arbitrary order between sequences. Considering a document collection in transactional form $\widetilde{D} = \{\widetilde{d_1}, \widetilde{d_2}, \ldots, \widetilde{d_N}\}$, the space storage needed by the top-down methods in the asymptotic analysis is

$O(|\widetilde{D}|\log(|\widetilde{D}|))$ and for the bottom-up approaches is $O(|\widetilde{D}|)$ which gives super-lineal and lineal order respectively. However, the total space is also dependant on a factor $|\bar{S}|$, that stands for the average size of documents. For the collection used in the experiments reported in [10], the Google Programming Contest collection, $|\bar{S}|$ has a value of 256 terms.

In this paper we propose a way to make the reassignment methods operational by arranging the input data into a lower dimensionality space, which reflects the major association patterns between documents and terms. Furthermore, the space storage needed can be parameterized so this technique has good behaviour also in collections where the average document size is high. To achieve this dimensionality reduction, we used the *Singular Value Decomposition* (SVD) technique. This way we built a representation of the document similarity matrix (the graph G). Instead of working with the original $d \times d$ similarity matrix (where d is the number of documents in the collection), we use a $d \times k$ matrix, where k is a chosen constant. Using the reduced dimension we can precalculate the amount of memory used by the reassignment algorithm. In addition it is possible to lower/upper the memory bounds, finding a compromise between space usage and performance. We tested our implementation with the *TSP* Greedy-NN algorithm and give evidence of the feasibility of the technique in some TREC collections. We also implemented and tested a more time efficient version, dividing the original problem in a number of similar sub-problems.

The rest of the paper is organised as follows. Section 2 describes the TSP algorithm. Section 3 shows the way of reducing the document similarity matrix dimensionality by computing its singular value decomposition and how we applied this result to the reassignment problem. Section 4 describes the experimental conditions and the tests results of our approach. In Section 5 we discuss the leading lines in further research derived from this work. Section 6 presents some conclusions from the experimental results.

2   The TSP Approach to the Document Reassignment Problem

Given that we will illustrate the use of the dimensionality reduction technique for document reassignment with the TSP algorithm, we briefly review the work in [9].

2.1   The Document Reassignment Problem as a TSP

An inverted file can be seen as a posting list set. Each list contains the information for a single term appearing in the document collection, expressed as a sequence of encoded d-gaps $G_t = \{g_1, \ldots, g_{f_t}\}$. The document reassignment problem tries to find the bijective function f that

- maps each document identifier into a new identifier in the range $[1 \ldots d]$
- minimizes the average document gap.

Similarity between documents is defined as the number of common terms, and maintained in a similarity matrix Sim, where Sim_{ij} represents the similarity between the document i and the document j.

Shieh et al. [9] proposed a gap-reduction strategy based in the transformation of the problem into a *Travelling Salesman Problem* (TSP). The TSP is stated as follows: given a weighted graph $G = (V, E)$ where $e(v_i, v_j)$ is the weight for the edge from v_i to v_j, find a minimal path $P = \{v_1, v_2, \ldots, v_n\}$ containing all the vertexes in V, such as if $P' = \{v'_1, v'_2, \ldots, v'_n\}$ is another path in G, $\sum_{i=2}^{n} e(v_i, v_{i-1}) \leq \sum_{i=2}^{n} e(v'_i, v'_{i-1})$.

Considering Sim an weighted adjacency matrix, it is possible to build a Document Similarity Graph (DSG) expressing the similarities between documents. This graph can be traversed by a gap-reduction strategy based on the similarity factor between documents. The idea is assigning close document identifiers to similar documents as this will likely reduce the d-gaps in common terms postings. This traversing problem can be transformed into a TSP just by considering the complement of the similarity as the weight in the TSP. The solution found by the TSP is the path that minimizes the sum of the distances between documents, therefore the algorithm is an appropriate strategy to the document reassignment problem.

2.2   Heuristic Approximations

The TSP is an *NP*-complete problem, so some polynomial-time heuristic approximations were modified for the reassignment problem. These algorithms were classified as greedy algorithms and spanning tree algorithms. We tested our low-dimension approximation with the Greedy-NN algorithm.

The Greedy-NN (Nearest Neighbor) expands the path by adding the closest vertex to the tail of the current path. In each iteration the algorithm adds a new

---

Greedy-NN algorithm

1: **Input:**
   The Graph G
   The Vertex set V
   The weighted Edges set E
2: **Output:**
   A global path P maximizing the similarity between vertexes
3: Select the edge $e(v_i, v_j) \in E$ with the largest weight;
4: Add v_i and v_j to P;
5: $v_{last} \leftarrow v_j$;
6: **while** $(|P| \neq |V|)$ **do**
7:     Choose $v_k \in V$ and $v_k \notin P$ such that $e(v_{last}, v_k)$ is maximal;
8:     Add v_k to P;
9:     $v_{last} \leftarrow v_k$;
10: **end while**
11: **return** P;

Table 1. Statistics of the pure TSP approach on two TREC collections reported by Shieh et al. [9]

Collection	FIBS	LATimes
Size of the Collection	470 MB	475 MB
Number of distinct terms	209,782	167,805
Number of distinct documents	130,471	131,896
Temporal Cost	19.63 h	23.28h
Space Cost	2.10 GB	2.17 GB

vertex (document) chosen that its similarity is the largest with the last vertex in the path. This approximation is high time consuming. Each vertex is inserted only once in the path P and at iteration i the algorithm does $d - i$ comparisons (the remaining documents) involving the term size t of both documents. Therefore the overall complexity is $O(d^2 t)$.

2.3   Implementation Considerations

The TSP approximation for the identifier reassignment problem was evaluated in [9]. The solution demonstrated good improvements in the compression ratio, although it presented some design challenges and poor performance time and space results.

First, this approach requires a big amount of space. The similarity matrix is symmetric ($Sim_{ij} = Sim_{ji}$) and the elements in the diagonal are not relevant, so it is easy to prove that we need to store $\frac{d(d-1)}{2}$ *similarity pointers* ($O(|d^2|)$). Even with a suitable coding schema this amount can become unmanageable, so a matrix partitioning technique has to be developed. Second, building this matrix can be very expensive if it does not fit into memory, as each update has to access the disk twice, involving big delays.

Experimental results were presented for two medium sized collections (FIBS and LATimes in TREC disk 5), to prove the effectiveness of this mechanism. These tests are summarized in table 1.

It is important to remark that the work in [9] provides bar graphs that show an approximated gain of one bit per gap when reassigning with the Greedy-NN for delta and gamma coding. The temporal costs include the process of building the similarity matrix, greeding and recompressing the inverted file. However, the results show that this full TSP approach may be unacceptable for very large collections, as it takes 23 hours and 2.17 GB to process a 475 MB collection.

3   Document Reassignment by Dimensionality Reduction

Approaches proposed so far aimed at reducing the d-gaps using different representations of the full inverted file. Shieh et al. [9] and Blandford and Blelloch [2] built a full document similarity graph and traversed it by different algorithms such as the TSP and recursive splitting. Silvestri et al. [10] used an *on the fly* assignment technique with temporal and spacial complexity linear or super-linear on the number of documents, but also dependant on the average document length.

We propose a new approach based on dimensionality reduction in which reordering algorithms can operate efficiently. We aim at:

- allowing a controlled and efficient memory usage for such algorithms
- giving consistent results through different document and collection sizes and heuristics
- not being outperformed by the original working framework.

We tested our approach with the TSP reassignment algorithm described in section 2 with good results (section 4). In this section, the application of SVD to the document identifier reassignment problem is presented.

3.1   Single Value Decomposition

Singular Value Decomposition (SVD) is a well known mathematical technique used in a wide variety of fields. It is used to decompose an arbitrary rectangular matrix into three matrices containing singular vectors and singular values. This matrices show a breakdown of the original relationships into linearly independent factors. The SVD technique is used as the mathematical base of the Latent Semantic Indexing (LSI) IR model [3].

Analytically, we start with X, a $t \times d$ matrix of terms and documents. Then, applying the SVD X is decomposed into three matrices:

$$X = T_0 S_0 D_0' \tag{2}$$

T_0 and D_0 have orthonormal columns, and S_0 is diagonal and, by convention, $s_{ii} \geq 0$ and $s_{ii} \geq s_{jj} \forall i \geq j$. T_0 is a $t \times m$ matrix, S_0 is $m \times m$ and D_0' is $m \times d$ where m is the rank of X. However it is possible to obtain a k-ranked approximation of the X original matrix by keeping the k largest values in S_0 and setting the remaining ones to zero obtaining the matrix S with $k \times k$ dimensions. As S is a diagonal matrix with k non-zero values, the corresponding columns of T_0 and D_0' can be deleted to obtain T, sized $t \times k$, and D', sized $k \times d$, respectively. This way we can obtain $\hat{X}$ which is a reduced rank k approximation of X:

$$X \approx \hat{X} = TSD' \tag{3}$$

$\hat{X}$ is the closest rank k approximation of X in terms of the Euclidean or Frobenious norms, i.e. the matrix which minimizes $||X - \hat{X}||_N^2$ where $|| \cdot ||_N^2$ is the involved norm.

The i-th row of DS gives the representation of the document i in the reduced k-space and the similarity matrix $\Theta(X)$ is k-approximated by $\Theta(\hat{X})$:

$$\Theta(X) \approx \Theta(\hat{X}) = \hat{X}'\hat{X} = DS^2 D', \tag{4}$$

where $\hat{X}'$ is the transposed matrix of $\hat{X}$ and D' is the transposed of D.

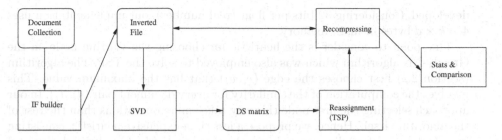

Fig. 1. Block diagram for the indexing and reassignment system

If $D_{d \times k} = \{z_{ij}\}$ and $\{s_i\}$ is the set of diagonal elements of S, it is easy to prove that

$$\Theta(\hat{X})_{ij} = \sum_{\gamma=0}^{k-1} z_{i\gamma} z_{j\gamma} s_\gamma^2 \tag{5}$$

Therefore it is possible to calculate $\Theta(\hat{X})_{ij}$ only storing the set of k elements $\{s_i\}$ and the $d \times k$ matrix D instead of computing and writing the full rank matrix $\Theta(X)_{d \times d}$.

The output of the SVD of X, $\hat{X}$ has been used in the computation of $\Theta(\hat{X}) = \hat{X}' \cdot \hat{X}$. The same result could be obtained by calculating the SVD of $\Theta(X) = X' \cdot X$ due to the uniqueness property of SVD [1]. Since SVD computes the best rank k approximation, it is proved that the best rank k approximation of $\Theta(X)$ is obtained starting from X and without the need of computing $\Theta(X)$.

3.2   SVD in the Document Reassignment Problem

Figure 1 describes the system built for testing this approach. The inverted file builder mechanism outputs the X data matrix to a SVD module. This module produces the matrices $D_{d \times k}$ and $S_{k \times k}$ that allow the computation of $\Theta(\hat{X})$, therefore there is no longer needed to store the similarity matrix $\Theta(X)_{d \times d}$. The reassignment module uses the SVD output matrix to compute the TSP approach described in section 2.2. As k is a constant factor, we can conclude that the space usage of the algorithm now is $O(d)$, i.e., linear in collection size and not dependant on document size. The output of the TSP reassignment module is used by an inverted file recoding program which exploits the new locality of the documents to enhance the d-gaps compression. Finally, some statical information is taken to make suitable comparisons between compression ratios achieved by the original encoding and those obtained after reassignment.

The main difference in this model is that computing the similarity between two documents d_i and d_j involves k operations ($\sum_{\gamma=0}^{k-1} (DS)_{i\gamma} (DS)_{j\gamma}$) and storing k real pointers per document, making a total of $k \times d$ for the full matrix. This representation can fit smoothly into memory by adjusting the parameter k and uses considerably less space than the original $d \times d$ matrix. Even more, the space usage can be precalculated so suitable scalable algorithms can be easily developed. Considering 32 bits per float (real number), our implementation uses $4 \times k \times d$ bytes of main memory.

One point to consider is the heuristic for choosing the starting node on the Greedy-NN algorithm which was also employed to solve the TSP. The algorithm (section 2.2) first chooses the edge (v_i, v_j) that has the maximum value. This involves the computation of the similarity for every document pair (d_i, d_j). In our approach selecting the first node this way takes more operations than the rest of the algorithm itself. Hence, we propose a less time-expensive heuristic, consisting in calculating, after dimensionality reduction, each (d_i, d_i) self-similarity and choosing the document (node) with the largest value.

4   Experiments and Results

We performed several experiments for testing the low-dimension approach on the two TREC document collections described in table 1. These collections were not preprocessed, so indexing and reordering did include stop words and terms were not stemmed. The machine used was a 2.5 GHz AMD with 40 GB ATA disk and 1GB of main memory, running Linux OS. The original index file was built with MG4J [6] from the University of Milan, a free Java implementation of the indexing and compression techniques described in [12] and originally implemented in the MG software [5]. For the SVD module we used the SVDLIBC [11], a C library based on the SVDPACKC library. We wrote the reassignment, recoding and statistical software in Java. It should be pointed that we needed to modify the MG4J software to output data directly to the SVDLIBC module. Also some modifications were made that allowed us to encode document pointers with interpolative coding.

The first experiment assessed the performance of the system with the Greedy-NN algorithm, in terms of average bits per compressed document pointer (d-gap). The document collections were inverted, the IF was inputted to the SVD module and the program computed the Greedy-NN in the reduced dimension for the reassignment task. After reordering the collection, the inverted file was recompressed. The software measured the average bits per gap in the inverted file, before and after reordering and recompressing, which reflects the amount of compression gained by reordering the document collection. We ran several tests varying the following parameters:

- the parameter k which reflects the desired dimensionality reduction
- coding schemes for document pointers: delta coding, gamma coding or interpolative coding [7][12].

Best results are obtained considering X as a binary matrix in the reassignment process. The elements of X represent the presence or absence of a term in a given document. The recompressing module acts over the original index file which contains in-document term frequency and frequency of the term in the collection values. Results are given in bits per document gap because it is a measure independent of these indexing options. As stated in 3.2, the memory usage leads

Table 2. LATimes bits per gap results

	Random	Original	k						
			200	100	50	20	10	5	1
Gamma	8.15	7.77	6.71	6.75	6.79	6.89	6.99	7.13	7.44
Delta	7.65	7.25	6.29	6.36	6.39	6.48	6.57	6.73	7.02
Interpolative	6.08	5.88	5.25	5.26	5.28	5.29	5.33	5.44	5.57

Table 3. FIBS bits per gap results

	Random	Original	k						
			200	100	50	20	10	5	1
Gamma	7.84	6.74	6.20	6.24	6.31	6.46	6.63	6.81	7.07
Delta	7.35	6.35	5.80	5.86	5.92	6.07	6.23	6.42	6.69
Interpolative	5.83	5.25	4.98	4.99	5.01	5.06	5.17	5.21	5.33

to $4 \times d \times k$ bytes, concretely $0.497707 \times k$ MB for the FBIS and $0.503143 \times k$ MB for the LATimes (for $k = 200$ less than 101 MB in both collections).

Tables 2 and 3 show the results for the different coding schemes. Columns refer to bits per document gap results for: random reassignment, original document identifiers and reassignment after reducing the dimensionality with different k values. Assigning values to k similar to those used in retrieval [4], the low-dimension algorithm operates with gains that give good benefits in bits per gap. As expected, the method behaves better as the k value increases. Also, the figures seem to have an asymptotic behaviour. With k=200, for the LATimes collection (FIBS collection) we achieved a 13.65% (8.02%) gain in compression ratio respect to the original document identifier order with the gamma encoding, 13.2%(8.7%) for the delta encoding, and 11.32% (5.15%) for the interpolative coding. These values are 17.67% (21.92%), 17.8%(21.1%) and 13.66% (14.58%) repetively for both collections and the three encoding schemes, respect to a random reassignment. Computing the Greedy-NN TSP with the reduced space approximation $\Theta(\hat{X})$ gives worthy compression ratios in every case. The gains in the FBIS collection are worse than the ones in the LATimes, although starting from a randomized order the result is inverted. This is the expected behaviour if the FBIS collection exhibits a better original document order. One point to remark is that even in tha case of interpolative coding, where the starting point is much better, the method is able to produce gains in bit per document gap. Our tests did not include the computation of the full dimension solution as presented in [9], because it requires the development of matrix partition techniques and partial reading/writing, which is the task that we want to avoid. Shie et al [9] provided bar graph results for gamma and delta encoding in the LATimes and FBIS collections. However, exact compression values depends on the indexing software and particular indexing options. This information is not explicitly provided, thus it is not possible to make exact comparisons between their published full-dimension results and the k-dimension solutions.

Table 4. FIBS running times

	k						
	200	100	50	20	10	5	1
SVD	34m 58s	15m 01s	5m 42s	3m 18s	2m 09s	1m 33s	58s
Reorder and recompress	8h 30m	4h 20m	1h 48m	58m 20s	31m 13s	17m 55s	7m 5s

Table 5. LATimes running times

	k						
	200	100	50	20	10	5	1
SVD	42m 31s	20m 37s	11m 25s	4m 5s	2m 33s	1m 55s	1m 09s
Reorder and recompress	8h 33m	4h 24m	2h 15m	58m 18s	32m 05s	18m 31s	7m 30s

Time measurement is divided in three parts: inverted file construction, SVD running time and reordering and recompressing time. As the system was built upon different modules, the different software pieces employ a lot of temporal I/O transfer time, which also is measured, so results are given in *elapsed time* in tables 4 and 5. Inversion takes 5m 20s for the FIBS collection and 6m 03s for the LATimes collection and it is not shown in the tables. Although the SVD software performs well for the collections and k values used, the TSP greedy algorithm running time still rises to high values. Anyway, we conclude that it is possible to achieve good compression ratios with reasonable time performance with our technique.

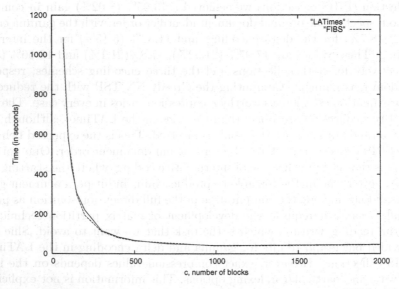

Fig. 2. Running times for the c-GreedyNN with the LATimes and FIBS collections under k=200 and delta coding

Table 6. LATimes bits per gap and running time (k=200 and delta coding)

	c								
	70	100	150	200	300	400	500	1000	2000
Bits per gap	6.68	6.72	6.77	6.81	6.87	6.92	6.95	7.02	7.09
c-GreedyNN & recompress	18m8s	9m50s	5m8s	3m21s	1m57s	1m25s	1m7s	42s	47s

Table 7. FIBS bits per gap and running time (k=200 and delta coding)

	c								
	70	100	150	200	300	400	500	1000	2000
Bits per gap	5.98	6.00	6.02	6.05	6.09	6.12	6.14	6.22	6.3
c-GreedyNN & recompress	17m37s	9m35s	4m59s	3m15s	1m53s	1m21s	1m5s	40s	45s

Another advantage of the approach is that it is possible to propose more efficient reordering algorithms in time performance. We developed a simple new algorithm based on the division of the original problem in c subproblems, hereinafter c-GreedyNN. It operates as follows: first, it divides the DS matrix (which represents the document similarities in the k space) in c blocks of $\lceil d/c \rceil$ documents each. Then, each block is reordered by running the greedy algorithm. Finally, a block order is decided by running another greedy with c documents each one selected from different blocks. For a simpler explanation we consider d an exact multiple of c. Analytically, the Greedy-NN after dimensionality reduction does d comparisons to select the first document, and $\frac{d(d-1)}{2}$ for reordering, resulting in $\frac{d}{2}(d+1)$ comparisons involving k multiplications each. The new approach chooses c block-representatives and then performs c greedy runs with d/c documents, resulting in $d + c(\frac{\frac{d}{c}(\frac{d}{c}-1)}{2}) = \frac{d}{2}(\frac{d}{c}+1)$ comparisons, so the overall number of operations is reduced in a $1/c$ factor. Experimental results with different values of the number of blocks c are presented in figure 2 and tables 6 and 7. Results are provided for the LATimes and FIBS collections, $k = 200$ and delta coding. Tables 6 and 7 also show that the compression factor increases as the number of blocks decreases, with a goal value of 6.29 (5.80) for the LATimes (FIBS) collection, which is the value of considering the matrix as one whole block.

Running times are as expected from the analytical form and comparable as the ones presented in [10], and they give acceptable compression values. The method enhances the original compression ratio 7.25 (6.35) and the randomly ordered collection ratio 7.65 (7.35) with a minimum time usage, which can also be parametrized by selecting the c and k values.

5   Future Work

In a first experimental line, immediate research involves three task:

- experimentation with different heuristics for selecting the first document in the Greedy-NN algorithm

- experimentation with web collections
- implementation of the solutions presented in [10] using the low-dimension scaling presented here and analysis of the behavior in collections with more than 600 terms per document in average, such as the LATimes or FIBS.

Another future working line is the following: as long as the TSP in the reduced dimension space performs well, we may pursue a formal characterization to the distance of the optimal solution reached, with this sort of heuristic solutions. On the other hand, dividing the TSP graph into c blocks allows effective reordering without compromising the index reduction. So, it is necessary to study different block-reordering strategies.

6   Conclusions

We presented a smart approximation for the document identifier reassignment problem by using a previous dimensionality reduction with SVD. Results presented provide time-efficient methods that yields good inverted file reduction gains. Concretely, we implemented the TSP Greedy-NN approach in the reduced dimension space and one variant, that applies this solution to sub-collections of the original data, reordering them next. It is possible to emphasize that the obtained data allows the exposition of future lines of work, as the design of algorithms and heuristics that could provide a better characterization of the result respect to the optimum compressed inverted file.

Acknowledgements. The work reported here was co-founded by the "Secretaría de Estado de Universidades e Investigación" and FEDER funds under research projects TIC2002-00947 and Xunta de Galicia under project PGIDT03PXIC10501PN.

References

1. B. T. Bartell, G. W. Cottrel and R. K. Belew. Latent Semantic Indexing is an optimal special case of Multidimensional Scaling. In *Proceeding of the 15th Annual International ACM SIGIR Conference on Research and Development in Information Retrieval*, pp. 161-167, 1992.
2. D. Blandford and G.Blelloch. Index compression through document reordering. In *Proceedings of the IEEE Data Compression Conference (DCC'02)*, pp. 342-351, 2002.
3. S. Deerwester, S. T. Dumais, G. W. Furnas, T. K. Landauer and R. Harshman. Indexing by Latent Semantic Analysis. In *Journal of the American Society for Information Science*, 41(6):391-407, 1990.
4. S. T. Dumais. Latent Semantic Indexing (LSI): TREC-3 Report. In *NIST Special Publication 500-225: Proceedings of the Third Text REtrieval Conference (TREC-3)*, November 1994.
5. http://www.cs.mu.oz.au/mg/ Managing Gigabytes.
6. http://mg4j.dsi.unimi.it/ MG4J (Managing Gigabytes for Java).
7. A. Moffat, A. Turpin. *Compression and Coding Algorithms*, Kluwer 2002.

8. R. Rivest, RFC 1321: The md5 algorithm.
9. W.-Y. Shieh, T.-F. Chen, J. J.-J. Shann and C.-P. Chung. Inverted file compression through document identifier reassignment. *Information Processing and Management*, 39(1):117-131, January 2003.
10. F. Silvestri, S. Orlando and R. Perego. Assigning identifiers to documents to enhance the clustering property of fulltext indexes. In *Proceeding of the 27th Annual International ACM SIGIR Conference on Research and Development in Information Retrieval*, pp. 305-312, 2004.
11. http://tedlab.mit.edu/~dr/SVDLIBC/ SVDLIBC.
12. I. H. Witten, A. Moffat and T. C. Bell. *Managing Gigabytes - Compressing and Indexing Documents and Images*, 2nd edition. Morgan Kaufmann Publishing, San Francisco, 1999.

Scalability Influence on Retrieval Models: An Experimental Methodology

Amélie Imafouo and Michel Beigbeder

Ecole Nationale Supérieure des Mines de Saint-Etienne,
158 Cours Fauriel - 42023 Saint-Etienne, Cedex 2, France
{imafouo, beigbeder}@emse.fr

Abstract. Few works in Information Retrieval (IR) tackled the questions of Information Retrieval Systems (IRS) *effectiveness* and *efficiency* in the context of scalability in corpus size.

We propose a general experimental methodology to study the scalability influence on IR models. This methodology is based on the construction of a collection on which a given characteristic C is the same whatever be the portion of collection selected. This new collection called uniform can be split into sub-collection of growing size on which some given properties will be studied.

We apply our methodology to WT10G (TREC9 collection) and consider the characteristic C to be the distribution of relevant documents on a collection. We build a uniform WT10G, sample it into sub-collections of increasing size and use these sub-collections to study the impact of corpus volume increase on standards IRS evaluation measures (recall/precision, high precision).

1   Former IR Works on Scalability

The information retrieval process consists in providing, in response to a user request, documents which as well as possible meet his information need (relevant documents). This process is divided in several steps: collection construction, indexing, querying and evaluation. In the following sections, after some brief recalls on these phases, we will review works which were interested in scalability.

1.1   Collection Construction

IR experiments are usually based on static collections which are composed of a set of documents, a set of information needs or topics, and a set of relevance judgments on those documents using the topics. The techniques currently used (pooling) described in the case of TREC [1] come up against many limits with the growth of information volume [2]. Some pooling improvements were proposed without resolving all the limits [2], [3], [4]. But [2] showed that using the pooling techniques to identify documents to be assessed introduces a skew that does not have a significant impact. He also showed that the relevance judgments obtained by the pooling technique provide a credible base for the evaluation of

D.E. Losada and J.M. Fernández-Luna (Eds.): ECIR 2005, LNCS 3408, pp. 388–402, 2005.

IRS that did not take part in TREC campaign.[5] showed the impact of judges disagreements on the reliability of relevance judgments can be neglected.

In the case of IRS using several distributed sources, [6] propose to scale in corpus size by reducing the duplication of identical documents coming from different sources. [7] are interested in replicating the Web hyperlinks structure features on a collection of reduced size. This relates to collection sampling: determine some properties of a large collection, build a collection of reduced size which has the same properties and make studies on the reduced collection (what should be easier than on the whole collection) and defer the results obtained on this reduced collection on the whole collection.

1.2   Indexing and Querying

The average time to index collections increases in a very significant way according to their size [8]. Solutions suggested for this scalability limit are based on the physical information compression but their impact on the retrieval performance remains not significant [9]. A track that will allow the reduction of the representation space is the increase in the information granularity (using aggregate concepts to represent information rather than low level information units like the terms or the n-grams).

The average time for processing requests also scale badly. Techniques that aim to reduce this time need better knowledge of the user information need, which makes it possible to identify sub-collections (i.e. to reduce the size) which would be enough to carry out search and meet the user's need. The question is then how to segment the collection (collection segmentation based on questions answered by users, segmentation based on a users profile [10]). Other works rely on additional metadata related to the user information need and/or to the documents allowing a better classification of documents [8].

1.3   Evaluation

Two measures generally help to carry out IR evaluation: precision is the proportion of retrieved documents that are relevant; recall is the proportion of relevant documents that are retrieved. Precision and recall put forward two different aspects of an IRS performance. Hitherto, few work tackled the collection size impact on effectiveness. The relevance evaluation of retrieval results depend neither on collection size nor on corpus diversity, and this can generate biases when comparing different IRS performance. This is one of the main goal of the TeraByte task introduced at TREC in 2004. Heterogeneity is more important in large collections. Thus [11] showed that for large collections, the terms discrimination is amplified : the number of frequent terms does not increase in relation with the collection size and the proportion of discriminating terms decreases. The use of these collections for IRS evaluation will require new measures that put forward the precision on the first retrieved documents. Our work focuses on precision in first retrieved documents; they determine the users satisfaction particularly in the Web context.

1.4   Former Research Work on the Scaling Impact

Following the 5 assumptions put forth by the TREC-6 VLC task participants
(they noticed a significant increase of high precision when the collection size
increases) [12]. [13] studied the impact of the collection (size) on attribution of a
score to a document and used various forms of relevant documents distribution
and irrelevant documents distribution. He carried out experiments by building
three types of samples of the collection:

- *Uniform samples*: One creates N primary disjoint samples of equal size and
  compose them to have several sub-collections of a certain size (e.g 3/7). The
  tests are done on each of these sub-collections and the result deferred for the
  sample of this size (e.g. 3/7) corresponds to an average of the results on all
  these sub-collections and takes into account all the data.
- *Replicated samples*: One takes the primary samples of size 1/10 of the whole
  collection and replicate them a desired number of times.
  Example: $(0), (0,0), \cdots, (0,0,0,0,0,0,0,0,0,0), (1), \cdots, (1,1,1,1,1,1,1,1,1,$
  $1), (9), \cdots, (9,9,9,9,9,9,9,9,9,9)$.
- *Biased samples*: the TREC6 data is subdivided in 5 disjoined sub-collections
  according to their origin. Each of the 5 sub-collections is considered as a
  sample, but these sub-collections have neither the same number of documents
  nor the same size and their documents do not have the same probabilities of
  relevance.

Both our methodology and Hawking's work aim to sample a given collection to
allow experiments on the scalability influence in a reproducible way.

2   Our Methodology

2.1   Assumptions and General Methodology

We want to study the influence of collection growth on IR models. To achieve
this goal, we have to carry out experiments on collections of growing size and
analyze the behavior of different IR models when the collection size increases.
The question is how to build collections of growing size that will be used to carry
out experiments and obtain reliable results on scalability influence? Let C be
a characteristic of a collection and $\{P_i\}$ be some properties. The methodology
goal is to obtain a collection on which the characteristic C is the same whatever
be the portion selected in the collection. If we have such a collection, we can
split it into portions of different size, study properties $\{P_i\}$ on different portions
and analyze the influence of portion size on these properties. The way the initial
collection is split must not be a constraint. This mean we want to allow any
splitting of the collection, the only constraint is that the characteristic C must
be the same whatever be the portion of the collection selected. Our methodology
is divided in 4 steps:

1. We suppose in this step that we have an collection. We study the character-istic C on this collection. If the constraints we want on C are satisfied, we move to step 3;else we continue to step 2. In the same way, if we do not have an initial collection, move to step 2.
2. (Re)build the collection to have a new one on which the characteristic C remain unchanged whatever be the portion of the collection selected
3. Split (sample) the new collection into portions of growing size
4. Study the properties $\{P_i\}$ on different portions and analyze the influence of portion size on these properties.

We apply this general methodology on retrieval evaluation. Given the fact that IR evaluation is based on relevant documents retrieving, we assume that for a study on scalability influence, the way relevant documents are distributed within collections of growing size is important. For two collections of different size, the relevant documents distribution must not change. We have an initial large collection and want to split it into sub-collections of growing size. We want to allow any splitting of the collection, the only constraint is that the distribution of relevant documents must be the same whatever be the portion of the collection selected. So, we apply the general methodology explained above with characteristic C chosen to be the distribution of relevant documents on the collection and the properties $\{P_i\}$ are evaluation measures.

2.2   Step 1: Study the Characteristic C

The first step of our methodology is to study the characteristic C (in this case, it is the distribution of relevant documents among the collection) to notice if this distribution has a particular shape. If the distribution is unspecified, we move to next step and our goal is to have a uniform collection.

2.3   Step 2: Build a Uniform Collection

This step aims to obtain a collection that can be split in different ways, by respecting our assumptions. In this new collection (called uniform), whatever be the portion selected, the number of relevant documents for a given topic is proportional to the portion size and the total number of relevant documents (for all topics) is proportional to the portion size. We can obtain such a collection if relevant documents for a topic are distributed uniformly on the collection. This means that relevant documents for a given topic t must be separated by the same number of documents. To carry out this distribution, we first of all compute $E(t)$which is the wished distance between two documents relevant to the topic t. Let $R(t)$ be the set of the relevant documents for topic t, T the set of all topics and D the set of all the documents of the collection. We have

$$E(t) = \frac{\mid D \mid - \sum_{k \in T} \mid R(k) \mid}{\mid R(t) \mid}$$

Thus within the new collection, for each topic t we want its relevant docu-ments to be separated by $E(t)$ irrelevant documents (i.e. documents which are

not considered to be relevant for any topic) and possibly by documents considered to be relevant for some topics different from t. For documents considered to be relevant for several topics, they are inserted only once in the new collection, with the position defined by the first of the concerned topics that is processed. This can possibly change the real distance between two relevant documents of a topic t. So for a topic t, the real distance between two relevant documents is
$E_r(t) \leq E(t) + \sum_{k \in T, k \neq t} | R(k) |$

This introduces a skew on the uniform collection. We assume that our collection is large and that $\sum_{k \in T} | P(k) | <<< | D |$: the total number of relevant documents is much smaller than the collection size. The skew on the real distance between two relevant documents for a topic t is then not significant; it does not affect the uniformity we wanted on the collection.

Let us look at this on an example. Let us suppose that we have a collection made up of 30 documents ordered as follows:
$D = \{d_1, \cdots, d_{30}\}$ and $T = \{t_1, t_2\}$. Let us suppose $R(t_1) = \{d_1, d_7, d_{18}\}$ and $R(t_2) = \{d_7, d_{21}\}$. Document d_7 is relevant for both t_1 and t_2.

We compute $E(t_1) = \frac{|D| - \sum_{k \in T} |R(k)|}{|R(t_1)|} = \frac{(30-4)}{3} \approx 8$ and $E(t_2) = \frac{(30-4)}{2} \approx 13$

In the uniform collection, the documents are ordered as follows:

$$\{d_2, d_3, d_4, d_5, d_6, d_8, d_9, d_{10}, \underbrace{d_1}, d_{11}, d_{12}, d_{13}, d_{14}, d_{15}, \overbrace{d_7}, d_{16}, d_{17}, d_{19},$$

$$d_{20}, d_{22}, d_{23}, d_{24}, d_{25}, \underbrace{d_{18}}, d_{26}, d_{27}, d_{28}, d_{29}, d_{30}, \overbrace{d_{21}} \}$$

We envisaged that the relevant documents for topic t_1 will be separated by $E(t_1)$ irrelevant documents. In the worst case for our example, two relevant documents for topic t_1 will be separated by $E(t_1) + | R(t_2) |= E(t_1) + 2$.

Notice that the document d_7 is inserted once. Because this document is relevant for more than one topic, the real distance between 2 relevant documents of topic t_1 is different from our envisaged distance. This skew is not significant if we assume that the collection is large.

2.4   Step 3 : Sample the Collection

With the methodology explained above, we obtain a uniform and reusable collection for various types of experiments. This collection can be split out in portions of different sizes using various ways since the number of relevant documents on a portion is proportional to the portion's size. The choice of the way the collection will be split can vary according to experiments needs. One could split out the whole collection into N sub-collections of equal size and then put those N sub-collections together in various ways to obtain collections of various sizes since it is known that the number of relevant documents on a portion is proportional to the portion's size.

For the example we showed previously, to obtain sub-collections of growing size, one can split the collection in $N = 3$ portions of size $\frac{|D|}{N} = 10$

- A first portion is $D_1 = \{d_2, d_3, d_4, d_5, d_6, d_8, d_9, d_{10}, d_1, d_{11}\}$
- A second portion is $D_2 = \{d_{12}, d_{13}, d_{14}, d_{15}, d_7, d_{16}, d_{17}, d_{19}, d_{20}, d_{22}\}$
- A third portion is $D_3 = \{d_{23}, d_{24}, d_{25}, d_{18}, d_{26}, d_{27}, d_{28}, d_{29}, d_{30}, d_{21}\}$

Then one can build sets of sub-collections $\{S_1 = D_1, S_2 = D_1 \bigcup D_2, S_3 = D_1 \bigcup D_2 \bigcup D_3\}$ or $\{S_1 = D_2, S_2 = D_1 \bigcup D_3, S_3 = D_1 \bigcup D_2 \bigcup D_3\}$. In the two cases, we obtain three sub-collections of growing size with the same distribution of relevant documents.

2.5   Step 4: Study the Influence of Collection Size on IR Models Properties

In this step, we have sub-collections of growing size with the same distribution of relevant documents and want to study the scalability impact on a given property of an IR model (for example evaluation measure like recall, precision, high precision). We study the property for each-sub collection and analyze the property's behavior as the collection size grows.

3   Using Our Methodology with WT10G

3.1   Relevant Document Distribution on WT10G

Data. We worked on the TREC test collection WT10G [14]. Information needs for our tests are topics 451-500. This test collection contains 1,692,096 doc-

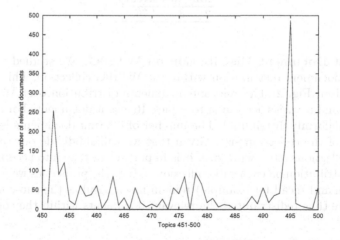

Fig. 1. Number of relevant documents per topic in WT10G

Table 1. Collection WT10G: statistics on the number of relevant documents per topic

Min	Max	Median	Average(Avr)	Topics $t/ \mid R(t) \mid < Avr$	Topics $t/ \mid R(t) \mid > Avr$
0(topics 485 and 486)	487	25	47.42	35	15

uments including 2,371 documents considered to be relevant for topics 451-500 and distributed among those topics as the Fig. 1 shows.

Table 1 gives some statistics on relevant documents in the WT10G collection. The characteristic C is the relevant document distribution.

$T = \{451, \cdots, 500\}$, D is WT10G and $\mid D \mid= 1,692,096$, $\sum_{t \in T} \mid R(t) \mid= 2,371$

Query Building. From the TREC9 topics, we manually built a request set for querying the collection. A request is a list of key-words based on the topic title, the description and the narrative of the relevant documents awaited for this topic as provided by TREC. For the topic 460 for example:

<top>
<num> Number: 460
<title> Who was Moses?
<desc> Description: Find documents that discuss the biblical figure of Moses.
<narr> Narrative: A relevant document includes any information concerning Moses and his deeds regarding the Israelites.
</top>

We built the request "*Moses Israelites bible biblical*" (title (Moses), description (biblical, bible) and narrative (Israelites)). Table 2 shows the statistics on the number of key-words for the queries we built.

Table 2. Some statistics on our queries: number of words per topic

Min	Max	Average
2	8	4.76

Relevant Document Distribution on WT10G. We studied the per topic relevant document distribution within the WT10G collection. This distribution is plotted on Fig. 2. The relevant documents distribution over WT10G is unspecified and it varies according to topics. Relevant documents For a given topic are not uniformly distributed. The number of relevant documents is not a linear function of the collection size. Given that we will subdivide our test collection in sub-collections of growing size, it is important to take into account the documents distribution on each sub-collection so that the properties we want to study (precision and recall for example) remain meaningful as the sub-collections size grows. We thus redistributed the relevant documents within the collection.

3.2   The Uniform WT10G

We redistributed the relevant documents within WT10G collection to obtain a uniform collection. In this new collection, the number of relevant documents for a given topic is a linear function of the collection size and the total number of relevant documents (for all the topics) is also a linear function of the collection size.

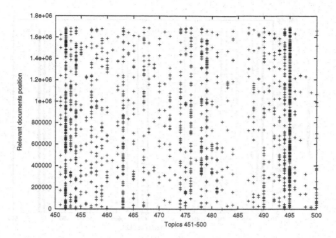

Fig. 2. Relevant documents per topic distribution (initial collection)

For example, the topic number $t = 495$ has 487 documents considered to be relevant, then $E(t)$ is equal to $\frac{(1,692,096-2,371)}{487} = 3,469$

For the WT10G collection, $E_r(t) \leq E(t) + 2,371$. This introduces a skew on the uniformity of our distribution but given the total number of documents in the collection (1,692,096 documents), this skew is not significant. This skew has no influence on the uniformity of the distribution of relevant documents which we want to draw up on the test collection. When the whole collection is split into sub-collections, the size of these sub-collections remains big enough to allow us to continue neglecting the skew. Moreover, this skew is a compromise to obtain a collection within which the relevant documents are at the same time distributed uniformly for each topic and are distributed uniformly (with little near) if the whole set of the topics is considered.

Figure 3 shows the distribution of relevant documents on the uniform collection. In the uniform collection, the relevant documents for a given topic are distributed in a uniform way on the collection and the relevant documents (all topics fused) are distributed in a uniform way on the collection. Thus, whatever the collection portion selected, the number of relevant documents (either all topics fused or topic by topic) is proportional to the portion size.

3.3   Sampling Uniform WT10G

Within the framework of our experiments, we built portions of increasing size with a variation of 200,000 documents by taking the documents in the order of appearance in the collection. We obtained 8 portions and we worked on 7 of them (The portions we worked on are size 200,000 documents to size 1,400,000 documents). However, the choice of the variation can be modified according to experiments needs. One could split out the whole collection into N sub-collections of equal size and then mix those N sub-collections in various ways to obtain col-

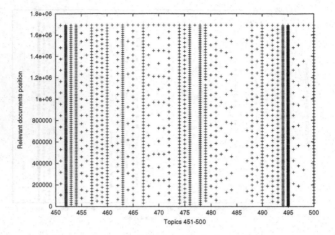

Fig. 3. Relevant documents per topic distribution (uniform collection)

Table 3. Uniform WT10G: statistics on documents size for every sub-collection

Sub-collection size	Min size	Max size	Empty doc	Average size(Avr)	doc size <=Avr	doc size>Avr
200,000	3	2,326,790	3	3,875.22	155,090	44,910
400,000	3	2,326,790	14	4,103.59	314,199	85,801
600,000	3	2,326,790	21	3,902.08	468,430	131,570
800,000	3	2,344,747	29	3,876.66	628,158	171,842
1,000,000	3	2,344,747	33	3,857.18	785,360	214,640
1,200,000	3	2,344,747	34	3,766.91	943,802	256,198
1,400,000	3	2,344,747	36	3,773.19	1,101,592	298,408
1,600,000	3	2,344,747	38	3,790.24	1,260,289	339,711

lections of various sizes since it is known that the number of relevant documents on a portion is proportional to its size.

4   Using Uniform Collection to Study Scalability Impact

4.1   IR Models Used

We used five IR models for our experiments:

- The LUCY tool [15] we used implements the Okapi model, which is an extension of the probabilistic model.
- We used the tool MG [16] which is based on the vector model.

The 3 other models are based on the proximity between the request term; the implementations we used are described with more details in [17].

- The Cover Density Ranking method [18] rank the relevant documents according to "the density of cover" of the request keywords in the documents. We call this method *Clarke model*.

- For the method proposed in [19], a request is a set of tuples (U, A) composed of a set of terms U and an importance coefficient A. Each element of $I(U, A)$ (set of documents intervals which contains all terms of U) takes part in the relevance score of the document. We call this method *Hawking model*.
- The method in [20] allots to each document, for a given request, a score computed by adding the Okapi model score and a proximity score. We call this method *Rasolofo model*.

4.2   Precision /Recall Graphs

Assumptions. When the relevant documents are not distributed in a uniform way on the collection, it is difficult to evaluate the impact of increasing the collection size on precision and recall. If the relevant documents are distributed in a uniform way on the collection, then the precision for a given level of recall is the same never mind that one works on the whole collection or on one of its samples.

Recall/precision curves for the 5 IR models we used are plotted on Fig. 4 (Clarke model), Fig. 5 (Hawking model), Fig. 6(Okapi model as implemented in the Lucy tool), Fig. 8 (vector model as implemented in MG tool) and Fig. 7 (Rasolofo model).

Hawking model and Clarke model : for the first recall level, recall/precision curves for big collections are very close. For high recall level, the curves remain close. This means that those models have a certain *stability* regarding the precision/recall measure when the collection size increase. For the two models, the retrieval status value (RSV) for a document does not depend on the collection; it depends only on the document content and on the query.

For the OKAPI model (Fig. 6), the precision/recall ratio is much better for big collections than for small ones for the first recall level. When recall level

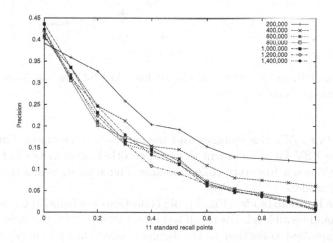

Fig. 4. Recall/Precision curves on the uniform WT10G for our 7 collection sizes - Clarke IR model

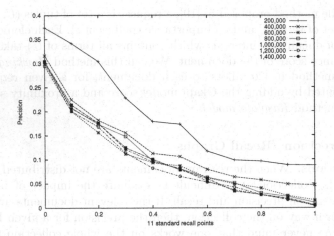

Fig. 5. Recall/Precision curves on the uniform WT10G for our 7 collection sizes - Hawking IR model

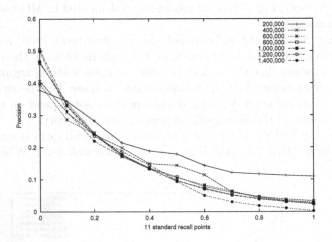

Fig. 6. Recall/Precision curves on the uniform WT10G for our 7 collection sizes - Okapi IR model from Lucy Tool

increases (up 10%), this changes and the curves become closer. For the OKAPI model, the RSV for a document depends on others documents in the collection. So the RSV is not free from collection size. The *stability* is less than for the two preceding models.

For the Rasolofo model (Fig. 7), big collections are below the small collections for very small recall level. For recall level from 10% to 30%, the curves are ordered from the smallest collection to the biggest collection and curves are not close. For big collections, curves start to be close from 30% recall. This model combines the proximity between query's terms in a document and the Okapi model to give

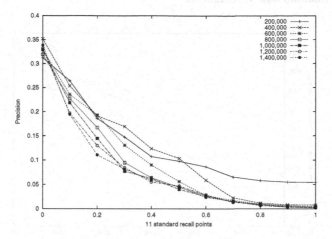

Fig. 7. Recall/Precision curves on the uniform WT10G for our 7 collection sizes - Rasolofo IR model

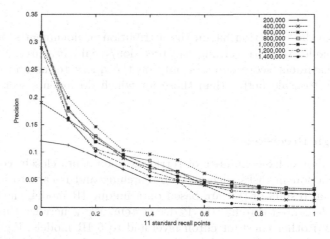

Fig. 8. Recall/Precision curves on the uniform WT10G for our 7 collection sizes - Vectorial IR model from MG tool

an RSV to a document. So, it combines a method for which a document's RSV depend on the collection and a method for which a document's RSV depend only on the document and the query. Its *stability* starts at high recall level.

For the vector model (Fig. 8), big collections curves are close for small recall level (until 10%). The order between curves according to the collection size changes from a recall level to another. This implies a certain *instability* regarding the precision/recall measure when the collection size increase. The RSV given to a document by this model depends on query's term frequency in the document (*tf*) and on inverse document frequency (*idf*). The *idf* depends on the collection.

400   A. Imafouo and M. Beigbeder

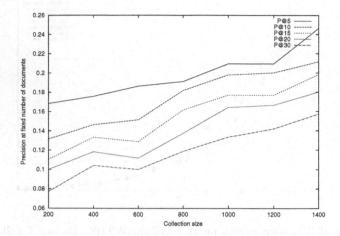

Fig. 9. Precision on first documents retrieved on the uniform WT10G for our 7 collection sizes (Collection size/1000) - Clarke IR model

The role the collection has in the attribution of document scores affect the way the model scale (regarding the precision/recall measure). IR models for which a document score depends only on the query terms and on the document seam to scale better than those for which documents score depends on collection.

4.3   High Precision

Precision after a fixed number of retrieved documents closely correlates with user satisfaction in tasks such as Web searching and is easy to interpret. The experimental results of [13] are based on a unique IR model, the Okapi BM25 model implemented through the Padre system. We generalize this results to 4 (5, 10, 15, 30) other constant cutoff level and to 5 IR models. Figure 9 (Clarke model)show the evolution of these precisions when the collection size grows. For the four others model we used, the curves shape are similar to those of Clarke model Fig.9. These results show that the precision on the first retrieved documents increases with the sample size selected. [13] conclude that this increase is due to two main factors: the number of relevant documents in a portion of the collection (This number increases with the portion size) and to the ability of the couple (E, Q) (where E is the search engine and Q the query)to rank relevant documents ahead of irrelevant ones.

We also notice that for a given sub-collection, $P@n \leq P@m$ if $n < m$. Thus for each one of the studied sub-collection, $P@5 \leq P@10 \leq P@15 \leq P@20 \leq P@30$ for all the IR models on which we experimented contrary to what one would have expected intuitively.

5   Discussion and Conclusions

The methodology proposed in this work build a collection on which a given characteristic C is the same whatever be the portion of collection selected. This new collection is called uniform (according to the characteristic C) and can be split in sub-collection of growing size on which some given properties will be studied. This methodology is general and reproducible.

We apply our methodology and consider the characteristic C to be the distribution of relevant documents on a collection. We uniformize WT10G, sample it into sub-collections of increasing size and study the impact of corpus volume increase on some standards IRS evaluation measures. We noticed that IR models for which a document score depends only on query terms and on the document seam to scale better than those for which documents score depends on collection. We are interested to know more about how the collection role on the attribution of document RSV influences the IR models scalability. Our results for precision at a constant cutoff level(5, 10, 15, 30) generalize those of [13] and we extend them to various IR models.

We are now using the uniform WT10G collection to study the scalability impact on others IR models properties, like the position of the first relevant document retrieved, other IR measures (R-precision, the Mean Average Precision) or new measure like bpref [21] that seam to be robust to incomplete relevance judgments.

While information grows continuously, it becomes important to know what impact the scalability has on retrieval models to improve these models and ensure they scale correctly. The methodology we propose is a general one. We believe it can be used to build others "uniform" collections according to some others characteristics (proportion of query terms when evaluating relevance feedback algorithms for example) and to use these new collections to study the scalability impact on IR models.

References

1. Voorhees, E., Harman, D.: Overview of the sixth text retrieval conference (trec-6). In: NIST Special Plublication 500-420-The Sixth text retrieval Conference. (1997)
2. Zobel, J.: How reliable are the results of large scale information retrieval experiments. In: Proceedings of the 21th ACM SIGIR Conference on research and development in information retrieval. (1998) 307–314
3. Cormack, G., Palmer, C., Clarke, C.L.A.: Efficient construction of large test collections. In: Proceedings of the 21st annual international ACM SIGIR conference on Research and development in information retrieval. (1998) 282–289
4. Soboroff, I., Nicholas, C., Cahan, P.: Ranking retrieval systems without relevance judgments. In: Proceedings of the 24th annual international ACM Conference on research and Development in Information Retrieval. (2001) 66–73
5. Voorhees, E.: Variations in relevance judgments and the measurement of retrieval effectiveness. Information and Processing Management (2000) 697–716

6. Frieder, O., Grossman, D.: On scalable information retrieval systems. In: Invited Paper, 2nd IEEE International Symposium on Network Computing and Applications., Massachusett, Cambridge (2003)
7. Gurrin, C., Smeaton, A.: Replicating web structure in small-scale test collections. Information retrieval **7** (2004) 239–263
8. Chevallet, J.P., Martinez, J., Boughanem, M., Lechani-Tamine, L., Calabretto, S.: Rapport final de l'AS-91 du RTP-9 'passage à l'échelle dans la taille des corpus' (2004)
9. Witten, I.H., Moffat, A., Bell, T.C. In: Managing Gigabytes - Compressing and indexing documents and images. Second edn. Morgan Kaufman Publishers (1999) 451–468
10. Newby, G.B.: The science of large scale information retrieval. Internet archives (2000)
11. Beigbeder, M., Mercier, A.: Etude des distributions de tf et de idf sur une collection de 5 millions de pages html. In: Atelier de recherche d'informations sur le passage à l'échelle Congrès INFORSID 2003, Nancy, France (2003)
12. Hawking, D., Thistlewaite, P.: Scaling up the trec collection. Information retrieval **1** (1999) 115–137
13. Hawking, D., Robertson, S.: On collection size and retrieval effectiveness. Information retrieval **6** (2003) 99–105
14. Bailey, P., Craswell, N., Hawking, D.: Engineering a multipurpose test collection for web retrieval experiments draft. In: Proceedings of the 24th annual international ACM SIGIR conference. (2001)
15. (http://www.cs.mu.oz.au/mg/)
16. (http://www.seg.rmit.edu.au/lucy/)
17. Mercier, A.: Etude comparative de trois approches utilisant la proximité entre les termes de la requête pour le calcul des scores des documents. In: INFORSID 2004 - 22ème congrès informatique des organisations et des systèmes d'information et de décision. (2004)
18. Clarke, C.L.A., Cormack, G., Tudhope, E.: Relevance ranking for one to three term queries. Information Processing and Management **26** (2000) 291–311
19. Hawking, D., Thistlewaite, P.: Proximity operators - so near and yet so far. In: Proceedings of the Fourth Text Retrieval Conference TREC-4. (1995) 131–143
20. Rasolofo, Y., Savoy, J.: Term proximity scoring for keyword-based retrieval systems. In: Proceedings of European Conference on Information Retrieval Research. (2003) 207–218
21. Voorhees, E., Buckley, C.: Retrieval evaluation with incomplete information. In: Proceedings of the 27th annual international conference on Research and development in information retrieval. (2004) 25–32
22. Lyman, P., Varian, H.R., Swearingen, K., Charles, P., Good, N., Jordan, L.L., Pal, J.:   How   much   informations   2003. http://www.sims.berkeley.edu/research/projects/how-much-info-2003/ (2003)
23. (http://trec.nist.gov/)

The Role of Multi-word Units in Interactive Information Retrieval

Olga Vechtomova

Department of Management Sciences, University of Waterloo,
Waterloo, Canada
ovechtom@engmail.uwaterloo.ca

Abstract. The paper presents several techniques for selecting noun phrases for interactive query expansion following pseudo-relevance feedback and a new phrase search method. A combined syntactico-statistical method was used for the selection of phrases. First, noun phrases were selected using a part-of-speech tagger and a noun-phrase chunker, and secondly, different statistical measures were applied to select phrases for query expansion. Experiments were also conducted studying the effectiveness of noun phrases in document ranking. We analyse the problems of phrase weighting and suggest new ways of addressing them. A new method of phrase matching and weighting was developed, which specifically addresses the problem of weighting overlapping and non-contiguous word sequences in documents.

1 Introduction

Multiword units (MWUs), also commonly referred to in IR literature as 'phrases'[1], received much attention in information retrieval research throughout its more than 30-year old history. This interest can be partially attributed to the fact that phrases typically have a higher information content and specificity than single words, and therefore represent the concepts expressed in text more accurately than single terms. Ideally document and query representations should be mapped directly and unambiguously to the underlying concepts conveyed in text. However, at present, this still remains a difficult goal to reach. Most of the leading statistical IR models, such as probabilistic [1,2] and vector-space [3] rely on the use of single terms and are based on strong term independence assumptions to make them computationally tractable. Experimentally these models have consistently demonstrated high performance results with a variety of large test collections in the evaluation exercises such as TREC [4]. Nevertheless, many attempts have been made to introduce phrases into the retrieval process, but so far with mixed results.

MWUs comprise a wide variety of lexical associations with various degrees of idiomaticity or compositionality, such as named entities ('Tony Blair', 'United Nations'), nominal compounds ('amusement park', 'free kick') and phrasal verbs

---

[1] We will use these terms interchangeably throughout the paper.

D.E. Losada and J.M. Fernández-Luna (Eds.): ECIR 2005, LNCS 3408, pp. 403–420, 2005.

('reach out', 'kick the bucket'). Although MWUs can belong to different lexical categories, our focus is on nominal MWUs, primarily because nouns and noun phrases are considered to be the most content-bearing syntactic category. Also, there is some evidence from previous research that noun phrases hold more promise for query expansion in IR [5].

Query expansion is a widely used technique in IR. In automatic query expansion (AQE) additional terms or phrases are added to the original query by the system, whereas in interactive query expansion (IQE) users select terms or phrases manually. Terms and phrases for query expansion can be retrieved using statistical or linguistic methods from a variety of sources, the most common being top-ranked documents in the retrieved set (blind or pseudo-relevance feedback) and documents judged relevant by the user in the retrieved set (relevance feedback). Single-term interactive query expansion techniques were extensively evaluated in the past [24, 25]. Some researchers investigated the use of phrases in IQE (see section 2.3), however no systematic comparison of different types of phrases in IQE has been conducted so far. In this work we are interested in studying how different types of phrases can help users to interactively enhance their initial search formulation.

This paper has two foci:

1. To investigate the utility of multiword units (MWUs) in interactive query expansion;
2. To study the effectiveness of MWUs in the document ranking.

The main goal of the first focus of this study was to investigate the following hypotheses:

Hypothesis 1: Nominal MWUs are better candidates for interactive query expansion than single terms.

Hypothesis 2: Nominal MWUs which exhibit strong degree of stability in the corpus are better candidates for interactive query expansion than noun phrases selected by the frequency parameters of the individual terms they contain.

We used a combined syntactico-statistical approach for selecting nominal MWUs for interactive query expansion. In the first selection pass, noun phrases were obtained using a part-of-speech (POS) tagger and a noun phrase chunker. In the second pass, statistical measures were applied to select strongly bound MWUs. In particular, we have experimented with two statistical measures to select MWUs from text: the C-value [6] and the Log-Likelihood [7]. Selected MWUs were then suggested to the user for interactive query expansion. Techniques developed for the selection of MWUs are presented in section 3. Experiments investigating the above hypotheses and evaluation results are described in section 5.

The goal of the second focus of this work is to study the effectiveness of noun phrases in document ranking. We contribute to the previous findings in the field by further analysing the problems of phrase matching and weighting and suggesting new ways of addressing them. The following hypothesis was investigated:

Hypothesis 3: Ranking documents using phrases leads to better performance than ranking documents by single terms.

We have developed a new method of phrase-based document ranking, which specifically addresses the problem of weighting overlapping phrases in documents, which in statistical IR models like probabilistic ones [2] leads to the problem of the artificial over-inflation of the document score. The method is described in detail in section 4.

2 Previous Research

2.1 Statistical Versus Syntactical Phrases

Hypotheses claiming that phrases are better contents discriminators than single terms have been studied since the beginning of research on automated IR in the 60s. Simple statistical co-occurrence based techniques for identification of phrases have always been rivalled by NLP-based techniques. The main considerations in favour of NLP were: (1) it may have better tools to uncover meaningful linguistic phrases and (2) it can capture the syntactical relationships between words.

Statistical phrases are typically short-span collocations extracted from text using different modulations of their frequency parameters. Syntactical phrases are identified using a variety of NLP methods ranging from low-level techniques such as part-of-speech tagging, aimed at identifying word-sequences of a certain syntactic pattern like adjective + noun, to more complex methods like extended N-grams and shallow syntactic parsing, attempting to discover uniform semantic units underlying various forms of expression.

At the early stages the motivation for research on automatic phrase generation came from the determination to emulate human indexing. The belief was that complex normalising descriptions of the kind assigned to documents by human indexers are more useful than simple terms. One of the early experiments on phrase indexing was carried out by Bely [8], who used very elaborate NLP techniques to identify instantiations of thesaurus concepts and their semantic relationships in documents. Despite the fact that no retrieval evaluation was conducted, the research suggested that the relational structure of the descriptions was not flexible enough for sufficient matching. Another historically important piece of research was undertaken by Salton [11], whose technique consisted in identification of thesaurus terms in text supported by syntactic analysis. The comparison of performance results for syntactic phrases and for statistical phrases, defined as within-sentence co-occurrences of thesaurus descriptor constituents, showed that there was no performance improvement in using syntactical phrases over simple statistical phrases.

One of the most comprehensive early evaluations of phrases in IR was undertaken by Fagan [9,10]. The main focus of his experiments was systematic evaluation of statistical phrases under different parameter settings, such as distance between their constituents and their frequency values. The evaluation results showed that performance for statistical phrases was in general better than for single terms. He then compared performance for statistical phrases with performance for syntactical phrases, which he obtained using syntactic parsing, stemming and normalisation to head-modifier pairs. The evaluation showed that linguistically-derived phrases gave results similar to or worse than statistically extracted phrases. When he analysed earlier work taking into account his findings, he concluded that the same pattern, statistical phrases ≥ syntactical phrases ≥ single terms, was evident in all the experiments. The performance gains from the use of statistical phrases obtained in his experiment were in the range of 17% to 39%. He concluded that syntactical phrases gave poor performance because queries and documents did not share exactly the same phrases. Among the reasons for the systems' inability to match documents and queries by syntactic phrases, Fagan pointed out the low collection frequency of the best phrases and the fact that the documents involved were abstracts. Stzalkowski et al. [12] pointed to another main reason for this, namely, the limited amount of information about the user's information need conveyed by the queries.

It is worthwhile to note that the above earlier studies of phrases in IR were undertaken on rather small collections (for example Fagan used a 10MB CACM collection of abstract-length documents). The last decade in IR research saw two major changes: (1) statistical models using single term weighting have been refined to achieve very high and robust performances; (2) the size of test collections has grown dramatically. Some of the phrase indexing and search techniques which used to work well with the old retrieval techniques on small collections, no longer give positive results.

More recent study of syntactic and statistical phrases was undertaken by Mitra et al. [13]. By statistical phrases they understood contiguous bigrams of non-stopwords which occur in at least 25 documents. Syntactical phrases were defined in their experiments as specific POS-tag sequences (e.g. Noun-Noun, Adjective-Noun). Their studies demonstrate that overall both statistical and syntactical phrases have very little effect on performance. Syntactical phrases showed marginally better performance than statistical phrases when used on their own (i.e. without single terms) in retrieval. An interesting finding, which emerged from their study, is that phrases tend to improve precision at higher recall levels, and have little or no effect on precision at lower recall levels. This suggests that phrase search may not prove to be a "precision-enhancing technique", but rather a "recall-enhancing technique".

2.2 Phrase Weighting

We consider that one of the major and yet unsolved problems of phrase-based techniques is weighting. Phrases like single terms vary in their contents-discriminating ability, so it may be possible to treat a phrase in the same way as a single term, and calculate, for example, its inverse document frequency (idf) in the same manner. However phrases also have other characteristics, which single terms do not have, and which may need to be reflected in their weighting. One of the most prominent characteristics of phrases is the degree of the stability in the corpus. We distinguish the following types of phrases by their stability in the corpus:

1. Combinations of terms which occur only with each other in many document collections, for example "Burkina Faso".
2. Combinations of terms which frequently occur together as a phrase and whose syntactic structure does not permit any changes (i.e. intervening words, change of word order), for example "amusement park", "stainless steel", "acrylic paint". Typically, one or all terms in such phrases may form lexical-syntactic constructions with other terms as well. If the expression has some degree of idiomaticity (i.e. the phrase as a whole has a different meaning than the combination of individual meanings of its parts), for example "Mad Cow Disease", we may not be able to substitute all or some of the words with related or synonymous words without the radical change of meaning. For example we cannot substitute "mad" with "crazy" in the above example.
3. And finally combinations of terms which have strong degree of flexibility, namely allow intervening words, change of word order, substitution of phrase components with synonyms, hypernyms or hyponyms. For example the exact meaning underlying the phrase "animal protection" can be also represented in text as "protection of animals". The word "animal" can be substituted with hyponyms, such as "reptile" or "mammal".

The above categorisation of phrases has the following implications for IR:

– If the search on one term is highly likely to match on the entire phrase (what is typically the case with the phrases of the first category and some phrases of the second category above), then applying phrase search techniques will not be useful.
– If we search by a phrase belonging to the third category, it may be beneficial to relax search constraints to accommodate possible lexical-syntactic variations of the phrase. With this category of phrases, it may even be useful to relax search constraints to allow match on terms separated by longer distances, in order to capture within-topic relations between terms, rather than only phrasal relations.

The integration of phrase-search into the IR models, which were designed for single-term indexing and searching, is problematic. For example a probabilistic model of IR [2] calculates the document score by non-linearly combining weights of query term occurrences in the document. Phrases may be treated by the model in the same way as single terms, however Robertson et al. [14] pointed at the following problem: considering that a query may contain both single terms and phrases, and that some of the single terms may also be part of phrases, then the document matching on the phrase will also match on the single term. As a result both the weight of the phrase occurrence and the weight of the term occurrence will contribute to the document score, artificially inflating it. The solution suggested in [14] was to subtract the weight of the single term occurring in the query from the weight of the phrase, containing that term.

In this paper we examine phrase-weighting further and point at another problem that needs to be addressed, namely when the query contains two or more phrases which share one/more terms. In particular this situation can happen following query expansion, where the user or the system selects a number of phrases to be added to the original query. An example of such phrases is: "stainless steel" and "steel manufacturing". If these phrases match the contiguous string "stainless steel manufacturing" in text, then we face a similar problem of over-inflating the document score as pointed at in [14]. This problem, however, cannot be solved using their technique. We propose a new method of phrase matching and weighting in the document, which attempts to address this problem. The technique is presented in section 4.

2.3 Use of Phrases in Interactive Query Expansion

Phrases can play a useful role in interactive query expansion by helping the users to formulate their information need, in particular when the information need is vague, and the users do not know what exactly they are trying to find. Marchionini [15] and Smeaton and Kelledy [16] have argued that the process of formulating the query is more cognitively demanding on the part of the user than the process of selecting terms and phrases from the list, as the former involves recall, while the latter – recognition. According to cognitive psychology findings, recall is more demanding than recognition. Therefore in real-world search applications users prefer to formulate terse search statements, which tend to produce poor results, and then browse through the retrieved documents, finding more words and phrases and manually reformulating their queries. Extracting related terms/phrases from the documents retrieved by the original query and showing them to the user facilitates this process as the user does not have to go through large amounts of text.

Smeaton and Kelledy [16] have experimentally studied the usefulness of statistically-selected phrases in interactive query expansion. In particular they compared the effectiveness of user-selected phrases in search with the user-selected single terms and their combinations. They also looked at the differences between these techniques when used by novice and expert searchers. The best results are obtained when phrases are used in combination with single terms. Also phrase-based query expansion tends to be less effective with the novice searcher than the expert searcher.

The contribution of our study to the field of interactive query expansion is that we systematically evaluated the effect of different types of phrases and single terms on retrieval performance in the large-scale TREC experimentation settings.

3 Query Expansion Methods

In this section we describe the developed techniques for interactive query expansion using MWUs following blind feedback. The idea of blind (pseudo-relevance) feedback is to take top-ranked documents, retrieved using the original user's query and extract query expansion terms/phrases from them. Our approach is to extract query expansion phrases from query-biased summaries of the n top-ranked documents. We used a method proposed in [17] of building query-biased summaries which are composed of m sentences selected using two main factors: (1) the idf weights of the original query terms present in the sentence, and (2) information value of the sentence, i.e. the combined $tf.idf$ value of its words.

In our experiments we used 2-sentence summaries of the 25 top-retrieved documents[2]. We then apply Brill's rule-based tagger [18] and the BaseNP noun

---

[2] These parameters showed good performance in the past experiments [17].

phrase (NP) chunker [19] to extract noun phrases from the document summaries. Multi-word units are then selected from the list of obtained noun phrases using the C-value and the Log-Likelihood. The two subsections below describe these techniques.

3.1 Selection of Query Expansion Phrases Using the C-Value

MWUs are characterised foremost by relative stability in the corpus. Some of the noun phrases output by the NP chunker are chance word groupings, and not stable MWUs. We were interested in exploring the value of MWUs compared to all noun-phrases in representing useful query expansion concepts to the user. The method of selecting stable MWUs from noun phrases using C-value is outlined below.

Noun phrases output by the NP chunker are ranked by the average *idf* of their constituent terms. For each phrase we generate the list of all phrases that it subsumes, i.e. contiguous or non-contiguous combinations of words in forward order, including the original complete phrase. For each subphrase, the C-value is calculated. The C-value is a measure of stability of an n-gram in the corpus [6]. The C-value formula we used is as follows [26]:

$$C - value\ (a) = (length\ (a) - 1)(\ freq\ (a) - \frac{t(a)}{c(a)})\qquad(1)$$

Where:
$t(a)$ – frequency of the phrase a in longer phrases;
$c(a)$ – number of longer phrases including a;
$freq(a)$ – frequency of the phrase a in the corpus;
$length(a)$ – number of words in the phrase a.

All subphrases for a given phrase are ranked by the C-value. The top-ranked subphrase is then used to replace the original phrase in the list of candidate query expansion terms. The original complete phrase may get a higher C-value than any of its subphrases, in which case it is kept without changes.

For example, in our experiment, the bigram "World Cup" received the highest C-value out of all its subphrases generated from the phrase "grueling IAU 100-kilometer World Cup" and as a consequence was selected for the phrase list.

Some of the original noun phrases may contain intervening modifiers which are too specific. The reason why we considered non-contiguous word combinations is to eliminate such modifiers and to obtain the most stable and recurrent word combinations. The problem, however, is that some of the resulting phrases are too general (e.g. original phrase: *freak training accident*, selected sub-phrase: *freak accident*), or may have weak or no semantic relatedness to the original phrase (e.g., original phrase: *Moroccan born American runner Khalid Khannouchi*; selected sub-phrase: *born American*). As a result we may have strong topic drift and precision loss at the expense of having linguistically correct MWUs. We did not experiment with using only contiguous word combinations, which might help avoid some of the above problems, but remain for future work.

The obtained phrases are then ranked by their C-value, top n of which are shown to the user for interactive query expansion. Table 1 shows the 15 top-ranked phrases selected for the topic 404 "Marathon Training".

Table 1. Top 15 subphrases ranked by C-value and the original phrases from which they were derived (topic "Marathon Training")

Selected sub-phrase	Original phrase
World Cup	grueling IAU 100-kilometer World Cup
web site	marathon's web site
San Diego	San Diego Rock Roll Marathon
York City	York City Marathon
Olympic Games	Athens Olympic Games
training camp	training camp
world title	world half marathon title Paula Radcliffe
Athens Olympics	Athens Olympics
Medical Association	International Marathon Medical Directors Association
World Athletics	World Masters Athletics
Training Center	Duoba National Plateau Training Center
Olympic team	Olympic marathon team Athletics Kenya
training base	altitude training base
world's fastest	world's fastest
Road Race	25-kilometer 10-kilometer Road Race

3.2 Selection of Query Expansion Phrases Using the Log-Likelihood Ratio

The Log-Likelihood [20] has been extensively used for the identification of statistically significant word collocations in text and has shown good results for English.

$$Loglike\ (a,b) = 2 \times (\log \theta_1^{s1}(1-\theta_1)^{n1-s1} + \log \theta_2^{s2}(1-\theta_2)^{n2-s2}$$
$$- \log \theta^{s1}(1-\theta)^{n1-s1} - \log \theta^{s2}(1-\theta)^{n2-s2}) \tag{2}$$

Where:

$$s1 = f(a,b) \qquad s2 = f(b) - f(a,b)$$
$$\theta_1 = \frac{s1}{n1} \qquad \theta_2 = \frac{s2}{n2} \qquad n1 = f(a) \qquad n2 = N - f(a)$$
$$\theta = \frac{f(b)}{N}$$

N – number of words in the corpus;
$f(a,b)$ – frequency of words a and b appearing together in text;
$f(a)$ – frequency of a; $f(b)$ – frequency of b.

The phrase weighting is done as follows: first, from each phrase output by the NP chunker all contiguous bigrams are derived. For each bigram, its Log-Likelihood score is calculated using the Ngram Statistics Package [21]. The highest Log-Likelihood score of any bigram derived from the phrase is taken as the phrase weight. Top n phrases ranked using this weighting scheme are shown to the user for interactive query expansion. This is a rather crude phrase weighting method, but it does reward phrases which contain a strongly bound collocation which stands as a focus of our experiment.

4 Phrase-Based Document Retrieval

Following the interactive query expansion stage where the users select query expansion phrases, the next step is to use them in search. Intuitively using them as phrases in search should lead to better precision than if we split them into single words. One problem associated with the use of phrases in a statistical IR model, such as probabilistic [2] is that some terms may occur in multiple phrases. For example, we assume there are two phrases in the expanded query: *"air traffic"* and *"traffic control"*, and two documents: the first containing one phrase *"air traffic control"*, and the second – two phrases *"air traffic"* and *"traffic control"*. How should they be weighted? If we calculate weights of each phrase in the document separately and then add them up to get the document score, as is currently done in the probabilistic model for single terms, then both documents would get equal scores. That obviously should not be the case. But then how should the phrase weight be calculated for the first document? The situation gets more complex if we allow for non-contiguous word combinations, i.e. matching the following: *"1 air 2 traffic 10 control"* (where numbers denote positions of the words in text). Allowing match on non-contiguous word combinations is good for recall as it relaxes search constraints, but the distance between the phrase elements should be inversely related to the phrase weight. Therefore, the two main issues to be addressed by the phrase search algorithm are:

- remove the problem of overlapping phrases;
- reflect the distance between the phrase elements in the phrase weight.

We have developed the following phrase search algorithm, which attempts to address the above problems:

The first step is to retrieve a set of documents using a best-match document retrieval function[3] and a query which consists of all single terms extracted from the query expansion phrases. The next step is to re-rank these documents by using phrase information. We take the top 1000 documents per topic in the retrieved set, stem the terms in each document and create a document representation, consisting only of the stemmed occurrences of terms from the query in their original order and their sequential position number in text.

For each query phrase, all possible subphrases (i.e. contiguous and non-contiguous, ordered and non-ordered combinations of words) are generated and recorded in the list ranked in the descending order of their length. For each subphrase in the list we use *cgrep* – a pattern matching program for extracting minimal matching strings [22] to extract the minimal spans of text in the document containing the subphrase. Each time cgrep returns matching strings, they are removed from the document representation and the procedure is repeated with the same phrase. If no matching

---

[3] We used the Okapi BM25 search function [2].

string is found, the program attempts to match the next phrase in the list, and so on. In this way we can match progressively longer spans containing the phrase or its subphrases. An example of extracted windows for the phrase "practical implementation" is given in figure 1 (the number preceded by the '#' sign is the sequential position of the following word in the original document text).

```
# 106 implementation # 120 practical
# 120 practical # 186 implementation
# 4 implementation
# 21 implementation
# 43 implementation
# 59 implementation
```

Fig. 1. An example of windows extracted from a document

As we can see, windows extracted using the above method might overlap. Our approach to eliminating overlaps in windows is a two-step process: (1) rank the windows by their weight and (2) remove overlapping words from the lower ranked windows.

4.1 Window Weighting

In this approach the window weight is calculated from the combination of *idf* weights of individual terms occurring in it. The following formula was used:

$$WindowWeight(w) = \sum_{i=1}^{n} idf_i \times \frac{n}{(span+1)^p} \qquad (3)$$

Where:
i – word in the window w;
n – number of words in the window w;
$span = pos(n) - pos(1)$
where: $pos(i)$ – position number of the ith word in the window w;
p – tuning parameter[4].

So, the more informative the words in the window are, the shorter the span is, and the more words there are in the window, the higher is the weight of the window.

4.2 Removing Duplicate Windows

After the windows are ranked, we remove overlapping words by doing pairwise comparison of all windows. If two windows have overlapping word(s), these words are removed from the lower ranked window. The windows shown in figure 1 after the removal of overlapping words are illustrated in figure 2.

---

[4] Experiments showed that 0.2 gives the best performance on the HARD track 2003 corpus.

```
# 106 implementation # 120 practical
# 4 implementation
# 21 implementation
# 43 implementation
# 59 implementation
# 186 implementation
```

Fig. 2. An example of windows after the removal of overlapping words

All windows extracted for every phrase from the document are then added to the same list, weighted using the formula (3) above and have the overlapping words removed. For each window we also keep the index of the phrase which was used to extract it.

4.3 Calculating Document Scores

The next step is to calculate document scores. First, for each phrase in the query we calculate its weight in the document as follows:

$$PhraseWeight(a) = \frac{(k+1) \times \sum_{w=1}^{n} WindowWeight(w)}{k \times NF + n} \qquad (4)$$

Where:
  w – window, extracted for the query phrase a;
  n – number of windows extracted for the phrase a;
  NF – document length normalisation factor (see equation 5 below).
  k – phrase frequency normalisation factor[5].

The document length normalisation factor was calculated in the same way as in the BM25 document ranking function [2]:

$$NF = (1-b) + b \times \frac{Doclen}{AveDocLen} \qquad (5)$$

Where:
  $Doclen$ – document length (word count);
  $AveDoclen$ – average document length in the corpus;
  b – tuning constant[6].

Document score is then calculated as the sum of *PhraseWeight* values for all query phrases that occur in the document:

$$DocumentScore(d) = \sum_{a=1}^{n} PhraseWeight(a) \qquad (6)$$

---

[5] Experiments showed that k=1.2 gives the best performance on the HARD track 2003 corpus.
[6] Spärck-Jones et al. have experimentally determined that 0.75 gives best results on TREC data [2].

Where: a – the query phrase occurring in the document d;

   n – number of query phrases occurring in the document d.

Finally the top 1000 documents in the originally retrieved set are re-ranked by the new document scores.

5   Evaluation

The testbed for our experiments is the Okapi IR system based on the Robertson/Spärck Jones probabilistic model of retrieval [2]. The evaluations of the developed techniques were conducted within the framework of the HARD (High Accuracy Retrieval from Documents) track of TREC 2004 [23, 27]. The HARD track evaluation framework includes an interactive component, which allowed us to test interactive query expansion techniques. The interactive evaluation experiment consists of the following steps:

1. TREC organisers release the search statements (topics) formulated by the annotators (users) in the traditional TREC format (Title, Description and Narrative) to the participating sites.
2. Participating sites use any information from the topics to produce the initial (baseline) document sets and compose clarification forms for the user to fill in. The purpose of clarification forms is to clarify or refine the annotator's search statement.
3. The annotator fills out clarification forms (with a 3-minute time limit per form).
4. Participating sites use the annotator's feedback to the clarification forms to improve the search (for example by query expansion). The end result is a new document set.
5. The annotator performs relevance judgements of the retrieved sets[7].

The HARD track test collection includes the document corpus (635,650 documents from eight newswire collections) and 50 topics. In addition to the traditional TREC topic fields of Title, Description and Narrative, the topics also contained several Metadata fields, describing various additional search criteria, such as "genre", "retrieval element" and "familiarity". We did not use any of the metadata except "retrieval element" in the runs reported here. In all expansion runs for topics with the retrieval element "Document" we used the Okapi document retrieval function BM25, and for topics with the retrieval element "Passage" we used the Okapi passage retrieval function BM250.

We conducted two baseline runs using only the information available in the TREC topics: in the run *baseTD*, we used all non-stopword terms extracted from the Title and Description fields of the topic and in *baseT*, we used all terms from the Title field only. For both runs we applied Okapi BM25 search function.

---

[7] Top 75 documents from two runs per site were added to the relevance judgement pool. Each document in the pool was assigned a binary relevance judgement. The same annotator who formulated the topic provided feedback to all clarification forms for that topic and performed relevance judgements.

Four clarification forms were generated for each topic. Phrases for each clarification form were extracted from 2-sentence query-biased summaries [17] of the top 25 documents retrieved in the run *baseTD*, as Title+Description gave higher performance than Title on HARD 2003 data.

- 1st *clarification form:* top n phrases selected using the C-value method (section 3.1 above);
- 2nd *clarification form:* single terms from the phrases displayed in the 1st clarification form;
- 3rd *clarification form:* top n phrases output by the NP chunker and ranked by the average *idf* of their constituent terms;
- 4th *clarification form:* top n phrases selected using the Log-Likelihood ratio (section 3.2 above).

The 2nd clarification form was introduced in order to investigate Hypothesis 1 (section 1), which suggests that users select better terms when they are shown to them in the context of phrases (in the 1st clarification form), than separately. By comparing the phrases selected from the 3rd clarification form with the 1st and 4th we aim to investigate Hypothesis 2, which suggests that the application of the measures of phrase stability in the corpus leads to better phrases for query expansion.

Five query expansion runs were conducted. Runs 1, 2, 3 and 4 used the feedback provided by the users to the 1st, 2nd, 3rd and 4th sets of clarification forms accordingly. In each run the query was constructed by splitting the phrases selected by the user from the corresponding clarification form into single terms and adding them to the original query terms. Each term in the expanded query was weighted in Okapi using pseudo-relevance data[8]. The BM25/BM250 search function was then used to search the query against the database. Run 5 was conducted using the developed phrase search algorithm. Here for each topic we take the top 1000 documents retrieved in the run 1 (i.e. using single terms from the user-selected phrases from the 1st clarification form) and re-rank them using the method presented in section 4.

6 Results

The results of the evaluation are presented in table 1. All expanded runs significantly improve the performance over the baseline run BaseTD (t-test at .05 significance level).

Retrieval performance of the expanded queries created from the user feedback to clarification forms 1 and 2 is very similar. This suggests that users tend to select similarly good terms whether they are shown to them in the context of phrases or on their own. Hypothesis 1, formulated in the beginning of the paper, is therefore not supported. On average users selected 21 phrases from the 1st clarification form and 27 single terms from the 2nd form. There were 675 phrase-terms selected only from the 1st form, 384 terms selected only from the 2nd form and 921 terms selected from both forms.

---

[8] The number of documents used in the blind feedback was used as the number of known relevant documents.

Table 2. Results of the runs, averaged over all topics

Run	Precision at 10 documents	Average Precision
Baseline, Title terms (**BaseT**)	0.3089	0.2196
Baseline, Title + Description (**BaseTD**)	0.42	0.2693
Single-term search, Query expansion with phrases from clarification form 1 (**ExpRun1**)	0.4889	0.3176
Single-term search, Query expansion with terms from clarification form 2 (**ExpRun2**)	0.48	0.3026
Single-term search, Query expansion with phrases from clarification form 3 (**ExpRun3**)	0.4911	0.3191
Single-term search, Query expansion with phrases from clarification form 4 (**ExpRun4**)	0.4689	0.3019
ExpRun1 reranked using the phrase-search algorithm (**ExpRun5**)	0.4422	0.3233

There is also negligible difference between the performance of the queries from phrases selected using the average *idf* of their terms (ExpRun3) and queries from phrases selected using the measures of phrase stability in the corpus: the C-value (ExpRun1) and the Log-Likelihood ratio (ExpRun4). This suggests that the statistical component of phrase selection does not play an important role when it is combined with syntactical phrase selection techniques, such as POS-tagging and NP-chunking. Hypothesis 2 is, therefore, not supported.

Table 3. Precision at various recall levels of the single-term search method (ExpRun1) and the phrase search method (ExpRun5)

Recall level	ExpRun1	ExpRun5
at 0.00	0.6606	0.6259
at 0.10	0.5713	0.5182
at 0.20	0.4852	0.4614
at 0.30	0.4263	0.4316
at 0.40	0.3782	0.3882
at 0.50	0.3392	0.3553
at 0.60	0.2749	0.3027
at 0.70	0.2222	0.25
at 0.80	0.1671	0.188
at 0.90	0.096	0.1241
at 1.00	0.0456	0.0774

The phrase search algorithm (ExpRun5) did not demonstrate improvement in the average precision or precision at 10 documents over the performance of the single-term search method (ExpRun1). While average precision increased slightly (1.8%), precision at 10 documents dropped by 9%. The use of phrases improved average precision in 17 topics and degraded precision in 28 topics. The average gain was 56%, while the average loss was 24%. More interesting results, however, emerge from the analysis of precision at various recall levels (table 3).

At low recall levels, precision of the single-term run is higher, but beginning from 30% recall, the precision of the phrase-based run starts to exceed the precision of the single-term run. These results are consistent with the results evidenced in the earlier studies [13]. The likely explanation of this pattern, suggested in [13], is that in the single-term retrieval documents at high ranks tend to contain a large number of different single terms with high *idf*, therefore the likelihood is high that they cover the topic of the query. However, at lower ranks the number of single term matches is much lower and, therefore, there are more possibilities for topic drift. Phrases usually have much higher weight than single terms, therefore they tend to dominate the document match. At higher ranks this may have a negative effect of over-emphasising a single aspect of the query, whereas at lower ranks phrase-match helps to promote documents with few good matches on phrases and demote documents with matches on single terms which can be peripheral to the query topic.

The results of the phrase-based search experiments partially support Hypothesis 3: precision at high recall levels is better than in the single-term search, whereas precision at low recall levels is inferior.

We performed a detailed analysis of phrase search in one topic (429) "Biodynamic and organic farming". The user has selected 38 phrases with an average length of 2 words. The single-term search retrieved 31 relevant documents with the average precision of 0.46. Re-ranking the retrieved document set by phrases improved average precision to 0.56. Upon detailed examination of the results it was observed that 17 relevant documents were promoted on average 70 ranks higher in the ranked set, whereas 14 documents were demoted on average 127 ranks lower. The phrase search method tends to rank higher those documents which match few phrases completely and ranks lower the documents which match more phrases, but mostly by one term. The rationale of this approach to ranking is that in the latter case we have less supporting evidence that the matching single term is related to the concept expressed in the query phrase. In some documents, however, this approach fails. For example, one of the relevant documents retrieved for the topic 429 was demoted from rank 53 to 349 because it matched predominantly one term per query phrase. For example the phrase "sustainable development" matched only instances of "sustainable", which however was used in related context in phrases such as "sustainable growing" and "sustainable production". Another document, however, was promoted from rank 542 to 62 because it matched many complete phrases either in contiguous positions or separated by a few words.

We are currently experimenting with various parameters of the phrase-search algorithm in order to understand its behaviour better and possibly to obtain better results. One of the parameters is the maximum span for phrase match. In the reported experiments we did not set any span limit. The rationale for this was to capture not only phrasal, but also within-topic relations between terms. So, a document which contains two terms from the same phrase in one paragraph is possibly more likely to be relevant than a document which contains these terms in different sections. However, this approach may be more useful with long multi-topic documents, rather than short documents. Since HARD track collection consisted mainly of short news articles, this aspect of the phrase search method is unlikely to help distinguish between relevant and non-relevant documents more than single-term match would do. So, setting the span limit to only capture phrasal relations between terms may be sufficient.

7   Conclusions

In this paper we presented a comparative evaluation of different phrase selection techniques in interactive query expansion and a phrase-based document ranking method. A combined syntactico-statistical method was used for the selection of phrases. First, noun phrases were selected using a part-of-speech tagger and a noun-phrase chunker, and secondly, different statistical measures were applied to select phrases for query expansion. Three selection methods were used: C-value, Log-Likelihood ratio and the average *idf* of phrase terms to select phrases, which were then shown to the user for interactive query expansion. Evaluation experiments did not demonstrate substantial difference between these statistical methods in their effect on retrieval performance.

We also studied whether users select better terms when they are shown in the context of phrases, than separately. The users were asked to select query expansion items from two clarification forms: one with the complete phrases selected by the C-value, and the other with the single terms from these phrases. The two query expansion runs gave very similar results, which suggests that presenting terms in the context of phrases does not provide more help to the users in selecting good query expansion terms.

The phrase-based document ranking method demonstrated high precision gains at higher recall levels and losses in precision at lower recall levels as compared to single-term document ranking. We are currently working on improving our phrase-weighting formulae. As discussed earlier in the paper, phrases differ by their stability in the corpus, therefore they should not be treated uniformly in search. For example, a document which has a partial match on a non-compositional or idiomatic phrase (e.g. "Salt Lake City") is more likely to be non-relevant, than a document that has a partial match on a non-idiomatic expression (e.g. "organic product"). Therefore the weight of the partially matching phrase should be reduced more in the first case than in the second. One of the extensions of this work will be to use measures of phrase stability to estimate phrase weight in the documents.

References

1. Robertson S.E., Spärck Jones K. Relevance Weighting of Search Terms. Journal of the American Society for Information Science, 27 (1976) 129–146
2. Spärck Jones, K., Walker, S. and Robertson, S.E. A probabilistic model of information retrieval: development and comparative experiments. Information Processing and Management, Vol. 36, n. 6, (2000) 779–808 (Part 1); 809–840 (Part 2)

3. Salton, G; Wong, A.; Yang, C. S. A vector space model for information retrieval. Communications of the ACM, Vol. 18, n.11 (1975) 613–620
4. Voorhees E. and Buckland, L. (Eds.) Proceedings of the Twelfth Text Retrieval Conference, NIST, Gaithersburg, MD, 2004
5. Xu J. and Croft B. Query expansion using local and global document analysis. In Proceedings of the 19th International Conference on Research and Development in Information Retrieval (SIGIR '96), Zurich, Switzerland (1996) 4–11
6. Frantzi, K.T. and Ananiadou, S. Extracting nested collocations. In Proceedings of the 16th Conference on Computational Linguistics, COLING (1996) 41–46
7. Dunning, T. Accurate methods for the statistics of surprise and coincidence. Computational Linguistics, Vol. 19, n. 1 (1993) 61–74
8. Bely, N., Borillo, A., Virbel, J. and Siot-Decauville, N. Procédures d'analyse sémantique appliquée à la documentation scientifique. Paris: Gauthier (1970)
9. Fagan J.L. Automatic Phrase Indexing For Document Retrieval: An Examination Of Syntactic And Non-Syntactic Methods. In Proceedings of the Tenth ACM SIGIR Conference on Research and Development in Information Retrieval, New Orleans (1987) 91–108
10. Fagan J.L., The effectiveness of a nonsyntatic approach to automatic phrase indexing for document retrieval, Journal of the American Society for Information Science, Vol. 40 n. 2 (1989) 115–132
11. Salton, G. and Lesk M.E. Computer Evaluation of Indexing and Text Processing Journal of the ACM (JACM), Vol. 15 , n. 1 (1968) 8–36
12. Strzalkowski T. Perez-Carballo J. Evaluating natural language processing techniques in information retrieval. In: Strzalkowski, T. (Ed.) Natural language information retrieval. Kluwer Academic Publishers (1999) 113–145
13. Mitra, M., Buckley, C., Singhal, A. and Cardie, C. An Analysis of Statistical And Syntactic Phrases. In Proceedings of RIAO97, Computer-Assisted Information Searching on the Internet, Montreal, Canada (1997) 200–214
14. Robertson, S.E., Zaragoza, H. and Taylor, M. Microsoft Cambridge at TREC-12: HARD track. In Proceedings of the Twelfth Text Retrieval Conference, Voorhees, E. and Buckland, L., (Eds.), NIST, Gaithersburg, MD, (2004) 418–425
15. Marchionini, G. Interfaces for End-User Information Seeking. Journal of the ASIS Vol. 43, n. 2 (1992) 156–163
16. Smeaton, A. F. and Kelledy, F. User-Chosen Phrases in Interactive Query Formulation for Information Retrieval, In Proceedings of the 20th BCS-IRSG Colloquium, Grenoble, France, Springer-Verlag Workshops in Computing (1998)
17. Vechtomova, O., Karamuftuoglu, M., Lam, E. Interactive Search Refinement Techniques for HARD Tasks. In Proceedings of the Twelfth Text Retrieval Conference, Voorhees, E. and Buckland, L., (Eds.), NIST, Gaithersburg, MD, (2004) 820–827
18. Brill, E. Transformation-based error-driven learning and natural language processing: a case study in part of speech tagging. Computational Linguistics, Vol. 21, n. 4 (1995) 543–565
19. Ramshaw, L. and Marcus, M. Text Chunking Using Transformation-Based Learning. In Proceedings of the Third ACL Workshop on Very Large Corpora, MIT (1995)
20. Manning, C.D., Schütze, H. Foundations of Statistical Natural Language Processing. The MIT Press, Cambridge, Massachusetts (1999)
21. Banerjee, S. and Pedersen, T. The Design, Implementation and Use of the Ngram Statistics Package. In Proceedings of the Fourth International Conference on Intelligent Text Processing and Computational Linguistics, Mexico City (2003)

22. Clarke, C.L.A. and Cormack, G.V. On the use of Regular Expressions for Searching Text. University of Waterloo Computer Science Department Technical Report number CS-95-07, University of Waterloo, Canada (1995)

23. Allan, J. HARD Track Overview in TREC 2003 High Accuracy Retrieval from Documents. In Proceedings of the Twelfth Text Retrieval Conference, Voorhees, E. and Buckland, L., (Eds.), NIST, Gaithersburg, MD, (2004) 24-37

24. Beaulieu, M. and Jones S. Interactive searching and interface issues in the Okapi best match probabilistic retrieval system. Interacting with Computers. Vol. 10, n. 3 (1998) 237–248

25. Ruthven I. Re-examining the potential effectiveness of interactive query expansion. Proceedings of the 26th ACM-SIGIR conference, Toronto, Canada (2003) 213–220.

26. Vintar Š. (2004) Comparative Evaluation of C-Value in the Treatment of Nested Terms. In Proceedings of MEMURA 2004 Workshop (Methodologies and Evaluation of Multiword Units in Real-world Applications), Language Resources and Evaluation Conference (LREC), Lisbon, Portugal (2004) 54-57.

27. Vechtomova O., Karamuftuoglu M., Approaches to High Accuracy Document Retrieval in HARD Track. To appear in Proceedings of the Thirteenth Text Retrieval Conference, Voorhees, E. and Buckland, L., (Eds.), NIST, Gaithersburg, MD (2005).

Dictionary-Based CLIR Loses Highly Relevant Documents

Raija Lehtokangas, Heikki Keskustalo, and Kalervo Järvelin

Department of Information Studies,
FIN-33014 University of Tampere, Finland
{Raija.Lehtokangas, Heikki.Keskustalo, Kalervo.Jarvelin}@uta.fi

Abstract. Research on cross-language information retrieval (CLIR) has typically been restricted to settings using binary relevance assessments. In this paper, we present evaluation results for dictionary-based CLIR using graded relevance assessments in a best match retrieval environment. A text database containing newspaper articles and a related set of 35 search topics were used in the tests. First, monolingual baseline queries were automatically formed from the topics. Secondly, source language topics (in English, German, and Swedish) were automatically translated into the target language (Finnish), using both structured and unstructured queries. Effectiveness of the translated queries was compared to that of the monolingual queries. CLIR performance was evaluated using three relevance criteria: stringent, regular, and liberal. When regular or liberal criteria were used, a reasonable performance was achieved. Adopting stringent criteria caused a considerable loss of performance, when compared to monolingual Finnish performance.

1 Introduction

A lot of CLIR research has been carried out during the last years, see, e.g., TREC [15], CLEF [3], and NTCIR [10]. The research is, however, mainly based on binary relevance assessments. So there is not sufficient knowledge on how CLIR methods treat documents of various relevance levels. In this paper, we concentrate on this aspect of CLIR performance evaluation. At NTCIR, empirical results with graded relevance assessments have been presented (see, e.g., [17], [4]), but these results have not been interpreted from the point of view we have in this paper. We compare dictionary-based CLIR performance between different levels of relevance and also analyze failures in retrieving highly relevant documents.

Using binary relevance assessments (documents are either relevant or non-relevant) ignores the fact that documents are to different degrees relevant with respect to search requests - considering a marginally relevant document as valuable as a highly relevant one. This is a real problem since a majority of documents relevant in a database may be only marginally relevant [14]. Normally, searchers prefer documents with a higher degree of relevance. In the present information overload it is more vital than ever to be able to pick the best documents. So, degrees of relevance should be taken into account when evaluating IR systems and

D.E. Losada and J.M. Fernández-Luna (Eds.): ECIR 2005, LNCS 3408, pp. 421–432, 2005.
© Springer-Verlag Berlin Heidelberg 2005

methods, and systems and methods able to retrieve the most valuable documents should be credited for this.

Evaluation of IR methods and systems by various relevance levels has recently become possible for two reasons. First, evaluation methods for handling graded relevance data have been developed [6], [7]. Secondly, test collections exist that provide graded relevance assessments [13], [14], [8], [9], [16].

This paper presents novel CLIR results based on graded relevance assessments. Our main research question is how well dictionary-based CLIR is able to find documents relevant to different degrees, in particular highly relevant documents. A four-point relevance scale is used in the tests: documents in the test database are highly, fairly or marginally relevant, or non-relevant. CLIR performance is evaluated under three conditions: 1) *stringent* (only highly relevant documents are accepted) 2) *regular* (both highly and fairly relevant documents accepted), 3) *liberal* (highly, fairly and marginally relevant documents accepted). Moreover, performance is evaluated by generalized precision and recall [7] using varying weighting schemes for documents of different levels of relevance.

CLIR performance is evaluated in a laboratory setting, using a best match retrieval system (InQuery) and a test database consisting of Finnish newspaper articles. CLIR queries, having English, German and Swedish as source languages, are translated into the target language by an automated process using morphological analyzers, machine-readable dictionaries and stopword lists. *n*-Gram techniques are applied to words that are untranslatable by the dictionaries. Both structured and unstructured target queries are used.

We are able to show the graded relevance assessment performance for dictionary-based CLIR. Likewise we are able to show that CLIR performs on a reasonable level when *liberal* or *regular* relevance criteria are used. When *stringent* criteria are used to evaluate the same queries, a loss of performance is observed.

The paper is organized as follows: test design is presented in Section 2 and findings in Section 3. In Section 4 findings are further discussed. Section 5 concludes the paper.

2   Test Design

2.1   Test Collection

The target database consists of 53,893 Finnish newspaper articles from three newspapers [13] [7]. As Finnish is a highly inflectional language and rich in compounds (words written together as singular units), a morphological analyzer was used in index building. Words recognized by the analyzer were normalized into their basic forms in the index, and in addition to this, compounds were split. Finally, all words not recognized by the analyzer were put into the index as such (thus typically in inflected forms). The resulting index contains about

241,000 unique recognized words (or compound components) in basic forms and about 118,000 unique unrecognized word forms.

There are 35 test topics, each expressing a search request in 1-4 sentences. The themes of the topics are distributed as follows: person (5 topics), organisation (12), geographical place (10), general theme (8). The topics are originally expressed in Finnish, but have been translated by professional translators into English, German and Swedish.

2.2   Graded Relevance Assessments

A recall base has been collected for the 35 topic requests by extensive pooling. With respect to the 35 requests, altogether 17,338 documents have been evaluated by human assessors using a 4-point relevance scale. Four relevance judges were employed, and the relevance of 20 requests was assessed by two persons, and the remaining 15 requests by one person. [13], [6]

A 4-point scale was used in the relevance assessments. Relevance level 0 is used to denote non-relevant documents not about the subject of the request. Relevance level 1 denotes marginally relevant documents – documents referring to the request but not giving more information than the request itself. Relevance level 2 is used to denote fairly relevant documents – documents that contain some new facts with regard to the request. Finally, relevance level 3 is used to denote highly relevant documents - documents that contain valuable information with regard to the request. [13]

The relevance assessors agreed in 73 % of the parallel assessments. In 21 % of the cases the difference was one point. In the remaining 6 % of the cases the difference was two or three points. Disagreements in judgments were resolved in the following way: if the difference was one point, the assessment was selected from each judge in turn. If the difference was two or three points, the researcher made the final decision about the relevance level. [6]

As a result of the relevance evaluations for the 35 requests, 444 documents are considered highly relevant (relevance level 3), 829 documents fairly relevant (level 2), and 993 documents marginally relevant (level 1). Thus, the recall base contains 2,266 documents evaluated as relevant for the 35 topics. The rest of the database is considered to contain only non-relevant documents with respect to the topics (relevance level 0).

2.3   Resources Used

The retrieval system used in the experiments was *InQuery*, a probabilistic retrieval system provided by the Center for Intelligent Information Retrieval at the University of Massachusetts [2].

Inquery queries are either natural language queries (e.g. English sentences) or structured queries. Structured queries are constructed by using, e.g., the operator *syn*, which treats all of its arguments as instances of one search key. All operators are preceded by the hash sign #, and the arguments are delimited by parentheses, e.g. *#syn(ship vessel boat)*. If no operator is given, the operator *sum* is used as default. This treats all of its arguments as having an equal influence on the result.

Large machine-readable dictionaries, provided by Kielikone plc., Finland, were used for the word-by-word translations in the language routes *English to Finnish*, *German to Finnish*, and *Swedish to Finnish*. For normalizing source and target language words, morphological analyzers provided by Lingsoft plc., Finland, were used in the respective languages. Novel stop word lists were designed for the present study. Number of words in the stop word lists are as follows: English (402 words), Finnish (737), German (637), Swedish (658).

2.4   Monolingual Queries

The monolingual queries used as the baseline of the study were formed automatically from the topics by normalizing each word into its basic form by using a morphological analyzer and forming an *InQuery* synonym set (*#syn*) from the normalized forms (each word having possibly multiple lemmas). If a word was not recognized by the analyzer, approximate string matching was applied to find the most similar strings from the target index. We used skip-grams (see [12]) for selecting the two best matching strings. Finally, stop words were removed.

As an example, after processing the Finnish topic *OPEC:n öljyn hintaa ja tuotantomääriä koskevat päätökset (The decisions of OPEC concerning oil prices and production levels)* the following baseline query (in *InQuery* syntax) was formed:

> *#sum(#syn(opec) #syn(n) #syn(öljy) #syn(hinta) #syn(tuotantomääri) #syn(tuotantomäärä) #syn(päätös))*

In the example above, the words *OPEC, öljyn* (inflected word form referring to *oil*), *n* (genetive suffix), *hintaa* (inflected word form referring to *price*), *tuotantomääriä* (inflected form referring to *production volume*) and *päätökset* (inflected form referring to *decision*) are normalized successfully. (Note that the word *tuotantomääriä* generates two normalized word forms, *tuotantomääri* and *tuotantomäärä*.) The remaining query words are stopwords (*ja* meaning *and, koskevat* - inflected form referring to *related*). Thus they are removed from the query.

2.5   Translated Queries

The translated queries were formed automatically by translating the topics in English, German and Swedish into Finnish. The query translation framework UTACLIR is based on ideas presented originally in [5]. In the present study, the details of the translation process were fine-tuned using training data. The basic idea of the processing is to utilize morphological analysis for normalizing source words into basic forms, split the untranslatable source compounds into components, and utilize machine-readable dictionaries for bilingual word-by-word translations for translatable words. For untranslatable words, approximate string matching is used for finding, with respect to the source word, the most similar words from the target database index. As in the monolingual case, stop words are removed. Stop word lists are applied for both source and target language words during the translation process. [11]

As an example, after translating the Swedish topic *OPEC:s beslut om priset och produktionsmängderna för olja* the following translated query (in *InQuery* syntax) is formed:

#sum(#syn(opec roope) #syn(päätöksenteko päätös ratkaisu tuomio) #syn(arpoa arvo hinta kunnia palkinto ylistys) #syn(produktio tuotanto valmistua valmistus) #syn(ainemäärä erä joukko määrä paljous suuruus) #syn (rasvata voidella öljy öljytä))

In the example above, the untranslatable Swedish word *OPEC* is replaced in translation by the first synonym set containing approximate string match results *opec* and *roope*. The source word *beslut* (*decision*) is translatable and is translated by the second synonym set containing the correct dictionary translations (*päätöksenteko*, etc.) for the word. The next word is a stopword (*om* meaning *about*) and is removed. The source word *priset* (inflected form of *pris* meaning *price*) can be normalized and translated, and it is replaced by the third synonym set of the query above. The next source word is a stopword (*och* meaning *and*) and is removed. The next word *produktionsmängderna* is an inflected compound which is untranslatable as a whole. It is automatically split into components (*produktion, mängd*) which are individually translated (corresponding fourth and fifth synonym sets in the translated query). Next word is a removable stop word (*för* meaning *for*). Finally, the word *olja* (*oil*) is translated. Compared to the monolingual case, the synonym sets formed by the translations typically include several words (see Section 3).

2.6   Source Query Word Types

The following source query word types are automatically recognized and processed accordingly in query translation [5]:

- Stop words: source query words belonging to the source stop lists are omitted first. Also, a target stop word list (Finnish) was used to remove remaining stop words from the translated query in each translation route.
- Recognized translatable words: these source words are recognizable (included in the lexicon of the morphological analyzer) and translatable (included in the translation dictionary). They are translated, and the translations are treated as synonyms (connected with *InQuery's* synonym operator).
- Recognized untranslatable and unsplittable words: these source word are untranslatable and cannot be split by the morphological analyzer. Typically, this kind of words include proper names and they occur because of the relatively large lexicon of the morphological analyzer. As translation is not possible, approximate matching is performed instead to find the most similar strings from the target index.
- Recognized and untranslatable but splittable words: source words belonging to this type are compounds not included in the translation dictionary as

whole words. These words are split and translation is attempted for the components.

- Unrecognized but translatable words. These words are rare, because typically the morphological analyzers do recognize translatable words. In case such source words exist, they are translated.
- Unrecognized and untranslatable words: typically these words are proper names, acronyms, scientific terms, rare words or new words of the language. As direct translation is not possible, approximate matching is performed as in the third case above.

3 Findings

3.1 Structured Runs

General properties with respect to the number of words and synonym sets in the (structured) target queries are presented in Table 1. As we can see, the number of synonym sets varies. Also, in some language routes, the average number of words in a synonym set is larger. On the average, English as a source language produced the largest synonym sets.

The effectiveness results of the monolingual and bilingual structured runs are presented in Table 2, separately for highly relevant (*stringent* relevance criteria accepting relevance level 3 - *Rel = 3* in Table 2), fairly and highly relevant (*regular* criteria: *Rel = 2,3*), and marginally, fairly and highly relevant (*liberal* criteria: *Rel = 1,2,3*) documents. When all the levels are studied together, difference between the baseline monolingual run and the bilingual runs ranges from -11 % to -19 %. As for the levels 2 and 3, the difference between the monolingual and the bilingual runs is slightly greater, ranging from -14 % to -21 %. The results of the relevance level 3 are clearly the worst, -21 % to -35 % below the monolingual baseline.

Above effectiveness was evaluated using binary relevance (yet separately for different relevance levels or their combinations). Performance of the runs was also evaluated using generalized precision and recall [7]. By this measure effectiveness can, taking the different degrees of relevance into account, be expressed in one single value. Relevance values originally given to the documents can be reweighted, thus allowing experiments with different user scenarios.

Weighting reflects how documents at different levels of relevance are valued in relation to each other (e.g., if highly relevant documents are valued 10 times

Table 1. General properties of the structured queries (monolingual and translated)

Language route	Topics	Words	Synonym sets	Words/Synonym set
Finnish to Finnish	35	479	459	1.04
English to Finnish	35	5390	517	10.4
German to Finnish	35	2479	616	4.02
Swedish to Finnish	35	1959	647	3.03

Table 2. Effectiveness of structured target queries at three relevance tresholds (non-interpolated average precision)

Language route, Rel = 3	Average precision	Difference	Difference (%)
Finnish-Finnish	28.4	-	-
Swedish-Finnish	20.7	-7.7	-27.1
English-Finnish	22.5	-5.9	-20.8
German-Finnish	18.5	-9.9	-34.9
Language route, Rel = 2,3	Average precision	Difference	Difference (%)
Finnish-Finnish	36.9	-	-
Swedish-Finnish	31.9	-5.0	-13.6
English-Finnish	31.3	-5.6	-15.2
German-Finnish	29.2	-7.7	-20.9
Language route, Rel = 1,2,3	Average precision	Difference	Difference (%)
Finnish-Finnish	37.6	-	-
Swedish-Finnish	33.4	-4.2	-11.2
English-Finnish	32.8	-4.8	-12.8
German-Finnish	30.3	-7.3	-19.4

Table 3. Effectiveness of structured target queries using different weighting schemes for relevance levels (generalized interpolated average precision (GP) over 11 recall points)

Language route	GP (w=1,1,1)	Difference (%)	GP (w=3,2,1)	Difference (%)
Finnish-Finnish	39.5	-	31.5	-
Swedish-Finnish	34.9	-11.6	26.2	-16.8
English-Finnish	34.5	-12.7	26.8	-14.9
German-Finnish	32.5	-17.7	24.5	-22.2
Language route	GP (w=10,4,1)	Difference (%)	GP (w=100,10,1)	Difference (%)
Finnish-Finnish	27.8	-	26.2	-
Swedish-Finnish	21.6	-22.3	18.7	-28.6
English-Finnish	23.2	-16.6	20.7	-21.0
German-Finnish	20.5	-26.3	17.3	-34.0

as much as marginally relevant, the former get the weight 10, the latter 1). If all the relevance levels is given the same weight, we have the normal binary relevance situation.

Results using generalized precision and recall are presented in Table 3. We experimented by giving different weights to the relevance levels, first having the original weights 3, 2 and 1 (3 for highly relevant, 2 for fairly relevant and 1 for marginally relevant documents), then valuing the highly relevant ones more (weights 10,4,1, and 100,10,1). The table presents also the binary relevance situation where all the levels are weighted equally (1,1,1), and for each

Table 4. Effectiveness of unstructured target queries at three separate relevance tresholds (non-interpolated average precision)

Language route, Rel = 3	Average precision	Difference	Difference (%)
Finnish-Finnish	28.1	-	-
Swedish-Finnish	15.0	-13.1	-46.6
English-Finnish	14.5	-13.6	-48.4
German-Finnish	12.1	-16.0	-56.9
Language route, Rel = 2,3	Average precision	Difference	Difference (%)
Finnish-Finnish	36.8	-	-
Swedish-Finnish	25.5	-11.3	-30.7
English-Finnish	18.1	-18.7	-50.8
German-Finnish	17.9	-18.9	-51.4
Language route, Rel = 1,2,3	Average precision	Difference	Difference (%)
Finnish-Finnish	37.6	-	-
Swedish-Finnish	26.3	-11.3	-30.1
English-Finnish	18.3	-19.3	-51.3
German-Finnish	19.0	-18.6	-49.5

language pair the difference to the monolingual baseline. It can be seen that the more the highly relevant documents are weighted in relation to the less relevant ones, the bigger is the difference to the baseline. This is in line with what was observed about the lower performance for the highly relevant documents (Table 2).

3.2   Unstructured Runs

The results of the unstructured translated queries are presented in Table 4. (The only distinction between the structured and unstructured runs is the non-use of synonym sets in the target queries in the latter.) On the whole, the performance level of the unstructured queries is lower, measured both in absolute figures and in relation to the the monolingual baseline. However, differences between the relevance levels are smaller in comparison to the structured queries when measured as a difference to the baseline (and averaged over the three runs at each level). At all relevance levels, runs with English as source language are most affected by not using query structuring in the target queries. There is a clear connection here to the number of words in the different runs: the number of words is by far the largest in the English-Finnish run (see Table 1). Runs with Swedish as source language are remarkably less affected, again the number of words in the Swedish-Finnish target query is clearly smaller than elsewhere.

4   Discussion

In our experiments, dictionary-based CLIR was performed under three conditions: 1) *stringent* (only highly relevant documents are accepted), 2) *regular* (fairly and highly relevant documents accepted), and 3) *liberal* (marginally, fairly and highly relevant documents accepted). It was found that reasonable CLIR performance can be achieved if liberal or regular relevance criteria are used. Instead, if stringent criteria are used, i.e. when only highly relevant documents are accepted, as high performance cannot be achieved.

A random sample of 76 highly relevant documents ranked low (representing 30 topics) from the Swedish-Finnish run was selected for a further study. Rankings of these documents ranged from 51 to 983. The vocabulary of the documents was studied to find possible reasons why these documents did not match with the queries and were thus not retrieved earlier.

A quite common reason for a mismatch between a query and a newspaper article is that newspaper articles take up specific, concrete things whereas topics express the same on a more general level. For example, talking about environmental investments of the forest industry (the exact wording of a topic), articles may mention by name individual paper mills and real measures taken there - without at all telling that these measures are environmental investments or anything like that.

It was also noticed that the right sense may be expressed in the document but by a word not in a right form, e.g. a verb may be used in a document when a noun would be needed. Talking, e.g., about incidence of AIDS, all the studied documents (three) used only verb forms ('sairastavat', 'sairastavan' etc., meaning 'to suffer from a disease') referring to 'disease' whereas there was a noun ('sairaus') in the query. A normalized index requires the use of precisely the right part-of-speech in the query, as words representing different parts-of-speech normally get separate entries in the index (here: 'sairaus' and 'sairastaa, respectively). Also, the wording of topics is often quite scarce, so additional words might be needed in the query. Depending on the situation, these could be in hierarchical, associative or synonymous relationship to the words of the original query.

What was said above implies to modifications in queries. Of the two main components in the retrieval process - query and document - attention is here paid to the former because it is the query that is modifiable in the short run. To find out reasons for late rankings in our document sample, we experimented with modifications of the original target queries and tried to raise the rankings of the late retrieved documents. It was decided that the rankings should fall in the range of 1 to 50 after the modifications. There were 76 documents in the sample, and the ranking of all but three documents could be raised. Only modifications that could be carried out without hurting the overall performance of the query (measured in average precision) were accepted (i.e., the performance of the modified query needed to be higher than that of the original query). Sometimes one measure was enough, sometimes two or three different measures together were needed. For each document, all the measures (or combinations of them) that could be found were listed. These lists are, of course, not exhaustive, but could possibly be supplemented. Altogether, there were 196 occurrences of measures (occurring either separately or with others). In 59 % of the occurrences, a word or more had to be added to the query. In 16 % of the occurrences, the wording of the original topic had to be changed, and in 10 %, the dictionary had failed: either an entry or a translation equivalent was missing. In 8 % of the occurences, there was a special problem connected with a group of compound words, and in 7 %, there were problems with proper names (either proper names were incorrectly interpreted as common nouns of the source language and translated as such, or the inflected forms brought by the n-gram process were not exactly those present in the document).

Above, notable is the large proportion of word additions, over half of all occurrences. In 17 % of word additions, the added word and a word in the original query were words of the same root (e.g., one was a derivative of another, or both were derivatives of the same word). This kind of additions could be produced automatically, on the basis of the original query. However, an overwhelming majority of the words added (83 %) did not have a direct relation to the wording of the original target query. Words of this kind should be picked from external sources. Altogether, it should be noted that word additions in these experiments were done intellectually, knowing the vocabulary of the document in question and trying numerous word combinations. Without prior knowledge of the vocabulary in the documents it would have been, in most cases, impossible to know which words to add. It is possible that adding words automatically would not be as successful in raising the rankings of late retrieved documents. Therefore it remains an issue whether source or target language query expansion (see [1]) would increase query effectiveness regarding highly relevant documents.

Further research is needed to find out why retrieving highly relevant documents was not as successful as retrieving fairly and marginally relevant documents. When the same queries retrieve documents of other relevance levels quite successfully, it is an interesting question why they fail with respect to the highly relevant ones. Is there something inherent in the highly relevant documents that makes the difference?

5   Conclusion

In this paper, dictionary-based CLIR was tested in a best match retrieval environment, using graded relevance assessments. A 4-point relevance scale was used in the test database, which consists of newpaper articles. Source language queries in English, German and Swedish were translated by an automated process into the target language, using morphological analyzers, machine-readable dictionaries, stopword lists, n-gramming of untranslatable words, and structured and unstructured queries. Effectiveness of the translated queries was compared to that of the monolingual queries using *stringent, regular* and *liberal* relevance criteria (*stringent*: only highly relevant documents accepted ; *regular*: highly and fairly relevant documents together accepted; *liberal*: highly, fairly and marginally relevant documents together accepted). Reasonable CLIR performance was achieved when *liberal* or *regular* relevance criteria were used. Instead, when *stringent* criteria were used, i.e. when only highly relevant documents were accepted, equally high performance could not be achieved. When a sample of highly relevant documents ranked low were studied, reasons for the low rankings of these documents were found.

Acknowledgements

The InQuery search engine was provided by the Center for Intelligent Information Retrieval at the University of Massachusetts.

ENGTWOL (Morphological Transducer Lexicon Description of English): Copyright (c) 1989-1992 Atro Voutilainen and Juha Heikkilä. FINTWOL (Morphological Description of Finnish): Copyright (c) Kimmo Koskenniemi and Lingsoft plc. 1983-1993. GERTWOL (Morphological Transducer Lexicon Description of German): Copyright (c) 1997 Kimmo Koskenniemi and Lingsoft plc. SWETWOL (Morphological Transducer Lexicon Description of Swedish): Copyright (c) 1998 Fred Karlsson and Lingsoft plc. TWOL-R (Run-time Two-Level Program): Copyright (c) Kimmo Koskenniemi and Lingsoft plc. 1983-1992. MOT Dictionary Software was used for automatic word-by-word translations. Copyright (c) 1998 Kielikone plc., Finland.

This research was funded by the Academy of Finland, under Project Numbers 177033 and 1209960.

The authors thank the anonymous referees for useful suggestions.

References

1. L. Ballesteros, and W.B. Croft. Resolving Ambiguity for Cross-language Retrieval. In *Proceedings of the 21st Annual International ACM SIGIR Conference on Research and Development in Information Retrieval*, New York, ACM Press, 64–71, 1998.
2. J. Broglio, J. Callan, and W.B. Croft. INQUERY system overview. In *Proceedings of the TIPSTER text program (Phase I)*. San Francisco, CA: Morgan Kaufmann Publishers, 1994.
3. CLEF Homepage. Available: http://clef.iei.pi.cnr.it
4. A. Fujii, and T. Ishikawa. Cross-Language IR at University of Tsukuba: Automatic Transliteration for Japanese, English, and Korean. In *Working Notes of NTCIR-4*, Tokyo, 2-4 June, 2004. Available: http://research.nii.ac.jp/ntcir-ws4/NTCIR4-WN/index.html
5. T. Hedlund, H. Keskustalo, A. Pirkola, M. Sepponen, and K. Järvelin. Bilingual tests with Swedish, Finnish and German queries: dealing with morphology, compound words and query structure. In C. Peters (ed.) *Cross-language information retrieval and evaluation: Proceedings of the CLEF 2000 workshop*, Lecture Notes in Computer Science: 2069, 210–223, 2001.

6. K. Järvelin, and J. Kekäläinen. IR evaluation methods for retrieving highly relevant documents. In *Proceedings of the 23rd Annual International ACM SIGIR Conference on Research and Development in Information Retrieval*, New York, ACM Press, 41–48, 2000.
7. J. Kekäläinen, and K. Järvelin. Using Graded Relevance Assessments in IR Evaluation. *Journal of the American Society for Information Science and Technology*, 53(13): 1120–1129, 2002.
8. K. Kishida et al. Overview of CLIR Task at the Fourth NTCIR Workshop. In *Working Notes of NTCIR-4*, Tokyo, 2-4 June, 2004. Available: http://research.nii.ac.jp/ntcir-ws4/NTCIR4-WN/index.html
9. S. Lee et al. Characteristics of the Korean Test Collection for CLIR in NTCIR-3. In *Working Notes of NTCIR-3*, Tokyo, October 8-10, 2002. Available: http://research.nii.ac.jp/ntcir/workshop/OnlineProceedings3/index.html
10. NTCIR Homepage. Available: http://research.nii.ac.jp/ntcir/index-en.html
11. A. Pirkola, T. Hedlund, H. Keskustalo, and K. Järvelin. Dictionary-Based Cross-Language Information Retrieval: Problems, Methods, and Research Findings. *Information Retrieval*, 4 (3/4), 209–230, 2001.
12. A. Pirkola, H. Keskustalo, E. Leppänen, A.-P. Känsälä, and K. Järvelin. Targeted *s*-Gram Matching: a Novel *n*-Gram Matching Technique for Cross- and Monolingual Word Form Variants. *Information Research*, 7 (2), 2002. Available: http://InformationR.net/ir/7-2/paper126.html
13. E. Sormunen. A Method for Measuring Wide Range Peformance of Boolean Queries in Full-Text Databases. Dissertation. Tampere, University of Tampere, 2000.
14. E. Sormunen. Liberal Relevance Criteria of TREC - Counting on Negligible Documents? In *Proceedings of the 25th Annual International ACM SIGIR Conference on Research and Development in Information Retrieval*, New York, ACM Press, 320–330, 2002.
15. TREC Homepage. Available: http://trec.nist.gov/
16. E. Vorhees. Evaluation by Highly Relevant Documents. In *Proceedings of the 24th Annual International ACM SIGIR Conference on Research and Development in Information Retrieval*, New York, ACM Press, 74–82, 2001.
17. Y. Zhou, J. Qin, M. Chau, and H. Chen. Experiments on Chinese-English Cross-language Retrieval at NTCIR-4. In *Working Notes of NTCIR-4*, Tokyo, 2-4 June, 2004. Available: http://research.nii.ac.jp/ntcir-ws4/NTCIR4-WN/index.html

Football Video Segmentation Based on Video Production Strategy

Reede Ren and Joemon M. Jose

Department of Computing Science,
University of Glasgow,
17 Lilybank Gardens, G12 8QQ, UK
{reede, jj}@dcs.gla.ac.uk

Abstract. We present a statistical approach for parsing football video structures. Based on video production conventions, a new generic structure called 'attack' is identified, which is an equivalent of scene in other video domains. We define four video segments to construct it, namely *play, focus, replay* and *break*. Two middle level visual features, *play field ratio* and *zoom size*, are also computed. The detection process includes a two-pass classifier, a combination of Gaussian Mixture Model and Hidden Markov Models. A general suffix tree is introduced to identify and organize 'attack'. In experiments, video structure classification accuracy of about 86% is achieved on broadcasting World Cup 2002 video data.

1   Introduction

Many techniques have been developed in the literature for football video analysis, starting from shot classification[4] and scene reconstruction[15], to structure analysis[3][5][6], event extraction[9][14] and summarization[7][12]. These approaches primarily focus on visual cues. Ekin et al[12] categorized them into cinematic and object-based ones. Cinematic algorithms utilize features from video composition and production rules, while object-based turns to video object detection. Xu and Lei et al[6] proposed the cinematic feature 'dominant colour ratio' to segment video. They indicated that video reporters have to focus on play yard to convey game status. In [5], they used a set of HMMs to parse broadcasting video into *play* and *break*, where *break* presents a stop of game, while *play* contains normal game clips. Object-based features enable high-level domain analysis, but their extraction may be computationally expensive and sometimes needs manual supervision. Intille[7] and Gong et al[4] analyzed football trajectories and player interactions to detect a large set of semantic events. Both of their work rely on pre-extracted accurate object trajectories. Ekin[12] introduced a framework employing both cinematic and object-based features. It includes low-level football video processing algorithms, such as dominant colour region detection, shot boundary detection and shot classification, as well as some higher level algorithms for goal detection, referee detection and penalty-box detection.

D.E. Losada and J.M. Fernández-Luna (Eds.): ECIR 2005, LNCS 3408, pp. 433–446, 2005.
© Springer-Verlag Berlin Heidelberg 2005

A new trend is to combine audio and visual information under one framework [1, 2]. The idea has been examined in some recent papers, from event detection to scene boundary analysis. Baillie and Jose[9] detected game highlights by selected audio features, i.e. Mel-Frequency Cepstral Coefficients(MFCC). In [13], video segment detectors were developed for audio, colour and motion separately. Project 'Multiject'[14] fused audio sub-band data and colour histograms. The main problem behind this approach is asynchronism of audio and visual cues. It stands on two facts, (1) Audio and picture stream are independently encoded, transferred and replayed in most commercial video formats, i.e. H.263, MPGE-1/2 and AVI. There exists random delay between them when playing. (2) Audio and video are of different resolution. According to multi-sensor theory, an event in audio stream may carry on for several seconds and the resolution of audio is on coarse minute level, while video is updating at the speed of 25 frames per second with the resolution of finite second level.

Jurgen[3] discovered that there exists typical production styles and editing patterns, which make football video a loose simple-structured temporal sequence. These embedded repetitive structures are called video pattern or video structure. In this paper, we describe a new approach for video segmentation. We introduce a novel structure called 'attack' based on video making conventions. By close observation to football video production tactics, we first define the structure 'attack', an equivalent of scene in other video domains. Then we extend Lei's 'play' and 'break' detection framework[5] to 'play', 'focus', 'replay' and 'break' detection. These segments form the set of football semantic alphabets to construct 'attack'. Finally, we utilize 'attack' to setup a content-based video index and offer variable semantic summaries.

We select three salient features; field ratio, zoom size and image mean contrast. A two-pass classification system is employed to detect these video structures. Our goal is to parse continuous video stream into a sequence of 'attack'. Subsequently, we set up a hierarchical video content index to summarize the game and allow a nonlinear navigation of video content.

The rest of paper is organized as follows. Section 2 introduces the semantic sensitive video structure framework and provides a HMM football video model. In Section 3, we describe the video structure discrimination system and related feature extraction algorithms. Section 4 covers 'attack' scene construction. Experimental results are shown in Section 5. In 6, a brief of our nonlinear video browser and summarization system based on 'attack' segmentation is previewed. The final Section 7 comes with discussion and conclusion.

2   Football Video Structure

2.1   Video Production Strategy in Football Broadcasting

A football game is made up by a series of team movements called 'attack' in sports jargon[10]. They are mostly independent and sorted by time throughout the game. In some sense, 'attack' decides broadcasting strategy. During broadcasting, video reporters focus on two issues, (1) how to record the game or

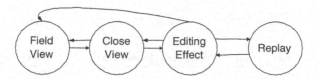

Fig. 1. The Video Making Sequence During Attack

'*attack*'s; (2) how to avoid missing interesting issues in an '*attack*'. They employ field view to describe team tactics and middle view or close-up view to catch players' detailed movement. When an important event or highlight takes place, such as goal, it will be replayed. The strategy (Fig.1) can be stated as following,

1. When an attack begins, a global view will be used until the ball passes the centre circle.
2. When the ball comes into front field, a middle view is going to be employed to show how groups of players attack and defend.
3. When the ball come into or close to the penalty area, a close-up view is here to catch possible highlights and players' action in detail.
4. When there is a highlight, such as shoot and foul, a close-up slow motion replay will come to state the event.

With these observations, we conjecture,

1. Video making methods in football game dictate the structure of video and compose semantics.
2. As a time sequence, a football game can be modelled by Hidden Markov Model with 'attack' video structure.
3. 'Attack' is an independent semantic video unit, which can be treated as a scene in football video domain. It is useful in video segmentation, indexing and summarization.

2.2   Four-Class Video Structure

'*Attack*' takes the role of **scene** in our framework. To detect it, we define a new video structure layer between shot and '*attack*'(Fig.2). It includes four mutually exclusive video structures in broadcasting video data(*play, focus, replay* and *break*). During **play**, video makers convey global status of the game and employ long and medium shots or field view in the general video terminology[10]. **Focus** is a short stop of game, in which the video maker traces a player to show his or her detailed actions. In video production terminology, it is called player close-up. **Replay** is for slow-replays. **Break** includes non-game video clips, such as interview and advertisement. These structures are useful in event detection[9] and helpful in shot boundary allocation. Moreover, they bring following advantages, (1) We can identify video segment with clear game content. It helps in video summarization and indexing, and promises a compact meaningful highlight set. (2) These video segments will not overlap in both time and semantics. It eases

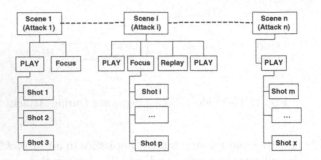

Fig. 2. Hierarchical Video Structure for Football

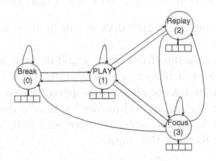

Fig. 3. Football Game Model

video indexing, which has developed complex index structure[16], such as X-tree and R+ tree, to keep overlapped video segments for retrieval. (3) These video structures maps actual film production skills, such as focus and replay, which can be detected automatically.

Given the repeat nature of '*attack*', a football game can be modelled by the hidden Markov Model(Fig.3). The model has four states: (0) Break, (1) Play, (2)Replay and (3) Focus, starting from *break* and ending in *break*.

3   Video Structure Detection System

In all four types, *replay* is ad hoc. It is a replenisher of prior frames, while *play, focus*, and *break* are characterized by view content. A two-pass classification(Fig.4) is proposed to deal with the difference. It identifies video structures and labels video frames with their video structure type, '*play*', '*focus*', '*replay*' and '*break*'. The first pass discriminates *play, focus* and *break* by a GMM classifier and its output label sequence is smoothed by dynamic programming process(Fig.5a). The second pass detects '*replay*'. From domain knowledge, *replay* is a slow motion video clip sandwiched by editing effects. So the process consists of a slow motion identification[8] and an editing effect detector. The HMM(Fig.5b) identifies slow motion clips among *play* and *focus*, while the editing effect detector looks for editing effect sequences before and after slow motion clips. Both of

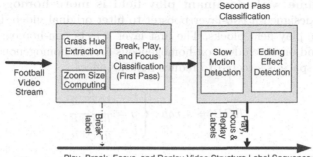

Fig. 4. Video Structure Identification System

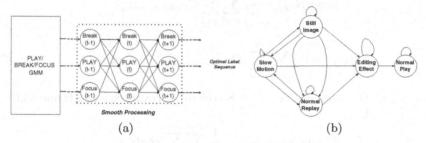

Fig. 5. (a) Mixed Classifier for Break,Play and Focus Discrimination (b) HMM for Replay Scene Detection([8])

them allocate 'replay'. After the classification, we get the video structure label sequence.

Three middle-level salient features are computed in current system for the first pass GMM classification, namely field ratio $R_{field}(t)$, zoom size $P(t)$ and image mean contrast $Con(t)$(Eq.3). In following subsections, we will introduce our algorithms for feature calculation and edit effect sequence detection.

3.1 Field Ratio

Xu[6] proposed *dominant colour ratio* to classify sports video. It is defined as play field area ratio over image, $R_{field}(t) = \frac{\|H_{field\_colour}(t)\|}{\|H(t)\|}$, where H is colour histogram of image blocks. Ekin[12] gathered grass pixels manually and calculated a prior grass colour model, in which grass occupies $65°$ - $85°$ hue interval in HSV colour space. However, we argue that play field hue varies greatly with light, weather and location, it is difficult for a unified model to abide these variations while keeping high precision. On the other hand, play field is not always the dominant area throughout a video. In test data, more than 37% sample frames are with a field ratio lower than 20%, i.e. those belonging to 'focus' and 'break'. In this work, we introduce an automatic pre-processing to detect play field colour distribution by two observations, **(1) play field is a homogeneous area; (2)**

A video frame with dominant play field is more homogeneous than others. We designed a two-layer booster to filter original video data to gather most possible play field blocks. The first layer rejects non-homogeneous frames and the second one excludes non-homogeneous area in homogenous frames. The s_rgb colour space is selected to reduce lighting effect.

$$RGB \Rightarrow s\_rgb : \begin{cases} r = \frac{R}{R+G+B} \\ g = \frac{G}{R+G+B} \\ b = \frac{B}{R+G+B} \end{cases}$$

Given MPEG block encoding, we define block mean hue(Eq. 1) and block covariance(Eq.2) of $n \times n(n = 8)$ image blocks to reduce noise,

$$mean(i,j) = \frac{1}{n^2} \sum_{x=1}^{n} \sum_{y=1}^{n} C_{(i*n+x,j*n+y)} \tag{1}$$

$$cov(i,j) = \frac{1}{n^2} \sum_{x=1}^{n} \sum_{y=1}^{n} |C_{(i*n+x,j*n+y)} - mean(i,j)| \tag{2}$$

where $C_{(i,j)}$ is the colour of Pixel(i,j). So the mean covariance of a frame will be,

$$MeanCov_{frames} = \frac{1}{IJ} \sum_{i=0}^{I-1} \sum_{j=0}^{J-1} cov(i,j) \tag{3}$$

where a frame contains $I \times J$ blocks. The threshold is calculated by maximum entropy,

$$threshold = arg \max_{N} \sum_{n=0}^{N} (-P_n \log(P_n)) \tag{4}$$

where P_n is the probability of frames whose mean block covariance is n.

All frames with a higher frame covariance than threshold will be rejected as the first layer of booster classifier. Another similar threshold is computed for every frame left, by which blocks with high covariance are removed as the second layer of booster. Fig.6 shows the effectiveness of this rejection stratagem, which keeps most of grass blocks while removing non-grass blocks. Then a GMM model is trained to simulate the grass colour distribution throughout the game by K-mean algorithm.

3.2   Zoom Size

Football uniform is an obvious domain feature. Compared with human face, it has following merits,

1. It is with bright colour and special pattern and can be easily discriminated.
2. it associates with the appearance of player only.
3. It is rotation robust.

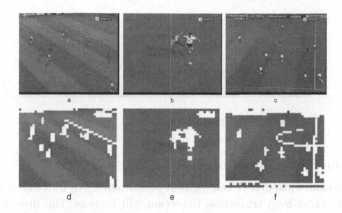

Fig. 6. Effect of Grass Area Booster(a,b,c is origin images and d,e,f is respective result after boosting)

Fig. 7. Training Samples for Polo-shirt Detection

In broadcasting, uniform size varies significantly from 9×13 pixel to more than 180×150 pixels in 352×288 video frame. We range it 13 scales, from 0 to 12, to measure zoom depth.

A FST(Foley-Sammon Transform) football uniform detector[11] is employed on multiple resolution from coarse to detail and decides its size. An 11-layer pyramid is built, in which every layer is 1.25 larger of the prior. The bottom one is of 352×288 pixels. The detector scans every layer from left to right and from top to bottom. If it finds a polo shirt on a certain layer, for example, the second layer, the frame will be labelled with zoom size 2. If a polo shirt is not discriminated in any layer, zoom size will be zero. The training set includes about 300 9×11 pixel samples(Fig.7) from different view.

Fig. 8. Log Transition Frames in World Cup 2002

3.3   Edit Effect Detection

'*Replay*' is sandwiched between logos of broadcaster. An automatic post-process of edit effects or logo transition detection will increase the precision of *replay* detection. Different from the algorithm in [8], we relies on colour histogram distance instead of pixel distance. It is robust on the presence of banners, which significantly changes the position of logo area and incapacitates the logo template detection algorithm[8].

A logo transition, usually 1-2 sec long or more than 30 frames in MPEG-1, is a set of consecutive frames that contain special logo. Fig.8 shows a logo transition sample for the football competition, World Cup 2002. It took place just before and after replay frames. A pre-log colour histogram array template is computed to detect edit effects before replay, while a post-log array template for these after replay. By slow-motion detection(Fig.5b), we build a '*replay*' candidate set. Pre-log frame array and post-log frame array are computed for every candidate. They include $n(n = 25)$ frames just before the start frame of the candidate or after the last frame, respectively. Then we align them. For two arrays u and v, the histogram array match measurement is defined as,

$$HC(u,v) = \min_{i \in [0,n)} \sum_{j=0}^{n} \|H_{i+j,u} - H_{i,v}\| + 1 \qquad (5)$$

where $H_{i,v}$ is the colour histogram of frame i in pre-log or post-log array of candidate v, and j is the match parameter. When the sum of i and j is greater than n, a large value will be assigned as a punishment. The algorithm seeking for the pre-log histogram array template can be described as,

1. Find two matching pre-log arrays with the smallest histogram array measurement in all;
2. Align them according to their match parameter j and compute histogram bin difference frame by fame;
3. The top 10 non-zero bins with smallest bin difference in every frame are characterized as eigen bins;
4. All eigen bins are sorted according to frame sequence to set up the n-j length histogram array template.

The histogram array template is employed to calculate the histogram match for all candidates. Mismatched candidate will be removed.

4   Attack Scene Construction

After video structure classification, we get the video structure label sequence "...BPFPFPRP...", where **B** is the abridgement for *'Break'*, **P** for *'Play'*, **F** for *'Focus'* and **R** for *'Replay'*. The string records the process of video making and keeps the information of 'attack'. So the job of 'attack' construction is to divide it into a serials of substrings, which contain only one 'attack' sequence each. But the string is too long for the attack model (Fig.1) to detect 'attack' scenes directly.

From domain knowledge, *'replay'* stands for game events and interrupts the game as *'break'*. The occurrences of *'replay'* and *'break'* divide the whole sequence into a set of strings. But they are still too long. Given following facts, (1)Such a string may contain more than one *'attack'* sequence; (2)'attack' is the largest video structure in our framework(Fig.2); (3)All 'attack' are similar in the video making sequence; video pattern of 'attack' can be treated as the longest common repetitive substring in these video making strings. This assumption also brings robustness to discrimination error and rouge artefact, such as a producer not using a slow motion as usual. Moreover, the attack model(Fig.1) will find the boundary between *'attacks'*.

Let alphabet $\Sigma = \{B, P, F, R\}$ and T be a string over Σ, the problem of longest common repetitive substring extraction can be stated as,

Definition 1 (Normal Repeat and Super Maximal Repeat). *A string p is called a normal repeat of T if $p = T[i..i + |p| - 1]$ and $p = T[i'..i' + |p| - 1]$ for $i \neq i'$. A super maximal repeat is a maximal repeat that never occurs as a substring of any other repeat.*

Definition 2. *Given a set of strings $U = \{T_1, T_2, ..., T_l\}$, the (k,l) longest common repeat problem is to find the longest normal repeat which is common to k strings in U for $1 \leq k \leq l$.*

A generalized suffix tree(GST)[17] stores all suffixes of a set of strings as a suffix tree(ST) does for a string. Fig.9 is an example of the generalized suffix tree for $T_1 = BBPFP$ and $T_2 = BPFPPFP$. Each leaf node has an ID representing the original string where the suffix came. The outline of our algorithm for the longest common repeat problem is as follows,

1. Build $ST(T_i)$ for each $1 \leq i \leq l$.
2. Build $GST(T_1T_2...T_l)$.
3. Find super maximal repeats T_i for each i in $GST(T_1T_2...T_l)$.
4. Remove super maximal repeat branch from $GST(T_1T_2...T_l)$ and build the GST of super maximal repeats.
5. Go to 3 unless the length of super maximal repeat is 1.
6. Find the longest common repeat among the super maximal repeat GST built in 4.

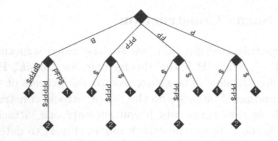

Fig. 9. The generalized suffix tree for $T_1 = BBPFP$ and $T_2 = BPFPPFP$

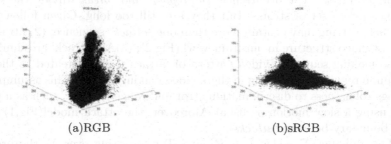

(a)RGB   (b)sRGB

Fig. 10. Mean Block Colour Distribution After Two-state Boost in Final Game

5   Experiment

The data set includes two MPEG-1 broadcasting videos in World Cup 2002 from BBC, the final game and the one Japan vs Turkey. It is about 320 minutes (more than 400000 frames@352 × 288) or 4.3GB, containing interview, celebration and commercial clips. Both games are divided into halves, Final I, Final II, Japan-Turkey I and Japan-Turkey II. The first half of Japan-Turkey and final game are labelled manually to set up ground truth. 13462 frames are sampled at the rate of 1/25, including 4535 'play' frames (33.7%), 4253 'focus' frames(31.6%) and 4674 'break' frames (34.6%). There are 33(19/14)[1] 'replay's in the final game and 34(18/16) in the Japan-Turkey game. Training set includes 2000 frames(about 15% in all, 400 from 'play', 1000 from 'focus', 600 from 'break'), which are randomly selected from marked samples. Remaining frames are kept for test.

The grass hue model is automatically calculated for every game. Fig.10 shows mean block colour distribution of the final game in RGB and $sRGB$ space. $sRGB$ space reduces light effect significantly and compacts data distribution. In order to find the optimal number of classes for the colour model, we experiment with 2,3,4, and 5 classes. Their effect on 'play','break' and 'focus' classification over training set is shown in Table.1. We set class number 4 in later experiments. The first pass classifier(Fig.5a, *play, break* and *focus* discrimination) is trained by training set while one entire half of game is used to train the smoothing HMM.

---

[1]   19 replays in the first half and 14 in the second half.

Table 1. Colour GMM With Different Classes Number

Class Number	Precision of Classification			Average Precision
	Play	Focus	Break	
2	74.5%	69.3%	74.6%	72.8%
3	80.2%	70.1%	76.0%	75.4%
4	84.0%	76.4%	75.2%	78.5%
5	81.7%	70.5%	74.3%	75.5%

Table 2. Play,Focus,Break Scene Classification Precision

Test Set	GMM			Training Set											
	Play	Break	Focus	Final I			Final II			Jap-Tur I			Jap-Tur II		
				Play	Break	Focus	Play	Break	Focus	Play	Break	Focus	Play	Break	Focus
Final I	0.894	0.840	0.823	*0.963*	*0.944*	*0.905*	0.913	0.852	0.830	0.948	0.920	0.877	0.933	0.917	0.891
Final II	0.786	0.664	0.708	0.824	0.730	0.721	*0.863*	*0.817*	*0.824*	0.835	0.713	0.773	0.824	0.711	0.765
Jap-Tur I	0.862	0.877	0.853	0.887	0.930	0.910	0.872	0.880	0.863	*0.890*	*0.952*	*0.917*	0.887	0.925	0.912
Jap-Tur II	0.880	0.861	0.836	0.905	0.892	0.870	0.897	0.870	0.845	0.930	0.905	0.887	*0.971*	*0.915*	*0.903*
avg-gen	0.856	0.811	0.805	0.894	0.874	0.852	0.886	0.855	0.840	0.898	0.873	0.864	0.904	0.867	0.868

Table 3. Mean Precision and Recall of Video Structure Classification

Test Set	Average Precision				Average Recall			
	Play	Break	Focus	Over All	Play	Break	Focus	Over All
Final I	0.931	0.896	0.866	0.898	0.941	0.926	0.883	0.917
Final II	0.827	0.718	0.753	0.766	0.894	0.879	0.864	0.879
Jap-Tur I	0.882	0.912	0.895	0.896	0.902	0.907	0.872	0.893
Jap-Tur II	0.930	0.889	0.867	0.895	0.955	0.896	0.875	0.909
Mean	0.893	0.854	0.845	0.864	0.923	0.902	0.873	0.899

Other three clips are employed for test. The process repeats for each video clips as the training set. We measure classification accuracy as the number of correctly classified samples over total number of samples. Training and testing accuracies are shown in Table.2. Average classification performance of each clip as test set (Table.3) is computed as the mean of the non-diagonal elements in Table.2. Average generalization performance (avg-gen) is computed for the clip as training set. Final II is noted for its lowest precision because the long celebration clip seriously garbles our classifier. A large group of people wearing uniform moved around in the play field. Those frames are compliant with 'play' and 'focus' in feature space, though we label them 'break'. Besides Final II, our skim-how average precision is 89.6% (91.4% in 'Play', 89.9% in 'Break', and 87.6% in 'Focus').

The replay detecting HMM is trained by five pre-marked slow motion clips. It runs through all focus segments to find possible candidates, from which the editing effect histogram template is drawn. All of replays are found in experi-

Table 4. Candidate Set Size and Template Length

	Candidate Set Size	Actual Replay Segment Number	Histogram Array Template Length
Final I	31	19	18
Final II	47	14	7
Jap-Tur I	22	18	21
Jap-Tur II	29	16	22

Table 5. Attack Detection Precision

	Attack Number	Precision	Recall
Final I	32	0.732	0.890
Final II	40	0.541	0.794
Jap-Tur I	31	0.762	0.846
Jap-Tur II	44	0.710	0.803

ment. The result is shown in Table. 4, where the candidate set size is the number of video clips found by the slow motion HMM.

We employ TRECVID2003[18] video segmentation precision and recall to measure 'attack' result. The precision is the ratio of total time of correctly identified segments over total time of videos and the recall is total time of correctly identified segments over total time of reference segment.

6   Application: Browser Index

We propose a new indexing scheme for football video, called *browser index*. It is built from *'attack'* and is organised along *'play'*, *'focus'* and *'replay'* structures, thus generating a hierarchical video index(Fig.2). *'Replay'* covers highlights during a game and their congregation can be treated as a brief summary[8]. It represents 'attack'. If it does not contain highlight, the *'attack'* may be discarded as a plain one. We assign all *'play'*'s and *'focus'*'s in the same 'attack' to *'replay'*, and set up the middle layer of index, for they contain game information around *'replay'*. All of them will be decomposed into shots, which is the bottom. Fig.11 shows the index structure.

A non-linear video browser and an interactive video summarization system are developed based on this browser index. They not only supplies brief highlight summary, but can be improved to fill variant requirements through interaction. Two major interfaces are included, **related video browser**(Fig.12a) and **summary browser**(Fig.12b).

Related video browser retrieves *'replay'* and its *'play'* and *'focus'* segments. It includes two regions in the panel, *'replay'* segment list and related segments panel. The related segments panel displays top n(n=3) closest *'play'* and *'focus'* to the selected *'replay'*. User chooses *'replay'* from the *'replay'* segment list and

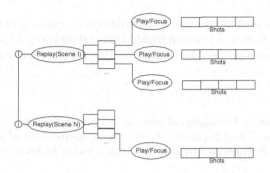

Fig. 11. Video Browser Index

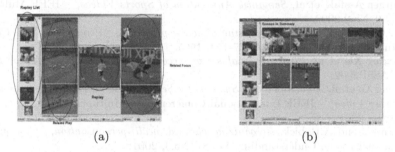

(a)   (b)

Fig. 12. (a) Related Video Browser (b) Summary Browser

decides whether to contain it and its related video segments in summary or not. A double-click on icons will play the video clip by a stand alone window.

Summary browser shows all video segments in the proposed summary, and grantees user the ability to insert and remove shots. The upper right region (Fig.12b) browses video segments, which are chosen in *related video browser*. All *'replay'*s will be included as default. If user selects a video segment in the list, shots belongs to the segment will be shown in the bottom right region so that user can decide whether to include the shot or not.

7   Discussion and Conclusion

In this paper, we identified a new semantic video structure called *'attack'* for football videos. It is based on video production conventions and helps in video summarization and indexing. In some sense, 'attack' is a semantic unit of football game and is an equivalent of scene in other video domains. The result shows those high-level video structures can be computed with high accuracy using middle-level features. We focus on video structure identification and how to merge these structures into *'attack'* scene. In the future work, we will measure accuracy of 'attack' boundary. The algorithm leaves much space for improvements: (1) Audio event detectors, such as goal and whistle detection, can be integrated; (2) Improve GST algorithm to search more embedded video structure; (3) It will be worthwhile to investigate unsupervised learning scenarios without extensive training.

References

1. Ricardo Lenardi, Pierangelo Migliorati and Maria Prandini, *Semantic Indexing of Soccer Audio-Visual Sequence: A multimodal approach based on controlled Markov chains*, IEEE Trans on Circuits&System for Video Technology, pp.634-643, Vol.14, No.5, 2004.
2. Ying Li, Shrikanth Narayanan and C.C.Jay Kuo, *Content-Based Movie Analysis and Indexing based on AuidoVisual cures*, IEEE Trans on Circuits&System for Video Technology, pp.1073-1085, Vol.14, No.8, 2004.
3. Jurgen Assfalg et al, *Semantic Annotation of Sports Videos*, IEEE MultiMedia Vol.9, No.2,2002.
4. Y. Gong et al. *Automatic parsing of soccer programs*, Proc. IEEE Intl. Conf. on Mult. Comput. and Sys, pp.167-174, 1995.
5. Lexing Xie et al. *Structure analysis of soccer video with Hidden Markov Models*, ICASSP2002.
6. Peng Xu et al. *Algorithms and Systems for Segmentation and Structure Analysis in Soccer Video*, IEEE International Conference on Multimedia and Expo, Tokyo, Japan, 2001.
7. S.Intille and A.Bobick, *Recognizing planned, multi-person action*, Computer Vision and Image Understanding, Vol.81, No.3, 2001.
8. H.Pan et al. *Detection of slowmotion replay segments in sports video for highlights generation*, ICASSP2001.
9. Baillie,M. and Jose J.M., *Audio-based Event Detection for Sports Video*, CIVR2003, pp.300-310, July 2003
10. Bob Burke and Frederik Shook, *Sports photography and reporting*, Chapter 12 in 'Television field production and reporting', 2nd Ed, Longman Publisher, 1996
11. Yue-Fei Guo and Lide Wu, *A generalized Foley-Sammon transform based on generalized fisher discriminant criterion and its application*, Pattern Recognition Letters 24(2003) 147-158.
12. A. Ekin, A. M. Tekalp, and R. Mehrotra, *Automatic soccer video analysis and summarization*, IEEE Trans. on Image Processing, vol. 12, no. 8, pp. 796-807, July 2003.
13. J.Huang, Z.Liu and Y.Wang, *Integration of audio and visual information for content-based video segmentation*, Proceedings of IEEE Conforence on Image Processing, Oct. 1998.
14. M.R.Naphade et al. *Probabilistic multimedia objects(MULTIJECTS): a novel apporach to video indexing and retrieval in multimedia systems*, Proceedings of IEEE Conforence on Image Processing, Oct. 1998.
15. D.You, M.Yeung and G.Liu,*Analysis and presentation of soccer highlights from digital video*, Proc. ACCV, Dec.1995.
16. Jianping Fan et al. *Class View: Hierarchical Video Shot Classification, Indexing and Acessing*, IEEE Trans. on Multimedia, Vol.6 No.1, 2004.
17. L.C.K Hui *Color set size problem with applications to string matching*, Proceedings of the Third Annual Symposium on Combinatorial Pattern Matching, pp.230-243. Springer-Verlag, 1992.
18. TRECVID 2003, http://www-nlpir.nist.gov/projects/tv2003/tv2003.html

Fractional Distance Measures for Content-Based Image Retrieval

Peter Howarth and Stefan Rüger

Department of Computing, Imperial College London,
South Kensington Campus, London SW7 2AZ, UK
{peter.howarth, s.rueger}@imperial.ac.uk

Abstract. We have applied the concept of fractional distance measures, proposed by Aggarwal et al. [1], to content-based image retrieval. Our experiments show that retrieval performances of these measures consistently outperform the more usual Manhattan and Euclidean distance metrics when used with a wide range of high-dimensional visual features. We used the parameters learnt from a Corel dataset on a variety of different collections, including the TRECVID 2003 and ImageCLEF 2004 datasets. We found that the specific optimum parameters varied but the general performance increase was consistent across all 3 collections. To squeeze the last bit of performance out of a system it would be necessary to train a distance measure for a specific collection. However, a fractional distance measure with parameter $p = 0.5$ will consistently outperform both L_1 and L_2 norms.

1 Introduction

The goal of Content-Based Image Retrieval (CBIR) is to provide the user with a way to browse or retrieve images from large image collections, based on visual similarity. At the heart of any CBIR system are visual features that have been extracted from images and distance measures that are used to quantify the similarity between these features. The combination of these two attributes will drive the overall performance of a system.

Visual features are a compact representation of a specific visual facet of an image, such as colour, texture or shape. They are often high-dimensional. Dimensionality of the order of 10^2 to 10^3 is common. Each feature has its own characteristics, such as sparsity, dimensionality and correlation between elements.

A distance (or similarity) measure is a way of ordering the features from a specific query point. These can take many forms. They can be described as a function that maps the $\mathbb{R}^n$ feature space to a one dimensional distance or similarity. The retrieval performance of a feature can be significantly affected by the distance measure used. Ideally we want to use a distance measure and feature combination that gives best retrieval performance for the collection being queried. Often the commonly used distance measures, such as the L-norms, are used as a matter of course. However, a lot can be gained by careful selection of a suitable measure.

D.E. Losada and J.M. Fernández-Luna (Eds.): ECIR 2005, LNCS 3408, pp. 447–456, 2005.
© Springer-Verlag Berlin Heidelberg 2005

In this paper we have applied a fractional distance measure proposed by Aggarwal et al. [1] to the CBIR domain. These measures are an extension of the commonly used L-norm metrics which include Manhattan and Euclidean distance measures. The authors demonstrated that the measures were effective when applied to high-dimensional database vectors for data mining problems, outperforming the more frequently used l_p norms.

This paper is organised as follows. Section 2 discusses the details of fractional distance measures. Section 3 describes how we devised experiments to evaluate the effectiveness of distance measures and Section 4 sets out the results and analysis.

2   Fractional Distance Measures

There are a large number of distance measures that have been used for CBIR. Common ones include: Manhattan, Euclidean, Mahalanobis, and histogram intersection. It is accepted that the choice of proximity measure can have a profound effect on local topology. This is significant for CBIR as when querying a multimedia database we are normally interested in the nearest neighbours. However, often the choice of distance measure is made without much thought. The Euclidean distance metric has its basis in 2 and 3 dimensional space and in this context it is the physical distance measured in a straight line. For higher dimensions it loses its significance, although it is often used as a matter of course.

Beyer et al. [2] set out the problem with nearest neighbour search in high dimensions. That is, that as the dimensionality increases, the distance to the nearest and farthest neighbours tend to converge to the same value. This occurs with most reasonable data distributions and distance measures. The implication of this is that the contrast between data points becomes insignificant as dimensionality increases. Correspondingly, nearest neighbour search may no longer be meaningful. It would therefore appear beneficial if we can use a distance measure that preserves the contrast between data points at higher dimensionality.

The L_p norm is usually induced by the distance,

$$\text{dist}_d^p(x, y) = \left[\sum_{i=1}^d \parallel x^i - y^i \parallel^p \right]^{1/p}, \tag{1}$$

where d is the dimensionality of the space and p is a free parameter, $p \geq 1$. Aggarwal et al. [1] extended this definition to allow $p \in (0, 1)$. Please note that strictly speaking the fractional measures defined by dist^p with $p \in (0, 1)$ are no longer distances in the mathematical sense as the triangle inequality is violated. The reason for this is that the a ball with radius one under dist^p is no longer convex for $p < 1$, see Figure 1. This can have an effect on some indexing and partitioning schemes that rely on the metric properties. Nevertheless dist^p still conveys a sense of closeness and we will refer to it as a fractional distance.

In [1] a relative distance measure was used to describe the characteristics of the distance space. This had been adapted from [2]; it is defined as:

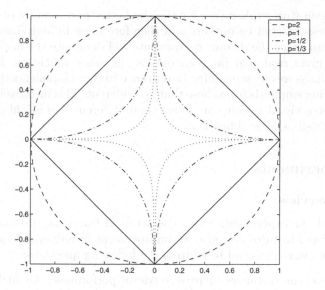

Fig. 1. Unit balls for $p = 2$, $p = 1$, $p = 1/2$ and $p = 1/3$

$$\frac{D\max_d^p - D\min_d^p}{D\min_d^p}, \tag{2}$$

where $D\max_d^p$ is the maximum dist^p between 2 points in a d dimensional distribution, and $D\min_d^p$ is the corresponding minimum distance. This can be used as a measure of the meaningfulness of a distance distribution. In particular [1] showed two results applicable to both ordinary ($p \geq 1$) and fractional ($p \in (0,1)$) distances.

The first was that the absolute difference between the maximum and minimum distances increases at the rate of $d^{1/p-1/2}$. Thus the smaller the value of p the greater the divergence. Secondly that the relative contrast has the following bounds:

$$C\sqrt{\frac{1}{2p+1}} \leq \lim_{d \to \infty} E\left[\frac{D\max_d^p - D\min_d^p}{D\min_d^p}\right] \leq C(n-1)\sqrt{\frac{1}{2p+1}}. \tag{3}$$

This is for a uniform distribution of n points and a constant C. It is an interesting result as it shows that fractional measures should have better relative contrast than ordinary distances.

These findings still leave some questions to be investigated. For fractional measures they were based on uniform distributions. They would indicate that the smaller the value of p the better the relative contrast. Whilst this may be the case, with CBIR systems we are interested in the retrieval performance. Altering the value of p may increase the contrast but could also adversely affect the local neighbourhood and therefore the retrieval performance. In addition the bounds are wide so the nature of the distribution of points may have a significant effect.

One qualitative explanation for the the better performance of L_1 over L_2 is that it is less affected by outliers and therefore noise in high dimensional data. In Euclidean space the distant components will dominate the distance measure. Using L_1 gives near and far components the same weighting. By moving to fractional measures we are adding importance to the components that are similar and removing emphasis from those that are different. This intuitively makes sense as the human visual system can detect small differences in neighbouring patches equally as well as large differences.

3   Experiments

3.1   Overview

The aim of our experiments was to ascertain if fractional distances can be applied to visual features and give an improvement in retrieval performance. Our experiments were designed to address the following questions:

- Do fractional distances increase retrieval performance for high dimensional visual features?
- How does the performance vary with the fractional parameter p?
- If there is an optimal p for a specific feature is this stable across different image data sets?
- Is it possible to predict the optimal setting for p from any characteristics of the feature or the resultant distance distribution?

We use mean average precision (m.a.p.) as a measure of performance of distance measures. This is because we are interested in performance in the context of a CBIR task. Whilst m.a.p. can be criticised for not being related to a specific user task it does give a good overall measure of performance that trades off between precision and recall. M.a.p. is widely adopted for information retrieval and we therefore feel justified in its use.

3.2   Data Sets

It is recognised with image retrieval that the data set used can have a large influence on results of any experiments and the resultant conclusions. To ensure that our results were not just a feature of the data set used we ran experiments using three different collections. Our primary experiments were done with a collection taken from the Corel image library. These were then followed up with further experiments using TRECVID 2003 and ImageCLEF 2004 collections. This enabled us to validate our results and draw conclusions about the general applicability across three very different collections. The collections and queries are described below.

Corel. We used a subset of Corel that was created by Pickering et al. [3] to evaluate visual features. 6,192 Corel images were carefully selected to give 63 categories that were visually similar internally, but different from each other. This was then split into two sets. The first, a set of 1,548 images, was used to query the remaining 4,644 images. From the query collection we generated single and multiple image queries across all categories. The number of images per query was varied from 1 to 6; for each number we created 630 queries. This made 3,780 in total. The results shown in Section 4 are the mean average precision across these queries.

TRECVID 2003. This collection is widely used. It is much larger than Corel but has drawbacks mainly due to the limited number of queries. It comprises of 32,318 key-frames from TRECVID 2003 video collection [4]. These were taken from ABC and CNN news broadcasts. The search task specified for TRECVID consists of 25 topics. For each topic a few example images were given as a query. The published relevance judgements for these topics were used to evaluate the retrieval performance for different combinations of features and distance measures.

ImageCLEF 2004. This is a medical image collection comprising of 8,725 images, 24 single image queries plus ground truth. It was created for evaluation on the image track of the Cross Language Evaluation Forum [5]. The dataset is quite different to others in that the images are mainly X-rays, CT-scans and medical photographs. The majority of images are monochrome and are carefully posed. It therefore provides an interesting contrast to the other collections.

3.3   Methods

For multiple image queries we used the k-nearest neighbour (k-nn) retrieval approach. Previous work in our group [3] has demonstrated that this outperforms the vector space models for multi-image queries. It is based on the idea that given positive and negative example images, the test images can be classified according to their proximity to these examples. A version of the distance weighted k-nn approach was used [6]. Positive examples (P) are supplied as the query and negative examples (N) randomly selected from the collection. To rank an image i in the collection we identify those images in P and N that are amongst the k-nearest neighbours of i. Using these neighbours we determine the dissimilarity:

$$D(i) = \frac{\sum\limits_{n \in N} (\text{dist}(i, n))^{-1}}{\sum\limits_{p \in P} (\text{dist}(i, p))^{-1}} . \tag{4}$$

A value of $k = 40$ was used for our experiments. A small positive constant value is added to the denominators to prevent division by zero.

3.4   Visual Features

We used a range of high dimensional visual features. These were based on colour, texture and structure. Full details are available in [3,7]. A brief summary is below:

- **RGB**, this is a joint colour histogram defined in RGB colour-space. It has 8x8x8 = 512 bins and is sparse.
- **HSV**, this is a joint colour histogram defined in the hue, saturation and value colour-space. The arrangement of bins used is 8x5x5, giving a relatively sparse 200 dimensional vector.
- **HDS**, this is the MPEG-7 colour structure descriptor. It has 184 non uniformly quantised bins and is relatively sparse.
- **Gabor**, this is a texture feature generated using Gabor wavelets. A bank of 2 by 4 filters are used to detect different scales and directions that characterise a texture. These are applied to image tiles to give additional discrimination. The resultant vector has dimensionality of 560 and is relatively densely populated.
- **Convolution**, this feature discriminates between low level structures in an image. It is created by filtering the image with 25 low level filters designed to detect primitive structures. The resulting feature maps are then re-filtered giving a 625 dimensional feature that is relatively sparse.
- **Thumbnail**, this is created from the pixel intensity values of a scaled down image. We used a size of 40 by 30 resulting in a dense vector of length 1200. This feature is a good discriminator for near identical images.

4   Results

4.1   Performance of Fractional Distances

Corel. The first set of experiments, with the Corel collection, were aimed at determining if fractional distance measures gave a significant retrieval performance gain across a range of visual features. We generated the visual features described in Section 3.4 and ran our query set against these. The results are plotted in Figure 2, which shows mean average precision retrieval against p.

The first thing to note from this graph is that all the features show an increase in m.a.p. for fractional distances. The most significant increases are for the RGB, HSV, HDS and convolution features. The Gabor and thumbnail features are both flat across the graph, showing only a slight improvement in retrieval performance for fractional distances. The position of the maxima vary from feature to feature but all fall between p values of 0.25 and 0.75.

The HDS feature shows the maximum relative gain in m.a.p.. It increases from 18.2% at $p = 1$ to 23.6% at $p = 1/4$, a relative gain of 30%.

TRECVID 2003. The larger TRECVID collection presents more of a challenge for image retrieval. We generated the same features as for Corel. The retrieval performance is shown in Figure 3. The results show a marked performance increase for fractional distance measures.

The overall results are very similar to those for Corel. RGB, HDS, HSV and convolution features show increased performance for fractional distances. Similarly, the performance for the Gabor and thumbnail features does not improve.

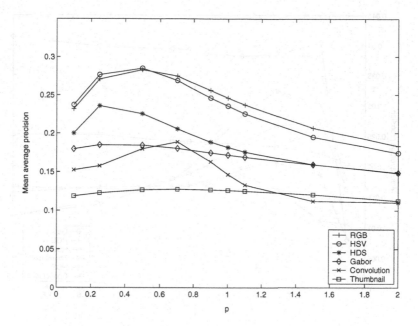

Fig. 2. Graph of retrieval results for Corel

The maximum gain in m.a.p. is shown by the RGB feature which increases from 2.0% at $p = 1$, to 3.3% at $p = 1/2$. This is a relative increase of 65%.

The plots from the 2 experiments have the same characteristic shape, with the maxima falling between 0.25 and 0.75. However, a detailed examination of the p values at maximum retrieval for each feature shows that they are different to the Corel collection. This demonstrates that the optimum value of p is not independent of the data collection.

ImageCLEF. Fewer colour features were used with the ImageCLEF collection due to its mainly monochrome nature. The results are plotted in Figure 4.

Examining the ImageCLEF results we can see that the general trend is similar to those from Corel and TRECVID. HDS and convolution features show performance gains for fractional p values. The convolution feature has a much larger relative gain than for TRECVID whereas HDS only has a slight gain. The performance of the Gabor feature reduces for fractional p values. The significant difference in the results is for the thumbnail feature. In contrast to the 2 previous experiments it shows a marked performance gain for fractional distances.

To explain these results we must consider the characteristics of the collection. It contains a large proportion of monochrome images and because of the medical subject contains groups of near identical images. For example X-rays of a specific part of the body will always be composed in exactly the same way. In addition the queries for this collection are single images.

The effect of the monochrome images on colour features will be to reduce the dimensionality. Qualitatively this explains the reduced gain for the HDS

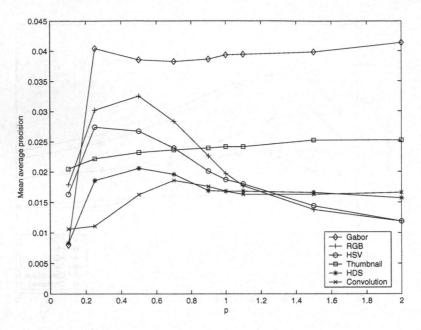

Fig. 3. Graph of retrieval results for TRECVID2003

feature. The increase in performance for thumbnail may be due to the groups of very similar images in the collection. This feature will discriminate these effectively and it appears that its performance is enhanced by the fractional distance measure.

4.2   Discussion of Results

Overall the results on Corel, CLEF and TRECVID show that the performance benefits of fractional distance measures are generally applicable across widely differing datasets, features and queries.

All the features, except Gabor and thumbnail, consistently show an increase in retrieval performance when used with fractional distance measures. The maximum gains appear at values of p between 0.25 and 0.75. The optimum value of p varies depending on the combination of feature and test collection.

In an attempt to find a predictor for the optimum value of p we investigated the statistical properties and dimensionality of the space defined by the features and test collection. No clear relationship was found. We intend to research this further.

Taking a more qualitative viewpoint, the 2 features that do not respond well to fractional distances are both dense vectors. The features with the greatest improvement are all sparse vectors. It would therefore appear that the sparsity of the feature vector may be a general indicator that use of a fractional distance measure will improve mean average precision retrieval.

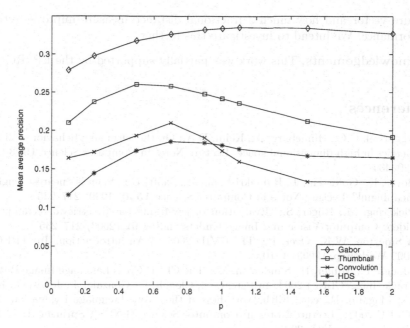

Fig. 4. Graph of retrieval results for ImageCLEF2004

Intuitively this makes sense as fractional distance measures give more weight to element comparisons where the values are similar, i.e. 2 zeros, or 2 non-zero values. With sparse features a large number of element-wise comparisons will be between zero and some value. The contribution of these to the total distance will add noise that may swamp the overall similarity. These will be given less importance with fractional distances than with higher norms.

5   Conclusion

We have shown that fractional distance measures give a significant improvement in mean average precision retrieval over the commonly used L_1 and L_2 norms. The performance gains were consistent when using high dimensional visual features over three different image collections.

By experimenting across very different data sets we have shown that the optimum value of value of p for a feature cannot be determined by training on a single collection. It is linked to the combination of both feature and dataset. However, we have demonstrated that a choice of $p \in (0.25, 0.75)$ improves mean average precision across nearly all features and datasets. To find the optimum p the distance measure would need to be learnt for each collection. However, a value of $p = 0.5$ will improve retrieval performance in nearly all circumstances.

We could not determine a reliable predictor for the optimum value of p. However, qualitatively there appears to be a link between the sparsity of the feature vector and how much a fractional distance measure improves retrieval performance. We intend to investigate this further.

Acknowledgements. This work was partially supported by the EPSRC, UK.

References

1. Aggarwal, C.C., Hinneburg, A., Keim, D.A.: On the surprising behavior of distance metrics in high dimensional space. Lecture Notes in Computer Science **1973** (2001) 420–434
2. Beyer, K., Goldstein, J., Ramakrishnan, R., Shaft, U.: When is "nearest neighbor" meaningful? Lecture Notes in Computer Science **1540** (1999) 217–235
3. Pickering, M., Rüger, S.: Evaluation of key-frame based retrieval techniques for video. Computer Vision and Image Understanding **92** (2003) 217–235
4. A Smeaton, W.K., Over, P.: TRECVID 2003 — An introduction. In: TRECVID 2003 Workshop. (2003) 1–10
5. Clough, P., Müller, H., Sanderson, M.: The CLEF Cross Language Image Retrieval Track (ImageCLEF) 2004. In Peters, C., Clough, P., Gonzalo, J., Jones, G., Kluck, M., Magnini, B., eds.: Fifth Workshop of the Cross–Language Evaluation Forum (CLEF 2004), Lecture Notes in Computer Science (LNCS), Springer, Heidelberg, Germany (in print) (2005)
6. Mitchell, T.M.: Machine Learning. McGraw Hill (1997)
7. Howarth, P., Rüger, S.: Evaluation of texture features for content-based image retrieval. In: Proceedings of the International Conference on Image and Video Retrieval, Springer-Verlag (2004) 326–324

Combining Visual Semantics and Texture Characterizations for Precision-Oriented Automatic Image Retrieval

Mohammed Belkhatir

Laboratoire CLIPS-IMAG,
Université Joseph Fourier, Grenoble, France
mohammed.belkhatir@imag.fr

Abstract. The growing need for 'intelligent' image retrieval systems leads to new architectures combining visual semantics and signal features that rely on highly expressive frameworks while providing fully-automated indexing and retrieval processes. Indeed, addressing the issue of integrating the two main approaches in the image indexing and retrieval literature (i.e. signal and semantic) is a viable solution for achieving significant retrieval quality. This paper presents a multi-facetted framework featuring visual semantics and signal texture descriptions for automatic image retrieval. It relies on an expressive representation formalism handling high-level image descriptions and a full-text query framework in an attempt to operate image indexing and retrieval operations beyond trivial low-level processes and loosely-coupled state-of-the-art systems. At the experimental level, we evaluate the retrieval performance of our system through recall and precision indicators on a test collection of 2500 photographs used in several world-class publications.

1 Introduction and Related Work

The first image retrieval systems (signal-based) [6,15,20,23,25] propose a set of still images indexing methods based on low-level features such as colors, textures... The general approach consists in computing structures representing the image distribution such as color histograms, texture features and using this data to partition the image; thus reducing the search space during the image retrieval operation. These methods are based on the computation of discriminating features rejecting images which do not correspond to the query image and hold the advantage of being fully automatic, thus are able to quickly process queries. However, aspects related to human perception are not taken into account. Indeed, an image cannot be sufficiently described by its moments or color histograms. The problem arising from invariants or discriminating features lies on the loss of semantic information conveyed by the image. These tools are used for restricting the search space during the retrieval operation but cannot however give a sound and complete interpretation of the content. For example, can we accept that our system considers red apples or Ferraris as being the same entities simply because they present similar color histograms? Definitely not, as shown in [13],

D.E. Losada and J.M. Fernández-Luna (Eds.): ECIR 2005, LNCS 3408, pp. 457–474, 2005.
© Springer-Verlag Berlin Heidelberg 2005

taking into account aspects related to the image content is of prime importance for efficient photograph retrieval.

Several frameworks dealing with the automatic extraction of the image semantic content have been proposed [5,9,12,27]. One of the early solutions presented a probabilistic framework based on estimating class likelihoods of local areas, labeled as either man-made vs. natural or inside vs. outside objects [5]. In [27], training sample regions of images are categorized into 11 clusters through a neural network mapping (e.g. *tree, fur, sand...*). To alleviate the restrained cardinality of the proposed previous sets of visual clusters, a richer index vocabulary consisting of 26 image labels called Visual Keywords (such as *sky, people, water...*) is specified in [12]. However, this solution relies on a query-by-example framework as far as image querying is concerned and no language able to manipulate the extracted semantics has been proposed. Also, a relevance-based model for keyword annotation and retrieval is presented in [9].

The main disadvantage of this second class of frameworks relies on the specification of restrained and fixed sets of semantic classes. Regarding the fact that several artificial objects have high degrees of variability with respect to signal properties such as texture variations, an interesting solution is to extend the extracted visual semantics with signal characterizations in order to enrich the image indexing vocabulary and query language. Therefore, a new generation of systems integrating semantics and signal descriptions has emerged and the first solutions [10,14,29] are based on the association of textual annotations with relevance feedback (RF). Prototypes such as iFind [14] and ImageRover [10] offer loosely-coupled solutions based on textual annotations to characterize semantics and on a RF scheme operating on low-level signal features. These approaches have two major drawbacks: first, they fail to exhibit a single framework unifying low-level data and semantics, which penalizes the performance of the system in terms of retrieval efficiency. Then, as far as the query process is concerned, the user is to query both textually in order to express high-level concepts and through several and time-consuming RF loops to complement his initial query. This solution for integrating semantics and low-level features, relying on a cumbersome query process does not enforce facilitated and efficient user interaction.

As an extension to our previous work in [2,3], we propose a unified multi-facetted framework unifying visual semantics and texture features for automatic image retrieval that enforces expressivity, performance and computational efficiency. After specifying a fully-automatic framework extracting the visual semantics, we enrich the description of images through the specification of processes establishing a correspondence between extracted low-level features and high-level texture concepts. E.g. with the semantic concept "sky" one might assign additional concepts such as "covered", "smooth" characterizing its texture. Therefore, not only do we characterize visual semantics, but also relations linking them to high-level texture concepts. For this, we consider an efficient operational model that allows relational indexing and is adaptable to symbolic image retrieval: **conceptual graphs** (CGs) [26]. However, contrarily to the EMIR^2 system [17] which was one of the early attempts at using CGs for image retrieval and limited its descriptive power to the basic semantics associated with these graphs (i.e. the conjunction of concepts and relations), we extend their operational semantics to handle a rich image query language consisting of the 3 major boolean operators (conjunction, disjunction and negation). Indeed, we are interested in dealing with non trivial queries involving the combination of visual semantics and high-level texture concepts and the possibility to associate boolean operators to these queries. This would allow the user to retrieve images with "bumpy **and** cracked roads", "a covered **or** a bright sky" or "**non**-interlaced flowers"...

In the remainder of this paper, we first present the general organization of our image retrieval architecture. We deal in sections 3 and 4 with the visual semantics and texture characterizations. Section 5 will specify the query framework. We finally present in section 6 the validation experiments conducted on a test collection of 2500 photographs used in several world-class publications.

2   A Strongly-Coupled Model for Texture/Semantics Integration

As far as state-of-the-art image retrieval systems are concerned, images cannot be easily or efficiently retrieved due to the lack of a comprehensive image retrieval framework that captures the structured abstractions, the signal information conveyed and the semantic richness of images. To remedy such shortcomings, we propose an architecture consisting of index and retrieval modules that integrate a comprehensive image model combining visual semantics and texture features (cf. figure 1).

The image model consists of both a physical image level representing an image as a matrix of pixels and a conceptual level. The latter is itself a multi-facetted framework supported by an expressive knowledge representation formalism: CGs.

- The **object facet** describes an image as a set of **image objects** (IOs) abstract structures representing visual entities within an image. Their specification is an attempt to operate image indexing and retrieval operations beyond simple low-level processes [15,20,23,25] or object-based techniques [6] since IOs convey the visual semantics and the signal texture information at the conceptual level. Formally, this facet is described by the set I_{IO} of IO identifiers.

- The **visual semantics facet** describes the image semantic content and is based on labeling IOs with a semantic concept. E.g., in figure 1, the first IO (Io1) is tagged by the semantic concept *Hut*. Its formal description will be dealt with in section 3.

- The **texture facet** describes the signal content in terms of symbolic texture features. E.g. the second IO (Io2) is associated with the texture keyword **lined**. The texture facet is detailed and formalized in section 4.

In order to instantiate this model within an image retrieval framework, we need a representation formalism capable to represent IOs as well as the visual semantics and signal information they convey. Moreover, this representation formalism should make it easy to visualize the information related to an image. A graph-based representation and particularly CGs are an efficient solution to describe an image and characterize its components. They have indeed proven to adapt to the symbolic approach of image retrieval [17,21]. CGs allow to represent components of our image retrieval architecture and to specify expressive index and query frameworks.

Formally, a CG is a finite, bipartite, connex and oriented graph. It features two types of nodes: concept and relation nodes. In the example graph [ECIR2005]←(Name)←[Conference]→(Location)→[Santiago de Compostela], concepts are between brackets and relations between parenthesis. This graph is semantically interpreted as: the ECIR2005 conference is held in Santiago de Compostela. Concepts and conceptual relations are organized within a lattice structure partially ordered by the IS-A ($\leq$) relation. For example, Person $\leq$ Man denotes that the concept

Man is a specialization of the concept *Person*, and will therefore appear in the off-spring of the latter within the lattice organizing these concepts. Within the scope of the model, CGs are used to represent the image content at the conceptual level.

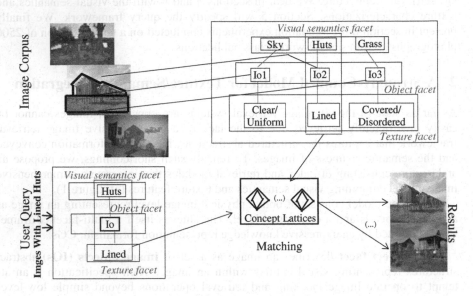

Fig. 1. System architecture and Image model

The indexing module provides a representation of an image document in the corpus with respect to the multi-facetted image model. It is a CG called document index graph. In figure 1, an image belonging to the corpus is characterized at the conceptual level by a multi-facetted representation. Also, as far as the retrieval module is concerned, a user full-text query is translated into an image conceptual representation: the image query graph corresponding to the multi-facetted image description. In figure 1, the query "Find images with lined huts" is translated into a multi-facetted conceptual representation. The image query graph is then compared to all conceptual representations of image documents in the corpus. Lattices organizing semantic and texture concepts are processed and a relevance value, estimating the degree of similarity between image query and index graphs is computed in order to rank all image documents relevant to a query.

3   The Visual Semantics Facet

3.1   Extracting the Semantics

Semantic concepts are learned and then automatically extracted given a visual ontology. Its specification is strongly constrained by the application domain [17]. Indeed dealing with corpus of medical images would entail the elaboration of a visual ontology that would be different from an ontology considering computer-generated images.

In this paper, our experiments in section 6 are based on a collection of color home photographs.

Several experimental studies presented in [18] have led to the specification of twenty categories or picture scenes describing the image content at a global level. Web-based image search engines (google, altavista) are queried by textual keywords corresponding to these picture scenes and 100 images are gathered for each query. These images are used to establish a list of semantic concepts characterizing objects that can be encountered in these scenes. A total of 72 semantic concepts to be learnt and automatically extracted are specified. Figure 2 shows their typical appearance.

Fig. 2. Semantic concepts: ground, sky, vegetation, water, people, mountain, building

A 3-layer feed-forward neural network with dynamic node creation capabilities is used to learn these semantic concepts from 375 labeled image patches cropped from home photographs. Color and texture features are computed for each training region as an input vector for the neural network.

Once the neural network has learned the visual vocabulary, the approach subjects an image to be indexed to a multi-scale, view-based recognition against these semantic concepts. An image to be processed is scanned with windows of several scales. Each one represents a visual token characterized by a feature vector constructed with respect to the feature vectors of semantic concepts previously exhibited. Recognition results are then reconciled across multiple resolutions and aggregated according to configurable spatial tessellation. Figure 3 presents the architecture for automatic extraction of semantic concepts (more details can be found in [12]).

E.g., the highlighted image in figure 1 is characterized by three semantic concepts, based respectively on top, center and bottom areas and linked to three IOs. The semantic concept *sky* is linked to the first IO *Io1*, the semantic concept *huts* to the second IO *Io2* and the semantic concept grass to the third IO *Io3*. We also consider left and right areas, which are not meaningful in this example image.

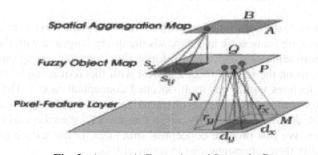

Fig. 3. Automatic Extraction of Semantic Concepts

3.2 Model of the Visual Semantics Facet

IOs are represented by *Io* concepts and the semantic concepts are organized within a lattice specified in the next section. An instance of the visual semantics facet is represented by a set of canonical CGs, each one containing an *Io* type linked through the conceptual relation *sct* to a semantic concept. The basic graph controlling the generation of all visual semantics facet graphs is: [Io]→(sct)→[SC]. E.g., graphs [Io1]→(sct)→[Sky], [Io2]→(sct)→[Huts] and [Io2]→(sct)→[Grass] are the representation of the visual semantics facet in figure 1 and can be translated as: the first IO (Io1) is associated with the semantic concept *huts*, the second IO (Io2) with the semantic concept *sky* and the third IO (Io3) with the semantic concept *grass*.

3.3 The Organization of the Lattice of Semantic Concepts

We use WordNet to elaborate a visual ontology that reflects the Is-A relationship among the semantic concepts. They are organized within a multi-layered lattice ordered by a specific/generic partial order (figure 4).

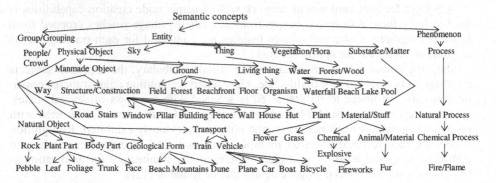

Fig. 4. Lattice organizing semantic concepts

4   The Texture Facet: From Low-Level Signal Texture Extraction to Symbolic Characterization

The integration of texture information within the conceptual level is crucial since it enriches the indexing framework and expands the query language with the possibility to query over both semantics and visual information. After presenting our formalism, we will now focus on the texture facet and deal with theoretical implications of integrating texture features within our multi-facetted conceptual model. This integration is not straightforward as we need to characterize low-level texture features at the conceptual level, and therefore specify a rich framework for conceptual signal indexing and querying. We first propose conceptual structures for the texture facet and then thoroughly specify their representations in terms of CGs.

4.1 Extracting Low-Level Texture Features

The study of texture in computer vision has lead to the identification of several low-level features used in texture computation as well as the development of computational models for texture measurement and analysis. Mainly three models are used in the framework of content-based image retrieval architectures. The statistical model, which categorizes textures according to statistical computation involving texture attributes such as regularity, directionality... is used in QBIC [20]. Photobook [23] proposes to combine two texture extraction and characterization models, one based on probability distributions in random fields and a spectral model based on Fourier transforms. Finally, Netra [15] uses a spectral model based on the decomposition of images into texture features using a bank of Gabor filters [8] that has proven to outperform other methods for content-based image retrieval [11].

Our computational model for texture extraction is to capture aspects related to human perception. It is therefore inspired by the work in [8] where a computational framework for texture extraction which is the closest approximation of the human visual system is proposed. The action of the visual cortex, where an object is decomposed into several primitives by the filtering of cortical neurons sensitive to several frequencies and orientations of the stimuli, is simulated by a bank of Gabor filters. However, as opposed to their work operating at a global level of an image, we will focus on computational texture extraction at the IO level. We therefore characterize each IO by its Gabor energy distribution within seven spatial frequencies covering the whole spectral domain and seven angular orientations. Each IO is then represented by a 49-dimensions vector, with each dimension corresponding to a Gabor energy.

4.2 Characterizing Textures Through High-Level Texture Concepts

As presented in the previous section, several works have proposed the identification of low-level features and the development of algorithms and techniques for texture computation. However, few attempts have been made to propose an ontology for texture symbolic characterization and naming. Rao and Lohse proposed a set of experimentations to identify symbolic features used in the perception of textures. Three orthogonal dimensions, namely repetitive vs non-repetitive, directional vs non-directional and granular vs non-granular are highlighted [24]. Further work was carried out to provide a texture lexicon, i.e. 11 high-level texture categories were identified, which constitute a basis for symbolic classification of textures [4]. In each of these categories, several texture words which best describe the nature of the characterized texture are proposed.

The first texture cluster C_1 gathers textures with random 3-dimensional imperfections and is characterized by the texture word **bumpy** (tw_1=**B**). C_2 comprises textures exhibiting random linear orientation and is represented by the texture word **cracked** (tw_2=**C**). Texture cluster C_3 gathers textures that do not present any structure nor any dominant orientation. It is represented by the texture word **disordered** (tw_3=**D**). C_4 gathers structured textures with a weave-like structure. This cluster is represented by the texture word **interlaced** (tw_4=**I**). C_5 consists of linearly oriented textures (the orientation is along a straight line). It is represented by the texture word **lined** (tw_5=**L**). Texture cluster C_6 consists of **marbled** (tw_6=**M**) textures. C_7 consists of texture with two-directional characteristic features, combined to form a weave. Textures in C_3 differ from textures in this category as they present a certain amount of variation and randomness. It is represented by the texture word **netlike** (tw_7=**N**). C_8 groups textures presenting some disfigurement. It is characterized by the texture word **smeared**, which denotes negative aesthetics (tw_8=**S**). C_9 consists of textures with representative features being small, blob-like and scattered over a plane. It is characterized by the texture word **spotted** (tw_9=**Sp**). C_{10} refers to **uniform** (tw_{10}=**U**) textures (here the nature of the repetition is not specified, which was the case for textures in cluster C_7). The last cluster C_{11} consists of circularly oriented textures. It is represented by the texture word **whirly** (tw_{11}=**W**).

These eleven high-level texture categories are the foundation of our framework for texture symbolic characterization. We study in the next section the mapping between automatically extracted low-level textures and these high-level texture categories.

4.3 Mapping with Support Vector Machines

4.3.1 Specification

Our architecture and its supported operational model make it possible for a user to combine texture characterizations with visual semantics in a full-text conceptual framework for indexing and querying. However, querying textually on texture features requires to implement a correspondence process between extracted low-level features and symbolic texture names. The naïve mapping from computational texture features to high-level symbolic texture features can be somewhat complex and difficult to derive. In the case of mapping these 49-dimensions vectors of Gabor energies to the 11 texture words, support vector machines [28] are trained to perform this mapping efficiently. We adopt the one-against-rest approach where a separate classifier is designed for each of the eleven texture words for reasons of optimized inter-class separation. We also associate a confidence value for the classification defined. For this, we use the distance from an IO i to be characterized with texture word t to the decision boundary $f_t(i)$ (where f_t is the trained discriminant function on the one-against-rest classification problem involving texture word t) and map it on posterior probabilities of recognition. In order to achieve this mapping, we use a 1D logistic classifier [1] which maximizes the likelihood of the classified training IOs.

Table 1. Cross-Validation Percentages

TW	B	C	D	I	L	M	N	S	S_p	U	W
%	83,7	85,2	88,9	91,9	94,5	98,0	86,8	83,4	90,0	97,3	81,4

Lined   Whirly   Netlike   Uniform   Disordered   Spotted   Interlaced   Smeared   Cracked   Bumpy

Fig. 5. Correspondence between texture images and texture words

4.3.2 Testing

The data set consists of 10000 texture images used in [11], each of the eleven texture words being represented by 900 to 1000 texture images. We propose in figure 5 example images for each of the specified texture words.

To determine the performance of our mapping through SVMs, we first use v-fold cross-validation. The training set is divided into v subsets of equal size. Sequentially, one subset is tested using the classifier trained on the remaining v-1 subsets. Thus, each instance of the whole training set is predicted once so the cross-validation accuracy is the percentage of data which are correctly classified. This procedure prevents the overfitting problem [7]. Then, we apply the grid-search procedure to find the optimal parameters achieving the best cross-validation accuracy. For each of the eleven texture words, the best cross-validation rate is given in table 1. Let us note that the SVMs are able to label new instances of unknown textures with corresponding texture words with a high accuracy, cross-validation percentages being all higher than 80%.

4.4 Conceptual Structures for the Texture Facet

4.4.1 Texture Index Structures

Texture index concepts (TICs) are supported by a vector structure **t** with eleven elements corresponding to texture words tw_i. Values $t[i]$, $i \in [1,11]$ are booleans stressing that the texture distribution of the considered IO is characterized by the texture word tw_i. E.g., the second IO (Io2) corresponding to the semantic concept *huts* in figure 1 is characterized by the texture index concept <B:0,C:0...I:0,L:1,N:0...>, which is translated by Io2 being characterized by the texture word **lined**.

4.4.2 Texture Query Structures

Our framework proposes an expressive query language which integrates visual semantics and symbolic texture characterization through boolean operators. A user shall be able to associate visual semantics with a boolean conjunction of texture words such as in Q1: "Find images displaying a road with both **bumpy** AND **cracked** textures", a boolean disjunction of texture words such as in Q2: "Find images with a **covered/disordered** OR **bright/uniform** sky" and a negation of texture words such as in Q3: "Find images with NON-**interlaced** flowers".

Three types of conceptual structures are specified to support the previously defined query types. *And* texture concepts (ATCs) represent the signal distribution of an IO by a conjunction of texture words; *Or* texture concepts (OTCs) by a disjunction of texture words and *No* texture concepts (NCCs) by a negation of texture words. The ATC <B:1,C:1...I:0,L:0,N:0...>$_{AND}$, the OTC <B:0,C:1...I:0,L:0,N:1...>$_{OR}$ and the NTC <B:0,C:0...I:1,L:0,N:0...>$_{NO}$ respectively correspond to the texture distributions expressed in queries Q1, Q2 and Q3.

4.5 Conceptual Specification for the Texture Facet

Texture concepts are elements of partially-ordered lattices organized with respect to the type of the query processed. We will propose in section 5 the organization of the lattice processing *And* texture concepts and *Or* texture concepts. There are 2 types of basic graphs controlling the generation of all the texture facet graphs. **Index texture**

graphs link an *Io* type through the conceptual relation ind_tx to a texture index concept: **[Io]→(ind_tx)→[TIC]**. **Query texture graphs** link an *Io* type through conceptual relations a_tx, o_tx, or n_tx to a texture query concept, respectively an *And, Or* or *No* texture concept: **[Io]→(and_tx)→[ATC]**; **[Io]→(or_tx)→[OTC]** and **[Io]→(no_tx)→[NTC]**. Eg, index graphs [Io1]→(ind_tx)→[<B:0,C:0,D:1,I:0...>], [Io2]→(ind_tx)→[<B:0,C:0...I:0,L:1, N:0...>] and [Io3]→(ind_tx)→[<B:0,C:0...U:1...>] are the index representation of the texture facet in figure 1 and are interpreted as: the first IO (Io1) is associated with the texture index concept <B:0,C:0,D:1,I:0...> (**i.e. disordered/covered**), Io2 with the texture index concept <B:0,C:0...I:0,L:1,N:0...> (**i.e. lined**) and Io3 with the texture index concept <B:0,C:0...U:1...> (**i.e. uniform**).

5 The Query Module

In image retrieval systems, the typical mode of user interaction relies on query-by-example: a user provides an image as an input to the system, which generates a query and then outputs images that are the most similar to the input image. This mode of interaction suffers from the fact that the user's need remains implicit, i.e. given the input images chosen by the user, the system has thus to use its knowledge of the image content to extract implicit information and build a query. This process can be very complex and lead to ambiguities and poor retrieval performance when dealing with high-level characterizations of an image. Our conceptual architecture is based on a unified full-text framework allowing a user to query over both the visual semantics and the texture facets. This obviously enhances user interaction since contrarily to query-by-example systems, the user becomes in charge of the query process by making his needs explicit to the system. We study next the transcription of queries within our conceptual framework and then deal with their processing.

5.1 Query Expression

The representation of a user query in our model is, like image index representations, obtained through the combination (joint operation) of CGs over the visual semantics and texture facets (query texture graphs).

E.g., the Q1 query "Find images displaying a road with both **bumpy** and **cracked** textures" is represented by the graph: **[Io1]→(sct)→[Road]**
→ (and_tx)→[<B:1,C:1,D:0,I:0...>$_{AND}$]

The Q2 query is represented by the graph: **[Io1]→(sct)→[Sky]**
→ (or_tx)→[<B:0...D:1,I:0...U:1...>$_{OR}$]

The Q3 query is represented by the graph: **[Io1]→(sct)→[Flowers]**
→ (no_tx)→[< B:0...I:1...W:0>$_{NO}$]

5.2 The Matching Process

The matching framework is based on an extension of VanRijsbergen's logical model proposed in [22]. The relevance of an image document ID with respect to a query Q is given by a combination of the exhaustivity and specificity measures:
Relevance(ID,Q) = F[P(ID→Q), P'(Q→ID)]

Exhaustivity measures to which extent the image document satisfies the query. It is given by the value of $P(ID \rightarrow Q)$, P being the exhaustivity function.

Specificity measures the importance of the query themes within the image document, it is given by the value of $P'(Q \rightarrow ID)$, P' being the specificity function.

The F function values are to be proportional to the values of the exhaustivity and specificity functions, we have chosen the trivial multiplication operation. We present in the next sections an instanciation of the exhaustivity and specificity functions.

5.2.1 The Exhaustivity Function P

The exhaustivity function P consists in two operations. It first checks that all elements described within the query graph are also elements of the index graph. For this, we use the CG projection operator to compare image query and index graphs. This operator allows to identify within the image index graph i all sub-graphs with the same structure as the query graph q, with nodes being possibly restricted, i.e. they are specializations of q nodes. $\Pi q(i)$ is the set of all possible projections of query graph q into image index graph i.

Then, for each selected image document, we provide an estimation of its relevance with respect to the query, which corresponds to the quantitative evaluation of the similarity between query and document. It is given by the exhaustivity value between query graph q and image index graph i:

$$EV(q,i) = MAX_{\Pi q(i)} \; \Sigma_{SCq \text{ concept of } q, \; SCi \text{ matching concept of } i} \; I(SC_i) + Cpt\_Match(SC_i, SC_q) +$$

$$\Sigma_{TCq \text{ concept of } q, \; TCi, \text{ matching concept of } i} \; Cpt\_Match(TC_i, TC_q) \tag{1}$$

The I function measures the 'importance' of a semantic concept within an image document. It is both proportional to the size of the corresponding IO and its global localization with respect to the image center, as corroborated by the user study in [16].

The *Cpt_Match* function is correlated to the importance of the recognition posterior probabilities of the matching semantic and texture concepts of graph i with respect to semantic and texture concepts of graph q. In our approach, the *Cpt_Match* function is the negative Kullback-Leibler divergence [9] between the probability of the image document semantic and texture concepts and the query concepts (which are themselves certain, ie. $P(SC_q)$ and $P(TC_q)$ equal 1).

Let us note that brute-force implementations of the projection operator would result in exponential execution times. Therefore, based on the work in [21], we use an adaptation of the inverted file approach for image retrieval. We specify indeed lookup tables associating semantic concepts to the set of image index representations that contain these concepts. Moreover, lattices organizing texture concepts are defined by mathematical partial orders and are consequently not stored in memory, which avoids traversing complex graph structures at retrieval time.

5.2.2 The Specificity Function P'

The specificity function takes into account the importance of the query terms within the image document. As a matter of fact, following the conclusions of the user study in [16], a user expects that retrieved image documents are strictly restricted to visual elements connected to his query terms. If not, we say that the image document 'degrades' the query. Indeed, if a user queries with "Find images with bumpy roads", he considers as the most relevant images displaying roads characterized by the texture word bumpy <u>only</u>. Other images are composed of roads characterized by a bumpy texture and at least one additional texture word not mentioned in the query. Lattices of texture concepts (cf. 5.3) take into account the query degradation phenomenon by relating more closely texture concepts with the most common number of texture words. Therefore, the evaluation of the query degradation is formally mapped to a path length evaluation problem in these lattices. Considering index and query texture graphs, the *Path_Tex* function computes path lengths in texture concept lattices between matching index and query concepts.

Also, if image documents include additional visual entities not mentioned in a user query, they are expected to be the most closely related to entities specified in this query [16]. E.g., if a user queries with "Find images with cars", he considers that images displaying cars and bicycles are more relevant for his search than images containing cars and buildings. This notion of 'close relationship' between semantic concepts is evaluated in the lattice of semantic concepts by the *Path_Sem* function. The latter computes the path length between a query and an index semantic concept. In our example, the path length between semantic concepts *car* and *bicycle* equals 0, since they are at the same level in the lattice of semantic concepts (figure 4). However, the path length between semantic concepts *car* and *building* equals 6.

The specificity value measures the importance of the query themes within the image document by minimizing path lengths between semantic and texture concepts of a query graph q and concepts of an index graph i:

$$SV(q,i) = MIN_{\Pi q(i)} \ [\Sigma_{SCq \ concept \ of \ q, \ SCi \ matching \ concept \ of \ i} \ \textbf{Path\_Sem(SC}_i,\textbf{SC}_q\textbf{)} +$$
$$\Sigma_{TCq \ concept \ of \ q, \ TCi, \ matching \ concept \ of \ i} \ \textbf{Path\_Tex(TC}_i,\textbf{TC}_q\textbf{)]} \tag{2}$$

As far as the computational load is concerned, path lengths in the lattice of semantic concepts are pre-computed and stored in an annex file. Also, to evaluate path lengths in texture concept lattices, there is no computationally-expensive lattice traversal performed. Indeed, path lengths within these lattices are computed on the fly through a mathematical relation that is not explicited in this paper due to space restriction. We specify next the lattices organizing *And* and *Or* texture concepts.

5.3 Fast Query Processing

5.3.1 Processing Queries with *and* Texture Concepts

Texture index concepts are organized within an *And* lattice (↓ corresponds to a specialization operation in figures 6 and 7) to process a query conveying a boolean conjunction of texture words such as "Find images with bumpy **and** cracked roads". When this query is formulated, it is translated in its graph representation (cf. 5.1). The semantic concept *road* is processed by the lattice of semantic concepts (cf. figure 4). The *And* texture concept <B:1,C:1...I:0,L:0,N:0...>$_{AND}$ is related to its equivalent index texture concept as highlighted in figure 6. There is a synonymy link between these two concepts as they convey the same boolean operator (i.e. a conjunction). The most relevant images provided by the system present bumpy and cracked roads, i.e. only texture concepts mentioned in the query. This symbolic texture distribution is represented by the highlighted texture index concept (t_1) in figure 6. Other images are composed of roads characterized by bumpy and cracked texture words with at least 1 additional texture word not mentioned in the query (called secondary). In the lattice, texture index concepts representing such distributions are sons of t_1.

The general organization of this lattice is such that texture index concepts with a unique non-zero component are sons of the maximum virtual element of the lattice T_{AND}.

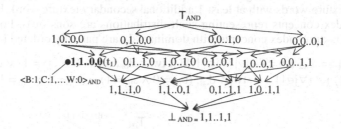

Fig. 6. Lattice Processing *And* Texture Concepts

They characterize IOs with a texture distribution represented by a unique texture word. The texture index concept with all non-zero components is at the bottom of the hierarchy, it is the minimum virtual element noted $\perp_{AND}$. This concept will be considered as a specialized concept of all index concepts presenting at least a non-zero component (it characterizes an IO with a texture distribution represented by all specified texture words!). A mathematical partial order noted $\leq_{AND}$, which allows to quickly evaluate the matching between index and query texture concepts at retrieval time, defines the lattice processing *And* texture concepts:

$$\forall a,b \in TICs \quad a \leq_{And} b \leftrightarrow [a = \perp_{And} \vee b = T_{And}] \vee [\neg \exists k \in [1,11], b_{[k]} = 1 \wedge a_{[k]} = 0] \quad (3)$$

5.3.2 Processing Queries with *or* Texture Concepts

Texture index concepts are organized within an *Or* lattice to process a query conveying a boolean disjunction of texture words such as "Find images with a covered **or** bright sky". When this query is formulated, it is translated in its graph representation (cf. 5.1). The semantic concept sky is processed by the lattice of semantic concepts. However, contrarily to the trivial synonymy relation between *And* texture concepts and texture index concepts previously exhibited, the link between the generated *Or* texture concept $<B:0...D:1,I:0...U:1...>_{OR}$ and its equivalent texture index concept is not straightforward. A new category of concepts eliciting this link by taking into account **dominant** texture words (i.e. texture words mentioned in a query as they have a higher importance in the ordering process of texture concepts within the lattice, other texture words are called **secondary**) shall be introduced. These concepts are texture index concepts **with dominant d_{OR}**, where d_{OR} is the set of dominant texture words. They are supported by a vector structure t_d with eleven elements corresponding to texture words tw_i Values $t_d[i]_{i \in [11]}$ such that $tw_i \in d_{OR}$ characterize the presence of dominant texture words and values $t_d[j]_{j \in [1,11]}$ such that $j \neq i$, the presence of secondary texture words within the texture distribution of the considered IO. Texture index concepts **with dominant d_{OR}** are specializations of *Or* texture concepts representing a boolean disjunction of texture words in a query and generalizations of texture index concepts. The *Or* texture concept $<B:0...D:1,I:0...U:1...>_{OR}$ is related to its equivalent index texture concept with dominant {disordered, uniform}: $<B:0...\underline{D:1},...,\underline{U:1},W:0>$ as highlighted in the lattice of figure 7. As a matter of fact, the most relevant images provided by the system present a covered/disordered or a bright/uniform sky, i.e. a sky with a texture distribution characterized only by dominant texture words. This symbolic texture distribution is represented by the highlighted texture index concept (t_2) in figure 7. Other images are composed of a sky characterized by disordered or uniform texture words with at least 1 additional secondary texture word. In the lattice, texture index concepts representing such distributions are sons of t_2. Formally, sub-lattices of texture index concepts with dominant d_{OR} are partially ordered by $\leq_{OR}$:

$$a \leq_{OR} b \Leftrightarrow [a = \perp_{OR} \vee b = T_{OR}] \vee [(\forall i \in [1,11], tw_i \in d_{OR}, (a_{[i]} = 0 \wedge b_{[i]} = 1) \vee (a_{[i]} = 1 \wedge b_{[i]} = 1)) \wedge (\forall j \in [1,11], tw_j \notin d_{OR}, (b_{[i]} = 0 \wedge a_{[i]} = 1) \vee (b_{[i]} = 1 \wedge a_{[i]} = 1))] \quad (4)$$

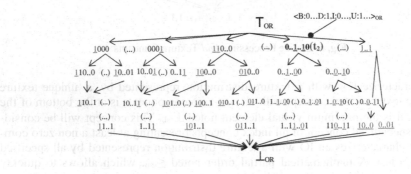

Fig. 7. Lattice Processing *Or* Texture Concepts

6   Validation Experiments: An Application to Home Photographs

The SIR prototype (its interface implemented in C++ is proposed in figure 8) implements the theoretical framework exposed in this paper and validation experiments are carried out on a corpus of 2500 personal color photographs used as a validation corpus in several world-class publications [2,12,13,19].

We choose to deal with a collection of home photographs instead of the Corel professional collection since it has been argued that the Corel dataset is much easier to annotate and retrieve; and in fact does not capture the difficulties inherent in more challenging datasets used in real world [19]. Indeed, our collection includes some pictures with inferior quality (fading black and white, flashy, blur, noisy, dark and over-exposed photographs) that are however kept in our test collection to reflect the complexity of original and realistic personal photographs. Let us note that they could affect any automatic indexing and retrieval processes. As a matter of fact, experiments reported in [19] confirmed that classification and retrieval results for home photographs are on the whole poorer than those for the Corel images since their quality and content are more varied and heterogeneous.

IOs within the 2500 photographs are automatically assigned a semantic concept as presented in 3. and are characterized with index texture structures presented in 4.

As opposed to state-of-the-art semantic frameworks allowing only single-word queries [5,9,12,27], we wish to retrieve photographs that represent elaborate image scenes and propose 24 queries involving semantic concepts with texture characterizations such as *lined people, interlaced foliage...* The evaluation of our formalism is based on the notion of *image relevance* which consists in quantifying the correspondence between index and query images. We compare SIR with a system based on a symbolic approach: the *Visual Keyword* system S_1 and a state-of-the-art loosely-coupled system S_2 combining a textual framework for querying on semantics and a RF process operating on low-level texture features.

Visual keywords (VKs) [2,12,13,19] are intuitive and flexible visual prototypes extracted or learned from a visual content domain with relevant semantic labels. A set of 26 specified VKs are learned using a neural network, with low-level features computed for each training region as an input for this network. An image is then represented through a set of local VK histograms with each bin corresponding to the aggregation of recognition results. The matching function of S_1 is computed as the weighted average of the similarities between the corresponding local VK histograms of index and query images.

The semantic framework of S_2 is an adaptation of the VK approach where the most probable label is kept, which allows to query textually over symbolic entities. It is associated with a RF process based on Gabor texture extraction [11]. The matching function of S_2 is computed as the weighted average of the similarities between the corresponding local most probable VKs and locally weighted Gabor energy matrices of index and query images.

For each proposed query in table 2, we construct relevant textual query terms using corresponding semantic and texture concepts as input to SIR (e.g. 'Find images with a lined crowd' for *lined people*). The retrieval results for this query are given in figure 8. S_1 processes three series of three random relevant photographs for each query (they correspond to lined people as far as our example query is concerned). Also each query in table 2 is translated in relevant textual data to be processed by the semantic framework of S_2 ('Find images with people' for *lined people*). Then to refine the results, three random relevant photographs are selected as input to the RF framework.

Table 2. Queries

Bumpy Roads	Field of Lined Flowers
Cracked Grounds	Lined Trees
Cracked Walls	Marble Floor
Covered Sky	Brick-like Ground
Interlaced Vegeta-	Smeared Buildings
Lined Huts	Dirt-smeared Roads
Lined People	Dirt-smeared Walls
Uniform Crowd	Spotted Fur
Smooth Sky	Spotted Floors
Uniform Floor	Cracked & Smeared Walls
Whirly Water	Non Interlaced Flowers
Netlike Windows	Netlike or Marble Floors

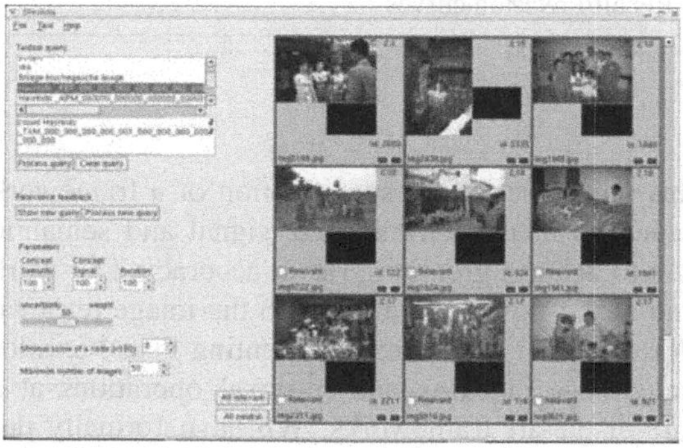

Fig. 8. SIR interface "Images with a lined crowd"

We determine all images which are relevant to the 24 defined queries within the corpus and each author evaluates the number of relevant documents found by the compared systems. Recall/precision curves of figure 10 illustrate the average results obtained for all queries considering the corpus of 2500 images: the curve associated with the *SIR* legend illustrates the results in recall and precision obtained by SIR, the curve associated with the *VK* legend by S_1 and the curve associated with the *SignSymb* legend by S_2. The average precision of SIR (0.4292) is approximately 78,54% higher over the average precision of the VK system (0.2404) and approximately 35,61% higher over the average precision of the loosely-coupled state-of-the-art system (0.3165). We notice that improvements of the precision values are significant at all recall values. This shows that when dealing with elaborate queries which combine multiple sources of information (here visual semantics and texture characterizations) and thus require a higher level of abstraction, the use of an "intelligent" and expressive representation formalism (here the CG formalism within our framework) is crucial. As a matter of fact, our system complements automatic keyword-based approaches (in this case the VKs) through the enrichment of their single-word query frameworks with texture characterization. Moreover, it outperforms state-of-the-art loosely-coupled solutions by proposing a unified full-text framework optimizing user interaction and allowing to query with precision over visual semantics and high-level texture features.

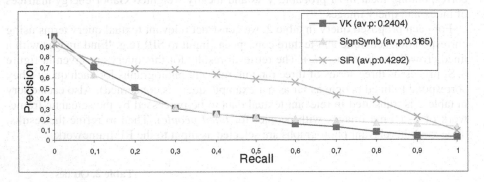

Fig. 9. Recall/Precision curves

7   Conclusion

We proposed within the scope of this paper the formal specification of a framework combining the two existing approaches in image retrieval, i.e. signal and semantic within a strongly-coupled architecture to achieve greater retrieval accuracy. Our work has contributed both theoretically and at the experimental level to the image retrieval research topic. We have specified IOs, abstract structures representing visual entities within an image in order to operate image indexing and retrieval operations at a higher level of abstraction than state-of-the-art frameworks. We have formally described the visual semantics and texture facets that define the conceptual information conveyed by IOs and have finally proposed a unified and rich framework for querying. At the experimental level, the obtained results allowed us to validate our approach and stress the relevance of integrating visual semantics and signal texture characterizations.

References

1. Anderson, J.: Logistic discrimination. (1982)
2. Belkhatir, M. & al.: Integrating Perceptual Signal Features within a Multi-facetted Conceptual Model for Automatic Image Retrieval. ECIR (2004) 267-282
3. Belkhatir, M. & al.: The Outline of an 'Intelligent' Image Retrieval Engine. ICWI (2004) 1228-1232
4. Bhushan, N. & al: The Texture Lexicon: Understanding the Categorization of Visual Texture Terms and Their Relationship to Texture Images. Cognitive Science 21(2) (1997) 219-246
5. Bradshaw, B.: Semantic based image retrieval: a probabilistic approach. ACM MM (2000) 167-176
6. Carson, C. & al.: Blobworld: A System for Region-Based Image Indexing and Retrieval. VISUAL (1999) 509-516
7. Hsu, C.W. & al.: A Practical Guide to Support Vector Classification.
8. Guyader, N. & al. "Towards the introduction of human perception in a natural scene classification system". NNSP (2002)
9. Jeon, J. & al.: Automatic image annotation and retrieval using cross-media relevance models. SIGIR (2003) 119-126
10. La Cascia & al.: Combining Textual and Visual Cues for Content-Based Image Retrieval on the World Wide Web. IEEE Workshop on Content-Based Access of Image and Video Libraries (1998) 24-28
11. Leow, W.K. & Lai, S.Y. "Invariant matching of texture for content-based image retrieval". MMM (1997) 53-68
12. Lim, J.H.: Explicit query formulation with visual keywords. ACM MM (2000) 407-412
13. Lim, J.H. & al.: Home Photo Content Modeling for Personalized Event-Based Retrieval. IEEE Multimedia 10(4) (2003)
14. Lu, Y. & al.: A unified framework for semantics and feature based relevance feedback in image retrieval systems. ACM MM (2000) 31-37
15. Ma, W. & Manjunath, B.: NeTra: A toolbox for navigating large image databases. ICIC (1997) 568-571
16. Martinet, J.: Un modèle vectoriel relationnel de recherche d'information adapté aux images. PhD Thesis (2004) Joseph Fourier University
17. Mechkour, M.: EMIR^2: An Extended Model for Image Representation and Retrieval. DEXA (1995) 395-404
18. Mojsilovic, A. & Rogowitz, B.: Capturing image semantics with low-level descriptors. ICIP (2001) 18-21
19. Mulhem, P. & Lim, J.H.: Symbolic photograph content-based retrieval. CIKM (2002) 94-101
20. Niblack, W. & al.: The QBIC project: Querying images by content using color, texture and shape. SPIE, Storage and Retrieval for Image and Video Databases (1993) 40-48
21. Ounis, I. & Pasca, M.: RELIEF: Combining expressiveness and rapidity into a single system. SIGIR (1998) 266-274
22. Nie, J.: An Outline of a General Model for Information Retrieval Systems. SIGIR (1988) 495-506

474   M. Belkhatir

23. Pentland, R. & al.: Photobook: Tools for Content-Based Manipulation of Image Databases. SPIE (1994) 34-47
24. Rao, A.R., & Lohse, G.L.: Towards a texture naming system: Identifying relevant dimensions of texture. Visualization, (1993) 220-227
25. Smeulders, A.W.M. & al.: Content-based image retrieval at the end of the early years. IEEE PAMI, 22(12) (2000) 1349-1380
26. Sowa, J.F. "Conceptual structures: information processing in mind and machine". Addison-Wesley publishing company (1984)
27. Town, C.P. & Sinclair, D.: CBIR Using Semantic Visual Categories". TR2000-14, AT&T Labs Cambridge (2000)
28. Vapnik, V.: Statistical Learning Theory. Wiley (1998)
29. Zhou, X.S. & Huang, T.S.: Unifying Keywords and Visual Contents in Image Retrieval. IEEE Multimedia 9(2) (2002) 23-33

Applying Associative Relationship on the Clickthrough Data to Improve Web Search

Xue-Mei Jiang[1], Wen-Guan Song[1], and Hua-Jun Zeng[2]

[1] Department of Information Management, Shanghai Business School,
2271 Zhongshan West Ave., 200235 Shanghai, P.R.China
xuemei.jiang@gmail.com, swg@21cn.com
[2] Microsoft Research Asia, 5F, Sigma Center,
49 Zhichun Road, Beijing 100080, P.R.China
hjzeng@microsoft.com

Abstract. The performance of web search engines may often deteriorate due to the diversity and noise contained within web pages. Some methods proposed to use clickthrough data to achieve more accurate information for web pages as well as improve the search performance. However, sparseness became the great challenge in exploiting clickthrough data. In this paper, we propose a novel algorithm to exploit the user clickthrough data. It first explores the relationship between queries and web pages to mine out co-visiting as the associative relationship among the Web pages, and then Spreading Activation mechanism is used to re-rank the results of Web search. Our approach could alleviate such sparseness and the experimental results on a large set of MSN clickthrough log data show a significant improvement on search performance over the DirectHit algorithm as well as the baseline search engine.

1 Introduction

The mainly approach in web search engines is to calculate the relevancy of web pages for a given query by counting the search keywords contained in the web pages. This method works well when users' queries are clear and specific. However, in real world, web search queries are often short (less than 3 words [1]) and ambiguous. On the other hand, web pages contain a lot of diverse and noisy information. These will very likely lead to the deterioration of the performance of web search engines, due to the gap between query space and document space [6][9]. This problem can be partially solved by using external evidence to enrich the content of existing web pages. One of such examples is to use anchor texts as additional description of target Web pages. Previous research [17][24][26] show that this method yields better search result than searching on Web page content alone. This is because anchor texts represent the view of a web page by other web editors rather its own author. Another solution is to introduce additional description by using clickthrough data, which has not been extensively studied.

User clickthrough data can be extracted from a large amount of search logs accumulated by web search engines. These logs typically contain user-submitted search queries, followed by the URL of Web pages which are clicked by users in the corre-

D.E. Losada and J.M. Fernández-Luna (Eds.): ECIR 2005, LNCS 3408, pp. 475–486, 2005.

sponding search result pages. Although these clicks do not reflect the exact relevancy, they provide valuable indications to the users' intention by associating a set of query terms with a set of web pages. If a user clicks on a web page, it is likely that the web page is relevant to the query, or at least related to some extent. Many valuable applications have been proposed along this direction, such as query expansion [6], term suggestion [3][18], and query clustering [7][13].

Derived from the co-citation and co-coupling methods [12][23] to find the similar papers, we propose to use an analogous method, called co-visiting, which is used to exploit the relationship between the Web pages and the queries in the clickthrough data and so, to find the association relationship among the Web pages; if the two Web pages are clicked by many same queries, they are assumed similar according to this co-visiting method... Additionally, we use a weight to represent the degree of the similarity between two Web pages, which can be spread among the Web pages pool thanks to a Spreading Activation approach

The rest of this paper is organized as follows. In Section 2, we first review the related work. The analysis of the characteristics about the Web graph structure is given in Section 3.. In Section 4, we show our ranking algorithm. Our experimental results are presented in Section 5. Finally, conclusions and future works are discussed in Section 6.

2   Related Work

Our approach has strong ties to what might generally be called "structure context analysis" [10] and bibliometrics [12][15]. The latter considers the citation patterns of scientific papers: relationships between papers are inferred from citations. Most notable works from this field are the works on co-citation [12] and bibliographic coupling [15]. In the co-citation scheme, similarity between two papers p and q is based on the number of papers which cite both p and q and on the other hand in bibliograpgic coupling, similarity is based on the number of papers cited by both p and q. These methods have been used to cluster scientific journals as described in [23]. Most recently, the co-citation method has been used to cluster web pages [7][13] as well. Jeh and Widom [10] proposed a generalized iterative technique to incrementally calculate the similarities of all pairs of web objects and linearly combine the final results.

Query log analysis is extensively investigated in recent years. [27] proposed to reuse past optimal queries to improve search by re-formulating new queries. Recently, Joachims [14] propose a method of utilizing clickthrough data in learning of a retrieval function (e.g., a meta-search function). Specifically, he introduces a new method for training a retrieval function on the basis of clickthrough data, which he calls Ranking SVM. His method is unique in that it takes the relative positions of the clicks in a rank as training data. New approaches [7][13] on query log analysis focus on query clustering and web pages clustering. The use of clickthrough data to measure similarity between objects was found to be better than calculating similarities using objects' content vector. For example, Beeferman and Berger proposed an innovative query clustering method [7] based on clickthrough data. Each record of clickthrough data consists of a user's query to the search engine and the URLs that user actually visited among the list provided by the search engine. Clickthrough data sets can be treated as a bipartite graph and the identification of similar web pages as result of a clustering of topology of this graph; but this process ignores the content features in both query and document, and the hyperlink interconnectivity information of web pages, either. Wen and al [13] describes a query clustering method using user logs, in which two queries are similar if they contain the same terms or leading to the selection of the same retrieved documents. Unfortunately, these methods do not consider the web pages and queries as an integrated fashion, where each feature could reinforce the similarity of the other.

DirectHit is more similar to our proposed algorithm. The method collects information on: (a) the queries of individual user submitted to search and (b) the pages they look at. This information is used to return pages that *most* users visit after performing the given query. However, this method just takes the frequency into account, while there are lot of information could not be discovered using this unique feature. So beyond only considering frequency, we developed an algorithm exploiting the relationship between the queries and Web pages and able to find the associative relationship in the clickthrough data.

3 Spreading Activation on the Clickthrough Data

In this section, we first define the problem of generating associative relationship among the Web pages from clickthrough data. Then, a co-visited algorithm is proposed to find the associative relationship. Finally, we propose the spreading activation approach to utilize the associative relationship to improve the quality of Web search.

3.1 Problem Description

We define clickthrough data as a set *Session*, whose element is defined as a pair of a query and a web page the user clicked on. Clickthrough data is generated from raw search logs, which may contain large amount of useless logs such as images and scripts, and random user behaviors. Through certain session split algorithm and noise filtering (which will be described in the experiment section), we could get more accurate clickthrough data. We further assume that the set of clicked web pages c is relevant to the query q. This assumption might be too strong in some cases because of some noisy clicks inside the data. But most users usually are likely to click on a relevant results, thus we can benefit from a large quantity of clickthrough data.

By merging same queries and web pages in the above sessions, clickthrough data could be modeled as a weighted directed bipartite graph $G=(V, E)$, where nodes in V represent web pages and queries and edges E represent the clickthroughs from a query to a clicked web page. We can divide V into two subsets $Q=\{q_1, q_2, ..., q_m\}$ and $D=\{d_1, d_2, ..., d_n\}$ where Q represents the queries and D represents the Web pages, as shown in Figure 1.

Then, the problem is to efficiently find the associative relationship between the nodes in D by mining the bipartite graph G. Here we propose a co-visiting mining algorithm to solve this problem.

Queries   Web Pages

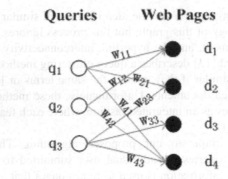

Fig. 1. Interrelations between queries and Web pages

3.2 Co-visiting Mining (CVM)

It is easy to demonstrate that DirectHit Method could achieve good performance if the query clickthrough data is complete, i.e. each query is associated with all the related documents. But unfortunately, we found that in the real world, each query will randomly be associated with only a few individual pages instead of whole list. This data incompleteness problem makes the performance of the naïve method drop significantly and that's why we derived methods of co-citation described in Section 1 to find similar web pages. As shown in Figure 2, if the two web pages are clicked by mostly the same queries, it is possible that these two web pages are similar. We define a term **co-visited** to represent such a relationship, which means that if two web pages are clicked by users with the same query, the two web pages are co-visited.

Queries   Web Pages

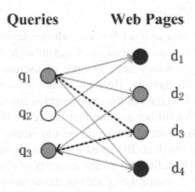

Fig. 2. Co-visited graph

Next we describe how to measure the similarity of two co-visited web pages using the clickthrough information. All possible pairs and their frequency are calculated from all the sessions. Precisely, the number of visit times of a web page d_i, denoted as *visited*(d_i), refers to the number of the sessions that the web page d is visited by all the related queries. The number of co-visited times of a two web pages pair (d_i, d_j), denoted *visited*(d_i, d_j), is defined in a similar way.

With the above definitions, the similarity S between two web pages d_i and d_j based on the co-visited relationship can be computed as:

$$S(d_i,d_j) = \frac{visited(d_i,d_j)}{visited(d_i)+visited(d_j)-visited(d_i,d_j)}$$

The measure is scaled to [0, 1].

For example, if we assume that each web page of Figure 1 is visited by the queries only once in the Figure 2, we can apply the above formula to compute the similarity of any two web pages. The result is shown as follows:

$$S(d_2,d_3) = \frac{1}{2+1-1} = 0.5$$

$$S(d_3,d_4) = \frac{1}{1+3-1} = 0.33$$

If the similarity value between two web pages is greater than a minimum threshold σ, the two web pages are treated as similar. So if σ is equal to 0.4, the web pages d_2 and d_3 are similar to each other and the web pages d_3 and d_4 are dissimilar by definition. Furthermore, if σ is set to 1, which means that two web pages are clicked by exact the same queries, this algorithm is the same as the naïve method; and if σ is set to 0, which means that any two pages that have one common query are similar to each other. Later experiments will show that the precision of queries associated with a given page is highest when σ is equal to 0.3. All the similar pages of a given page d is denoted as $Sim(d)$.

From above processes, the co-visiting relationship with a similarity values between the two Web pages could be mining out. Then, we could take such co-visiting relationship as the associative relationship among the pages and use such relationships to improve the Web search.

3.4 Spreading Activation on Web Search

Spreading activation techniques have been applied to associative retrieval both as a human cognition and information processing model [7] and as a computational mechanism to speed up the exploration process of networks of associations. Spreading activation techniques have also been applied recently to explore different types of networks, including the Web, citation networks, and content similarity networks [3][4][19]. In our study, we emphasized the use of spreading activation as a computational method to efficiently explore transitive associations among the Web pages.

Derived from the definition of spreading activation approach, we propose to use this method to re-rank the result of Web search by utilizing the co-visiting information among the Web pages.

First, the user submits the query Q to the search engine and the system returns the result set D that match the query terms. The degree of match between a Web page d_i in D and Q is computed by the retrieval system (In this paper, we take the BM2500 as relevance measurement between the query and Web pages). We denote the similarity between the d_i and Q as $sim(d_i, Q)$.

Then, we use the spreading activation approach to propagate the similarity between the d_i and Q to the co-visiting Web pages of d_i through a certain number of cycles using a propagation factor. To simplify the problem, we use a simplified version with only one cycle. In that case, the final retrieval status, called sim_{final}, value of a Web page d_i that co-visiting with m Web pages is computed according to the following equation:

$$sim_{final}(d_i, Q) = sim(d_i, Q) + \lambda \sum_{j=1}^{m} sim(d_j, Q)$$

Finally, the search result is re-ranked according to the final similarity values between the Web pages and query.

Through the active spreading, the associative relationship could be fully exploited to further solve the sparse problem.

4   Experiments

In this section, we introduce the experimental data set, our evaluation metrics, and the experimental result based on those metrics.

4.1   Data Set

In order to study the effectiveness of the proposed iterative algorithm for optimizing search performance, our experiments are conducted on a real clickthrough data which is extracted from the log of the MSN search engine [16] of August, 2003. It contains about 1.2 million query requests recorded over three hours. The log we obtained is already processed into a predefined format, i.e. each query request is associated with one clicked web page. We called it "query session", which can be defined as follows:

Query Session: = query text [clicked Web page *]

Table 1. A sample of the raw MSN query clickthrough data

Query	Clicked Web Page
patent	www.uspto.gov
maps	www.mapquest.com
www.teen+titan.com	www.cartoonnetwork.com/titans/
www.ikea.com	www.ikea-usa.com
cokemusic.com	www.cokemusic.com
motel6	www.motel6.com
pampered chef	www.pamperedchef.com
Weather	www.nws.noaa.gov

The average query length is about 2.8 words. A small sample of the raw data is shown in Table 1. Before doing experiment, some preprocessing steps are applied to queries and web pages in the raw log. All queries are converted into lower-case, stemmed by the Porter algorithm and stop words are removed. The query sessions sharing a same query are merged into a large query session, with the frequencies being summed up. We use a crawler to download the content of all web pages contained in this log and remove the dead links. After downloading the pages, Okapi system [22] is used to index the full text using BM25 formula. After preprocessing, the log contains 13,894,155 sessions, 507,041 pages and 862,464 queries.

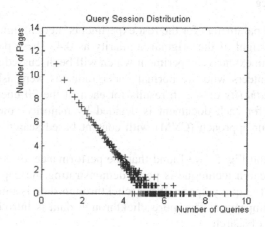

Fig. 3. Query session distribution (Logarithmic scale on X and Y)

Clickthrough data is very sparse, because web users are more likely to click top n (typically 10) web pages returned by a search engine. According to the statistics from the MSN clickthrough data, the average query frequency for a web page is 1.5. Furthermore, the distribution satisfied the Power Law. As shown in Fig. 3, most pages are only associated with few queries, while only a few pages are associated with a large number of queries. So it is necessary to exploit the clickthrough data and to mine out the latent association relationship between the web pages and the queries.

4.2 Evaluation Criteria

The *Precision* in IR is applied to measure the performance of our proposed algorithm. Given a query Q, let R be the set of the relevant pages to the query and $|R|$ be the size of the set; let A be the set of top 20 results returned by our system. *Precision* is defined as:

$$Precision = \frac{|R \cap A|}{|A|}$$

In order to evaluate our method effectively, we also propose a new evaluation metric *Authority*. Given a query, we ask ten volunteers to identify top 10 authoritative pages according to their own judgments. The set of 10 authoritative web-pages is denoted by M and the set of top 10 results returned by search engines is denoted by N. *Authority* is defined as:

$$Authority = \frac{|M \cap N|}{|M|}$$

Precision measures the degree to which the algorithm produces an accurate result; while *Authority* measures the ability of the algorithm to produce pages that are most likely to be visited by users. *Authority* measurement is more relevant to users' degree of satisfactory on the performance of a web search engine.

4.3 Performance

We fixed several parameters for the rest experiments. i.e. minimum similar threshold as 0.3 and the weight of the original similarity as 0.4. These parameters are determined based on an extensive experiment which will be discussed in section 4.5.

First, 10 volunteers who are normal undergraduates were asked to evaluate the *Precision* and *Authority* of search results for each of the 20 queries. The final relevance judgment for each document is decided by majority votes. Fig. shows the comparison of our approach (CVM) with content based search (CB) and DirectHit (DH).

From Fig. 4 and Fig. 5, we found that the performance of content based search, using full text search technique is poor, demonstrating the gap between the document space and the query space. When clickthrough data is introduced, the search performance is improved. The more clickthrough data is introduced, the higher is the performance of search.

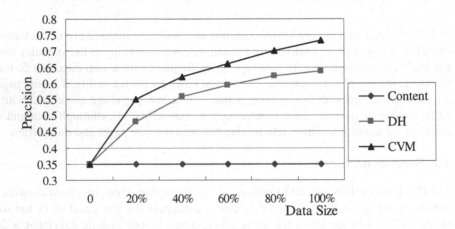

Fig. 4. The precision on different data size

In Fig. 4 and Fig. 5, Co-visited method has a good performance compared to other algorithms. Co-visited method outperforms the naive method because it takes the queries of the similar pages as its virtual queries. However some noise data is also introduced into the metadata of web pages.

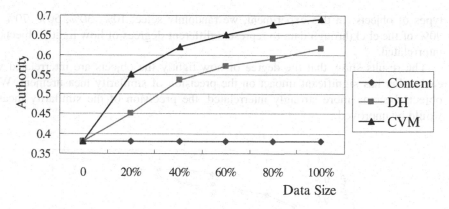

Fig. 5. The authority on different data sizes

4.4   Case Study

Table 2 shows the URLs contained in the results of co-visited method but not contained in the results of the naive method. From the table, we could find that such results are not so relevant with the query "Cribs". While these pages are co-visited with the pages that have a query "Cribs", the Table 2 shows that, many noise metadata are created by the co-visited method. This noise raises the problem of parameter selection which is discussed in the next section.

Table 2. Results of co-visited based method

URL	Topic
http://www.babysupermall.com/main/browse/crib-bedding-sets.html	Crib bedding
http://www.sears.com/sr/entry.jsp?keyword=Baby+Bedding&sid=I000460 7410000400085	Baby bedding
http://www.best-deals-baby-shopping.com/baby-bedding.html	Baby bedding
http://www.cheap-baby-stuff.com/toddler-bed-bedding-sets.html	Baby bedding
http://www.kids--bedding.com/	Baby bedding

4.5   Parameters Selection

As we mentioned, several parameters are used in the experiments, such as minimum co-visited threshold, the weight of linear combination, using result fusion and the iterative times of the IA. Here we provide experiments for setting those parameters.

The density of relationships between two types of objects has significant impact on the precision of similarity calculation. In Fig.6, we empirically analyze the precision of finding the similar queries, given different interrelationship density between two types of objects. In this experiment, we randomly select 10%, 30%, 50%, 70% and 90% of the clickthrough data to represent different degrees of how tightly objects are interrelated.

The results show that the degree of how tightly the objects are interrelated with each other has significant impact on the precision of similarity measurement. When objects become more strongly interrelated, the precision of the similarity measure would be improved.

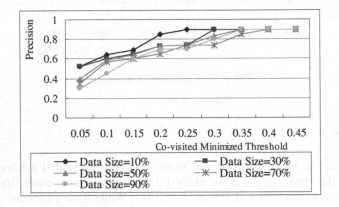

Fig. 6. Precision on different threshold

As stated previously in Section 3.3, the similar web pages of a given web page are generated by the restriction of the minimum co-visited similarity. The higher the co-visited similarity of two Web pages, the higher the probability of the two pages is similar. As shown in Figure 6, the precision monotonously increases as the minimum co-visited similarity increases where the δ increase from 0 to 0.3. When the threshold $\delta=0.3$, the precision is nearly the highest. A larger threshold will not lead to further increment of the precision. So we choose the minimum co-visited threshold as 0.3.

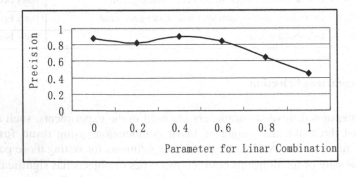

Fig. 7. The precision on different parameters

In order to measure the weight between the content and the clickthrough data, we tune the parameter of α (the weight for the content) and β (the weight for the meta-data from clickthrough data) from 0 to 1. Since $\alpha + \beta = 1$, we only change the α in our experiment. The experimental results on 10 selected queries are shown in Fig. 7. We found that the precision is improved while introducing some content. The system achieves the best precision when α=0.4 and β=0.6. If we continue to introduce more content into consideration, in increasing this parameters, precision drops down since there is too much noise embedded in the content.

5 Conclusions

Clickthrough data is supposed to add more accurate additional content for web pages, thus improve the relevance measurement. However, clickthrough data is often too sparse. In this paper, we propose a novel mining algorithm to utilize clickthrough data. The algorithm could fully explore the interrelations between heterogeneous data objects, and effectively find the associative relationship between web pages, thus deal with the above issue. Experiment results on a large set of MSN clickthrough data show a significant improvement of search performance.

Our work can be extended in several directions. For our problem, the content of the queries and the web pages is not considered to calculate the similarity of the web pages, so the future work should take the content into account to measure the similarity of the Web pages and to deal with the new queries and new Web pages. Another problem is that we now only consider the web pages which have been clicked by at least one query; in fact there are lots of web pages are not visited by users and so do not appear in clickthrough data. In the next step, we want to integrate the clickthrough data, hyperlink structure, anchor text and the content of the web pages and help users to go faster and more easily to the intended information.

References

[1] Bernard J. Jansen , Amanda Spink , Judy Bateman , and Tefko Saracevic. Real life information retrieval: a study of user queries on the Web, *ACM SIGIR Forum*, v.32 n.1, p.5-17, Spring 1998.
[2] Brian D.D., David, G.D., and David B.L. Finding Relevant Website Queries, in *Proceedings of the Twelfth International World Wide Web Conference*, 2003.
[3] Bollen, J., Vandesompel, H., and Rocha, L. M. 1999. Mining associative relations from web site logs and their application to context-dependent retrieval using spreading activation. In proceedings of the Workshop on Organizing Web Space (WOWS). ACM Digital Libraries 99.
[4] Crestani, F. and Lee, P. L. 2000. Searching the web by constrained spreading activation. Inf. Proc. Manage. 36, 585-605
[5] Chien-Kang Huang, Lee-Feng Chien, and Yen-Jen Oyang. Relevant term suggestion in interactive web search based on contextual information in query session logs. JASIST 54(7): 638-649,2003.
[6] Cui H., Wen J.R., Nie J.Y., and Ma W.Y., Query Expansion by Mining User Logs, IEEE Transaction on Knowledge and Data Engineering, Vol. 15, No. 4, July/August 2003.

[7] Collins, A. M and Loftus, E. F 1975. A spreading activation theory of semantic processing. Psych. Rev. 82, 6, 407-428.

[8] D. Beeferman and A. Berger. Agglomerative clustering of a search engine query log. In Proceedings of the sixth ACM SIGKDD International Conference on Knowledge Discovery and Data Mining, pages 407-415, 2000.

[9] Funas, G.W., Landauer,T.K., Gomez,L.M. and Dumais, S.T. 1987. The vocabulary problem in human-system communication. Communications of the ACM 20,11, Pages 946-971, Nov.1987.

[10] G. Jeh and J. Widom. SimRank: A measure of structural-context similarity. In Proceedings of the Eighth ACM SIGKDD International Conference on Knowledge Discovery and Data Mining, Edmonton, Alberta, Canada, July 2002.

[11] G. Salton and C. Buckley. On the use of spreading activation methods in automatic information, in Proceedings of the 11th annual international ACM SIGIR conference on Research and development in information retrieval, p.147-160, Grenoble, France, May 1988.

[12] H. Small. Co-citation in the scientific literature: A new measure of the relationship between two documents. Journal of the American Society for Information Science, 24:265–269, 1973.

[13] J.-R. Wen, J.-Y. Nie, and H.-J. Zhang. Clustering user queries of a search engine. In Proceedings of the Tenth International World Wide Web Conference, Hong Kong, May 2001.

[14] Joachims T. Optimizing Search Engine using Clickthrough Data. In Proceedings of the ACM Conference on Knowledge Discovery and Data Mining, 2002.

[15] M. M. Kessler. Bibliographic coupling between scientific papers. American Documentation, 14:10–25, 1963.

[16] MSN Search Engine, http://www.msn.com.

[17] Nick C., David H., and Stephen R. Effective Site Finding using Link Anchor Information, ACM SIGIR'01, New Orleans, 2001.

[18] Nicolas J. Belkin, Helping people find what they don't know, Communications of the ACM, v.43 n.8, p.58-61, Aug. 2000.

[19] Pirolli, P., Pitkow, J., and Rao, R.1996. Silk from a sow's ear: Extracting usable structures from the web. In Proceedings of the ACMCHI96 Conference on Human Factors in Computing Systems.118-125

[20] Porter, M. An algorithm for suffix stripping. Program, Vol. 14(3), pp. 130137, 1980.

[21] R. Baeza-Yates and B.Ribeiro-Neto. Modern Information Retrieval. Addison-Wesley, 1999.

[22] Robertson, S.E. et al. Okapi at TREC-3. In Overview of the Third Text REtrieval Conference(TREC-3), 109-126, 1995.

[23] R. R. Larson. Bibliometrics of the World-Wide Web: An exploratory analysis of the intellectual structure of cyberspace. In Proceedings of the Annual Meeting of the American Society for Information Science, Baltimore, Maryland, October 1996.

[24] S. Brin and L. Page, The Anatomy of a Large-Scale Hypertextual Web Search Engine, in Proceedings of the 7th international World Wide Web Conference. Vol.7, 1998.

[25] S. Chakrabarti et al., Automatic Resource Compilation by Analyzing Hyperlink Structure and Associated Text, in: Proceedings of the 7th International World Wide Web Conference, 1998.

[26] Thijs W., Wessel K., and Djoerd H., Retrieving Web Pages using Content, Links, URLs and Anchors, TREC10, 2002.

[27] V. V. Raghavan and H. Sever. On the reuse of past optimal queries. In Proceedings of the ACM SIGIR Conference on Research and Development in Information Retrieval, pages 344-350, Seattle, WA, July 1995.

Factors Affecting Web Page Similarity

Anastasios Tombros and Zeeshan Ali

Department of Computer Science, Queen Mary University of London, London, U.K
tassos@dcs.qmul.ac.uk, zeeshan@odl.qmul.ac.uk

Abstract. Tools that allow effective information organisation, access and navigation are becoming increasingly important on the Web. Similarity between web pages is a concept that is central to such tools. In this paper, we examine the effect that content and layout-related aspects of web pages have on web page similarity. We consider the textual content contained within common HTML tags, the structural layout of pages, and the query terms contained within pages. Our study shows that combinations of factors can yield more promising results than individual factors, and that different aspects of web pages affect similarities between pages in a different manner. We found a number of factors that, when taken into account, can result in effective measures of similarity between web pages. Query information in particular, proved to be important for the effective organisation of web pages.

1 Introduction

The World Wide Web provides large repositories of electronically stored information. The size, dynamic nature and diversity of content of this information necessitate the development of effective search tools. Web search engines are today one of the most frequently used tools for retrieving information from the web [18]. Apart from research into methods for effective retrieval of information on the Web, there has also been a considerable increase in research into methods for effective information organisation, access and navigation [16]. For such research problems, relationships (i.e. similarities) between web pages become important. Some contexts in which the notion of similarity finds uses include cluster-based search engines (e.g. Vivisimo, iBoogie[1]), web communities [23], the related pages function of search engines [5, 10], identification of duplicate web pages [1], collaborative filtering, and visualisation [17].

Given the importance of page similarity on the Web, it is essential to understand how similarity is determined in this context. Current similarity approaches typically use information from the hyperlink structure of web pages [5, 9], the textual content of the pages [1, 7], and from the structural layout of the pages [3, 14, 27]. A number of approaches combine different sources of information; the most typical combination is that of link and textual content [16, 19, 26].

---

[1] http://www.vivisimo.com, http://iboogie.tv

D.E. Losada and J.M. Fernández-Luna (Eds.): ECIR 2005, LNCS 3408, pp. 487–501, 2005.

The main motivation for this work has been to systematically look into factors that determine similarities between web pages. In past studies on page similarity, the effect of different aspects of web pages (e.g. content, layout, etc.) on the effectiveness of similarity measures has not been thoroughly investigated. In this study we focus on three aspects of information that is available from web pages: the textual information contained within common HTML tags, the structural layout of pages, and the query terms present in web pages. We systematically investigate the effect of these sources by varying their relative importance in the resulting similarity measures, and by examining the effect of the variations in the effectiveness of the similarity measures. Our approach for using multiple sources of evidence is motivated by results of previous research that have suggested that a single source of information for detecting web page similarity is unlikely to be the most effective [3, 7].

In the rest of this paper, we first present some related work on similarity measures on the Web in section 2, then in section 3 we present the details of our investigation, in section 4 we present and analyse the results and in section 5 we conclude and draw some pointers for taking this work further.

2   Related Work

Similarity between documents in information retrieval (IR) is typically measured as a degree of content overlap [24]. Inter-document similarities in IR have been extensively researched, due to their application to areas such as clustering, visualization, etc. [20]. The concept of similarity is also central to the Cluster Hypothesis [13], which states that documents relevant to the same queries tend to be more similar to each other than to non-relevant ones. The hypothesis has been investigated in a number of different contexts [12, 22] where it has been linked to the effectiveness of document clustering for IR.

In web IR, the success of link-based evidence for effective retrieval [15], has led researchers to look into using the same evidence to determine inter-page similarities [5, 9] (e.g. the more links two pages have in common the more similar they are, etc.). Haveliwala and his colleagues [10] have suggested that most web pages under link-based measures have orthogonal vectors. A further possible of link-based measures is that they make it difficult to discover similarity relations for relatively new web pages, which have not been cited enough.

A number of approaches have used evidence from the textual content of web pages to calculate similarities [1, 2, 6, 7, 10]. Different aspects of content have been used. For example, [2, 6, 10] have used hyperlinks and anchor text associated to hyperlinks as a succinct representation of the content of the target page. Referred pages are then typically indexed by some form of aggregation of the anchor texts of their incoming links [10]. In [6] it was also demonstrated that anchor text resembles query text in terms of length and term distribution and that it is also less ambiguous than query text, resulting in more coherent retrieval results. This evidence from past work demonstrates that anchor text is an important aspect of the content of a web page. Some other content-based approaches [7] have used proper names in web pages to "boost" the effectiveness of similarity measures. A widely used approach for detecting duplicate web pages was also proposed in [1], where a set of contiguous terms, or shingles, extracted from pages are considered, and the number of matching shingles determines the degree of similarity between pages.

A different source used to determine similarity is the structural layout of pages [3, 8, 14, 27]. The rationale of structure-based approaches is that pages containing similar information would also have a similar structure [27], or a similar layout and look-and-feel [14]. An approach that has utilised tag frequency information from web pages to determine their similarity is reported in [3]. This approach is based on the assumption that tag frequencies reflect some inherent characteristics of a web page and correlate with its structure. A number of measures of structural similarity between pages were developed in [3], and their effectiveness was compared to measures of similarity using the text of documents alone. The results showed that certain improvements are introduced by the structure-based approaches; however, the authors emphasise that it is unlikely that structure information alone will be an effective enough source of evidence. They also stress the importance of combining different sources of evidence for the calculation of inter-page similarities. Other approaches that make use of the hierarchical structure of web pages to calculate similarities, include [14, 27]. In such approaches a tree representation of the HTML structure of pages is used to calculate similarities. In general, tree-based approaches have proven to be computationally expensive [14].

A number of approaches have also used combinations of link and content-based approaches to page similarity [16, 17, 26]. Such approaches typically combine content and link similarities. Most of this work however, is limited in that the effectiveness of the resulting similarity measures is not evaluated.

Evidence from past work suggests that a single source of evidence is unlikely to provide the most effective input for measuring similarities. Based on this observation, in our approach we examine three different sources of evidence that are available to us from the content of web pages. First, we look into textual content that is contained within different HTML tags. This source has been investigated for its effect on retrieval effectiveness [4], but not on web page similarity. Second, we investigate how structural layout information can be used to detect similarity, and how it can be combined with other sources. The combination of structural information with other sources of evidence has not been investigated by previous research. Third, we use information provided by the query to increase the similarities between pages that are likely to be relevant to the same queries. This query-based approach to similarity has been shown to be effective for cluster-based document retrieval [20], but it has not been investigated in the context of web pages. In the next section we present the details of our research approach.

3   Research Approach

We first present the three different sources of evidence that we use in section 3.1. Then, in section 3.2 we outline the details of the experiments, and in section 3.3 we describe the evaluation approach used.

3.1   Sources of Evidence

We use three different sources of evidence to calculate similarities between pages, and we examine the relative effectiveness of each source by adjusting its importance in linear combination formulas. The main aim of this approach is not to establish optimal values for the weights of the different sources, but rather to investigate how the different sources affect similarities between pages.

HTML Tags. We use a number of the most common HTML tags typically found in web pages. We place tags in classes depending on their semantic connotations. In Table 1 we present the eight classes we used along with the tags contained within each class. Content within each individual class is indexed separately, and treated as the representation of each class. In [4] a similar approach was employed for indexing web pages: index terms were assigned different weights depending on the classes in which they occurred. This work demonstrated that a significant improvement in retrieval effectiveness is introduced when using tag information. We aim to examine whether the same holds when calculating similarities between web pages.

Titles and *headings* are deemed to be good author-provided representations of the main contents of a page [4]. *Tables* and *lists* offer both a good representation of the layout and general look of a page, and an effective means of capturing information that may be salient within a web page. When calculating similarities based on the table class, we do not take into account numbers, as this may lead to increased noise in the calculations. For the *font* class, we hypothesise that, similar to titles and headings, authors will use special font options for content they deem salient within a page. *Images* are also a significant source of information. We assume that pages that use images in a similar textual context will have some degree of topical relatedness. We implement this assumption by using the text contained within an image window (text withing the bounds of the P tag in which the image is used) and the text in the ALT option of the IMG tag as the representation of the image class.

For the *anchor* class, we follow a different approach to [2, 10]. We suggest that the anchor text coupled with the hyperlink can be a good measure of similarity

Table 1. The eight classes and associated HTML tags

Class name	HTML tags
Content	All legal tags
Title	TITLE
Heading	H1-H6
Table	TABLE, TR, TD, TH
List	LI, OL, UL
Anchor	A and anchor window
Font	STRONG, B, I, U
Image	IMG and image window

of web pages. We assume that in a situation where two pages P_1 and P_2 refer to the same page P_3, the two referring pages are likely to be about a related topic. We only consider this textual information if two pages point to the same page. We should however note that we do not take into account the referred page. Further, to enhance the semantic context in which pages are referred, we use both the text included within the bounds of the anchor tag, as well as the text included within an anchor window defined by the paragraph (P tag) in which the anchor appears.

We use the *content* class as a baseline, as it encompasses the entire textual content of a web page. We are therefore interested in examining how close to this baseline the other classes, or the combinations of the classes, can get.

This approach may be susceptible to some problems: not all authors use the same semantics with HTML tags, web page content may also contain spam content, pages generated automatically may follow different stylistic conventions, the anchor and image windows may introduce noise in the similarity calculations. However, we believe that this approach is general enough to provide us with evidence about the importance of different HTML tags at detecting similarity.

Structure. To determine the structural layout of a page, we examine the frequency with which tags occur in the page. We assume that this frequency will provide an indication of the page's general layout and structure, and may be an effective source of evidence for detecting the similarity of structurally-similar pages. For example, hub pages providing links to other pages will have similar distributions of the anchor and list-related tags.

To measure the structural similarity between pages, we use the tag frequency distribution analysis (TFDA) measure proposed in [3]. The frequency of HTML tags is used to calculate similarities as follows. Let $TagF_{ti}$ and $TagF_{tj}$ be the frequencies of the same tag t in pages P_i and P_j, n the total number of tags, w_t the weight for the t-th tag and $\sum_{t=1}^{n} w_t = 1$. Similarity can then be computed as:

$$S(P_i, P_j) = 1 - \sum_{t=1}^{n} (TagF_{ti} - TagF_{tj})^2 * w_t \tag{1}$$

Values are normalised to fall between zero and one. The weights w_t are calculated to be proportional to the ratios of the different tags.

A drawback of this approach is that it does not take into account the order in which tags appear in pages. On the other had, TFDA can be implemented efficiently for on-line calculations and is an effective means of detecting the broad categories to which pages belong (e.g. hub pages, etc.) [3]. In this paper we extend the work in [3] by combining structural similarity with other sources of evidence.

Query. Recent research in inter-document similarity [20, 21] has suggested that similarity measures that take the query into account are more effective than conventional measures. This class of similarity measures is called query-sensitive (QSSM). QSSM are based on the assumption that documents that are jointly relevant (*co-relevant*) to a query, display an inherent similarity that is dictated by the query itself. QSSM aim to detect this inherent similarity by viewing the query terms as the salient features that define the context under which similarity is examined for an IR task. Conventional similarity measures (e.g. cosine coefficient) are enhanced by the inclusion of a query-sensitive component which introduces a dynamic nature to similarity; similarity values for the same pair of documents are different for different queries. This dynamic component is shown in equation 2, which is based on the cosine coefficient formula:

$$Sim(D_i, D_j, Q) = \frac{\sum\limits_{k=1}^{n} c_k \cdot q_k}{\sqrt{\sum\limits_{k=1}^{n} c_k^2 \cdot \sum\limits_{k=1}^{n} q_k^2}} \qquad (2)$$

where $Q = \{q_1, q_2, \ldots, q_n\}$ is the query vector, D_i and D_j are the two document vectors, and $C = D_i \cap D_j = \{c_1, c_2, \ldots, c_k, \ldots, c_n\}$ is a vector which contains the common terms of documents D_i and D_j.

This equation essentially enhances the similarity of pairs of documents that have many query terms, as well as many other content terms, in common. The dynamic component is combined with a standard cosine coefficient measure between the two documents to yield the overall value for a QSSM, as equation 3 shows. Functions that were investigated in [20, 21] were a linear combination and the product of the two components.

$$Sim(D_i, D_j | Q) = f(Sim(D_i, D_j), Sim(D_i, D_j, Q) \qquad (3)$$

QSSM have been shown to be significantly more effective than conventional similarity measures at detecting the similarity of co-relevant documents, and have also been shown to significantly increase the effectiveness of cluster-based IR [20]. However, the effectiveness of these measures for web pages has not been investigated. In this paper, we use the query as a source of evidence, and we use equation 2 to measure the query component of similarity measures.

3.2   Experimental Environment

Our experimental approach consists of using a set of documents, queries and relevance assessments to evaluate the effectiveness of various similarity measures. We used the WT2g test collection, from the TREC-8 Web track [11], for our study. This collection includes about 250,000 web pages from a web crawl carried out in 1997. We also used TREC-8 topics 401-450.

It should be noted that the WT2g collection has shown to be inadequate for evaluating the retrieval effectiveness of link-based IR approaches. In [11] it was reported that this collection, which forms part of the larger VLC2 collection, does not contain a large enough number of inter-server links within its pages for link-based methods to be sufficiently evaluated. Although this limitation is significant for link-based approaches, it does not affect the validity of this study, as we do not use any form of link information.

With regards to the TREC queries used, we considered only the *title* part the queries, as we deem this to be more representative of the way searchers formulate queries. The average length of the *title* section was 2.7 terms. For each query, we retrieve the top 100 documents and use them for our study. In [12, 20, 21] it has been demonstrated that using relationships from among documents ranked high by an IR system in response to a query, is more effective than using relationships from entire document collections.

The IR system we used in this study is the Lucene system[2]. We applied standard stemming as provided by Lucene to preprocess the web pages, and we used an extended stop-word list by including non-meaningful terms that are commonly included in HTML pages. Standard *tf-idf* weights were used for document and query terms. Retrieval was performed using the cosine coefficient for matching between documents and queries. The cosine coefficient was also used as the basic formula for measuring page similarity.

3.3 Evaluation Measure

Our evaluation approach is based on the view that for IR tasks, effective similarity measures should structure the information space in such a manner that, for each query, co-relevant documents (web pages) should be closer to each other than to non-relevant documents. This evaluation approach is also reflected by the cluster hypothesis [13]. Based on this approach, the effectiveness of a similarity measure is gauged by its effectiveness at placing co-relevant documents close to each other; this also facilitates the direct comparison of the effectiveness between different similarity measures. The practical significance of the results of such an evaluation is that for applications such as the related pages function of search engines, for a given relevant web page, we can determine how many of its immediate neighbours are also relevant. Cluster-based IR systems would also benefit from similarity measures that result in an increased adherence to the hypothesis [13, 20, 25].

A test which is suited to this evaluation framework is the nearest neighbour (NN) test first proposed in [25]. This test consists of finding the N nearest neighbours (i.e. most similar pages) of each relevant page for a query, and of counting the number of relevant pages in this neighbourhood. The higher the number of relevant pages, the higher the adherence to the cluster hypothesis. A single value that corresponds to the number of relevant pages contained in the NN set (we used a value of 5 for the test, the same that Voorhees used for her experiments) can be obtained when averaging over all of the relevant pages for all the queries in the WT2g collection.

We use the Wilcoxon signed-ranks test to look at the statistical significance of results. This test does not make any assumptions about the distribution of the values that it is comparing. The test assumes that there is information in the magnitude of the differences between paired observations, as well as in the sign of the differences. We consider results to be statistically significant at $p < 0.05$.

---

[2] http://jakarta.apache.org/lucene

4   Results

In this section we present the results of our study. We begin by presenting results from the use of individual sources in 4.1, then in 4.2 we present results from the combination of sources, and in 4.3 we discuss the main findings.

4.1   Individual Sources

HTML Tags and Query Terms. In Table 2 we present the results of the 5NN test when each of the eight tag classes is considered on its own: similarity is calculated based only on matching terms between pages in the respective tag class in the table. The second column of the table contains the average 5NN values for each class, and the third column contains the average number of terms in each class, after stop-word removal.

The results demonstrate that the content class provides the most effective source of evidence. All differences between content and the other classes are significant at levels <0.02. The title class is the second most effective among the tags. What is surprising is that with an average of only 4.4 terms per page for this class, similarity calculations are relatively effective. This demonstrates that titles of web pages are good descriptors of the topical content of pages. The same, to a slightly lesser degree, applies to the heading class. A further observation from this table is that images and anchors are not particularly good sources of evidence. One potential reason for this is the amount of noise that may be introduced by the anchor and image windows used.

The last row of Table 2 presents the 5NN value for the QSSM given by equation 2. For this study we used a slightly expanded form of the TREC queries, by using the *description* section of the queries. This was based on findings in [21] which suggest that QSSM tend to be affected by query length. The new average length of the queries used is 7.2 terms (compared to 2.7 for the *title* section alone). The 5NN values given by the QSSM are the second most effective. The values obtained with the QSSM are significantly more effective than those obtained with all the tag classes, apart from the title class. Content is still signif-

Table 2. Average 5NN values and statistics for individual classes

Class	5NN	Avg. terms per page
Content	2.45	539.83
Title	2.13	4.39
Heading	2.07	8.92
Font	2.06	26.93
Anchor	1.98	63.10
List	1.97	33.02
Table	1.97	64.81
Image	1.88	13.64
Query	2.24	n/a

Table 3. Average 5NN values using tag frequency

Title	Heading	Font	Anchor	List	Table	Image
1.84	1.73	1.87	1.81	1.84	1.86	1.92

icantly more effective than QSSM. We view these results as providing evidence that the presence of query terms in pages is an effective source of evidence for page similarity.

Structural Layout. In Table 3 we present the average 5NN values resulting from the structural layout-based similarity between pages. Values in this table are calculated by matching the tag frequency of the individual classes using equation 1. No data are calculated for the content class, as this class includes all possible HTML tags.

The results based on tag frequency do not show a high degree of correlation to those in Table 2. The image class is the most effective source in this case, whereas headings and titles are less effective. Few of the differences between classes are statistically significant: the image, font, title and table classes provide significantly better results than the heading class, and the image class is also significantly more effective than the anchor class. It seems that information from tag distribution alone is not a good source for measuring page similarity. This result is in agreement to [3]. In the following section we combine tag frequency information with various other sources.

4.2   Combinations of Sources

When calculating the similarity $S(P_i, P_j)$ using combined sources, we use a linear combination of the sources: $S(P_i, P_j) = \alpha * S_{s1}(P_i, P_j) + \beta * S_{s2}(P_i, P_j)$, where α and β are adjustable parameters ($\alpha + \beta = 1$), and $S_{s_1}(P_i, P_j)$, $S_{s_2}(P_i, P_j)$ are the similarities of pages P_i and P_j according to sources s_1 and s_2. By varying α and β, we are interested in examining the relative effect that different sources have on the effectiveness of page similarity.

Combining Tag Classes. We combined pairs of tag classes and measured the average 5NN values of the resulting similarity measures. The rationale of these combinations is to examine whether specific pairs of tags provide better sources of evidence than individual tags. Our results showed that all classes benefit from combination with the title class. This result correlates with the high effectiveness of the title class reported in section 4.1. The combination with the title class has a "smoothing" effect, and the best 5NN values of the combined pairs of classes are now not significantly different to each other. The range of the best values is from 2.03 for images and titles to 2.2 for titles and tables. These improved values are generally significantly better than those obtained from individual classes. It should also be noted that, in general, the parameters α and β in these combinations were in a the region of 0.6 and 0.4, with the highest weight attributed to the title class.

Combinations of other tag classes apart from the title class, still improve the 5NN values obtained from the individual classes, but not to the same extent as the title class did. Some promising results are obtained by the combination of lists and fonts (2.13), tables and headings (2.12) and tables and fonts (2.09). We further combined the most effective class pairs with the content class. The rationale of this comparison is to examine whether certain tag classes are worth "promoting" when measuring page similarities. For example, if two pages have substantial overall content overlap which is focused on specific tags (e.g. lists or tables), then by appropriately rewarding the tag-specific similarity we can examine the effect on the 5NN values.

The results from this study are positive. The combinations of all possible pairs of classes with the content class yield 5NN values between 2.43 and 2.49. These values represent best average values, i.e. they have been obtained at optimal settings for the α and β parameters. In general, these parameters weighted the content class more than the other classes, in ratios of 3:2. Unlike the combination of pairs of classes where the title class yielded the most effective combinations, in these results there is no clear tendency for a single class to be optimally combined with other classes and with the content class. The highest best average values are obtained with combinations of table and images with content (2.49) and with table and lists with content (2.48). These results are not significantly better than the 5NN values attained by using the content class alone.

Combining Tag Frequencies. We split the seven tag classes for which we have tag frequency data into two groups: group A contains the anchor, list, table and image classes, while group B contains the title, heading and font classes. The first group corresponds to layout-oriented tags of a page, while the second to more content-oriented tags. We also used different settings of the parameters to assign weights to classes within each group (we used 4 parameters in this case, with the sum of the parameters equal to 1). These weights were representative of the effectiveness of the individual classes when using the TFDA-based similarity measure. We then calculated page similarities based on each of the two groups.

The best average 5NN values obtained in this study were 2.13 for group A and 2.06 for group B. For both groups, these values are significantly better than values from tag frequencies from individual classes. The difference between the two groups is not statistically significant; however, it is consistent. The consistency of the results provides evidence that the layout-oriented tags provide a better source for measuring page similarity using TFDA.

We also calculated 5NN values based on combinations of frequencies of pairs of classes. These results were not significantly better than those obtained from individual classes. However, all possible combinations of pairs consistently gave results that were higher than any of the individual parts of the pair. Further, combinations that included the image, list, table and to a lesser extent, the anchor classes, were consistently the most effective.

Table 4. Best average 5NN values for combinations of tag frequencies and tag classes

	Font	Heading	List	Title	Content
F_{image}	2.10	2.07	1.97	2.15	2.43
F_{list}	2.02	1.99	1.92	1.97	2.45
F_{anchor}	1.95	1.98	1.99	1.98	2.42
F_{table}	2.01	2.01	1.94	2.11	2.44

We also combined tag frequency information with tag classes. We calculated all combinations of individual tag classes and individual tag frequencies (including content). We present the most effective combinations in Table 4. Values in a cell of the table (5NN values) are derived by the combination of the respective row (tag frequency) and column (tag class), and correspond to the best average value attained.

The classes whose tag frequencies combined best with tag classes were the image, list, anchor and table classes. In general, combinations of tag frequencies with tag classes (except content) yield 5NN values which are significantly higher than values obtained by using individual tag frequencies. For example, using individual tag frequency from the image class, the average 5NN value was 1.92 (Table 3); combining image tag frequency with the font class the value significantly increases to 2.10. All these values are however significantly lower than those obtained by the content class alone (2.45, Table 2).

When combining tag frequencies with content, there is a significant increase in the 5NN values (compared to other tag frequency values), as this is demonstrated in column 6 of Table 4. These best values reported in the table are obtained at parameter settings that weight the content class four times more than the tag frequency information. These results are either slightly less than, or equal to, the 5NN value for the content class alone (2.45). These results are significantly higher than all other data using tag frequency information.

Combining Query with Other Sources. We combined the query-based measure given in equation 2 with the content class. This is equivalent to the linear combination function of the static and query-based similarities reported in [20, 21]. By varying the parameters α and β we vary the importance attributed to the static (i.e. cosine) and the dynamic (i.e. equation 2) components of the similarity, respectively. These results are reported in column 2 of Table 5. In columns 3, 4 and 5 we report the results from the combination of content and query sources (C+Q) with the font (F), heading (F) and title (T) tag classes respectively.

The results in Table 5 are generally higher than those obtained by using the content class alone (2.45 from Table 2). If we examine the results in column 2, we see that as the effect of the static component of the similarity increases, so does the 5NN value. The highest value in this column is achieved when the static component is weighted four times as much as the query component. These results do not agree with ones previously reported in [20, 21], where best results were

Table 5. Average 5NN values for combinations of query-based measures

$\alpha : \beta$	C+Q	(C+Q)+F	(C+Q)+H	(C+Q)+T
0.2 : 0.8	2.33	2.40	2.41	2.42
0.4 : 0.6	2.42	2.43	2.41	2.44
0.5 : 0.5	2.48	2.47	2.46	2.49
0.6 : 0.4	2.50	2.53	2.53	2.52
0.8 : 0.2	2.54	2.53	2.55	2.55

observed for higher weighting of the query component of the similarity. However, these results were obtained from different TREC test collections, and it is likely that the different properties of the collections have caused this difference. It should also be noted that in the case where $\alpha=0$ and $\beta=1$, the 5NN value is equal to that reported in Table 2 for query alone (2.24), and if $\alpha=1$ and $\beta=0$, it is equal to the value reported in Table 2 for content alone (2.45).

We also combined the results of the joint query and content similarity with different sources. In columns 3, 4 and 5 we report the most effective combinations with the font, heading and title classes respectively. The trend of these results is similar to those in column 2; by increasing the effect of the joint content and query similarity, we also increase the 5NN values. In a large number of cases, the values of the combinations are higher than those of content alone (2.45), or even higher of the respective values in column 2 of the same table.

There are few significant differences in these results, mainly for different settings of the parameters in the same similarity measure (same column of the table). There are also two significant differences, for $\alpha : \beta = 0.8 : 0.2$, between the content only value of 2.45 and the content and query value of 2.54 (column 2) and the content-query and title value of 2.55 (column 5).

4.3 Discussion

In the results reported in the previous sections, the effect of the content of web pages at determining similarity is significant. The baseline set by measuring similarity using content alone was exceeded by only a few cases. Most of these cases involved the use of the query as an additional source of evidence. The significance of query terms for determining the similarity between pages is an important finding of this study. Unlike previous studies of the effectiveness of QSSM, in this study the strong effect of overall content overlap weakens the effect of query terms on page similarity. Despite this, clear effectiveness gains are introduced by the incorporation of query information.

By looking at the results using evidence from tag classes and the query, there is a general trend for the title, heading and font classes to provide effective sources for measures of similarity. These three classes seem to capture a signifi-cant amount of information related to a page's semantic content. The incorpo-ration of content from these three classes in general improves the effectiveness of the similarity measures.

With regards to the structural-layout based similarity, results obtained with the TFDA measure were less effective than those obtained with other sources. In general, tag frequencies from single classes demonstrated low effectiveness. Improvements were introduced by combinations of classes, and by combinations of structural and content-based sources. The classes that consistently displayed a positive effect on similarity were those of anchors, images, lists and tables. The distribution of these classes within pages proved to be an effective source of evidence for calculating similarities. These tag classes may also be better at distinguishing different categories that pages belong to. For example, by looking at the distribution of anchor and list items within a page, we can infer whether this page is a hub page.

The TFDA-based similarity measures may also be introducing a certain level of noise in similarity calculations. For example, two pages may have similar tag frequency distributions but their actual topical content may be different. It would, however, be worthwhile to investigate how well structure-based similarity correlates with searchers' perception of page similarity. One can expect that structurally-motivated similarity may be better suited to searchers' intuitive interpretation of similarity than to TREC relevance assessments. This issue would need to be further investigated. Different methods for calculating structural similarity can also be investigated. Of particular interest would be measures that take into account the order of occurrence of tags in pages (e.g. [3]).

A further result from our study is that combinations of sources of evidence generally yield similarity measures that are more effective than the constituent sources alone. This was particularly evident in the case of the TFDA-based measures. When linearly combining different sources, results obtained within a region of the optimal parameter settings were also not significantly different to each other. It should be noted that the effectiveness of combination of evidence in IR is well-established [26].

The results of this study also suggest that certain query types are better suited to certain types of evidence for measuring similarity. This has been observed from a per-query analysis of the results, and has been a by-product of the current investigation. We aim to further analyse this behaviour in our data.

5   Conclusions and Further Work

In this paper we examined the effect that different aspects of web pages have on determining inter-page similarity on the Web. We looked into the textual content contained within common HTML tags, the structural layout of pages as defined by the distribution of HTML tags, and the presence of query terms in pages. The results of this study suggest that certain aspects of web pages are effective sources of information for calculating inter-page similarity. The presence of common query terms in pages was a particularly effective source of evidence. Further, the textual content of certain HTML tag classes (title, headings, font) and the tag frequency of the table, list, anchor and image classes also proved to be effective factors for similarity calculations. Combinations of factors were more effective than individual factors.

This study can be extended by looking into user-oriented factors that determine page similarity, by using a larger dataset, and by looking more thoroughly into the dependence of certain query types on certain sources of evidence for similarity calculations. Other types of similarity measures (e.g. link-based measures) can also be examined to establish whether similar factors affect their effectiveness. The results from this study can have implications for systems that rely on the effective calculation of web page similarity, such as systems that retrieve or recommend web pages. We view this study as an important step towards understanding how similarities between web pages are determined.

References

1. A.Z. Broder, S.C. Glassman, M.S. Manasse, and G. Zweig. Syntactic clustering of the web. In *Proceedings of the 6th WWW Conference*, pages 1157–1166, 1997.
2. S. Chakrabarti, B. Dom, P. Raghavan, S. Rajagopalan, D. Gibson, and J. Kleinberg. Automatic resource compilation by analyzing hyperlink structure and associated text. In *Proceedings of the 7th WWW Conference*, pages 65–74, 1998.
3. I.F. Cruz, S. Borisov, M.A. Marks, and T.R. Webb. Measuring structural similarity among web documents: preliminary results. In *Proceedings of the 7th International Conference on Electronic Publishing*, pages 513–524, 1998.
4. M. Cutler, H. Deng, S.S. Maniccam, and W. Meng. A new study on using html structures to improve retrieval. In *Proceedings of the 11th IEEE International Conference on Tools with Artificial Intelligence*, pages 406–409, 1999.
5. J. Dean and M. Henzinger. Finding related pages in the world wide web. In *Proceedings of the 8th WWW Conference*, pages 1467–1479, 1999.
6. N. Eiron and K.S. McCurley. Analysis of anchor text for web search. In *Proceedings of the 26th ACM SIGIR Conference*, pages 459–460, 2003.
7. N. Friburger and D. Maurel. Textual similarity based on proper names. In *Proceedings of the ACM SIGIR Workshop on Mathematical Formal Methods in Information Retrieval*, pages 155–167, 2002.
8. P. Ganesan, H. Garcia-Molina, and J. Widom. Exploiting hierarchical domain structure to compute similarity. *ACM Transactions on Information Systems*, 21(1):64–93, 2003.
9. M. Halkidi, B. Nguyen, I. Varlamis, and M. Vazirigiannis. Thesus: Organising web document collections based on link semantics. *VLDB Journal*, 12(4):320–332, 2003.
10. T.H. Haveliwala, A. Gionis, D. Klein, and P. Indyk. Evaluating strategies for similarity search on the web. In *Proceedings of the 11th WWW Conference*, pages 157–163, 2002.
11. D. Hawking, E. Voorhees, N. Craswell, and P. Bailey. Overview of the trec-8 web track. In *Proceedings of TREC-8*, pages 131–150, 2000.
12. M.A. Hearst and J.O. Pedersen. Re-examining the cluster hypothesis: Scatter/gather on retrieval results. In *Proceedings of the 19th ACM SIGIR Conference*, pages 76–84, 1996.
13. N. Jardine and C.J. van Rijsbergen. The use of hierarchical clustering in information retrieval. *Information Storage and Retrieval*, 7:217–240, 1971.

14. S. Joshi, N. Agrawal, R. Krishnapuram, and S. Negi. A bag of paths model for measuring structural similarity in web documents. In *Proceedings of the 9th ACM SIGKDD Conference*, pages 577–582, 2003.
15. J.M. Kleinberg. Authoritative sources in a hyperlinked environment. *Journal of the ACM*, 46(5):604–632, 1999.
16. D.S. Modha and W.S. Spangler. Clustering hypertext with applications to web searching. In *Proceedings of the 11th ACM Conferencei on Hypertext and Hypermedia*, pages 143–152, 2000.
17. S. Mukherjea. Organizing topic-specific web information. In *Proceedings of the 11th ACM Conference on Hypertext and Hypermedia*, pages 133–141, 2000.
18. S. Ozmutlu, A. Spink, and H.C. Ozmutlu. A day in the life of web searching: an exploratory study. *Information Processing & Management*, 40(2):319–345, 2004.
19. P. Pirolli, J. Pitkow, and R. Rao. Silk from a sow's ear: extracting usable structures from the web. In *Proceedings of ACM SIGCHI Conference*, pages 118–125, 1996.
20. A. Tombros. *The effectiveness of hierarchic query-based clustering of documents for information retrieval*. PhD thesis, Department of Computing Science, University of Glasgow, 2002.
21. A. Tombros and C.J. van Rijsebrgen. Query-sensitive similarity measures for information retrieval. *Knowledge and Information Systems*, 6(5):617–642, 2004.
22. A. Tombros, R. Villa, and C.J. van Rijsbergen. The effectiveness of query-specific hierarchic clustering in information retrieval. *Information Processing & Management*, 38(4):559–582, 2002.
23. M. Toyoda and M. Kitsuregawa. Creating a web community chart for navigating related communities. In *Proceedings of the 12th ACM Conference on Hypertext and Hypermedia*, pages 103–112, 2001.
24. C.J. van Rijsbergen. *Information Retrieval*. Butterworths, London, 2nd edition, 1979.
25. E. Voorhees. *The Effectiveness and efficiency of agglomerative hierarchic clustering in document retrieval*. PhD thesis, Department of Computer Science, Cornell University, 1985.
26. R. Weiss, B. Velez, and M. Sheldon. Hypursuit: A hierarchical network search engine that exploits content-link hypertext clustering. In *Proceedings of the 7th ACM Conference on Hypertext and Hypermedia*, pages 180–193, 1996.
27. W. Wong and A.W. Fu. Finding structure and characteristics of web documents for classification. In *Proceedings of ACM SIGMOD Workshop on Research Issues in Data Mining and Knowledge Discovery*, pages 96–105, 2000.

Boosting Web Retrieval Through Query Operations

Gilad Mishne and Maarten de Rijke

Informatics Institute, University of Amsterdam,
Kruislaan 403, 1098 SJ Amsterdam, The Netherlands
{gilad, mdr}@science.uva.nl

Abstract. We explore the use of phrase and proximity terms in the context of web retrieval, which is different from traditional ad-hoc retrieval both in document structure and in query characteristics. We show that for this type of task, the usage of both phrase and proximity terms is highly beneficial for early precision as well as for overall retrieval effectiveness. We also analyze why phrase and proximity terms are far more effective for web retrieval than for ad-hoc retrieval.

1 Introduction

An important aspect in which web retrieval differs from ad-hoc retrieval concerns the users needs. User studies and anecdotal evidence suggest that web users wish to spend as little time as possible going through the results, and are mostly interested in a small number of relevant documents in the topmost ranks. Most users look only at the first page of results (usually, containing 10 results) [20, 32], and this trend is strengthening over time [31]. Moreover, web search users usually have short search sessions, indicating that once a user followed a link to a document which she finds relevant, she will in most cases not return to the result list and examine further hits [7].

Accordingly, recent large-scale web search evaluations such as the web track at TREC [10, 11] have widened the traditional focus on evaluation measures such as Mean Average Precision (MAP) and Precision/Recall graphs to also include early precision based measures such as Precision@10, Precision@20 and Success@10; in some cases, even higher precision is evaluated, e.g., Mean Reciprocal Rank (MRR, mostly for tasks with a single relevant document) and Precision@5, Success@5 and Success@1. The latter measures are motivated by the fact that, due to physical limitations, the first 10 results are not always displayed in a single "screen page," requiring the user to scroll down the list.

The web continues to be an inspiring domain for retrieval research. For instance, the layout information embedded within HTML documents gave rise to numerous refinements and extensions of retrieval models that attempt to take non-content features of documents into account [8]. Our focus in this paper is not on web retrieval models but on web *queries*. How can we boost web retrieval

D.E. Losada and J.M. Fernández-Luna (Eds.): ECIR 2005, LNCS 3408, pp. 502–516, 2005.

effectiveness, measured using any of the measures just mentioned, by means of automatic operations on queries?

An important difference between web retrieval queries and typical queries in other retrieval tasks is the average query length. Web search user studies such as those mentioned earlier report on average lengths of 1.5 to 2.6 terms; similar numbers have recently been cited by top web search engines [25] and also emerge out of web query logs we are currently gathering. In contrast, closed-domain searches have significantly higher average lengths, e.g., 4.9 terms for the TREC 2004 Genomics track [18]. Given these observations on query length, it is obviously important to make the most out of what little information web queries give us. We examine the effect of automatic query rewrites, specifically phrasal and proximity-based retrieval, on the performance of web retrieval. A phrase match between a document and a query is usually an accurate indication that the document deals with the aspect of the query described by the phrase. Intuitively, the ability to detect overlap between a document and a query aspect is particularly important if queries are short and may have very few aspects.

We are especially interested in the effectiveness of "light-weight" query operations for web retrieval. Thus, we do not consider phrases as indexing units, but submit queries that exploit phrases or proximity terms against an index consisting of single terms only. Also, our phrases are not syntactic or even statistical in nature; we simply treat every word n-gram from the query as a phrase. For us, proximity based retrieval is a natural extension of phrasal retrieval where the restriction on the nearness of the terms is somewhat more relaxed.

Now, usage of proximity and phrases has been studied extensively for ad-hoc retrieval. Reports on their contribution are mixed, and it is generally accepted now that with a good basic ranking formula, the effectiveness of phrases is negligible or even negative [24], while recent evaluations of the use of automatically generated proximity terms suggest that term proximity may improve retrieval effectiveness especially at the top documents retrieved [28]. Our main research questions are:

- Given a good basic ranking scheme for web retrieval, how much additional benefit do phrases and proximity terms bring in retrieval effectiveness?
- To what extent are improvements gained by phrases and proximity terms dependent on the structured nature of web documents?
- Do phrases and proximity terms impact Mean Average Precision scores differently than high precision measures?
- Do phrases and proximity terms have a different impact on retrieval effectiveness for extremely short queries (2 or 3 terms) than for longer queries?

One of our main findings is that because of the structured nature of web documents, phrases and proximity terms can increase effectiveness for web retrieval. When using short (or very short) queries to retrieve HTML documents, significant improvements can be obtained if phrases and proximity terms are used, not only in terms of the high-precision measures mentioned above but, interestingly, also in terms of traditional measures such as Mean Average Precision.

The rest of the paper is organized as follows. In Section 2 we survey work on phrasal retrieval, discuss current web retrieval efforts, and describe state of the art techniques used for the latter task. In Section 3 we describe the phrase and proximity based methods we experimented with for boosting web retrieval effectiveness; we motivate them, and give examples. Next, in Section 4, we describe our experimental framework, largely based on the TREC web track retrieval evaluations. We follow with an account of our results, comparing them to the performance of other techniques for web retrieval. In Section 5 we provide a deeper analysis for some topics, aiming to understand where our methods are especially beneficial or detrimental to web retrieval effectiveness. Finally, our conclusions and ongoing work come in Section 6.

2   Background and Related Work

Web Retrieval. In recent years, web retrieval tasks were divided into two categories: *Named Page Finding* and *Topic Distillation.* Named page finding targets scenarios where a user searches for a specific page (which is known to exist, such as a personal home page); this task is often evaluated with MRR or Success@N for low values of N, since the user is known to be interested in only one result, and prefers it to be as high on the ranked list as possible. Topic distillation, on the other hand, involves finding key resources for a particular subject. Distillation is normally evaluated with traditional MAP and precision@N scores [10, 11].

We focus on retrieval for topic distillation. Why? First, current performance on the named page task is very high, making it almost a solved problem. In the 2003 edition of the TREC web track, top performing systems achieved 90% Success@10 and 0.7 MRR scores for this task [11], meaning that in most of the cases the single relevant document is returned at rank 1. Furthermore, the median scores over all participating systems are 80% for Success@10 and well over 0.5 for MRR. In contrast, the topic distillation task has lots of room for improvements: at TREC 2003, the best performing system scored less than 0.13 on Precision@10 and less than 0.16 on MAP.

Secondly, the good results on named page retrieval are partly due to the heavy usage of factors not directly related to the ranking formula (e.g., indegree information); this makes the task highly sensitive to these external factors, thus making it more complex to study the effects of changes in the ranking algorithm or query processing on retrieval performance.

Finally, we focus on topic distillation because we want to determine the impact of the use of phrases and proximity terms both in terms of the traditional MAP scores and in terms of (very) high precision measures such as MRR, Precision@1/Precision@5, and Success@1/Success@5. Topic distillation is unique as a task where both types of evaluation scores make sense.

Phrases and Proximity Terms. Intuitively, proximity and phrase operators are factors which improve retrieval effectiveness; indeed, lots of research was directed in this direction. The relative merits of statistical and syntactic phrases were extensively investigated by Fagan [14], and again by Hull *et al.* [19]. Until the late 1990s, usage of phrases and proximity operators—as well as a careful usage of boolean operators—did show varying degrees of improvements of retrieval results [17, 12, 22], but rarely anything substantial.

As retrieval models became more advanced, the usage of various query operators was questioned. Mitra *et al.* [24] investigate the effectiveness of using phrases for plain text retrieval (on a standard newswire text collection); they employ both linguistic and statistical methods for phrase extraction. Their conclusion is that when using a good, modern ranking algorithm, phrases have no effect on high precision retrieval (and sometimes negative effect from topic drift); for low precision, there is some marginal improvement from the usage of phrases. Similar conclusions have been reached for non-English IR, also on plain text [23].

Work on retrieval using a proximity framework is more scarce. Hawking and Thistlewaite explore the use of proximity scoring within the PADRE system [16]. Clarke and Cormack [9] show promising results, especially for manually-refined queries; it is unclear how this approach is combined with $tf \cdot idf$ based models, which constitute the majority of today's retrieval approaches (including Okapi and Language Modeling, which usually derive the estimations used in them from these factors). Rasolofo and Savoy [28] combine term-proximity scoring heuristics with the Okapi probabilistic model, obtaining 3%–8% improvements for Precision@5/10/20, with hardly observable impact on the MAP scores.

There has been relatively little systematic work on the effectiveness of phrases and proximity terms in the setting of web retrieval. At the TREC 2003 web track, however, several participants reported improvements based on proximity information, spans, and phrases [11]; two of the five top performing systems in the named page finding task used proximity in some way [30, 33]. However, we were unable to find systematic evaluations of the use of proximity terms in queries compared to the same ranking formula with no use of proximities.

Our work on query operations differs from earlier work because of our exclusive focus on web retrieval, exploiting the structure of web documents as well as the special content of some document fields (such as URLs and anchors), and because of our focus on "light-weight" phrases that are computationally cheap and robust against grammatical and spelling errors often found in web queries.

3   Query Refinement for Web Retrieval

In this section we describe the operations we use for query refinement and motivate their selection as an approach for improving web retrieval effectiveness.

3.1   Phrases and Proximity Terms

Previous research on the use of phrases for query refinement discusses statistical, syntactical, and lexical phrase detection [3, 14, 24, 27]. All approaches show mixed results on ad-hoc retrieval, with the maximal gain to precision being

5%–7%. We follow a different, shallow way of phrase detection: an "everything-is-a-phrase" approach. In our view, phrase terms need not necessarily be actual phrases, either in the syntactical or statistical sense; they can simply be words which appear consecutively in relevant documents, with high likelihood. For example, for topic WT04-58 from TREC 2004, "automobile emissions vehicle pollution," it seems that many subsets of consecutive words from the query are relevant as phrase terms, regardless of the statistical or syntactical evidence for their "phrasehood." Such subsets are "automobile emissions" and "vehicle pollution" but also "emissions vehicle" (which matches, after stopping and stemming, "emissions from a vehicle" or "emitted by vehicles"). While this also creates non-phrases, linguistically or statistically, the frequency of such word n-grams in the collection is virtually zero [6], preventing performance degradation. So, in our experiments, we choose to consider every word n-gram (of any length, inclusive single words and all words) which is part of the query, as a phrase. This naive approach carries with it some practical benefits: robustness, low computational overhead, no noise created by additional mechanisms and algorithms, etc.

For proximity operators, we employ a similar approach. We consider all word n-grams from the query as a proximity term; we then experiment with two query rewriting methods to exploit proximities: *fixed distance* and *variable distance*. Using the fixed distance method, every n-gram is a proximity term with a fixed distance, which depends on the length of the n-gram and an externally provided parameter. For example, if the parameter is $k = 2$, the n-gram is "emissions vehicle", and the method for combining the parameter and the length is multiplying them, the distance we have for this proximity is 4. We experimented with estimation methods for deriving the proximity distance from the external parameter and the n-gram length, e.g., linear combinations, products, squared combinations, and so on; we found no major differences in average performance (for both early precision and overall performance measures), provided that the values of k are tuned for the specific combination with the n-gram length. Hence, we use a simple sum of the external parameter and the size of the n-gram; the value of k was empirically set to 11. This type of combination allows longer proximity terms a larger distance, loosening the restrictions on longer terms which tend to be ungrammatical (e.g., "automobile emissions vehicle pollution").

With the fixed distance method, assuming the calculated distance is n, all occurrences of the term words in windows of n and less are scored equally. To reward terms according to the actual distance between the proximity terms, within the variable distance rewriting method we rewrote a proximity term into a series of proximity terms, each having a lower distance restriction. Terms which are found in smaller windows than n will match more than one term, effectively increasing the ranking of the document. Practically, this is done using the same method used to generate the fixed distance proximity terms, but with decreasing values of k. For example, the term "automobile emissions vehicle pollution" will be translated into 11 separate query terms, ranging from a fixed distance term with $k = 11$ down to the same term with $k = 1$.

In all our experiments, the result list was reranked using link indegree and URL length as reported in [1].[1]

3.2   Query Operators in the Vector Space Model

In our experiments, we focus on the vector space model, for which all advanced query operators are well researched; virtually any IR textbook (e.g., [4, 29]) contain a discussion of operators such as phrases, proximity, and wildcards. Rather than tuning up the retrieval formula, tweaking it to match the specific task that is addressed, we use a fixed, basic ranking formula. For this formula, we define the ranking of both simple terms and more complex ones (e.g., phrase terms). We then experiment with a range of transformation methods for deriving terms out of the original query; the definition given for ranking each term type is used to derive the final ranking formula.

Given a collection D, the basic similarity score between a document d and a query q containing terms t_i in our experiments is a common vector space variation:

$$sim(q, d) = \sum_{t \in q} \frac{tf_{t,q} \cdot idf_t}{norm_q} \cdot \frac{tf_{t,d} \cdot idf_t}{norm_d} \cdot coord_{q,d} \cdot weight_t,$$

where

$$tf_{t,X} = \sqrt{\text{freq}(t, X)} \qquad idf_t = 1 + \log \frac{|D|}{\text{freq}(t,D)}$$
$$norm_d = \sqrt{|d|} \qquad coord_{q,d} = \frac{|q \cap d|}{|q|}$$
$$norm_q = \sqrt{\sum_{t \in q} tf_{t,q} \cdot idf_t^2}$$

Terms can be either a single word, a phrase, or a proximity term. For single term words, the *tf* and *idf* calculation is straightforward. For a multiple-word term t (phrase or proximity), composed of the single word terms $t_0, t_1, \ldots, t_n$, the actual frequency counts in the collection of a phrase are not normally used, mainly for efficiency reasons. There are various ways to estimate these figures; previous experiments have shown little difference in performance between methods [24]. We experimented with the following estimation methods, testing early precision measures as well as MAP:

Sum: $idf = \sum_{i=0}^{n} idf_i$

Minimum: $idf = \min_i idf_i$

Maximum: $idf = \max_i idf_i$

Arithmetic Mean: $idf = \sum_{i=0}^{n} idf_i / n$

Geometric Mean: $idf = \prod_{i=0}^{n} idf_i^{\frac{1}{n}}$

The results, evaluated on the test set described in Section 4.1, are presented in Table 1; best scores (for a given evaluation measure) are in boldface. As may

---

[1] We note that similarly to the results obtained there, the reranking substantially improved all measures, up to 60% improvement in early precision scores. The improvements seemed consistent for all models—with or without usage of query operators—and we consider them orthogonal to the results of the various query reformulations.

Table 1. Comparison of *idf* estimation methods

Method	Phrases			Proximity		
	P@10	S@10	MAP	P@10	S@10	MAP
Sum	0.1576	0.7440	0.1438	**0.1888**	0.7600	**0.1569**
Minimum	**0.1712**	0.7680	0.1433	0.1832	**0.7840**	0.1502
Maximum	0.1688	0.7600	**0.1457**	0.1832	0.7840	0.1502
Arithmetic Mean	**0.1712**	**0.7760**	0.1450	0.1824	0.7760	0.1485
Geometric Mean	**0.1712**	**0.7760**	0.1433	0.1824	0.7760	0.1482

be seen from the results in Table 1, for some measures there are differences between estimation methods, but they are not dramatic. As an aside, phrase terms seem to display more variability than proximity terms. We choose the Minimum estimation, which seems to provide good performance both for early precision and for overall precision scores. The Minimum estimation also seems more intuitive, since phrase occurrences should be more restrictive than the occurrences of the words within them.

As for the *tf* figures for multiple-word terms, they remain the same as single-word ones, i.e. real frequencies of the multiple-word term in the document or the query. The frequency is calculated according to the multiple-word restrictions, e.g., if the term is a proximity term with two single word terms in a span of 10 words, an "occurrence" of it will be counted every time the two words appear in a window of 10 words or less. For example, in the document "dog cat mouse dog dog cat", the number of occurrences of the phrase "dog cat" is 2, and the proximity term "dog cat" with distance 3 has 4 occurrences.

3.3   Multiple Representations of Documents

When addressing web retrieval, most of the target documents are HTML documents containing markup, rather than simple plain text. This markup has been extensively used in the web retrieval setting, for example by top performers in the TREC web retrieval tasks, to form a more sophisticated document representation than a bag-of-words (see e.g., [2, 26]).

We make use of the markup by dividing each document into multiple "fields" which are indexed separately, providing separate frequency estimates for each field. The fields we identify in an HTML document are TITLE, DESCRIPTION, KEYWORDS, BODY, URL and ANCHOR TEXT. We experimented extensively with the use of different combinations of fields; our best results consistently appear when using only the TITLE, BODY and ANCHOR TEXT field. We attribute the lack of contribution of the DESCRIPTION and KEYWORDS fields to the relative sparseness of their usage: only 16% of the documents in our corpus (described in Section 4.1) contain the META keyword "description" and only 18% contain the "keywords" keyword.

Additionally, we experimented with methods for assigning term weights to the phrase terms according to the length of the *n*-gram, various external parameters and hard-coded assumptions (e.g., "TITLE is more important than URL"). For the

majority of the methods, the effect on performance was not substantial. We did
establish consistent if small improvements when using term weights derived from
the real frequencies of the term (as a phrase) in a certain field in the collection,
and report on this in Section 4.

4   Evaluation

In this section we describe our experiments and their outcomes.

4.1   Experimental Setting

We follow the experimental setup of the web tracks at TREC 2003 [11] and TREC
2004 [13]. The corpus used for the experiments is the .GOV corpus, which is a
crawl of a subset of the .gov domain performed in 2002. The corpus contains
18.1Gb of data in 1.25M documents, the vast majority of which are HTML
documents, and it preserves the link information between the documents. Our
test set consists of the two topic distillation topic sets released with TREC 2003
and 2004, containing 50 and 75 queries respectively, for a total of 125 queries,
with topic lengths as detailed in Table 2. We use the assessments provided by
the organizers of the web tracks.

4.2   Experiments and Results

First, we provide a brief description of the different query formulation methods
we experimented with.

- baseline: All words from the topic are single-word terms.
- phrases: All word n-grams from the topic are used as phrase terms, as
  described in Section 3.1.
- phrases-b Same as phrases, but every phrase term is given a term weight
  proportional to the real term frequency of the term phrase (as a phrase) in
  different fields.
- proximity All word n-grams from the query are used as proximity terms,
  with a fixed distance length.
- prox-v All word n-grams from the query are used as proximity terms, with
  a variable distance length.

The scores of the different experiments for early precision measures and additional measures are presented in Table 3 and Table 4, respectively.

On the TREC 2003 distillation topics, the baseline achieves scores which
would position it among the top 10 experiments (out of 93 experiments) for
all measures; for Precision@10, the baseline equals the best reported score. Our
non-baseline runs score better than any reported experiment.

Table 2. Distribution of topic lengths

Topic Length	1	2	3	4	5	6	Mean	2.38
Topic Count	10	64	25	11	4	2		

Table 3. Comparison of methods, early precision measures

Method	P@10	P@5	S@10	S@5	MRR
Single field representation					
baseline	0.1456	0.1840	0.7040	0.5440	0.4193
phrases	0.1456 (0%)	0.1888 (+2%)	0.7200 (+2%)	0.5520 (+1%)	0.4273 (+2%)
proximity	0.1528 (+5%)	0.1968 (+7%)	0.7280 (+3%)	0.5900 (+8%)	0.4126 (-2%)
prox-v	0.1488 (+2%)	0.2064 (+12%)	0.7200 (+2%)	0.5940 (+9%)	0.4283 (+2%)
Multiple field representation					
baseline	0.1720	0.2224	0.7520	0.6400	0.4811
phrases	0.1712 (-1%)	0.2288 (+3%)	0.7680 (+2%)	0.6240 (-2%)	0.5215 (+8%)
phrases-b	0.1912 (+11%)	0.2416 (+9%)	0.7600 (+1%)	0.6560 (+2%)	0.4992 (+4%)
proximity	0.1888 (+10%)	0.2512 (+13%)	0.7920 (+5%)	0.6560 (+2%)	0.5142 (+7%)
prox-v	0.1904 (+11%)	0.2496 (+12%)	0.7840 (+4%)	0.6560 (+2%)	0.5156 (+7%)

Table 4. Comparison of methods, additional measures

Method	R-Prec	MAP
Single field representation		
baseline	0.1157	0.1041
phrases	0.1235 (+6%)	0.1088 (+4%)
proximity	0.1282 (+10%)	0.1094 (+5%)
prox-v	0.1267 (+9%)	0.1101 (+5%)
Multiple field representation		
baseline	0.1578	0.1271
phrases	0.1687 (+7%)	0.1433 (+13%)
phrases-b	0.1607 (+2%)	0.1443 (+13%)
proximity	0.1791 (+13%)	0.1569 (+23%)
prox-v	0.1822 (+15%)	0.1559 (+22%)

4.3   Discussion

Mitra *et al.* [24] report that the use of phrases yields little or no improvement, provided that the basic ranking formula is a good one. When using a single field representation of the document, i.e., all text—title, body, propagated anchor text and so on—is indexed in the same field, we reach similar conclusions. Interestingly, however, for the multiple field representation of documents, we clearly see an improvement on all measures when using phrases and proximities, up to 23% on some measures. Observe, moreover, that these improvements cannot be attributed to a low baseline: as pointed out before, the baseline achieves state of the art performance on the 2003 topics, and well above median performance on the 2004 ones. Additionally, our non-baseline runs score better, on some early precision measures, than unrelated state of the art models we use for the task [21].

Concluding that our baseline is sufficiently high, we take a closer look at the results. A number of observations can be made. First, clearly, the less restrictive the additional operators are, the larger the improvement is to performance: fixed proximity terms outperform the more rigid phrase term, but are themselves generally not as good as the flexible proximity terms. Second, the use of plain phrases, without the additional term weights, yields unstable results—improving some measures but degrading others. Finally, the Success@10 measure is the most difficult to improve, possibly since it is high to start with.

Combinations. There is strong evidence suggesting that combinations of different retrieval techniques results in significant improvement of results (see, e.g., [5]). Since we used different query modifications, we had reason to believe that combinations of them are worthwhile; we therefore experimented with various ways to combine between our experiments. Additionally, we combined the results of our methods with a completely different set of experiments, based on the language modeling approach to IR and achieving in itself very good results for web IR at TREC 2003 and 2004 [1]. We observed that combinations yield consistent improvements of an additional 3%–5% percent both to early precision and to average precision measures. For space reasons, we do not report on the experiments here, and will give a more detailed account in [21].

5   Topic Analysis

In this section we provide a more detailed analysis of the impact of phrase and proximity operators on the retrieval effectiveness of individual queries. To save space, we restrict our discussions and comparisons to experiments using the multiple field representation; moreover, the results we obtained on the single field representation are similar to ones already reported by others.

5.1   Topic Length and Effectiveness

The most visible factor determining the effectiveness of the phrasal and proximity methods in our experiments is, not surprisingly, the query length. The mean length of the topics in our test set is 2.38, in line with the average query length for web retrieval mentioned earlier (Section 1). In Table 5 we examine the Precision@10 and MAP scores separately for different topics lengths, and their change from the baseline. We do not include topics of length 1 (for which there is no change in the ranking formula), and topics of length 5 and above, which constitute only 4% of the topics and are not statistically significant.

We can observe a strong correlation between the length of the queries and the effectiveness gain: the gain is significantly larger for topics of relative short (2–3) length. This is largely due to the fact that many of the shorter (2–3

Table 5. Performance comparison for most frequent query lengths

Topic Length	Topic Count	Phrases		Proximity	
		P@10	MAP	P@10	MAP
2	64	0.2286 (21%)	0.1392 (22%)	0.2254 (19%)	0.1451 (27%)
3	25	0.1640 (17%)	0.1295 (23%)	0.1520 (8%)	0.1658 (57%)
4	11	0.1273 (-18%)	0.1195 (-25%)	0.1455 (-6%)	0.1499 (-5%)

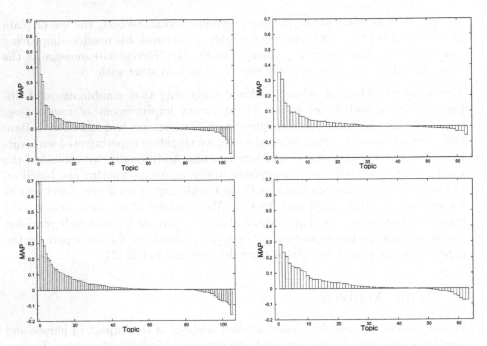

Fig. 1. Per-topic gain in Mean Average Precision compared to the baseline. (Top row): Using phrases, with all 106 topics longer than 1 word (left) and all 64 topics of length 2 (right). (Bottom row): Using proximity terms, with all 106 topics longer than 1 word (left) and all 64 topics of length 2 (right)

term) queries were formed of a single linguistic phrase, whereas longer queries are commonly just a collection of words. For longer lengths than those displayed in the table (such as 5 or 6 words) we observed an even larger drop in performance.[2]

A further breakdown of individual gain per topic is given in Figure 1 (effect on MAP for phrases and proximity) and Figure 2 (effect on Precision@10 for phrases and proximity). The histograms show similar behavior of both phrases and proximity terms. Improvements are generally far greater and far more frequent than degradations. When looking at topics of all lengths, 10% to 20% have a significant improvement, another 30%–40% some improvement, and for about 30% of the topics the usage of the query operators results in reasonably limited reduced effectiveness. Results for the 2-word topics are analogous, with larger percentages of topics achieving effectiveness gains.

---

[2] The results in Table 5 suggest that phrases and proximity should not be used for topics of length 4 or more. We experimented with the "best" setting for each group of topics (where topics are grouped by length). As topics of length 4 or more account for less than 14% of the topics, no dramatic differences could be observed with the results in Table 4.

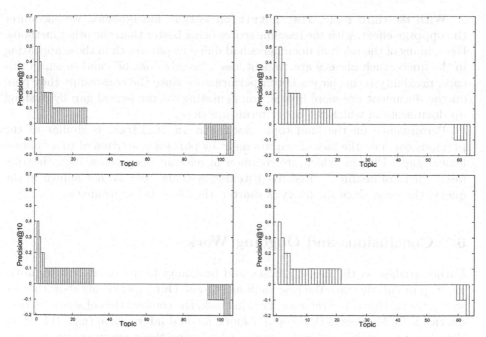

Fig. 2. Per-topic gain in Precision@10 compared to the baseline. (Top row): using phrases, with all 106 topics longer than 1 word (left) and all 64 topics of length 2 (right). (Bottom row): using proximity terms, with all 106 topics longer than 1 word (left) and all 64 topics of length 2 (right)

5.2   Examples

In Table 6 we take a closer look at the scores of a number of specific topics from the test set; in addition to Precision@10 scores, we list Average Precision (AP) scores per topic. A discussion regarding the causes for the differences in effectiveness for each topic follows.

The first two topics, skin cancer and homeland security, are somewhat classical examples of the effectiveness of using proximity between terms in the ranking. In the baseline model, the score is heavily dominated by the term cancer and security, which appear in short fields such as title and anchor text. In this case, both the usage of proximity and of phrases yields significant improvements.

Table 6. Individual topic examples

Topic	Baseline P@10	Baseline AP	Phrases P@10	Phrases AP	Proximity P@10	Proximity AP
skin cancer	0.2	0.1208	0.4	0.3350	0.4	0.3275
homeland security	0.1	0.0721	0.3	0.2065	0.3	0.2064
diet nutrition weight management	0.2	0.1107	0.0	0.0297	0.1	0.0840
deafness in children	0.2	0.0903	0.1	0.0917	0.1	0.1190

With the third topic, `diet nutrition weight management`, we encounter the opposite effect, with the baseline scores being better than the other methods. Here, many of the relevant documents had different phrases than those appearing in the query; such phrases are "weight loss", "weight control", and so on. In this case, proximity terms have a better performance since the constraints they pose on the document are more liberal, compensating for the lexical gap by pushing up documents in which the query terms are close.

Performance on the final topic, `deafness in children`, is similar to the previous one, i.e., the lack of improvement by phrases is attributed to a "phrase lexical gap." Phrases which are common in relevant documents, e.g., "hearing loss," "hard of hearing," "assistive listening systems," etc, do not appear in the query. However, since the query is shorter, the effect is less dramatic.

6   Conclusions and Ongoing Work

Earlier studies on the use of phrases and proximity terms show little improvement, particularly when the base ranking is good. Our experiments show that for web retrieval this is not the case. For this task, the combination of short, focused queries with documents that contain short, focused information (e.g., HTML titles) leads to significant improvements when using those query operators, even when applied in a naive fashion. The performance gains can be observed both for early precision mesures and for mean average precision.

The phrasal and proximity methods seem to help more the shorter the queries are; the queries that gain the most have, on average, the same length as the average length of web search engine queries. For longer queries, these methods cause topic drift, and need to be applied more carefully; we leave this issue for future work.

Returning to our main research questions, as formulated in Section 1, we have found that even on top of a good basic ranking scheme for web retrieval, phrases and proximity terms may bring improvements in retrieval effectiveness. While we observed improvements both when documents are represented as a single field, and as aggregates of multiple fields, the latter setting gave more substantial improvements. Somewhat suprisingly, we found that phrases and proximity terms improve scores for traditional mean average precision as well as for high precision measures, although the former tended to be more substantial. Another important finding was that phrases and proximity terms have a strong positive impact on web retrieval effectiveness for extremely short queries (2 or 3 terms), while they have less, or even negative, effects on longer queries.

We are currently exploring approaches to the usage of phrases and proximity terms in the language modeling framework for web retrieval. We expect that the theoretic foundations of language modeling will provide a better understanding of how and where usage of these operators improves effectiveness. Additionally, we will apply our current results to additional corpora where, similarly to web documents, multiple representations of documents exist: such corpora are XML documents [15] and biomedical document collections [18].

Acknowledgments

We wish to thank Jaap Kamps for many discussions and inspiration, and our referees for useful comments.

Both authors were supported by the Netherlands Organization for Scientific Research (NWO) under project number 220-80-001. Maarten de Rijke was also supported by NWO under project numbers 365-20-005, 612.069.006, 612.000.106, 612.000.207, 612.066.302, 264-70-050, and 017.001.190.

References

[1] D. Ahn, V. Jijkoun, J. Kamps, G. Mishne, K. Müller, M. de Rijke, and S. Schlobach. The University of Amsterdam at TREC 2004. In *TREC 2004 Conference Notebook*, Gaithersburg, Maryland USA, 2004.

[2] E. Amitay, D. Carmel, A. Darlow, M. Herscovici, R. Kraft, R. Lempel, A. Soffer, and J. Zien. Juru at TREC 2003 - Topic Distillation using Query-Sensitive Tuning and Cohesiveness Filtering. In *Proceedings of the 12th Text REtrieval Conference*, 2003.

[3] A.T. Arampatzis, Th.P. van der Weide, C.H.A. Koster, and P. van Bommel. An Evaluation of Linguistically-motivated Indexing Schemes. In *Proceedings of the 22nd BCS-IRSG Colloquium on IR Research*, 2000.

[4] R.A. Baeza-Yates and B.A. Ribeiro-Neto. *Modern Information Retrieval*. ACM Press / Addison-Wesley, 1999.

[5] B.T. Bartell, G.W. Cottrell, and R.K. Belew. Automatic Combination of Multiple Ranked Retrieval Systems. In *Research and Development in Information Retrieval*, pages 173–181, 1994.

[6] E. Brill, S. Dumais, and M. Banko. An analysis of the AskMSR question-answering system. In *Proceedings 39th Annual ACL*, 2002.

[7] F. Cacheda and A. Vina. Understanding how people use search engines: a statistical analysis for e-business. In *Proceedings of the e-Business and e-Work Conference and Exhibition*, pages 319–325, Venice, Italy, Oct 2001.

[8] S. Chakrabarti. *Mining the Web: Analysis of Hypertext and Semi Structured Data*. Morgan Kaufmann, 2002.

[9] C.L.A. Clarke and G.V. Cormack. Shortest-substring retrieval and ranking. *ACM Transactions on Information Systems (TOIS)*, 18(1):44–78, 2000.

[10] N. Craswell and D. Hawking. Overview of the TREC-2002 web track. In *Proceedings of TREC-2002*, Gaithersburg, Maryland USA, November 2002.

[11] N. Craswell, D. Hawking, R. Wilkinson, and M. Wu. Overview of the TREC-2003 web track. In *Proceedings of TREC 2003*, Gaithersburg, Maryland USA, November 2003.

[12] W.B. Croft, H.R. Turtle, and D.D. Lewis. The use of phrases and structured queries in information retrieval. In *Proceedings of the 14th annual international ACM SIGIR conference on Research and development in information retrieval*, pages 32–45. ACM Press, 1991.

[13] N. Craswell et al. Overview of the TREC-2004 web track. In *Proceedings 13th Text REtrieval Conference*, Gaithersburg, Maryland USA, To appear.

[14] J.L. Fagan. Experiments in automatic phrase indexing for document retrieval: A comparison of syntactic and non-syntactic methods. Technical report, Cornell University, 1987.

[15] N. Fuhr, M. Lalmas, and S. Malik, editors. *INEX 2003 Workshop Proceedings*, 2004.

[16] D. Hawking and P. Thistlewaite. Proximity operators—So near and yet so far. In *Proceedings TREC-4*, pages 131–143, 1996.

[17] D. Hawking and P. Thistlewaite. Relevance weighting using distance between term occurrences. Technical Report TR-CS-96-08, Department of Computer Science, Australian National University, 1996.

[18] W. Hersh and R.T. Bhupatiraju. TREC GENOMICS Track Overview. In *Proceedings TREC 2003*, pages 14–23, 2004.

[19] D.A. Hull, G. Grefenstette, B.M. Schultze, E. Gaussier, H. Schutze, and J. O. Pedersen. Xerox TREC-5 Site Report: Routing, Filtering, NLP, and Spanish Tracks. In *Proceedings TREC-5*, pages 167–180, 1997.

[20] B.J. Jansen, A. Spink, and T. Saracevic. Real life, real users, and real needs: a study and analysis of user queries on the web. *Information Processing and Management*, 36(2):207–227, 2000.

[21] J. Kamps, G. Mishne, and M. de Rijke. The University of Amsterdam at TREC 2004. In *Proceedings of the 13th Text REtrieval Conference*, to appear.

[22] E.M. Keen. Term position ranking: some new test results. In *Proceedings of the 15th annual international ACM SIGIR conference on Research and development in information retrieval*, pages 66–76. ACM Press, 1992.

[23] W. Kraaij and R. Pohlmann. Comparing the effect of syntactic vs. statistical phrase index strategies for Dutch. In *Proceedings of the Second European Conference on Research and Advanced Technology for Digital Libraries (ECDL)*, pages 605–617, 1998.

[24] M. Mitra, C. Buckley, A. Singhal, and C. Cardie. An analysis of statistical and syntactic phrases. In *Proceedings of RIAO-97*, 1997.

[25] V. Mittal, S. Baluja, and M. Sahami. Google tutorial on web information retrieval. In *RIAO-2004*, 2004.

[26] P. Ogilvie and J. Callan. Combining document representations for known-item search. In *Proceedings of the 26th annual international ACM SIGIR conference on Research and development in informaion retrieval*. ACM Press, 2003.

[27] J. Pickens and W.B. Croft. An exploratory analysis of phrases in text retrieval. In *Proceedings of RIAO-2000*, 2000.

[28] Y. Rasolofo and J. Savoy. Term proximity scoring for keyword-based retrieval systems. In *Proceedings 25th European Conference on IR Research (ECIR 2003)*, pages 207–218, 2003.

[29] G. Salton and M.J. McGill. *Introduction to Modern Information Retrieval*. McGraw-Hill, Inc., 1986.

[30] J. Savoy, Y. Rasolofo, and L. Perret. Report on the TREC-2003 experiment: Genomic and web searches. In *Proceedings TREC 2003*, pages 739–750, 2004.

[31] A. Spink, B.J. Jansen, D. Wolfram, and T. Saracevic. From e-sex to e-commerce: Web search changes. *Computer*, 35(3):107–109, 2002.

[32] A. Spink, D. Wolfram, B.J. Jansen, and T. Saracevic. Searching the web: the public and their queries. *Journal of the American Society for Information Science and Technology*, 52(3):226–234, 2001.

[33] J. Wen, R. Song, D. Cai, K. Zhu, S. Yu, S. Ye, and W.-Y. Ma. Microsoft Research Asia at the Web Track of TREC 2003. In *Proceedings TREC 2003*, pages 408–417, 2004.

Terrier Information Retrieval Platform

Iadh Ounis, Gianni Amati*, Vassilis Plachouras, Ben He, Craig Macdonald,
and Douglas Johnson

University of Glasgow, Glasgow G12 8QQ, UK
{ounis, gianni, vassilis, ben, craigm, johnsoda}@dcs.gla.ac.uk

Abstract. Terrier is a modular platform for the rapid development of
large-scale Information Retrieval (IR) applications. It can index various
document collections, including TREC and Web collections. Terrier also
offers a range of document weighting and query expansion models, based
on the Divergence From Randomness framework. It has been successfully
used for ad-hoc retrieval, cross-language retrieval, Web IR and intranet
search, in a centralised or distributed setting.

1 Introduction

Experience has shown that the evaluation and cross-comparison of IR models and
methods is best done on a common development platform. Hence, our aim for
building the Terrier (Terabyte Retriever) IR platform was to provide a publicly
available test-bed for the rapid development of IR applications.

Terrier offers a variety of IR models, based on the Divergence From Randomness (DFR) framework[1]. The DFR framework, which can be seen as a generalisation of Harter's 2-Poisson indexing model, is based on a simple idea: the
more the divergence of the within-document term-frequency of a term t from its
distribution within the collection, the more the amount of information carried
by t in the document. In addition to more than 50 parameter-free DFR models,
Terrier offers other IR models, such as tf-idf, BM25 and language modelling.

2 Overview of Terrier

The Terrier platform has been designed to efficiently scale up with the size of
document collections, operating in either a centralised or a distributed setting.
Its main data structures are the direct index, the document index, the inverted
index and the lexicon. The direct index stores the identifiers of terms that appear
in each document and the corresponding frequencies. It is used for automatic
query expansion, but can also be used for user profiling activities. The document index stores information about the document length and identifier, and a

---

* Gianni Amati is also affiliated to Fondazione Ugo Bordoni, Italy (gba@fub.it).
[1] More details can be found at http://ir.dcs.gla.ac.uk/terrier/description.html.

D.E. Losada and J.M. Fernández-Luna (Eds.): ECIR 2005, LNCS 3408, pp. 517–519, 2005.
© Springer-Verlag Berlin Heidelberg 2005

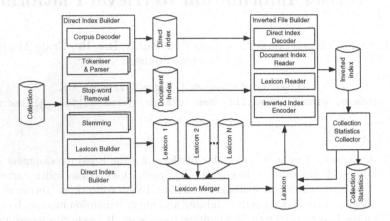

Fig. 1. Indexing process with Terrier

pointer to the corresponding entry in the direct index. The inverted index stores the posting lists, while the lexicon stores the collection vocabulary and the corresponding document and term frequencies. An additional data structure stores the collection statistics that are used for document ranking. While indexing, we compress the direct and inverted indices, using gamma and unary encodings.

In Figure 1, we outline the indexing process for a document collection. The double-framed boxes correspond to application-dependent modules. Each document in the collection is tokenised and parsed. Depending on the application, we remove stopwords and apply stemming. In this way, we build the direct and document indices. We also build in-memory temporary lexicons for parts of the collection, in order to reduce the required memory during indexing. These lexicons will be merged later, in order to form the lexicon of the whole collection. Next, the inverted index is built from the existing direct index, document index and lexicon. Finally, we collect statistics about the document collection and update the lexicon with information from the inverted file.

The retrieval process is outlined in Figure 2. A query is processed by removing stopwords and applying stemming, according to the application requirements. For a given query, Terrier is able to automatically select the optimal document weighting model and/or the appropriate retrieval approaches (e.g. query expansion, anchor text, or link analysis), using among other features, state-of-the-art query performance pre-retrieval predictors. If query expansion (QE) is applied, an appropriate term weighting model is selected and the most informative terms from the top ranked documents are added to the query. Furthermore, Terrier allows to easily fit the retrieval output to the application requirements (e.g. TREC or XML formats), and provides standard evaluation techniques.

Terrier provides a variety of features for indexing and retrieval. First, it uses state-of-the-art compression techniques for data structures. In a distributed setting, a full-text index of the TREC Terabyte track .GOV2 collection (the size of .GOV2 is 426GB) corresponds to only 4.1% of the total collection size (left part of Table 1). It can also use additional features, such as a retrieval approach

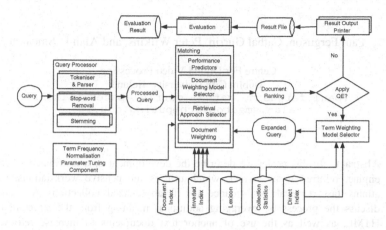

Fig. 2. Retrieval process with Terrier

Table 1. The size of data structures for a full-text index of the TREC .GOV2 collection, and the evaluation results for the corresponding TREC 2004 Terabyte retrieval task

Data Structures	Size	Run Description	MAP	bpref	P10
All structures	17.48GB	Short queries	0.2709	0.3026	0.5306
Inverted files	7.77GB	Short queries + anchor text	0.2690	0.3025	0.5245
Direct files	7.00GB	Long queries	0.3054	0.3356	0.6327
Lexicons	1.84GB	Long queries + QE	0.3075	0.3359	0.6163
Document indices	0.87GB	Participants' Median Run	0.1427	0.2015	0.4102

selector, position information for proximity and phrasal search, linkage information and HTML features. Terrier provides modular APIs for both indexing and querying, as well as an advanced query language.

Terrier has been successfully used in the Web, Robust and Terabyte tracks of TREC 2002–04. For the TREC 2004 Terabyte track, Terrier performed significantly better than the median of the participants' submitted runs (right part of Table 1). It has been also used for French and Italian retrieval in CLEF 2003–04, and it is currently used as an intranet search engine for various university and public organisations. A version of Terrier is available for download as open source software from http://ir.dcs.gla.ac.uk/terrier/.

Acknowledgements

This work is funded by a UK Engineering and Physical Sciences Research Council (EPSRC) project grant, number GR/R90543/01.

Físréal: A Low Cost Terabyte Search Engine

Paul Ferguson, Cathal Gurrin, Peter Wilkins, and Alan F. Smeaton

Centre For Digital Video Processing,
Dublin City University, Ireland
{paul.ferguson, cathal.gurrin, peter.wilkins,
alan.smeaton}@computing.dcu.ie

Abstract. In this poster we describe the development of a distributed search engine, referred to as Físréal, which utilises inexpensive workstations, yet attains fast retrieval performance for Terabyte-sized collections. We also discuss the process of leveraging additional meaning from the structure of HTML, as well as the use of anchor text documents to increase retrieval performance.

1 Introduction

As the size of the web increases, the task of developing a cost-effective search engine to deal with these large amounts of documents becomes a major engineering task. The presence of a new Terabyte track in TREC2004 is just one example of how important large-scale retrieval has become. The test collection used for the Terabyte track was the GOV2 collection, which consists of a large portion of the .GOV domain (25,205,179 documents). In this poster we describe an architecture for a distributed search engine which we have used to provide fast search facilities over collections including GOV2 and the even larger (94.5 million document) SPIRIT collection.

2 Retrieval Architecture

Físréal was designed to be a scalable, distributed search service. Our solution for this was to distribute the index across several machines and to provide a search engine or leaf server on each of these machines. These leaf nodes receive their queries from an aggregate engine which receives the initial query and distributes the query to each of the node engines, then combines the results from each before presenting a final ranked list. The hardware we employed consisted of DELL PowerEdge 600SC Servers, each with, one P4 2.4 Ghz CPU, 2GB RAM, 4x250GB IDE hard drives with RAID 0. The approximate cost of each server (Nov 2004) is €2,300.

One example implementation of Físréal (for the SPIRIT collection) required four leaf servers, with the collection being split arbitrarily into equal portions for each server. Experience gained in indexing SPIRIT suggested that retrieval performance was related to the number of leaf servers implemented, therefore when indexing the GOV2 collection (substantially smaller) we also employed four leaf servers.

D.E. Losada and J.M. Fernández-Luna (Eds.): ECIR 2005, LNCS 3408, pp. 520–522, 2005.
© Springer-Verlag Berlin Heidelberg 2005

Aggregate Server: The aggregate server provides the interface to the search service and handles all communication with the leaf servers. The aggregate itself does not directly reference any index.

Leaf Server: A leaf server is a single instance of the search engine and could be independently queried. As many leaf servers as required can be employed to produce the distributed search engine. Each of the leaf servers receives the same query from the aggregate server. A global lexicon and total number of occurrences for each term in the entire collection is held at each leaf server so that the correct ranking score for each document can be calculated as it would have been done if the entire index had been held on a single machine.

3 Indexing Issues

The following index structures are currently supported by the search engine:

Standard Index: The index employed by each leaf server is similar to a conventional inverted index. Essentially, for each term in a collection-wide lexicon, there is an object that contains the list of documents where that term occurs, and its corresponding TF. This object is sorted by the TF for each term normalised by the document length so as to allow the retrieval of the top subset of documents associated with each term. The effect of this on retrieval performance is currently under investigation and we will soon report concrete findings of the trade-off between precision, the proportion of the index examined and performance.

Weighted Index: It is believed that certain HTML tags contain text that is more representative of the content of the document than other text in the document. For example, text in the title tag would generally be more reflective of the content of the document than the body text of the document, and should therefore be given more weighting in retrieval. To infer these weightings, we defined what we considered to be the tags that would contain the most representative words, then we defined the extra weighting for terms in these tags based on previous work in TREC and elsewhere. These tags and their weightings are as follows:

Tag	TITLE	B	H1	H2	H3	H4	H5	H6	I	EM	U	A	ALT
Weight	6	4	4	4	2	2	2	2	2	2	2	4	6

These tags were identified in each document at indexing time, and each embedded term was given the appropriate weighting to be incorporated into the index during the indexing stage. The structure of the weighted index took on a similar structure to the conventional index, the difference being that along with the TF of the term the weighted TF was also held for each term in each document that it occurred in. This allows the same index to support either a weighted or non-weighted ranking for each query as specified at query time yet has a negligible effect on query processing time. This index has an average size of 12.6GB per leaf node, where each index is used to index over 23 million documents.

Anchor Text Index: It is believed that integrating anchor text into the retrieval process can be useful in improving retrieval performance for Web IR[1]. We generated anchor text surrogate documents by extracting the anchor text (with a window of 50 bytes either side, to the nearest word) from all documents that link to a given document. This creates a collection of documents which contains terms that the in-link authors used to describe the target document. We created an index from these documents with the same structure as the conventional index. This index has an average size of 1.86GB per leaf node.

URL Index: An index consisting of terms obtained by breaking up a document URLs into terms based on its domain and path. This index has a total size of 2.2GB.

4   Retrieval Performance and Conclusion

In order to examine the performance of Físréal we present results from experiments with the GOV2 collections and relevance judgements from the TREC 2004 TB track:

- A baseline BM25 run (BM25: k1=1.2, k3=1000, b=0.75).
- A BM25 run, using a weighted index (WBM25: k1=1.2, k3=1000, b=0.75).
- A run incorporating BM25 (k1=1.2, k3=1000, b=0.75), anchor text (k1=50, k3=1000, b=0), descriptions and URL text (k1=1.2, k3=1000, b=0.75).

All of our runs take only the title of the topic and use this as the query for all fifty queries.The following table presents the performance figures for these experiments.

RUN	MAP	Recall (10617 relevant)	Top 20 retrieval time (Note: same top 20 as top 10000)
BM25	0.1272	6765 (64%)	1.823 seconds
SWeighted BM25	0.1022	6284 (59%)	1.922 seconds
BM_Anchor_URL	0.1150	6765 (64%)	2.01 seconds

We have presented an architecture and preliminary results for a low cost distributed search engine. For a five-server implementation the cost is approximately €11,500, and for the GOV2 collection this equates to €450 per million documents indexed. As can be observed from the preliminary results further thought and refinement will need to be given to the weights selected for weighted BM25. We also plan to explore the cost-performance ratio for a larger number of leaf servers.

Acknowledgement. This work was supported by Science Foundation Ireland, under grant number 03/IN.3/I361.

References

1. N. Craswell and D. Hawking. (2003). *Overview of the TREC 2003 Web Track, Proceedings of the Twelfth Text Retrieval Conference, pg78-92, 2003.*

Query Formulation for Answer Projection

Gilad Mishne and Maarten de Rijke

Informatics Institute, University of Amsterdam,
Kruislaan 403, 1098 SJ Amsterdam, The Netherlands
{gilad, mdr}@science.uva.nl

Abstract. We examine the effects of various query modifications on the problem of answer projection — the task of retrieving documents that support a given answer to a question. We compare different techniques such as phrase searches and term weighting, and show that some models achieve significant improvements over unmodified queries.

1   Introduction

Largely spawned by the introduction of Question Answering (QA) tasks at evaluation forums such as TREC and CLEF, research on QA has intensified in recent years, with a strong focus on open-domain QA from a large collection of newspaper articles. As TREC and CLEF participants started moving to data-intensive (as opposed to knowledge-intensive) approaches, they discovered that for open-domain QA, consulting a much larger corpus — especially the web — often leads to improvements in performance. Efforts to move closer to shrink-wrapped trainable QA systems have brought with it a heavy usage of the web [1, 4] and other external resources, including gazetteers, WordNet and others [3, 5, 8].

Overall, users prefer a paragraph-sized chunk of text over just an exact phrase as the answer to their questions, and they generally prefer answers embedded in context, regardless of the perceived reliability of the source documents [7]. For QA systems that locate answers and partial answers in external resources, this creates a new challenge of *answer projection*, i.e., of finding a *supporting document*, one from which a human can deduce that the answer is correct.[1]

This, then, is the answer projection task we address in the paper: given an answer to a question, find supporting documents in a given collection for it. Phrased this way, the task resembles a known-item search task. Accordingly, answer projection has been addressed using the kind of high precision retrieval models that have typically been employed for known item search, such as specific Okapi settings [2], passage retrieval, and combinations of heuristics [6]. Instead of varying the retrieval model, in this paper we adopt a basic vector space model, for which various query operators are well understood, and

---

[1] As an aside, by the guidelines for QA evaluations at TREC and CLEF, with each answer, a supporting document has to be identified in a given corpus. Failure to return a supporting document with an otherwise correct answer is a significant problem [2, 5].

D.E. Losada and J.M. Fernández-Luna (Eds.): ECIR 2005, LNCS 3408, pp. 523–526, 2005.
© Springer-Verlag Berlin Heidelberg 2005

524 G. Mishne and M. de Rijke

explore different query formulation techniques and their effect on the projection task.

2 Query Formulation

In our experiments, the basic similarity between a document d and a query q is $sim(q,d) = \sum_{t \in q} \frac{tf_{t,q} \cdot idf_t}{norm_q} \cdot \frac{tf_{t,d} \cdot idf_t}{norm_d} \cdot coord_{q,d} \cdot weight_t$, where $weight_t$ is a user-assigned term weight term, $tf_{t,X} = \sqrt{(freq(t, X))}$, $idf_t = 1 + \log(|D|/freq(t, D))$, while $norm_q = \sqrt{(\sum_{t \in q} tf_{t,q} \cdot idf_t{}^2)}$, $norm_d = \sqrt{|d|}$ and $coord_{q,d} = |q \cap d|/|q|$. The terms in the query and the document may be phrases; in this case, the tf and idf scores for them are calculated accordingly. The following models were tested: **baseline** (the query is all words from the question and the answer), **boost-answer-N** (same as the baseline, but the answer words are weighted higher than other words, by a factor of N), **boolean-answer** (same as baseline, the answer words must be in the document), **phrases** (the query is all words from the question and answer; consecutive words that are phrases according to shallow analysis such as capitalization are phrased), and **phrase-answer** (all words from the question as single-word term, and the answer as a phrase). In addition, we consider combinations of the models, e.g., "**boolean-answer, boost-answer**" means that the answer words are required in the documents, and given higher term weights.

The models are based on simple "answer projection heuristics": it is *likely* that if the answer contains more than one word, it is a phrase; it is *likely* that all words in the answer must be in the supporting document, while not necessarily all words from the question will be there; and so on.

3 Evaluation

To evaluate the effectiveness of the different query formulation methods for answer projection, we used a collection of 786 factoid questions taken from the QA tasks at TREC 11 and 12; these consist of all factoid questions having an answer in the AQUAINT collection, according to the judgment set released by NIST. A question may have more than a single answer, and an answer may have more than a single supporting document; for example, for question *2378. How did Bob Marley die?*, both the answers "cancer" and "melanoma" are correct, and each is supported by more than one document. In total, there were 1814 correct answers to evaluate.

For each (question, answer)-pair we formulated queries according to the models presented in the previous section; we used standard stopping and Snowball stemming. To compare the models, we use both p@1 ("precision at rank 1") and MRR ("Mean Reciprocal Rank") measures; p@1 determines whether the top retrieved document is a supporting one, thus checking whether the method is useful in a real-life QA system, which looks only at the top retrieved document

Model	MRR	p@1
baseline	0.477	0.346
boost-answer-2	0.464 (-3%)	0.340 (-1%)
boost-answer-5	0.408 (-14%)	0.287 (-17%)
boost-answer-20	0.329 (-31%)	0.225 (-35%)
phrases	0.471 (-1%)	0.347 (0%)
boolean-answer	0.502 (+5%)	0.374 (+8%)
phrase-answer	0.525 (+10%)	0.398 (+15%)
phrases,phrase-answer	0.517 (+8%)	0.397 (+15%)
phrases,phrase-answer,boolean-answer	0.531 (+11%)	0.416 (+20%)

Fig. 1. Comparison of the query formulation models

during the justification stage; the MRR score shows how good the model is in pushing supporting documents higher in the ranking.

The results of the comparison are listed in Figure 1. All results are strongly statistically significant (using the sign test), except those of the **phrases** method. Usage of phrase and boolean operators results in a clear, gradual increase in performance, and combinations of them improve results further. On the other hand, the simple term weighting used degrades performance; this can be attributed to topic drift resulting from too much importance given to the answer, which is usually 1-2 terms and may have high *idf* values. We used shallow phrase recognition, and expect that deeper methods will improve the score further.

4   Conclusions

We address the answer projection task in Question Answering as a query formulation problem. Using a vector space model as a black box, we experiment with various methods of refining a query composed of the question, the answer, and various query operators as the building blocks. Our experiments show a consistent and significant improvement for some models and their combinations.

Acknowledgments. Both authors were supported by the Netherlands Organization for Scientific Research (NWO) under project number 220-80-001. De Rijke was also supported by NWO under project numbers 365-20-005, 612.069.-006, 612.000.106, 612.000.207, 612.066.302, 264-70-050, and 017.001.190.

References

1. E. Brill, S. Dumais, and M. Banko. An analysis of the AskMSR question-answering system. In *Proc. 39th Annual ACL*, 2002.
2. E. Brill, J. Lin, M. Banko, S.T. Dumais, and A.Y. Ng. Data-intensive question answering. In *Proc. 10th Text REtrieval Conference*, 2001.
3. C. Clarke, G. Cormack, G. Kemkes, M. Laszlo, T. Lynam, E. Terra, and P. Tilker. Statistical selection of exact answers. In *Proc. 11th Text REtrieval Conference*, 2002.

4. A. Ittycheriah, M. Franz, and S. Roukos. IBM's statistical question answering system. In *Proc. 10th Text REtrieval Conference*, 2001.
5. V. Jijkoun, G. Mishne, and M. de Rijke. How frogs built the Berlin Wall. In *Proc. CLEF 2003*. Springer, 2004.
6. J. Lin, A. Fernandes, B. Katz, G. Marton, and S. Tellex. Extracting answers from the web using knowledge annotation and knowledge mining techniques. In *Proc. 11th Text REtrieval Conference*, 2002.
7. J. Lin, D. Quan, V. Sinha, K. Bakshi, D. Huynh, B. Katz, and D.R. Karger. The role of context in question answering systems. In *CHI '03 Extended Abstracts on Human Factors in Computing Systems*. ACM Press, 2003.
8. L.V. Lita, W. Hunt, and E. Nyberg. Resource analysis for question answering. In *Proc. 42nd Annual ACL*, 2004.

Network Analysis for Distributed Information Retrieval Architectures

Fidel Cacheda[1], Victor Carneiro[1], Vassilis Plachouras[2], and Iadh Ounis[2]

[1] Dept. ICT, University of A Coruña, Campus de Elviña s/n, 15071 A Coruña, Spain
{fidel, viccar}@udc.es
[2] Department of Computing Science, University of Glasgow, Glasgow, G12 8QQ, UK
{vassilis, ounis}@dcs.gla.ac.uk

Abstract. In this study, we present the analysis of the interconnection network of a distributed Information Retrieval (IR) system, by simulating a switched network versus a shared access network. The results show that the use of a switched network improves the performance, especially in a replicated system because the switched network prevents the saturation of the network, particularly when using a large number of query servers.

1 Introduction

This study is a continuation of our previous work, introduced in [1] and extended in [2], on the choice of optimal architectures for building a distributed large-scale IR system. The SPIRIT collection (94,552,870 documents and 1 terabyte (TB) of text) [3] was used in these previous studies to simulate a distributed IR system using a local inverted file strategy, with the aim of measuring the performance for different configurations (distributed, replicated and clustered systems). In the local inverted file strategy, each query server is responsible for a disjoint subset of documents and has an independent local index. Tomasic and Garcia-Molina [6] proved that this strategy uses the system resources effectively and provides a good query throughput while being more resilient to failures.

The main objective of this work is to improve the interconnection network of a distributed system, by defining a switched network in order to analyse the improvements in performance as compared to the shared access network from our previous study.

2 Simulation Model

To explore the performance of different architectures for a distributed large-scale IR system, we implemented a discrete event-oriented simulator using the JavaSim simulation environment [4]. The simulated distributed IR system is an extension of the Terrier IR system described in [5]. Moreover, we use the analytical model described in [1] and [2] for the simulation of the querying process in the distributed IR system. The SPIRIT collection [3] is simulated (94,552,870 documents and on average 456

D.E. Losada and J.M. Fernández-Luna (Eds.): ECIR 2005, LNCS 3408, pp. 527–529, 2005.

words per document). In order to test the performance, we generate 50 queries, following the skewed query model [1] [2]. The performance is measured using 5 different simulations and calculating the corresponding average throughput.

In our previous studies in [1] and [2], the simulated distributed IR system contained a single shared access LAN, which had certain limitations that reduced the capacities of the simulated IR systems. To improve these limitations, we have defined a new network model equivalent to a switched network FastEthernet 100BASE-T at 100Mbps. This new model represents the interconnection using switches, assuming that each switch has a capacity for 64 hosts. Furthermore, the network overhead is analysed exhaustively, considering the network protocol headers, IP fragmentation, and even the propagation delay.

We analyse the similarity between the proposed model and a real network, by measuring the time to send messages between two PCs (AMD Athlon, 2 GHz and 512 MB RAM), through a switched LAN. According to the Mann-Whitney and Kolmogorov-Smirnov two sample tests, the correspondence between the real and estimated transmission times is statistically significant, with p-values higher than 0.90.

3 Network Experiments

We examine the differences in performance between a switched and a shared access network (both operating at 100 Mbps), for both a distributed system and a replicated system. In these experiments, the collection of documents is distributed using the local inverted file strategy over N query servers ($N = 1, 2, ..., 1024$).

Table 1. Throughput (queries/second) for different replicated IR systems with the optimal number of bropokers using a shared (*sh*) and switched (*sw*) LAN. The obtained improvement is also indicated (%)

Query servers	R=1			R=2			R=3			R=4		
	sh	Sw	%	sh	sw	%	sh	sw	%	sh	sw	%
1	0.02	0.05	170.6%	0.03	0.09	179.1%	0.05	0.13	177.7%	0.06	0.19	212.6%
2	0.03	0.09	161.7%	0.06	0.17	183.1%	0.09	0.25	183.2%	0.11	0.32	179.4%
4	0.06	0.16	147.7%	0.11	0.30	171.1%	0.15	0.42	180.3%	0.19	0.53	176.1%
8	0.11	0.25	129.1%	0.20	0.46	132.0%	0.27	0.71	166.3%	0.36	0.90	152.9%
16	0.18	0.37	103.8%	0.34	0.72	108.8%	0.47	1.00	114.2%	0.64	1.39	118.9%
32	0.29	0.49	69.7%	0.53	0.95	77.4%	0.77	1.38	79.1%	0.99	1.85	87.0%
64	0.41	0.58	38.9%	0.78	1.15	46.1%	1.18	1.67	41.6%	1.48	2.17	46.2%
128	0.53	0.64	21.4%	0.98	1.26	29.0%	1.42	1.83	29.0%	1.93	2.38	23.4%
256	0.60	0.67	11.8%	1.16	1.33	14.9%	1.70	1.93	13.8%	2.18	2.51	14.9%
512	0.64	0.69	6.6%	1.24	1.35	9.4%	1.78	1.95	9.5%	2.05	2.53	23.0%
768	0.66	0.69	3.9%	1.24	1.34	8.4%	1.42	1.93	35.4%	1.45	2.46	69.8%
1024	0.66	0.69	3.4%	0.99	1.32	33.9%	1.09	1.89	73.9%	1.13	2.40	112.0%

In Table 1 we detail the throughput obtained for a distributed and replicated IR system (with R replicas) with the optimal number of brokers, using both a shared and a switched network (obtained empirically as $2R + 1$ and $3R$, respectively). In a distributed system ($R=1$), the switched network improves the performance in all cases. However, this improvement is reduced when more query servers are added to the system, because the brokers, merging all the partial results, become the bottleneck [1] [2] and the network has a less significant impact on the final performance.

In a system with more replicas ($R=2$, 3 and 4), the percentage of improvement decreases as the number of query servers increases (following the pattern described for the distributed system), except for the maximum number of query servers where this percentage augments. This is motivated by the fact that, in a replicated system using a shared LAN, the bottleneck is the network, which becomes saturated as the number of query servers increases [1] [2]. The switched network prevents this saturation and therefore increases considerably the performance.

4 Conclusions

This paper is the continuation of our previous work on different architectures for a distributed IR system [1] [2]. In this work, we show that the use of a switched network for a distributed system improves the throughput performance in all cases. However, this improvement in performance is more important in replicated systems, as in these cases the bottleneck is the interconnection network. In our future work, we intend to apply these results to the clustered system analysis and we will study different techniques to reduce the brokers' bottleneck.

References

1. Cacheda, F., Plachouras & V., Ounis, I.: Performance Analysis of Distributed Architectures to Index One Terabyte of Text. In *Proceedings of 26th European Conference on Information Retrieval Research (ECIR'03)*, (2003), pp. 394-408.
2. Cacheda, F., Plachouras, V. & Ounis, I.: A Case Study of Distributed Information Retrieval Architectures to Index One Terabyte of Text. *Information Processing and Management Journal*, Articles in Press, (2004).
3. Jones, C. B., Purves, R., Ruas, A., Sanderson, M., Sester, M., van Kreveld, M. & Weibel, R.: Spatial information retrieval and geographical ontologies an overview of the SPIRIT project. In *Proceedings of the 25th ACM-SIGIR Conference on Research and Development in Information Retrieval*, pp. 387-388 (2002). New York: ACM Press.
4. Little, M. C.: *JavaSim User's Guide. Public Release 0.3, Version 1.0*. University of Newcastle upon Tyne. http://javasim.ncl.ac.uk/manual/javasim.pdf (2001).
5. Plachouras, V., Ounis, I., Amati, G. & van Rijsbergen C.J.: University of Glasgow at the Web track of TREC 2002. In Voorhees E.M. & Buckland, L.P. (Ed.), *Proceedings of The Eleventh Text REtrieval Conference*, 645-651. (2002) NIST Special Publication 500-251.
6. Tomasic, A. & Garcia-Molina, H.: Performance of inverted indices in shared-nothing distributed text document information retrieval systems. In *Proceedings of the 2nd International Conference on Parallel and Distributed Information Systems*, pp: 8-17 (1993).

SnapToTell: A Singapore Image Test Bed for Ubiquitous Information Access from Camera

Jean-Pierre Chevallet[2], Joo-Hwee Lim[1], and Ramnath Vasudha[1]

[1] Institute for Infocomm Research (I2R),
21 Heng Mui Keng Terrace, Singapore 119613
[2] IPAL-CNRS I2R-NUS joined Laboratory,
21 Heng Mui Keng Terrace, Singapore 119613
{joohwee, viscjp}@i2r.a-star.edu.sg

Abstract. With the proliferation of camera phones, many novel applications and services are emerging. In this paper, we present the SnapToTell system, which provides information directory service to tourists, based on pictures taken by the camera phones and location information. We present also experimental results on scene recognition based on a realistic data set of scenes and locations in Singapore which form a new original application oriented image test bed freely available.

1 Introduction

Imagine you are at a tourist spot looking at a beautiful monument and instead of searching through your travel guide books to learn more about the scene, you snap a picture of the scene using your camera phone. You phone send it to a service provider via Multimedia Messaging Service (MMS), and little time later you receive an audio clip (MMS) and/or a text message (SMS) that provides you more information about the scene. You can continue to enjoy the scene while your fingers carry out this information retrieval task. We promote this kind of picture-driven information access scenario, known as *SnapToTell* in this poster. As the saying goes "A picture is worth thousand words", you can forget about the hassle of looking up scene description in document that distracts you from enjoying the scene to access a text-driven information directory. We feel that camera mobile phones will become pervasive personal devices beyond the role of traditional voice communication.

From the technological point of view, obtaining location-based information is already possible with the GPS devices or the GSM cellular network infrastructure [1]. However, knowing the location of a mobile phone user is not sufficient to determine what he or she is interested in (or looking at). The location-based information certainly helps to refine the user's context, but fails to capture his or her intention. The image retrieval aspect is still complementary to the context localization information.

---

[1] We use only GSM cell id in our current prototype.

D.E. Losada and J.M. Fernández-Luna (Eds.): ECIR 2005, LNCS 3408, pp. 530–532, 2005.

2   SnapToTell Paradigm

The application scenario proposed here is similar to the one in [1] : the client device used is a PDA system connected to internet through WLAN. It supposes that this wireless access point is installed in the area in which the system is going to work. The system includes an iPAQ 3870, a NexiCam PDA camera, an orientation sensor, and a GPS receiver. The position detection is ensured by a GPS attached to the PDA. However, the direction and tilt sensor is connected to the PDA via a laptop computer due to technical difficulty. In our case, we have chosen a camera mobile phone (Nokia 7650) which is a lighter and more ubiquitous device. The camera is integrated into the communication device and localization is provided by the telecommunication operator.

In the PDA prototype [1], the image taken from the connected camera together with GPS and orientation data are sent to a server. The server then runs the 3DMax program to generate a reference image from the same position and angle in a 3D model built In SnapToTell, our approach of scene recognition is different. Instead of unnatural matching between a real image and a synthesized image from 3D model, our server will match the query image with *different images of a scene*, taken using different angles and positions. We think that 3D model construction is costly and not applicable to all kinds of scenes.

In essence, our scene indexing and matching strategy assumes that *a set of images of the same object or scene* have in common some characteristic recurrent local features that are discriminative enough to correctly detect the object among other possible ones in a given area. The location information about where the picture was taken reduces the search space and tends to simplify the problem as can be seen in our experiments.

3   Scene Database

Using Singapore as a test, we have set up an original data set of image and descriptions. We have divided the map into 6 zones, 15 locations and 88 scenes. A zone includes several locations, each of which may contain a number of scenes. A scene is characterized by images taken from different viewpoints (average of 17 images per scene), distances, and possibly lighting conditions. Besides a location ID and image examples, a scene is associated with a text description, an audio description which is send to the user an answer to his query.

Using only 530 images in our base [2], we have conducted an empirical study on scene recognition. We have adopted color histograms [2] to characterize and index the images. They are known to be invariant to translation and rotation about the viewing axis and change only slowly under change of angle of view, change of scale, and occlusion.

We have experimented with both global and local color histograms, i.e. using image blocs. Spatial locations are sometimes important for discriminating more

---

[2] The current state of the base includes 1600 images from 7 camera.

localized objects. Then local histograms will provide good sensitivity to spatial specificity. Furthermore, we can attach different weights to the blocks to emphasize the focus of attention: in our case we have emphasis the center. That is, the similarity λ between a query q (with m local blocks Z_j) and an image x (with m local blocks X_j) is defined as:

$$\lambda(q, x) = \frac{\sum_j \omega_j \cdot \lambda(Z_j, X_j)}{\sum_k \omega_k}, \tag{1}$$

where ω_j are weights, and $\lambda(Z_j, X_j)$ is the similarity between two image blocks defined as

$$\lambda(Z_j, X_j) = 1 - \frac{1}{2} \sum_i |H_i(Z_j) - H_i(X_j)|. \tag{2}$$

We obtain 71% for precision of scene recognition, using 11 bins and 3x3 blocs, and 82% using location, witch is enough in practice.

4   Conclusion

In this poster, we present an experimental but fully functional system for mobile and ubiquitous multimedia information retrieval. The histogram is computed in the phone itself, reducing the amount of data to be transferred. As the phone we use does not have floating point, only the raw histogram computation is send, final normalization is computed on the server. Our approach deals with *real situation* and *real access device* in order to measure the feasibility of such a system. It turns out that we have stretched the limit of currently available wearable technology, but we are convinced that ubiquitous computing is going to have rapid development in the very near future: that will solve some of the technical limitations uncounted.

Results obtained shows that simple matching, based on color histograms, combined with localization information, seems powerful enough to solve this particular image matching problem mainly because of task we have: retrieving among a set of images describing one object, the one that is closed to user one. It is not a usual IR querying task, and the poor value of the precision at full recall is not that significant in this case. The complete test collection is freely available under http://ipal.imag.fr/SnapToTell.html.

References

1. W. Mai, G. Dodds, and C. Tweed. Mobile and ubiquitous information access: Mobile hci 2003 international workshop, udine, italy. In *Lecture Notes in Computer Science*, volume 2954 / 2004, pages 143–157. Springer-Verlag Heidelberg, Sept 2003.
2. M. Swain and D. Ballard. Color indexing. *Intl. J. Computer Vision*, 7(1), 1991.

Acquisition of Translation Knowledge of Syntactically Ambiguous Named Entity

Takeshi Kutsumi[1], Takehiko Yoshimi[2,3],
Katsunori Kotani[3], Ichiko Sata[1], and Hitoshi Isahara[3]

[1] SHARP Corporation,
492 Minosho-cho, Yamatokoriyama-shi, Nara, 639-1186, Japan
[2] Ryukoku University,
1-5 Yokotani, Setaoe-cho, Otsu-shi, Shiga, 520-2925, Japan
[3] National Institute of Information and Communications Technology,
3-5 Hikaridai, Seika-cho, Soraku-gun, Kyoto, 619-0289, Japan

1 Introduction

Bilingual dictionaries are essential components of cross-lingual information retrieval applications. The automatic acquisition of proper names and their translations from bilingual corpora is especially important, because a significant portion of the entries not listed in the dictionaries would be proper names.

Previous work on the acquisition of translation knowledge of English named entity [1, 2, 3] dealt with mainly a simple and non-recursive noun phrase, and had a little discussion about a complex proper noun phrase defined as a proper noun phrase with prepositional phrases and/or coordinated phrases. Complex proper noun phrases (hereafter CPNP) like *the U.N. International Conference on Population and Development* are often seen in a corpus of newspaper articles.

This paper addresses the acquisition of translation knowledge of CPNPs. Since a CPNP might be syntactically ambiguous, it is necessary to find the correct prepositional attachment and/or the correct scope of coordination. We propose a method of resolving the syntactic ambiguities.

2 Extraction of Complex Proper Noun Phrases and Japanese Noun Phrases

Sequences of words matching the pattern (1) are extracted as a noun phrase candidate from an English sentence. Note that we do not use a syntactic parser.

$$SimpleNP \ ((Prep|Conj) \ SimpleNP)^+ \qquad (1)$$

$SimpleNP$, P and C denote a simple and non-recursive noun phrase, a preposition and a conjunction respectively. $SimpleNP$ is a sequence of words beginning with capital letters.

From a Japanese sentence which corresponds to the English sentence, sequences of words matching the pattern (2) are extracted.

D.E. Losada and J.M. Fernández-Luna (Eds.): ECIR 2005, LNCS 3408, pp. 533–535, 2005.

$$(JN\ F)^*\ JN \tag{2}$$

JN and F denote a compound noun and a function word respectively.

3   Alignment of CPNP and Japanese Noun Phrase

An extracted CPNP is translated into a Japanese noun phrase by a machine translation system. Matching between a machine-translated CPNP (hereafter MTNP) and a Japanese noun phrase (translation candidate) is examined.

3.1   Measurement of Semantic Similarity

Examination of whether two noun phrases are matched or not is made by a character-based method, as Japanese characters represent semantic primitives. We use the Jaccard coefficient to estimate the similarity for the two noun phrases. Let X be the number of characters of a MTNP, and Y be the number of characters of a Japanese noun phrase, and Z be the number of matching characters between them. Then the semantic similarity score for the pair S_{sem} is calculated according to the formula (3).

$$S_{sem} = \frac{Z}{X + Y - Z} \tag{3}$$

3.2   Improved Measurement of Semantic Similarity

Japanese is made up of multiple character types such as Kanji and Kana. While a single Kanji character often represent a semantic primitive, a single Kana character does not. The matching method described in Section 3.1 does not take the difference into account. This sometimes leads to incorrect alignments. We propose to vary a matching unit according to the character types, namely to use a character-based method for Kanji and a word-based method for Kana.

3.3   Measurement of Phonetic Similarity

Semantic similarity can not be measured properly when a part or whole of a CPNP is not listed in the dictionary of a machine translation system. In this case, we transliterate the not-listed words and measure the phonetic similarity between the transliteration of the CPNP and a Japanese noun phrase. We again choose the Jaccard coefficient to calculate the phonetic similarity score S_{pho}.

3.4   Overall Measurement of Similarity

Our method calculates the overall similarity score S for a pair as the weighted sum of the semantic and phonetic scores according to the formula (4), and outputs the pair if its overall score is greater than or equal to a threshold θ.

$$S = \begin{cases} (1 - \beta) \times S'_{sem} + \beta \times S_{pho} & \text{if a CPNP contains not-listed words} \\ S'_{sem} & \text{otherwise} \end{cases} \tag{4}$$

β and θ are currently set to 0.5 and 0.1 respectively.

3.5   Judgement of Semantic Well-Formedness

The method described in Section 2 might extract a semantically ill-formed CPNP. Such a CPNP as *the United States into World* extracted from the following sentence (E1) should not be aligned with any Japanese noun phrase.

(E1)   The attack on Pearl Harbor drew the United States into World War II.

The judgement of the well-formedness of a CPNP depends on whether a counterpart of the CPNP exists or not. We assume that there is such a Japanese noun phrase if and only if the MTNP and the Japanese noun phrase meet the condition (C1).

(C1)   A constituent of a MTNP, is said to "participate" in the correspondence between the CPNP and the Japanese noun phrase if their overall similarity score S is greater than or equal to the threshold θ. The rate of participants among all constituents should be greater than a threshold θ_{part} (currently set to 0.5).

4   Experiment

We evaluated 200 sentence pairs selected randomly from the experimental results. Table 1 shows the performance of our method described in Section 3.2 through 3.5, and that of the baseline method described in Section 3.1. The F value of our method surpasses that of the baseline method. Precision, to which we attach greater importance than to recall, is improved by incorporating the condition (C1).

Table 1. Experimental Result

	Correct	Noise	Misses	Precision	Recall	F value
baseline	113	116	46	0.4934	0.7107	0.5825
our method	97	30	62	0.7638	0.6101	0.6783

References

1. Y. Al-Onaizan and K. Knight. Translating Named Entities Using Monolingual and Bilingual Resources. In *Procs. of the 40th Annual Meeting of the ACL*, pages 400–408, 2002.
2. F. Huang, S. Vogel, and A. Waibel. Automatic Extraction of Named Entity Translingual Equivalence Based on Multi-feature Cost Minimization. In *Procs. of the ACL Workshop on Multilingual and Mixed-language Named Entity Recongnition*, pages 9–16, 2003.
3. R. Moore. Learning Translations of Named-Entity Phrases from Parallel Corpora. In *Procs. of the 10th Conference of the EACL*, pages 259–266, 2003.

IR and OLAP in XML Document Warehouses

Juan M. Pérez[1], Torben Bach Pedersen[2], Rafael Berlanga[1], and María J. Aramburu[1]

[1] Department of Computer Science, Universitat Jaume I Castellón, Spain
{martinej, berlanga, aramburu}@uji.es
[2] Department of Computer Science, Aalborg University, Denmark
tbp@cs.aau.dk

Abstract. In this paper we propose to combine IR and OLAP (On-Line Analytical Processing) technologies to exploit a warehouse of text-rich XML documents. In the system we plan to develop, a multidimensional implementation of a relevance modeling document model will be used for interactively querying the warehouse by allowing navigation in the structure of documents and in a concept hierarchy of query terms. The facts described in the relevant documents will be ranked and analyzed in a novel OLAP cube model able to represent and manage facts with relevance indexes.

1 Introduction

During the last years, enterprises have successfully applied data warehouse and OLAP [1] technologies to analyze the structured data they produce. OLAP databases rely on a *multidimensional* view of data, where data is divided into *facts*, the central entities/events for the desired analysis, e.g., a sale, and hierarchical *dimensions*, which provide contextual information for the facts, e.g., the products sold and the grouping of products into categories. Typically, the facts have associated numerical measures (e.g., profit) and queries aggregate fact measure values up to a certain level, e.g., total profit by product category and month, followed by either *roll-up* (further aggregation, e.g., to year), or *drill-down* (getting more detail, e.g., looking at profit per day) operations.

Text, emails or web documents also contain highly valuable information and are beginning to be available in XML format. However the structured approach of OLAP databases cannot directly be applied to these documents. IR techniques have proven to work for querying large repositories of text documents. Our goal is to combine IR and OLAP approaches to provide analysis capabilities in an XML warehouse.

2 Application Scenario

We consider a warehouse with a large collection of text-rich XML documents. Figure 1 shows a piece of such a document. Since the facts are described in the textual contents of the documents, information extraction mechanisms have to be applied to identify these facts. The paragraph shown depicts the fact (Club=/Spain/ Real-Madrid, Player="David Beckham", Cost=25,000,000, Date=/2003/07/17).

D.E. Losada and J.M. Fernández-Luna (Eds.): ECIR 2005, LNCS 3408, pp. 536–539, 2005.

In this example, it could be interesting to analyze the average contractual expenses per football club and year. By rolling up, the average costs per country could be studied. A drill down operation would allow the analysis of the different players that joined the clubs at each particular year. By drilling down further, we could obtain the original articles were the details of each contract are described.

```
<NEWSPAPER NAME="El País" PUBLICATION_DATE="17th July 2003"> ...
<SPORTS><ARTICLE> <TITLE>Real Madrid contracts Beckham</TITLE>
<PARAGRAPH>David Beckham has been contracted by Real Madrid for the
four next seasons. The club will pay 25 million euros ... </PARAGRAPH>
...</ARTICLE> ... </SPORTS> ... </NEWSPAPER>
```

Fig. 1. An article at the sports section of the Spanish newspaper *El Pais*

In [5] we presented a document model that supports analysis in a warehouse with the characteristics discussed above. The typical tree representation of XML documents is chosen. Thus, each element of the original document is mapped into a tree node. Query processing is divided into two stages: First, we build the set *RQ* (nodes Relevant to the Query) with the document nodes that satisfy the stated conditions. During this stage, we calculate a relevance index for each node $n \in RQ$. Second, we apply relevance modeling [2] to estimate the set of facts relevant to the query. The relevance of a fact f_i is calculated by the probability $P(f_i|RQ)$ of observing the fact f_i in a relevant node $n \in RQ$. The result of a query is a set of facts ranked by relevance.

3 System Overview

Figure 2 shows a multidimensional implementation of the document model discussed in [5]. We propose to build two OLAP cubes, namely the *RQ-cube* and the *R-cube*. The aim of the *RQ-cube* is to help users to interactively specify the set of document nodes relevant for their particular analysis purposes, *RQ*. *R-cube* stands for Relevance-cube, as its objective is to analyze the factual information described in the documents of *RQ* by managing uncertainty (facts with a relevance index).

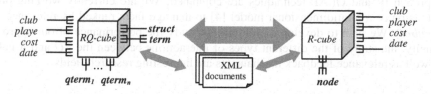

Fig. 2. Multidimensional implementation of the document model

The *RQ-cube*. The facts in the *RQ-cube* represent document nodes. Each document node is characterized by the terms of its textual contents (*term* dimension), its position in the logical structure of the document (i.e. sports section, article, title, etc., called the *struct* dimension) and all the dimension values found in the factual information de-scribed by the node (*club*, *player*, *cost*, *date*, etc. in the example of Section 2). The *RQ-cube* has as many *qterm_i* dimensions as query terms the corresponding IR condi-tion. The *qterm_i*'s and *term* dimensions share the same value domain.

In order to restrict the analysis to articles in the sports section about football con-tracts with a cost greater than 10,000€, the user may state the conditions: *qterm_1*='contract', *qterm_2*='football', *struct*='/newspaper/sports/article', *cost*> 10,000.

We propose to build a concept hierarchy over the *term* (*qterm_i*) dimension. In this way, when the user rolls-up to the "contract" concept in the *qterm_1* dimension, the terms below this concept (e.g. "labor contract", "purchase agreement", etc.) are automatically considered as query term occurrences for the *qterm_1* dimension.

The document nodes that satisfy the specified conditions are shown in the *RQ-cube*. For each document node in the resulting cube, its index of relevance to the stated conditions is presented as a measure. This OLAP approach provides a highly interactive way of refining queries. The hierarchical nature of OLAP dimensions provides a very intuitive general-to-specific (or vice versa) method to specify *RQ*.

The *R-cube*. The *R-cube* contains the facts described by the nodes in *RQ*. Each fact in the *R-cube* is characterized by its dimension values (*club*, *player*, etc.) and by the document nodes in which the fact is described (*node* dimension). In this cube we measure the relevance of each fact [5] and provide all the traditional OLAP operations to analyze them. An example of analysis was discussed in Section 2.

Related work. In [3] a multidimensional implementation for an IR system was pro-posed. The resulting system is intended to analyze the distribution of documents through a concepts hierarchy that allows their categorization. We additionally propose to use this hierarchy as term dimensions and as a query expansion mechanism, at the same time that we support the document structure dimension. In [3] the documents are ranked by relevance but the facts derived from them are not. No mechanisms for fact analysis (R-cubes) were provided.

4 Conclusions

In this paper we have presented a system to analyze text-rich XML documents. In our approach IR and OLAP techniques are combined. We are currently working on an extension of a multidimensional model [4] to manage facts ranked by relevance (i.e. *R-cubes*). We plan to develop a prototype to study the performance of our approach. Finally, the study of the different types of interactions between the *RQ* and *R* cubes, as well as relevance feedback mechanisms are interesting research fields.

References

1. Codd E. F., Codd S. B. and Salley C.T.: Providing OLAP to user-analysts: An IT mandate. Technical Report, E.F. Codd & Associates, 1993.
2. Lavrenko V. and Croft W. B.: Relevance-based language models. Proc. of ACM SIGIR' 2001 conference, pp. 267-275, 2001.

3. McCabe M.C. et al.: On the Design and Evaluation of a Multi-dimensional Approach to Information Retrieval. Proc of ACM SIGIR' 2000 conference, pp. 363-365, 2000.
4. Pedersen T.B., Jensen C.S. and Dyreson C.E.: A foundation for capturing and querying complex multidimensional data. Information Systems 26(5): 383-423, 2001.
5. Pérez J.M., Berlanga R. and Aramburu M.J.: A Document Model Based on Relevance Modeling Techniques for Semi-Structured Warehouses. Proc. of DEXA 2004, pp. 318-327, 2004.

Manipulating the Relevance Models of Existing Search Engines*

Oisín Boydell[1], Cathal Gurrin[2], Alan F. Smeaton[2], and Barry Smyth[1]

[1] Adaptive Information Cluster,
Smart Media Institute, Department of Computer Science,
University College Dublin, Belfield, Dublin 4, Ireland
{Oisin.Boydell, Barry.Smyth}@ucd.ie
[2] Adaptive Information Cluster,
Center for Digital Video Processing, Dublin City University,
Glasnevin, Dublin 9, Ireland
{Alan.Smeaton, cgurrin}@computing.dcu.ie

Abstract. Collaborative search refers to how the search behavior of communities of users can be used to influence the ranking of search results. In this poster we describe how this technique, as instantiated in the I-SPY meta-search engine can be used as a general mechanism for implementing a different relevance feedback strategy. We evaluate a relevance feedback strategy based on anchor-text and query similarity using the TREC2004 Terabyte track document collection.

1 Introduction

The I-SPY Web search engine [1] proposes an approach to search known as collaborative search. The basic intuition is that the world of web search can be both repetitive and regular. For example, an I-SPY search box located on a motoring Web site will attract motoring related queries and result selections so that ambiguous queries such as "jaguar" will result in the selection of car-related sites rather than those relating to cats or operating systems of the same name.

To achieve this, I-SPY operates as a meta-search engine (see Figure 1), dispatching queries to multiple traditional search engines and merging their result-lists. However, I-SPY also tracks the results that are selected by users for given queries and stores this information in a so-called hit-matrix. The importance of the hit-matrix is that it allows I-SPY to estimate the relevance of a page p_i for a query q_j in terms of the relative proportion of times that p_i has been selected for those queries that are similar to q_j. Crucially, this relevance information can be used directly as a means to promote the rank of those results that have been previously selected for q_j or related queries; see [2] for additional detail.

---

* This material is based on works supported by ScienceFoundation Ireland under Grant No. 03/IN.3/I361.

D.E. Losada and J.M. Fernández-Luna (Eds.): ECIR 2005, LNCS 3408, pp. 540–542, 2005.

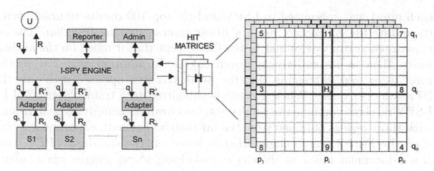

Fig. 1. The I-SPY system architecture and hit-matrix

2   Modelling Relevance

The I-SPY approach is not only limited to the use of user selection information as a source of relevance. In fact, we can view the hit-matrix as a general
mechanism for implementing any arbitrary relevance model on top on any existing search engine without impacting the operation of the existing search engine.
For example, in the work in this poster we applied I-SPY to two different search
collections, both of which use the Físréal search engine [3], with a view to demonstrating how I-SPY can be trained to incorporate a model of relevance based on
the terms that occur in hyperlinks in web documents, as well as on the standard
document terms.

The first collection is a standard TREC2004 Terabyte track document index
for a collection of 25,205,179 documents. The second is the link anchor texts
associated with target documents within this collection. To apply I-SPY to these
document collections we first train its hit-matrix to reflect our relevance model
of choice. This involves the following steps:

1. A set of training queries must be generated. We derive these queries by
   selecting sets of terms from the narrative and description sections of each
   TREC2004 Terabyte topic.
2. These queries are submitted to I-SPY and the results are processed for entry
   into the hit-matrix according to a suitable selection model.

3   Evaluation

We conducted two separate experimental runs of I-SPY which differ in terms of
both the underlying search engines that I-SPY calls upon, and in the manner in
which hit-matrix training occurs.

For the first experimental run, we configured I-SPY to operate with both the
standard document index and the anchor-text index as underlying search engines. We generated 500 training queries for each of the 50 TREC2004 Terabyte
topics with each query being between 2 and 8 terms in length. During training,

each query was submitted to I-SPY and the top 100 results returned were used to update the hit-matrix using a linear inverse ranking function. The second experimental run was similar to the first except that it relied on the anchor-text index alone as its underlying search engine. In addition only 250 queries per topic were used in training, and the hit-matrix was updated with only the top 20 results per query. When a query is submitted to a trained version of I-SPY, I-SPY needs to combine the results obtained from its underlying search engine(s) with those results obtained from the hit-matrix. For both experimental runs, we used the Físréal search engine that is based on the standard TREC Terabyte track document index as the single underlying search engine when submitting the test queries. Each query was used to probe the hit-matrix, retrieving the entries associated with all similar queries (above a set similarity threshold with the original query) and ranking these results according to the weighted relevance metric used by I-SPY.

In both of our experimental runs we actively promoted those hit-matrix results which also appear in the top 10,000 results returned from the underlying search engine, ahead of the other results, and ranked them by their weighted relevance.

4   Results and Conclusions

In this paper we have outlined how we have used I-SPY's collaborative search approach as a means to impose new relevance models on top of existing 'black-box' search engines. Our results have been evaluated as part of the TREC2004 Terabyte Track and our experimental runs were ranked 54th and 56th respectively out of 71 submitted runs. Further analysis is needed to determine improvements to this technique, particularly in the methods used to combine the results obtained from the underlying search engine(s) with those results obtained from the hit-matrix.

References

1. Freyne, J., Smyth, B., Coyle, M., Balfe, E., Briggs, P.: Further Experiments on Collaborative Ranking in Community-Based Web Search. AI Review: An International Science and Engineering Journal 21(3-4) (2004) 229–252
2. Balfe, E., Smyth, B.: Case Based Collaborative Web Search. In: Proceedings of the 7th European Conference on Cased Based Reasoning. (2004) 489–503
3. Blott, S., Boydell, O., Camous, F., Ferguson, P., Gaughan, G., Gurrin, C., Murphy, N., OConnor, N., Smeaton, A.F., Smyth, B., Wilkins, P.: Experiments In Terabyte Searching, Genomic Retrieval And Novelty Detection For TREC-2004. In: Draft Proceedings of the Thirteenth Text REtrieval Conference. (In Print). (2004)

Enhancing Web Search Result Lists Using Interaction Histories*

Maurice Coyle and Barry Smyth

Smart Media Institute, Department of Computer Science,
University College Dublin, Dublin 4, Ireland
{maurice.coyle, barry.smyth}@ucd.ie
http://ispy.ucd.ie

1   Introduction

As a method for information retrieval (IR) on the Web, search engines have become the tool of choice for most online users. However, despite the variety of next generation approaches to Web search we have recently seen (e.g. [1, 2]), the problems of information overload, vague user queries and spam still have the effect that many search sessions end in user frustration. Generally search engines are criticised for returning result lists that have low precision, where the user's information need is not satisfied by any of the returned result pages.

However, what has largely been ignored are situations in which the particular result page that the user is looking for is not in the result list, but can be navigated to from a page that is in the result list. In our analysis of live user search sessions, 36% of all page accesses are for pages such as these, which can be reached by a particular *navigation sequence* starting at a result list page.

I-SPY (see [3]) is a search engine that records the *interaction histories* (see [4, 5]) of its users. That is, when a user enters a query and selects a result, I-SPY records this information in a *hit matrix* and uses it to improve future result lists for a community of online users. Then when a community member enters a new query, I-SPY looks in the hit matrix, identifies related or similar queries to the current one and retrieves their relevant results. These results are then promoted in the result list. Experiments indicate that this approach significantly improves result list precision and recall. Other research has used the results of previous queries to improve result list relevance (see [6]), though generally these approaches are limited to the previous results for the current user rather than a community of like-minded users.

In this paper we look to track user interactions beyond the initial results page. We capture navigation sequences that a user initiates by selecting a result list url. We call the first page of a navigation sequence (i.e. one that appears in a result list) a *direct result* and we refer to subsequent pages which are navigated to beginning at a direct result but which may not themselves appear in the result list as *indirect results*. We will show in this paper that by promoting these

* The support of the Informatics Initiative of Enterprise Ireland is gratefully accepted.

D.E. Losada and J.M. Fernández-Luna (Eds.): ECIR 2005, LNCS 3408, pp. 543–545, 2005.
© Springer-Verlag Berlin Heidelberg 2005

indirect results or inserting them into result lists, further improvements in result list precision and recall are possible. See [7] for an introduction to this approach.

2   Result List Enhancement Using Live Search Session Log Data

We performed our analysis by extracting search sessions out of 9 weeks' worth of web access logs which were generated by 45 users. When a search engine query url was encountered (e.g. 'http://www.google.com?q=jaguar'), we parsed out the query, obtained the search engine's result list for that query and used the pages requested subsequent to the query url to determine which direct results were clicked. We downloaded the content of each of these direct results to see which links from within that page were clicked and so on. In this way we recorded user interactions which started at a result list url and proceeded by selecting links from within this and subsequent pages.

From the web access logs we extracted 2235 search sessions which had 1 or more result list urls clicked on. We identified 4934 urls that were requested as part of a session. 1785 (36%) of these urls didn't occur in a result list but rather were navigated to from a result list page. These urls were not considered relevant to the user's query by the search engine but the user navigating to them is an indication that they considered them in some way relevant, further reinforcing the notion that recording these navigation sequences could be useful in guiding future searches. With this in mind, it seems natural to assume that inserting these urls into the result list could increase the list's overall relevance and aid the user in finding their required information more rapidly.

Our approach to the insertion/promotion of indirect urls was to insert the last page in a navigation sequence into the result list. This was based on the assumption that in a search situation, a user will end a navigation sequence when they find what they are looking for. To test this method of result list augmentation an enhanced version of I-SPY was implemented which promoted/inserted indirect results. In each case, an indirect result was inserted into a result list beneath the result list url which a user clicked on to begin their navigation.

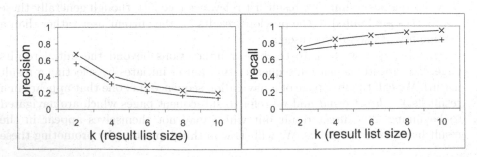

Fig. 1. Precision and Recall characteristics for standard I-SPY (+) vs. enhanced I-SPY (x) result lists

For each of the 2235 search sessions, the session's query was submitted and a result list obtained for both the standard and enhanced versions of I-SPY. The set of direct and indirect results for the session in question was used as the set of relevant results for that session, allowing the calculation of result list precision and recall. In Fig. 1, the precision and recall values for the standard and enhanced I-SPY's result lists are graphed for various result list sizes. Fig. 1 shows that this method of recording users' browsing patterns and using them to add new urls to a result list, though simple, can help to increase the overall relevance of the list.

3   Conclusions and Future Work

We have argued that ending the interaction between user and search engine when the user leaves the search results page is insufficient to help users to rapidly locate specific items of interest. We have suggested that accompanying the user past the initial results page and recording their click behaviour provides us with useful information which can be used to guide future searches. We have shown that enhancing result lists using this information can increase result list relevance.

In future work, we plan to perform a more comprehensive and extensive evaluation of our technique using more sophisticated methods for result promotion and relevance calculation. We will show that our approach complements the existing Web search paradigm and enhances user experience by reducing the time it takes to locate information items of interest on the Web.

References

1. Selberg, E., Etzioni, O.: Multi-Service Search and Comparison Using the MetaCrawler. In: Proceedings of the 4th International World-Wide Web Conference, Darmstadt, Germany, pages 195–208 (1995)
2. Brin, S., Page, L.: The Anatomy of a Large-Scale Hypertextual Web Search Engine. In: Computer Networks and ISDN Systems, 30(1–7), pages 107–117 (1998)
3. Freyne, J., Smyth, B., Coyle, M., Balfe, E., Briggs, P.: Further Experiments on Collaborative Ranking in Community-Based Web Search. In: AI Review: An International Science and Engineering Journal, 21(3–4), pages 229–252 (2004)
4. Hill, W., Hollan, J., Wroblewzki, D., McCandless, T.: Edit Wear and Read Wear. In: Proceedings of the SIGCHI Conference on Human Factors in Computing Systems, California, USA, pages 3–9 (1992)
5. Wexelblat, A., Maes, P.: Footprints: History-Rich Web Browsing. In: Proceedings of the 3rd International Conference on Computer-Assisted Information Retrieval, Montreal, Canada, pages 75–84 (1997)
6. Mitra, M., Singhal, A., Buckley, C.: Improving Automatic Query Expansion. In: Proceedings of the 21st Annual International ACM-SIGIR Conference on Research and Development in Information Retrieval, Australia, pages 206–214 (1998)
7. Coyle, M., Smyth, B.: SearchGuide: Beyond the Results Page. In: Proceedings of the 3rd International Conference on Adaptive Hypermedia and Adaptive Web-based Systems, Eindhoven, The Netherlands, pages 296–299 (2004)

An Evaluation of Gisting in Mobile Search

Karen Church, Mark T. Keane, and Barry Smyth

Adaptive Information Cluster,
Smart Media Institute, Department of Computer Science,
University College Dublin, Belfield, Dublin 4, Ireland
{Karen.Church, Mark.Keane, Barry.Smyth}@ucd.ie

1   Introduction

Mobile devices suffer from limited screen real-estate and restricted text input capabilities. In the recent past these limitations have greatly effected the usability of many mobile Internet applications [1], largely because little effort has been typically made to take account of the special features of the mobile Internet. These limitations are especially problematic for mobile search-engines: they restrict the number of results that can be displayed per screen and impact the type of queries that are likely to be provided. Nevertheless, most attempts to provide mobile search engines have involved making only simplistic adaptations to standard search interfaces. For example, fewer results per page are returned and the 'snippet' text associated with each result may be truncated [2]. We believe that more fundamental adaptations are necessary if search technology is to succeed in the mobile space. In this paper we focus on the snippet text issue and we argue that providing paragraphs of descriptive text alongside each result is a luxury that does not make sense in the context of mobile device limitations. We describe how the I-SPY system [3] can track and record past queries that have resulted in the selection of a given result page and we argue that these related queries can be used to help users understand the context of a search result in place of more verbose snippet text.

2   Snippets Versus Related Queries for Result Gisting

The I-SPY search engine focuses on community-based search by recording the search histories—queries and result selections—of communities of like-minded individuals. This information is stored in a query-result *hit-matrix* that records the number of user selections that a result p_j has received in response to a query q_i and the information is used to adapt future result-lists for similar queries by promoting results that have been selected in the past. Thus, I-SPY gradually adapts to the learned needs of communities of individuals and this has been previously shown to significantly improve overall search performance [3].

Another distinctive feature of I-SPY is that it facilitates the recommendation of related queries alongside any individual search results. Very briefly, for each search result p_k, that is associated with some target query q_T, I-SPY can

D.E. Losada and J.M. Fernández-Luna (Eds.): ECIR 2005, LNCS 3408, pp. 546–548, 2005.

generate a set of related queries from those queries, $q_1, ... q_n$, that have also led to the selection of p_k. Unlike general Web search, a significant overlap exists between queries executed by users in community-based search [3]. Therefore, a high number of related queries will be generated for the majority of communities. Different strategies for ranking these related queries according to the likelihood that they match the user's current requirements is described in [4]. The point is that these queries serve as meaningful yet compact summaries of their associated search results. For example, a 'jaguarcars.com' result page might be associated with queries such as 'jaguar photos' or 'sports cars'; see Figure 1. Given the screen limitations of mobile devices it is interesting to consider whether these related queries might provide a viable alternative to snippet text as a way to gist search results.

3   Evaluation

We were given access to search logs generated from a recent I-SPY trial. To evaluate the usefulness of related queries as an alternative to result snippets, these search logs are used as a source of related query data; see [3]. For each result page p we compare the effectiveness of its related queries and its snippet text at capturing the essence of the page. To do this we use each alternative (related queries and snippet text) to generate a new *test* query and then evaluate this query according to how well it captures the content of p. To perform this evaluation we submit the test query to an independent search-engine (in this case Google) and compare the position of p in the result-lists produced; we consider the top 100 Google results only. The higher p is in the result-list the more representative the test query must be as a indicator of p's content, and hence the more representative the related queries or snippet text. Ideally some type of relevance judgements or feedback strategies would be used to enhance these related queries. However, this type of query enrichment is difficult to implement in a mobile scenario but it is an area we want to explore as part of future work.

There are a number of ways to convert the related queries and snippet text for p into test queries. Strategy $RQ1$ produces a test query by simply concatenating the related queries into a single query. Strategy $RQ2$ is similar but with duplicate terms removed. Converting snippet text into a test query is slightly more complex. To ensure a fair comparison we produce a test query from the snippet text that has the same number of terms as the test queries produced from the related queries. To produce the test query we parse the snippet text by removing stop-words and special characters and then select terms from the remaining snippet text using two different strategies. In strategy $S1$ we select a random set of k terms; where k is the number of terms in the corresponding test query produced by $RQ1$. Strategy $S2$ selects the top k most common terms in the snippet text.

We generated queries for 51 result pages using the 4 strategies outlined above; these 51 queries had 2 or more related queries associated with them in the search logs. Our results are summarised in Figure 2 as a graph of the average position

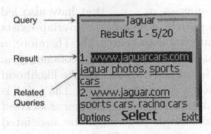
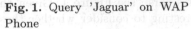
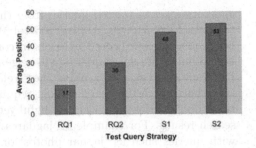

Fig. 1. Query 'Jaguar' on WAP Phone

Fig. 2. Average Position of p in Result-List

of each p in the result-lists produced. There is a clear benefit to the related query strategies, $RQ1$ and $RQ2$, when compared to the snippet-text strategies, $S1$ and $S2$, with the former strategies locating its target results much higher in Google's result-lists than the latter. For example, $RQ1$ locates each p at an average position of 17 compared to the best performing snippet-based strategy, which locates p at an average position of 48. Interestingly $S1$ performs better than $S2$ indicating that selecting random terms from the filtered snippet text is preferable to selecting the most popular terms; we leave this as something to be examined as part of future work.

4   Conclusions

Mobile Internet search engines need an economic way to summarise the contents of their search results. Traditional snippet text is simply too verbose. In this paper we have suggested using previously successful queries as an alternative and we have provided some preliminary empirical evidence that suggests these queries may be as informative as snippet text. These resultant queries take up less than half the space of snippet text and can also be used as a simple way for users to launch further more elaborated searches. All of these benefits suggest that related queries could be quite valuable in the mobile search realm.

References

1. Ramsay, M., Nielsen, J.: The WAP Usability Report (2000)
2. Jones, M., Buchanan, G., Thimbleby, H.: Sorting Out Searching on Small Screen Devices. In: Proceedings of the 4th International Symposium on Human Computer Interaction with Mobile Devices, MobileHCI'02, Pisa, Italy, Springer-Verlag (2002) 81–94
3. Smyth, B., Balfe, E., Freyne, J., Briggs, P., Coyle, M., Boydell, O.: Exploiting Query Repetition & Regularity in an Adaptive Community-Based Web Search Engine. User Modeling and User Adapted Interaction (Forthcoming)
4. Balfe, E., Smyth, B.: Collaborative Query Recommendation for Web Search. In: Proceedings of 16th European Conference on Artificial Intelligence, IOS Press (2004) 268–272

Video Shot Classification Using Lexical Context

Stéphane Ayache, Georges Quénot, and Mbarek Charhad

1 Introduction

Associating concepts to video segments is essential for content-based video retrieval. We present here a semantic classifier working from text transcriptions coming from automatic speech recognition (ASR). The system is based on a Bayesian classifier, it is fully linked with a knowledge base which contains an ontology and named entities from several domains. The system is trained from a set of positive and negative examples for each indexed concept. It has been evaluated using the TREC VIDEO protocol and conditions for the detection of visual concepts. Three versions are compared: a baseline one, using only word as units, a second, using additionally named entities, and a last one enriched with semantic classes information.

2 Associating Visual Concepts in Video by Lexical Analysis

Detection of visual concepts in video documents is usually achieved by categorizing key images from signal information. These approaches use low-level extraction processes for color, texture and motion features and a supervised learning phase such as KNN, SVM, or NN methods. The audio stream can also help to identify concepts. The approach studied here is based on the idea that a lexical context (word distribution) is associated to the presence of a concept in a video document. This kind of approach has been used with success for emotion detection in oral dialogues [2]. We have thus developed and experimented a classifier based on a lexical analysis of transcribed speech. Since our approach is supervised, we must train the system for each concept. This is done by the following 3 steps:

- Extract text from ASR around instances of concepts: in order to catch lexical context of concepts, we define temporal offsets around the shots containing a concept. We choose offsets for each concept by computing cross validation in the development data.
- Textual analysis: the simplest way to analyze textual information is to extract every 1-gram terms. This approach is our baseline model for textual analysis. Experiments compare models enriched using a knowledge base with this approach.
- Compute the probability p_{we} of each term w being in the class e.

Learning a semantic class by lexical analysis aim to perform a co-occurrence-like process between semantic and lexical information. In this way, the following lines are the top 6 entries of the "Madeleine Albright" model:

During the detection process, the system assigns a score value V_{se} for each shots s being in semantic class e according to a matching function, for example:

D.E. Losada and J.M. Fernández-Luna (Eds.): ECIR 2005, LNCS 3408, pp. 549–551, 2005.
© Springer-Verlag Berlin Heidelberg 2005

550   S. Ayache, G. Quénot, and M. Charhad

Table 1. Top 6 entries from basic "Madeleine Albright" model

0.029062	State	0.022457	U.S.
0.027741	Secretary	0.013210	Iraq
0.026420	Albright	0.013210	Madeleine

$$V_{se} = \frac{1}{L} \sum_w \frac{P(w|e)}{P(w)} \tag{1}$$

where $P(w)$ is the probability of w being in the general model computed on a development set), and $P(w|E)$ is the probability of having w known a model e. L is the length of the filtered text.

3   Toward a Lexical and Semantic Analysis

Based on the idea that semantic information can enhance the detection process, we simply merge lexical entities and ontology leaves or nodes. With this approach, the textual extraction process aims to tag the text using our specific knowledge base by finding named-entities, class information, or applying stemming and stop-lists. We also define a set of entities referring the same concept or very closed entities, such as train and locomotive.

3.1   Ontology Design

We are interested in named entities with the point of view of Information Retrieval. Named entities can improve topic classification and text desambiguisation. Thus, we designed a named entities extraction tool based on a domain specific ontology and patterns to identify persons, locations, acronyms etc. The ontology contains about 10000 instances of concepts organised in three specific classes : people (with activities), geography (with continents) and organization (full names or acronyms). This choice is justified by the kind of video document that we use as corpora (TRECVID 2003 and 2004 collections contain TV broadcast news).

3.2   Named Entities Enriched Model

We enrich the basic class model by adding named entities, which have been extracted from text data. Thus, a model is not only defined by 1-gram terms, but also by N-grams terms, like: "Madeleine Albright" and "Secretary of State".

3.3   Semantic Class Label Enriched Model

Semantic classes label are node names (not leaves) of the ontology, such as "European-Politics", "Middle-East-Places", "Actors", "Football Players", etc. Since semantic classes are specialized enough and obviously domain dependent, we expect them to improve the accuracy of the classifier. Thus, we construct a semantic class label model by adding node names probabilities of the extracted named entities. Also, in order to evaluate this approach, we build a model containing only node names entries.

4   Experiments and Results

We have experimented our classifier using the TREC VIDEO corpus and protocol. Learning and tuning was done using the TRECVID 2003 collection and the evaluation was done using the TRECVID 2004 collection. Lexical context based classification was performed using the LIMSI ASR transcription [1]. In order to our approach, we computed the classification with just 1-gram terms (Baseline), enriched models with named entities, enriched models with semantic classes information only, and enriched models with named entities and classes information. We experiment on TRECVID 2004 corpus the first six high-level features. Table 2 shows a comparison of our 4 runs.

Table 2. Mean Average Precision on TREC VID 2004 high level features

Feature	Baseline	Named Entity	Class Info	NE + CI
Ship/Boat	0.0024	0.0611	0.0013	0.0563
Madeleine Albright	0.0338	0.0702	0.0192	0.0715
Bill Clinton	0.1082	0.1144	0.0687	0.1200
Train	0.0613	0.2029	0.00	0.1530
Beach	0.0024	0.0145	0.0006	0.0139
Basket scored	0.0436	0.0548	0.0202	0.0353

The named entities enriched model approach perform globally better than the baseline approach, since the semantic feature appears in a well established context. For instance, we saw on the development set that trains appears frequently in broadcast news to report a train accident. Such events are well modeled by enriched lexical analysis. However, classes label don't contribute to a good accuracy. Since our domain specific ontology is not sufficiently rich of information (there are few node names), it can't enhance accuracy of classification. The global performance is quite low but the searched concepts are quite difficult and the approach considered here uses information only from tha audio track. It could be fused with other approaches using information from the image track.

References

[1] The LIMSI broadcast news transcription system. *Speech Communication, 37(1-2):89-108*, 2002.
[2] I. Vasilescu L. Devillers. Détection des émotions à partir dindices lexicaux, dialogiques et prosodiques dans le dialogue oral. *TALN-JEP, Maroc*, 2004.

Age Dependent Document Priors in Link Structure Analysis

Claudia Hauff[1] and Leif Azzopardi[2]

[1] University of Magdeburg, Magdeburg, Germany
hauff@student.uni-magdeburg.de
[2] University of Glasgow, Glasgow, United Kingdom
leif@dcs.gla.ac.uk

Abstract. Much research has been performed investigating how links between web pages can be exploited in an Information Retrieval setting [1, 4]. In this poster, we investigate the application of the Barabási-Albert model to link structure analysis on a collection of web documents within the language modeling framework. Our model utilizes the web structure as described by a Scale Free Network and derives a document prior based on a web document's age and linkage. Preliminary experiments indicate the utility of our approach over other current link structure algorithms and warrants further research.

1 Introduction

Recently, Scale Free Networks (SFN) have been proposed to account for the evolving nature of many real networks based on two factors; the growth of the network and preferential attachment [2]. Such networks are characterized by a power law distribution. It was shown that the World Wide Web is a SFN where the number of links pointing to (in-links) and from a web page (out-links) follow power law distributions [3]. We attempt to utilize the SFN when estimating a document's importance given its age and link information, by exploiting the property that as a page ages (and more pages enter the network) it would attract more links (preferential attachment). Our approach is unlike the traditional link structure analysis algorithms, such as HITS and PageRank, which view the web as a static structure not evolving over time. Whilst a modified version of the PageRank algorithm, that heuristically boosts younger pages with higher scores has been proposed [1], under the SFN approach page age is accounted for in a principled manner. We present a brief overview of our approach and provide some experimental results.

2 Popularity Within a SFN

Briefly, the web as a SFN: starting at time $i = 0$ with $m_i > 0$ web pages, at each time step $i = j$ a new web page $d_{i=j}$ is introduced to the network with m links pointing to different pages already in the network. The probability that an

D.E. Losada and J.M. Fernández-Luna (Eds.): ECIR 2005, LNCS 3408, pp. 552–554, 2005.
© Springer-Verlag Berlin Heidelberg 2005

existing page d attracts one of these new links is denoted by $\prod(d)$ and depends on the number of links l_d that d has already acquired, such that:

$$\prod(d) = \frac{l_d}{\sum_{d'} l_{d'}} \qquad (1)$$

This allows us to derive a function that determines the number of in-links a web page "should" have collected at any given time step i, given the page's age. The expected number of in-links $e_j(i)$ at time i for a page d_j introduced to the network at time j is given by:

$$e_j(i) = m\sqrt{\frac{i}{j}} - m \qquad (2)$$

For a collection of web pages the constant m is the average number of out-links and the order in which the pages enter the network is established by ranking the pages according to their age. This expectation can be exploited in deriving a popularity score based on comparing the actual number of in-links with the expected number of in-links for a particular page. The rationale is that we would anticipate a popular page to have more in-links than expected and vice versa for an unpopular page. We obtained the popularity score based on a smoothed ratio of actual over expected number of in-links and normalized to a range between 1 and 3.

3   Experiments and Results

The Language Modeling framework [4] offers a principled way to incorporate query-independent knowledge in a retrieval model. In this framework, a document d is sampled with the prior probability $p(d)$, then from d the query q is drawn with probability $p(q|d)$. Essentially, the joint probability of d and q is used to rank the documents and the prior $p(d)$ allows us to encode its importance. In this study, we compare several different priors in an ad hoc retrieval web task - the Uniform prior, the Document Length prior, the Laplace-smoothed In-link prior, and the PageRank based prior (see [4, 5] for more details) - against our SFN prior. The SFN prior was created by normalizing the popularity scores. The age of each web page was defined as the difference between the last modified date and the current date. Of course, this is not the true age of the page, but a reasonable estimate given the data available. We performed this pilot study on the WT2g Collection, and used the titles of TREC topics 401-450 for evaluation purposes. To compute the query likelihood $p(q|d)$, we used Bayes Smoothing with a Dirichlet prior fixed at 1000.

We report the mean Average Precision for each of the document priors (Table 1). Besides clear ranking $p(q, d)$, the best performing interpolated retrieval value is also presented, where α is the interpolation ratio: $\alpha p(q|d) + (1 - \alpha)p(d)$. The percentage change was computed relative to the uniform prior.

Table 1. Performance of variable document priors on WT2g

Document Prior	Clear mAP	±%	Interpol. mAP	α	±%
Uniform	29.325	-	-	-	-
Document Length	31.395	+7.01	32.544	0.60	+11.02
In-Link	22.918	-21.82	29.277	0.95	-0.13
PageRank	22.639	-22.77	29.270	0.90	-0.15
SFN	29.625	+1.06	29.718	0.60	+1.37

4   Discussion and Conclusions

From our results it is clear that the performance of link priors based on a static view of the network (In-Link and PageRank) is substantially (clear ranking) or slightly worse (interpolation ranking) than the Uniform prior. However, whilst not statistically significant, the SFN prior shows promise with over one percent increase in mean Average Precision over the Uniform prior and other link priors[1]. We believe this provides an encouraging platform from which to develop the model further. Future research will be aimed at addressing several key issues of the proposed method and the limitation of this study. These include: testing on larger web collections where the link structure is more representative of the true web, different ways to generate popularity scores given the expected number of in-links, improvement in the estimation of document age, and application to web retrieval tasks other than ad-hoc retrieval. [2]

References

1. R. Baeza-Yates, F. Saint-Jean, and C. Castillo, *Web structure, age and page quality*, 2nd International Workshop on Web Dynamics (WebDyn 2002), 2002.
2. A.-L . Barabási, R. Albert, and H. Jeong, *Mean-field theory for scale-free random networks.*, Physica A **272** (1999), no. 173; cond-mat/9907068.
3. A.-L. Barabási, R. Albert, and H. Jeong, *Scale-free characteristics of random networks: the topology of the world wide web*, Physica A **281** (2000), no. 69.
4. W. Kraaij and T. Westerveld, *Tno/ut at trec-9: How different are web documents?*, Proceedings of the ninth Text Retrieval Conference TREC-9, 2001, pp. 665–671.
5. D. R. H. Miller, T. Leek, and R. M. Schwartz, *A hidden markov model information retrieval*, 22nd Annual International ACM SIGIR conference on Research and development in information retrieval (California, US), ACM Press, 1999, pp. 214–221.

---

[1] For brevity we ignore any discussion about the document length prior. However, a report containing full details about this study is available from the first author's web site (http://www.uni-magdeburg.de/hauff).

[2] This work was performed during a 6 month visitation to the Glasgow IR Group and the authors would like to thank Professor C.J. van Rijsbergen for his support and input.

Improving Image Representation with Relevance Judgements from the Searchers

Liudmila V. Boldareva

University of Twente,P.O.Box 217, 7500 AE Enschede, The Netherlands
l.boldareva@utwente.nl

Keywords: Image retrieval, relevance feedback, long-term learning.

1   Introduction

In visual information retrieval, a *semantic gap* exists due to the poor match between machine-understood content of an information object and the user-percepted one. The mismatch of perception results in difficulties for a user in formulating the query, and consequently in inability for the retrieval system to produce satisfactory answers. Adding searcher's relevance judgements for (intermediary) search results is known to improve the retrieval. With relevance feedback the system learns the user's information need through interaction.

There is a large body of work to extend the learning capabilities of a retrieval system beyond a single interactive session, in both collaborative filtering and information retrieval communities, to name a few examples [5, 4, 3].

This paper discusses a generic approach to making use of learning, within and across retrieval sessions, from user's judgements about relevance of the presented documents to his/her information need. The advantage of the proposed framework is that it fully supports similarity search based on low-level features along with relevance notions based on user judgements. In the first place, this allows the system to operate from the beginning, and an extended training phase is not needed. The training data is collected on the way in the form of history of successful retrieval sessions.

2   Unified Framework for Learning from User Feedback

2.1   Learning Within a Search Session

We use a probabilistic framework to model a single search session. It is described in more detail in [1]. Given the user's query and relevance feedback $\{\delta_x\}$, the probability of relevance $P(T)$ of each object is estimated. Assuming conditional independence of user judgements, the following formula retrieves the objects most likely relevant to the user's information need:

$$P^{\mathrm{new}}(T) = P(T|\delta_{x_1} \ldots \delta_{x_n}) = \frac{P^{\mathrm{old}}(T) \prod_{s=1}^{n} P(\delta_{x_s}|T)}{P(\delta_{x_1} \ldots \delta_{x_n})} \ . \tag{1}$$

D.E. Losada and J.M. Fernández-Luna (Eds.): ECIR 2005, LNCS 3408, pp. 555–557, 2005.
© Springer-Verlag Berlin Heidelberg 2005

$P(\delta_x|T)$ is probability of a certain user action in assessing relevance of x given hypothesised search target T. At the beginning of the system's lifetime the values of $P(\delta_x|T)$ are based on low-level features. Any available feature set may provide similarity values. By fitting the distribution of these pair-wise values with the Normal distribution, $P(\delta_x|T)$ are estimated as probabilities that the user's perception of similarity between two objects matches the feature-based one. Such definition suggests the use of an appropriate α-*value* under which this probability of the match is insignificant and can be replaced with a constant. The pair-wise conditional probability estimates, derived from low-level features, above the level of significance are stored as the index to access the object at search time.

When a vast history of user interactions is available, these probabilities for each pair can be computed from frequencies of the observed events of relevance feedback. Because the access index is supported by the low-level features, a separate training phase is not needed.

2.2   Learning Between Search Sessions

What is learned from a single search session, serves as input data for long-term learning, or learning across queries. The event of x marked by the user as relevant should result in a more accurate estimate of the corresponding $P(\delta_x|T)$. The actual user information need T often remains hidden,therefore the retrieval session, in which $P(T)$ is learned, can be interpreted as the "E"-step in the Expectation Maximisation algorithm [2].

To update the involved conditional probability estimates, we use the maximum likelihood principle, which boils down to counting events. Suppose $P(\delta_x|T)$ should be updated. The following equation will correspond to frequency-based update when δ represents binary choice (relevant or not):

$$P^{\text{new}}(\delta_x|T) = \frac{\kappa \cdot P^{\text{old}}(\delta_x|T) + iP(T)}{\kappa + P(T)} \ , \quad i = \begin{cases} 1 \text{ for positive feedback} \\ 0 \text{ otherwise} \end{cases} \quad (2)$$

Here κ can be seen as is weight for prior observations.

2.3   Experiments on TRECVID Data

We performed preliminary study on key frames from TRECVID collection [6, 7]. To compare performance in a controlled environment, automated experiments were used. That is, relevance judgements of real users were substituted with the TRECVID ground truth for the collection. The training data to improve feature-based similarities, however, came from sessions with real users and contained erroneous input: on average 75% of human's positive judgements were relevant according to the ground truth and in some sessions up to 50% of all relevant items displayed were not marked as such by the humans. Search logs of six users that took part in TRECVID 2003 experiments, were used to update the probabilities from the access index, as described in Section 2.2.

In Figure 1 two curves are plotted showing mean average precision after 45 iterations, each consisting of 12 key frames, for purely feature-based access index

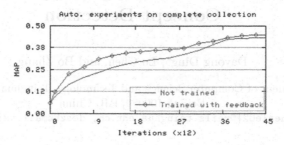

Fig. 1. Trained vs. not trained access index

and the trained version of it. The observed improvement is significant at 5% level, tested with the Sign test.

3   Discussion

In this paper a framework is presented to unify short-term (intra-query) learning from user feedback with long-term learning across the queries in visual information retrieval, illustrated by a small experiment. Within a retrieval session the information need of the user is learned through interaction. The interaction history is used to improve the general objects representation.

Because the proposed framework is supported by lower-level features, it has advantages over a pure collaborative learning system:

(1) The system can be directly used for retrieval; The training takes place in parallel with the system working.
(2) Each user can start a retrieval session with an arbitrary query. The prior probability of relevance resulting from the query forms a context for the search, where current probability of relevance can be seen as a weighting factor for the existing associations between the objects stored in the access index.

References

1. L. Boldareva and D. Hiemstra. Interactive content-based retrieval using pre-computed object-object similarities. In *Proceedings CIVR-2004*, Dublin, 2004.
2. A. P. Dempster, N. M. Laird, and D. B. Rubin. Maximum likelihood from incomplete data via the EM-algorithm. *J. Royal Statistical Society*, 39(B):1–38, 1977.
3. D. R. Heisterkamp. Building a latent semantic index of an image database from patterns of relevance feedback. In *ICPR 2002, vol.4, p.134–145, Canada, 2002.*
4. T. Hofmann and J. Puzicha. Latent class models for collaborative filtering. v. 2, p.688–693. Morgan Kaufmann Publishers, 1999.
5. T. Minka. An image database browser that learns from user interaction. Master's thesis, Cambridge, MA, 1996.
6. A. Smeaton, W. Kraaij, and P. Over. TRECVID 2003 - an introduction. In *TRECVID Workshop*. Washington, 2003.
7. T. Westerveld, T. Ianeva, L. Boldareva, A. de Vries, and D. Hiemstra. Combining information sources for video retrieval. In *TRECVID Workshop*. Washington, 2003.

Temporal Shot Clustering Analysis for Video Concept Detection

Dayong Ding*, Le Chen, and Bo Zhang

Department of Computer Science and Technology, Tsinghua University,
Beijing 100084, P.R. China
{ddy01, chenle02}@mails.tsinghua.edu.cn, dcszb@mail.tsinghua.edu.cn

Abstract. The phenomenon that conceptually related shots appear together in videos is called *temporal shot clustering*. This phenomenon is a useful cue for video concept detection, which is one of basic steps in content-based video indexing and retrieval. We propose a method, called *temporal shot clustering analysis*, to improve results of video concept detection by exploiting the temporal shot clustering phenomenon. Two other methods are compared with temporal shot clustering analysis on the TRECVID 2003 dataset. Experiments showed that temporal shot clustering is of much benefit for video concept detection, and that temporal shot clustering method outperforms the other methods.

1 Introduction

As a basic step to effective content-based video retrieval and indexing, video concept detection is an emerging research direction [1]. Multi-modal technologies, which try to integrate information from various cues, are widely used for video concept detection. Text, visual modality and aural modality are conventional modalities that have been widely studied. However, properties of temporal distribution of video shots have been received relatively less attention.

Temporal clustering phenomenon of video shots is an interesting and useful cue for video concept detection. In this paper, we discuss the temporal clustering property of video shots in Section 2, and a new method, called *shot clustering analysis* method, to expoit this property for boosting video concept detection in Section 3, followed by experiments and conclusions in Section 4 and 5.

2 Temporal Shot Clustering and Its Exploitation

Due to requirement of understandability of videos, conceptually related shots often appear in temporal clusters. If a shot with certain concept is found, it is very likely to find more with the same concept nearby. Contrarily, if a shot is

---

* Supported by National Natural Science Foundation of China(60135010,60321002), Chinese National Key Foundation Research & Development Plan(2004CB318108).

D.E. Losada and J.M. Fernández-Luna (Eds.): ECIR 2005, LNCS 3408, pp. 558–560, 2005.

predicted to have some concept but no similar shot is in its neighborhood, the prediction may be of doubt. This is *temporal shot clustering* phenomenon.

Temporal shot clustering may be a useful cue to improve video concepts detection. Usually a result of concept detecting is a list of probable shots, descending-sorted by their confidence values given by the concept detecting procedure. Using original detection result and temporal shot clustering property, we can estimate the time spans where clusters of probable shots lie in, according to which the list of detection result can be adjusted to include more shots covered by clusters, or exclude isolated shots. Thus the effectiveness of the original concept detection, measured by *average precision (AP)* [2], may be improved.

3   Temporal Shot Clustering Analysis Method

Temporal shot clustering analysis is a method that exploits the temporal shot clustering property to improve results of concept detection. Basic steps of temporal shot clustering analysis are as follows: 1) measure the clustering degree; 2) estimate clusters in the results and 3) adjust the result list. Hereafter, shots that contain certain concept in a detecting process are called *positive shots*. Correspondingly, those that do not contain the concept are *negative shots*.

The improvement that clustering analysis may bring to the result of concept detection is largely determined by the degree that positive shots actually cluster. So *Long Cluster Coverage (LCC)*, defined as the percentage of positive shots that are in long clusters, is chosen as a measure of the degree of shot clustering. For example, positive shots of the *Basketball Match* concept have a 3-shot LCC of 0.8745 when MICG=800, which means 87.45% of the positive shots are in clusters that contains at least 3 shots. Here MICG, abbreviation of *Maximum Intra-Cluster Gap*, is a threshold to perform clustering judgement, which is defined as maximum possible time span between boundaries of two shots in a cluster.

When detecting a concept, the actual clusters of positive shots can only be estimated from original detecting result. However wrongly detected shots in the result will disturb the estimation greatly. In order to minimize the affection of negative shots in the result list, only highly confident shots are used for cluster estimation. So *Highly Confident Shot Range (HCSR)*, defined as the range in a result list within which shots are highly confident and be suitable for cluster estimation, is another parameter to be chosen during clustering analysis.

Given MICG and HCSR, clusters of result shots can be determined. During analysis, those non-highly confident shots, including those outside the result list, that are near to shots within HCSR, are absorbed to clusters. Then we have four kinds of shots: 1) a result shots that is not absorbed by any cluster is called an *isolated shot*; 2) any non-isolated result shot is called a *clustered shot*; 3) any non-result shot that lies within the range of a cluster is called a *stuff shot* of this cluster; and 4) any non-result shot that is near to a cluster, according to MICG, is called an *attachment shot* of this cluster.

Finally, the result list is rearranged in the following order: clustered shots, stuff shots, attached shots and isolated shots. Within each type, keeping the original order for result shots and using chronological order for non-result ones.

4   Experimentals and Results

Two typical concepts, *Aircraft(A)* and *Basketball Match(B)*, are detected on
the TRECVID 2003 development data [3] from only visual features by SVM
classifiers. Then these original results are improved by three different methods
using temporal clustering properties: 1) *Feature Combination* method, which
combines the above-mentioned visual features and shot time feature before the
classifiers are trained; 2) *Lists Merging* method, which merges the result list
detected from only shot time feature, denoted as *Only Time Feature* result,
with the the original ones, by AP-based Borda voting [4]; and 3) temporal shot
Clustering Analysis method. Goodness of the results are measured by the average
precision (AP). Experiment results are listed in Table 1.

Table 1. Experiments summary: properties of concepts and APs of different results

Concepts	3-shot LCC (MICG=800)	Only Time Feature	Original Result AP	Feature Combination	Lists Merging	Clustering Analysis
Aircraft	0.3855	0.0040	0.1141	0.1244	0.1143	0.1249
Basketball	0.8793	0.0285	0.4896	0.5347	0.4903	0.5743

From LCCs we can see that most of positive shots of concept B are in long
clusters, whereas those of A are NOT. This can partly explain why temporal
clustering properties brought much less improvement to A than to B. For the
same reason, the differences between the result of A and that of B, only by
time feature, is understandable. On the other hand, much lower original AP
of A make it more difficult to exploit the temporal clustering property, which
is another reason for the weaker results of A. Finally, among three methods,
temporal clustering analysis method performed the best because it utilizes the
clustering property explicitly, whereas other methods use it implicitly.

5   Conclusions and Discussions

Temporal clustering of shots in video clips is a useful cue to boost the concept detection. Temporal shot clustering analysis method is very effective. The
generalization of this method is an interesting topic for further research.

References

1. Naphade, M.R., Smith, J.R.: On the detection of semantic concepts at trecvid. In:
   ACM Multimedia 2004. (2004) 660
2. NIST: Trec-10 appendix on common evaluation measures. Technical report (2001)
3. Smeaton, A.F., et al.: Trecvid: An introduction. Technical report (2003)
4. Chen, L., et al.: Ap-based borda voting method for feature extraction in trecvid-
   2004. In: 27th European Conference on Information Retrieval. (2005)

IRMAN: Software Framework for IR in Mobile Social Cyberspaces

Zia Syed and Fiona Walsh

School of Computing, The Robert Gordon University,
Aberdeen, AB25 1HG, Scotland
{zs, fw}@comp.rgu.ac.uk

Abstract. With the increasing popularity of *blogs* (online journals) as a medium for expressing personal thoughts and advice, and users becoming more mobile, we foresee an opportunity for such opinionated content to be utilised as information sources in the mobile arena. In this short paper, we present IRMAN (Information Retrieval in Mobile Adhoc Networks), a software framework for Peer-to-Peer (P2P) IR over Mobile AdHoc Networks (MANET). A Java based prototype system has been developed based on the aforementioned framework for creating, retrieving, and sharing user blogs on handhelds in mobile social cyberspaces.

1   Introduction

Consider the scenario; you have just arrived in an unfamiliar city planning to do your shopping. Faced with a multitude of gift shops and with no idea where to start, you use your handheld to seek out other shoppers' opinions about the best places to shop. Your device receives relevant opinions and advice by people within your physical proximity. Using this personal knowledge as your guide, you set off on your shopping trip. Although this scenario may sound slightly futuristic, with the recent advances in wireless communication technologies, particularly in Personal Area Networking (PAN) [1], coupled with the ever-increasing rate of mobile device adoption, we see this scenario becoming a reality, sooner rather than later. This scenario setting, typically attributed as a Mobile Social Cyberspace [2] , we believe will be realised through the combination of user interactive technologies, such as blogs, and mobile computing.

Blogs are user's online journals containing posts, typically, expressing personal opinions and/or documenting experiences of past events i.e. a holiday. Currently, they are gaining widespread popularity as the latest form of online communication[3]. Pair this statement with the fact that mobile devices are becoming an integral part of our everyday lives and it is not hard to envision a setting where people will use their handhelds to read, write and share blogs while on the move in the near future. In order to accomplish this setting, it would be necessary to implement a system, which supports information exchange in an ad hoc P2P fashion in mobile environments.

In our research, we have built such a system using our developed framework based on the P2P communication model.

D.E. Losada and J.M. Fernández-Luna (Eds.): ECIR 2005, LNCS 3408, pp. 561–563, 2005.

2   The IRMAN Framework

IRMAN is a framework which enables the development of software applications for mobile evironments. It incorporates an information processing engine which uses context-awareness (user and device context) for effective IR in such evironments. The framework, as shown in Fig. 1(a) provides application layer connectivity between wireless devices in a P2P fashion, and enables content searching and sharing in an adhoc manner. The modular design of the framework supports component based development of a variety of P2P applications (e.g. File swapping, Instant Messaging etc.) for handheld devices irrespective of wireless communication, information processing and presentation technologies.

A typical IR scenario in the IRMAN system is as follows: Peer x submits a query q, to the system, which is then broadcast to all other proximal participating peers pn. Upon receiving q, each peer attempts to find relevant documents (*blogs*) in their (previously indexed) local datasets. Each peer in pn, selects their top five matching documents and sends them back as a query result to peer x. A query result comprises of relevant document summaries and the host device information i.e. address. After accumulating query results from pn, peer x displays the results to the user. Upon selection (by the user) of a particular search result, peer x makes a direct request for a specific document from the hosting peer.

Following are the five main components in the IRMAN framework. The **Application Communication Layer (ACL)** provides a standardised interface between the higher level application software and the underlying wireless technology. It includes several sub-packages, which are responsible for device connectivity and data transfer. The **Network Interface** handles the software-to-physical layer network connectivity. The **Information Processor** unit accesses, manages and operates on the local dataset. The main sub-component of the Information Processor unit is the *Query Processor*, which handles query requests made by the peers (including local host) and then executes them on the local dataset. The query results are then relayed back to the requesting peer via the ACL. The **Context Processing** unit maintains the user and device context.

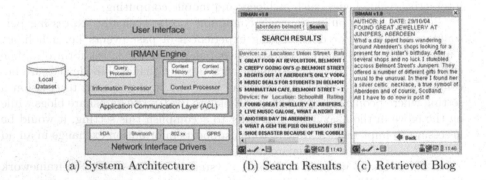

(a) System Architecture   (b) Search Results   (c) Retrieved Blog

Fig. 1. IRMAN Software Architecture and Screenshots of Experiment System

It periodically updates contextual data values by making requests to relevant sources i.e. GPS unit etc. Other software components such as the Information Processor and the **User Interface Layer** (houses the GUI components of the system), interact with this module to acquire current contextual data.

3   Experimental Setup and Method

A prototype application, which targets Personal Java (Java platform for hand-held devices), was developed based on the IRMAN framework. Fig. 1(b) and 1(c) show screenshots of the prototype running on a WiFi (Adhoc mode) enabled Sharp Zaurus PDA. We carried out some initial experiments in order to evaluate the performance of the developed prototype. We were interested in recording the time taken for query broadcasts (searching), query replies (retrieval) and the direct request and receipt of specific documents (blogs). Our experiments were repeated, as per normal practice for system performance testing, and the following results were observed. The average time taken for results to be received after a query was broadcasted was 1453 milliseconds and for a specific document to be retrieved was 26 milliseconds. These values are acceptable for the prototype system to be used in future user experiments.

4   Conclusion and Future Work

In this paper we presented IRMAN, a software framework which supports Peer-to-Peer IR in mobile settings. Through an evaluation of the performance of our framework, we found that its services (search and retrieval) were reliable and that their speed (or time taken) was reasonably quick. Our future aims for the system are as follows: to perform user testing in order to evaluate the usability of our prototype; to extend the system to incorporate other types of content; and finally, to include features for automatic query generation which supports proactive Information Retrieval.

Acknowledgments. The authors would like to thank Ayse Göker and Stuart Watt for their advice and support. Also thanks are due to the AmbieSense project (EU-IST 2001-34244) for enabling access to mobile equipment.

References

1. Kortuem, G., Schneider, J., Preuitt, D., Thompson, T.G.C., Fickas, S., Segall, Z.: When peer-to-peer comes face-to-face: Collaborative peer-to-peer computing in mobile ad hoc networks. In: Proceedings of the First International Conference on Peer-to-Peer Computing (P2P'01), IEEE Computer Society (2001) 75
2. Rheingold, H.: SMART MOBS: The Next Social Revolution. Number ISBN 0-7382-0608-3. Perseus Publishing (2003)
3. Nardi, B.A., Schiano, D.J., Gumbrecht, M., Swartz, L.: "i'm blogging this": A closer look at why people blog. In: In submission to Communications of the ACM. (2004)

Assigning Geographical Scopes To Web Pages*

Bruno Martins, Marcirio Chaves, and Mário J. Silva

Departamento de Informática da, Faculdade de Ciências da,
Universidade de Lisboa, 1749-016 Lisboa, Portugal

1   Introduction

Finding automatic ways of attaching geographical scopes to on-line resources, also called "geo-referencing" documents, is a challenging problem, getting increasing attention [1, 5, 3]. Here we present a system architecture and a process for identifying the geographical scope of Web pages, defining a scope as the region where more people than average would find that page relevant. We rely on typical Web IR heuristics (i.e. feature weighting, hypertext topic locality, anchor description) and assumptions on how people use geographical references in documents. The method involves three major steps. First, geographical named entities are identified in the text. Next, we propagate the found named entities through the Web linkage graph. Finally, a geographical ontology is used to disambiguate among the named entities associated to a document, this way selecting the most likely scope. In the future, we plan on using scopes in new location-aware search tools.

2   System Architecture

The proposed architecture relies on Semantic Web standards such as RDF and Dublin Core. Documents are harvested into XMLBase, our Web data management system which contains a crawler, data/meta-data repositories, and several document analysis components (i.e. language identification, document parsing). The sequential processing stages of the scope assignment algorithm take RDF representations of the documents and augment them with additional information. In the end, a geographical scope is assigned to each document. The geographical information used by the algorithm is kept in GKB [2], a common knowledge base integrating data from multiple external resources (i.e. public gazetters and databases). GKB essentially includes place names and the ontological relationships between them (i.e. broader/narrower geographical entities), supporting mechanisms for storing, maintaining and exporting this information.

---

* This research was partially supported Fundação para a Ciência e Tecnologia, under grants POSI/SRI/40193/2001 and SFRH/BD/10757/2002.

D.E. Losada and J.M. Fernández-Luna (Eds.): ECIR 2005, LNCS 3408, pp. 564–567, 2005.
© Springer-Verlag Berlin Heidelberg 2005

3   Step 1 - Geographic Named Entity Recognition

After low level document processing operations (text extraction and tokenization) we identify the geographical named entities (toponyms) present in the text through a simple named entity recognition (NER) approach. This is based on list lookups (using place names from GKB) and heuristics such as capitalization and surrounding text. Surrounding text is also used to disambiguate the types of places mentioned in the text (i.e. "city of Lisbon", "Setubal district"). Mikheev et al. showed that a NER system could perform well without gazetteers for most entity classes, but not for place names [6]. The same study found that simple list lookup performs reasonably well for locations. Previous studies have also shown that geographic name types are commonly disambiguated in the text itself [4]. The discovered named entities are weighted according to their occurrence frequency and HTML markup information (i.e. text from the title of the documents or from hypertext anchors is considered more important). These weights are used afterwards as disambiguating properties, since the same document may reference several different geographic entities.

4   Step 2 - Web Graph Propagation

Weights for the entities recognized in document d are divided between all linking documents associated with d in the Web graph ($\frac{d}{|inlinks(d)|}$). The value is then assigned to the same entity in the linking documents. This "propagation" procedure is applied only once for each page, and therefore entities contribute only to pages that are one hyperlink away from the source. We also use heuristics to guide this propagation stage. For instance, documents hosted on the same site are considered more likely to relate to the same geographical concept, and therefore weights propagated through these links are given extra credit.

5   Step 3 - Assigning Scopes to Documents

Named entity recognition in itself does not derive the meaning of the expressions recognized. A major problem concerns ambiguity, as for instance "Odivelas" refers to both a city near "Lisbon" and another in "Alentejo" (the referent ambiguity problem). The same location can also have more than one name (reference ambiguity) and this latter problem has another twist: the same name can be used for locations as well as for other class of entities such as persons (referent class ambiguity). Our final stage involves disambiguating the entities associated with a document from the previous steps, and the semantic relationships between these entities, to decide (if possible and reasonable) on the scope to be assigned to each page. Information from the GKB is used to build a geographical ontology (essentially a place hierarchy). Each node is "activated" with the weight associated to its defining named entity in the document. These values are then propagated across the ontological relationships between the entities, using inference methods from probabilistic graphical models. For instance, if "Lisbon" is associated with a page, some weight is also given to all the entities corresponding to sub-regions of "Lisbon". Again, heuristics are used to guide the process, as different ontological relationships (i.e. narrower/broader, equivalent) propagate weights in different ways. Finally, we select the highest weighted entity as the most probable scope for the document, or none if all entities are weighted below a given threshold.

6   Conclusions

Statistics collected through our Web search engine tumba! (www.tumba.pt) motivated this research, in the sense that geographic information is pervasive on both documents and queries. A prototype system currently implements most of the ideas described here, and we are now starting evaluation experiments in tandem with additional software development. Since many parameters are combined, a very important step concerns tuning the "importance" given to each of them. For now, we are essentially relying on empirical tests and on published results from other IR experiments. In the future, we plan on separately evaluating the different aspects involved in our approach. The geographical named entity recognition step will be more thoroughly evaluated through the participation on a joint evaluation promoted by Linguateca (www.linguateca.pt). As for the evaluation of the system as a whole, we intend to use a test collection built from the following sources:

- Pages from sites for Portuguese municipalities, under the assumption that all the pages in a site belong to a geographic scope covering the area of the municipality.
- Pages from the Open Directory Project located under the branch devoted to Portuguese pages with a coherent geographic scope.
- Pages under the RCTS network (public infrastructure hosting sites for schools, museums, and other institutions) under the assumption that all the pages in the same Web site belong to the geographical scope of the institution. From these pages, we only considered the ones from public schools, where the scope is well defined.

Although this collection cannot accurately model the linkage information found on a large sample of the Web, it will nonetheless allows us to automatically test the algorithm on a relatively large sample of Web pages.

References

1. E. Amitay, N. Har'El, R. Sivan, and A. Soffer. Web-a-where: Geotagging Web content. In *Proceedings of SIGIR-04, the 27th annual international conference on Research and developement in information retrieval*, pages 273–280. ACM Press, 2004.
2. M. Chaves, B. Martins, and M. J. Silva. Grease Knowledge Base. DI/FCUL TR 04–XX, Department of Informatics, University of Lisbon, November 2004.

3. J. Ding, L. Gravano, and N. Shivakumar. Computing geographical scopes of web resources. In *Proceedings of VLDB-00, the 26th International Conference on Very Large Data Bases*, pages 545–556. Morgan Kaufmann Publishers Inc., 2000.
4. L. L. Hill, J. Frew, and Q. Zheng. Geographic names - the implementation of a gazetteer in a georeferenced digital library. *D-Lib Magazine*, 5(1), January 1999.
5. C. B. Jones, R. Purves, A. Ruas, M. Sanderson, M. Sester, M. van Kreveld, and R. Weibel. Spatial information retrieval and geographical ontologies: An overview of the SPIRIT project. In *Proceedings of SIGIR-02, the 25th Annual International ACM SIGIR Conference on Research and Development in Information Retrieval*, pages 387–388. ACM Press, August 2002.
6. A. Mikheev, M. Moens, and C. Grover. Named entity recognition without gazetteers. In *Proceedings of EACL-99, the 9th Conference of the European Chapter of the Association for Computational Linguistics*, 1999.

AP-Based Borda Voting Method for Feature Extraction in TRECVID-2004

Le Chen*, Dayong Ding, Dong Wang,
Fuzong Lin, and Bo Zhang

Department of Computer Science and Technology,
Tsinghua University, Beijing 100084, P.R. China
chenle02@mails.tsinghua.edu.cn

Abstract. We present a novel fusion method — AP-based Borda voting method (APBB)— for rankings. Due to its adaptive weighting scheme, APBB outperforms many traditional methods. Comparative experiments on TRECVID 2004 data were carried out and showed the robustness and effectiveness of this method.

1   Introduction

Fusion methods based on rank have been extensively studied for more than a decade, but it is still far from finding a robust and effective fusion methods. In this paper, we introduce a novel fusion method — *AP-based Borda voting method (APBB)* , which is more robust and effective than various fusion methods including the standard Borda voting method (Std), median Borda (Median)[1], the highest rank method (HR) [2], and AP-weighted Borda (APw)[3].

Our study and methodology are motivated by the feature extraction task in TRECVID-2004 [4]. This task is a two-class classification problem, as each semantic feature or concept is assumed to be binary in each video shot. The performance measure is *Average precision (AP)*, which is a single-valued measure that reflects the performance over all relevant shots [5]. Our final goal is to maximize the AP value.

In this paper, APBB is introduced in Section 2. Then two suits of comparative experiments, one for fusion of consistent models (EXP1), the other inconsistent ones (EXP2), are described in Section 3. Finally, we give a conclusion in Section 4.

2   AP-Based Borda Voting Method

The AP-based Borda voting method can be formulated as follows: Suppose we have n classifiers, and there are m samples to classify. For ith sample, the rank

---

* Supported by National Natural Science Foundation of China(60135010,60321002), Chinese National Key Foundation Research & Development Plan(2004CB318108).

D.E. Losada and J.M. Fernández-Luna (Eds.): ECIR 2005, LNCS 3408, pp. 568–570, 2005.

value ranked by classifier j is denoted as Υ_i^j, and its final confidence $-\Upsilon_i^{APb}$ [1].
Then,

$$\Upsilon_i^{APBB} = \sum_{j=1,...,n} -\exp(C(\overline{w}_j - 1)) \cdot \Upsilon_i^j, \qquad i = 1,...,m, \tag{1}$$

where $\overline{w}_j$ is the normalized AP values w_j by $\overline{w}_j = w_j/w_{max}$, $w_{max} = \max\{w_i | i = 1,...,n\}$. C is non-negative variable determining the degree of difference among the weights. As C increases, the difference of the weights is amplified. The method degenerates to standard Borda method when $C = 0$, and to HR when C is large. Logistic regression (LR) [3][6] can also be used to determine the different weights. But estimating weights by LR is suitable for multi-class classification problems, rather than two-class ones.

3   Comparative Experiments

In TRECVID-2004 [4], we compared the standard Borda voting method (Std) and its various variants, e.g. median Borda[1], the highest rank method (HR) [2], AP-weighted Borda (APw)[3], with APBB in detecting "Basket Scored" concept. Two suits of experiments, EXP1 and EXP2, one for 20 consistent models and the other 20 inconsistent ones. The consistency of these models can been seen from the individual APs as listed in Table 1. The best result of individual models (Sbest) can be used as a base line. As Fig.1 shows, APBB outperforms any other fusion methods.

On average, it provides about 3.1% gain over Std and 9.4% over Sbest in EXP1. Corresponding gains in EXP2 are 21.1% and 6.5%. Compared with the results of Sbest, which are the same in the two experiments, results of Std and APw are not so robust to poor lists while results of APBB are steadily high.

The performance of APw is higher than Std by using AP as its weight, but it is still less than APBB because the latter adjusts the gap between the APs, which act as initial weights. As can be seen in the last row of Table 1, the weights for extremely poor lists are adjusted to 0, while only a few of top lists remain valid in final decision with non-zero weights.

Table 1. A sample of weights in our experiments. "AP" is estimated on training data, and "Wt" is the final weights by our method. Due to the limit of space, the weights are round to hundreds place here, which are round to ten-thousands in our experiments

	Lists	1	2	3	4	5	6	7	8	9	10	11	12	13	14	15	16	17	18	19	20
EXP1	AP	.65	.51	.45	.51	.39	.66	.67	.67	.68	.66	.67	.67	.63	.60	.68	.65	.67	.63	.64	.61
C=7	Wt	.66	.11	.05	.10	.02	.81	.86	.90	.98	.78	.92	.90	.50	.37	**1.0**	.69	.84	.51	.64	.38
EXP2	AP	.06	.07	.12	.17	.24	.39	.46	.51	.61	.61	.63	.65	.65	.66	.67	.67	.68	.68	.68	.68
C=137	Wt	.00	.00	.00	.00	.00	.00	.00	.00	.00	.00	.00	.00	.00	.02	.10	.08	.21	.33	.74	**1.0**

---

[1] Since lower rank means higher confidence, the negative rank is used as the confidence.

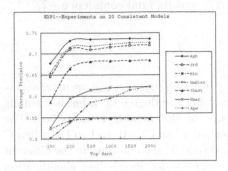 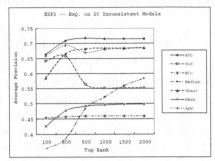

Fig. 1. Comparative experiments of different fusion methods with both consistent and inconsistent models. 20 lists were used in each experiment. The X axis represents the length of rankings from different models

4 Conclusion

The AP-based Borda voting method is a robust and effective fusion method for rankings, which outperforms many traditional methods. The effectiveness of APBB is mainly due to its adaptive weighting scheme. In fact, our results on "Basket scored" detection submitted to TRECVID-2004 are based on this method and achieves No.1 in all runs. Further work will include more sophisticated deal with rank values and applying APBB to detecting more concepts.

References

1. Erp, M.V., Schomaker, L.: Variants of the borda count method for combining ranked classifier hypotheses. In: Proceedings of IWFHR7, the seventh International Workshop on Frontiers in Handwriting Recognition, Amsterdam, The Netherlands. (2000) 443–452
2. Ho, T.K., Hull, J.J., Srihari, S.N.: On multiple classifier systems for pattern recognition. In: Proc. of the 11th Int'l Conference on Pattern Recognition, The Hague, The Netherlands (1992) 84–87
3. Aslam, J.A., Montague, M.H.: Models for metasearch. In: SIGIR. (2001) 275–284
4. NIST: The home page of trec video retrieval track. http://www-nlpir.nist.gov/projects/trecvid/ (2004)
5. NIST: Common evaluation measures. appendix in Special Publication (TREC 2001), NIST, Gaithersburg, MD, http://trec.nist.gov/pubs/trec10/appendices/measures.pdf **22** (2001) 500–250
6. Melnik, O., Vardi, Y., Zhang, C.H.: Mixed group ranks: Preference and confidence in classifier combination. Ieee Transactions on Pattern Analysis and Machine Intelligence **26** (2004) 973–981

Author Index

Lecture Notes in Computer Science

For information about Vols. 1–3321

please contact your bookseller or Springer

Vol. 3369: V.R. Benjamins, P. Casanovas, J. Breuker, A. Gangemi (Eds.), Law and the Semantic Web. XII, 249 pages. 2005. (Subseries LNAI).

Vol. 3368: L. Paletta, J.K. Tsotsos, E. Rome, G.W. Humphreys (Eds.), Attention and Performance in Computational Vision. VIII, 231 pages. 2005.

Vol. 3366: I. Rahwan, P. Moraitis, C. Reed (Eds.), Argumentation in Multi-Agent Systems. XII, 263 pages. 2005. (Subseries LNAI).

Vol. 3365: G. Mauri, G. Păun, M.J. Pérez-Jiménez, G. Rozenberg, A. Salomaa (Eds.), Membrane Computing. IX, 415 pages. 2005.

Vol. 3363: T. Eiter, L. Libkin (Eds.), Database Theory - ICDT 2005. XI, 413 pages. 2004.

Vol. 3362: G. Barthe, L. Burdy, M. Huisman, J.-L. Lanet, T. Muntean (Eds.), Construction and Analysis of Safe, Secure, and Interoperable Smart Devices. IX, 257 pages. 2005.

Vol. 3361: S. Bengio, H. Bourlard (Eds.), Machine Learning for Multimodal Interaction. XII, 362 pages. 2005.

Vol. 3360: S. Spaccapietra, E. Bertino, S. Jajodia, R. King, D. McLeod, M.E. Orlowska, L. Strous (Eds.), Journal on Data Semantics II. XI, 223 pages. 2005.

Vol. 3359: G. Grieser, Y. Tanaka (Eds.), Intuitive Human Interfaces for Organizing and Accessing Intellectual Assets. XIV, 257 pages. 2005. (Subseries LNAI).

Vol. 3358: J. Cao, L.T. Yang, M. Guo, F. Lau (Eds.), Parallel and Distributed Processing and Applications. XXIV, 1058 pages. 2004.

Vol. 3357: H. Handschuh, M.A. Hasan (Eds.), Selected Areas in Cryptography. XI, 354 pages. 2004.

Vol. 3356: G. Das, V.P. Gulati (Eds.), Intelligent Information Technology. XII, 428 pages. 2004.

Vol. 3355: R. Murray-Smith, R. Shorten (Eds.), Switching and Learning in Feedback Systems. X, 343 pages. 2005.

Vol. 3353: J. Hromkovič, M. Nagl, B. Westfechtel (Eds.), Graph-Theoretic Concepts in Computer Science. XI, 404 pages. 2004.

Vol. 3352: C. Blundo, S. Cimato (Eds.), Security in Communication Networks. XI, 381 pages. 2005.

Vol. 3351: G. Persiano, R. Solis-Oba (Eds.), Approximation and Online Algorithms. VIII, 295 pages. 2005.

Vol. 3350: M. Hermenegildo, D. Cabeza (Eds.), Practical Aspects of Declarative Languages. VIII, 269 pages. 2005.

Vol. 3349: B.M. Chapman (Ed.), Shared Memory Parallel Programming with Open MP. X, 149 pages. 2005.

Vol. 3348: A. Canteaut, K. Viswanathan (Eds.), Progress in Cryptology - INDOCRYPT 2004. XIV, 431 pages. 2004.

Vol. 3347: R.K. Ghosh, H. Mohanty (Eds.), Distributed Computing and Internet Technology. XX, 472 pages. 2004.

Vol. 3346: R.H. Bordini, M. Dastani, J. Dix, A.E.F. Seghrouchni (Eds.), Programming Multi-Agent Systems. XIV, 249 pages. 2005. (Subseries LNAI).

Vol. 3345: Y. Cai (Ed.), Ambient Intelligence for Scientific Discovery. XII, 311 pages. 2005. (Subseries LNAI).

Vol. 3344: J. Malenfant, B.M. Østvold (Eds.), Object-Oriented Technology. ECOOP 2004 Workshop Reader. VIII, 215 pages. 2005.

Vol. 3343: C. Freksa, M. Knauff, B. Krieg-Brückner, B. Nebel, T. Barkowsky (Eds.), Spatial Cognition IV. Reasoning, Action, and Interaction. XIII, 519 pages. 2005. (Subseries LNAI).

Vol. 3342: E. Şahin, W.M. Spears (Eds.), Swarm Robotics. IX, 175 pages. 2005.

Vol. 3341: R. Fleischer, G. Trippen (Eds.), Algorithms and Computation. XVII, 935 pages. 2004.

Vol. 3340: C.S. Calude, E. Calude, M.J. Dinneen (Eds.), Developments in Language Theory. XI, 431 pages. 2004.

Vol. 3339: G.I. Webb, X. Yu (Eds.), AI 2004: Advances in Artificial Intelligence. XXII, 1272 pages. 2004. (Subseries LNAI).

Vol. 3338: S.Z. Li, J. Lai, T. Tan, G. Feng, Y. Wang (Eds.), Advances in Biometric Person Authentication. XVIII, 699 pages. 2004.

Vol. 3337: J.M. Barreiro, F. Martin-Sanchez, V. Maojo, F. Sanz (Eds.), Biological and Medical Data Analysis. XI, 508 pages. 2004.

Vol. 3336: D. Karagiannis, U. Reimer (Eds.), Practical Aspects of Knowledge Management. X, 523 pages. 2004. (Subseries LNAI).

Vol. 3335: M. Malek, M. Reitenspieß, J. Kaiser (Eds.), Service Availability. X, 213 pages. 2005.

Vol. 3334: Z. Chen, H. Chen, Q. Miao, Y. Fu, E. Fox, E.-p. Lim (Eds.), Digital Libraries: International Collaboration and Cross-Fertilization. XX, 690 pages. 2004.

Vol. 3333: K. Aizawa, Y. Nakamura, S. Satoh (Eds.), Advances in Multimedia Information Processing - PCM 2004, Part III. XXXV, 785 pages. 2004.

Vol. 3332: K. Aizawa, Y. Nakamura, S. Satoh (Eds.), Advances in Multimedia Information Processing - PCM 2004, Part II. XXXVI, 1051 pages. 2004.

Vol. 3331: K. Aizawa, Y. Nakamura, S. Satoh (Eds.), Advances in Multimedia Information Processing - PCM 2004, Part I. XXXVI, 667 pages. 2004.

Vol. 3330: J. Akiyama, E.T. Baskoro, M. Kano (Eds.), Combinatorial Geometry and Graph Theory. VIII, 227 pages. 2005.

Vol. 3329: P.J. Lee (Ed.), Advances in Cryptology - ASIACRYPT 2004. XVI, 546 pages. 2004.

Vol. 3328: K. Lodaya, M. Mahajan (Eds.), FSTTCS 2004: Foundations of Software Technology and Theoretical Computer Science. XVI, 532 pages. 2004.

Vol. 3327: Y. Shi, W. Xu, Z. Chen (Eds.), Data Mining and Knowledge Management. XIII, 263 pages. 2005. (Subseries LNAI).

Vol. 3326: A. Sen, N. Das, S.K. Das, B.P. Sinha (Eds.), Distributed Computing - IWDC 2004. XIX, 546 pages. 2004.

Vol. 3325: C.H. Lim, M. Yung (Eds.), Information Security Applications. XI, 472 pages. 2005.

Vol. 3323: G. Antoniou, H. Boley (Eds.), Rules and Rule Markup Languages for the Semantic Web. X, 215 pages. 2004.

Vol. 3322: R. Klette, J. Žunić (Eds.), Combinatorial Image Analysis. XII, 760 pages. 2004.